The Activist Impulse

The Activist Impulse
Essays on the Intersection of Evangelicalism and Anabaptism

Edited by
Jared S. Burkholder and David C. Cramer

With a foreword by
George M. Marsden

and an afterword by
Sara Wenger Shenk

◌PICKWICK *Publications* • Eugene, Oregon

THE ACTIVIST IMPULSE
Essays on the Intersection of Evangelicalism and Anabaptism

Copyright © 2012 Wipf and Stock Publishers. All rights reserved. Except for brief quotations in critical publications or reviews, no part of this book may be reproduced in any manner without prior written permission from the publisher. Write: Permissions, Wipf and Stock Publishers, 199 W. 8th Ave., Suite 3, Eugene, OR 97401.

Pickwick Publications
An Imprint of Wipf and Stock Publishers
199 W. 8th Ave., Suite 3
Eugene, OR 97401

www.wipfandstock.com

ISBN 13: 978-1-60899-350-5

Cataloging-in-Publication data:

The activist impulse : essays on the intersection of Evangelicalism and Anabaptism / edited by Jared S. Burkholder and David C. Cramer ; foreword by George M. Marsden ; afterword by Sara Wenger Shenk.

xvi + 428 p. ; 23 cm. — Includes bibliographical refernces and index.

ISBN 13: 978-1-60899-350-5

1. Evangelicalism — United States. 2. Anabaptists — History. I. Burkholder, Jared S. II. Cramer, David C. III. Marsden, George M., 1939– IV. Shenk, Sara Wenger, 1953– V. Title.

BR1640 .A25 2012

Manufactured in the U.S.A.

Contents

Foreword by George M. Marsden / vii
Acknowledgments / xi
List of Contributors / xiii

    Introduction: The Activist Impulse / 1

Part I   **Intersecting Stories: Historical Reflection on the Nexus of Evangelicalism and Anabaptism**

    Introduction to Part I / 9

  1 Activist Impulses across Time: North American Evangelicalism and Anabaptism as Conversation Partners—STEVEN M. NOLT / 11

  2 Anabaptism and Evangelicalism Revisited: Healing a Contentious Relationship?—JOHN D. ROTH / 45

  3 Intellectual Hospitality as Historical Method: Moving beyond the Activist Impulse—JOHN FEA / 74

Part II   **Intersecting Challenges: Anabaptism and the Fundamentalist-Modernist Controversy**

    Introduction to Part II / 101

  4 Fundamentalists, Modernists, and a Mennonite "Third Way": Reexamining the Career of Bishop Daniel Kauffman—BENJAMIN WETZEL / 104

  5 "I Submit": Daniel Kauffman and the Legacy of a Yielded Life—NATHAN E. YODER / 129

Contents

    6 A Cord of Many Strands: Reexamining Grace Brethren Identity and the Fundamentalism of Alva J. McClain
—M. M. Norris / 156

    7 Misfits and Fundamentalists: The Question of Evangelicalism and Defection among Lancaster and Franconia Mennonites
—Jared S. Burkholder / 185

Part III **Intersecting Concerns: Anabaptist and Evangelical Public Witness**

  Introduction to Part III / 215

    8 Practicing Peace, Embracing Evangelism: Missional Tensions in the Mennonite Brethren in Christ Church
—Matthew Eaton and Joel Boehner / 217

    9 "Pool Tables are the Devil's Playground": Forging an *Evangelico-Anabautista* Identity in South Texas
—Felipe Hinojosa / 237

  10 Re-Baptizing Evangelicalism: American Anabaptists and the 1970s Evangelical Left—David R. Swartz / 262

  11 The Evangelical-Anabaptist Spectrum: The Political Theologies of Francis Schaeffer, John Howard Yoder, and Jim Wallis—Geoffrey C. Bowden / 292

Part IV **Intersecting Trajectories: Toward an Evangelical Anabaptist Theology and Praxis**

  Introduction to Part II / 323

  12 "Go Tell that Fox!" Evangelical Anabaptist Reflections on Religion and the
Public Square—Timothy Paul Erdel / 325

  13 Beyond Anselm: A Biblical and Evangelical Case for Nonviolent Atonement—Kirk R. MacGregor / 350

  14 Evangelical Hermeneutics, Anabaptist Ethics: John Howard Yoder, the *Solas*, and the Question of War
—David C. Cramer / 379

Afterword by Sara Wenger Shenk / 407
Index / 409

Foreword

"EVANGELICAL," AS IT IS used regarding American religious life, is a peculiar term. According to sociologists, "evangelical" designates the largest religious grouping in the United States today, yet most of the members of that group do not identify themselves as such. In their recent major study, *American Grace: How Religion Divides and Unites Us*, Robert D. Putnam and David E. Campbell tell us that people with evangelical affiliations overwhelmingly designate themselves as "Christian" and not as "evangelical," or in many other cases they identify as belonging to a particular sub-denomination. Putnam and Campbell determine who belongs to their category of "evangelical" on the basis of a list of churches that they regard as teaching evangelical doctrines, and that list includes Mennonite and various Brethren groups. These Anabaptist evangelicals, then, have in common with most other American evangelicals that they do not typically think of themselves as "evangelicals." They are also not alone in wondering what their proper relationship is to the larger category.

Those who wish to explore the interactions between Anabaptists and evangelicalism are particularly blessed by a generation of fine scholars who can guide them in that exploration. One of the encouraging developments that seems to be accelerating in recent decades has been a renaissance of evangelical scholarship. Not every sub-group within evangelicalism has been equally represented in this scholarly surge. Anabaptists, however, seem to be especially well represented, as this volume testifies. Such scholars are well trained academically, but their scholarship is far more than "academic." Particularly conspicuous among these Anabaptist scholars is that they are openly committed and are characteristically engaged not only with issues of principle but also with the actions that should result from principle.

When Anabaptist observers think of their relationships to evangelicalism, it is probably safe to say that they are usually thinking not so much of all of the many other sub-groups that might be classed as "evangelical," but rather of a core tradition in which it has been more likely that people might actually classify themselves as "evangelical." This interdenominational or nondenominational group of what might be called "card-carrying" evangelicals was particularly influential during the twentieth century in shaping a trans-evangelical coalition. That was the sort of evangelicalism associated with Billy Graham (and similar evangelists and evangelistic organizations) and with institutions such as Moody Bible Institute (and a network of similar Bible Institutes), Wheaton College, Dallas Theological Seminary, Fuller Theological Seminary, Gordon-Conwell Theological Seminary, and *Christianity Today*. As the histories of these would suggest, this sort of evangelicalism was shaped by a prior "fundamentalism" growing out of the controversies of the 1920s.

The changing face of this core evangelicalism during the past century is particularly significant for thinking of the relationships between Anabaptists and other evangelicals. During the decades from the 1920s through the 1950s when "fundamentalism" was still a common term to designate those who are now classed as "evangelical," fundamentalist-evangelicals and Anabaptists were often drawn together by their common biblicism and also by their sense of opposition toward many trends in modern culture and modern theology. Most of the core American fundamentalist-evangelicals, however, had a very different relationship to the American cultural mainstream than did most Anabaptists. On the one hand, such fundamentalist-evangelicals typically were members of strong local church communities that cultivated a sensibility of being outsiders to the mainstream culture. They spoke of being "strangers and pilgrims" and emphasized that Christians should live self-consciously separated from the vices of the surrounding culture. Typically they were premillennialists who said that politics would not solve human problems and that the only hope for modern civilization was the imminently expected return of Jesus to set up his kingdom. But on the other hand, these same fundamentalist-evangelicals were also heirs to an older tradition of revivalist evangelicalism that went back to times and places in which evangelicalism was almost the default American religion. In that tradition American evangelicals assumed that piety and patriotism went hand in hand, particularly in times of war. America was in some sense God's chosen nation with a national mission that would be aided by its military strength. In that tradition evangelicals aspired to Christianize, to shape, and even to control mainstream American culture. Mid-twentieth-century fundamentalist-evangelicals, shaped by these two heritages, were often highly ambivalent when it came to thinking about their relationship to modern American civilization.

During the past sixty years or so evangelicalism has changed from being noted for its fundamentalist separatism to becoming the leading religious grouping in the country, a transmutation that has important implications for Anabaptists who relate to evangelicalism. Evangelicalism as a whole no longer includes a very large culturally separatist impulse. Its residual "fundamentalist" wing, though separatist in some respects, often seems more militant about "taking back" American culture than about remaining pure from its temptations, including its political temptations. But perhaps the most important point to note regarding contemporary evangelicalism is that the movement has become so wide and so diverse that it is difficult to identify any core when it comes to cultural issues. What unites the movement is broad agreement on some doctrinal issues and many widely shared practices of worship and expressions of piety. But no one today can plausibly claim to represent or speak for evangelicalism as a whole. So with regard to the majority within this amorphous evangelical grouping, it would be difficult to generalize as to what their stance toward the mainstream culture is. They are, like most Americans with religious commitments, selective as to what they accept as a matter of course and what they reject. That is not to say that they are not pious or thoughtful. It is just to say that most (there are important exceptions among some other sub-groups, such as the Reformed) have not thought systematically about the relationship of Christianity to the cultural mainstream and its political and economic order.

Anabaptists come from a very different heritage in which thinking about their relationship to the cultural mainstream has always been a fundamental matter. Anabaptists are also, like other ethno-religious communities, coming to be closer to the cultural mainstream than they once were. That naturally raises the question as to what their relationship should be to their fellow evangelicals with whom they share many (if not necessarily all) traits in theology, but who have very different heritages regarding how Christians should relate to the complex set of practices that constitute contemporary culture. The present volume is a wonderful contribution to that enterprise. Not only are these essays helpful guides for people of Anabaptist allegiances who are seeking to assess how best to relate to their fellow evangelicals, they also offer excellent resources for other evangelicals who may wish to see what might be learned by looking at the larger evangelical movement from Anabaptist perspectives.

George M. Marsden
Francis A. McAnaney Professor of History Emeritus
The University of Notre Dame

Acknowledgments

THE IDEA FOR THIS volume initially took shape while mingling with other participants at the 2008 biennial meeting of the Conference on Faith and History, an organization comprised mostly of evangelical historians. Held that year at Bluffton University, an Anabaptist institution in northwest Ohio, the program included several sessions on Anabaptist topics, including a plenary address by Mennonite historian, John Roth. At such a gathering, it seemed only natural to reflect on the historical and theological relationship between evangelicals and Anabaptists. Since that time, a number of gifted individuals have contributed their time, friendly advice, and expertise. Conversations with Roth and his colleague at Goshen College, Steve Nolt, proved especially fruitful and brought us, a historian and a theologian, together in conversation. Steve was especially insightful during the early stages, serving as a sounding board and advisor, as well as suggesting names of potential contributors. Eric Miller helped with the proposal stage as did Doug Sweeney, who offered comments and challenged us to think with greater creativity. We received much encouragement from colleagues at Grace College, including Mark Norris, and Bethel College and Keller Park Missionary Church, including Matt Eaton, Joel Boehner, and especially Tim Erdel, who not only supported the project but graciously agreed to proof the entire manuscript. Bethel College reference librarian Mark Root also provided helpful assistance tracking down some last minute sources, as did the staff at the Mennonite Historical Library at Goshen College. We must also thank the editorial team at Wipf and Stock for taking on this book in the first place and for following through with patient and skillful editorial assistance.

We owe much to the School of Arts and Sciences at Grace College and to the Provost, Bill Katip, who has brought a fresh emphasis on scholarship to the Grace campus. Bill provided persistent and tangible encouragement and graciously agreed to fund part of the project despite the economic recession. The Grace College Department of History and Political Science provided such essentials as office supplies and work space, while Sarah Rice's assistance with departmental operations proved especially helpful and allowed for greater focus on the project at hand. Carrie Halquist, Connor Park, and Hillary Burgardt also assisted in the final stages.

Of course this volume would not exist without the authors whose insightful essays fill the pages of this book, and we are grateful for the many helpful conversations we have had with each of them. Somehow, these individuals managed to fit this project in around heavy teaching loads, academic responsibilities, and other research and writing projects. We also appreciate the support of George Marsden and Sarah Wenger Shenk, who provided the foreword and afterword respectively. Throughout the process of writing and revision, these contributors, along with their work, proved to be engaging companions. Lastly, we owe a great debt to our families, and especially our spouses, Connie and Andrea. Without their longstanding and loving encouragement, this project would never have materialized.

Jared S. Burkholder and David C. Cramer
Lent 2012

Contributors

Joel Boehner (MLS, Indiana University) is Instructor of Writing and Director of the Writing Center at Bethel College (Mishawaka, IN). He has previously written on the history of the Missionary Church and recently presented a paper on Anabaptist missiology at a conference of the Evangelical Missiological Society.

Geoffrey C Bowden (PhD, University of Notre Dame) is Associate Professor of Political Science at Savannah State University (Savannah, GA). He has articles in *The Cresset*, *Christian Scholar's Review*, and *Christian Reflections*, and has given scholarly papers on the political philosophies of John Locke, Elisha Williams, and Joseph Raz. In addition to speaking for groups including the Malone College Writer's Group and local community groups, Bowden has been working on a monograph on the history of American political theology as well as a book entitled *The Project and Prospects of Perfectionist Liberalism*.

Jared S. Burkholder (PhD, University of Iowa) is Associate Professor of History at Grace College (Winona Lake, IN) where he also serves as the director of the Office of Faith, Learning, and Scholarship. He has published several pieces on evangelicalism in America as well as articles on colonial Moravians in Pennsylvania for such journals as *Fides et Historia* and *The Pennsylvania Magazine of History and Biography*. He has also presented academic papers at meetings of the American Academy of Religion, American Society of Church History, and the Conference on Faith and History.

David C. Cramer (MDiv, Trinity Evangelical Divinity School; MA, Trinity International University) is a PhD student in Religion with a concentration in theological ethics at Baylor University. He previously taught in the Religion and Philosophy Division at Bethel

College (Mishawaka, IN). He has published articles and reviews in *The Mennonite Quarterly Review, Priscilla Papers, Philosophia Christi,* and elsewhere, and has presented numerous conference papers on evangelical Anabaptist theology and ethics. He has served on the editorial team for various journals and is currently Editor of the historical journal of the Missionary Church, *Reflections,* as well as a licensed minister of the Missionary Church.

Matthew Eaton (MA, Wheaton College; MATS, Associated Mennonite Biblical Seminary) is a PhD student in Theology with a concentration in ecological ethics at the University of St. Michael's College in the Toronto School of Theology. He has published articles in *The Mennonite Quarterly Review, Conrad Grebel Review,* and elsewhere.

Timothy Paul Erdel (PhD, University of Illinois at Urbana-Champaign) teaches religion, philosophy and other courses in the humanities at Bethel College (Mishawaka, IN). Reared in Ecuador, he lived in Jamaica and has published in a variety of disciplines. He is a licensed minister of and the denominational archivist for the Missionary Church.

John Fea (PhD, State University of New York at Stony Brook) is Associate Professor of History and Chair of the History Department at Messiah College (Grantham, PA). He is the author of *The Way of Improvement Leads Home: Philip Vickers Fithian and the Rural Enlightenment in Early America* (University of Pennsylvania Press) and *Was America Founded as a Christian Nation?: A Historical Introduction* (Westminster John Knox), and he is co-editor of *Confessing History: Explorations in Christian Faith and the Historian's Vocation* (University of Notre Dame Press).

Felipe Hinojosa (PhD, University of Houston) is Assistant Professor of History at Texas A&M University. He has given numerous scholarly presentations on race, religion, and social movements and has received awards and research grants including the Hispanic Theological Initiative dissertation grant in 2008 and most recently the Louisville Institute's "First Book Grant for Minority Scholars" in 2010. Currently he is working on a manuscript entitled "Quiet Riots: Faith, Activism, and Identity Among Latino/a Mennonites, 1932–1982."

Kirk R. MacGregor (PhD, University of Iowa) is Visiting Assistant Professor of Theology at Quincy University (Quincy, IL). He is the author of *A Central European Synthesis of Radical and Magisterial Reform: The Sacramental Theology of Balthasar Hubmaier* (2006) and *A Molinist-Anabaptist Systematic Theology* (2007), and he is co-editor of *Perspectives on Eternal Security* (2009). He has published articles in the *Journal of the American Academy of Religion*, *Bibliotheca Sacra*, *Journal of the Evangelical Theological Society*, *The Mennonite Quarterly Review*, and *Westminster Theological Journal*.

Steven M. Nolt (PhD, University of Notre Dame) is Professor of History at Goshen College (Goshen, IN) where he also serves as the chair of the Department of History and Political Science. He has written numerous books and scholarly articles on Mennonite history, Amish communities, and issues related to ethnicity and religion. He has also served on various editorial boards including those of *The Mennonite Quarterly Review*, *Pennsylvania History*, *Journal of Mennonite Studies*, and *Pennsylvania Mennonite Heritage*.

M. M. Norris (PhD, University of Edinburgh) is Professor of History at Grace College (Winona Lake, IN) where he also serves as chair of the Department of History and Political Science. He has given presentations at various professional conferences including a paper on Helen ("Ma") Sunday and American evangelicalism. He currently has a forthcoming book on Tudor England and is working on an edited volume on the history of Grace Theological Seminary.

John D. Roth (PhD, University of Chicago) is Professor of History at Goshen College (Goshen, IN) where he also serves as Director of the Mennonite Historical Library. He has served as the Editor of *The Mennonite Quarterly Review* since 1994 and has published extensively on Anabaptism and the history of the Radical Reformation. Additionally, he speaks regularly to lay and professional audiences on issues of Anabaptist-Mennonite history and theology, reconciliation, and peacemaking.

David R. Swartz (PhD, University of Notre Dame) is Assistant Professor of History at Asbury University. His writing has appeared in *The Mennonite Quarterly Review*, *Religion and American Culture*, *Journal for the Study of Radicalism*, *Communal Societies*, and *Books & Culture*. His book on the evangelical left is forthcoming from the University of Pennsylvania Press.

Benjamin Wetzel (MA, Baylor University) is a PhD student in History at the University of Notre Dame. He has presented academic papers at numerous professional meetings, including the Conference on Faith and History. He previously received the Guittard Fellowship in History (Baylor), completed an internship at the Lancaster Mennonite Historical Society, and has articles on Anabaptist history in the *Baker Handbook of Denominations and Ministries* as well as *Pennsylvania Mennonite Heritage*.

Nathan E. Yoder (PhD, University of Notre Dame) is Professor of Church History at Eastern Mennonite Seminary and Archivist for Eastern Mennonite University (Harrisonburg, VA). He is an ordained minister who has integrated scholarship with pastoral work, speaking regularly to both academic and lay audiences. In addition to his publications in Mennonite journals, Yoder is working on a critical history of the Conservative Mennonite Conference.

Introduction

The Activist Impulse

JARED S. BURKHOLDER and DAVID C. CRAMER

IN 1979, AS JIMMY Carter—a self-identified evangelical—sat in the oval office, Anabaptist scholars contemplated the rising prominence of the evangelical movement in American politics. Prior to the 1970s, there were few substantial responses by Anabaptists to American evangelicalism, but with mainstream media outlets bantering about the significance of a "born again" president and the rise of influential movements, such as Jerry Falwell's new "Moral Majority," consideration of the evangelical movement seemed especially apt.[1] In recognition of this, a handful of Mennonites and a few representatives from what would come to be called the "evangelical left" weighed in on the issues surrounding the Anabaptist-evangelical relationship during the Carter years. Under the editorial guidance of prominent Goshen College professor, C. Norman Kraus, the group brought together a collection of essays entitled simply, *Evangelicalism and Anabaptism*. The contributors hoped to clarify for their constituents the new evangelical identity and what, if anything, evangelicals and Anabaptists had to talk about. Published by Herald Press, the official publishing outlet of the (Old) Mennonite Church, the main themes in the volume serve to identify the primary topics of discussion in the late 1970s: fundamentalism, Pentecostalism, American politics, biblical inerrancy, and eschatology were all areas of focus. The book constitutes an

---

1. For a treatment of Carter, the response to his identification as "born again," and the significance of evangelical leaders, such as Falwell, for American politics, see Martin, *With God on our Side*.

important part of the evangelical-Anabaptist conversation and with reprints available since 2001, its relevance remains.[2]

Three decades later, evangelicals and Anabaptists continue to wrestle with the question of their relationship, even as the social and political context of their activity has evolved. Evangelical leaders have continued, in increasing numbers, to enter the fray of partisan politics and popular culture. At the same time, the evangelical rank and file has exerted a surprising strength of influence at the polls in recent elections. Anabaptists, too, have made their mark. Many have fleshed out their commitment to nonviolence by protesting American wars in the Middle East, while others have inspired the nation with radical forgiveness in the face of senseless domestic violence.[3]

The last thirty years have shown that both evangelicals and Anabaptists, while sharing space on the margins of American society, have manifest a shared commitment—an "impulse"—to engage American society through religiously motivated activism. This is not to say that all Anabaptists or every evangelical would consider themselves an activist in the popular sense of the word. But it is certainly the case that many members of both traditions have participated in vigorous efforts, on both the right and the left, in support of Christian ideals as they have interpreted them. As one would expect, however, evangelicals and Anabaptists have very distinct visions of how that activism ought to look. These unique visions flow directly from their particular heritage, theological framework, and shared experience, which have essentially formed a cluster of overarching characteristics that define each tradition.

This volume operates with broad definitions of these two traditions and leaves the individual authors to offer more precision if they so choose. In general, however, evangelicals in America have always emphasized the doctrine of divine redemption and the necessity of personal conversion. They have defended traditional definitions of biblical orthodoxy, encouraged mission, and in recent years, gravitated toward a vision of Christian service that includes significant political involvement and participation in America's "culture wars."

2. Kraus, *Evangelicalism and Anabaptism*. Reprints are available through Wipf and Stock Publishers.

3. We are, of course, thinking primarily of the murder of five Amish school children in Nickel Mines, Pennsylvania in October of 2006. On the Amish response to this tragedy, see Kraybill, Nolt, and Weaver-Zercher, *Amish Grace*.

Anabaptists are situated within the Historic Peace Church tradition and foster an identity that has coalesced around the creation of close-knit communities and the value of living separate from "the world" and its loyalties. Owing to a distinct two-kingdom theology, Anabaptists, especially in recent years, have nurtured a commitment to global nonviolence and social justice as they make the radical teachings of Jesus relevant for the twenty-first century.

While members of both traditions have sought to engage the society around them, they have not always agreed on how best to respond to each other. The traditional interpretation has oversimplified the relationship between evangelicals and Anabaptists, offering something of a "declension thesis," whereby the growing influence of evangelicalism is eroding distinctive Anabaptist teachings and ethnic identity. Such is the argument suggested by another collection published in 1979, *Mission and the Peace Witness*,[4] in which a number of prominent Anabaptist theologians and practitioners reflected on the influence of evangelicalism—notably the "Church Growth Movement" and its accompanying "homogenous unit principle"—on Anabaptist missions and evangelism.[5] While such arguments still carry some weight, and some Anabaptists continue to resent the appeal of popular evangelicalism, others see plenty of opportunity for integrating the two traditions.[6]

For their part, many evangelicals have been disillusioned with what they perceive to be Anabaptist "liberalism" with regard to theology and culture, and in a time when conservative evangelicals have often melded their faith with nationalistic sentiment, the Anabaptist critique of American action around the world does not engender much affection towards Anabaptists. Still, a growing number of evangelical leaders have found in Anabaptism a robust alternative to the program of political involvement employed by the leaders of the Religious Right within their midst.[7] Indeed, Anabaptist themes offer an attrac-

---

4. Ramseyer, *Mission and the Peace Witness*.

5. Ramseyer, "Introduction," 7; cf. Showalter, "Church Growth Principles," 104–13.

6. Indeed, while there is criticism of contemporary evangelical practice in *Mission and the Peace Witness*, there is also a tone of hope for the possibility of mutually enriching integration. See, e.g., Sider, "Call for Evangelical Nonviolence," and Yoder, "Contemporary Evangelical Revival," 52–103.

7. Among scholarly authors, Hughes' *Christian America* is a good example while

tive option for those on the left-of-center edges of evangelicalism and especially among the growing number of "Neo-Anabaptist" religious leaders and scholars, from Shane Claiborne to Scot McKnight, who have perhaps most successfully integrated the activist impulse of both evangelicalism and Anabaptism.[8]

Throughout these developments, the issues raised in *Evangelicalism and Anabaptism* remain as relevant as they were in the 1970s. But given the changing political, religious, and social environment, it would seem there is room for fresh perspective. *The Activist Impulse* seeks to offer such new insights on this ongoing conversation. At the heart of this volume is the notion that, though complex, the intersection of evangelicalism and Anabaptism, both in its historical and contemporary contexts, is rich and dynamic; and by exploring this relationship, new avenues for scholarly inquiry, reflective dialogue, and most of all, greater clarity and understanding will emerge.

The contributors to this volume are professionals from a variety of settings. The majority work in small church-affiliated schools. A number have pastoral experience and speak regularly to both popular and professional audiences. But regardless of their background or professional experience, each of the fifteen writers included below has either professional or personal experience with both the evangelical and Anabaptist traditions. Some are Anabaptist scholars who have pursued topics of research in American evangelicalism. Others are evangelicals who have been influenced or attracted by the richness of the Anabaptist heritage. Several would identify with both the Anabaptist and evangelical traditions.[9] What unifies the contributors

Boyd's *Myth* is representative of a popular espousal of the same position.

8. Claiborne is a popular speaker and writer as well as a founding member of the Simple Way, a religious community in Philadelphia situated within the "New Monastic" movement. McKnight is a New Testament scholar at North Park University. Both Claiborne and McKnight incorporate elements of evangelical and Anabaptist perspectives within their thought and praxis.

9. Given the diversity of backgrounds among the contributors, we have retained certain stylistic features of the individual authors, choosing to provide consistency when needed, but opting not to impose strict conformity on every matter. For example, one chapter may refer to the "Anabaptist-evangelical" relationship while another may mention the "evangelical-Anabaptist" relationship without any substantial difference in meaning. There also may be small variations in the capitalization of certain terms, such as F/fundamentalism or M/modernism. Moreover, instead of assuming a common definition of evangelicalism and Anabaptism from the outset, we allow each author to describe these complex traditions from their own perspective

to this volume is the notion that the evangelical-Anabaptist conversation, and the activist impulse found within it, is worthy of scholarly attention and fresh examination.

The essays offered below are divided into four sections, organized around the various ways evangelicalism and Anabaptism intersect. The first section, "Intersecting Stories," provides a broad overview by leading Anabaptist historians on the historical nexus of evangelicalism and Anabaptism, while the last section, "Intersecting Trajectories," provides three proposals for how an evangelical Anabaptist theology and praxis might look going forward. These sections serve as bookends, therefore, which frame the essays included in the center sections. The second and third sections—"Intersecting Challenges" and "Intersecting Concerns"—are both historical in nature, offering essays on the challenges Mennonites faced during the era of American fundamentalism at the beginning of the twentieth century (which in some ways mirror the challenges evangelicals faced during the same period) as well as examinations of evangelical Anabaptist "experiments" throughout the rest of the twentieth century. The reader will find more specific introductions to the individual chapters at the beginning of each of the four sections.

It goes without saying that, given the complexity of the issues related to the evangelical-Anabaptist intersection, the essays included here will not constitute the final word on this ongoing conversation. Taken together, however, it is our hope that these essays demonstrate the potential for fresh scholarly inquiry, continued conversation, and greater clarity regarding the activist impulse at the intersection of evangelicalism and Anabaptism. Moreover, though we would not presume to speak for the others who have contributed to this volume, as both of us have been profoundly shaped personally and spiritually by the evangelical-Anabaptist intersection, it is our hope that these essays will offer a glimpse into the richness of Kingdom living that is at once irreducibly evangelical and unabashedly Anabaptist.

---

with the hope that definitions of these terms will be arrived at inductively while reading through this volume; though, when necessary, we have provided clarifications or definitions of key terms.

The Activist Impulse

BIBLIOGRAPHY

Boyd, Gregory. *The Myth of a Christian Nation: How the Quest for Political Power Is Destroying the Church*. Grand Rapids: Zondervan, 2006.

Hughes, Richard T. *Christian America and the Kingdom of God*. Champaign, IL: University of Illinois Press, 2009.

Kraus, C. Norman. *Evangelicalism and Anabaptism*. Scottdale, PA: Herald, 1979.

Kraybill, Donald B., Steven M. Nolt, and David L. Weaver-Zercher. *Amish Grace: How Forgiveness Transcended Tragedy*. San Francisco: Josey-Bass, 2007.

Martin, William. *With God on our Side: The Rise of the Religious Right in America*. New York: Broadway, 1997.

Ramseyer, Robert L. "Introduction." In *Mission and the Peace Witness: The Gospel and Christian Discipleship*, edited by Robert L. Ramseyer, 7–8. Scottdale, PA: Herald, 1979.

———, editor. *Mission and the Peace Witness: The Gospel and Christian Discipleship*. Scottdale, PA: Herald, 1979.

Showalter, Richard. "Church Growth Principles and Christian Discipleship." In *Mission and the Peace Witness: The Gospel and Christian Discipleship*, edited by Robert L. Ramseyer, 104–13. Scottdale, PA: Herald, 1979.

Sider, Ronald J. "A Call for Evangelical Nonviolence." In *Mission and the Peace Witness: The Gospel and Christian Discipleship*, edited by Robert L. Ramseyer, 52–67. Scottdale, PA: Herald, 1979.

Yoder, John Howard. "The Contemporary Evangelical Revival and the Peace Churches." In *Mission and the Peace Witness: The Gospel and Christian Discipleship*, edited by Robert L. Ramseyer, 68–103. Scottdale, PA: Herald, 1979.

PART I

Intersecting Stories

Historical Reflection on the Nexus of Evangelicalism and Anabaptism

Introduction to Part I

REFLECTING ON THE PAST is a fitting place to begin an exploration of the intersection of Anabaptism and evangelicalism and the activist impulse found in both traditions. A strong sense of history has been a significant part of Anabaptist and evangelical identity, and narratives of the past continue to play an important role in shaping their respective communities. Not only can we observe significant points of intersection within the past, but the telling of their stories has significantly affected the way Anabaptists and evangelicals have viewed each other. Steven M. Nolt's engaging essay both opens this initial section and serves as a foundation for the volume as a whole. Nolt begins by offering a clear description of Anabaptism's and evangelicalism's activist impulse, setting it in historical context. Nolt then offers several short case studies, which illustrate patterns of evangelical-Anabaptist interaction.

John D. Roth then offers a historical assessment of evangelical-Anabaptist encounter, including a critical overview of Anabaptist historiography on the matter. He highlights the shortcomings of the traditional story and proposes a new paradigm for future conversation—one that reminds us that evangelicals and Anabaptists are both children of the Reformation and therefore share certain tensions and possibly even internal contradictions. Roth finishes by turning our attention to Pilgram Marpeck, the sixteenth-century lay theologian, whose sacramental theology and views on the church offer a model for healthy dialogue between Anabaptists and evangelicals.

John Fea concludes the section with reflections on the limits of the activist impulse for the faithful study of history, arguing that evangelicals and Anabaptists alike often have trouble understanding the past on its own terms as their views can become clouded by political or theological agendas. Fea argues for a method of historical inquiry that seeks more nuanced and empathetic understanding by extending "intellectual hospitality" to the past and the individuals we find there. In so doing, we embrace virtues, such as humility, that both evangelicals and Anabaptists value, and in the process become better Christians as well as better historians.

1

Activist Impulses across Time

North American Evangelicalism and Anabaptism as Conversation Partners

STEVEN M. NOLT

IN THE LAST FIVE decades, Anabaptists and evangelicals have engaged in a conversation, both literal and figurative, that has been enlivening and engaging, cautious and contentious. Consider the following:

- Thousands of Mennonite youth, packing their denominationally-sponsored convention, sing "Come, Now is the Time to Worship," "Your Love is Amazing," and other songs by contemporary Christian artist Brian Doerksen—who in his own youth had left the Mennonite Brethren church for John Wimber's Vineyard Fellowship.[1]

- Connections made at the 1989 National Prayer Breakfast, a Washington DC event often seen as blending evangelical faith and crass nationalism, pave the way for Mennonite peacebuilding work in apartheid-era South Africa.[2]

- During the 1960s, Brethren in Christ educator Arthur M. Climenhaga becomes the second executive director of the National

---

1. More recently Doerksen left Vineyard Fellowship to cofound an independent Bible church in Abbotsford, British Columbia.

2. Sampson and Lederach, *From the Ground Up*, 36–38.

Association of Evangelicals, and Wilbur D. Benedict, who was raised in an Old German Baptist Brethren family, serves as the publisher of *Christianity Today*.³

- In a 1991 fundraising letter, evangelical radio speaker and author John MacArthur appeals to supporters for help in presenting the gospel in creative ways to unsaved people groups, such as the Amish.⁴

- In 1974 more than a dozen Old Colony Mennonite families living near Osler, Saskatchewan, organize Osler Mission Chapel, a church championing assurance of salvation and embracing evangelicalism as liberation from Mennonite tradition.⁵

- In 2007, after participating in a Mennonite conference on ministry in contemporary society, Greg Boyd, an evangelical writer and megachurch pastor, tells readers of his popular blog, "It turns out I'm a Mennonite!" As Mennonites explained their "conviction that the Kingdom of God is radically different from all versions of the Kingdom of the World," Boyd was "excited, because I felt like I found a tribe I could passionately embrace," and "on a deep level, it kind of felt like coming home."⁶

These examples illustrate not only the diversity of the evangelical-Anabaptist conversation, but also some of the distinctive voices, connections, tensions, and choices that exist at the center of this ongoing, historically-rooted relationship. Both traditions, in different ways, are at home in North America, and both share an activist impulse—a desire to convert their Christian convictions into lived religion and a refusal to regard faith as private or merely otherworldly. At the same time, evangelicalism and Anabaptism embody somewhat different

---

3. Climenhaga served 1964–1967; Benedict, 1963–1970.

4. Fundraising letter from "John MacArthur, Jr., Pastor-Teacher," 16 September 1991, author's files. MacArthur told of an Amish man who surreptitiously owned a radio and, thus, could hear MacArthur's "Grace to You" broadcast: "You and I would probably never have an opportunity to share God's truth with the Amish farmer—his sheltered lifestyle prevents that. Yet a simple radio made all the difference in the world.... And right now [because the Amish man can hear "Grace to You"] he is in a strategic position to share God's living Word with others in his village!"

5. Guenther, "Living with the Virus," 237–39.

6. Boyd, "It Turns out I'm a Mennonite!" Online: www.gregboyd.org.

emphases and inclinations, even as each stream encompasses a degree of diversity within itself.

By many measures, Anabaptists and evangelicals are religious kin—although whether the metaphor runs more in the direction of supportive siblings or fraternal feuding is not always clear. What is clear is that members of these branches of the Christian family tree have carried on a vital conversation during their years in North America and especially so in recent decades. If that conversation sometimes took the form of argument and dispute, it was just as often a discourse of shared convictions, imitation, or mutual longing.

To be sure, the shape of this relationship has often been asymmetrical: A numerically small and "sectarian" tradition, on the one hand, and a wide and socially influential movement, on the other. Large numbers of North American evangelicals have little knowledge of Anabaptist theology, nor any direct contact with the Mennonites, Brethren, or Amish who represent it. In contrast, most Anabaptists find themselves in regular interaction with evangelical neighbors, institutions, and ideas, and often have to define themselves religiously in relationship to evangelicalism. Perhaps this asymmetry explains the suspicion and misunderstanding that has sometimes marked this conversation, even as it suggests that the conversation is sure to continue.

Moving past such misunderstanding requires listening to one another's stories. Several years ago Associated Mennonite Biblical Seminary president J. Nelson Kraybill said, "I have resolved to stop comparing the best of my Anabaptist heritage with the worst of evangelicalism."[7] In that spirit, the stories here introduce both traditions and then heed specific exchanges between them, seeking the outlines of the conversation by listening for common and prominent themes.

THE ACTIVIST IMPULSE IN AMERICAN EVANGELICAL HISTORY

In theological terms, evangelicalism is a stream of Protestant Christianity marked by emphases on religious conversion, active and overt expression of faith, the authority of the Bible, and Christ's death on the cross.[8] These hallmarks, as British historian David

---

7. Kraybill, "Is Our Future Evangelical?" 15. The essay was reprinted in several Mennonite venues.

8. Bebbington, *Evangelicalism in Britain*, 2–17.

Bebbington has shown, were common across the north Atlantic world among those who called themselves evangelicals in the 1700s, and they have served as a minimal definition of evangelicalism in the centuries that followed. As a starting point for an *American* evangelical story, this sort of theological definition is necessary but incomplete. These four traits emerged as a cluster in reaction to staid and rational state church systems in the British Isles and defined evangelicalism as a renewal impulse. In early America, by contrast, English-speaking evangelicals were almost everywhere a majority, and in the absence of an official church against which to rebel, shifted from being a protest movement of theological outsiders to being an unofficial establishment. That turn of events did not dull key convictions, but it placed them in a new context, a context in which evangelicalism's impulse to renewal turned from reviving an ailing state church to invigorating the nation itself.[9] Indeed, by the early 1800s evangelicalism, flanked to the right by Catholicism and to the left by Unitarianism, was the dominant religious expression in the United States—an expression marked as much by its earnest sense of responsibility for the nation as by particular doctrines.

Indeed, differences in doctrine and temperament drove the development of evangelicalism along two branches.[10] A Reformed branch, given to systematic theological reflection and institution-building, flourished in most sections of the country, but especially in the North, and fostered an impressive intellectual and organizational world that gave it influence beyond its substantial numbers. Meanwhile, a Wesleyan-Holiness branch, oriented to the work of the Holy Spirit, tended toward emotive (and often emotional) worship, favored revivalism over catechesis, and had a greater openness to women's ministry. The Holiness branch often seemed strongest in cultural and geographical borderlands and also encompassed most African-American evangelicals.

To be sure, both branches shared many things in common, and certain emphases cut across lines. Some in the Reformed camp, such

---

9. Noll, *American Evangelical Christianity*. A helpful collection of essays comparing evangelicalism in various Anglo contexts is *Evangelicalism*, edited by Noll, Bebbington, and Rawlyk. For a different definition of evangelicalism in terms of Continental European concerns and context, see Ward, *Protestant Evangelical Awakening*.

10. See Noll, *America's God*, 161–364.

as Charles Finney and Dwight Moody, adapted revivalism to suit their needs, and some members of both groups made sense of the Bible and human history via premillennial eschatology or dispensational theology, which systematized the Bible's prophetic language and explained society's moral deterioration as a precursor to Christ's second coming. As well, both branches saw themselves as responsible for the vitality of the United States and the spread of the gospel throughout the world—responsibilities they saw as intertwined.[11] (In Canada, evangelicalism more often functioned as an outsider renewal movement, as in Britain, although evangelicalism in the Maritime Provinces often mirrored its American cousin.[12])

In the late nineteenth and early twentieth centuries, both evangelical branches experienced crises—crises that, given the central role of evangelicals in American society, had broad social and political implications. On the Holiness side, Pentecostalism emerged as a dramatically Spirit-infused movement of signs and wonders.[13] It also sparked theological and social reaction from many evangelicals who saw Pentecostalism as sectarian or anti-intellectual or simply unbiblical. Others were uncomfortable with the interracial fellowship that Pentecostalism pioneered, and the way Pentecostal theology seemed to diminish the role of the visible church or undercut male leadership.

Meanwhile, tensions brewing within the Reformed branch eventually became known as the Modernist-Fundamentalist Controversy and reflected different responses to an increasingly pluralist America. For modernists, a desire to maintain Protestantism's leading role in a society being reshaped by immigration and intellectual inquiry led them to redefine beliefs in more generic terms with which few people would be likely to object.[14] For those who came to be known as fundamentalists, however, the crisis created by American pluralism and an impending sense of becoming religious and cultural minorities engendered a militant style of conservative theology defined in

---

11. This was true even of premillennialists, who in the twentieth century were often more pessimistic about the value of social reform.

12. See Rawlyk, *Canada Fire*, and Rawlyk, *Protestant Experience*.

13. Wacker, *Heaven Below*.

14. Marsden, *Understanding*, 44.

even more specific terms, often matched by an impassioned defense of traditional mores.[15]

The battles between fundamentalists and modernists played out in denominational conventions, seminary board rooms, and mission board offices, and were sharpest in the northern United States (and to a certain extend in Canada) where the institutions of Reformed America were concentrated. By 1924 Fundamentalist forces had largely been outflanked and expelled from the centers of influence in the North and Midwest. Coincidentally, in 1925, Tennessee science teacher John Scopes attracted national media attention as he stood trial for teaching evolution. The jury convicted Scopes, but the publicity and the intellectual weakness of the prosecution tarnished traditionalists in every branch of the evangelical family tree.[16]

During the next quarter century, northern fundamentalists and conservative evangelicals of all stripes cast a much lower public profile. Instead—and in a way that diverged from their historic role as cultural custodians—the heirs of nineteenth-century evangelicals turned inward. Those in the Reformed tradition reconstructed new institutions—seminaries and foreign mission agencies, for example—to replace the ones they had lost to the modernists, and they joined Holiness and even Pentecostal groups in building new networks among youth workers, missionaries, and pastors. Charles Fuller and others created mass media alternatives to mainstream commercial outlets they ruefully conceded would be secular. Despite setbacks, the activist impulse had not diminished.[17]

ACTIVIST IMPULSES TODAY

Today evangelicalism is a movement whose identity is both theological and social. Traditional convictions remain at the core of evangelical belief, but evangelicals also define themselves through a loose network

---

15. Marsden, *Fundamentalism*. Following Sandeen in *Roots of Fundamentalism*, some commentators treat dispensationalism as central to Fundamentalism; Marsden's approach is a more complex reading of the developments and debates within the Reformed wing of the American evangelical tradition.

16. Lienesch, *In the Beginning*.

17. See Carpenter, *Revive Us Again*, and Carpenter and Shenk, *Earthen Vessels*.

of often overlapping institutions, affiliations, and personalities that represent their convictions in public ways.[18]

One face of evangelicalism is represented by institutions founded in the 1940s and 1950s by a group of self-identified "neo-evangelicals." These leaders, who had come out of northern fundamentalist circles, questioned the inflexible style of fundamentalism and sought to reengage society in positive ways.[19] These new evangelicals, many of them based in Boston and Philadelphia, such as Carl F. H. Henry and Harold J. Ockenga, formed the National Association of Evangelicals (1942), National Religious Broadcasters (1942), Youth for Christ (1942), Fuller Theological Seminary (1947), World Vision (1950), Evangelical Theological Society (1956), and *Christianity Today* (1956), among others. When these Northern institutions teamed up with Southern preacher Billy Graham in 1949, their efforts began to attract attention outside conservative Christian circles. Graham's 1956 crusade in Los Angeles, for example, grabbed headlines across the country, and Graham was soon a presidential confidant. For many Americans, this collection of names and organizations still defines the evangelical movement.[20]

Another face of contemporary evangelicalism took shape in the 1960s in southern California, where migrants from the Ozarks and the Midwest, such as Pat Boone and Tim LaHaye, had combined their "plain folk" religion with West Coast pragmatism and a firm belief that the political order should reflect those values.[21] Although never confined to Southern California, this impulse surfaced in support for California governor Ronald Reagan's rhetorical attacks on atheistic communism and Berkeley liberals. Matched with dispensational theology, this version of evangelicalism energized support for the State of Israel. Combined with a concern for the vulnerable, it fueled the pro-

18. A dated, but still helpful, collection in this regard is Dayton and Johnston, *Variety*, which includes a chapter on Mennonites (245–73) by C. Norman Kraus.

19. After the mid-1940s self-identified Fundamentalists remained, but they were a more isolated lot, represented by the likes of Carl McIntyre, Bob Jones University, and King James-only Baptist churches.

20. Wuthnow, *Restructuring*, 173–214. One very helpful window into this side of evangelicalism, from the 1940s–1980s, is Marsden, *Reforming Fundamentalism*, which focuses on the role of Fuller Seminary in the evolution of American fundamentalism. Although Fuller Seminary developed in southern California, for much of its early history its president resided, in *absentia*, in Boston.

21. Dochuk, *Bible Belt*. See also Miller, *Billy Graham*.

life movement. In 1976 reporters were perplexed by Jimmy Carter's claim to being "born again," but by the 1980s evangelicals were widely regarded as a major force in politics.[22]

The charismatic movement has shaped yet another expression of contemporary evangelicalism. This 1960s movement brought the Spirit-inspired signs of Pentecostalism—healing, speaking in tongues, and so on—into churches that had traditionally looked askance at Pentecostalism or questioned its spiritual legitimacy. Although the charismatic movement was at times associated with particular groups, such as the Jesus People in the 1970s, televangelists in the 1980s, or Vineyard Fellowship in the 1990s, the influence of the charismatic movement was more often its style and informality than its pneumatology. Raising hands in worship and guitar-chord "praise songs" that diverged from traditional hymns came to define large portions of the evangelical landscape.[23]

By the twenty-first century evangelicalism was increasingly diverse, and worship style and musical tastes are only one measure. There are mega-churches and alternative communities, evangelical environmentalists and those drawn to the ancient church. Meanwhile, a new era of mass immigration has brought millions of Latino, Asian, and African Christians and would-be converts into evangelical circles. Today thousands of churches comprised of new immigrants, many undocumented, embrace an evangelical identity, even as polls reveal that many white evangelicals are among the most ardent supporters of tighter borders.[24] And north of the border, Canadian evangelicals share theological commitments with co-believers to the south but live in a context that has tempered their style and spirituality.[25]

Despite the diversity, identifiable traits continue to mark the evangelical family and have sometimes even trended toward greater coherence. For example, in recent years megachurch pastor and author Rick Warren has used the language of a "purpose driven life"

---

22. Consult Weber, *Road to Armageddon*; Koop and Schaeffer, *Whatever Happened*; and Brint and Schroedel, eds., *Evangelicals and Democracy*.

23. Burgess, *New International Dictionary*; Harrell, *All Things Are Possible*.

24. Carroll, *Christians at the Border*; and the UnDocumented.tv project of World Relief, an arm of the National Association of Evangelicals. See also the related work by Emerson and Smith, *Divided by Faith*.

25. Reimer, *Continental Divide*, uses comparative cross-border survey data, including data on Mennonite Brethren.

to popularize the doctrine of predestination among evangelicals who had not previously claimed it.[26] But perhaps the most common traits are those that express the activist impulse—the impulse to act on beliefs, to evangelize the world, and to transform society, through preaching, acts of mercy, and loving solidarity with others. Indeed, a careful study of evangelicals' charitable giving—a fair measure of the animating values of any group—reveals that their chief concerns are not funding domestic political causes, but supporting food pantries, homeless shelters, crisis pregnancy centers, and international relief and reconstruction ministries.[27]

AN ACTIVIST IMPULSE AMONG NORTH AMERICAN ANABAPTISTS

Despite its small size, the North American Anabaptist family has been far from monolithic. Its Mennonite and Amish branches stem from the Radical Reformation of the sixteenth-century, and its Brethren branches trace roots both to the Radical Reformation and to Radical Pietism of the late seventeenth-century. The Anabaptist radicals of the 1520s and 1530s refused infant baptism, rejected the state-church system, and sought to follow New Testament teaching—especially the words of Jesus—even when civil and religious authorities told them that doing so was illegal. Anabaptists' refusal to take up the sword or swear oaths, coupled with their determination, in many cases, to spread their beliefs, earned them the opprobrium of officials and resulted in the martyrdom of perhaps twenty-five hundred forebears of today's Mennonites and Amish.[28] By the late 1600s persecution was less often lethal, but when a group of Radical Pietists, who began calling themselves Brethren, absorbed Anabaptist ideas and broke with their respective Lutheran and Reformed churches, they were socially and economically stigmatized. Undeterred, in 1708 they acted to es-

---

26. Thuesen, *Predestination*, 12, 209–16. By dint of its influential institutions and intellectual strength, the historic Reformed wing of evangelicalism has also had considerable influence in evangelical discussions of women's leadership, even among groups stemming from the historic Holiness wing of the movement.

27. Hamilton, "More Money," 130–32.

28. Snyder, *Anabaptist History*. The first Anabaptist baptisms took place in 1525 in Switzerland and in 1530 in the Netherlands.

tablish a visible church renewed through the right practice of baptism and the Lord's Supper and the ethical commands of Christ.[29]

The activist impulse among Anabaptists was apparent in their commitment to applying their faith in everyday ethics and doing so in the social context of a believers church whose collective way of life was visibly different from worldly society. Adult baptism was the gateway into this church and collective discipline kept the boundaries of behavior clear. Disagreement among Anabaptists, compounded by their lack of centralized ecclesial authority, resulted in a variety of groups, including, after 1693, the Amish, whose discipline and sense of separation from society was often keener than that of the Mennonites. Among the Brethren these Anabaptist sensibilities combined with a legacy of mystical Pietism to heighten the importance of the church as the Bride of Christ "without spot or wrinkle."[30]

As with Anglo-evangelicals, these theological roots and expressions—while essential—explain Anabaptist identity in North America only in part. As Mennonites began immigrating to North America (after 1683), along with Brethren (after 1719), their Anabaptist activist impulse played in a new environment in which their particular Christian practices earned them an ethnic niche instead of martyrdom. So although Anabaptist theology affirmed that blood was not thicker than baptismal water, Mennonite and Brethren communities practiced their faith in concrete ways and in specific settings that often ended up nurturing ethnic identities.[31]

In the relatively tolerant atmosphere of nineteenth-century North America, Mennonites, Brethren, and Amish practiced what they termed a "nonconformed, nonresistant faith of the New Testament." Nonconformity might express itself in a humility theology that eschewed expensive dress and home décor, higher education, and conspicuous production. But nonconformity to the world was often most pointed in nonresistance. Drawing on Jesus' words in the Sermon on the Mount to "resist not evil" (Matt 5:39), nonresistance included a refusal to participate in warfare or defend one's rights through litigation.

---

29. Meier, *Schwarzenau Brethren*. The first Brethren baptism took place in 1708.

30. Snyder, *Footsteps*; Bowman, *Brethren Society*, 46–50.

31. Schlabach, *Peace, Faith, Nation*, 19–116; Bowman, *Brethren Society*, 23–92; and Nolt, "'Two-Kingdom' People."

For some Anabaptists nonresistance also implied an unwillingness to hold public office, serve on juries, or vote.

CONVERSATIONS OVER TIME

Emphasizing nonconformity and pacifist dissent can obscure the many ways Anabaptists have been integrated into North American society, living much of their lives as farmers, daughters, professionals, husbands, students, or shopkeepers very much like their neighbors. They have interacted socially and economically with others and exchanged ideas. And evangelicalism has often been a partner in that exchange.

As heirs of the Protestant Reformation, Anabaptists shared basic theological convictions with most Anglo-evangelicals. True, an influential Mennonite leader such as bishop Benjamin Eby (1785–1853) could summarize the Christian message without mentioning the cross and barely noting the resurrection (focusing instead on obeying divine commands), but most nineteenth-century Mennonite religious writings reflected evangelical convictions concerning God's grace, Christ's atoning death, and other matters.[32] The Pietist heritage of Brethren churches ensured that their discourse more often matched, in vocabulary and tone, the English-speaking evangelical mainstream even as Brethren retained distinctive teachings on immersion baptism, nonresistance, and plain living.[33]

Anabaptists typically engaged the Wesleyan-Holiness wing of evangelicalism, attracted to its bias for personal ethics but at the same time ambivalent about its more individualist and emotional character. In the 1780s Anabaptist-Holiness interaction birthed a new group that blended both traditions, the so-called River Brethren, later renamed Brethren in Christ. In the mid-nineteenth century Mennonites in Pennsylvania, Indiana, and Ontario who sought to infuse their churches with Holiness-inspired revivalism found themselves excommunicated. They formed the core of what eventually became the Mennonite

---

32. B. Eby, *Kirchen-Geschichte*, 7–10. Weaver, *Keeping Salvation Ethical*, shows that Mennonite writers had a distinctive ethical cast to their theology, but that its content was broadly evangelical even if it was sometimes pointedly anti-Calvinist.

33. Miller, *Doctrine Defended*.

Brethren in Christ, a forerunner of today's Missionary Church.[34] In contrast, an Old Order movement in Anabaptist circles emerged in the 1850s–1880s in part as a reaction against evangelical innovations and alliances. The Old Order Amish, Old Order Mennonites, and Old German Baptist Brethren strengthened their sense of nonconformity in the face of evangelical overtures and defined themselves in opposition to revivalism, Sunday school, foreign mission work, and the like.[35]

But schism and reaction were not the only byproducts of the conversation with evangelicalism. More common were Mennonites or Brethren who remained committed to the distinctive tenets of their tradition, yet also read books from Fleming Revell's Colportage Association or organized Sunday schools by taking cues from Methodist and Presbyterian neighbors. During the later nineteenth and early twentieth centuries, a significant slice of North American Anabaptists engaged in a burst of organizational activity—launching schools, foreign mission work, and publishing concerns—that often drew inspiration from sources such as Dwight Moody, the Student Volunteer Movement, the Christian and Missionary Alliance, and other evangelical pioneers.[36]

During the twentieth century, however, the relatively comfortable place many Anabaptists had found in society was shaken by the nationalistic patriotism of two world wars and the cold war that followed. The quest to find alternatives to military service, or to resist conscription, became new hallmarks of Anabaptist identity. So too became efforts to ease human suffering—providing "a cup of cold water" to refugees from warfare, for example—through organizations such as Mennonite Central Committee and Brethren Voluntary Service.[37] Some key Anabaptist leaders began to question trends toward cultural assimilation, and they articulated a new sort of sectarian theology, positioning Anabaptism as a "third way" that was neither Catholic nor conventionally Protestant. In an influential 1943 essay entitled "The Anabaptist Vision," Mennonite historian Harold S.

---

34. Wittlinger, *Quest for Piety*; Lageer, *Merging Streams*.

35. Hostetler, "Old Orders," 5–25.

36. Schlabach, *Gospel Versus Gospel*. Interestingly, although this book's critique of Fundamentalist influences on Mennonite mission work drew criticism from some evangelically-inclined Mennonites, old order readers—or at least those old orders who read academic history—warmly endorsed its message.

37. Bush, *Two Kingdoms*; Kreider, *Cup of Water*.

Bender (1897–1962) argued that the sixteenth-century radicals had accomplished a more thoroughgoing Reformation than had mainstream Protestantism, and he called on Mennonites to embrace discipleship, community, and nonresistance as the distinctive genius of Anabaptism. In a somewhat different and much more sophisticated way, Mennonite theologian John Howard Yoder (1927–1997) offered a contemporary neo-Anabaptist theology in his 1972 book, *The Politics of Jesus*, which introduced these themes to a much wider audience.[38]

In his early career, Bender had presented theological liberalism as the major threat to contemporary Anabaptism, and in the "Anabaptist Vision" he spoke of Anabaptism as sharing much in common with orthodox, evangelical faith. But soon, Bender and other Mennonites who had worked with Anabaptist conscientious objectors during World War II began to shift their rhetoric. Bender had overseen the collection data on conscientious objection, and the data were startling.[39] Almost half of drafted men from Mennonite churches (and a much higher percentage in Brethren groups) had gone to war. As they parsed the draft census, these leaders saw a clear correlation between the influence of fundamentalism and a lack of peace conviction. Bender shifted from fingering liberalism to identifying fundamentalism as the greatest threat to Anabaptist faithfulness. During the 1950s he struggled to nuance his view, publicly approving of the neo-evangelical Fuller Seminary while becoming more critical of evangelicals to that school's right.[40] Bender's influence was wide-ranging, and for generations of Mennonite academics and denominational leaders the message was often one of wariness toward evangelical encounters.

Nevertheless, the neo-Anabaptist theological revival (from Bender to Yoder and beyond) had minimal impact in many parts of the North American Anabaptist world. In groups such as the Conservative Mennonite Conference or in pockets of the Church of

---

38. Bender, "Anabaptist Vision," 3–24; Hershberger, *Recovery*; Yoder, *Politics*. For more context, see Toews, *Mennonites in American Society*.

39. One summary of the data is Hershberger, *Mennonite Church*, 34–48.

40. Bender, "Outside Influences," 45–48, esp. "Note by Author," 48, in which Bender distinguished "The term 'Fundamentalism' (with a capital 'F')" from the "conservative evangelical Protestantism" of Harold J. Ockenga and his "new evangelicalism (the Fuller self-definition of its position)" that is orthodox "in doctrine but manifests a social consciousness and responsibility." Bender cited David C. Cook publications, Fundamentalist radio broadcasts, *Sunday School Times*, the Scofield Reference Bible, and other examples as negative influences.

the Brethren, the 1960s were marked by debates over plain dress and other nonconformity issues, rather than the relevance of the politics of Jesus. For these Anabaptists, evangelicalism provided a fresh way to talk about salvation and discipleship in terms other than the culture of plainness that now seemed like a stale badge of ethnicity rather than an expression of faith. At the same time, a persistent cultural conservatism made these folk sympathetic to mainstream evangelicals' concerns about changing public mores.[41]

Meanwhile, for those in the neo-Anabaptist camp, the political muscle that evangelicals began exercising in the 1970s—first noticeable in the work of Jerry Falwell and others in opposing the United States' return of the Panama Canal Zone to Panama—seemed to confirm their fear that involvement with evangelicals would be an exercise in exchanging serious discipleship for shallow nationalism.[42]

In a context of escalating "culture wars," conversation partners on all sides ran the risk of stereotyping or imposing simplistic categories that skew an understanding of the historically nuanced exchange among Anabaptists and evangelicals. The encounters that follow offer three windows into complex conversations that have been congenial and conflicted, driven by ethnic commitments and theological convictions, and played out in homes, church meetinghouses, and school campuses.

EVANGELICAL BIBLE STUDY IN MANHATTAN (1920s–1960s)

Biblicism has been central to both evangelicals and Anabaptists, so it might not be surprising that Bible study would bring members of both traditions together. Yet the sorts of fruitful connections that

---

41. See the forthcoming history of the Conservative Mennonite Conference by Nathan E. Yoder; see also a wide variety of Mennonite-authored books that drew on evangelical authors and sources for practical advice on evangelism and church life, such as Stutzman, *Welcome*. See also a deeply-documented summary of Mennonite participation in "Probe '72" and "Key '73," in Bush, "Anabaptism Born Again," 37–38. For Mennonite and Brethren in Christ views on social and cultural issues in the 1970s, see the survey data in Kauffman and Harder, *Four Centuries Later*.

42. For a collection of thoughtful critiques from Mennonites at the time, see Kraus, ed., *Anabaptism and Evangelicalism*. Whether Falwell should be considered an evangelical or a Fundamentalist has been a point of debate; Harding, *Book of Falwell*, argues that he was able to appeal politically to people in both camps.

developed between Mennonite students and a group of evangelicals associated with Biblical Seminary in New York in the mid-twentieth century helped transform Mennonite Bible teaching and understanding of biblical authority.[43]

Unlike many evangelicals, Mennonites in the early twentieth century did not possess a long-standing or well-defined theology of inspiration or biblical authority.[44] Mennonites were thoroughgoing biblicists, to be sure, but they used the Bible in a piecemeal, nonsystematic way, mixing literalism and figurative reading. With "a certain loose artistry" they looked to biblical texts not only for their common-sensical, historical meaning but also for simple "practical insights and guidance," regardless of the wider context of a passage.[45] For example, Jesus' post-resurrection words to Mary, "touch me not," could be both an historical statement of the risen Christ and a practical directive that women and men should sit separately during worship services. Likewise, God's separating light from darkness in Genesis 1 was an account of creation, but more often in Mennonite preaching it served as evidence of God's desire that the church be a separate people, visibly different from "the world."

In the early twentieth century such approaches to the Bible still suited Old Order Mennonites and Amish, but for the Anabaptist majority eager to engage in mission work and whose business and educational experience led them to accept more rational categories of historically-conscious thought, these older approaches to Scripture became implausible. Which teachings were historically conditioned, and how could one decide? In what sense was Scripture inspired, and how could one logically talk about that? Mennonite tradition offered little guidance and few resources for coming to terms with the Bible in contemporary ways or applying Scripture in ways that made sense to others.

Few Mennonites found the approach of the new higher criticism appealing, but the alternatives offered by the theory of inerrancy or of

---

43. For detail and documentation on the story summarized here, see Nolt, "Evangelical Encounter," 389–417.

44. The 1632 Dordrecht Confession, used by many North American Mennonites through the 1920s, had no article on Scripture, but simply assumed biblical authority.

45. Schlabach, *Peace, Faith, Nation*, 108. Mixing literal and figurative rendering of Scripture had been common among pre-modern Protestants—see Frei, *Eclipse*, 17–50.

dispensationalism were also less than satisfactory. Although a handful of American Mennonites attended schools, such as Westminster Seminary, that espoused those doctrines, and more from the Midwest attended Moody Bible Institute, a good number of leaders and lay members remained puzzled, or even suspicious. They found the collection of philosophical affirmations and axioms that were necessarily presuppositions to inerrancy to be a curious distraction from simply reading the Bible, and dispensationalism projected Jesus' teaching into the future in ways that shortchanged obedience. And yet, given liberal alternatives, these fundamentalist resources at least signaled a serious regard for Scripture, which Mennonites appreciated.[46]

It was in this time of unsettledness, during the 1920s, that members of the two largest Mennonite bodies—the Mennonite Church and the General Conference Mennonite Church—discovered Biblical Seminary in New York, an interdenominational evangelical school in midtown Manhattan. From 1930 to 1970, evangelicals at Biblical Seminary provided a new way to understand biblical authority and make the Bible relevant in the modern world, offered a path between fundamentalism and modernism, trained a generation of leaders, and supplied a model for Mennonite theological education.

Chartered in 1900, Biblical Seminary in New York was known for promoting inductive Bible study.[47] Although many American evangelicals celebrated induction, Biblical Seminary founders and faculty believed that few actually practiced it. Coming to the text with doctrinal commitments in mind, students read with an eye for passages that supported their dogmatic categories. So Biblical Seminary rejected dispensationalism, Calvinist systematics, and precise theories of inspiration as deductive accoutrements that hindered Bible study. Similarly, they eschewed liberal theories of the evolution of religion and higher criticism's demand that scholars suspend faith in favor of skepticism. The school purposely had an evangelically diverse set of trustees and faculty, and sought to teach "in such a way as to avoid provoking the spirit of controversy and to foster unity among all students" so as to graduate "constructive, nondisputatious" alumni. Its brand of

---

46. See, for example, E. Miller, "Moody, Fundamentalism and Mennonites." For context, see Noll, *Between Faith and Criticism*.

47. For a history of BSNY as an evangelical school, see Nolt, "Avoid Provoking," 318–40 (322–23 provide archival citations for the quotations in this paragraph).

evangelicalism was, one faculty member observed, "regarded as too conservative for the liberals and too radical by the conservatives."

The first Mennonites to enroll at Biblical were missionaries on furlough, who presumably had learned of the school from colleagues overseas. By the 1930s Mennonite attendance was steady and continued so through the 1960s. At one point twenty-two Mennonites were enrolled at the same time, comprising a sizable portion of the school's roughly one hundred and fifty-member student body. During the middle decades of the twentieth century, it is likely that no graduate seminary attracted more Mennonites than Biblical Seminary, and from 1943 to 1968 the school's trustees included influential Mennonite administrator, Orie O. Miller (1892–1977), who heightened the seminary's visibility in the church.

Mennonite student Stanley C. Shenk (1919–2010) recalled that "the seminary was conservative in interpretation and doctrine—and yet relaxed and tolerant." When Shenk had briefly studied at Eastern Baptist, he was troubled by professors who "rammed Second Isaiah down our throats." At Biblical, hard questions about how to interpret Isaiah also emerged, but they emerged out of inductive study and not from modernist theories.[48] The school's curriculum was built around Bible book study courses in which students worked inductively through one text after another. The "biblio-centric" approach, as it was called, created a level playing field among an interdenominational student body that regularly included more than thirty groups—Free Methodists, United Brethren, Swedish Baptists, and Nazarenes, as well as evangelical members of Presbyterian and Episcopalian bodies. For Mennonites unsure of where they belonged in America's larger ecclesiastical scheme, there was safety in a group of minorities. The school took diversity in stride. Students elected Mennonite George Smoker, conspicuous for his adherence to plain garb, as student body president, and supported pacifist convictions (if arrived at inductively!) during World War II. The school was also known for its openness to female faculty and students—often from Holiness traditions in which women's ministry had a long history—and the generation of Mennonite leaders who attended Biblical warmed to women's leadership as they studied under and alongside evangelical women.

---

48. Stanley C. Shenk, interview by author, February 3, 1995.

When General Conference and Mennonite Churches opened their own small seminaries in 1945 and 1946, in Chicago and in Goshen, Indiana, they modeled their curriculum on Biblical Seminary by requiring an inductive Bible sequence of courses and downplaying systematic theology. What is more, the Mennonite school's first generation of faculty included at least ten members with strong ties to Biblical Seminary, and who assigned textbooks by Biblical Seminary teachers and alumni.[49]

Evangelicals at Biblical Seminary also provided Mennonites with a new language for talking about biblical authority that bypassed the fundamentalist inerrancy arguments of J. Gresham Machen and Charles Trumbull and instead focused on "the instrumental worth of holy Scripture in forming responsible Christian character." Simply put, the Bible was authoritative because it changed lives. Such an approach fit Mennonite concern to gauge faithfulness in terms of discipleship, and bridged traditional convictions and modern contexts.[50] As the "Battle for the Bible" raged among conservative Christians in the 1970s, the inductive-instrumental framework gained from evangelicals in New York grounded a Mennonite response that upheld biblical authority without recourse to inerrancy.[51]

The influence of Biblical Seminary came at a critical time for Mennonites caught in a period of historic transition.[52] It is easy to imagine the bitter turmoil that might have ensued as they struggled to translate their traditional biblicism into a contemporary idiom. Instead, evangelicals in New York played a key role in saving Mennonites from such a fate.

---

49. The Church of the Brethren's Bethany Biblical Seminary (today, Bethany Theological Seminary) had something of a connection to B.S.N.Y., as well, through Bethany's founder, Albert C. Wieand, who had taught briefly at B.S.N.Y. in the early 1900s; see Kostlevy, *Bethany Seminary*, 20–23.

50. Kuist, *These Words*; Traina, *Methodical Bible Study*. See, for example, the influence of the inductive-instrumental framework in *A Christian Declaration*.

51. Lindsell, *Battle for the Bible*; Swartley, *Mark*, 235–38; and Zehr, *Biblical Criticism*, 65, 73, 81, 100–104.

52. Mennonite ties to the school ended in the early 1970s when intense financial pressures forced the seminary to close. Reopened as New York Theological Seminary, the school had a new and smaller faculty, a new curriculum, and a new location—and it lost most of its original evangelical constituency.

ETHNICITY AND REVIVAL ON THE PRAIRIES (1950S)

Despite evangelicals' often sharp criticism of popular culture and mainstream mores, evangelicalism as a movement has often been a means of acculturation for ethnic minority churches, from Swedish Covenanters to Korean Presbyterians. Immigrant groups seeking to navigate the unfamiliar often found that "militant anti-modernists' ambivalence toward aspects of American culture resembled" their own misgivings, and "there is little doubt that many independent Bible churches attracted considerable numbers of northern European ethnics, who found a congenial form of Americanism" in evangelical circles.[53] And many others who never considered joining an independent church, nevertheless thought it wise to take cues from long-established English-speaking neighbors who were cultural insiders yet harbored religiously-informed reservations about mainstream morals.

During the 1940s and 1950s these themes played out among Mennonites on the Canadian prairies. Without dismissing religious conviction, observers recognized the appeal of innovative, interdenominational, English-speaking evangelicalism to Mennonite town dwellers, businessmen, and entrepreneurially-oriented young pastors looking for ways to make religious sense of their environment. Descendants of 1870s and 1920s arrivals from Russia and the Soviet Union, Manitoba's Mennonites were divided into at least ten subgroups. In most of these, bishops vested with broad authority preached in German and oversaw catechism classes that served as a gateway to baptism and, in effect, marriage and participation in the adult world. That world was further regulated by the *bruderschaft* (brotherhood meeting) of male adult baptized members, which often made decisions that limited both churchly and economic innovation. In their own ways, Sunday schools, the accumulation of wealth, and moving to the city posed threats that the bishops and *bruderschaft* guarded against. Following World War I, the most tradition-minded Mennonites had moved to Mexico in reaction to an aggressive program of anglicization in the province's public schools, but by the 1940s and 1950s those who had remained in Canada faced new questions of how to be in, but not of, the world.[54]

---

53. Marsden, *Fundamentalism*, 194–95. See also Alumkal, *Asian American Churches*.

54. Epp, *Mennonites in Canada*, 94–297, 421–29.

For the Mennonite Brethren and some other Mennonite groups, schools such as Prairie Bible Institute in Three Hills, Alberta, Briercrest Bible Institute in Caronport, Saskatchewan, and Winnipeg Bible College offered places for young people to become familiar with English variations on the themes of conversion and foreign missions that Mennonite Brethren had hummed in a German key. In turn, recruiters and evangelists tied to these schools itinerated in Mennonite circles, preaching in German as necessary, but including messages of dispensationalism and child evangelism that were novel even to Mennonites sympathetic to the missionary programs the Bible institutes represented.[55]

For other Mennonites, the challenge of acculturation was more than linguistic. During the 1950s, for example, rural members of the Kleine Gemeinde Mennonites in southeastern Manitoba moved into the town of Steinbach. There the entire system of social separation on which a traditional notion of the church had rested seemed uncomfortable, if not nonsensical, to younger members. Alarmed by the increasing lure of assimilation to Canadian consumer society, some rural Kleine Gemeinde members had moved to Mexico in 1948, bolstering the relative influence of the new town-dwelling members and setting the stage for those remaining in Canada to negotiate their "way in a wider English-speaking world through the language of evangelicalism."[56]

Led by civic-minded pastor Ben D. Reimer (1909–1994), the Steinbach congregation in 1952 pressed to change its name to Evangelical Mennonite Church, purchased a piano, diminished distinctive dress, and rejected shunning and other practices that Reimer took to be defensive church discipline, in favor of aggressive church growth and the planting of a new church in the city of Winnipeg.[57]

In the summer of 1957 a coalition of evangelically-oriented leaders and laymembers staged perhaps the most publicly dramatic example of their agenda, inviting a U.S. Mennonite evangelist named George R. Brunk II to a four-community, English-language preaching campaign to light "revival fire" in Mennonite communities. Based

---

55. Regehr, *Mennonites in Canada*, 208, 239–40. Briercrest Bible College had been founded by Mennonite-reared Henry Hildebrand (1911–2006).

56. Loewen, *Diaspora*, 102–16; quotation, 112.

57. Ibid., 116–22.

in Virginia, Brunk employed a sophisticated system of tents, trucks, and amplification that mimicked, on a smaller scale, the methods that Billy Graham had catapulted to prominence in 1949. Since 1951, in the eastern United States, Brunk had preached a message that, for complex reasons, had legitimated aspects of East Coast Mennonite tradition and authority. But when Reimer and other progressive ministers and businessmen invited Brunk to preach in their towns, the effect was anything but traditional.[58]

In June Brunk's tent went up for three weeks in Steinbach, then moved on for similar periods in Winker, Altona, and Winnipeg. Night after night, Brunk offered an English message of "severe criticism" of churches "trapped in linguistic, social, cultural, and religious traditions."[59] A sympathetic newspaper reporter summarized a key feature of Brunk's preaching as "faith superseding tradition." "Tradition can be either master or servant to the Christian faith," the journalist explained, and "In the lives of many Mennonites in southern Manitoba tradition was definitely assuming the master role. This expressed itself in various ways . . . That the mission of the church was cultural, rather than spiritual, was the opinion of others. The practices of the past were authority enough for the individual, said some." But now, "In all of the campaigns these falsehoods were exposed. The exposure struck deep into the heart of a formalistic and traditionalistic Mennonite community life, but thus became part of the ongoing revival," which others described as "revival fire" burning away both sin and Germanic ethnicity.[60]

Reimer and other organizers were heartened by the "Scores of lost [people who] found forgiveness of sin and peace for their souls, as they . . . surrendered to the Lord," and the reported conversions (approximately one thousand) and renewed commitments (at least sixteen hundred), yet they admitted that not everyone in the community was "always in full agreement with the method and the message employed."[61] Here were conversions legitimated by "a neutral

58. See [Epp, ed.], *Revival Fires in Manitoba*, [5, 7, 12]. See also [Klassen, ed.], *Revival Fires in British Columbia* for a similar report from the next year, when Brunk preached among Mennonites in that province. [Editors and page numbers are not printed in original documents but have been supplied here.]

59. Regehr, *Mennonites in Canada*, 210.

60. [Epp, ed.], *Revival Fires in Manitoba*, [15–16].

61. Ibid., [12, 17–18]. Ben Reimer labeled 1957 "a new era in the history of the

outsider" and witnessed by an interdenominational audience—quite unconnected to a baptismal catechism class and unaccountable to the *bruderschaft*. Not only did revivalism displace communal religious authorities, its supporters began immediately to mimic the evening and midweek programming of neighboring English churches. Indeed, although the planning committee had employed a revivalist who shared something of their Anabaptist heritage, a result of the campaign was a sense of ecumenicity that extended beyond the Mennonite pale.[62]

Significant, too, was the role that businessmen had taken in promoting the revival, through advertising sponsorship, strategic use of CFAM radio news, and revival program booklets that emphasized that "the Southern Manitoba Mennonite community is progressive and fast developing in the economic, educational, and cultural areas."[63] Mennonite traditionalists who moved to Mexico had carefully limited household production and consumption, but those who remained in Canada embraced evangelicalism and entrepreneurship as twin blessings. A theology that blessed individual conversion and personal religious authority not only reduced the role of the bishop, it also sanctified the individual initiative and authority that was at the heart of agribusiness and entrepreneurship, providing a potent combination of faith and enterprise.[64]

Certainly ethnicity was not entirely burned away by the "revival fires" of 1957, nor was acculturation the only dynamic among earnest Christians that summer. But in both obvious and more subtle ways evangelicalism—its language, methods, and way of making sense of the world—were slowly providing Mennonites with tools "for drawing new cultural and moral boundaries in the unfamiliar territory of Canadian culture."[65]

Mennonite churches," because eight different groups "united in a warm, co-operative effort to reach the lost for the Lord Jesus Christ" and sponsored Brunk, who alone "could have stimulated such genuine co-operation among the established groups" (18). Three highly traditionalist Mennonite groups in the region (Chortitzer, Sommerfelder, and Old Colony) did not participate.

62. [Epp, ed.], *Revival Fires in Manitoba*, [5–6]; Loewen, *Diaspora*, 118–22.
63. [Epp, ed.], *Revival Fires in Manitoba*, [4, 16].
64. Moreton, *To Serve God and Wal-Mart*; Loewen, *Diaspora*, 59–70, 169–201.
65. Guethner, "Virus," 239.

CONFLICT AND CONCORD OVER THE AIRWAYS (1960s–2000s)

Evangelicals have often been innovative communicators, and during the middle decades of the twentieth century they used radio and other mass media to create alternatives to secular broadcasts, build parachurch networks among believers, and spread their message to unbelievers.[66] During those same years, some Mennonites were battling the influence of broadcasting in any form.[67] Opposition to radio (and later television) stemmed from the secular or simply frivolous nature of programming on the newly-organized Columbia and Mutual networks, and few Mennonites were as resolute in their anti-radio stance as leaders of the Lancaster Mennonite Conference, a 15,000-member group centered in eastern Pennsylvania. The conference had a long tradition of trying to limit the influence of worldliness in members' lives, and its pronouncements against radio as a medium of popular music and secular drama seem to have been effective in keeping radios out of members' homes. In many congregations, ownership was a "test of membership," and one could be excommunicated for owning a receiver set.

In 1954 the Conference softened its stance a bit. Still certain that "the influence of the use of the radio in its entirety is not conducive to the spiritual upbuilding of the Christian home and church," the Conference forbade ordained ministers from having radios in their homes. But ownership would no longer be a test of membership for laity—though the conference continued to strongly "discourage its use and distribution," and in most congregations a radio listener would not be trusted to be a Sunday school teacher or hold any other position of influence.[68] (Television remained off-limits for everyone.)

Then, in 1959, Youth for Christ evangelist and broadcasting pioneer Percy B. Crawford (1902–1960) launched a Christian radio station, WDAC, in the heart of Lancaster Conference.[69] "This posed

---

66. E.g., Blumhofer, *Aimee Semple McPherson*.

67. See "Radio Broadcasting" and "Radio" for context and examples of Mennonites who embraced radio.

68. "Statement of Christian Doctrine and Rules and Discipline of the Mennonite Church, Lancaster Conference, Approved September 16, 1954," 22.

69. The Canadian-born Crawford spent most of his ministry in the Philadelphia area. A graduate of Wheaton College, he was also one of the early graduates of Fundamentalist-inspired Westminster Theological Seminary. He had begun a regular radio program (from Philadelphia) in 1931. An entrepreneur, he began a number

a real dilemma for the [Lancaster Conference] bishops," recalls John Eby, a Mennonite and long-time program director at WDAC. The presumption against radio had been its secular influence, "but here was a station that broadcast hymns and gospel preaching." WDAC was a commercial station, but did not run advertisements on Sundays, and its announcers frequently included words of Scripture along with station identification.[70]

Understanding that Mennonites were a large share of the station's potential market, and that Mennonite leaders might reasonably fear that if they endorsed listening to WDAC some members would soon be scanning the entire radio dial, WDAC management "bought and distributed hundreds, if not several thousand, fixed-tuned radios which could pull in only WDAC's 94.5 FM signal." Mennonites snapped up the fixed-tuned receivers, allowing them to listen exclusively to Christian radio, which both appeased the bishops' anxiety and created a remarkably loyal listener base for the next half century.[71]

In some ways, WDAC is an unusual station. It consistently ranks in the top five (and sometimes claims the number one spot) in Arbitron market ratings, which is unprecedented in Christian radio. In other ways, the station is typical of Christian broadcasters with a lineup of noted evangelical speakers—Charles Swindoll, James Dobson, David Jeremiah—and Christian music, although the music style tends to be traditional rather than contemporary. Recent surveys reveal that about one quarter of today's listeners are Mennonites—the largest share of any denomination—and suggest that a large portion of Mennonites in the region listen to WDAC.[72] Influence is always difficult to measure, but presumably the inspirational format, doctrinal teaching, and perspective on current events (for example, *Family News in Focus*) shape listeners in important

---

of camps, radio stations, a Bible college, a periodical, and the nation's first Christian television station (WPCA Philadelphia in 1958); see Crawford, *Thirst for Souls*.

70. John Eby, Interview by author.

71. Ibid.; *WDAC 2010 Program Guide*, 47. The *2010 Program Guide*, as a fiftieth-anniversary issue, includes a good deal of history of the station, although not as an organized narrative.

72. *WDAC 2010 Program Guide*, 27. This percentage is a disproportionately large share since Mennonites represent less than 10 percent of the population in the station's listening area. A *national* survey of Mennonite Church USA members, conducted in 2006, revealed that 47 percent of the denomination's members listen to Christian radio; see Kanagy, *Road Signs*, 106.

ways. No doubt the station's style of music holds special appeal for those culturally-conventional Mennonites who have not warmed to the contemporary Christian music or Christian rock music scene.[73]

Yet, there have always been Mennonite critics of the station. From the beginning, some Lancaster Conference leaders were suspicious of WDAC. If they did not object to the wholesome music, they worried about the speakers. During the 1930s and 1940s Lancaster Mennonites had experienced small but painful schisms. Members forbidden by the bishops to attend dispensational Scofield Bible classes or to sit under the preaching of Calvinist itinerates from Philadelphia, had left the Mennonite fold for congregations such as Calvary Independent Church and Word of Life Chapel.[74] The wounds were still sore, and now those forbidden voices would have a direct and private channel into members' homes. It is difficult to sort the complex mix of social and cultural changes that swept over Lancaster Mennonites during the 1960s, but WDAC was surely part of the mix. If some bishops were cool to the station, some members may have been all the more ready to tune in. In any case, centralized church authority was falling on hard times, and by 1968 even the rule against television collapsed.[75]

Meanwhile, Mennonite interests have mattered to the station and its evangelical owners. Through the years the station has carried more than a dozen different Anabaptist-originated programs—more programs than from any other particular tradition—and in 2010 added "Shaping Families," produced by Mennonite Church USA's ThirdWay Media.[76] Program director John Eby makes a point of including press

---

73. The Lancaster market is also home to WJTL, a station with a contemporary Christian playlist.

74. Ruth, *Earth*, 906–8, 930–32, 1049–50. WDAC's very first broadcast was a live service from Calvary Independent Church (now Calvary Church).

75. "Statement of Christian Doctrine and Rules and Discipline of the Mennonite Church, Lancaster Conference, Approved July 17, 1968," 25.

76. Programming on WDAC from Anabaptist-linked sources has included: "The Mennonite Hour," "Heart to Heart," "Your Time," "Moments of Glad Tidings," "Gospel Tide Hour" [Brethren in Christ], "Calvary Hour," and "Guidelines for Today," along with institutional update spots "Highlights from the Mennonite Home" and "Provident [Bookstore] Prism." None of these programs are currently produced or broadcast, but WDAC carried all of them for as long as they were in production. In 2010 the following programs from Mennonite sources were on the air: "Life with God," "Sunday School Meditations," "Voice of Hope," "Shaping Families," and "Focus" (weekly information spot from Eastern Mennonite Missions).

releases from Mennonite Central Committee and Mennonite Disaster Service in the station's news reporting, and has offered radio time to these organizations in the form of interviews that likely would not come from other broadcasters. The station's staff has always been solidly evangelical, but denominationally mixed. Eby, who began as an announcer in 1965, later left for two years to complete a term of voluntary service in Washington DC as a conscientious objector during the Vietnam War. Station management held his job and welcomed him back, despite their personal support of Christian service in the military. In contrast to the negative image of evangelicals as exclusive, Eby characterizes the ecumenical atmosphere of the station as one that respects different convictions and does not play into a stereotype of evangelical exclusivity.[77]

During his tenure at the station, Eby has heard from many grateful Mennonite listeners, often wanting to let him know "how a particular song we played spoke to them in a special way" or thanking him in a general way for the programming the station provides and the witness it offers to the community.[78] But beyond the inspiration they receive, listeners are also participating in a powerful parachurch network that defines much of contemporary American evangelicalism—a network of teachers, commentators, and music that parallels without completely replacing traditional church life.[79]

Eby also hears from Mennonites who fear the station's theological influence, and who are sometimes quite blunt in their appraisals. Recognizing the station's widespread listenership, some critics have suggested that WDAC will be "the downfall of the Mennonite church." Although WDAC has never aired controversial programming, such as so-called health-and-wealth preachers or programs that promote exclusive faith healing, the dispensational theology of some teachers present biblical interpretation and political agenda that differ substantially from neo-Anabaptist emphases. Station critics tend to be pastors trained in Mennonite seminaries, while loyal listeners are

77. Eby, interview by author. Longtime station owner and general manager, Paul Hollinger, was raised in the United Zion Church, a nineteenth-century offshoot of the Brethren in Christ Church, but for most of his adult life he has been a member of Lancaster's Calvary Church.

78. Ibid.

79. This network is what Marsden has called the "evangelical denomination"; see Marsden, *Understanding Fundamentalism and Evangelicalism*, 62–82.

often ordinary lay members.[80] As such, tensions over WDAC continue a divide between leadership and laity that has been a frequent theme in Lancaster Mennonite history. In that respect, despite critics' fears, WDAC has not changed the Lancaster Mennonite world all that much, even as it has been a significant voice in the dialogue between Anabaptism and evangelicalism in its community.

CONTINUING A WIDENING CONVERSATION

These stories and the ones that fill the following chapters testify to a lively and enlivening conversation that suggests three interrelated longings among members of these Christian communities. First, is a desire for spiritual renewal. For Anabaptists, connections with evangelicals at times offered opportunities to distinguish theological convictions from ethnic conventions, or to assert deeply personal faith in the midst of a smothering religious community. In such circumstances, evangelicalism was a means of reviving or reforming a stale tradition. For some evangelicals, in turn, Anabaptism's long-standing witness of discipleship, even when such a stance is unpopular, has served as a critique of American evangelicals' ease with the cultural status quo and, thus, has been a source of prophetic renewal. Those who assert Anabaptism's revitalizing possibilities include pastor and writer Brian McLaren, Simple Way founder Shane Claiborne, and New Testament teacher Scot McKnight, and their calls to renewal stand alongside the witness of Ron Sider, Myron Augsburger, and other Mennonites who have deliberately engaged evangelical audiences with Anabaptist messages.[81]

Second, the conversation between evangelicals and Anabaptists also highlights the uncomfortable, or at least ambivalent, relationship that both traditions have with American culture. For socially marginal

---

80. Eby, interview by author. See, for example, the sharp critique of Adams, "Addicted to Radio Preaching," 6. Adams is a Mennonite pastor in Lancaster City.

81. Sider, raised in an Ontario Brethren in Christ home, has been active in the Mennonite Church while serving as a professor at Palmer Theological Seminary (formerly Eastern Baptist) and, since 1978, as president of Evangelicals for Social Action. See Sider, *Good News and Good Works* and *I Am Not a Social Activist*. Augsburger was president of Eastern Mennonite College (now University) from 1965–1980 and president of the evangelical Council of Christian Colleges and Universities from 1988–1995.

Anabaptists, embracing evangelicalism was sometimes a safe way to merge with the religious mainstream and move past embarrassing particularity. Yet the possibility of sacred assimilation was often what spurred Mennonite critics of evangelicalism, critics who feared its influence would leach distinctive conviction and leave behind a generic and nationalistic faith.[82] In 2010, for example, Richard Kyle, a historian of evangelicalism and a convert to the Mennonite Brethren Church, critiqued evangelicals' propensity to "pander unashamedly to the popular tastes of American culture" and urged Mennonites to hold on to "the lordship of Christ, discipleship, social justice, the believers' church, peace, separation of church and state, and community as an alternative to rampant individualism."[83]

But Anabaptists are not the only ones who are uneasy. Certain evangelicals find the influence of Anabaptism threatening their agenda of calling committed Christians to deeper involvement in the messy and, they would say, sometimes necessarily violent work of civil government, which they see as a divine mandate.[84] Meanwhile, other evangelicals, such as theologian and megachurch pastor Greg Boyd, are troubled for precisely the opposite reason. They are increasingly uneasy with evangelicals' desire for partisan political power, and they are drawn to Anabaptism as an antidote. "Millions are waking up to the truth that followers of Jesus are called to love the unlovable, serve the oppressed, live in solidarity with the poor, proclaim Good News to the lost and be willing to lay down our life for our enemies," Boyd wrote in 2008, and "the only tradition that embodies what this rising breed of Kingdom radicals is looking for is the Anabaptist tradition."[85] Whatever their specific concern, the unease that both Anabaptists

---

82. Perhaps the sharpest critique is Redekop, *Leaving Anabaptism*.

83. Kyle, "Inconsistent Evangelicals," 18. Kyle's article was published in *Christian Leader*, a publication of the U.S. Conference of Mennonite Brethren churches. Among his publications on evangelical history is the title *Evangelicalism: An Americanized Christianity*.

84. A recent example is Leithart, *Defending Constantine*, esp. chapters 12 and 13, which are a sustained critique of neo-Anabaptist theology from a traditional Reformed standpoint.

85. Boyd, "A Word to My Mennonite Friends." Boyd also notes the irony that "just as millions like myself are running toward this treasure, many Mennonites are running away from it. In the name of becoming culturally relevant, the distinctive, radical aspects of the Anabaptist tradition are being downplayed." See also Boyd, *Myth of a Christian Nation*.

and evangelicals feel with their real or imagined status in American society has shaped their mutual conversation.

The very fact that Anabaptists and evangelicals have often turned to one another as they sought spiritual renewal or as they sorted out their place in contemporary society points to a third feature of their relationships: On some level, both traditions recognize that they are an incomplete representation of the Kingdom of God. They long for broader connections among the Christian family, and they have often found it in one another. The necessity of thinking beyond one's own tradition has often become all the clearer to both evangelicals and Anabaptists engaged in mission and who come face-to-face with new believers who bring fresh perspectives, question theological and cultural assumptions, or present creative new ways of witness. In a world of globalizing and multicultural Christianity, conversations between evangelicalism and Anabaptism are certain to become more common. And that is a fact that bears keener attention from faithful evangelicals and Anabaptists alike.

In North America, evangelicalism is already the vanguard—though often unrecognized—in many Anabaptist groups. A 2006 survey of Mennonite church members found that although only 18 percent of white members chose "evangelical" as one of two terms that best describe their theology, 30 percent of so-called racial/ethnic members did so, and another 16 percent of racial/ethnic members chose "charismatic/Pentecostal."[86] A church that finds it growing edge among people of color who are happy to claim both evangelical *and* Anabaptist identities needs to concentrate more on a conversation that has and is taking place between these traditions. Meanwhile, evangelicals outside North America are increasingly apt to cast their faith in terms that resonate with Anabaptist themes or that call into question common political assumptions of American evangelicals.

Perhaps a gathering of evangelicals in October 2010 suggests the future of the conversation. They had come to Cape Town, South Africa, for the third Lausanne Congress on World Evangelization, a global mission consultation first convened thirty-six years earlier by Billy Graham. Mennonite and Brethren in Christ leaders from all continents were among the four thousand participants from 198 countries. Stanley Green, a South African Anabaptist who now heads the

---

86. Kanagy, *Road Signs*, 149–50.

North American-based Mennonite Mission Network reported that "with the preponderance of southern voices there was a fresh framing of the gospel in terms of transformation that impacted people's social, physical, material and spiritual circumstance," and evangelicals from the Global South pressed Western Christians to move "beyond the conflicts that have plagued the Western church, often framed by the fundamentalist and social gospel controversies of the post-World War II era." "Given the shape of the conversations at the event," Green concluded happily, "Anabaptists would have had little difficulty feeling at home."[87]

BIBLIOGRAPHY

Adams, Ron. "Addicted to Radio Preaching." *The Mennonite*, July 2010, 6.

Alumkal, Antony W. *Asian American Evangelical Churches: Race, Ethnicity, and Assimilation in the Second Generation*. El Paso, TX: LFB Scholarly Publishing, 2003.

Bebbington, David W. *Evangelicalism in Modern Britain: A History from the 1730s to the 1980s*. London: Unwin Hyman, 1989.

Bender, Harold S. "The Anabaptist Vision." *Church History* 13 (1944) 3–24.

———. "Outside Influences on Mennonite Thought." *Mennonite Life*, (1955) 45–48.

Biblical Interpretation in the Life of the Church: A Summary Statement. Scottdale, PA: Mennonite Publishing House, 1977.

Blumhofer, Edith L. *Aimee Semple McPherson: Everybody's Sister*. Grand Rapids: Eerdmans, 1993.

Bowman, Carl F. *Brethren Society: The Cultural Transformation of a "Peculiar People."* Baltimore: Johns Hopkins University Press, 1995.

Boyd, Gregory A. Christus Victor Ministries blog. Online http://www.gregboyd.org/.

———. *The The Myth of a Christian Nation: How the Quest for Political Power Is Destroying the Church*. Grand Rapids, MI: Zondervan, 2006.

Brint, Steven and Jean Reith Schroedel, eds. *Evangelicals and Democracy in America*, 2 vols. New York: Russell Sage, 2009.

Burgess, Stanley M., ed. *The New International Dictionary of Pentecostal and Charismatic Movements*, Rev. ed. Grand Rapids, MI: Zondervan, 2002.

Bush, Perry. *Two Kingdoms, Two Loyalties: Mennonite Pacifism in Modern America*. Baltimore: Johns Hopkins University Press, 1998.

———. "Anabaptism Born Again: Mennonites, New Evangelicals, and the Search for a Useable Past, 1950-1980." *Fides et Historia* 25 (Winter/Spring 1993): 37–38.

Carpenter, Joel A. *Revive Us Again: The Reawakening of American Fundamentalism*. New York: Oxford University Press, 1999.

——— and Wilbert R. Shenk, eds. *Earthen Vessels: American Evangelicals and Foreign Missions, 1880–1980*. Grand Rapids, MI: Eerdmans, 1990.

---

87. Green, "Third Lausanne Gathering," 45.

Carroll R., M. Daniel. *Christians at the Border: Immigration, the Church, and the Bible.* Grand Rapids: Baker Academic, 2008.

Christian Declaration on the Authority of the Scriptures. Newton, KS: General Conference Mennonite Church, [1962].

Crawford, Dan D. *A Thirst for Souls: The Life of Evangelist Percy B. Crawford.* Selinsgrove, PA: Susquehanna University Press, 2010.

Dayton, Donald W., and Robert K. Johnston, editors. *The Variety of American Evangelicalism.* Knoxville: University of Tennessee Press, 1991.

Dochuk, Darren. *From Bible Belt to Sunbelt: Plain-Folk Religion, Grassroots Politics, and the Rise of Evangelical Conservatism.* New York: W. W. Norton, 2010.

Eby, Benjamin. *Kurzgefaßte Kirchen-Geschichte und Glaubenslehre der Taufgesinnten Christen oder Mennoniten.* Berlin, ON: B. Eby, 1841.

Eby, John. Interview by author, August. 12, 2010.

Emerson, Michael O., and Christian Smith. *Divided by Faith: Evangelical Religion and the Problem of Race in America.* New York: Oxford University Press, 2001.

Epp, Frank H. *Mennonites in Canada, 1920-1940: A People's Struggle for Survival.* Scottdale, PA: Herald Press, 1996.

Frei, Hans W. *The Eclipse of Biblical Narrative: A Study in Eighteenth and Nineteenth Century Hermeneutics.* New Haven: Yale University Press, 1974.

Green, Stanely. "Third Lausanne Gathering Nets Capetown Commitment." *The Mennonite,* December 2010, 45.

Guenther, Bruce L. "Living with the Virus: The Enigma of Evangelicalism among Mennonites in Canada." In *Aspects of the Canadian Evangelical Experience,* edited by George A. Rawlyk. Montreal: McGill-Queen's University Press, 1997.

Hamilton, Michael S. "More Money, More Ministry: The Financing of American Evangelicalism since 1945." In *More Money, More Ministry: Money and Evangelicals in Recent North American History,* edited by Larry Eskridge and Mark A. Noll, Grand Rapids: Eerdmans, 2000.

Harding, Susan Friend. *The Book of Jerry Falwell: Fundamentalist Language and Politics.* Princeton, NJ: Princeton University Press, 2001.

Harrell, David Edwin Jr. *All Things Are Possible: The Healing and Charismatic Revivals in Modern America.* Bloomington: Indiana University Press, 1979.

Hershberger, Guy F., editor. *The Recovery of the Anabaptist Vision: A Sixtieth Anniversary Tribute to Harold S. Bender.* Scottdale, PA: Herald, 1957.

———. *The Mennonite Church in the Second World War.* Scottdale, PA: Mennonite Publishing House, 1951.

Hostetler, Beulah Stauffer. "The Formation of the Old Orders." *Mennonite Quarterly Review* 66 (1991): 5–25.

Kanagy, Conrad L. *Road Signs for the Journey: A Profile of Mennonite Church USA.* Scottdale, PA: Herald, 2007.

Kauffman, J. Howard, and Leland Harder. *Anabaptists Four Centuries Later: A Profile of Five Mennonite and Brethren in Christ Denominations.* Scottdale, PA: Herald, 1975.

Koop, C. Everett, and Francis A. Schaeffer. *Whatever Happened to the Human Race?* Old Tappan, NJ: Revell, 1979.

Kostlevy, William C. *Bethany Theological Seminary: A Centennial History.* Richmond, IN: Brethren Journal Association, 2005.

Kraus, C. Normal, editor. *Anabaptism and Evangelicalism.* Scottdale, PA: Herald, 1979.

Kraybill, J. Nelson. "Is Our Future Evangelical?" *The Mennonite*, March 5, 2002, 15.
Kreider, J. Kenneth. *A Cup of Cold Water: The Story of Brethren Service*. Elgin, IL: Brethren, 2001.
Kuist, Howard. *These Words Upon Thy Heart: Scripture and the Christian Response*. Richmond, VA: John Knox, 1947.
Kyle, Richard. *Evangelicalism: An Americanized Christianity*. New Brunswick, NJ: Transaction Publishers, 2006.
———. "Inconsistent Evangelicals." *Christian Leader*, June-July 2010, 18.
Lageer, Eileen. *Merging Streams: Story of the Missionary Church*. Elkhart, IN: Bethel, 1979.
Leithart, Peter J. *Defending Constantine: The Twilight of an Empire and the Dawn of Christendom*. Downers Grove: IVP Academic, 2010.
Lienesch, Michael. *In the Beginning: Fundamentalism, the Scopes Trial, and the Making of the Antievolution Movement*. Chapel Hill: University of North Carolina Press, 2007.
Lindsell, Harold. *The Battle for the Bible*. Grand Rapids: Zondervan, 1976.
Loewen, Royden. *Diaspora in the Countryside: Two Mennonite Communities and the Mid-Twentieth-Century Rural Disjuncture*. Urbana: University of Illinois Press, 2006.
MacArthur, John. "John MacArthur Jr., Pastor-Teacher." Fundraising letter (Sept. 16, 1991) in author files.
Marsden George M. *Understanding Fundamentalism and Evangelicalism*. Grand Rapids, MI: Eerdmans, 1991.
———. *Fundamentalism and American Culture: The Shaping of Twentieth-Century Evangelicalism, 1870-1925*. 2nd ed. New York: Oxford University Press, 2006.
———. *Reforming Fundamentalism: Fuller Seminary and the New Evangelicalism*. Grand Rapids: Eerdmans, 1987.
Meier, Marcus. *The Origins of the Schwarzenau Brethren*. Trans. by Dennis L. Slabaugh. Philadelphia: Brethren Encyclopedia, 2008.
Miller, Elizabeth M. "Moody, Fundamentalism and Mennonites: The Struggle for Particularity and Engagement in Illinois Mennonite Churches, 1900-1955." *Illinois Mennonite Heritage Quarterly* 24 (Winter 2007) 96–101, and 25 (Spring 2008) 1–8.
Miller, R. H. *The Doctrine of the Brethren Defended* . . . Indianapolis: Printing and Publishing House, 1876.
Miller, Steven P. *Billy Graham and the Rise of the Republican South*. Philadelphia: University of Pennsylvania Press, 2009.
Moreton, Bethany. *To Serve God and Wal-Mart: The Making of Christian Free Enterprise*. Cambridge: Harvard University Press, 2009.
Noll, Mark A. *American Evangelical Christianity: An Introduction*. Malden: Blackwell, 2001.
———. *America's God: From Jonathan Edwards to Abraham Lincoln*. New York: Oxford University Press, 2002.
———. *Between Faith and Criticism: Evangelicals, Scholarship, and the Bible in America*. Grand Rapids: Baker, 1991.
Noll, Mark A., David W. Bebbington, and George A. Rawlyk, editors. *Evangelicalism: Comparative Studies of Popular Protestantism in North America, the British Isles, and Beyond, 1700-1990*. New York: Oxford University Press, 1994.

Nolt, Steven M. "'Avoid Provoking the Spirit of Controversy': The Irenic Evangelical Legacy of The Biblical Seminary in New York." in *Re-forming the Center: American Protestantism, 1900 to the Present*, edited by Douglas Jacobsen and William V. Trollinger, Jr. Grand Rapids: Eerdmans, 1998.

———. "An Evangelical Encounter: Mennonites and The Biblical Seminary in New York." *Mennonite Quarterly Review* 70 (1996) 389–417.

——— "A 'Two-Kingdom' People in a World of Multiple Identities: Religion, Ethnicity, and American Mennonites." *Mennonite Quarterly Review* 73 (1999) 485–502

"Radio Broadcasting, Mennonite." In *Mennonite Encyclopedia*, v. 4.

"Radio." In *Mennonite Encyclopedia*, v. 5.

Rawlyk, George A. *The Canada Fire: Radical Evangelicalism in British North America, 1775–1812*. Kingston, ON: McGill-Queen's University Press, 1994.

———, editor. *The Canadian Protestant Experience, 1760–1990*. Burlington, ON: Welch, 1991.

Redekop, Calvin W. *Leaving Anabaptism: From Evangelical Mennonite Brethren to Fellowship of Evangelical Bible Churches*. Telford, PA: Pandora, 1998.

Regehr, T. D. *Mennonites in Canada, 1939-1970: A People Transformed*. Toronto: University of Toronto Press, 1996.

Reimer, Sam. *Evangelicals and the Continental Divide: The Conservative Protestant Subculture in Canada and the United States*. Montreal: McGill-Queen's University Press, 2003.

Revival Fires in Manitoba: A Report on the Work of the Brunk Revivals, Inc., in four Manitoba Communities, Summer of 1957. Denbigh, VA: Brunk Revivals, [1957?].

Revival Fires in British Columbia: A Report on the Work of the Brunk Revival Campaigns in the Fraser Valley, Summer of 1958. Denbigh, VA: Brunk Revivals, [1958?].

Ruth, John L. *The Earth Is the Lord's: A Narrative History of the Lancaster Mennonite Conference*. Scottdale, PA: Herald Press, 2001.

Sampson, Cynthia and John Paul Lederach, eds. *From the Ground Up: Mennonite Contributions to International Peacebuilding*. New York: Oxford University Press, 2000.

Sandeen, Ernest R. *The Roots of Fundamentalism: British and American Millenarianism, 1800-1930*. Chicago: University of Chicago Press, 1970.

Schlabach, Theron F. *Gospel Versus Gospel: Mission and the Mennonite Church, 1863-1944*. Scottdale, PA: Herald Press, 1980.

———. *Peace, Faith, Nation: Mennonites and Amish in Nineteenth-Century America*. Scottdale, PA: Herald, 1988.

Shenk, Stanley C. Interview by author, February 3, 1995.

Sider, Ronald J. *Good News and Good Works: A Theology for the Whole Gospel*. Grand Rapids, MI: Baker, 1999.

———. *I Am Not a Social Activist: Making Jesus the Agenda*. Scottdale, PA: Herald Press, 2008.

Snyder, C. Arnold. *Anabaptist History and Theology*. Kitchener, ON: Pandora Press, 1995.

———. *Following in the Footsteps of Christ: The Anabaptist Spirituality*. Maryknoll, NY: Orbis Press, 2004.

"Statement of Christian Doctrine and Rules and Discipline of the Mennonite Church, Lancaster Conference. Approved September 16, 1954."

"Statement of Christian Doctrine and Rules and Discipline of the Mennonite Church, Lancaster Conference. Approved July 17, 1968."

Stutzman, Ervin R. *Welcome! A Biblical and Practical Guide to Receiving New Members.* Scottdale, PA: Herald, 1990.

Swartley, Willard M. *Mark: The Way for All Nations.* Scottdale, PA: Herald, 1979.

Thuesen, Peter J. *Predestination: The American Career of a Contentious Doctrine.* New York: Oxford University Press, 2009.

Toews, Paul. *Mennonites in American Society, 1930-1970: Modernity and the Persistence of Religious Community.* Scottdale, PA: Herald Press, 1996.

Traina, Robert A. *Methodical Bible Study: A New Approach to Hermeneutics.* New York: Ganis & Harris, 1952.

UN: UnDocumented.tv. Jesse Oxford, producer. Wheaton, IL: World Relief. Online: http://undocumented.tv/.

Wacker, Grant. *Heaven Below: Early Pentecostals and American Culture.* Cambridge: Harvard University Press, 2001.

Ward, W. Reginald. *The Protestant Evangelical Awakening.* New York: Cambridge University Press, 1992.

Weaver, J. Denny. *Keeping Salvation Ethical: Mennonite and Amish Atonement Theology in the Late Nineteenth Century.* Scottdale, PA: Herald, 1997.

Weber, Timothy P. *On the Road to Armageddon: How Evangelicals Became Israel's Best Friend.* Grand Rapids: Baker Academic, 2004.

WDAC Program Guide, 2010. Quarryville, PA: WDAC, 2010.

Wittlinger, Carlton O. *The Quest for Piety and Obedience: The Story of the Brethren in Christ.* Nappanee, IN: Evangel Press, 1978.

Wuthnow, Robert. *The Restructuring of American Religion: Society and Faith since World War II.* Princeton, NJ: Princeton University Press, 1988.

Yoder, John Howard. *The Politics of Jesus.* Grand Rapids: Eerdmans, 1972.

Zehr, Paul M. *Biblical Criticism in the Life of the Church.* Scottdale, PA: Herald, 1986.

Anabaptism and Evangelicalism Revisited

Healing a Contentious Relationship?

JOHN D. ROTH

IN THE FALL OF 1832, Samuel Froehlich, an itinerant Swiss revival preacher, held a series of meetings in the Bernese region of the Emmental that attracted great attention among the Mennonites living there. For a brief period of time, following the completion of his theological studies at Basel in 1828, Froehlich had served as a Reformed pastor in his home town of Leutwil. But his emotional sermons on the themes of repentance and sanctification—though popular among the local townsfolk—had aroused the ire of local civic and church authorities. In October of 1830, after repeated warnings to desist from criticizing a new Reformed confession and to refrain from "preaching salvation," authorities rescinded Froehlich's ordination and forced him to resign his pastorate. Undeterred, he traveled to London where he fellowshipped for a time with the Baptist Continental Missionary Society. Early in 1832 he returned to Switzerland, received baptism as an adult in a pietist fellowship in Geneva (*Société évangélique de Genève*), and embarked on a series of itinerant missionary journeys throughout Switzerland.[1]

Froehlich's sojourn among the Mennonites in the Emmental produced much fruit. In the fall of 1832 some sixty members of the Mennonite church in Langnau, led by Christen Gerber and

---

1. Weber, "Über die Anfänge der Neutäufer," 3–21.

Christen Baumgartner, left the congregation. In March of 1835 the group formally organized on the Giebel farmstead close to Bärau and became part of the Evangelisch-Taufgesinnter Gemeinde (Evangelical Baptism-Minded Church),[2] more commonly known as the *Neutäufer*. For the next century Mennonites and Neutäufer lived uneasily alongside each other in Switzerland until a rapprochement among church leaders following World War II ushered in a new era of friendship and cooperation.[3]

The story of Samuel Froehlich and the church division of 1832 among the Mennonites in the Emmental is a theme that runs very deeply in Anabaptist-Mennonite history. Wherever Mennonites have settled—be it in Europe, South Russia, or the Americas—remarkably similar patterns of ecclesial boundary maintenance and renewal have unfolded. In each of these settings, the Mennonite reluctance to swear oaths, bear arms or integrate fully into the surrounding culture frequently resulted in an identity of nonconformity and separation. At times political authorities reinforced this separatist mentality by imposing special taxes, restricting their freedom of movement, or making toleration conditional on promise that Mennonites would not proselytize. At other times, Mennonites voluntarily adopted habits of cultural separation. In south Russia and North America, for example, the persistence of the German language, combined with deep memories of persecution, strong family networks, an emphasis on intermarriage, and tightly-knit community settlement patterns, all contributed to their sense of being "a people apart."

At its best, this impulse toward a separatist ecclesiology testified to the seriousness of Christian conversion as expressed in a transformed way of life and a visible, corporate witness to the world. As a voluntary gathering of earnest Christians, committed to practices

---

2. The link to the Anabaptist tradition is unmistakable in the phrase "Evangelisch-Taufgesinnter." Already in the sixteenth century Dutch Mennonites were known as the *Doopsgezinde* (baptism-minded). German-speaking Mennonites adopted the parallel label of *Taufgesinnten* as their preferred named over the more common *Wiedertäufer* (Anabaptist = rebaptizer), which in the European context had a very negative connotation due to its close association in the sixteenth century with Pelegianism and with the Münster debacle of 1535. In the United States the group is known as the Apostolic Christian Church. See Klopfenstein, *Marching to Zion*.

3. For a closer examination of the on-going themes of renewal within the *Neutäufer* (or Apostolic Christian Church) see Pfeiffer, "Between Remnant and Reviewal."

of church discipline and mutual aid, Mennonite communities were a "light on the hill" to the world around. Anyone attracted to this form of committed Christianity was welcome to join. At their worst, however, traditional Mennonite communities became spiritually inert ethnocentric enclaves, focused primarily on their own survival. Traditional patterns of mutual accountability and the call to Christian discipleship easily ossified into legalistic, and sometimes oppressive, forms of church discipline. The principle of voluntary baptism became a routinized rite of passage into adulthood, tied to a specific age. A commitment to communal consensus squelched the charismatic gifts of the Spirit and threatened to reduce Christian faith to a joyless conformity to group expectations. According to a contemporary witness in Switzerland, Samuel Froehlich and his followers were, "trying to bring new life into the fellowship, because they saw what a lukewarm condition the *Alttäufer* [Mennonites] found themselves in. To be sure, the external forms were still intact, but there was almost no evidence of an inner spiritual life."[4]

In the context of this persistent sociological pattern, spiritual renewal in Anabaptist-Mennonite communities almost always came in the form of evangelical revival.[5] Although circumstances varied significantly from community to community, the catalyst of renewal frequently took the form of an itinerant minister from outside the Mennonite tradition. As in the case of Samuel Froehlich's visit to the Emmental, the visiting preacher would begin with informal gatherings in a private home. In sharp contrast to the routine recitations of their own lay preachers, the tone of those meetings was almost always heartfelt, personal and emotional; and the substance of the message inevitably focused on the atoning work of Christ, whose love relativized all human ordinances and whose unmerited gift of grace freed Christians from the burden of works-righteousness. Included in the renewal message were appeals to active Bible reading as an encounter with the living word of God, admonitions to renewed zeal in Christian

---

4. Quoted in Zürcher, "Herausforderungen für die Schweizer Mennoniten durch die Erweckungsbewegung," 22–35.

5. Another, quite different, form of renewal within the Anabaptist-Mennonite tradition can be seen in the emergence of Old Order groups seeking to enliven Christian commitment by recalling the humility and suffering of Christ and by renewing and reinforcing lines of separation between church and world. I describe this form of renewal in J. Roth, "Introduction," 1–17.

devotion, calls for a fresh yielding to the inner movement of the Spirit, and a new sense of urgency about missionary outreach, beginning with a true conversion experience prior to baptism.

Thus, even before Froehlich's missionary journey through Switzerland in the early 1830s, Moravian missionaries from Herrnhut had long targeted Mennonite communities in their regular missionary itineration through South Germany after 1750, preaching a conversionist gospel of heartfelt devotion to Christ that transcended denominational barriers. The Church of the Brethren—which emerged out of an eighteenth-century Pietist conventicle led by Alexander Mack—promoted similar teachings of warm, engaged piety and attracted numerous Mennonite converts, especially after the group found a foothold in the New World. In the 1820s Mennonites in south Germany—who had long been avid readers of Pietist devotional tracts—hosted William Henry Angas, a Baptist missionary from England, for several mission conferences. The initiative eventually sparked a church division, but it also prompted numerous Mennonites in Palatinate to offer financial support to the Baptist mission school in nearby Basel and to introduce more expressive forms of hymnody and prayer into their worship. Across the Atlantic, immigrant Mennonites in Pennsylvania were deeply moved by the revivalist preaching of Jacob Engle in the late eighteenth century, with many leaving to help form the Brethren in Christ church in a quest for a more vibrant expression of faith. A few decades later, in 1859, John Holdeman led in the formation of the Church of God in Christ Mennonites, a group stressing the necessity of the new birth, baptism of the Holy Spirit, and missionary outreach. At about the same time, the influence of the Lutheran revivalist preacher, Edward Wüst, among Mennonites in South Russia played a crucial role in the formation of the Mennonite Brethren church, with a strong focus on a conversion experience, mission outreach, and a personal relationship with God that went beyond the formalities of church membership. In 1866 a dynamic Amish preacher by the name of Henry Egly established the Defenseless Mennonite Church, with a similar emphasis on conversion, assurance of salvation, and missions. The group later adopted the name Evangelical Mennonite Church, and is now known as the Fellowship of Evangelical Churches. For similar reasons, in 1874 Daniel Brenneman, a Mennonite preacher in Indiana, together with Solomon Eby in Ontario, created the Reformed Mennonites, a group that later became part of the Mennonite Brethren in Christ Church (now part of the Missionary Church). The Evangelical Mennonite Brethren Conference traces its beginnings to 1889 with the revivalist preaching of Isaac Peters and Aaron Wall and the formation of a mission-oriented movement among Russian Mennonite immigrants in the areas around Mountain Lake, Minnesota and Henderson, Nebraska. In 1899, Joseph Stucky was instrumental in promoting a renewal movement that led to the formation of the Central Illinois Conference. Several years later that conference joined with the Defenseless Mennonites (or Evangelical Mennonite Conference) to establish its own foreign mission venture in the Belgian Congo as the Congo Inland Mission Board. In 1952 the Kleine Gemeinde, a Russian Mennonite group who had immigrated to Canada in the 1870s, changed its name to the Evangelical Mennonite Church, and then—in an attempt to distinguish itself from a group in the U.S. with the same name—to the Evangelical Mennonite Conference in 1959.

This long litany of Mennonite divisions sparked by encounters with evangelical forms of renewal has continued until the present. Thus, for example, in 1983 a group of Mennonites in the eastern U.S., concerned about perceived liberal theological tendencies in the Mennonite Church, formed the Association of Evangelical Mennonites who joined with like-minded congregations from Virginia in 1992 to create the Evangelical Anabaptist Fellowship. In 2002 the group was reconstituted as the Alliance of Evangelical Mennonite Congregations, with some twenty congregations among its members.[6] In a similar fashion, the Conservative Mennonite Conference's Rosedale Bible College in Irwin, Ohio has made its intention to be both "evangelical" and "Anabaptist" an explicit part of its identity and has sponsored a series of annual conferences—the "Evangelical Anabaptist Symposium"—to explore what this might mean.[7]

Hidden within this litany of renewal movements, of course, are dozens of distinct stories, each with its own unique context, leadership, goals, and outcomes. But all of them reflect similar impulses of

---

6. For more on the history and context of this group see their website: http://www.aemc2000.org.

7. Summaries of the various symposia are posted on the Rosedale Bible College website: http://www.rosedale.edu/leaders/.

renewal within the Anabaptist-Mennonite tradition marked by an encounter with "evangelicalism" of one sort or another.[8]

TRADITIONAL ASSESSMENTS OF ANABAPTIST-MENNONITE ENCOUNTERS WITH EVANGELICALISM

During the first half of the twentieth century, Mennonite church leaders generally regarded the evangelical impulse as a positive influence within the broader Anabaptist-Mennonite tradition. Although it was clear that many of these renewal movements disrupted traditional patterns of ecclesial order and often led to painful church division,[9] Mennonites were rarely critical of the evangelical impulse. The emerging Mennonite mission movement in the early twentieth century, for example, adopted the language of a crisis conversion, focused on Christ's atoning sacrifice, along with a strong emphasis on devotional life and practices of personal piety. Mennonite doctrinal statements during the first half of the twentieth century frequently echoed the classic themes of evangelical theology.[10] For young Mennonites who had

---

8. The challenge of defining "evangelical" with any precision is on-going. In his now classic formulation, British historian David Bebbington defined the hallmarks of evangelical religion as: conversionism; activism; biblicism; and crucicentrism (an emphasis on the sacrifice of Christ on the cross).—Bebbington, *Evangelicalism in Modern Britain*, 2–17. A second definition focuses much more narrowly on a cluster of groups—frequently associated with people like Billy Graham, institutions like Wheaton College or Youth for Christ, or membership in the National Association of Evangelicals—that emerged in North America in the middle decades of the twentieth century somewhat in reaction against fundamentalist movement in the 1920s and 1930s. Yet a third definition regards "evangelical" more as a style or set of emphases than a precise list of beliefs. That style includes such things as an emphasis on outreach and mission, focused on a conversion experience; an expressive worship style; a warm, practical piety; and a tendency to minimize denominational distinctions to find common cause with other Christians of a similar orientation.—cf. Institute for the Study of American Evangelicals at: http://isae.wheaton.edu/defining-evangelicalism/defining-the-term-in-contemporary-times/. I am using "evangelical" primarily in the last sense.

9. Today, there are as many as fifty-five different Anabaptist-Mennonite groups in Lancaster County, Pennsylvania alone—and at least 20 different groups in Holmes County, Ohio—all of whom trace their spiritual lineage in one way or another to the Anabaptist tradition, but each formally separated from the others in a quest for faithful renewal.

10. Harold Bender's description of Mennonite churches in the 1930s, for example, included the following phrase: "All the American Mennonite groups without

begun to leave their rural communities for college or Civilian Public Service, general evangelical themes—rooted as they were in a voluntarist, free church ecclesiology—provided a welcome point of connection with the broader Christian world.[11] By mid-century, Mennonite evangelists were borrowing explicitly from the Billy Graham crusades to create a new sub-culture of tent revival meetings bringing the gospel of salvation to dozens of established Mennonite communities.[12] Even Harold Bender—whose own approach to church renewal focused on the recovery of a distinctive "Anabaptist Vision" rooted in the Radical Reformation of the sixteenth-century—was quick to label "genuine" sixteenth-century Anabaptists as "evangelical Anabaptists," in order underscore their biblicism, conversion-oriented, and theologically orthodox approach to the gospel, and to distinguish them from Christian humanists or other, more radical, reformers who were advocating political or economic revolution.[13]

By the second half of the twentieth century, however, Mennonite scholarly opinion regarding "evangelicalism"—especially within the (Old) Mennonite Church—shifted dramatically. One obvious reason for this new assessment was the long legacy of division associated with evangelical renewal. As the Mennonite church developed more rationalized forms of church polity, the defenders of these new, centralized structures looked askance at any form of renewal that promoted congregational autonomy and encouraged division.

But alongside pragmatic arguments were a host of deeper theological concerns. The first to sound the alarm in a systematic way was the historian, Robert Friedmann, a close colleague of Bender. In 1949 Friedmann's *Mennonite Piety Through the Centuries* leveled a resounding critique of the way revivalist, spirit-centered expres-

---

exception stand upon a platform of *conservative evangelicalism* in theology, being thoroughly orthodox in the great fundamental doctrines of the Christian faith. . . ."—Bender, "Mennonites of the United States," 79 (emphasis added).

11. The standard discussion on free church ecclesiology is Littell, *Free Church*. Cf. Durnbaugh, *Believers' Church*; Garrett, Jr., *Concept of the Believers' Church*.

12. Cf. Lehman, *Mennonite Tent Revivals*.

13. Bender described the first Anabaptists in Switzerland as "the culmination of the Reformation, the fulfillment of the original vision of Luther and Zwingli," and went on to argue that the movement was best understood as "a *consistent evangelical Protestantism* seeking to recreate without compromise the original New Testament church, the vision of Christ and the Apostles."—Bender, "Anabaptist Vision," 72 (emphasis added).

sions of Christianity—which he labeled collectively as "Pietism"—had negatively affected the Anabaptist-Mennonite tradition. On the surface, Friedmann noted, Anabaptism and Pietism appeared to have much in common. But these parallels were deceptive. In his analysis, Anabaptism and Pietism began from fundamentally different premises and invested significantly different meanings into the terminology which they shared. The starting point for Anabaptists, Friedmann argued, was a *corporate* goal—that of bringing about the Kingdom of God. By contrast, Pietism's primary focus was on the *individual* experience of grace and personal blessedness. If Anabaptism stressed the "bitter" Christ of suffering, obedience, and martyrdom, Pietism emphasized the "sweet" Christ of forgiveness of sin and the enjoyment of one's relationship with God. Whereas discipleship (*Nachfolge*) was the central theme of Anabaptism, Pietists celebrated an inner yieldedness to the will of God (*Gelassenheit*).[14]

Friedmann's intention was to expose Pietism as the Trojan Horse of true Anabaptism. Sometimes consciously, often unwittingly, Mennonite leaders allowed Pietist language to enter the walls of the Mennonite community—always with disastrous consequences. Wherever its influence was felt, a new mood of pious inner devotion supplanted an earlier commitment to suffering discipleship. Mennonite churches who opened themselves to Pietist influences increasingly became mere aggregations of saved individuals—"generic" Christians who were easily absorbed into the Protestant mainstream. In short, Friedmann argued, Pietism robbed the Anabaptist movement of its essential core.

During the half-century which followed, Friedmann's provocative claim that expressive forms of spirituality were somehow antithetical to authentic Mennonite identity became a generalized assumption within Mennonite historiography.[15] Whether in Europe or in North

14. Friedmann, *Mennonite Piety Through the Centuries*, esp. 72–77. For more biographical material on Friedmann, see the Robert Friedmann memorial issue of *The Mennonite Quarterly Review*. I have explored these themes in more detail in J. Roth, "Pietism and the Anabaptist Soul," 182–202.

15. In retrospect, the sustained influence of *Mennonite Piety Through the Centuries* is rather remarkable. Friedmann has been especially popular among the New Order Amish, a group which recently had *Mennonite Piety Through the Centuries* reprinted. For a fascinating example of how some people among the New Order have appropriated Friedmann's argument (without acknowledgement), see Burkholder, *The Inroads of Pietism*. In this small pamphlet, Burkholder understands

America, it seems that Mennonites have always been willing to sell their birthright of rugged discipleship for the soggy porridge of pious devotion. Whenever Mennonite leaders could be documented as speaking of religious experience, wherever Mennonite hymnbooks included songs that spoke of the passion of Christ, wherever preachers emphasized the centrality of God's grace, or wherever the boundaries of Mennonite community were weakened by some form of acculturation, modern Mennonite historians invariably could demonstrate that Pietism—or, in the North American context, evangelicalism—in one form or another, was the precipitating cause.

Already in the late 1950s, Harold Bender worried that the disturbing erosion of the peace witness among Mennonites during World War II could be attributed to the influence of Fundamentalism and conservative evangelicalism in some quarters of the church.[16] In 1980 Mennonite historian Theron F. Schlabach echoed these concerns in *Gospel Versus Gospel*, a landmark history of the (Old) Mennonite Church mission movement.[17] As the title of the book suggested, Schlabach recast the story of North American Mennonite missions as a struggle between two competing—and fundamentally different—versions of the gospel. One version, borrowed directly from the broader theological currents of conservative American Protestantism, focused on a crisis conversion experience and the inner drama of personal salvation. The heart of the gospel, early Mennonite missionaries insisted,

---

Pietism and evangelicalism to be one and the same thing, which he describes as "an overly sentimental or emotional devotion to religion" with "a heavy, individualized emphasis on inner experience and devotion to God." He sets this in sharp contrast to the Anabaptist emphasis on the "call to discipleship" and the "binding authority" of the fellowship of believers. Pietism, claims Burkholder, was "born in the palled stillness of a religious graveyard. . . . Experience became an end in itself rather than the springboard to obedience and service. There was no emphasis on the brotherhood of believers being the Body of Christ. . . . Persecution was rare for Pietists because of their avoidance of conflict." "The success of Pietism in the broader Mennonite circles is quite evident. . . . Where Pietism has taken root the church has lost its disciplinary power over her membership. The door for participation in communion has been flung wide open and group responsibility and authority have been replaced by personal liberty and judgment. The deciding factor about one's spiritual standing has become personal testimony or lip service rather than personal life and obedience" (6–7).

16. See, e.g., Bender, "Outside Influences on Mennonite Thought," 45–48.

17. Schlabach, *Gospel Versus Gospel*. It is also the central theme in the collection of essays edited by Kraus entitled *Evangelicalism and Anabaptism*.

was not to be found in traditional doctrines of nonconformity and nonresistance, or in distinctive ordinances like plain dress or the devotional covering. To the contrary; these were mere cultural trappings that stood in the way of true conversion. Missions were about "saving souls." Over against this understanding of the gospel, Schlabach posited an alternative gospel—a "full orbed" vision of shalom, which refused to separate conversion from the transformed life of the believer and the witness of the gathered Christian community. In his reading, the gospel as traditionally understood within the Anabaptist-Mennonite tradition—in which salvation was inseparably joined to an ethic of love, a commitment to follow Christ in daily discipleship, and a community of believers—had been diminished, if not replaced, by an alternative gospel.

Schlabach was clearly a careful and nuanced scholar, who himself raised critical questions about the Friedmann thesis.[18] But *Gospel Versus Gospel* served as a microcosm of a much larger argument embraced by Mennonite church leaders, theologians, historians, and missiologists in the second half of the twentieth century that pitted "genuine" Anabaptism over against various expressions of American evangelicalism that had infiltrated the Mennonite church. Whereas Bender could still identify sixteenth-century Anabaptists as "evangelical" without embarrassment, the generation of scholars who succeeded him tended to regard evangelicalism as a foil over against which an authentic Anabaptist-Mennonite theology could be defined. Thus, theologians like C. Norman Kraus and J. Denny Weaver argued that evangelical atonement theology was incompatible with Anabaptist-Mennonite understandings of nonresistance, hermeneutics, and ecclesiology.[19] Mennonite sociologists worried that traditional Mennonite communities were embracing evangelical theology in order to legitimate their acculturation into mainstream American society.[20] And

18. Cf. Schlabach, "Mennonites and Pietism in America," 222–40.

19. Weaver has put forward this general argument in numerous publications, but the most systematic version can be found in Weaver, *Keeping Salvation Ethical*; see also Kraus, "Interpreting the Atonement in Anabaptist-Mennonite Tradition," 291–311; Kraus, "American Mennonites and the Bible," 309–29.

20. See, e.g., Kauffman, "Boundary Maintenance," 227–40, and Schlabach, "Reveille for 'Die Stillen im Lande,'" 213–26. A more general expression of a similar concern can be inferred in the findings of a sociological survey presented in Kauffman and Harder, *Anabaptists Four Centuries Later*, 83–100, and in a subsequent study, Howard and Driedger, *Mennonite Mosaic*, 210–30, 253.

defenders of the Mennonite tradition of a capella hymnody bemoaned the influence of evangelical "praise and worship" music. By the late twentieth century, "evangelicalism" for many Mennonite denominational leaders had become synonymous with the aggressively patriotic, and often militaristic, political agenda of the Moral Majority, the high-profile lifestyles of flamboyant televangelists, the dispensationalist apocalypticism of the "Left Behind" series, and the kitsch culture of the spiritual self-help industry.[21] On the basis of these impressionistic stereotypes, any form of evangelical influence in Mennonite communities was inherently negative. Far from being a source of renewal, "evangelicalism" had become a problem from which the Mennonite Church needed to be saved.

MENNONITES AND EVANGELICALS: A NEW APPROACH TO AN OLD QUESTION

Problems with the Mennonite Critique

Although the concerns raised by Friedmann, Schlabach, and others were certainly not without merit, the critical posture toward evangelicalism by Mennonite church leaders has also been deeply problematic. Too often, the term "evangelical" was reduced to a negative caricature that, not surprisingly, was found wanting when compared with the very best qualities of the Anabaptism-Mennonite tradition. Furthermore, the allergic rejection to all things "evangelical" by some leaders reinforced a long-standing tendency among Mennonites to foster an identity of opposition—that is, defining who they were by focusing on what they rejected. Thus, Mennonites were *"neither Catholic nor Protestant"*; they were *not conformed* to the world; and they were emphatically *not* evangelicals.[22] Yet to dismiss evangelical forms of renewal out of hand as alien to the Anabaptist-Mennonite

---

21. Things reached a point where Nelson Kraybill, then president of Associated Mennonite Biblical Seminary, found it necessary to publicly defend the term "evangelical" in an essay, "Is Our Future Evangelical?" 6–7, which was then frequently reprinted in a number of Mennonite periodicals.

22. Although the historian Walter Klaassen has since backed away from this language, his highly popular book, *Anabaptism: Neither Catholic nor Protestant*, went a long way to reinforce this impulse to ground Mennonite identity in oppositional language.

faith is to ignore the deep debts that the movement owes to the Protestant reformers.

Perhaps the most troubling aspect of this anxious rejection of evangelicalism was the fact that it avoided serious engagement with the spiritual hunger in Mennonite congregations which evangelicalism seemed to satisfy. Simply rejecting evangelicalism out of hand as a blight on "genuine" Anabaptist-Mennonite faith does not adequately address the various internal problems Mennonites have consistently had to confront in their history—a tendency toward legalism and works-righteousness, for example, or a posture of collective arrogance, or an inclination toward joylessness—for which evangelical renewal has frequently served as something of an antidote. All living traditions are constantly in the process of renewal. The very persistence of the evangelical impulse within Anabaptist-Mennonite history suggests that it offers Mennonite communities some elements of the Christian faith that is lacking in their own tradition.

A Confessional Approach to Future Dialogue

In light of this complex, somewhat tortured relationship between Anabaptist-Mennonites and evangelicalism, how might Anabaptist-Mennonites approach future interaction with evangelicals? In the past, those of us in the Anabaptist-Mennonite side of the conversation have often begun by attempting to define the "essence" of each tradition, and then to negotiate appropriate boundaries by comparing and contrasting the two groups.[23] Not surprisingly, the result has often been a tendency to retreat to theological abstractions and idealized versions of both sides. In a more charitable approach, the conversation partners are inclined to negotiate a rhetorical compromise by identifying several distinctive emphases in each tradition, pronounce them to be "strengths," and then call for a friendly rapprochement in which both groups agree to borrow the best elements from the other.[24]

For the remainder of this essay, I would like to propose the framework of a different approach to future conversations between evangelicals and Mennonites. Rather than refining yet another list of

23. See, for example, Kraus's essays, "Introduction: What is Evangelicalism?" and "Anabaptism and Evangelicalism," 9–22, 169–82.

24. See, for example, Sider's essay, "Evangelicalism and the Mennonite Tradition," 149–68.

distinctive theological characteristics, I suggest that future conversations between Anabaptist-Mennonites and evangelicals be framed in a *confessional* mode, focusing on a set of theological blindspots, contradictions, or conundrums that both traditions share and which neither has resolved very well. I recognize that my invitation to frame the dialogue between our two traditions from a shared posture of humility and vulnerability may initially seem unattractive, especially for Mennonite scholars and church leaders who have grown accustomed to thinking of American evangelicalism in antagonistic terms. But I think such an approach has the potential to open a path to renewal in both traditions and could help to check—and possibly even reverse—the long history of division that seems so deeply entrenched in our shared history.

A Shared Reformation/Free Church Legacy

After all, despite their distinctive historical and theological trajectories in the nineteenth and twentieth centuries, Anabaptist-Mennonites and evangelicals share much in common. Both are children of the Protestant Reformation, born in that maelstrom of religious debate and division whose legacy has deeply shaped their identity ever since. Almost all of the first generation Anabaptists, for example, began their theological journey as part of the broader evangelical (*evangelisch* / Protestant) reformation movement. Along with the other reformers of the day—and with later evangelicals—the Anabaptists rejected papal authority and the sacramental system of Catholicism; they embraced a high view of Scripture as the Word of God, freed from its "captivity" to the medieval hermeneutical tradition; and they linked salvation to an individual encounter with Jesus, in which repentance and conversion were inseparably joined to God's initiative and the free gift of grace. Beyond these general themes, both the Anabaptist-Mennonite and the evangelical traditions have embraced believer's baptism and the voluntary nature of the church; they regard the sacraments as symbols rather than efficacious rituals; they share a deep concern for personal morality and a rich devotional life; and they have generally favored congregationalist-oriented models of church polity.

Clearly, these shared emphases have borne enormous fruit—the strengths of both traditions are abundantly clear. But embedded within these distinctive markers of identity are several persistent theological and ecclesial tensions—part of our shared Reformation legacy—that neither the Anabaptist-Mennonite nor the evangelical tradition have fully resolved. Although we encounter these tensions or contradictions in different ways, their enduring persistence in both traditions could serve as a useful point of departure for shared conversation.

SHARED THEOLOGICAL TENSIONS, CONTRADICTIONS, AND CONUNDRUMS

In the remainder of this essay I briefly identify four potential themes for future Anabaptist-Mennonite/evangelical dialogue, and then propose a constructive theological framework for engaging that conversation.

The Gift and the Burden of Religious Voluntarism

Like most evangelicals, Anabaptist-Mennonites are deeply committed to the principle of "conversion" and voluntary baptism. To be sure, the gift of God's salvation is completely unmerited—it is not something we earn. Yet we have also taught that God does not coerce faith. The offer of salvation must be freely received. As a consequence, Anabaptist-Mennonites have advocated for the principle of believer's baptism and the freedom of religious conscience. These convictions, we believe, are theologically coherent, consistent with Scripture, and in accord with the witness of the early church.[25]

At the same time, however, the strong emphasis on voluntarism within our traditions has also led to several unintended consequences that merit closer reflection. What, for example, is an appropriate age of baptism? If the only thing at stake in conversion is a young child's conscious remorse for an inherent inclination to disobedience, then baptism could occur at age five or six. If the emphasis is on a Christian maturity sufficient to meaningfully participate in the baptismal vow to "give and receive of counsel," then a somewhat older age for baptism would seem more appropriate, perhaps sixteen or eighteen. But if the central concern is a genuinely "free" decision—independent of outside pressure or subtle forms of coercion—then baptism should prob-

---

25. See, for example, the recent encyclopedic study by Ferguson, *Baptism in the Early Church*.

ably wait until a child has left the parental home and is fully capable of choosing a life outside the Christian community.[26]

Another obvious question raised by the principle of believer's baptism is the lingering critique of works-righteousness. If coming to Christ requires a conscious act of individual volition, some in the Christian tradition have argued, then it must inevitably follow that we believe that the individual *initiates* salvation—that we are somehow "responsible" for our own salvation. This illusion that the will is truly free in matters of salvation, the argument continues, enslaves rather than liberates the Christian. The "voluntary" believer is forced to confront an endless cycle of anxious uncertainty about the assurance of salvation that call for repeated rounds of introspection and recommitment. The result is a perpetual, low-grade anxiety about the state of one's soul that leads to weekly altar calls and serial "conversions."[27]

An equally challenging consequence of our shared emphasis on a voluntary faith is the extent to which our focus on "free choice" has fed into the pervasive individualism of the modern world, making the decision to follow Christ simply one more consumer-oriented decision that comes with a promise of enhancing my life. "While there is no inherent conceptual tension between discipleship and voluntary church membership," writes Stanley Hauerwas, ". . . in liberal cultures too often voluntary church membership is translated into the right to make up one's own mind." In the modern context of religious pluralism, voluntary baptism can easily be confused with the secular commitment to individualism and autonomy. "Such a church," Hauerwas concludes, "too often reproduces ethnic, class, and national identification in the name of freedom."[28]

I do not believe that the solution to these challenges lies in a return to infant baptism or the doctrine of double-predestination. But Anabaptist-Mennonites would benefit by more intentional conversa-

---

26. I treat these questions more carefully in J. Roth, *Beliefs*, 59–73.

27. In his early magisterial history of the Mennonite Brethren church, P. M. Friesen described this tendency among Russian Mennonite circles as "Mennonite melancholia."—Friesen, *Mennonite Brotherhood in Russia*, 212. See also Gundy, "Scatter Plots," 5–27.

28. "Accordingly," Hauerwas continues, "the church as a disciplined body becomes a community of like-minded individuals who share the conviction that they should respect each other's right to make up his or her own mind."—Hauerwas, "Whose Church?" 71, 73.

tions with evangelicals about how they have wrestled with the theological and psychological tensions inherent in a voluntaristic tradition.

The Ambiguities of Biblical Hermeneutics

Children of the Reformation tend to look fondly on that stirring moment at the Diet of Worms in 1521 when Martin Luther stood before the assembled temporal and ecclesial authorities of Europe and defiantly defended the freedom of individual conscience in matters of biblical interpretation. For free church heirs of the Protestant tradition, the principles of "Scripture alone" and the "priesthood of all believers" are foundational. Like most evangelicals, Anabaptist-Mennonites understand themselves to be a tradition rooted deeply in the authority of Scripture. The Bible is accessible to ordinary Christians; its meaning is plain; and its word sufficient for guiding the church in all matters of faith and practice. Moreover, we believe that the authority to interpret Scripture resides not in the papacy, or in the teaching office of the Catholic church, or in the ancient traditions of biblical interpretation established by the Church Fathers. Rather, the task of interpreting Scripture is shared by all Christians who come to the task with pure hearts, ready to be led in their reading by the Holy Spirit.

On the surface, these principles sound quite appealing. But when it comes to the real work of biblical hermeneutics, claiming the authority of "Scripture alone" almost always begs the question. After all, Scripture is always interpreted in a context. Scripture is always read through the lens of a particular theological tradition—elevating some texts above others, resolving apparent contradictions according to some set of larger principles, and applying texts to the realities of daily life by some sort of active interpretation. It should not be surprising that all groups emerging out of the Reformation quickly adapted extra-biblical "lenses" to guide the interpretation of Scripture: the introduction of authoritative confessions of faith, for example, or the creation of a teaching office in the form of "ordination" or, as with the Anglicans, a return to the principle of apostolic succession.

Most Anabaptist-Mennonite groups have been reluctant to explicitly frame biblical hermeneutics in these formalistic ways. But in the absence of clearly articulated principles of biblical hermeneutics, rhetorical claims that the "word of God is clear" or that we are "simply a Bible-believing church" begin to ring hollow. I do not mean to suggest that our traditions have read Scripture arbitrarily or randomly. In point of fact, both groups have given an enormous amount of attention to the question of hermeneutics.[29] But our suspicion of tradition and the learned exegesis of erudite scholars have sometimes blinded us to the richness of Scripture, or made us susceptible to the eccentric teachings of charismatic individuals, or even, at times, cynical about the authority of Scripture itself. Insisting that the Bible is our sole authority, while ignoring the way that we have also been shaped by tradition or context, has frequently been the source of deep division.

Anabaptist-Mennonites would be well served to engage in more conversation with evangelicals about the principles of biblical hermeneutics—including our understandings of tradition, the place of the teaching office, and the role of "dictates of conscience"—as we seek to discern God's Word in our time and context.

The Ecclesial Confusions of a Congregationalist Polity

None of the reformers in the sixteenth century set out to create a new "denomination." But they were convinced that the institution of the Roman Catholic Church had become encrusted with human innovations that had no basis in Scripture or the early church. If the "true church" was to be restored, they believed, a millennium of theological and institutional accretions would need to be swept away in order to recover a more faithful form of Catholicism by restoring the true faith of the apostolic church.[30]

As children of the Reformation, both Anabaptist-Mennonites and evangelicals are united in their rejection of Roman Catholic claims to be the "universal" church and the principle of "apostolic succession" as the basis for papal authority. Yet one of the most frequent questions addressed to the Anabaptists in the sixteenth century was: what is the *basis* for your ecclesial authority? Who ordained your preachers to teach the Word of God? By what right do you set up your teachers

---

29. For some sense of the range of this literature see, e.g., Murray, *Biblical Interpretation*; Swartley, *Essays on Biblical Interpretation*; or Swartley, *Slavery, Sabbath, War, and Women*.

30. For an incisive, provocative reflection on the consequences of rejecting the legacy of the medieval Catholic tradition, see Martin, "Nothing New under the Sun?" 1–27. Williams explores a similar set of questions from the evangelical side in his *Evangelicals and Tradition*.

and your churches over against the established church? Or are your teachers simply self-designated?

Although these questions may seem trivial on the surface—especially for modern Christians who are quite accustomed to thinking about faith as a personal right—at stake here are substantive matters that have had significant consequences for our traditions. If it is true, as Luther argued, that the "dictates of one's conscience" are authoritative in matters of biblical interpretation, then it inevitably follows that *all* Christians have the right to speak with authority about their own reading of Scripture, provided that they are following the imperative of their conscience. Not surprisingly, the end result of this logic has been not merely a divided church, but a splintered church. Today some fifteen thousand independent religious organizations are registered with the IRS in the United States alone, with a total of more than forty thousand Christian denominations scattered around the world.

In the absence of an overarching framework for ecclesial authority—such as that provided by the Catholic sacerdotum, the Anglican episcopacy, or the Lutheran Augsburg Confession—the principles of ecclesial unity in free church settings are often determined by the local congregation. In some settings this takes the form of a clearly defined set of doctrines (Fundamentalism) or a list of ethical practices (as in the Ordnung, or discipline, of the Amish). Often, however, the real source of church unity is grounded in the personal charisma of the individual pastor. Anabaptist-Mennonite congregations may speak of their pastor's authority in terms of a "calling," and there may be mechanisms in place for formal "ordination"; yet to a significant degree, ecclesial authority is centered not in the office per se, but rather in the personal abilities, charms, persuasiveness, and occasionally manipulation, of the pastor.[31] When tensions emerge within the congregation, the resolution is often division.

A closely-related corollary of a congregationalist ecclesiology is a persistent lack of clarity regarding the relationship of the individual congregation to other like-minded congregations or to the larger Christian church. From the beginning, free church groups have always tended to create networks of associations. During the

---

31. Or, as is often the case in contemporary Mennonite circles, we take the opposite tact and repress any expressions of charismatic authority so as to reduce the concept of spiritual leadership to that of a group facilitator.

nineteenth and twentieth centuries many of these groups in the North American context adopted the organizational model of the mainstream Protestant denominations, sometimes with district or conference intermediary structures. Yet the relationship of the local congregation to other congregations or to a larger, transregional fellowship of like-minded groups has often remained theologically and functionally ambiguous. As a result, the witness of the church remains deeply divided. And ecumenical conversations are rendered almost impossible since it is not clear who speaks—and with what authority—on behalf of "the church."[32] All this does not even begin to address the larger question of how our individual conferences, or our respective traditions, envision themselves in relation to the larger Christian world or to the universal church.

Anabaptist-Mennonites would benefit by engaging in conversation with evangelicals about our relationship to the "people of the promise" who God called out already in the book of Genesis to be a light unto the nations, and our mutual understanding of the millennium of church history that connects the early church with the Protestant Reformation. We would be well-served by reflecting more carefully together about our understandings as to what constitutes the basis for the unity of the church.

Anxieties about the Sacraments

Like most evangelicals, Anabaptist-Mennonites emphatically rejected medieval Catholic sacramental theology. For those in the free church tradition, the Catholic view of the sacraments seemed to promote a mechanistic view of grace (*ex opera operato*) that turned salvation into a commodity, reduced believers to passive recipients, and transformed the clergy into all-powerful intermediaries of God's presence in the lives of ordinary believers. Yet the wholehearted rejection of these perceived abuses within the Catholic church has left our traditions with a very ambiguous understanding of the sacraments.

---

32. This is not to detract from the significant conversations recently undertaken by the Mennonite World Conference with Catholics and Lutherans, resulting in the publication of W. Roth and Schlabach, *Called Together to Be Peacemakers*, and *Healing Memories*. But since the Mennonite World Conference is not a church body, the ecclesial status of these statements remains rather ambiguous.

At the heart of all theological reflection is a fundamental question: how do heaven and earth meet? How does the transcendent world of the Spirit intersect with the ordinary material world of time and space? In short, how are humans reconciled with God? For medieval Catholics, the answer to these questions would have been unimaginable apart from the sacraments—that is, formal rituals within the church initiated by the clergy in which God's grace and living presence was mediated to human beings in time and space. In the most common sacrament, the celebration of the Mass, ordinary human beings entered into the living presence of the divine as they ingested the communion wafer—bread that literally had been transformed into the body of Jesus.

Anabaptist-Mennonites are generally very quick to assure those present at communion that the bread and wine are "merely" symbols—that Christ is present "only" in spirit; that the water of baptism is "just" water. While bread and wine and water may be helpful tangible reminders of our covenant with Christ, what really matters to God is the inner transformation of our heart. This spiritualized language of the sacraments squares with a view of salvation anchored in the doctrine of substitutionary atonement. Through the shedding of his innocent blood, Christ paid the debt of our sins. All we need to do is to accept this gift by inviting Jesus into our hearts as our Lord and personal Savior. For many Christians, these phrases are so familiar that we scarcely give them a second thought.

Yet this view of salvation, combined with our unease about the sacraments—that is, the physical, tangible, embodied expressions of God's presence in our midst—can easily leave us with an abstract, subjective understanding of faith that is ultimately disconnected from daily life.[33] Christian faith in this mode is tethered to emotional feelings, the recitation of certain words, or expressive forms of worship, but not necessarily "embodied" in a concrete, material, or physical form. God is present, we insist—but our reluctance to embrace the tangible expressions of God's presence in the created world suggests that we are, in the end, not very clear just how God is made visible in the world.

Such reluctance can easily lead to a view of worship focused on ourselves—our performance, our feelings and emotions, our words—

---

33. I explore this tendency in more detail in J. Roth, *Practices*, 193–211.

that is disembodied. Yet God imbues the world of his creation; the doctrine of the incarnation affirms the reality of God's presence in physical form. We should not be too quick to dismiss ritual expressions of God's presence as "just" symbols or "merely" bread/water.

None of these theological conundrums have crippled the church; many of our congregations are thriving. Yet these issues continue to lurk at the edges of our church life as barely hidden contradictions or as tensions that remain unresolved. They are often ignored—despite their negative impact—because opening them up seems to threaten so much that is a given. One way forward in relations between Anabaptist-Mennonites and evangelicals would be to enter into conversation about our shared struggles with these themes.

A FRAMEWORK FOR CONVERSATION? THE INCARNATIONAL THEOLOGY OF PILGRAM MARPECK

One potential beginning point for a constructive conversation could focus on the life and thought of Pilgram Marpeck, a creative sixteenth-century Anabaptist lay theologian who anticipated many of these theological tensions in his writings and spent much of his life working toward a coherent solution. Marpeck's writings, recently the subject of a great deal of scholarly attention, are of particular interest to this conversation because Marpeck was explicitly evangelical in his basic theological orientation, while also attentive to elements of Catholic theology that he thought merited reform rather than dismissive rejection. Less sectarian than other radical reformers, Marpeck has attracted the interest of theologians across the free church theological spectrum, including both evangelicals and Mennonites.[34]

Pilgram Marpeck began his career as a civil official in the Catholic mining town of Rattenberg, where he first encountered Anabaptism in the form of itinerant preachers who were summarily executed for their convictions.[35] In 1528, when Archduke Ferdinand

---

34. For several recent and very thoughtful Baptist engagements with Marpeck's thought see Yarnell, *Formation of Christian Doctrine*, 73–106, and Rothkegel, "Pilgram Marpeck," 7–36.

35. The literature on Marpeck has expanded enormously in recent years. The best entré into his life and thought is a recent biography by Klaassen and Klassen, *Marpeck*. Almost all of Marpeck's writing is now available in English translation. I

ordered Marpeck to assist in hunting down other Anabaptists in the region, he resigned his office and fled to Strasburg where he found steady work as a civil engineer and a safe haven for conversation with other religious radicals who had also found refuge there. In Strasburg Marpeck began a long career as an energetic defender of Anabaptist theology, especially in response to the Spiritualists who rejected all outward ceremonies and in response to civil authorities who were ready to defend the Christian faith with violence. By 1532, those same civil authorities forced Marpeck to flee Strasbourg. After a decade of itinerant leadership, he eventually found employment as a city engineer in Augsburg, where he lived for the last fourteen years of his life in relative peace, even as he continued to support the underground Anabaptist fellowship there.

Although Marpeck had no formal theological training and was not a highly systematic thinker, he took the classic questions of Christian theology very seriously. In his response to the Spiritualists, who wanted to get rid of all rituals like baptism and the Lord's Supper, he vigorously defended the humanity of Christ and the necessity of ceremonies in the life of the church. On the other hand, in response to the Lutheran focus on "salvation by grace alone," Marpeck insisted that God's gift of grace—the transformation of the inner person— could not be understood or rightly received apart from a transformation of Christian behavior. And in conversation with Anabaptist groups whose quest for the pure church had led to legalism and endless disputes, Marpeck repeatedly emphasized the centrality of the Holy Spirit in the life of the church.

The key to thinking about God, Marpeck argued, begins with a proper understanding of the Incarnation, the wondrous mystery that "Christ became a natural man for natural human beings."[36] As God Incarnate—fully human and fully divine—Christ marked a fundamental break in human history that had consequences for every aspect of Christian faith and practice. In terms of biblical hermeneutics, the incarnation served Marpeck as the grounding for the essential unity of letter and spirit. Thus, he repeatedly challenged the Spiritualists to heed the concrete meaning of the text, while admonishing the biblical

---

have also written on Marpeck's thought, and some of what follows is taken from J. Roth, "Marpeck and the Later Swiss Brethren," 360–63; J. Roth, *Practices*, 201–9.

36. Klassen and Klaassen, *Writings of Pilgram Marpeck*, 85.

literalists to allow the Spirit and the principle of love to breathe life into the external word.

Even more central for the development of Marpeck's ethics, the incarnation marked a significant break between the Old Testament and the New Testament: in Christ, the promise of the Old Testament finds its fulfillment; the light of Christ illuminates what had previously been understood only as a shadow, revealing fully God's will for humanity. This conviction became the basis for Marpeck's insistence that regenerated Christians will follow Christ in life—most visibly in their willingness to participate in Christ's suffering rather than to take up the carnal sword to defend their lives. But Marpeck did not overlook the spiritual Christ. The world is full, he wrote, of Christians "who confess only the mortal and physical Christ, but very few believe and confess the risen Christ with their lives." True believers participate fully in the humanity of Christ—"his words, works, deeds and ceremonies"—but they do so "no longer according to the standard of carnal, but of spiritual, understanding."[37] Elsewhere, Marpeck described Christ's body in participatory language: because the Word was made flesh, our own flesh and bone is no longer tainted by that of Adam, but is renewed through our participation with Christ.[38]

This view of the incarnation also grounded Marpeck's understanding of the sacraments. Like most of his fellow Anabaptists, Marpeck rejected Catholic arguments for the bodily presence of Christ in the sacraments (transubstantiation)—he did not believe that the physical properties of the bread and wine changed in communion. Yet he was not willing to describe baptism and Lord's Supper as "merely" symbols. Whereas many Anabaptists regarded ceremonies as "outward signs of an inner transformation," Marpeck went further to argue that the water of baptism or the bread and wine of communion were "of one being with the inward reality they represented."[39] In his view, the physical, material elements of water, bread, and wine were essential to the Spirit's transformative presence in worship. Because we can only know God through tangible and material forms—seen most dramatically in the humanity of Christ—God continues to be revealed in history in ways that are si-

37. Ibid., 90.
38. Ibid., 76.
39. Rempel, *Lord's Supper in Anabaptism*, 97.

multaneously spiritual and material. Indeed, for Marpeck, the Spirit could not be mediated apart from the material elements—the physical, material elements were essential to the Spirit's transformative presence. Ceremonies like baptism and the Lord's Supper, Marpeck thought, were the means by which we encounter, participate in, and are transformed by the presence of God. When the outward signs of bread, wine or baptism were received with true inward faith, they "are no longer signs," Marpeck argued, "but are one essence in Christ."[40] In the person of Jesus—fully human and fully divine—created reality became the mediator of human participation with God. In partaking of the elements, believers participate in Christ's "unglorified" historical body, a body that struggled and suffered, so that they might be conformed to his "most holy, deified flesh and bone."

In developing his understanding of ceremonies, Marpeck drew heavily on the Christian doctrine of the Trinity. Through Christ's humanity, God is revealed in humble, material substances like water, bread, wine. But when the water, bread, and wine are received with true inward faith—when the Spirit is present in the believer—the ceremony of baptism or communion becomes an external "co-witness" (*Mitzeugnis*) of the Spirit's work. Thus, God the Father acts internally in the hearts of humans, through the Holy Spirit, so that the outward elements of the sacraments "are no longer signs but are one essence in Christ."[41] Insofar as these rituals carry on the presence of Christ in the world, participation in them transforms the believers. In baptism and communion we participate in a new reality. "Whoever has the truth in the heart," wrote Marpeck, "the truth which is pointed to and signified by the external sign, for him it is no sign at all, but rather one reality with the inner. . . . For that which the Father does, the Son does simultaneously: the Father, as Spirit internally; the Son, as the church, externally."[42]

Marpeck's view of the sacraments was also closely tied to his understanding of the church. In partaking of the outward elements of communion, believers participate in Christ's body. But just as the Word of God, Jesus Christ, became incarnate in human flesh, so the words of God must also become incarnate in physical reality. This

40. Klassen and Klaassen, *Writings of Pilgram Marpeck*, 195.
41. Ibid.
42. Ibid.

means that communion is indeed a memorial service—a service of remembering. To share in communion is to actively recall the suffering and self-emptying of the human Christ. But because Christ is also spiritually present in the Holy Spirit, this is not "merely" a symbolic event. Christ's victory over evil in the resurrection and the gift of the Holy Spirit at Pentecost have made possible a new social reality. Through the redemptive activity in Christ in history, those who have become "sons and daughters of God" receive a new nature and participate in this new reality in real time and space. Therefore, as we participate in Christ's "most holy, deified flesh and bone" in communion, we also—though the presence of the Holy Spirit—are being "re-membered," re-formed into the living body of Christ. The church thus "embodies" the living Spirit of God. In its worship and in its life together, the church becomes "the prolongation of the incarnation." It is the living Body of Christ.

> At the same time, Marpeck was emphatic that this transformation of Christian life was possible only through the presence and power of the Holy Spirit: "Without the artistry and teaching of the Holy Spirit, who pours out the love, which is God, into the hearts of the faith, and which surpasses all reason and understanding, everything is in vain. The Holy Spirit proceeds from the Father and Son, and He witnesses to the Father and Son in the hearts of all the faithful. He copies and repeats the perfect law of liberty of Christ. The faithful look into this law of liberty in order that they may fervently do what Christ spoke and commanded.[43]

The result of Marpeck's theology was a firm rejection of the sort of Spiritualism that focused primarily on a glorified, transfigured Christ, and a clear affirmation of a visible church that witnessed to the living Christ through the ordinances of baptism and the Lord's Supper, the practice of church discipline, and the morally regenerated lives of its members. At the same time, Marpeck offered an important corrective to those tendencies among some second-generation Anabaptists that vitiated the movement's spiritual core—a mechanistic "theology of suffering," for example, that could equate physical suffering with Christian faithfulness; an inclination to "works righteousness" that separated ethics from a living union with Christ; an absolute dualism

---

43. Ibid., 458.

between church and world that artificially isolated the church from its social and political context; or overly harsh disciplinary practices that had lost sight of the goal of love and restoration.

Marpeck's leadership in various Anabaptist communities spanned four decades, bridging the tumultuous early years of intense persecution with the growing stability that came to characterize most Anabaptist groups by the middle of the century. In an era given to extremes, Marpeck's was a voice of moderation. Though he was more of an apologist than a systematic theologian, more than any other leader of the time, he integrated Anabaptist thought within the categories of classical theology. His focus on the Incarnation could provide a useful beginning point for conversations between Anabaptist-Mennonites and evangelicals.

CONCLUSION

The world in which we live is broken and divided. One expression of that brokenness, tragically, is the divided nature of Christ's body, the church. As children of the Reformation, both Anabaptist-Mennonite and evangelical groups are deeply indebted to the theological legacy of the sixteenth-century reformers. But part of that legacy is also the reality of division. When we recall the history of Anabaptist-Mennonites and evangelicals alike, we remain participants in that division. In this essay, I have suggested that the path to healing is not to be found primarily in a reaffirmation of some ideal form of our distinctive identities. Rather, healing results when Christians come together to bear witness to the reality of the Incarnation.

The Good News of the Gospel is that Jesus has come to break down "the dividing wall of hostility" (Eph 2:14). In Jesus, God took on human form—the Word became flesh. We are called to "remember" this broken body, not because Christians are in danger of forgetting Christ. The opposite of remembering in the Bible is not necessarily forgetting. Rather, the opposite of remembering is "dis-membering"—that is, the persistent human impulse to pull apart, to divide. That is why the Bible so often shows us a God who re-members. The focus of God's activity in the world is that of making things whole, of restoring people, of re-membering communities, of re-membering us who are so often dis-membered. Right remembering calls us to acknowledge the broken body of Christ even as, paradoxically, it invites us to also participate in His restored and resurrected body.

At the heart of the "gospel of peace" is a conviction that the fear and violence that led to Christ's death on the cross will not have the last word. Rather in "humbling himself even unto death," God has "exalted him to the highest place" (Phil 2:8–9) so that, in the words of the Apostle Paul, "power is made perfect in weakness" (2 Cor 12:9). This is why "right remembering" matters in our conversations: that in our remembrance of Christ's body—broken and resurrected—we might find healing for our own brokenness and together bear witness to a watching world that love is indeed more powerful than death. And, in so doing, Anabaptist-Mennonites and evangelicals together might invite all those who are broken, divided, lonely, and alienated into the joy of new life, nourished by the vine of Christ, and bearing fruit of reconciliation and wholeness.

BIBLIOGRAPHY

Alliance of Evangelical Mennonite Congregations. No pages. Online: http://www.aemc2000.org.

Bebbington, David W. *Evangelicalism in Modern Britain: A History from the 1730s to the 1980s*. London: Unwin Hyman, 1989.

Bender, Harold S. "The Anabaptist Vision." *The Mennonite Quarterly Review* 18 (April 1944) 67–88.

———. "Mennonites of the United States and Canada." *The Mennonite Quarterly Review* 11 (January 1937) 50–75.

———. "Outside Influences on Mennonite Thought." *Mennonite Life* (January 1955) 45–48.

Burkholder, David G. *The Inroads of Pietism*. Baltic, OH: Amish Brotherhood, n.d.

Durnbaugh, Donald. *The Believers' Church*. Scottdale, PA: Herald, 1968.

Ferguson, Everett. *Baptism in the Early Church: History, Theology, and Liturgy in the First Five Centuries*. Grand Rapids: Eerdmans, 2009.

Friedmann, Robert. *Mennonite Piety Through the Centuries: Its Genius and its Literature*. Goshen, IN: Mennonite Historical Society, 1949.

Friesen, P. M. *The Mennonite Brotherhood in Russia, 1789–1910*. Winnipeg, MB: Christian, 1978.

Garrett, James Leo, Jr., ed. *The Concept of the Believers' Church*. Scottdale, PA: Herald, 1969.

Gundy, Jeff. "Scatter Plots: Depression, Silence, and Mennonite Margins." *Conrad Grebel Review* 18 (Winter 2000) 5–27.

Hauerwas, Stanley. "Whose Church? Which Future? Whither the Anabaptist Vision?" In *In Good Company: The Church as Polis*, 65–78. Notre Dame, IN: University of Notre Dame Press, 1995.

Healing Memories: Reconciling in Christ. Report of the Lutheran-Mennonite International Study Commission. Strasbourg: The Lutheran World Federation and The Mennonite World Conference, 2010.

Institute for the Study of American Evangelicals. No pages: http://isae.wheaton.edu/defining-evangelicalism/defining-the-term-in-contemporary-times/.

Kauffman, J. Howard. "Boundary Maintenance and Cultural Assimilation of Contemporary Mennonites." *The Mennonite Quarterly Review* 51 (July 1977) 227–40.

Kauffman, J. Howard, and Leland Harder. *Anabaptists Four Centuries Later: A Profile of Five Mennonite and Brethren in Christ Denominations*. Scottdale, PA: Herald, 1975.

Kauffman, J. Howard, and Leo Driedger. *The Mennonite Mosaic: Identity and Modernization*. Scottdale, PA: Herald, 1991.

Klaassen, Walter. *Anabaptism: Neither Catholic nor Protestant*. Waterloo, ON: Conrad, 1981.

Klaassen, Walter, and William Klassen. *Marpeck: A Life of Dissent and Conformity*. Scottdale, PA: Herald, 2008.

Klassen, William, and Walter Klaassen, editors. *The Writings of Pilgram Marpeck*. Scottdale, PA: Herald, 1978.

Klopfenstein, Perry A. *Marching to Zion: A History of the Apostolic Christian Church of America, 1847–2007*. 2nd ed. Eureka, IL: Apostolic Christian, 2008.

Kraus, C. Norman. "American Mennonites and the Bible, 1750–1950." *The Mennonite Quarterly Review* 41 (October 1967) 309–29.

———. "Anabaptism and Evangelicalism." In *Evangelicalism and Anabaptism*, edited by C. Norman Kraus, 169–82. Scottdale, PA: Herald, 1979.

———. "Interpreting the Atonement in Anabaptist-Mennonite Tradition." *The Mennonite Quarterly Review* 66 (July 1992) 291–311.

———. "Introduction: What is Evangelicalism?" In *Evangelicalism and Anabaptism*, edited by C. Norman Kraus, 9–22. Scottdale, PA: Herald, 1979.

Kraus, C. Norman, editor. *Evangelicalism and Anabaptism*. Scottdale, PA: Herald, 1979.

Kraybill, J. Nelson. "Is Our Future Evangelical?" *Canadian Mennonite*, 11 February 2002, 6–7. Reprinted in *The Mennonite*, 5 March 2002, 14–16; *Die Brücke: Täuferisch-mennonitische Gemeindezeitschrift*, May 2002; *Our Faith*, Summer 2002.

Lehman, James O. *Mennonite Tent Revivals: Howard Hammer and Myron Augsburger, 1952–1962*. Kitchener, ON: Pandora, 2002.

Littell, Franklin. *The Free Church*. Boston: Starr King, 1957.

Martin, Dennis D. "Nothing New under the Sun? Mennonites and History." *Conrad Grebel Review* 5 (1987) 1–27.

Murray, Stuart. *Biblical Interpretation in the Anabaptist Tradition*. Kitchener, ON: Pandora, 1999.

Pfeiffer, Joseph F. "Between Remnant and Reviewal: A Historical and Comparative Study of the Apostolic Christian Church among Neo-Anabaptist Renewal Movements in Europe and America." MA thesis, Associated Mennonite Biblical Seminary, 2010.

Rempel, John. *The Lord's Supper in Anabaptism: A Study in the Christology of Balthasar Hubmaier, Pilgram Marpeck, and Dirk Philips*. Scottdale, PA: Herald, 1993.

Robert Friedmann memorial issue of *The Mennonite Quarterly Review* 48 (April 1974).
Rosedale Bible College. No pages: http://www.rosedale.edu/leaders/.
Roth, John D. *Beliefs: Mennonite Faith and Practice*. Scottdale, PA: Herald, 2005.
———. "Introduction." In *Letters of the Amish Division: A Sourcebook*, translated and edited by John D. Roth, 1–17. 2nd ed. Goshen, IN: Mennonite Historical Society, 2002.
———. "Marpeck and the Later Swiss Brethren." In *A Companion to Anabaptism and Spiritualism, 1521–1700*, edited by John D. Roth and James M. Stayer, 347–88. Boston: Brill, 2007.
———. "Pietism and the Anabaptist Soul." *Pietismus und Neuzeit: Ein Jahrbuch zur Geschichte des neueren Protestantismus* 25 (1999) 182–202.
———. *Practices: Mennonite Worship and Witness*. Scottdale, PA: Herald, 2009.
Roth, Willard, and Gerald W. Schlabach, editors. *Called Together to Be Peacemakers: Report of the International Dialogue between the Catholic Church and Mennonite World Conference, 1998–2003*. Kitchener, ON: Pandora, 2005.
Rothkegel, Martin. "Pilgram Marpeck and the 'Fellows of the Covenant': The Short History of the Rise and Decline of an Anabaptist Denominational Network." *The Mennonite Quarterly Review* 85 (January 2011) 7–36.
Schlabach, Theron F. *Gospel vs. Gospel: Mission and the Mennonite Church, 1863–1944*. Scottdale, PA: Herald, 1980.
———. "Mennonites and Pietism in America, 1740–1880: Some Thoughts on the Friedmann Thesis." *The Mennonite Quarterly Review* 57 (1983) 222–40.
———. "Reveille for 'Die Stillen im Lande': A Stir Among Mennonites in the Late Nineteenth Century." *The Mennonite Quarterly Review* 51 (July 1977) 213–26.
Sider, Ronald J. "Evangelicalism and the Mennonite Tradition." In *Evangelicalism and Anabaptism*, edited by C. Norman Kraus, 149–68. Scottdale, PA: Herald, 1979.
Swartley, Willard M. *Slavery, Sabbath, War, and Women: Case Issues in Biblical Interpretation*. Scottdale, PA: Herald, 1983.
Swartley, Willard M., editor. *Essays on Biblical Interpretation: Anabaptist-Mennonite Perspectives*. Elkhart, IN: Institute of Mennonite Studies, 1984.
Weaver, J. Denny. *Keeping Salvation Ethical: Mennonite and Amish Atonement Theology in the Late Nineteenth Century*. Scottdale, PA: Herald, 1997.
Weber, Beat. "Über die Anfänge der Neutäufer." In *"Alt- und Neutäufer"—Gemeinsame Vergangenheit!? Gemeinsame Zukunft?!* Referate der Tagung vom 19–20 June 1993, 3–21. Liestal: Europäischen Mennonitischen Bibelschule Bienenberg, 1993.
Williams, D. H. *Evangelicals and Tradition: The Formative Influence of the Early Church*. Grand Rapids: Baker Academic, 2005.
Yarnell, Malcolm. *The Formation of Christian Doctrine*. Nashville: B. & H. Academic, 2007.
Zürcher, Isaac. "Herausforderungen für die Schweizer Mennoniten durch die Erweckungsbewegung." In *Gemeinsame Vergangenheit!? Gemeinsame Zukunft?!* Referate der Tagung vom 19–20 June 1993, 22–35. Liestal: Europäischen Mennonitischen Bibelschule Bienenberg, 1993.

3

Intellectual Hospitality as Historical Method

Moving beyond the Activist Impulse

JOHN FEA

LAUREN IS A HISTORY major and a Mennonite who is taking my course in Civil War history. Early in the semester I give the class a series of documents, most of them written in the 1850s, by southerners who passionately defended the institution of slavery. I ask the class to write a short paper interpreting these documents. One of the document authors claims that the New Testament does not condemn the institution of slavery and thus concludes that the South was justified in holding Africans in bondage. Another writer asserts that God was on the side of the Confederacy during the Civil War *because* of its commitment to slavery, which is a biblical, God-inspired institution. Lauren finds these documents foreign, strange, and morally reprehensible. She uses most of the space in her paper to argue with these slaveholding authors (quoting often from books she read in her Bible and theology classes), condemn their beliefs, and prove that they were wrongheaded and corrupt. As a young Anabaptist committed to fighting for social justice in the world, Lauren's natural reaction is to criticize these southerners, basing her moral assault on the teachings of Jesus. In the process, she engages the past, but fails to gain authentic historical understanding.

James is a political science major who grew up in the Evangelical Free Church, a denomination which might be described as mainstream evangelical. He is taking my course on the American Revolution, and on this particular day we are having an intense discussion about whether or not the United States was founded as a Christian nation. James grew up learning that the United States was indeed a Christian nation. In fact, this has inspired him to pursue a career in politics. He wants to work in a think tank, or perhaps even run for office, so he can help to advance the Christian values that he believes have long defined the country. When I suggest that one is hard-pressed, based upon the beliefs of the founding fathers, to call the creation of the American republic a uniquely Christian event, James has a brief vocational crisis. After class he comes into my office and says to me, "If America was not founded as a Christian nation, I don't think I can go into politics. What motivation would I have to engage in political activism if I am not fighting for the Christian beliefs that define our country?" As an evangelical who was raised in a culture of Christian nationalism, James cannot separate his belief in a Christian America from his vocational plan for a life of engagement with the world. His "activist impulse" has been based on a faulty view of American history.

Both Lauren and James (I have changed their names) were former students of mine at Messiah College, a unique kind of Christian college that has strong roots in both American evangelicalism and the Anabaptist tradition. As a professor of American history at Messiah, I have run into dozens of Anabaptist and evangelical students who are just like Lauren and James. My greatest challenge in teaching American history to serious Anabaptist students is to get them to lay aside their well-meaning Christian and moral criticism in order to seek understanding. My greatest challenge in teaching evangelical students is to get them to try to understand American history apart from the Christian nationalist ideas through which they tend to view most of the nation's past.

This essay explores the limits of the activist impulse within the Anabaptist and evangelical traditions as it relates to the study of the American past. Here I am less concerned with the numerous historians from both traditions who practice the historical method with skillful sophistication (such as those represented in this volume), but rather with the way that history often enters the public arena as just one of any number of rhetorical weapons marshaled in service of theological and political agendas. I write from the perspective of an educator and a champion of the essential role that the discipline of history plays in a Christian liberal arts education. Based on evidence from ten years of teaching history to undergraduates, it is my contention that the activist tendencies both in Anabaptism (particularly neo-Anabaptism) and evangelicalism (particularly of the conservative Christian nationalist variety) can, and often do, get in the way of deep historical learning. I am not suggesting that the views of the undergraduate population in our Christian colleges are somehow representative of everyone in the traditions, no matter how reflective or educated they are, with which these students identify. But I *am* suggesting that the approach to the past that we find among students such as Lauren and James may well reflect certain tendencies or expectations that have been cultivated within Anabaptist or evangelical circles in recent decades.

In this essay, I have two purposes in mind. First, I argue that both Anabaptists and evangelicals have been guilty of using history without submitting to the guiding principles of the historical discipline, thus exploiting the past for their respective agendas. On the Anabaptist side, this has amounted to a prophetic critique of American identity that highlights systemic injustice and then lays a foundation for social activism that is often built on dualistic presuppositions. On the evangelical side, this use of history has tended toward nationalistic sentiment and providentialist interpretations that lay a foundation for activism meant to somehow steer America back to its supposed Christian origins. Both of these approaches, I argue, are misguided. Second, I offer something of a solution—one that seeks to avoid the inherent pitfalls of these two traditions while tapping into some of the best features of both. I argue that when we approach the past on its own terms, and not ours, we not only find greater understanding, but we become better Christians, embodying virtues—such as humility, love, and hospitality—that both Anabaptists and evangelicals wholeheartedly embrace.

Since this essay attempts to offer something to scholars and non-scholars alike, I provide a more technical analysis of historiography while also offering principles for gaining historical understanding that will guide non-scholars as they negotiate the complexities of the past. Finally, this essay seeks to challenge both Anabaptists and evangelicals to move beyond the activist impulse to an approach we might call "intellectual hospitality."[1]

A PEACE CHURCH HISTORIOGRAPHY?

Part of Messiah College's heritage is found in the Anabaptist tradition. The denomination that founded the college—the Brethren in Christ Church—has roots that run deep into the history of American Anabaptism. As a result, Messiah gets its fair share of students from Anabaptist groups, including the Brethren in Christ Church, the Church of the Brethren, and the Mennonite Church. Other students tend to incorporate Anabaptist teaching, especially in the area of pacifism, social justice, and a suspicion of nationalism, into the Christian traditions that they brought with them to college. In the last decade I have found that many of the more socially active students at Messiah College are taking their marching orders not from the writings of traditional Anabaptists, but from those theologians and writers who, as Stuart Murray has described them, "identify with the Anabaptist tradition and are happy to be known as Anabaptists, but have no historic or cultural links with any Anabaptist-related denomination."[2] Many, if not all, of these "neo-Anabaptists" have been influenced by the late Mennonite theologian John Howard Yoder, and particularly his 1972 book, *The Politics of Jesus*. Yoder's work has inspired many of today's leading theological voices, including Stanley Hauerwas, Richard Hays, and Craig Carter, to name a few.[3]

As radical followers of the teachings of Jesus, neo-Anabaptists believe that the Church has the responsibility of proclaiming and living the gospel of Jesus Christ in the world. The Church should be made up of "resident aliens" who worship together, participate in the sacraments together, proclaim the Word of God together, and resist

---

1. Elsewhere I have proposed that such an approach is useful when considering the debate over whether or not American was founded as a Christian nation. See the introduction to Fea, *Was America?*, xxi–xxvii.

2. Murray, *Naked Anabaptist*, 18.

3. Hunter, *To Change the World*, 152. Hunter also suggests that there is much overlap between the teaching of the Anabaptists and the "radical orthodoxy" of theologians such as John Milbank, Graham Ward, and William Cavanaugh, to name a few.

violence together, all for the purpose of making devout disciples of Jesus Christ. The Church is an outpost—a distinctively Christian culture in the midst of American society. It confronts society with the claims of the gospel and serves as a countercultural alternative to the values of the world. All true Christians should thus find their citizenship in the Church, not in the nation. As Hauerwas and William H. Willimon write, "the church doesn't have a social strategy, the church *is* a social strategy."[4]

At first glance, neo-Anabaptists envision the Church as a separatist sect removed from the world—a sort of utopian movement reminiscent of the Amish or other religious groups that have been known for their agricultural pursuits, devout Christian faith, and otherworldly lifestyles. But they have also articulated a deliberate model of cultural engagement with the world unlike that of the historic Anabaptists from whom they draw some inspiration. As sociologist James Davison Hunter writes, Christian ethics for the neo-Anabaptists "comes down to 'the politics of Jesus.' Jesus himself was a 'political figure' and the 'model of radical political action.'" This kind of political action manifests itself in the neo-Anabaptist opposition to war, consumerism, global capitalism, materialism, and a host of other social injustices. Their dissent from nationalism, especially as articulated in the United States (which they believe promotes a Constantinian blend of religion and politics that confuses the church with the forces of the world), makes the neo-Anabaptists overtly political.[5] They understand the Church as a kind of monastic enclave—the "community of the cross"—that speaks "prophetically" to the larger culture.

It is precisely the "prophetic" nature of the neo-Anabaptist mission in the world that has drawn some of them, and their followers—including many young and thoughtful evangelicals who find their way to Christian colleges like Messiah—to a certain kind of historiography. As an Anabaptist historical theologian, John Howard Yoder once called for a "peace church historiography" that approaches the past from a self-avowed peach church perspective and thus interprets the past through what Christian historian Richard C. Goode has called "the lens of Radical faith." While such a peace church historiography can serve an important corrective role in historical *theology*, which

---

4. Hauerwas and Willimon, *Resident Aliens*, 43–47.
5. Hunter, *To Change the World*, 160–66.

often has been dominated by a "Constantinian" or Christendom narrative, Yoder nonetheless admits that it would likely occasion a "horror-struck reaction from professional historians." Taking off from Yoder's starting point,[6] Goode offers a scathing attack on Christian historians and the historical profession—and one that is fitting with a neo-Anabaptist prophetic stance—in which he accuses many Christian historians of going "about their professional work as if Easter had not occurred." If Christians took up Yoder's call, Goode argues, their approach to history would be "scandalous" and "prophetic." A true Christian historian would "study the non-religious world of ideas, culture, and politics for the express purpose of having their religious perspective bear judgment on the world's faulty assumptions." Christian historiography would be a form of "resistance literature."[7]

While Goode's call for a prophetic historiography is certainly inspiring, and I am sure his approach to the past attracts a large following of young neo-Anabaptists who want more from their history courses than facts, dates, and stories of "irrelevant" historical movements and people, I would argue that it is more suited for a historical theology or ethics classroom than a history classroom. In my view it confuses the role of the church with the role of the academy. The church, according to neo-Anabaptist theology, operates from the margins of society and takes upon the work of critiquing the moral failures of the world from the perspective of New Testament faith. But the academy—Christian or otherwise—is responsible for understanding the world.

---

6. An interesting question, but one that cannot be explored at great length here, is to what extent Goode's use of the concept of a "peace church historiography" builds on, or diverges from, Yoder's. To begin to answer this question, one would need to consult Yoder's numerous essays dealing with historiography, including but not limited to "Burden and Discipline," 21–37; "Anabaptism and History," 123–34; "To Serve Our God," 127–40; "'It Did Not Have to Be,'" 43–66; and various ad hoc discussions in *Christian Attitudes*. For Yoder, the fundamental axioms of a peace church historiography include (a) the historian's conviction that "It did not have to be," i.e., the rejection of historical determinism, and (b) the historian's stance of reading history from the perspective of the "underdog." The primary objective of Yoder's historical revisionism is thus not to be a contrarian per se, though that is often the outcome. Rather, the objective is to be "evangelical," i.e., to proclaim "good news" ("Burden and Discipline," 22), and "doxological," i.e., "to describe the cosmos in terms dictated by the knowledge that a once slaughtered Lamb is now living" ("To Serve Our God," 128). Cf. the Spring 2006 issue of *The Conrad Grebel Review* devoted to the topic, "John Howard Yoder as Historian."

7. Goode, "Radical Idea," 227–41.

By constantly decrying the ways in which American society has failed to model truly Christian values, very little historical learning takes place. For example, everyone knows that slavery is wrong and morally reprehensible. But what kind of historical education would take place if a professor took a fifty minute lecture to condemn this institution as it was practiced by nineteenth-century slaveholders? Such a lecture would only confirm what most students already know. Instead, by trying to understand the world of a slaveholder and doing one's best through the documents left behind to walk for a moment in his shoes, we can learn something about a world that is foreign to our own and, as we will see below, may even learn how to show compassion and even love for those with whom we disagree.

Political propaganda and theological criticism often utilize the past, but I would argue that little of it should be called history. For example, my students frequently ask me for my opinion of Howard Zinn's well-known, *The People's History of the United States*. This is a favorite among young neo-Anabaptist students because Zinn, writing from a left-wing, radical (but not Christian) perspective, offers many of the same critiques of American life that one finds among neo-Anabaptist theologians and writers. According to this work of historical revisionism, American history is best understood as a conflict between the elites and the masses. The elites oppress and exploit the masses to satisfy their own desires for fame, wealth, and glory. Europeans have destroyed Native American societies; slavery is a scar on the American past; and laborers have always struggled against capitalists.

Perhaps the most scathing critique of *A People's History of the United States* came in 2004 from Michael Kazin, a professor of history at Georgetown University, scholar of American populism, and currently the editor of the leftist magazine *Dissent*. Kazin concludes that Zinn's book is "quite unworthy of such fame and influence" because it "reduced the past to a Manichean fable." Kazin goes on to describe *A People's History* as "bad history," "history as cynicism," and a work that treats American elites as something "akin to the medieval church's image of the Devil." For Zinn, Kazin writes, "a governing class is motivated solely by its appetite for riches and power—and by its fear of losing them. Numerous historians may regard George Washington, Thomas Jefferson, James Madison, and Alexander Hamilton, as astute, if seriously flawed, men who erected a structure for the new nation that has endured over two centuries. But Zinn curtly dismisses them as 'leaders of the new aristocracy' and regards the nation state itself as a cunning devise to lull ordinary folks with the 'fanfare of patriotism and unity.'" And Kazin concludes:

> No work of history can substitute for a social movement. Yet intelligent, sober studies can make sense of how changing structures of power and ideas provide openings for challenges from below, while also shifting the basis on which a reigning order claims legitimacy for itself. These qualities mark the work of such influential (and widely read) historians on the left as Eric Hobsbawm, E. P. Thompson, Gerda Lerner, C. L. R. James, and erstwhile populist C. Vann Woodward. Reading their work makes one wiser about the obstacles to change as well as encouraged about the capacity of ordinary men and women to achieve a degree of independence and happiness, even within unjust societies. In contrast, Howard Zinn is an evangelist with little imagination for whom history is one long chain of stark moral dualities . . .[8]

Indeed, Howard Zinn is a champion of social justice. But he is not a historian. Readers of his book, which is assigned in colleges and universities throughout the country (even in some Christian colleges), will receive a one-sided view of American history that is more political propaganda than a rich treatment of the complexity of the past. Yet Christian historians from the Anabaptist tradition continue to praise Zinn. Perry Bush, for example, a fine historian of Mennonite pacifism in modern America, endorses Zinn's belief that "the historian has been embarrassed by his own humanity. Touched by the sight of poverty, horrified by war, revolted by racism, indignant at the strangling of dissent, he has nonetheless tried to keep his tie straight, his voice unruffled, and his emotions to himself." Bush builds off of Zinn's words as he writes to his fellow Christian historians: "We have erected a kind of protective antiseptic canopy around the writing of history so we might render it immune from any relevance to the needs of a globe reeling from an epidemic of violence and injustice. My goal here is to puncture that canopy, to rip great holes in it and tear it down." Bush makes no bones about his willingness to bring "political perspectives" into his writing of history and rails against his fellow historians who

---

8. Kazin, "Howard Zinn."

are concerned with objectivity.⁹ But one must ask: Is the historian in the business of promoting social movements and using their scholarship as a form of activism? Should history be considered "resistance literature?" It seems to me, as I will argue below, that the study of history has more limited goals.

John Howard Yoder is correct when he says that "peace church historiography" will "occasion a horror-stricken reaction from professional historians." He is right because this kind of approach to the study of the past—especially as it has been appropriated by those following Yoder—is not the discipline of history. Not everyone who studies the past is a historian; the past can be studied by theologians and ethicists for their purposes as well. But while contemporary neo-Anabaptists may believe that their ethical approach to the study of the past is prophetic, its net effect, to cite Hunter, "is overwhelmingly a message of anger, disparagement, and negation." America has "just not [been] Christian enough," they believe, and it is the role of the historian to make that fact clear.¹⁰

AMERICAN HISTORY AND CHRISTIAN NATIONALISTS

If the activist impulse informs the way that neo-Anabaptists approach the study and teaching of the past, the same might be said of Christians, including certain evangelicals, who use the past to exalt the exceptionalism, uniqueness, and Christian origins of the American republic. Unlike the neo-Anabaptists, Christian nationalist historiography operates not from the margins of American life, but from the center. It draws upon the longstanding relationship in American history between evangelical religion, nationalism, and citizenship. According to this view, the purpose of studying history is not to explore the American past in all its complexity, but to produce patriotic citizens committed to the furtherance of American nationalism. Such an approach, especially as it is employed by many Christians writing about the American past today, has the danger of becoming

---

9. Bush, "What Would History Look Like?" 49–56.
10. Hunter, *To Change the World*, 165.

what historian Bernard Bailyn has described as "indoctrination by historical example."[11]

History has always been a means of promoting patriotism. The study of the past can inculcate the members of a nation with civic pride and national unity. In the early part of the twentieth century, American historians were occasionally accused of treason for arguing, as in the case of historian Albert Bushnell Hart, that before the Stamp Act crisis of 1765 the colonists thought of themselves as part of England and were proud to be considered British. The relationship between history and national identity is why debates over history standards in American schools have been so heated in recent years.[12] As historian Gary Nash writes, "For some Americans, history that dwells on unsavory or even horrific episodes in our past is unpatriotic and likely to alienate young students from their country. 'Grim and gloomy' history is seen as undermining the national goal to educate loyal, proud Americans rather than pessimists and cynics."[13] Historians, however, believe that the story of the past must be told warts and all. Christian historians believe that all human beings are created in the image of God and thus have a story that is worthy to be told regardless of whether that story fits well into the kind of patriotic narrative conducive to producing good American citizens. Thus if neo-Anabaptists can be accused of focusing on everything that is wrong with America, Christian nationalist historians might be accused of focusing on everything, at least from their perspective, that is right with America. Both approaches allow political, religious, and cultural agendas to be their lens for understanding the past, rather than letting the past stand on its own terms.

Patriots have long extolled the virtues of American nationalism on Christian grounds. Some of the first American historians, writing in the decades following the American Revolution, did not shy away from trying to discern the hand of God in American history. Many of these historians believed that God had intervened on behalf of the United States during the American Revolution. David Ramsey, the author of *History of the American Revolution* (1789), described the events of the Revolutionary War through the grid of divine providence.

11. Bailyn, quoted in Wood, "Reading the Founders' Minds."
12. See, for example Nash, Crabtree, and Dunn, *History on Trial*, 15.
13. Ibid.

Mercy Otis Warren, in *History of the Rise, Progress and Termination of the American Revolution* (1805), was also overtly providential in her approach. She thought that the overthrow of English dominion by a band of colonial soldiers, and the creation of a government based on freedom, was so momentous that it could only be attributed to a "superintending Providence" or "the finger of divine Providence." As the nineteenth century rolled on, George Bancroft's multi-volume *History of the United States* (1834–1874) promoted the idea that America was a Christian nation established and sustained by God for the purpose of spreading liberty and democracy to the world.[14] God's providence in American history was also a dominant theme in school textbooks. Historian Jonathan Boyd's close study of nine of the early nineteenth century's most popular American history schoolbooks confirms that authors used providential language to teach students how to be good citizens of a Christian nation. In this sense, they look very different from the kinds of American history textbooks that schoolchildren read today.[15]

Today, this approach to the past has been taken up by Christian writers eager to promote the United States as a Christian nation. The most prolific of these voices is David Barton, the founder of WallBuilders, a ministry devoted to "presenting America's forgotten history and heroes with an emphasis on our moral, religious and constitutional heritage."[16] It is hard to separate the work of these historical writers from their political passions. Barton, for example, served eight years as the vice chair of the Texas Republican Party, the same political organization whose 2004 platform included the line: "the United States of America is a Christian nation."[17] Barton's books and videos about America's Christian heritage have sold thousands of copies, and he speaks widely on the subject to large evangelical audiences, both in person and through his radio and television ministry. In 2005 *Time* named Barton one of the twenty-five most influential evangelicals in America.

---

14. Warren, *History*, 97, 641, 505; Boyd, "This Holy Hieroglyph," 105, 106, 110, 118–19.

15. Boyd, "This Holy Hieroglyph," 206.

16. See WallBuilders website: http://www.wallbuilders.com/.

17. Young, "GOP's 'Christian Nation.'"

Christian nationalists such as Barton seek to accomplish many things with their tapes and books about America's past, but teaching readers how to be good historians is not one of them. By focusing only on references to God, Jesus Christ, and Christian morality in the past, they fail to provide anything close to a thorough and complex treatment of American history. One of their greatest fears is revisionism. Christian nationalist writers believe that professional historians, through the textbooks that they write, are out to indoctrinate American children in a "secular humanist" view of the American past. Barton defines "historical revisionism" as "a process by which historical fact is intentionally ignored, distorted, or misportrayed in order to maneuver public opinion toward a specific political agenda or philosophy."[18] It has probably never occurred to Barton that his approach to the American past is doing just that.

The fear of revisionism is why the defenders of Christian America strongly emphasize grounding their research in primary sources. If a historian makes an argument based upon the ideas of another historian's work, rather than the primary sources, then she has succumbed to revisionism. Barton calls his historical method a "best evidence" approach, a research strategy that is often used in law schools. This way of dealing with evidence allows him to let the founders speak for themselves, but it rarely explores deeply the context in which the words were uttered.[19] Such an approach to evidence is suitable for a lawyer. After all, a criminal lawyer's responsibility is to selectively pick from the past in order to find a legal precedent that will win the case for his client. A historian, as we will see below, does not approach the past this way.

Why focus on these Christian nationalists and their revisionist brand of American history? These writers are worth the attention because their approach to America's past has become the dominant way in which many American evangelicals understand the nation's history. It is also the way that most of the students, as with the story of James mentioned above, think about history when they arrive at Messiah College from their Christian high schools and youth groups. As many of the readers of this essay will know, there have been sophisticated scholarly attempts to debunk these Christian nationalist views of

---

18. Barton, *Original Intent*, 279.
19. Ibid., 5, 316.

the American past, but few of them are reaching evangelicals in the pews in the way that David Barton and other writers of his ilk are doing.[20] Few mainstream evangelicals read monographs published by university presses or serious books published by reputable Christian presses. In the last thirty years, as James Davison Hunter has shown in *To Change the World*, evangelicals have tried to "change the world" by working through the political system. As a result, much of the so-called "history" that they produce for popular readers has been driven by such an "activist impulse."

ANOTHER CHRISTIAN APPROACH TO THE PAST

It is my judgment that the activism of both neo-Anabaptists and contemporary evangelicals is not conducive to the kind of historical thinking that we need in the Christian academy today. If this is the case, however, then just what is the purpose of studying history? What do historians do? Does everyone who conducts a serious study of the past qualify as a historian? "In my opinion," writes Pulitzer Prize winning historian Gordon Wood, "not everyone who writes about the past is a historian. Sociologists, anthropologists, political scientists, and economists frequently work in the past without really thinking historically."[21] Could we add theologians to this list? Is there a difference between "the past" and "history," two terms that we often assume are synonymous?

Many people look to the past for something useable. They want to find inspiration in the actions of heroic figures, continuity with the present, or a sense of civic identity. Yet historians do not approach the past with the *primary* goal of finding something relevant. Those who pursue the past for the purpose of inspiration, familiarity, and civic identity *alone* are not really practicing history at all. Historians know that there exists a constant tension between the familiarity of the past and the strangeness of the past. They must always operate with this tension in mind. Historians Thomas Andrews and Flannery Burke have boiled down the task of historical interpretation into what they call the "5 Cs of Historical Thinking."[22]

---

20 For one example of a scholarly attempt to counter the way Christian nationalists approach the past, see Noll, Marsden, and Hatch, *Search for Christian America*.

21. Wood, *Purpose of the Past*, 276.

22. Andrews and Book, "What Does it Mean?"

First, historians must see *change over time*. While some things stay the same over the course of generations, many things change. For example, the United States changed considerably between 1776 and 1900. The country moved from an agricultural to an industrial society. The meaning of the Constitution was defined more clearly by a bloody Civil War. The demographic make-up of the country changed immensely with the arrival of new immigrants. The historian's task is to chronicle these changes. As historian John Tosh puts it, "There may be a gulf between 'us' and 'them,' but that gulf is actually composed of processes of growth, decay and change which it is the business of the historian to uncover."[23]

Second, historians must interpret the past in *context*. They examine the documents of the past in light of the time and the place in which they were written. Words ripped from their cultural and chronological context provide useful material for the compilers of quotation books, but they are useless to the historian. The words of the founding fathers, for example, must always be interpreted from the perspective of the eighteenth-century world in which they were uttered or written. There is a wide chasm that separates the past from the present. Context helps us to realize that more often than not people in the past do not think and behave the same way that we do.

Third, historians are always interested in *causality*. I remember a few years ago when the talk radio host Rush Limbaugh announced that "history is real simple. You know what history is? It's what happened. Now if you want to get into why what happened, that's probably valid too, but why what happened shouldn't have much of anything to do with what happened."[24] Limbaugh could not have been more wrong about what historians do. They are not only interested in facts, but always ask why a particular event in the past happened the way it did. What "caused" the American Revolution? Why did the Civil Rights movement emerge when it did? What motivated Hitler to form the Nazi party?

Historians are concerned, fourthly, with *contingency*. This is the notion that "every historical outcome depends upon a number of prior conditions."[25] Contingency celebrates the ability of humans to

---

23. Tosh, *Pursuit of History*, 12.
24. Quoted from Nash, *History on Trial*, 6.
25. Andrews and Burke, "What Does it Mean."

shape their own destiny. Every historical moment is contingent upon another historical moment which, in turn, is contingent upon yet another moment. Taking contingency seriously may lead the historian to ask "what if" questions. For example, what if Robert E. Lee's Special Orders 191 did not fall into the hands of George McClellan shortly before the battle of Antietam in 1862? How might the Civil War have been different if this event did not happen? Historians are thus concerned about the big picture—how events are influenced by other events.

Finally, historians realize that the past is *complex*. It often resists our efforts to simplify it or cut it up into easily digestible pieces. Most students of history are exposed to the past through textbooks which offer rather straightforward narratives of how a particular era unfolded. While often necessary for overviews and syntheses of the past, textbooks often fail to reveal that the past can be messy, complicated, and not easily summarized in a neatly constructed paragraph or two. Once again, the debate over whether or not America is a Christian nation is instructive here. On the one hand, the opponents of Christian America draw the conclusion that, just because the Constitution does not mention God, it must hold true that the framers did not believe that religion was important to the success of the republic. On the other hand, defenders of Christian America conclude that if the founders were men of Christian faith, then they must have set out to establish a uniquely Christian nation. Logicians call these assertions "non-sequiturs." Historians would argue that those who draw such conclusions lack an appreciation for the complexity of the past.

The task of the historian is to use these five "Cs"—change, context, causality, contingency, and complexity—to reconstruct the past and make her findings available to the public. As Tosh puts it: "All the resources of scholarship and all the historian's powers of imagination must be harnessed to the task of bringing the past back to life—or *resurrecting* it."[26] Historians make the dead live. They bring the past to an audience in the present. If we think about the vocation of the historian in this way, then we must distinguish between "history" and "the past." The past is the past—a record of events that occurred in bygone eras. But history is a discipline—the art of reconstructing the past.

---

26. Tosh, *Pursuit of History*, 7.

Most human beings tend to be present-minded when it comes to confronting the past. The discipline of history was never meant to function as a means of getting one's political point across or convincing people to join a cause. Yet Americans use the past for these purposes all the time. Such an approach to the past can easily degenerate into a form of propaganda or, as we have already seen, "indoctrination by historical example."[27] When we engage in the careful reconstruction of the past we will find that it is often strange when compared to our present-day sensibilities. There were some people in the past who burned witches, while other engaged in human sacrifice. As historian David Lowenthal, echoing the late L. P. Hartley, reminds us: "the past is a foreign country, they do things differently there."[28] It is the strangeness of the past that turns many off to its study. What if the past does not inspire us? What if we are required to investigate an era or a movement that, at first glance, does not seem to teach us anything about ourselves or our society? How does knowledge of the medieval feudal system help us live better lives? Will our lives be enriched by a thorough knowledge of the causes of World War I?

Gordon Wood has said that if someone wants to use the study of the past to change the world he should forgo a career as a historian and run for office.[29] While it is certainly a worthwhile exercise to use the past to critique a particular dimension of contemporary society, historians, by vocation, are not primarily cultural critics. Nor should they be in the business of using the past to promote a particular political or cultural agenda. The task of the historian is to pursue the truth, wherever it may lead. She works with original or primary documents to reconstruct the past in all its complexity and fullness. While the historian might choose the subject she will study based upon current events or personal interest, she must always let the evidence speak, even if that evidence leads her toward a conclusion that may not be useful.

Christians have suggested multiple ways of studying the past. One of the more popular approaches—among both neo-Anabaptists and evangelicals—is the belief that the past be critiqued from the perspective of Christian orthodoxy, a body of biblical teaching and

27. Quoted from Wood, "Reading the Founders Minds."
28. Lowenthal, *The Past*, xvi.
29. Wood, *Purpose of the Past*, 308.

church tradition that has always guided Christians in judging right from wrong. This approach to history offers ethical judgments on characters from the past, the ideas they defended, and the movements to which they affiliated. Indeed, the past provides us with moral lessons, making the historian—sometimes overtly, but most times subtly (but no less powerfully)—a critic by nature. Historian Robert Gleason has argued that historians have a three-fold task: to explain what happened, to ask why it happened, and to ask if what happened was "good." Those who embrace this vision of history find it imperative to add an additional moral dimension to their study of the past, one that is informed by their Christian convictions.[30] The validity of Gleason's approach depends in large measure on how the place of moral criticism is employed. There is, after all, a difference between a historian and a moral philosopher. Gleason's first two steps are certainly well within the role of the historian, but to ask if what happened in the past was "good" leads to a blurring of the disciplinary boundaries between history and ethics and, if we are not careful, can replace sound historical thinking with moral criticism. This is exactly what happened to Lauren, the student mentioned in the opening paragraph of this essay.

Moral criticism can be a vital part of Christian liberal arts curriculum, but it is not primarily the part of the curriculum that a history course should deliver. Historians are after understanding. They must avoid what historian James LaGrand has described as "preaching through history."[31] The case of Lauren and the pro-slavery documents are instructive here. Before condemning these pro-slavery advocates, history students need to know why someone from the nineteenth century would see the need to make such a defense of slavery. What was the context in which these documents were written? Who is the intended audience? What are the main issues at stake in the author's arguments? It is important that students enter into the world of a slaveholder and make an effort to empathize with him, no matter how repulsed they are by his words. In the end, engaging the past in this way could eventually result in a much more nuanced and rich critique of pro-slavery views. These principles apply not only to undergraduate history students, but to all of us who wrestle with the past and consider the role that history has for the present.

30. Gleason, *Keeping the Faith*, 216–20.
31. LaGrand, "Preaching Through History," 187–216.

TOWARD THE VIRTUES OF INTELLECTUAL HOSPITALITY

While I am not opposed to using the past to sharpen student's skills in moral criticism, I want to offer Christians, including Anabaptists and evangelicals, a slightly different approach to thinking about the past. It offers a more practical benefit for Christians in studying the past and, at the same time, intersects with some of the best and most recent scholarship in historical thinking. My argument is this: The study of history can help us mature *spiritually*.

Scholars of historical thinking, particularly Sam Wineburg in his masterful, *Historical Thinking and Other Unnatural Acts,* have argued convincingly that it is the very strangeness of the past that has the best potential to change our lives in positive ways. Those who are willing to acknowledge that the past is a foreign country—a place where they do things differently than we do in the present—set off on a journey of personal transformation. Wineburg writes, "It is this past, one that initially leaves us befuddled, or worse, just plain bored that we need most if we are to achieve the understanding that each of us is more than the handful of labels described to us at birth."[32]

An encounter with the past in all of its fullness, void as much as possible of present-minded agendas, can cultivate virtue in our lives. Such an encounter teaches us empathy, humility, selflessness, and hospitality—virtues prized by Anabaptists and evangelicals alike. By studying history we learn to listen to voices that differ from our own. We lay aside our moral condemnation about a person, idea, or event from the past in order to understand it. This is the essence of intellectual hospitality. The act of interpreting a primary source with students becomes the equivalent of inviting a person from the past into our classroom. By taking the time to listen to people from a "foreign country" we rid ourselves of the selfish quest to make the past serve our needs. The study of the past reminds us that we are not autonomous individuals, but part of a human story that is larger than ourselves. Wineburg sums it up well:

> For the narcissist sees the world—both the past and the present—in his own image. Mature historical understanding teaches us to do the opposite: to go beyond our own image, to go beyond our brief life, and to go beyond the fleeting moment in human history into which we have been born. History educates ("leads

---

32. Wineburg, *Historical Thinking,* 7.

outward" in the Latin) in the deepest sense. Of the subjects in the secular curriculum, it is the best at teaching those virtues once reserved for theology—humility in the face of our limited ability to know, and awe in the face of the expanse of history.[33]

Are we willing to allow history to "educate" us—to lead us outward?

Wineburg's reference to theology is worth further exploration. In his book, *A Theology of Public Life*, Charles Mathewes argues that Christians today are afflicted by the sin of escapism—the desire to flee from God and each other. God wants us to turn toward Him, but he also wants us to turn toward each other. In the process of loving our neighbor—for Mathewes such a practice goes to the heart of civic life—we grow as Christians. "Through the virtues' cultivation through engagement with public life," Mathewes writes, "the souls of Christians may be purified in and through their public engagements...."[34]

What if we viewed the study of the past as a form of public engagement? Even if the person we engage is dead, we can still enter into a conversation with the sources that he or she has left behind. In a passage strikingly familiar to Wineburg's thoughts on the discipline of history, Mathewes argues that when we encounter people in all their strangeness we "find ourselves decentered, we find that we are no longer the main object of our purposes, but participate in something not primarily our own. This confession then, is itself a turning to the other, not in the interests of mutual narcissism, which makes the other only a consolidation prize for having to be already ourselves—but as an openness to transforming and being transformed by the other."[35] If we take the *Imago Dei*—the notion that all human beings are created in the image of God—seriously, then we should also take seriously the idea that those who lived in the past were also created in God's image. The very act of studying humanity—past or present—can be what Mathewes calls an "exploration into God, a mode inquiring God...." An encounter with the past thus becomes an act of spiritual devotion. This kind of encounter "provides more than enough opportunities for humility and penance, recognition of one's sin and the sins of others, and a deepening appreciation of the terrible awe-fulness of God's providential governing

---

33. Ibid., 24.
34. Mathewes, "Author Meets His Critics."
35. Mathewes, *Theology of Public Life*, 87.

of the world. Indeed, involvement in public life today may itself increasingly need some such ascetical discipline."[36]

In other words, history is not only a discipline, in the sense that philosophy and literary criticism and sociology are disciplines. It is also a discipline in the sense that it requires patterns of behavior, such as the denial of the self, that are necessary in order to meet the "other" in a hospitable way. Doing history is not unlike the kind of "disciplines" we employ in our spiritual lives—disciplines that take the focus off of us and put it on God or others. If this is true, then prayer, a reliance on the Holy Spirit's power, and other spiritual practices should provide help in the pursuit of the kind of self-denial, hospitality, charity, and humility needed to engage the past in this way and allow ourselves to be open to the possibility of it transforming us.

Like any type of public engagement, an encounter with the strangeness of the past "inevitably leads to contemplation of the mysteries of providence, the sovereignty of God, and the cultivation of the holy terror that is integral to true piety."[37] It forces us to love others—even a nineteenth-century slaveholder—when they at first glance seem to be unlovable. Failure to respect the people in the past is ultimately a failure of love. It is a failure to recognize the common bond that we share with humanity. It is a failure to welcome the stranger. Moreover, when we uncover sinful behavior in the past, it should cause us to examine our own imperfect and flawed lives. This kind of engagement, as Mathewes puts it, "brings us repeatedly against the stubborn, bare there-ness of the people we meet in public life; it teaches us again and again the terrible lesson that there are other people, other ideals, other points of view that we can see and appreciate, even if we cannot inhabit them and remain ourselves."[38]

The discipline of history requires us to apply James 1:19 to our lives: We must be "quick to hear, slow to speak, and slow to become angry." This does not mean that we have to agree with every idea we encounter in the past. Sometimes we cannot inhabit an idea and still remain ourselves. But education—"to be led outward"—does require a degree of risk. Without taking a risk, without being open to transformation, liberal education cannot happen. "Self-denial," writes

36. Ibid., 166.
37. Ibid., 259–60.
38. Ibid., 304.

historian Mark Schwehn, "is a willingness to surrender ourselves for the sake of a better opinion. Wisdom is the discernment of when it is reasonable to do so."[39] A Christian who studies the past must be prudent. She must be slow to speak and quick to listen to the people she meets in the past. And she must pray for wisdom.

In order to illustrate what this might look like in a classroom, I return to my example about teaching texts written by nineteenth-century pro-slavery intellectuals. As with everyone else in my class, Lauren was appalled at the arguments contained in these documents. But by entering into a conversation with their authors, and being opened to letting these writers change her, she became a better Christian. Lauren learned that plantation owners often argued that slavery was justified because slaveholders treated their labor force (slaves) better than the burgeoning capitalists of the North treated their immigrant laboring class. Slaves were clothed, fed, Christianized, and usually worked ten hours a day. Northern industrial laborers, living in an age before the usual benefits afforded to workers today, worked sixteen hour days, were paid so poorly that they could not feed themselves or their families, and generally lived lives that were much worse than those of southern slaves. How dare the northern abolitionists and capitalists claim the moral high ground! How dare they accuse slaveholders of immorality while all the while turning a blind eye to the plight of the working-class "slaves" in their midst! The South's anti-capitalist feudalism offered, as historians Elizabeth Fox-Genovese and Eugene Genovese have shown, one of the most powerful critiques of industrialization in nineteenth-century America.[40]

Lauren was convinced that the slaveholders' criticism of northern industry did not take them off the moral hook. Slavery was still a reprehensible and sinful practice. Nor was Lauren sure that this defense of slavery was valid. The northern workers may have had it rough, perhaps even rougher than slaves, but at least they were free. Lauren did, however, learn to be cautious about condemning others before hearing their side of the story. Her response to these writers was not a knee-jerk moral criticism, but a thoughtful engagement with historical texts that taught her a valuable lesson about removing the log from your own eye before taking the speck out of the eye of

---

39. Schwehn, *Exiles from Eden*, 49.
40. Fox-Genovese and Genovese, *Mind of the Master Class*.

another. Lauren listened to the slaveholders. She understood them. She empathized with them. She saw them as fellow human beings. She realized that some of their flaws were also present in her own life and her relationships with others. And in the process she was, in a small way, changed. Are not these the kinds of transformative encounters that we want Christian college students to experience? It seems likely that dozens and dozens of such encounters would collectively contribute to making an educated person.

I wish I could say that Lauren is representative of the way students approach historical texts. But her case reveals that real transformation is possible when we are exposed to opinions that we naturally find uncomfortable. History students do not have to agree with slaveholders to learn something from them, even if it only reminds them that we, like the authors of these texts, are flawed, imperfect creatures in need of improvement and redemption. This is what history can do, and this is why Christians must study it. In my view it contributes to the mission of Christian higher education more than any other discipline. We need to practice history not because it can win us political points or help us push our social and cultural agendas forward. Nor should we be using history as a tool for promoting a prophetic Christianity or a Christian political platform. Whether we consider ourselves Anabaptists, evangelicals, or identify with both traditions or neither, we should be studying history because it has the amazing potential to transform our lives and even, perhaps, to make us better conversation partners—partners whose lives are defined by virtues such as humility, empathy, and hospitality.

BIBLIOGRAPHY

Andrews, Thomas, and Flannery Book. "What Does it Mean to Think Historically?" *AHA Perspectives* (January 2007) 32–35. Online: http://www.historians.org/Perspectives/issues/2007/0701/0701tea2.cfm.

Barton, David. *Original Intent: The Courts, the Constitution, & Religion*. 3rd ed. Aledo, TX: WallBuilders, 2000.

Boyd, Jonathan Tucker. "This Holy Hieroglyph: Providence and Historical Consciousness in George Bancroft's Historiography." PhD diss., Johns Hopkins University, 1999.

Bush, Perry. "What Would History Look Like If 'Peace and Justice' Really Mattered?" *Fides et Historia* 34 (Winter/Spring 2002) 49–56.

Fea, John. *Was America Founded as a Christian Nation?: A Historical Introduction*. Louisville: Westminster John Knox, 2011.

Fox-Genovese, Elizabeth and Eugene Genovese. *The Mind of the Master Class: History and Faith in the Southern Slaveholders' World View*. New York: Cambridge University Press, 2005.

Gleason, Philip. *Keeping the Faith: American Catholicism Past and Present*. Notre Dame, IN: University of Notre Dame Press, 1987.

Goode, Richard C. "The Radical Idea of Christian Scholarship: Plea for a Scandalous Historiography." In *Restoring the First-Century Church in the Twenty-First Century: Essays on the Stone-Campbell Restoration Movement in Honor of Don Haymes*, edited by Warren Lewis and Hans Rollman, 227–42. Eugene, OR: Wipf & Stock, 2005.

Hauerwas, Stanley, and William H. Willimon, *Resident Aliens*. Nashville: Abingdon, 1989.

Hunter, James Davison. *To Change the World: The Irony, Tragedy, & Possibility of Christianity in the Late Modern World*. New York: Oxford University Press, 2010.

"John Howard Yoder as Historian." Themed issue of *Conrad Grebel Review* 24.2 (2006) 3–83.

Kazin, Lauren. "Howard Zinn's History Lessons." *Dissent* (Spring 2004) 81–85. Online: http://www.dissentmagazine.org/article/?article=385.

LaGrand, James B. "Preaching Through History." In *Confessing History: Christian Faith and the Historian's Vocation*, edited by John Fea, Jay Green, and Eric Miller, 187–213. Notre Dame, IN: University of Notre Dame Press, 2010.

Lowenthal, David. *The Past is a Foreign Country*. New York: Cambridge University Press, 1999.

Mathewes, Charles. "Author Meets His Critics: A Theology of Public Life, Opening Remarks." Boisi Center for Religion and American Public Life. 11 October 2007. Boston College, Chestnut Hill, MA. Online: http://www.bc.edu/centers/boisi/meta-elements/pdf/furtherreadings/Mathewes_opening_comments.pdf.

Murray, Stuart. *The Naked Anabaptist: The Bare Essentials of a Radical Faith*. Scottsdale, PA: Herald, 2010.

Nash, Gary B., Charlotte Crabtree, and Ross E. Dunn. *History on Trial: Culture Wars and the Teaching of the Past*. New York: Vintage, 1997.

Noll, Mark A., George M. Marsden, and Nathan O. Hatch. *The Search for Christian America*. Expanded ed. Colorado Springs: Helmers & Howard, 1989.

Schwehn, Mark. *Exiles from Eden: Religion and the Academic Vocation in America*. New York: Oxford University Press, 1993.

Tosh, John. *The Pursuit of History: Aims, Methods, and New Directions in the Study of Modern History*. 4th ed. New York: Longman, 2006.

WallBuilders. Online: http://www.wallbuilders.com/.

Warren, Mercy Otis. *History of the Rise, Progress and Termination of the American Revolution*. 2 vols. 1805 reprint. Indianapolis: Liberty Fund, 1989.

Wineburg, Sam. *Historical Thinking and Other Unnatural Acts: Charting the Future of Teaching the Past*. Philadelphia: Temple University Press, 2001.

Wood, Gordon. *The Purpose of the Past: Reflections on the Uses of History*. New York: Penguin, 2008.

———. "Reading the Founder's Minds." *New York Review of Books* 54, 28 June 2007. No pages. Online: http://www.nybooks.com/articles/archives/2007/jun/28/reading-the-founders-minds/.

Yoder, John Howard. "Anabaptism and History." In *The Priestly Kingdom: Social Ethics as Gospel*, 123–34. Notre Dame, IN: University of Notre Dame Press, 1984.

———. "The Burden and the Discipline of Evangelical Revisionism." In *Nonviolent America: History through the Eyes of Peace*, edited by Louise Hawkley and James C. Juhnke, 21–37. Cornelius H. Wedel Historical Series. Newton, KS: Mennonite, 1993.

———. *Christian Attitudes to War, Peace, and Revolution*. Edited by Theodore J. Koontz and Andy Alexis-Baker. Grand Rapids: Brazos, 2009.

———. "'It Did Not Have to Be.'" In *The Jewish-Christian Schism Revisited*, edited by Michael G. Cartwright and Peter Ochs, 43–66. Scottdale, PA: Herald, 2008.

———. "To Serve Our God and to Rule the World." In *The Royal Priesthood: Essays Ecclesiastical and Ecumenical*, edited by Michael G. Cartwright, 127–40. Scottdale, PA: Herald, 1998.

Young, Cathy. "GOP's 'Christian Nation.'" *Boston Globe*, 13 July 2004. No pages. Online: http://www.cathyyoung.net/bgcolumns/2004/nation.html.

Zinn, Howard. *A People's History of the United States*. New York: Perennial Classics, 2010.

PART II

Intersecting Challenges

Anabaptism and the Fundamentalist-Modernist Controversy

Introduction to Part II

AMERICAN PROTESTANTS FROM MANY different religious traditions and denominations both contributed to and felt the effects of the controversy between conservative evangelicals and modernists in the early decades of the twentieth century. Anabaptists were no exception. While fundamentalists within small, outsider traditions, such as the Mennonites and Brethren, had much in common with other fundamentalists, patterns of development within these contexts were complicated by the fact that Anabaptists cherished certain distinctive features, such as nonviolence, strong discipleship, and community bonds, as well as simple lifestyles that made for unique manifestations of the fundamentalist phenomenon. The importance of these distinctive features can be seen by the persistent questions that emerged during these decades and that continue to facilitate historiographical debate, especially among Anabaptists. Could Anabaptists adopt the attitudes, concern for rigid orthodoxy, and the theological orientation of American fundamentalism while preserving core Anabaptist virtues and distinctives? Did aggressive efforts by traditionalist-minded Anabaptists to maintain the "right fellowship" constitute its own form of fundamentalism? These questions are complicated further by the fact that in the Anabaptist context, fundamentalism often constituted cultural innovation and even progressive tendencies, not necessary the ultra-conservatism to which it is often equated today.

The essays in this section seek to address some of these complex issues. It is safe to say that figures that make an appearance in this section—such as Daniel Kauffman, Alva J. McClain, John S. Hiestand, and William Anders—are anything but household names, even in Anabaptist circles. Yet these individuals are noteworthy because the tensions and paradoxes that characterized both their private and public lives are representative of the complex cultural negotiations that Anabaptists felt during these years and the way that American fundamentalism served both to challenge tradition among ethnic Protestants as well as provide new avenues for refashioning faith for a modern American context.

The first two essays below are devoted specifically to Mennonite bishop, Daniel Kauffman, a significant historical figure for the Anabaptist-evangelical relationship. Serving as editor of the *Gospel Herald*, the primary serial for the (Old) Mennonite Church, from 1908 to 1943, Kauffman was one of the most influential Mennonite leaders during the first half of the twentieth century. In this capacity Kauffman guided American Mennonites through the fundamentalist-modernist debates of the 1920s and 1930s. Because of his role in these decades, he since has become a figure that represents Anabaptist accommodation to American fundamentalism. Benjamin Wetzel and Nathan E. Yoder effectively counter this interpretation of Kauffman, asserting instead that his response to the broader currents of American religious culture is more nuanced than previously represented.

Since Kauffman's era Anabaptists have made various attempts to integrate the evangelical and Anabaptist traditions in intentional and creative ways. One such example is the founding of Grace Theological Seminary, the denominational seminary for the Fellowship of Grace Brethren Churches. M. M. Norris argues that the origins of the Fellowship of Grace Brethren Churches are more complex than is often assumed and that American fundamentalism was only one of several forces that shaped the seminary's founder, Alva J. McLain. A popular teacher, McClain attempted to find a workable synthesis of dispensationalism and Brethren piety.

Jared S. Burkholder then moves the focus to an examination of the Lancaster and Franconia (Pennsylvania) Mennonite conferences during the first half of the twentieth century. He considers the relationship between evangelical influence and Anabaptist defection, tracing dissenting movements led by local ministers John S. Hiestand and William Anders who journeyed from conservative Mennonite circles to conservative evangelicalism. While it is tempting to interpret theses schisms purely as a result of outside fundamentalist encroachment, Burkholder suggests that the controversy was a product of competing fundamentalisms and that the dissenters merely traded one form of conservative religiosity for another.

Fundamentalists, Modernists, and a Mennonite "Third Way"

Reexamining the Career of Bishop Daniel Kauffman

BENJAMIN WETZEL

ON JANUARY 27, 1998, the *Gospel Herald*, the denominational organ for the (Old) Mennonite Church, published its last issue.[1] The paper was being discontinued in anticipation of the 1999–2002 merger between the Mennonite Church and the General Conference Mennonite Church, whose new leadership combined the two groups' papers into a revamped publication, *The Mennonite*. In this final issue of the *Gospel Herald*, professor and author J. Daniel Hess reflected on the one hundred years of the *Gospel Herald* and assigned each one of its five editors a label. Hess described Daniel Kauffman (1865–1944), the *Herald*'s first editor, as someone who "lived with a strong suspicion of the world around him" and manifested "very little humor." Noting sardonically that "Kauffman was at the ready to expose errors of which there seemed to be many," Hess compared Kauffman's *Gospel Herald* to the notoriously partisan American political journals of the

---

1. An earlier version of this chapter was printed in *Pennsylvania Mennonite Heritage* and is used by permission. I would like to thank the Lancaster Mennonite Historical Society for sponsoring part of the research for this project during an internship conducted in the summer of 2008. I would especially like to thank Carolyn Wenger, Beth Graybill, and Steve Ness for their help.

late eighteenth century. For Hess, Kauffman could be summarized in one word: "Judge."[2]

A number of Mennonite historians have shared this negative view of Kauffman. Indeed, several scholars have contended that Kauffman's appropriation of American Fundamentalism damaged the Mennonite Church's identity. Leonard Gross, for example, has labeled the period of Kauffman's decisive leadership (1898–1944) as an "ahistorical era" in the Mennonite Church, while J. Denny Weaver has argued that Kauffman's separation of salvation from ethics was a departure from traditional Mennonite practice.[3] Most importantly, Kauffman has also been criticized by historians for failing to articulate a uniquely Mennonite "third way" during the Fundamentalist-Modernist Controversy of the early twentieth century. Theron Schlabach, Beulah Hostetler, and C. Norman Kraus, for example, have all argued that Kauffman capitulated to mainstream Protestant Fundamentalism and, in one way or another, betrayed historic Anabaptism.[4]

In contrast to these interpretations, I argue that Kauffman did in fact demonstrate a genuinely Mennonite "third way" during the theological controversies in the early twentieth century. Fundamentalism was not a monolithic movement within the Mennonite Church, and although Kauffman vigorously opposed modernism, his brand of fundamentalism was temperate in comparison with the actions of other Mennonite fundamentalist leaders.[5] Moreover, through his opposition to modernism *and* certain features of Protestant Fundamentalism (both in the Mennonite church and the culture at large), and through his strong defense of distinctive Mennonite teachings, Kauffman upheld the principles of sixteenth-century Anabaptism and articulated an authentic Mennonite third way for a church grappling with the Fundamentalist-Modernist Controversy.

2. Hess, "Judge to Statesman," 2. The labels given to the other four editors were rather more complimentary. These were: "Statesman," "Pastor," "Scholar," and "Provocateur" respectively.

3. Gross, "Doctrinal Era," 83. Kauffman published his *Manual of Bible Doctrines* in 1898 and died in 1944. Weaver, *Keeping Salvation Ethical*, 218–19.

4. Schlabach, *Gospel Versus Gospel*, 116; Hostetler, ["Eastern Pennsylvania Mennonites"], 2:2; Kraus, "American Mennonites," 324.

5. Throughout this chapter I have adopted the traditional Mennonite pattern of using "Fundamentalism" with a capital "F" to refer to the mainstream Protestant movement and "fundamentalism" with a lower-case "f" to designate Mennonite versions of this movement.

Before going further, a word concerning Kauffman's personal background is in order. Kauffman was born June 20, 1865 in Juniata, Pennsylvania, the son of Bishop David Kauffman. When he was quite young, his family moved west to Indiana and then again to Missouri, where Kauffman was raised.[6] He married Ota Bowlin in 1887 and she gave birth to their son James in June of the following year. Encouraged by his older brother Sam, Kauffman made a failed attempt to enter politics in 1890 and about the same time experienced a crisis of faith brought on by the death of his wife and newborn daughter. Faced with the awesome responsibility of raising his son alone, Kauffman was converted through the preaching of revivalist J. S. Coffman (1848–1899), after which he joined the Mennonite Church and was baptized in the fall of 1890.[7] Ordained in 1892, Kauffman became a bishop four years later, at the age of 31. Thereafter in a position of influence, Kauffman threw his support behind the creation of the Mennonite General Conference, which he moderated in 1898. From there he soon began his work as editor of the *Gospel Witness*, serving from 1905–1908, and of the *Gospel Herald*, which he oversaw from 1908–1943.[8] It was in his capacity as editor that Kauffman exercised unparalleled influence in the Mennonite Church during the first half of the twentieth century.[9]

MODERNISM, FUNDAMENTALISM, AND THE MENNONITE CHURCH

Updating Christianity to make it relevant for the current era was the hallmark of modernism, also known as the New Theology. Its principle exponents, including Horace Bushnell (1802–1876), Shailer Matthews (1863–1941), and Harry Emerson Fosdick (1878–1969) believed that the only way for Christianity to maintain respectability in light of new scientific, historical, religious, and philosophical theories was through a pattern of accommodation. Hence, modernists embraced evolutionary theory, higher criticism of biblical texts, the "experiential" religion of German theologian Friedrich Schleiermacher (1768–1834), and

6. Erb, "Kauffman," 3:156; Gingerich, *Life and Times*, 2.
7. Gingerich, *Life and Times*, 16–18.
8. Erb, 3:157.
9. For more on Kauffman, consult Nathan Yoder's essay in the present volume; on fundamentalism among Mennonites in other contexts, see Jared Burkholder's essay.

a progressive view of history.¹⁰ Specifically, as American intellectual elites became conversant with scientific ideas and the critical methodologies of German universities, modernist theologians questioned the Bible's supernatural accounts of miracles, Jesus' virgin birth, and literal resurrection. Instead, they applied the methods of textual criticism to the Bible itself and maintained that its contents could contain errors.[11] All in all, modernists proposed serious changes to the way that many Christians had historically understood their faith.

Most historians have asserted that the Mennonite church remained relatively untouched by the New Theology.[12] Indeed, Theron Schlabach, long-time professor of history at Goshen College, has concluded that anti-modernists in the Mennonite Church, such as John Horsch, were needlessly "aiming elephant guns to kill flies."[13] Consequently, these interpreters have tended to view Kauffman's codification of Mennonite orthodoxy and consolidation of power (epitomized by the 1923-1924 closing of Goshen College) primarily as an attempt to gain personal and cultural control rather than a legitimate response to genuine theological drift within the church.[14] While it is true that there was essentially no full-blown modernism in the Mennonite Church in the first few decades of the twentieth century, "moderate" forms of modernism certainly did exist, most prominently among the leadership of Goshen College. In particular, presidents Noah E. Byers and J. E. Hartzler advocated a moderate form of the New Theology from the classrooms of Goshen.

Noah E. Byers (1873-1962) assumed the presidency of Elkhart Institute (the forerunner of Goshen College) in 1898. One of the best-educated Mennonites of his generation, his extensive training had taken him to institutions where new philosophical and theologi-

10. Longfield, "Liberalism/Modernism, Protestant," 646-648. See also, Hutchison, *The Modernist Impulse*.

11. Ibid., 647-48.

12. Schlabach, *Gospel Versus Gospel*, 114; Toews, *Mennonites in American Society*, 66; Toews, "Fundamentalist Conflict," 244.

13. Schlabach, *Gospel Versus Gospel*, 114.

14. For example, Gross, "Doctrinal Era," 92-94; Schlabach, *Gospel Versus Gospel*, 110; Kraus, "American Mennonites," 326-27; Ainley, "Mennonite Cultural Wars," 147-49; Redekop, "Mennonite Defection and Fundamentalism," 24-28. Additionally, Perry Bush has discussed similar liberal/conservative conflicts at Bluffton College through the framework of power struggles in, "'United Progressive Mennonites,'" 357-80.

cal ideas were taught, such as the University of Chicago and Harvard University.[15] At Harvard, for example, Byers studied with the renowned pragmatist philosopher William James. Historian Nathan E. Yoder believes that Byers's view of religion was shaped by James's philosophical commitments, "whose focus upon the social influences in human experience relativized religious faith."[16] In addition to his studies at institutions traditionalists considered suspect, Byers promoted modernism in the classroom at Goshen. Reflecting on her experience at Goshen and advising the president (at his request) on how the college could improve, Anna Kauffman Hess, a student at Goshen from 1902–1905, advised Byers that he should "keep the average student thoroughly orthodox" while expressing his "most liberal views in private only to inquiring students."[17] What were Byers's "liberal views?" Hess recalled that Byers's theological views, along with those of Professor Paul E. Whitmer, allowed her to be "thoroughly in sympathy with the modern trend."[18] She admitted to being "far more liberal" than many of her classmates at Indiana University, where she matriculated after studying at Goshen, and found herself especially prepared for a class on William James's *Varieties of Religious Experience* (1902).[19] Hess was explicit, telling Byers on one occasion that her acceptance of the New Theology was due specifically to her time spent at Goshen under his guidance. His classes in Psychology and Ethics, she remembered, were especially "revolutionary."[20] This frank admittance on the part of an alumnus demonstrates that, at least in some capacities, Byers was transmitting to students the modernist sympathies he had gained through his own studies.

Another source of modernist-leaning teaching at Goshen College was Byers's successor John E. Hartzler (1869–1963), who served as president from 1913–1918. Like Byers, Hartzler's educational background also included studies at institutions with liberal reputations—

15. Miller, *Culture for Service*, 26 and 305.

16. Yoder, *Mennonite Fundamentalism*, 183 and 197.

17. Anna Kauffman Hess to Noah E. Byers, 22 November 1909, quoted in Yoder, *Mennonite Fundamentalism*, 187–88. This correspondence can be found in the Byers presidential papers, located at Goshen College. On this correspondence, see also Miller, 100–101.

18. Hess to Byers, quoted in Yoder, *Mennonite Fundamentalism*, 188.

19. Ibid.

20. Ibid.

such as Union Theological Seminary (NY) and the University of Chicago.[21] Initially, Kauffman, who counted Hartzler a personal friend, considered him orthodox enough to write chapters for *Bible Doctrine* (1914), Kauffman's popular book on Mennonite teachings. But by the time Hartzler became president of Goshen, conservative opponents were increasingly attacking the hapless president. Hartzler, in fact, invited such criticism in his inaugural address by rejecting the "erroneous view" that Christianity was "one unchanging body of dogma." Instead, echoing the ideas of Schleiermacher, Hartzler affirmed that "Religion is a matter of experience."[22] Moreover, Hartzler endorsed William Newton Clarke (1841–1912), a well-known Baptist minister and modernist, by assigning his *Outline of Christian Theology* (1898) for his classes. Although Hartzler discontinued using the Clarke text in the classroom after 1912, he continued to defend Clarke and even used him as a source for his chapters in *Bible Doctrine* in 1914. Perhaps more troubling for Hartzler's opponents, Goshen students "continued to cite Clarke as an authority" on theological matters.[23]

Although Hartzler was practically forced to resign the presidency of Goshen in 1918 due in part to the college's financial disarray, he continued to exert influence within the Mennonite church. As president of the short-lived Witmarsum Theological Seminary, located at Bluffton College, Hartzler penned *Education Among the Mennonites of America* (1925). In a chapter titled "The Outlook," Hartzler surveyed three current "tendencies among Mennonites" and contrasted "extreme conservatism" with "a more liberal philosophy of life." Recycling an analogy that would be used again and again by progressive Mennonites, Hartzler compared Mennonite ultra-conservatives to the sixteenth century Roman Catholic Church, which derived its power from "fear" and "penalty of excommunication." He criticized fundamentalists who believed "that virtue lies in exact, formal and literal statements and doctrines, good for all time and for all men, unalterable and unchangeable" and argued that the "major premise"

---

21. Weaver, "Hartzler, John Ellsworth," 5:363.

22. Quoted in Juhnke, *Vision, Doctrine, War*, 264. For a synopsis of the inaugural address, see *Goshen College Record* 16, 7–12.

23. Yoder, *Mennonite Fundamentalism*, 281–83. On Clarke's liberalism, see Weber, "Clarke, William Newton," 292.

of their argument was "wrong."[24] In contrast, Hartzler praised the liberalism that he believed was then penetrating Mennonite education: "The scientific spirit of the 19th and the 20th centuries has found its way into the life of the denomination in a remarkable way. The psychological tendencies so evident in the educational world during the past quarter or one-half century is working with tremendous force, overthrowing much of the religious tradition, and most of the religious educational method. This over-turning of things is not entirely unwelcome to the rising generation."[25]

Although it would be wrong to label Hartzler and Byers as unqualified modernists, each demonstrated sympathy for the New Theology.[26] As Yoder puts it, the liberals at Goshen "were absorbing and passing on more from modernist voices than they would or could acknowledge."[27] Thus, far from being a straw man of Kauffman's imagination, modernism in one form or another was being taught at Goshen in the early twentieth century.

Like modernism, fundamentalism, in various forms, could also be found among American Mennonites. Those of the broader Fundamentalist movement in America, which was comprised of members of different denominations, were united in a desire to defend what they perceived as the truth of historic Christianity against the inroads modernism was making in American Protestantism. Presbyterian theologian J. Gresham Machen, for instance, arguably Fundamentalism's ablest spokesman, referred to "modern liberalism" as "un-Christian" and as "a different religion from Christianity."[28] Likewise, *The Fundamentals* (1910–1915), published by California laymen Lyman and Milton Stewart and distributed to pastors, educators, and seminarians across the country, contained articles attacking modernist positions on inspiration, biblical authorship, and higher

---

24. Hartzler, *Education Among the Mennonites of America*, 181.

25. Ibid.

26. Kenneth Cauthen, for example, has distinguished between "evangelical liberals" and "modernistic liberals." In his view, the former were less radical than the latter. See Cauthen, *Impact of American Religious Liberalism*, 27–30.

27. Yoder, *Mennonite Fundamentalism*, 206.

28. Machen, *Christianity and Liberalism*, 7. On Machen, see Hart, *Defending the Faith*.

criticism, while they defended Christ's virgin birth and divinity, biblical archeology, and a score of other controversial issues.[29]

Mennonite forms of fundamentalism were varied and complex. The late Rodney Sawatsky, a Mennonite historian who served as president of Messiah College (Grantham, PA) created a helpful typology for understanding the various kinds of fundamentalists within Anabaptism in the early twentieth century. First were "radical fundamentalists" who, despite being Mennonites, accepted Calvinism, dispensationalism, and C. I. Scofield's "postponement theory." Although no major leaders fall into this category, the virulence with which George R. Brunk and Ira D. Landis attacked these positions suggests that some Mennonite laity may have adopted these ideas.[30] The second category, "moderate fundamentalists," was much more common. Including George R. Brunk (1871–1938), A. D. Wenger (1867–1935), John H. Mosemann (1877–1938), Jacob B. Smith (1870–1951), and John L. Stauffer (1888–1959), this school of thought rejected aspects of mainstream Fundamentalism, but retained others, notably a commitment to premillennialism. To be sure, it is their place in the spectrum of fundamentalism, not the level of their opposition to modernism, which should be termed "Moderate." Sawatsky included only Kauffman in his next category, "conservative fundamentalists." Recognizing Kauffman's desire for unity rather than division, Sawatsky saw Kauffman as being to the theological left of the "moderate fundamentalists." Finally Sawatsky identified a group of "fundamental conservatives," including Harold S. Bender (1897–1962), S. C. Yoder (1879–1975), Guy F. Hershberger (1896–1989), and Noah Oyer (1891–1931).[31] These men, according to Sawatsky, also strove for unity, though some such as Harold Bender gained most of their influence in the years following Kauffman's death in 1944.

KAUFFMAN'S THIRD WAY

The first way that Kauffman created a distinctly Mennonite response to the Fundamentalist-Modernist Controversy was through his

---

29. Dixon and Torrey, eds., *The Fundamentals*; Marsden, *Fundamentalism*, 119.
30. Sawatsky, "Fundamentalism, Liberalism, and Anabaptism," 8.
31. Ibid., 8–12.

opposition to modernism. To be sure, Kauffman was no friend of modernism. Even a cursory glance at the three books that he wrote or edited on biblical doctrines over a period of thirty years demonstrates convincingly that Kauffman opposed any tampering with traditional conceptions of orthodoxy. His steadfast opposition to Darwinism, "erroneous views" of the atonement, and higher criticism, for example, indicates his refusal to appropriate any part of the New Theology.[32] In fact, Kauffman's views on science, Scripture, and Christology were very much in line with mainstream Protestant Fundamentalists.[33] The Fundamentalist agenda served as a bridge between Kauffman's Mennonite Church and mainstream Protestantism. In addition to holding many of the same positions as mainstream Fundamentalists, Kauffman explicitly relied on their works as he edited the books on Bible doctrines. In the preface to *Doctrines of the Bible*, Kauffman listed R. A. Torrey, a contributor to *The Fundamentals*, and William Evans, author of the Fundamentalist *Great Doctrines of the Bible* as sources that he and the committee consulted in preparation for their project.[34] In fact, on all of the issues regarding Christology and the nature of Scripture, Kauffman was sympathetic to Fundamentalism.

Despite his continuity with certain segments of Protestant Fundamentalism, however, Kauffman remained aloof from the movement as a whole, believing Anabaptism should remain largely distinct from these broader trends. In fact, just as Kauffman opposed modernists at Goshen on the theological left, he also found himself at odds with Mennonite fundamentalists on the right. "We are," he said, referring to the Mennonite Church, "fundamentalists with a small 'f.'"[35]

By not adopting the Fundamentalist movement wholesale, Kauffman set himself apart from other Mennonites who appropriated Fundamentalism more fully, which is one reason Sawatsky placed Kauffman in a category by himself. Indeed, not all Mennonite lead-

---

32. For example, Kauffman, *Doctrines of the Bible*, 42 and 248–50; Kauffman, ed., *Bible Doctrine*, 113–28.

33. On Protestant Fundamentalism, see Marsden, *Fundamentalism and American Culture*; Carpenter, *Revive Us Again*; Longfield, *Presbyterian Controversy*; and Sandeen, *Roots of Fundamentalism*. For older, more negative conceptions of Fundamentalism, see Cole, *History of Fundamentalism*; and Furniss, *Fundamentalist Controversy*.

34. Kauffman, ed., *Doctrines of the Bible*, 8.

35. Quoted in Wenger, "Inerrancy Controversy," 112.

ers distinguished between Fundamentalism and historic Mennonite belief as clearly as Kauffman did. A number of these leaders, for example, adopted the premillennialism of the broader Fundamentalist movement. Although premillennialism was not a view that orthodox Anabaptists had historically accepted, American Mennonites' increasing familiarity with Protestant theological movements, such as dispensationalism, led some to accept this eschatological vision.[36] Premillennialists teach that the world will gradually degenerate until Christ's Second Advent, when He will banish the Antichrist and reign for a literal thousand years on earth before finally destroying Satan and taking believers to heaven.[37] The movement was popular among Mennonite fundamentalists because its adherents claimed to interpret the Bible literally. Likewise, because no modernists supported premillennialism, those who advocated it were free from suspicion of being tainted with modernism.[38] As early as 1898, revivalist A. D. Wenger (who had studied in 1894 at Moody Bible Institute) was advocating this view. At a Johnstown, Pennsylvania Bible Conference, Wenger noted that the world would "grow worse in the last days" after which he anticipated "a glorious reign on the earth of Christ and his saints for 1000 years."[39] While John S. Coffman, the moderator of the Bible Conference, cautioned that Wenger's view was "by no means the generally accepted view of the Mennonite people," in the next few decades premillennialism gained increasing sway among Mennonite conservatives.[40]

Far from remaining a theological hobbyhorse for conservative intellectuals, premillennialism was successfully imported into several Mennonite institutions. First, although Kauffman—who held the traditional amillennialist position—had tried to avoid eschatological controversy in the pages of the *Gospel Herald*, by July 1934 the premi-

36. Menno Simons, for example, specifically repudiated it, although Melchior Hofmann, Hans Hut, and the Munsterite Movement were dedicated to a chiliastic vision. This latter group, however, is not generally held up for admiration by Mennonites today. See Wenger, "Chiliasm," 1:557–58.

37. Wahlen, "Premillennialism," 332.

38. John L. Stauffer's defense of premillennialism exhibits both of these concerns. See Stauffer, *Premillennialism*. For a scholarly analysis of the movement, see Weber, *Living in the Shadow*.

39. Wenger and Kratz, *A.D. Wenger*, 10; Wenger, "Unfulfilled Prophecies," 53, 57.

40. Coffman, "Preface," to *Outlines*, 4.

lennial movement had gained enough strength to win an open forum in the *Herald* where its adherents (and the movement's opponents) were free to advocate their views.[41] Accordingly, John Thut, John H. Mosemann, S. F. Coffman, and Oscar Burkholder each argued for premillennialism in a special issue of *Christian Doctrine*—a quarterly supplement of the *Herald*— devoted to the subject.[42] Besides advocating their views in the *Herald*, the "moderate fundamentalists" created their own institutions of higher learning to combat the perceived liberalism at Goshen. The founding of Eastern Mennonite College in 1917 and the installment of ardent premillennialist John L. Stauffer as president assured conservatives that their views would be taught to Mennonite youth. Hesston College (founded 1909) also leaned towards premillennialism.[43] Thus, "moderate fundamentalists" in the Mennonite Church successfully advocated premillennialism through newspapers, pamphlets, Bible conferences, and colleges.

In addition to premillennialism, "moderate fundamentalists" also evinced attitudes of uncompromising militancy against modernism that further set them apart from Kauffman. Although many of these leaders were eager to expose modernism in the Mennonite church, none went so far as John Horsch (1867–1941), whose *The Mennonite Church and Modernism* (1924) created a stir of controversy following its publication. Instead of expressing his concerns in private letters as others had done, Horsch publicly named those whom he believed to be modernists. Not surprisingly, most of Horsch's targets were members of the "Old Goshen" faculty—many of whom had gone to Bluffton—such as Hartzler, Byers, S. K. Mosiman (1867–1940), and C. Henry Smith (1875–1948).[44] *The Mennonite Church and Modernism* was not Horsch's only assault on liberalism, however. Four years earlier, Horsch had fired the opening salvo with *Modern Religious Liberalism* (1920). Carrying an introduction by James M. Gray, president of Moody Bible Institute, and used as a textbook in that institution, *Modern Religious*

---

41. See Kauffman, *Vision of the Future*.

42. Consult the eight articles in the *Gospel Herald* supplement, "Christian Doctrine," 337–55.

43. Hostetler, ["Eastern Pennsylvania Mennonites"], 4:9.

44. Horsch, *Mennonite Church and Modernism*. See also Bush, "United Progressive Mennonites," 370–72.

Liberalism found favor among Protestant Fundamentalists at large in addition to its Mennonite audience.[45]

Other "moderate fundamentalists" demonstrated even more militancy in attacking modernism. In fact, Virginia bishop George R. Brunk epitomized the belligerent attitude inherent in Fundamentalism.[46] Considering Kauffman's *Gospel Herald* to be insufficiently vigilant in exposing the errors of the New Theology, Brunk inaugurated his own paper, the quarterly *Sword and Trumpet*, ostensibly "Devoted to the Defense of a Full Gospel, With Especial Emphasis upon Neglected Truths, and to an Active Opposition of the Various Forms of Error that Contribute to the Religious Drift of the Times."[47] In the publication's first issue, Brunk and Lancaster, Pennsylvania bishop John Mosemann contended to see who could denounce modernism in stronger terms. For Brunk, modernists in the church not only denied the "full inspiration" of the Bible and other fundamentals of the faith, but were

> flirting with Darwinism, which makes monkeys the progenitors of man, and Christ a lineal descendent of the brute! Such doctrines are no more Christian than a stinking carcass-eating buzzard is a dove! The monumental fraud of palming off this soul-damning modernism on the people for saving Christianity is only possible by their lack of enlightenment and the cunning, crafty camouflage of conscience-hardened liberals who practice deception in the name of God, and secretly glory in their shame; *and through the neglect of the Church to warn, enlighten, expose, and discipline.*[48]

Mosemann, for his part, gave Satan the credit for modernism's origin, arguing that "This God-contradicting doctrine first fell from the lips of the Devil when he said, 'Yea, hath God said?'" Furthermore, Mosemann saw modernism as "the Devil's handmaiden," while its proponents were alternately "wolves in sheep's clothing," thieves disguised as friends, and "satanic spirits coming as Angels of Light." "What are the aims of the Modernists?" Mosemann queried: "There is no ques-

---

45. Gray, "Introduction" to Horsch, *Modern Religious Liberalism*, 3–4. Horsch's book attracted enough attention to be reviewed by the *Princeton Theological Review*.

46. On militancy as a defining component of Fundamentalism, see Marsden, *Fundamentalism*, 4.

47. *Sword and Trumpet* 1.1.

48. Brunk, "The Drift" (emphasis is in the original).

tion about the fact that they are seeking to deceive all Christendom." With confident judgment, Mosemann proclaimed, "There is no true enlightened Christian in this Modernistic camp . . ."[49]

"Moderate fundamentalist" rhetoric was not limited to the *Sword and Trumpet*, however. Four years before, Brunk's zeal had taken him to the pages of the *Christian Exponent*, where he attacked the modernist heresy. The short-lived *Exponent*, which lasted only four years, was created in 1924 as a forum for the "Old Goshen" men to express their views. Constantly pleading for tolerance and individual conscience, the *Exponent* was in fact a temperate publication that protested the consolidation of authority by the bishops and occasionally reprinted statements of or reviews of books authored by proponents of modernism, such as Harry Emerson Fosdick or Henry Ward Beecher.[50] Yet its views were to the left of both the *Gospel Herald* and *Sword and Trumpet*, and Brunk feared its appeal to the church's youth. Responding in the *Exponent*'s "Open Forum" to articles such as Rudy Senger's February 27, 1925 piece entitled "Tolerance," Brunk blasted the paper from its own pages. He accused the editors of "scatter[ing] the seeds of suspicion, prejudice, and doctrinal looseness" and warned "the little Red Riding Hood of the Mennonite Youth" that the creature they took to be grandmother was in reality a dangerous wolf waiting to devour them.[51]

The extreme nature of much of the Mennonite fundamentalist attack became apparent when Brunk turned on Kauffman himself. According to Nathan Yoder, Brunk "regularly criticized Kauffman's editorial policies as pro-Goshen."[52] Brunk also complained in 1918 that, under Kauffman's leadership, the Mennonite Publishing House in Scottdale, Pennsylvania was "three fourths Goshenized."[53] Brunk characterized those like Kauffman who failed to separate fully from

---

49. Mosemann, "Fundamentalism *Versus* Modernism," 20–21.

50. See, for example, the piece in the *Christian Exponent* entitled, "Fosdick on War," 62; and Fosdick, "Does War Protect the Weak?" 66. Consult as well an anonymous review of Beecher, *Twelve Lectures* in the *Christian Exponent*, 126. It should be noted, however, that the *Exponent* advertised at least one anti-evolutionary book by William Jennings Bryan in the 15 February 1924 issue.

51. Brunk, "Mennonites and Modernism," 127–28.

52. Yoder, *Mennonite Fundamentalism*, 290.

53. Brunk to Smith, Wenger, and Kauffman, quoted in Juhnke, *Vision, Doctrine, War*, 263.

those in the liberal camp and did not oppose modernism vigorously enough for his tastes as "Laxitarian."[54] Such a characterization must have come as a surprise to Kauffman, who, as we have seen, could be quite adamant in his denunciations of modernism.[55]

The militancy demonstrated by Brunk and Horsch was largely foreign to the traditional practices of *die Stille im Lande*. Brunk's choice of a militaristic title for his paper was both ironic for a proponent of nonresistance and indicative of his larger departure from traditional Mennonite belief and practice. We have already discussed the nontraditional nature of his premillennialism; in addition to this, his militancy stood in marked contrast to Kauffman's civility. When a young, zealous Harold S. Bender recommended that Kauffman create an anti-modernist publication to combat the *Christian Exponent*, Kauffman demurred, opting instead to add a "Doctrinal Supplement" to the *Gospel Herald*.[56] Likewise, throughout his life John Horsch remained disappointed that Kauffman never endorsed his work to the extent that he wished.[57] Although Kauffman was certainly no friend of modernism, the tone he used was ultimately better suited for unity rather than division. He was, as Stephen C. Ainley writes, "caught in the middle" between the forces of modernism and Fundamentalism.[58] His middle ground—strikingly different from that of the "moderate fundamentalists"—was in fact an authentically Mennonite "third way" that offered a nuanced path through the Fundamentalist-Modernist Controversy.

Unlike those Mennonites who subscribed to premillennialism or adopted militant language in opposition to modernism, Kauffman believed he had good reason to distance himself from "large F" Fundamentalism. Although Fundamentalism was not a monolithic movement, many of its adherents subscribed to certain theological tenets that neither Kauffman nor historic Anabaptism accepted. For instance, according to historian C. Norman Kraus, mainstream "Fundamentalism's concern was . . . the maintenance of the conservative Puritan (Calvinistic) religious ethos of America as a Christian

---

54. Ainley, "Mennonite Culture Wars," 151.
55. See Kauffman, "Two Standards," 690–91.
56. Sawatsky, *History and Ideology*, 83–84.
57. Juhnke, "Theological and Social Boundaries," 20.
58. Ainley, "Mennonite Culture Wars," 151.

nation."⁵⁹ The Calvinism espoused by many Fundamentalists stood in stark contrast to Kauffman's emphasis on people's free will. Following historic Anabaptist teachings, Kauffman argued that human beings were "free" and that some would "willfully reject" God's grace.⁶⁰ Moreover, the *Mennonite Cyclopedic Dictionary* (1937), edited by Kauffman, declared Calvinist teaching to be "contrary to the teaching of the Word" and singled out the doctrine of eternal security for special condemnation.⁶¹ Thus, although many Fundamentalists were Calvinists, Kauffman did not capitulate to Reformed theology, choosing instead to maintain the historic Mennonite position.

On the subject of patriotism as well, Kauffman stood on firm Anabaptist ground. Historian Beulah Hostetler writes that Fundamentalism relied "heavily on the Old Testament for its conceptions of nationalism"—an understanding directly linked to the militant Christian nation rhetoric that Kraus has identified with Protestant Fundamentalism.⁶² Kauffman, on the other hand, opposed these notions of patriotism and nationalism. When an Eastern Mennonite School board member suggested moving the school to a site near Hayfield, Virginia, Kauffman "counseled against it because of its proximity to Mount Vernon, with its political, military and patriotic atmosphere."⁶³ In addition, Kauffman criticized the popular Spanish-American War and lamented that so few were concerned about the souls of the thousands of soldiers who had died since its duration.⁶⁴ Clearly, though Kauffman shared with Fundamentalists concerns about maintaining the integrity of historic Christian positions on Scripture and Christology, he did not simply adopt Protestant Fundamentalism wholesale—a fact recognized by others as well as himself. Harold S. Bender, for instance, stated as much in a memorial issue of the *Gospel Herald* dedicated to Kauffman: "While he was staunch in his opposition to modernism in any form, he frequently raised his voice against those who were ready to link up with

---

59. Kraus, "Evangelical Coalition," 54.

60. Kauffman, *One Thousand Questions and Answers*, 169.

61. Kauffman, "Calvinism," 50. On the issue of eternal security, see also Jared Burkholder's essay in this volume.

62. Hostetler, ["Eastern Pennsylvania Mennonites"], 2:20.

63. Gingerich, *Life and Times*, 78. Gingerich is quoting J. Irvin Lehman.)

64. Kauffman, "Points for Reflection," 146.

'fundamentalism' at the price of ignoring certain basic scriptural and Mennonite doctrines, such as nonconformity and nonresistance."[65]

More than simply distancing himself from the larger Fundamentalist movement, however, Kauffman charted a third way that displayed his unwavering commitment to traditional Anabaptist ways. Throughout his career as a bishop, committeeman, and editor, Kauffman consistently stressed the importance of uniquely Mennonite doctrine and practice. Among the more notable Mennonite "ordinances" that Kauffman defended were nonconformity to the world, nonresistance, the necessity of believers' baptism, and the devotional covering for women. Kauffman also opposed the taking of oaths, worldly fashion, and membership in secret societies.[66] In addition to these, Kauffman also defended other less well-known, though equally distinctive Mennonite practices. These included feet washing, the Christian salutation (holy kiss), anointing oil, self-denial, and opposition to life insurance, musical instruments, and birthday celebrations.[67] The Anabaptist ideals of nonresistance and nonconformity, however, arguably constitute the *sine qua non* of Anabaptism and, for this reason, Kauffman's views on these two points tell us much about his firm commitment to traditional Mennonite thought and practice.[68]

On the subject of nonresistance, Kauffman wrote in *Manual of Bible Doctrines* (1898) that "The doctrine of peace is so inseparably connected with the religion of Jesus, that it is difficult to conceive how any professing Christian can get the idea that it is right for any one under any circumstances to harm his fellowman."[69] Five years later, Kauffman again passionately argued against war, referring to it as "wholesale butchery" and "a baptism of bullets."[70] In August of

65. Bender, "Daniel Kauffman," 963.

66. A defense of these beliefs can be found in any of Kauffman's three volumes on Bible doctrine.

67. The opposition to birthday celebrations is found in Question 529 of *One Thousand Questions and Answers*. Specified as a "worldly amusement," the birthday party is prohibited along with "church entertainments," "banquetings, revelings, etc.," "foolish talking and jesting," and "carnal feasts," 101. For a detailed argument against the use of musical instruments, see Brunk, "Musical Instruments," 482–84.

68. On the importance of nonconformity and nonresistance to Mennonite identity as well as the multifarious ways in which these ideas have been practiced, see Kniss, *Disquiet*.

69. Kauffman, *Manual of Bible Doctrines*, 205.

70. Kauffman, "Why Oppose War?" 99.

1914, as the Great War erupted in Europe, Kauffman denounced the conflict in unqualified terms from the pages of the *Gospel Herald*. The war itself was an "institution of murder" that would bring only "savage fury" and "fields . . . drenched in blood." In the face of war, "socalled [sic] Christian nations" quickly degenerated into barbarism and ordinary men and women felt the full force of conflict and suffering. Times like these, Kauffman declared, called for faithfulness and a willingness to suffer "rather than inflict sufferings upon others, dying rather than to kill."[71]

Kauffman also demonstrated the importance of traditional Anabaptist teachings through his advocacy of the doctrine of nonconformity. He devoted considerable attention to the subject in *Manual of Bible Doctrines*, including under its heading everything from intemperance and licentiousness, to politics and "worldly adornment."[72] Nonconformity for Kauffman meant the necessity of a transformed life and its consequent—"an entire separation from the world."[73] Again in 1928, Kauffman reiterated the importance of nonconformity, calling it "an extensively taught Bible doctrine."[74] Perhaps Kauffman was most emphatic about this doctrine in his later life. In 1941, reflecting on his fifty years of service in the church, Kauffman remained unambiguous about the need for separation from the world:

> Worldly conformity is a sin that was in evidence in apostolic days, in every generation since that time, and is still in evidence. Notwithstanding the fact that the Bible is clear and emphatic in its teaching that the people of God should be a people who are distinct and separate from the world . . . the majority of churches (and some members in churches that are still clinging to Gospel standards) have chosen to conform to the world's standards rather than to obey the plain teachings of God's Word.[75]

Rather than simply paying lip-service to Mennonite distinctives, Kauffman upheld their importance throughout his life. Indeed, as

---

71. Kauffman, "Militarism Unchained," 313–14.
72. Kauffman, *Manual of Bible Doctrines*, 186–204.
73. Ibid., 201.
74. Kauffman, ed., *Doctrines of the Bible*, 490.
75. Kauffman, *Fifty Years*, 74–75.

Chester K. Lehman wrote in 1944: "The most important contribution to Mennonite thought made by Bro. Kauffman, I believe, is his presentation of the distinctive Mennonite principles and practices, such as Feetwashing, the Devotional Covering, the Christian Salutation, Anointing with Oil, Marriage, Nonconformity, Nonresistance, and so forth."[76]

This insistence on Mennonite distinctives coupled with his support for historic understandings of the fundamentals of Christianity served as the foundation for Kauffman's "third way."

FINAL THOUGHTS ON KAUFFMAN'S PLACE IN MENNONITE HISTORIOGRAPHY

The above notwithstanding, recent Mennonite historiography has continued to portray Kauffman as a rigid dogmatist, whose appropriation of Fundamentalism contributed to a profound shift away from traditional Anabaptist teaching and practice. Specifically, Kauffman's soteriology and his emphasis on doctrine have been interpreted as capitulations to Fundamentalism, rather than as the development of historically Mennonite teaching. It is the purpose of the final part of this chapter, then, to address in greater detail these interpretations of Kauffman.

First, former Bluffton University historian and theologian J. Denny Weaver has given one of the most compelling critiques of Kauffman's view of salvation in his monumental work *Keeping Salvation Ethical*. One of Weaver's central claims, if we accept his historical argument, is technically correct: that Kauffman, following his mentor J. S. Coffman, "separated salvation from ethics" by dividing the experience of conversion from that of Christian living.[77] Thus, for Kauffman and those like him, "Ethics was now something to be discussed at a later point, as a consequence of being saved."[78] Weaver bases these claims—that Kauffman introduced a new theological strain into Anabaptism—on his studies of early American

76. Lehman, "Thinker and Theologian," 966.

77. Weaver, *Keeping Salvation Ethical*, 218–19. Juhnke also makes this claim, but acknowledges that the separation was unintentional. Juhnke, *Vision, Doctrine, War*, 116.

78. Weaver, "Quickening of Soteriology," 42.

Mennonite and Amish leaders such as Jacob Stauffer (1811–1855) and Christian Burkholder (1746–1809). In Weaver's assessment, these leaders drew their sense of ethics (like nonresistance) to a large degree from Jesus' nonviolent atonement. Modifying the traditional Protestant "satisfaction theory" of atonement that Kauffman also advocated, Stauffer, Burkholder, and others believed that Jesus' nonviolence was intrinsically tied to atonement and salvation. Kauffman, on the other hand, admittedly advocated nonresistance as an ethic that Jesus preached, but did not link it explicitly to His atonement.[79] Moreover, according to Weaver, Kauffman's heavy emphasis on assent to correct doctrinal and Christological formulations represented a departure from historic Anabaptism's penchant for prioritizing correct living over propositional truth claims. Hence, Kauffman pushed Anabaptism toward a modified form of Fundamentalism and undermined—albeit unconsciously—the Anabaptist commitment to nonresistance.[80]

Despite the strengths of Weaver's study overall, there are two crucial errors with regard to Kauffman. First, Weaver exaggerates the extent to which Kauffman separated salvation from ethics and appropriated Fundamentalist terminology at the expense of historic Mennonite theology. Second, both Weaver and historian Leonard Gross underestimate the historic importance given to correct doctrine in the Mennonite church. It should be noted, as Weaver contends, that Kauffman did not, in fact, link ethics to atonement theology in the way that his American predecessors did. But to acknowledge this claim is not to conclude automatically that Kauffman did not see nonresistance or similar Mennonite distinctives as an integral part of the gospel, as Weaver asserts.[81] In fact, one of the most compelling characteristics of Kauffman's "third way" was his insistence on the necessity of the transformed life and his defense of the distinctives.

The crucial piece of evidence for this claim lies in Kauffman's 1930 work, *The Way of Salvation: Including Thoughts on What to Do*

---

79. Weaver, *Keeping Salvation Ethical*, 138, 219; "Quickening of Soteriology," 9–14.

80. Weaver, "Quickening of Soteriology," 37–42; *Keeping Salvation Ethical*, 218–19. See also Kraus, "Forward" to Weaver, *Keeping Salvation Ethical*, 14.

81. Weaver, "Quickening of Soteriology," 41; Gross, 83. According to Weaver, nonresistance was moved to "the periphery of the gospel" in Kauffman's works.

After We Are Saved. While Weaver might look at this work as the epitome of separating "getting saved" from "what to do after we are saved," in reality the work affirms Kauffman's strong commitment to ethics. Indeed, Kauffman explains the way of salvation and exhorts the reader concerning ethical living in the same breath. Mere intellectual assent to correct doctrine without evidence of regeneration in one's daily life (embodied in the practice of the distinctives) is unthinkable. Instead, "If we have really been saved from sin we walk 'in newness of life.' This means that our former sins . . . must now be kept out of our lives."[82] To be sure, Kauffman does not locate ethics in atonement theology, but his palpable commitment to the transformed life vitiates Weaver's claim that, with Kauffman's theological modifications, one could now "discuss the essence of salvation based on atonement without dealing with the nature of the saved life."[83] While Kauffman may have opened the door to a salvation divorced from ethics, he himself, in charting a Mennonite "third way," unswervingly maintained his commitment to ethics, traditional Mennonite teachings, and the necessity of a transformed life.

Second, both Weaver and Gross underestimate the historic importance assigned to doctrine in the Mennonite church, specifically in the sixteenth century. According to Weaver, American Mennonites and Amish in the nineteenth century "did not define the true church in terms of abstract beliefs, and measure faithfulness on the basis of wholehearted assent to particular doctrinal formulations. It is this non-creedal and nondogmatic orientation and the stress on a *lived faith* that has sometimes been interpreted as the absence of a recognizable Mennonite theology. While they had a theology, it was the obedient life that comprised and expressed the distinct dimensions of their theology."[84]

Likewise, Gross contends that Kauffman's doctrinal focus was "ahistorical" and represented an "extended interlude" with few roots in the Mennonite tradition.[85] Anyone familiar with Anabaptist history will recognize the truth of Weaver's claim that the concept of a "lived faith" was integral to Anabaptists' understanding of Christianity. Yet,

---

82. Kauffman, *Way of Salvation*, 27–28.
83. Weaver, *Keeping Salvation Ethical*, 219.
84. Ibid., 225.
85. Gross, "Doctrinal Era," 83.

for Menno Simons (1496–1561), founder of the Mennonite Church, "lived faith" defined as an obedient life was not enough. Menno debated with and eventually excommunicated fellow Anabaptist David Joris (1501–1556) not for Joris's failure to live righteously, but for his incorrect doctrinal claims.[86] Even more telling, Menno excommunicated Joris despite the fact that Joris consistently advocated and practiced nonresistance.[87] For Menno, Christianity consisted of more than simple obedience to Jesus' teachings; fundamental doctrines that were not negotiable also constituted an important part of the faith. Accordingly, Menno opposed Adam Pastor over the latter's denial of the true deity of Christ. After reconciliation attempts failed, Dirk Phillips and Menno excommunicated Pastor in 1547.[88] Menno's own painstaking attempts to clarify his Christology in the face of magisterial Protestant criticism indicate that correct doctrine, while in itself insufficient, was important to him and the early leaders of the Anabaptist movement. Although historically Mennonites did not develop systematic theologies concerning "fundamental" issues, writes Paul Toewes, nevertheless, they took "orthodox positions for granted" on "issues such as creation, virgin birth, resurrection, and the saving efficacy of Christ's shed blood."[89] Doctrine was also important for the earliest emigrant Mennonites to the United States, whose first printed book was a confession of faith (1727).[90] Kauffman's insistence on correct doctrine, then, is best viewed not only in light of the significance of the era in which he lived, but also in the context of the whole of Anabaptist history.

With Kauffman's death in 1944, his brand of consolidation and commitment to propositional truth claims gave way (with a sigh of relief on the part of some) to Harold S. Bender's advocacy of the less doctrinal "Anabaptist Vision." Kauffman and his leadership, in turn, faded into memories of an unpleasant, "ahistorical era." Perhaps one of the reasons for the widespread misunderstanding of Kauffman is

86. Joris believed that readers should passively let the Spirit interpret the Scriptures for them, rather than engage in rational thought concerning their meaning. See Waite, *David Joris*, 94.

87. Ibid., 100.

88. See Simons, "Confession of the Triune God," 489–98. See also Wenger's note on page 488 of *Complete Writings* for the background on Pastor.

89. Toews, *Mennonites in American Society*, 66.

90. Ainley, "Mennonite Culture Wars," 148.

the lack of attention paid to him in scholarly studies. While historians such as Schlabach, James C. Juhnke, Beulah Hostetler, Paul Toewes, and Nathan E. Yoder have done important and necessary work on the nature of Mennonite fundamentalism as a whole, there currently exists no critical monograph dedicated exclusively to Kauffman. As historians continue to examine, however, the Fundamentalist-Modernist Controversy as it played out within the context of religious enclaves such as American Mennonitism, they no doubt will gain a greater appreciation for the decisive role that mediating figures such as Kauffman played. Responding to the competing ideologies of modernism and Fundamentalism while keeping Anabaptist tradition in view required judgment, conviction, and compassion. Through his strong opposition to modernist deviations from orthodoxy and his emphasis on correct doctrine, Kauffman led the church away from beliefs that were not part of its history. At the same time, his defense of the Mennonite distinctives and his unwillingness to join rank with "moderate fundamentalists" such as Brunk helped the Mennonite church to avoid capitulation to Protestant Fundamentalism. As Susan Fisher Miller writes, "Kauffman himself, the arbiter and image of Mennonite correctness, stayed a relatively moderate course within the conservative spectrum."[91] Such was his authentically Anabaptist "third way."

BIBLIOGRAPHY

"Advertisement." *Christian Exponent*, 15 February 1924, 64.
Ainley, Stephen C. "Mennonite Cultural Wars: Power, Authority, and Domination." In *Power, Authority, and the Anabaptist Tradition*, edited by Benjamin W. Redekop and Calvin W. Redekop, 136–54. Baltimore: Johns Hopkins University Press, 2001.
Bender, Harold S. "Daniel Kauffman and His Times." *Gospel Herald*, 10 February 1944, 962–63.
Brunk, George R. "The Drift." *Sword and Trumpet* 1.1, January 1929, 3.
———. "Mennonites and Modernism." *Christian Exponent*, 10 April 1925, 127–28.
———. "Musical Instruments." *Gospel Witness* 1:51, 21 March 1906, 482–84.
Brunk, George R. to J. B. Smith, A. D. Wenger, and Daniel Kauffman. 18 December 1918. Box 2, I-20. Kauffman papers. Mennonite Church USA Archives, Goshen College.
Bush, Perry. "'United Progressive Mennonites': Bluffton College and Anabaptist Higher Education." *The Mennonite Quarterly Review* 74 (July 2000) 357–80.

---

91. Miller, *Culture for Service*, 95.

Burkholder, Jared S. "Fundamentalism and Freedom: The Story of Congregational Mennonite Church and Calvary Mennonite Church, 1935–1955." MA thesis, Trinity Evangelical Divinity School, 2000.

Carpenter, Joel A. *Revive Us Again: The Reawakening of American Fundamentalism*. New York: Oxford University Press, 1997.

Cauthen, Kenneth. *The Impact of American Religious Liberalism*. New York: Harper & Row, 1962.

Coffman, John S., editor. *Outlines and Notes Used at the Bible Conference Held at Johnstown, Pennsylvania, from Dec. 27, 1897–Jan. 7, 1898*. Elkhart, IN: Mennonite, 1898.

Cole, Stewart G. *The History of Fundamentalism*. New York: R. R. Smith, 1931.

Dixon, A. C., R. A. Torrey, et al., editors. *The Fundamentals: A Testimony to the Truth*. 4 vols. Chicago: Testimony, 1910–1915.

Erb, Paul. "Kauffman, Daniel." In *Mennonite Encyclopedia: A Comprehensive Reference Work on the Anabaptist-Mennonite Movement*, edited by Harold S. Bender and C. Henry Smith, 3:156–57. Scottdale, PA: Mennonite Publishing House, 1957.

Fosdick, Harry Emerson. "Does War Protect the Weak?" *Christian Exponent*, 29 February 1924, 66.

"Fosdick on War." *Christian Exponent*, 15 February 1924, 62.

Furniss, Norman F. *The Fundamentalist Controversy, 1918–1931*. New Haven, CT: Yale University Press, 1954.

Gingerich, Alice K. *The Life and Times of Daniel Kauffman*. Scottdale, PA: Herald, 1954.

Goshen College. *Goshen College Record* 16, November 1913.

Gray, James M. "Introduction." In *Modern Religious Liberalism: The Destructiveness and Irrationality of Modernist Theology*, by John Horsch. 2nd ed. Scottdale, PA: Mennonite House, 1924.

Gross, Leonard. "The Doctrinal Era of the Mennonite Church." *The Mennonite Quarterly Review* 60 (1986) 83–103.

Hart, D. G. *Defending the Faith: J. Gresham Machen and the Crisis of Conservative Protestantism in Modern America*. Grand Rapids: Baker, 1995.

Hartzler, John E. *Education Among the Mennonites of America*. Danvers, IL: Central Mennonite Board, 1925.

Hess, J. Daniel. "From Judge to Statesman to Pastor to Scholar to Provocateur: One Magazine, Five Editors, and 90 Years of Journalism." *Gospel Herald*, 27 January 1998.

Horsch, John. *The Mennonite Church and Modernism*. Scottdale, PA: Mennonite House, 1924.

Hostetler, Beulah Stauffer. ["Eastern Pennsylvania Mennonites and Fundamentalism, 1890–1950."] Unpublished paper, typescript, [1981]. Copy in Lancaster Mennonite Historical Society.

Hutchison, William R. *The Modernist Impulse in American Protestantism*. Durham, NC: Duke University Press, 1992.

Juhnke, James C. "Mennonite Church Theological and Social Boundaries, 1920–1930—Loyalists, Liberals, and Laxitarians." *Mennonite Life* 38 (1983) 18–24.

———. *Vision, Doctrine, War: Mennonite Identity and Organization in America, 1890–1913*. The Mennonite Experience in America 3. Scottdale, PA: Herald, 1989.

Kauffman, Daniel, editor. *Bible Doctrine: A Treatise on the Great Doctrines of the Bible pertaining to God, Angels, Satan, the Church, and the Salvation, Duties and Destiny of Man.* Scottdale, PA: Mennonite House, 1914.

———. "Calvinism." In *Mennonite Cyclopedic Dictionary.* Scottdale, PA: Mennonite House, 1937.

———, editor. *Doctrines of the Bible: A Brief Discussion of the Teachings of God's Word.* Scottdale, PA: Mennonite House, 1928.

———. *Fifty Years in the Mennonite Church, 1890-1940.* Scottdale, PA: Mennonite House, 1941.

———. *Manual of Bible Doctrines.* Elkhart, IN: Mennonite House, 1898.

———. "Militarism Unchained." *Gospel Herald*, 13 August 1914, 313-14.

———. *My Vision of the Future: A Brief Statement Setting Forth the Amillennialist's View of the Great Events Yet to Come, Including the Destiny of Man.* 2nd ed. Scottdale, PA: Mennonite House, 1939.

———. *One Thousand Questions and Answers on Points of Christian Doctrine.* Scottdale, PA: Mennonite House, 1908.

———. "Points for Reflection." *Herald of Truth*, 15 May 1898, 146.

———. "The Two Standards." *Gospel Herald*, 7 December 1922, 690-91.

———. *The Way of Salvation: Including Thoughts on What to Do After We are Saved.* Scottdale, PA: Mennonite House, 1930.

———. "Why Oppose War?" *Herald of Truth*, 26 March 1903, 99.

Kniss, Fred. *Disquiet in the Land: Cultural Conflict in American Mennonite Communities.* New Brunswick, NJ: Rutgers University Press, 1997.

Kraus, C. Norman. "American Mennonites and the Bible, 1750-1950." *The Mennonite Quarterly Review* 41 (1967) 309-29.

———. "Forward." In *Keeping Salvation Ethical: Mennonite and Amish Atonement Theology in the Late Nineteenth Century*, by J. Denny Weaver, 13-15. Scottdale, PA: Herald, 1997.

———. "The Great Evangelical Coalition: Pentecostal and Fundamentalist." In *Evangelicalism and Anabaptism*, edited by C. Norman Kraus, 39-61. Scottdale, PA: Herald, 1979.

Lehman, Chester K. "A Thinker and Theologian." *Gospel Herald*, 10 February 1944.

Longfield, Bradley J. "Liberalism/Modernism, Protestant (c. 1870s-1930s)." In *Dictionary of Christianity in America*, edited by Daniel G. Reid et al. Downers Grove, IL: InterVarsity, 1990.

———. *The Presbyterian Controversy: Fundamentalists, Modernists, and Moderates.* New York: Oxford University Press, 1991.

Machen, J. Gresham. *Christianity and Liberalism.* New York: Little & Ives, 1923; Grand Rapids: Eerdmans, 1946.

Marsden, George M. *Fundamentalism and American Culture.* 2nd ed. New York: Oxford University Press, 2006.

Mennonite Church USA Archives. Noah Byers Papers. Goshen, IN.

———. Daniel Kauffman Papers. Goshen, IN.

Miller, Susan Fisher. *Culture for Service: A History of Goshen College.* Goshen, IN: Goshen College, 1994.

Mosemann, John H. "Fundamentalism *Versus* Modernism." *Sword and Trumpet* 1 (1929) 20-21.

Redekop, Calvin W. "Mennonite Defection and Fundamentalism." *Pennsylvania Mennonite Heritage* 31 (2008) 24-28.

Review of Henry Ward Beecher, *Twelve Lectures to Young Men on Various Important Subjects*. *Christian Exponent*, 10 April 1925, 126.

Sandeen, Ernest R. *The Roots of Fundamentalism: British and American Millenarianism, 1800–1930*. Chicago: University of Chicago Press, 1970.

Sawatsky, Rodney James. "Fundamentalism, Liberalism, and Anabaptism: Mennonite Choices in the 1920's and 1930's." Speech at Lancaster Mennonite Historical Society, 4 December 1978. Located in vertical file of the Lancaster Mennonite Historical Society. Lancaster, PA.

———. *History and Ideology: American Mennonite Identity Definition through History*. Kitchener, ON: Pandora, 2005.

Schlabach, Theron. *Gospel Versus Gospel: Mission and the Mennonite Church, 1863–1944*. Scottdale, PA: Herald, 1980.

Simons, Menno. "Confession of the Triune God." In *The Complete Writings of Menno Simons*, edited by J. C. Wenger and translated by Leonard Verduin, 487–98. Scottdale, PA: Herald, 1956.

Stauffer, John L. *Premillennialism*. Harrisonburg, VA: Sword & Trumpet, 1952.

Toews, Paul. "Fundamentalist Conflict in Mennonite Colleges: A Response to Cultural Transitions?" *The Mennonite Quarterly Review* 57 (1983) 241–56.

———. *Mennonites in American Society: 1930–1970*. Scottdale, PA: Herald, 1996.

Wahlen, Robert K. "Premillennialism." In *Encyclopedia of Millennialism and Millennial Movements*, edited by Richard A. Landes. New York: Routledge, 2000.

Waite, Gary K. *David Joris and Dutch Anabaptism, 1524–1543*. Waterloo, ON: Wilfred Laurier University Press, 1990.

Weaver, J. Denny. "Hartzler, John Ellsworth." In *Mennonite Encyclopedia: A Comprehensive Reference Work on the Anabaptist-Mennonite Movement*, edited by Cornelius J. Dyck and Dennis D. Martin, 5:363. Scottdale, PA: Herald, 1990.

———. *Keeping Salvation Ethical: Mennonite and Amish Atonement Theology in the Late Nineteenth Century*. Scottdale, PA: Herald, 1997.

———. "The Quickening of Soteriology: Atonement from Christian Burkholder to Daniel Kauffman." *The Mennonite Quarterly Review* 61 (1987) 5–45.

Weber, Timothy P. "Clarke, William Newton (1841–1912)." In *Dictionary of Christianity in America*, edited by Daniel G. Reid et al., 292. Downers Grove, IL: InterVarsity, 1990.

———. *Living in the Shadow of the Second Coming: American Premillennialism, 1875–1982*. Enlarged ed. Chicago: University of Chicago Press, 1987.

Wenger, A. D. "Unfulfilled Prophecies." In *Outlines and Notes*, edited by John S. Coffman. Used at the Bible Conference held at Johnstown, Pennsylvania, from 27 December 1897 to 7 January 1898. Elkhart, IN: Mennonite Publishing.

Wenger J. C. "Chiliasm." In *Mennonite Encyclopedia: A Comprehensive Reference Work on the Anabaptist-Mennonite Movement*, edited by Harold S. Bender and C. Henry Smith, 1:557–59. Scottdale, PA: Mennonite Publishing House, 1955.

———. "The Inerrancy Controversy within Evangelicalism." In *Evangelicalism and Anabaptism*, edited by C. Norman Kraus, 101–24. Scottdale, PA: Herald, 1979.

Wenger, J. C., and Mary W. Kratz. *A.D. Wenger, 1867–1935*. Harrisonburg, VA: Park View, 1961.

Wetzel, Benjamin. "A Third Way: The Role of Daniel Kauffman in Mennonite Fundamentalism." *Pennsylvania Mennonite Heritage* 32 (2009) 12–17.

Yoder, Nathan E. "Mennonite Fundamentalism: Shaping an Identity for an American Context." PhD diss., University of Notre Dame, 1999.

"I Submit"

Daniel Kauffman and the Legacy of a Yielded Life

NATHAN E. YODER

IN OCTOBER 1890, JOHN S. Coffman (1848–1899), the most prominent Mennonite evangelist of the period, was conducting revival services at Mt. Zion Mennonite Church near Versailles, Missouri. A charismatic itinerant who was particularly successful in drawing young people into the Mennonite fold, Coffman held meetings for three weeks. Among those who walked the aisle during the Mt. Zion meetings was Daniel Kauffman (1865–1944), who had lost both his wife and an infant daughter earlier that year. Now, in response to Coffman's invitation, the young widower pledged his loyalty to Jesus and to the Mennonite church. He would later go on to serve as one of the key leaders of the (Old) Mennonites during the early decades of the twentieth century, playing a dominant role in shaping the infrastructure of the denomination. Fellow activists who celebrated what they called the "Mennonite Great Awakening" even lauded him as a pioneer.[1]

Kauffman was not without detractors, however. Traditionalists who opposed the institution building of Kauffman's generation decried these developments as innovative compromises. Kauffman also faced criticism for introducing Mennonites to American fundamentalism, which, when applied within a Mennonite context, turned out to be

---

1. Daniel Kauffman was part of the Mennonite Church, also known as the (Old) Mennonite Church. In 2002 this denomination merged with the General Conference Mennonite Church to form Mennonite Church USA. For more on Kauffman, see also Benjamin Wetzel's essay in this volume.

an uneasy mixture of both conservative activism and progressive innovation. Kauffman's legacy remains contested as various Mennonite historians have assessed his career in light of Anabaptist values and tradition. One cause for the diversity of views was the fact that Kauffman functioned as a mediating figure whose career straddled a pivotal time in Mennonite history—when American Anabaptists felt acutely the tensions between modern and traditional impulses. In this respect, American Mennonites were not unlike evangelicals who were experiencing their own tensions with mainstream America and grappling with modernity. In many ways, in fact, Kauffman was situated in the space between the Anabaptist and evangelical traditions, hoping to make use of broader American trends, including fundamentalism, in an attempt to carve out an Anabaptist identity that engaged both tradition and the modern world. Even as Kauffman contributed to institutional innovation, he also appealed to the traditional Anabaptist virtue of submission, or "yieldedness" (*Gelassenheit*).[2] Indeed, in recalling his conversion at the Mt. Zion church, Kauffman described the experience as one of yielding.[3] With his conversion serving as precedent for the rest of his career, "I submit" became a formative mantra.

Kauffman's commitment to the yielded life, along with his own perceptions of his career, comes into clear focus when contrasted with two other Mennonite leaders who were his contemporaries, namely C. Henry Smith and George R. Brunk. In the juxtaposition of these men's experience, Kauffman's reflection on submission as a prerequisite for leadership provides a relief for Smith's celebration of individualism and for Brunk's more insistent demand for surrender. Finally, Kauffman's motto continues to hold currency in ways that both Anabaptists and evangelicals can appreciate.

DANIEL KAUFFMAN IN CONTEXT

Daniel Kauffman was a leading figure in a generation of young leaders at the helm of cultural changes moving the Mennonite Church

---

2. Ironically, Anabaptists were noted for their stubborn tenacity in their insistence upon being non-deferential on matters of conscience while also teaching and practicing the yielding and letting go associated with *Gelassenheit*. Snyder, *Footsteps of Christ*, 39–43. See also Cronk, "Gelassenheit"; and Friedmann, "Gelassenheit."

3. Kauffman, *Fifty Years*, 2–3.

beyond sectarian ethnicity into a fuller engagement with modernity.[4] These leaders, many of whom experienced religious conversion through the itinerant ministry of John S. Coffman, began to assume leadership roles in the 1890s.[5] Kauffman's peers in ministry included entrepreneur and financier Aaron Loucks (1864–1945), urban missionary Menno Simons Steiner (1866–1911), revivalists and future college presidents Daniel H. Bender (1866–1945) and Amos D. Wenger (1867–1935), scholar and chiliast J. B. Smith (1870–1951), and preacher, editor, and polemicist George R. Brunk (1871–1938).

This generation established and ran what became the Mennonite Church's denominational bureaucracy. John F. Funk had begun publishing the *Herald of Truth* from Chicago during the Civil War as an entrepreneurial venture targeting Mennonite audiences. After he moved to Elkhart, Indiana, he founded the Mennonite Publishing Company as his own private endeavor. During the final decades of the century he recruited a cadre of young activists to Elkhart who not only edited text and ran presses but also initiated missionary and benevolent work. These northern-Indiana-based Mennonite ventures into publications, missions, and education provided much of the footprint for what would become a denominational Board of Education (1905), Board of Missions and Charities (1906), and Publication Board (1908).

The activism which nurtured Kauffman and many of his peers became manifest in a variety of specific ways. One of the most illustrative examples was the push for higher education. Where earlier generations had assumed that those of the church's youth who enrolled in college were lost to the Mennonite cause, this generation took up church-sponsored higher education. Talented young adults drawn to these new ventures in Elkhart, Indiana, were instrumental in founding

---

4. Schlabach, "Reveille"; Schlabach, *Gospel Versus Gospel*, chapter 1: "New Dreambeats"; Juhnke, *Vision, Doctrine, War*.

5. Coffman, who was celebrated for his ability to navigate both the boundary waters of progressive innovation and traditional adherence, preached in English rather than German. He connected easily with the youth of the church and had the ability to attract people on the margins of church fellowship, including Kauffman, who, at the time of his conversion, was running for political office (Mennonites frowned on political ambition). Coffman conveyed confidence and promoted education, becoming a figurehead for the Elkhart Institute in Indiana. His 1896 "Spirit of Progress" speech inspired highly optimistic assertions about the importance and relevance of higher education. For a documented, fuller version of this narrative, see Yoder, "Mennonite Fundamentalism."

the Elkhart Institute during the 1890s as an educational spoke in the progressive Mennonite wheel.[6] Despite the fact that John S. Coffman and Daniel Kauffman communicated as colleagues experimenting with Mennonite education both in Elkhart, Indiana, and Garden City, Missouri, later critics crafted an iconic version of Coffman's idealism as a foil to Kauffman's leadership.[7]

Establishing church-affiliated schools presented institutional challenges. Management, public relations, and finance stretched a people who had only nascent denominational structures. Furthermore, the intellectual and theological framework of most Mennonites tended to be traditional, pre-critical, and informal. Indeed, C. Norman Kraus has characterized this generation's approach to Scripture as "pre-theological Biblicism."[8] Not only were certain Mennonites engaging streams in the broader European and American context which they had for some centuries avoided, but higher education in the United States had itself been undergoing a profound shift. University-based education with graduate programs intent upon producing new knowledge were challenging constituent-based liberal arts education focused on passing the tradition of its sponsors to a younger generation.[9]

Turn-of-the-century Mennonite activism not only engaged modernity but also coincided with the emergence of the fundamentalist movement in broader American Protestantism. During the first three decades of the twentieth century, debate between fundamentalists and modernists became increasingly vitriolic. In 1921 the Mennonite Church's general conference passed its own affirmation of the "Christian Fundamentals," signaling their affinity with the concerns of fundamentalist evangelicals. The closing of Goshen College two years later illustrated the extent to which the school had become a lightning rod for conservative and fundamentalist concerns. Questions about authority and submission on multiple levels were foundational to confrontations both in broader Protestant and Mennonites circles.[10]

---

6. See especially chapter 2 in Miller, *Culture for Service*.

7. Miller, *Culture for Service*, 4–10, 89, 102. For examples of scholarship contrasting Kauffman unfavorably with Funk or Coffman, see Gross, "Doctrinal Era," 91–92; Epp, *Mennonites in Canada*, 248; Kniss, *Disquiet*, 43–45.

8. Kraus, "American Mennonites," 317.

9. Jencks and Riesman, *Academic Revolution*.

10. Yoder, "Mennonite Fundamentalism."

Also in line with broader evangelical currents, Kauffman and others adopted an understanding of conversion which highlighted a specific individual experience—something that was especially emphasized during "protracted meetings." Although various district conferences had articulated regulations against such meetings, certain itinerants were particularly skillful in communicating to young people, and the restrictions were increasingly relaxed toward the end of the nineteenth century in attempts to retain the youth.[11] Daniel Kauffman, as described above, was himself converted in his twenties during protracted meetings under the preaching of Coffman.

Kauffman's own leadership within this new generation of activists and fundamentalist-minded Mennonites who emerged during these transformational times was significant. He became an educational pioneer, for example, working with Coffman to spearhead the effort to establish a Mennonite school west of the Mississippi River. When insufficient funds made a denominational school unfeasible, however, Kauffman was persuaded to establish the Garden City (Missouri) Normal School and Business Institute on a nondenominational basis.[12] Kauffman also established and administered institutions to promote what he understood to be the church's vision. This can be seen in his advocacy for the general conference, organized in 1898 as a national assembly of the Mennonite Church. In 1905 he became the founding editor of the *Gospel Witness*, a competitor to Funk's *Herald of Truth*. Three years later, after the denomination sanctioned the merger of the two magazines into the *Gospel Herald*, Kauffman began his thirty-five year tenure as editor of that periodical. Of his books the most influential were the various editions on Bible Doctrine—in 1898, 1914, and 1928. Kauffman's most conflicted role was his appointment to the presidency of Goshen College for the 1922–1923 academic year in what proved to be a last ditch effort

---

11. Protracted meetings referred to revival or evangelistic services held in the same location for more than two or three successive nights. Prohibitions against such meetings were meant to guard against conversions which critics feared were fueled more by emotional revivalism then thoughtful discipleship. Some of the itinerants, however, were particularly skillful in communicating with young people. Hostetler, *American Mennonites*, 167–75.

12. Kauffman, *Conservative Viewpoint*, 21. Archival sources indicate that Coffman, who was linked to the Elkhart Institute in Indiana, engaged the younger Kauffman in Missouri through conversation and correspondence as a junior colleague. The Garden City school opened in September 1896.

to restore confidence before the denominational Board of Education closed the school for reorganization.¹³

His outlook was optimistic and modern as he shared, for example, the penchant of educators in the Progressive Era for standardizing curriculum and textbooks. Through modern analytical methods, he articulated and systematized the religious identity of a traditional people who for centuries passed their values through inter-generational practices.¹⁴ In short, Kauffman was a respected administrator, codifying systematizer, and influential arbiter.

Kauffman's historiographical reputation over the decades has shifted from complimentary appreciation for his influence in the decades following his death to later assessments which have been more critical. Particularly telling has been the interpretation of Kauffman's legacy as reflected on his extensive committee involvement within the emerging institutional structure of the denomination. Kauffman died in 1944, and ten years later his daughter published a biography with a laudatory reference to his dedication to the church, substantiated by the fact that "at one time he was a member of twenty-two different committees and boards of the Mennonite Church."¹⁵ Paul Erb, who succeeded Kauffman as editor of the *Gospel Herald*, several times recalled the twenty-two committees as a positive reminder of Kauffman's dedication and contribution to the church.¹⁶ This detail went on to become a stock phrase in references to Kauffman's work and influence—in the 1967 institutional history of Eastern Mennonite College¹⁷ and through several editions of a survey text in Mennonite history.¹⁸ These writers particularly conveyed an appreciation for Kauffman's authoritative leadership, portraying him as acting on behalf of the larger tradition.

Over time, the reputation evoked through references to Kauffman's twenty-two committee assignments lost its luster. In the early 1980s James Juhnke was relatively gentle in calling attention to the irony that "Kauffman, who had rejected worldly power, at one

13. Miller, *Culture for Service*, chapter 4: "Academics and Ecclesiastics."
14. Hauerwas and Wells, "How the Church Managed."
15. Gingerich, *Life and Times*, 48.
16. Erb, "Daniel Kauffman," 3:157; Erb, *South Central Frontiers*, 103.
17. Pellman, *Eastern Mennonite College*, 41.
18. Dyck, *Introduction to Mennonite History*, 2nd ed., 222; 3rd ed., 225–26.

time was a member of twenty-two church committees and boards."[19] J. Denny Weaver bypassed quantitative precision and simply generalized that Kauffman "served on all [of the Mennonite Church's] important committees during the first four decades of the twentieth century."[20] For Frank Epp the "22 committees and boards" offered proof that Kauffman and John Horsch "fashioned the official policy and polity of the Old Mennonite Church in the mould of their own conservative, authoritarian, and also very decisive preferences."[21] Susan Fisher Miller's 1994 centennial history of Goshen College repeated the increasingly infamous number "twenty-two" while portraying Kauffman as a quite benevolent president during his one year at the college.[22] However, a reviewer protested Miller's sympathetic treatment of such leaders as Kauffman, citing the number "twenty-two" as a signal of power grabbing and demanding harsher judgment of leaders who "wrecked pastoral and professorial careers when convenient and intimidated the church membership when possible."[23] Another writer termed Kauffman "an energetic and skilled bureaucratic organizer and infighter."[24] In recent decades there has been a tendency to echo such critique rather than to compliment the style of the man whose few photographs portray him as an elderly, dour looking bishop and editor.[25]

The nuance between affirming authoritative leadership and critiquing authoritarian imposition was a fine yet critical distinction, sometimes easily ignored.[26] Many Mennonites in Kauffman's day valued his authoritative direction. Others accused him of being authoritarian. Some of the most intractable battles between fundamentalists and modernists were fought over these same fault lines, in fact, and these patterns can be seen in the Mennonite context. Mennonites had a long tradition of embodying Anabaptist concerns for community in

19. James, "Gemeindechristentum and Bible Doctrine," 219.
20. Weaver, *Keeping Salvation Ethical*, 31.
21. Epp, *Mennonites in Canada*, 58.
22. Miller, *Culture for Service*, 82.
23. Ramseyer, review of Miller, *Culture for Service*, 350.
24. Kniss, *Disquiet*, 43.
25. For reproductions of two of the extant poses of Kauffman, see Erb and Gross, "Kauffman."
26. This distinction appears in the title of Owen, Wald, and Hill, "Authoritarian or Authority-Minded?"

practices which embodied authority and mutuality. As described below, regardless of how others viewed him, Kauffman believed himself to be guided by the principle of submission.

SUBMISSION REMEMBERED

Often remembered simply for his role as an assertive Mennonite leader, much of the literature on Kauffman neglects his own self-reflections on his spiritual life. These reflections reveal a person who sought first and foremost to align his career with the Anabaptist virtue of submission. This is illustrated particularly well by Kauffman's autobiographical writings, in which he utilizes the language of yieldedness, describing times he determined to submit to what he understood to be the expectations of the church and its tradition. Fifty years after his conversion and decision to become a Mennonite, he wrote an account of those decades, recalling that early in 1890 he lost his wife Ota Bowlin to typhoid pneumonia. In this retelling, he made no mention of the daughter born in January and predeceasing her mother.[27] Kauffman described having being left "with a twenty-month-old boy on my hands, and with it there came a deep sense of responsibility that I could not shake off." Further complicating Kauffman's sorting out of his loyalties were political ambitions. Political operatives put him forward as a candidate for county office in an election to be conducted that fall.[28]

Kauffman placed great emphasis on submission as he described his conversion. In his autobiography, Kauffman recalled the scene that took place in October of 1890 and is described in the opening of this chapter. "At the close of a three-week revival," he wrote, "while the last verse of the last hymn was being sung, I came forward and gave my hand to the evangelist and my heart to the Lord."[29] In the 1950s, following Kauffman's death, his daughter wrote a book-length biography of her father. Her account of Kauffman's conversion heightened the dramatic effect: "Night after night Daniel attended these meetings. What time he could spare from the school room was occupied with

---

27. Gingerich, *Life and Times*, 17.
28. Kauffman, *Fifty Years*, 2–3.
29. Ibid., 2.

his campaign, which grew more and more distasteful to him as the time wore on and the conflict within increased. The three weeks of meetings were almost over; the last night arrived, the last sermon was preached, and the final song of invitation was nearly ended when Daniel Kauffman, with the sleeping boy in his arms, rose to his feet."[30]

Kauffman's own telling tracks the debate within himself as to whether he would join the Mennonite congregation and conform to its prohibition against holding political office. Responding to evangelist Coffman's invitation did not settle this question of church affiliation. Kauffman recalled, "After yielding myself to the Lord, another struggle began." His decision did not come easily. Finally, he was convinced by the perspective that "having yielded myself to Him I cannot do otherwise than to yield myself in full obedience." He would express this obedience through baptism and affiliation with that expression of the Christian faith in which he had been raised in November. Kauffman's half-century account of his conversion and church affiliation appeared under the subheading "Yielding to the Lord."[31]

Kauffman's retelling of his conversion was not the only time that he invoked the themes of yielding and submission. In 1918, as the Great War ground on in Europe and ecclesial conflict mounted in the Mennonite Church, Kauffman drafted a book titled *The Conservative Viewpoint*.[32] The book included chapters on "Educational Problems," "Mission Problems," and "Publication Problems." The multiple references to "problems" reflected a growing sense of embattlement which church leaders felt in responding to challenges on multiple fronts.

Thus writing under a sense of crisis, Kauffman turned autobiographical in implicitly justifying his own exercise of authority. He recalled his willing submission as a young leader in the 1890s. Two years following his conversion and baptism, his fellow members in the Mt. Zion Mennonite congregation unanimously selected him for ordination as a minister.[33] Four years after this, however, as he labored at the new normal school in Garden City, he found he would need

30. Gingerich, *Life and Times*, 17–18.

31. Kauffman, *Fifty Years*, 2–3.

32. Kauffman, *Conservative Viewpoint*, 27. Internal evidence within the book—Kauffman's statement that the Eastern Mennonite School was still in its first year of operation—points to the author's writing in the spring of the year in which the book was published.

33. Gingerich, *Life and Times*, 22.

to choose between his duties as minister and his responsibilities at the school. One of the older ministers had urged that ordained leaders who were also schoolteachers resign their educational posts and dedicate themselves wholly to the welfare of the church. In Kauffman's mind, he, not yet thirty years old, was one of the young leaders to whom the proposal was addressed. Kauffman reached a difficult decision. In remembering the situation, he described his response as "a speech of two words." Before that regional conference he offered a resolute, "I submit." Although Kauffman's yieldedness received no notice in the conference minutes, twenty years later its significance was riveted in his own memory. In recalling these events, Kauffman said simply, "The next spring I quietly disposed of my interests in the school and it passed into other hands."[34]

AUTONOMY IDEALIZED: C. HENRY SMITH

Daniel Kauffman's delivery of his two-word speech and the elevated place that his submission occupied in his memory twenty-some years later take on added significance when contrasted with the autobiographical reflections of another Mennonite scholar. C. Henry Smith (1875–1948), ten years Kauffman's junior, also made his peace with the Mennonite tradition, but on different terms than did Kauffman. Smith's memory was one of celebrating individualism and autonomy rather than submission and yielding. He grew up Amish Mennonite in Woodford County, Illinois, among some of the more progressive Amish Mennonites in North America. Personally, he welcomed Coffman's English sermons in his German-speaking community, and admiration for Coffman prompted him to take up studies at the Mennonite-related Elkhart Institute in Indiana. Later he attended the University of Illinois and earned admission to the honor society of Phi Beta Kappa as an undergraduate. Graduate studies took him to the University of Chicago where he earned a doctorate.[35]

Smith was more interested in credentials legitimized by submission to the protocols of the academy than he was in observing the nuances of traditional Mennonite community. He chafed at the

---

34. Kauffman, *Conservative Viewpoint*, 21–22.
35. For autobiographical information on Smith, see his *Mennonite Country Boy*.

particularities of his tradition. Giving voice to the sentiments of many of the youth whom John S. Coffman was intent upon reaching, Smith wrote,

> No one, and least of all a boy of sixteen, cares to be ridiculed by his associates. The unusual dress regulations imposed on the girls, the big ungainly homemade bonnets and prayer caps, the ceremony of footwashing practiced at Communion, the custom among the preachers of greeting one another with a kiss when they met in church or on the streets . . . an uneducated farmer ministry, the German services in an English environment—all these religious practices so different from those of other religious groups I felt sure marked us as a queer people.[36]

Smith's impatience with what he experienced as incompetence and constraint carried over to some of his colleagues when he was part of the faculty at Goshen College in Indiana. He recalled, "The old leaders could not keep up with the procession. There was a wide gap, therefore, between the Harvard and Chicago graduates on the faculty attempting to make Goshen a progressive college abreast of the times and the board of farm preachers who were afraid to let go of the old traditions."[37] There was little point in deference to church leaders judged to be inferior or even incompetent.

At the University of Chicago, Smith had discovered an interpretation of the Anabaptist tradition which he found easier to stomach. Discovering that some scholars celebrated his spiritual ancestors for their insistence upon freedom of conscience, Smith reclaimed this interpretation of the heritage as his birthright. "The Bible alone is the all-sufficient standard and infallible guide," wrote Smith, "and each individual is left to decide for himself how the Bible shall be interpreted."[38] The Mennonites he described were harbingers of the individualism celebrated as part of the American ethos. Shrewd and thrifty, they thrived in the rough-and-tumble of the frontier. His 1910 article titled "The Mennonites as Pathfinders in American History" made this case in the Mennonite Publishing House's *Christian Monitor*.[39]

36. Ibid., 136, 109.
37. Ibid., 210.
38. Ibid., 19.
39. Smith, "Mennonites as Pathfinders," 435. See also Smith, *Mennonites in History*, 32.

By 1918, when Daniel Kauffman offered *The Conservative Viewpoint* as his corrective to what he believed was at risk in his denomination, C. Henry Smith was already five years beyond Goshen College. He had joined the exodus of faculty to Bluffton College in Ohio. Bluffton's ecclesiastical links were to the General Conference Mennonite Church rather than to the (Old) Mennonite Church which oversaw Goshen College. Furthermore, the (Old) Mennonite Church exercised more direct oversight and control over Goshen than Bluffton received. The émigrés from Goshen had looked to Bluffton as an academic haven.[40]

Like Daniel Kauffman, C. Henry Smith was making choices about how to engage a culture characterized as modern. Smith's flight from his Amish Mennonite tradition, infatuation with American individualism, immersion into higher education, and reinterpretation of Anabaptism all reflect his quest for autonomy. Historian Paul Toews assessed Smith's quest as one prodded by his individualism and refers to this impulse as "a graft, introduced by modernity."[41] Scholars have highlighted a sharply critical stance toward tradition as one of the tenets of modernity. The title of Jeffrey Stout's book, *The Flight from Authority: Religion, Morality, and the Quest for Autonomy*, invokes both the antipathy for authority and the pursuit of autonomy.

It was more than a coincidence that in putting forward his agenda for the church, Kauffman highlighted his experiences of submitting. He recalled these experiences as having paved the way to his own roles of influence. Yielding to God and the church was not only the means by which individuals claimed a Mennonite heritage and became a part of a congregation. The yielding associated with submission was also what legitimated those who provided leadership, speaking and acting on behalf of the corporate body with its tradition. Kauffman maintained that loyalty and submission were key criteria by which institutions claiming to serve the church were to be evaluated. In outlining essentials for educational success, he wrote, "The schools should stand as active, avowed, out-spoken champions of the tenets of the

---

40. Bush, *Dancing with the Kobzar*.
41. Toews, *Mennonites in American Society*, 105.

faith peculiar to their Church."[42] "Loyalty," elaborated Kauffman, "is an essential to success."[43]

SURRENDER IMPOSED: GEORGE R. BRUNK

For many of the same reasons that C. Henry Smith looked to Bluffton as a haven, conservative or fundamentalist critics such as George R. Brunk viewed not only that school but education in general with grave concern. For most of Brunk's childhood, his widowed mother was a single mother, faring for herself and her children on the Kansas prairies. Brunk was self-educated, reportedly at times studying through the night until dawn marked the beginning of a new work day. Converted, like Kauffman, under the preaching of John S. Coffman, Brunk also drank deeply of an emphasis on second-work-of-grace sanctification promoted by Wesleyan and holiness preachers and camp meetings. After being ordained first a minister and later a bishop, both while still single and still in his twenties, Brunk did marry and in 1910 moved to Virginia.[44]

The pursuit of academic respectability and elevation of scholarly authority were new within these streams of the traditional Mennonite community. They seemed to challenge ecclesial authority. What infuriated the sharpest conservative critics such as Brunk even more than Bluffton's presence was their fear that Goshen would follow in its path. Particularly irritating to them were assumptions by promoters of Goshen that the school would submit to the criteria for being a standardized school—accredited by the state and acknowledged by prestigious universities who would accept alumni for further study. Brunk insisted that the school conform not only to the broader academy, but also to his interpretation of the church's standards.[45]

After 1928 the bishop from Virginia was the unapologetically polemical editor of the independently published *Sword and Trumpet*. He elaborated on the significance of the periodical's title: "We shout through this Trumpet the importance of fulfilling all Bible conditions

---

42. Kauffman, *Conservative Viewpoint*, 35.
43. Ibid., 36.
44. Yoder, "Mennonite Fundamentalism," 125–43.
45. Ibid., 351.

in order to have robust new-born converts," and, "We slash right and left with the sword of God's truth" against half-heartedness and compromise.[46] From time to time, Brunk had chided Kauffman for imposing his editorial prerogative and muzzling some of his most strident critiques and exuberant flourishes in the denominational press. Now with his own independent mouthpiece, Brunk could warn the church on his own terms.

The manner in which George R. Brunk insisted upon the necessity of surrender to particular versions of ecclesial oversight underscores the critical nature of the authority side of the submission equation. At the opposite end of the spectrum from those views promoted by C. Henry Smith, Brunk made explicit the authority which demanded submission. In 1920 he contended in a letter, "We have a closed policy as to all that the Bible teaches, all that the Church rules that does not militate against the word—all that a Bishop rules in the interests of spiritual welfare."[47] In his periodical, Brunk echoed his emphasis on the Mennonite version of episcopal authority. He wrote, "Church government partakes largely and definitely of an episcopal nature from the fact that God through His Spirit, Word, and Church calls overseers to rule, be obeyed, and to administer the affairs of the Church in accordance with the principles and requirements of His Word." Congregationalism smacked of democracy, and Brunk was emphatic that "if the church were a democracy then it could overrule God and impeach him." Such godlessness, he wrote, was demonstrated in Russia, "where democracy has gone to seed."[48]

Smith and Brunk invoked different polities in their appeals. Smith had emphasized the democratic and individualistic impulses he found in Anabaptism. Brunk retorted that episcopal prerogative had "fallen altogether too much into obscurity" through the influence of "democratic Propaganda" as well as the "the popular demand to nullify episcopal authority." Brunk directed his intended corrective as much at his colleagues in the bishopric as he did at perceived democratic malcontents. "A bishop out of loyalty to God and the welfare of the Church must have courage enough to face the flood of hostile,

---

46. Brunk, "Editorial," 3.

47. Brunk to Harold S. Bender, 16 June 1920, quoted in Yoder, "Mennonite Fundamentalism," 255.

48. Brunk, "Church," 13.

democratic sentiment, and to magnify and justify his office."[49] Brunk described an exchange with an unnamed interlocutor whom he labeled "a liberal Mennonite propagandist of democracy." His correspondent had argued that the possibility of a congregation deposing its ordained leaders confirmed that power ultimately relies with the members of the church. Such challenge to ministerial authority stirred Brunk's ire. Decades before the advent of desktop publishing, he used the print fonts at his disposal to register his disapproval:

"My reply is that there is *divine authority* and *provision* by which an unfaithful bishop may be deposed by a *Scripturally organized church acting in harmony with the Word and Spirit* but that there is no democratic authority in an unscripturally organized group of a million religious democrats either to set up a bishop or minister, or to set him down."[50]

As Daniel Kauffman's "I submit" speech had profound personal consequences, so Brunk spelled out the implications of the sort of authority he advocated. While Kauffman recalled submitting, for Brunk, the operative word was *surrender*. He editorialized: "God is to give us a new heart and a new spirit and take away the stony heart out of our flesh. This is a major surgical operation which demands that we fully surrender ourselves upon the divine operating table—God cannot do his saving work if we are unsurrendered and go on our own disobedient way. Surgeons perform wonderful operations nowadays with marvelous success even upon the heart, but a condition of absolute surrender on the part of the patient is required."[51]

Editor Brunk frequently relied upon cartoonist Ernest G. Gehman to make his case even more vividly. Brunk's January 1933 verbal illustration of the unsurrendered surgical patient was one of those times. With Brunk's coaching, Gehman sketched a graphic image showing a patient fleeing an operating room. Pursuing the patient was the surgeon with a syringe in his left hand and a scalpel flailing menacingly in the right. The patient had an expression of obvious terror on his face, and blood flowed from multiple lashes or incisions on his back. Brunk narrated the scene: "Imagine an operation in which

---

49. Ibid.

50. Ibid. The italicized portions of this quote were, in the original, bolded for emphasis and the last part was not only bolded but printed in all caps.

51. Brunk, "Editorial," 3.

the patient is unsurrendered and resisting; on the operating table, and then off; with the surgeon chasing him from room to room and upstairs and down, cutting at him as he runs! Folly! But not more so than the common expectation that God should perform the work of grace upon the heart of such as are unsurrendered and disobedient." The caption for the cartoon instructed, "Surrender to Be Saved."[52]

The appearance of the *Sword and Trumpet* was a marker of a conservative or fundamentalist ascendency which would become entrenched toward mid-century in the Mennonite Church. C. Henry Smith himself might still seem a threat, but from 1913 onward that threat came from the ideologically more distant Bluffton rather than Goshen. The 1921 passage of the Christian Fundamentals and the 1923–1924 closing of Goshen College with the related purge of liberal congregations and leaders positioned conservatives within the Mennonite Church well on their way to dominating. By the time Brunk established his *Sword and Trumpet* magazine, the *Christian Exponent*, privately published during the mid-1920s from the progressive end of the Mennonite spectrum, was defunct.[53] Elsewhere I have risked the assessment, "Mennonite fundamentalists should not so much be faulted for winning during the 1920s as for failing to realize in the 1930s that they had won."[54]

Brunk's continued graphic insistence upon surrender undercut legitimate appeal to submission and echoed hollow on several fronts. Given the extent to which the conservatives had their way in the 1920s, it was disingenuous to insist that others surrender to them. Brunk's form of submission was based too much on his personally dominating discernment as bishop. His depiction would strike later sensibilities as less grotesque had he intended parody. He did not. Even those who agreed with the agenda he promoted at times urged him to muffle his strident tone. For those who came to regard Brunk as dogmatic and dictatorial, the cartoon confirmed some of the worst traits which they suspected to lurk in the repeated emphasis upon submission.

Daniel Kauffman and his peers shaped the denominational institutions, which they then administered and oversaw well into their senior years. Engineers of the conservative ascendency that

---

52. Ibid.
53. Juhnke, *Vision, Doctrine, War*, 267–69.
54. Yoder, "Mennonite Fundamentalism," 430.

dominated the church through mid-century, they comfortably associated many aspects of fundamentalism and evangelicalism with their own Anabaptist Mennonite tradition. That their generation continued to hold power when a rising generation began looking for places to exert their influence factored in a more restive mood. The reaction to Kauffman's influence—reflected in disparaging treatment of that piece of trivia about twenty-two committees—would later also dump cold water on glowing assessments of turn-of-the-century developments. A major plank in that revisionist platform was the contention that during the Awakening Kauffman's generation of young leaders had unwittingly diluted and soiled a pristine version of Anabaptism by borrowing uncritically from fundamentalist sources.[55]

ANABAPTISTS, EVANGELICALS, AND THE YIELDED LIFE

According to scholarly consensus, efforts to revitalize the Anabaptist tradition via revivalism and fundamentalism in the early decades of the twentieth-century were consistent with the cultural dynamics of modernity.[56] In their own context, Kauffman and his peers were part of a transition from a traditional, pre-critical cultural orientation to one that participated in many aspects of modern American society. Yet Kauffman's emphasis on submission has relevance for a twenty-first century context as well. Indeed, his two-word speech can serve as a framework through which we can view Anabaptist "ways of being"[57] in their relationship to their cultural context, knowledge of their theology, and the transmission of their values.

First, Anabaptist ways of being have always been framed by their identity as an alternative society that has existed in relationship to a host culture. Traditions less radical in their ethical expectations and more magisterial in their willingness to rely on civil authorities softened the impact of Christian identity as an alternative community or way of life. Luther, for example, drew a distinction between private ethics

55. Yoder, "Mennonite Scholars."

56. Schlabach, "Mennonites, Revivalism, Modernity," 415; Juhnke, *Vision, Doctrine, War*, 112–16; Toews, *Mennonites in American Society*, 32–34, 66, 82–83, 218–21; Schlabach, *War, Peace, and Social Conscience*, 273.

57. This phrase is an adaptation of the book title, *Anabaptist Ways of Knowing*, by Sara Wenger Shenk.

and public obligation. With this distinction he encouraged individual Christians to conform to the ethical expectation of the sphere in which they happened to find themselves.[58] A contemporary expression of this expectation is the justification that certain offensive behaviors are not immoral because they are merely part of conducting business and not meant to harm anyone personally. Applied on a more macro plane, such thinking might not only justify but even obligate Christians to act violently to maintain civil order or even to pursue military conquest. This magisterial version of a two-kingdom ethic was foundational to the late medieval context from which Anabaptism emerged. It maintained a dichotomy between an ordinary or secular sphere and another religious or holy one—the religious sphere differed markedly from the ordinary. A special set of words in Latin, the distinctive religious language, reconstituted elements into sacred emblems, and the host was consecrated at the altar by priests in distinctive vestments.

In contrast, Anabaptists' version of two-kingdom ethics assumed the distinction between the earthly kingdom and the heavenly, but stipulated that Christians consistently follow the example and teaching of Jesus in whichever sphere they find themselves. Their worship thus contrasted with medieval sacramental worship, to take one example. According to historian Walter Klaassen, "Anabaptism testifies uniformly that sacredness or holiness does not attach to special religious words, objects, places, persons, or days." Klaassen goes on to draw the ethical parallel: "A disciple's relationships are governed by love and truth, even as Christ's were; the command to love and be truthful is unconditional. No condition of religion or society, of church or state, may in any way qualify these demands."[59]

The Mennonite awakening and the broader encounter with modernity that Daniel Kauffman helped to facilitate necessitated that Mennonites rethink their ways of being in social and cultural relationships. It is not insignificant that the generation of young activists described above were frequently more comfortable with the English language than their German-speaking parents had been. For them, preaching in English and adapting revivalist methods associated with American evangelicalism were matters of both effectiveness and faithfulness. The decision to establish and sponsor Mennonite

---

58. George, *Theology of the Reformers*, 98–102, 132–36.
59. Klaassen, *Anabaptism*, 11, 22.

colleges for the purpose of educating and keeping young people within the church was a radical reversal of an earlier assumption that departure for college marked departure from the Mennonite community. Engagement with fundamentalism also loosened the ties to the immediate faith community.[60]

Such renegotiating of the boundaries defining faithfulness strained the tradition and its acknowledged authority structures. John S. Coffman mediated many of the strains as Mennonites adapted revivalism for their own congregations and ventured into high school and commercial training. They lacked a tradition in formal higher education and had virtually no ministerial leaders who knew the meaning of submitting to the rigors of the graduate education which legitimized authority in this arena. In making Kauffman president of Goshen when it was temporarily closed in 1922, the college's Board of Education was relying on his professional experience in the educational field three decades earlier. They looked to Kauffman to lead the school through the controversy, which was, to a large extent, the culmination of a crisis in authority and revolved around the question of how to be in relationship to the host culture.

Second, changes in an Anabaptist way of being entailed changes in knowing and believing as well. The integral link between the religious and the mundane was pivotal to theological integrity. Anabaptists have always been adamant that how people live gives evidence of what they believe. Stuart Murray has argued convincingly that for early Anabaptists, the reliability of a hermeneutical approach for making sense of the future depended on the interpreters themselves being obedient to truth already revealed.[61] Theological consideration and ethical living were thus coterminous. The primitive Anabaptist tradition did not consider Christian ethics as a separate discourse or discipline; this was rather a consequence of modernity's penchant for compartmentalization.

This shift can be illustrated through Kauffman's life. Soon after his conversion and baptism, Kauffman requested from John Funk, the well-known Mennonite printer, literature about what it meant to be a Mennonite. Funk had no literature to satisfy Kauffman's inquisitiveness, which was itself representative of modern impulses. Years later,

---

60. Kraus, "Evangelicalism," 198–99.
61. See chapter 6 in Murray, *Biblical Interpretation*.

Kauffman took up his own pen and provided, in modern fashion, what Funk was unable to do—offer his fellow Mennonites a compartmentalized collection of their own doctrine and the distinctive theology that legitimized their unique identity and the tradition to which he himself had become committed.[62] Similarly, building and regulating Mennonites' institutional life reflected Kauffman's application of impulses which he had learned as an educator, administrator, and aspiring politician. The fact that Kauffman and his colleagues called their undertaking an "awakening" and even "the Mennonite Great Awakening" signaled their optimism about their project.

Anabaptists and evangelicals alike, if they are concerned about ontological consistency in both the academy and the church, do well to reassess such a sanguine analysis. Stanley Hauerwas and Samuel Wells have argued that modernity undercuts those Christian habits which inform ethical behavior.[63] Mennonite theologian J. Denny Weaver has found this argument compelling. In parsing Mennonite writings across the nineteenth century, he describes a trajectory that consists of a "latent impulse toward the separation of ethics from salvation."[64] Not surprisingly then, in assessing Kauffman's books on doctrine, the "latent impulse" among earlier writers gives way to an indictment of Kauffman that makes him responsible for providing a new framework whereby "one could discuss the essence of salvation based on atonement without dealing with the nature of the saved life."[65] Indeed, Weaver went on to charge Kauffman with formulating "a complete separation of atonement and nonresistance."[66]

Weaver's analysis may well be oversimplified, however, since interpreting the separation of atonement from ethics in this manner

---

62. Kauffman, *Manual of Bible Doctrines* (1898); Kauffman, ed., *Bible Doctrine* (1914); Kauffman, ed., *Doctrines of the Bible* (1928).

63. Hauerwas and Wells, "How the Church Managed," 37–50.

64. Weaver, *Keeping Salvation Ethical*, 23; see also 27.

65. Ibid., 219.

66. Ibid., 218. Weaver's historical methodology and analysis merits a more in depth examination than is possible here. Suffice it to note several elements to be included in such a reassessment. First, a careful chronology of the compilation and publication of each of Kauffman's books on doctrine will reveal a far more complex authorial process, involving a wider range of writers and perspectives than Weaver describes. Second, a more adequate treatment of historical context will fault a broader range of voices for justifying violent conduct through theological machination, particularly during World War I. See also Juhnke, *Vision, Doctrine, War*, 114–16.

loads a tremendous amount of freight on the theological constructs of American evangelicalism. Although Hauerwas and Wells perceive a similar marginalization of religious practice as Weaver, they attribute this development to a much broader context than American evangelicalism. They write, "Desperate to find a substitute for the habits that make us Christians, Protestants as well as many Catholics have assumed that they can think their way out of the challenges that face being Christian in modernity."[67] (Ironically, as Hauerwas and Wells demonstrate, the very categories of ethics and soteriology, which scholars such as Weaver have utilized, are themselves markers of modernity.[68]) Not only did the turn toward modernity transcend American evangelicalism, but reading Kauffman carefully in his context reveals that he did, in fact, understand the critical link between theology and practice and between ethics and soteriology, especially when compared with others such as C. Henry Smith.[69] Kauffman's "I submit" speech was a proclamation and an act laced with the Anabaptist virtue of *Gelassenheit*. Submission embodied the values of a formative faith community and carried possibilities for being an antidote to the disintegrative acids of modernity.

For this reason, it is not only appropriate but also expedient to revisit the impact Kauffman had through articulating what his church knew and believed. It is also appropriate to assume that his work and that of C. Henry Smith and of George R. Brunk would all need corrective revisiting. Kauffman's writing merits particular scrutiny due to how influential his published work remained for well over a generation. We should analyze both the trajectories that systematic theologians map and the practices Kauffman himself would recall.

As euphoria with the modern experiment wanes, Anabaptist traditions that embody ways of knowing offer insights with

---

67. Hauerwas and Wells, "How the Church Managed," 48.

68. Ibid., 37–50.

69. While Daniel Kauffman's position with regard to modernity and Anabaptist tradition is complex, C. Henry Smith represents a more explicit accommodation of modernity. His interpretation of Anabaptism celebrated the movement's impulses for democratic individualism at the expense of communal identity, ecclesial cohesion, or ethical consistency. Historian Toews concludes that Smith's individualism "seemed appropriate for persons such as Smith who were seeking freedom from the authoritarianism in the Mennonite past. In the end, however, their approach was too ecumenical and too loose to give clear direction to a drifting people." See Toews, *Mennonites in American Society*, 105.

particular relevance. Mennonite theologian and educator Sara Wenger Shenk highlights the work of chemist-turned-philosopher Michael Polanyi as particularly instructive.[70] In re-examining the assumptions of modernity, Polanyi offer a lens which, when directed toward Anabaptism, can yield an appreciative perspective for that movement's contributions. He describes, for example, the value of knowledge and wisdom that is accessed through a community's elders rather than through critical analysis and appraisal. Particularly relevant for our discussion of Daniel Kauffman, Polanyi explicitly invokes the necessity of submitting. "When referring to such superior knowledge," he writes, "we are not laying down standards for judging the persons to whom we attribute this knowledge; we are submitting, on the contrary, to the standards laid down by them for our own guidance."[71] Shenk finds in Polanyi's writing a call for knowing through relationship. She writes, "That knowing must involve apprenticeship to a tradition and a teacher finds an enormous amount of resonance with Anabaptist distinctives."[72]

Mark T. Mitchell, a student of Polanyi's thought, elaborates on the link between belief, or knowing, and submission. He writes,

> If belief necessarily underlies all thought, it follows that authority, submission, and trust precede knowing, for belief entails submitting in trust to an authority and only subsequently understanding fully the content of that to which one submitted. Thus, for Polanyi, belief—that is, a fiduciary framework—is an essential component of all knowing, and although one can deny that this is the case, such denials reflect a blatant error that requires affirming in practice that which is being denied in theory.[73]

Mitchell goes on to stress the importance of the relational components of Polanyi's thought. He writes, "Knowledge embodied in practice cannot be acquired except through a personal relationship between a master and an apprentice" whereby apprentices submit themselves to the authority of their masters and in so doing acquire "the skills necessary to master the particular field of inquiry. Such

---

70. Shenk, *Anabaptist Ways of Knowing*, 81–94, 119–32.
71. Polanyi, *Personal Knowledge*, 376.
72. Shenk, *Anabaptist Ways of Knowing*, 93.
73. Mitchell, "Personal Participation," 77.

practical, unformulatable knowledge exists only in traditions which exercise authority by requiring a degree of submission by those who seek to become full practicing members." Mitchell emphasizes that submission is crucial: "Engaging fully in a tradition requires submission to an authority in the form of a master to an apprentice. Knowing is an art that requires skill. The skill necessary to know requires a relationship with a master whereby one can learn the unspecifiable elements of any skill and thus eventually become a connoisseur."[74]

In making a case for concepts such as commitment and submission, Polanyi pushes terminology beyond conventional blinders. Shenk notes, for example, his emphasis upon commitment as *a priori* to knowing. "Commitment," she writes, "as it's often been used, means commitment to one particular view—the opposite of open-mindedness." She goes on to argue that "Polanyi repudiated this impersonal, dogmatic, and rule-bound approach."[75] If the term *commitment* is in need of first aid, one can only imagine the resuscitation called for by insisting upon the necessity of *submission*. Yet Polanyi is not alone in reframing the significance of submission. Harvard theologian and Christian feminist Sarah Coakley also engages the possibilities of bringing fresh meanings to the term.[76]

Thus discussion of Daniel Kauffman and the yielded life is relevant for ongoing conversations about the virtues of *Gelassenheit*. Working from his autobiography toward a working definition of submission highlights the way Kauffman redirected personal ambition into a corporate enterprise. He also surrendered the autonomy of an illusive self determination and yielded to the wisdom of elders in the tradition. Of critical importance is that this experience was one of empowerment rather than subjugation. He understood his decision to trust and yield to the perspective of an elder to provide clarity for his own vocation.

In Kauffman's telling of the story, one hears his submission as laying the groundwork for legitimizing and validating his own emerging role and influence as a leader within Mennonites' alternative community. The earliest references to his serving on the twenty-two committees were appreciative of his leadership with the understanding that he moved authoritatively on behalf of his tradition and

74. Mitchell, "Michael Polanyi and Michael Oakeshott," 28.
75. Shenk, *Anabaptist Ways of Knowing*, 87.
76. Coakley, *Powers and Submissions*.

community. Responsibility did bring with it conflict. Fisher Miller portrays Kauffman's accepting the Goshen presidency itself as more an act of submission than an assertion of ego. She writes that he left "the pleasant order of his editor's life for a plunge into the Goshen maelstrom" at the behest of the Board of Education, making him "a victim of his own indispensable officialdom."[77] According to Fisher Miller, the unrest on campus during the 1922–1923 academic year were reactions to "the symbolic portent of Kauffman occupying the president's office, more than anything enacted by Kauffman himself."[78]

The yielded life is not only relevant to the Anabaptist tradition, however, but finds significant connections with evangelicalism as well. Evangelicals, both on the right and the left, have, like Anabaptists, struggled to navigate the waters of modernity, and this has included tensions over authority and submission similar to those that Daniel Kauffman could not escape. Ironically, fundamentalist evangelicals have demanded submission to the religious authority of orthodox doctrine, biblical literalism, and fundamentalist leaders while often encouraging the rejection of established denominational authority.[79] At least in this context, evangelicals believe that separation from one's immediate religious community or denomination is sometimes required to maintain continuity with (or submission to) what they believe to be a broader tradition of orthodoxy. The submission to orthodoxy found among conservative evangelicals is, admittedly, a far cry from the Anabaptist notion of *Gelassenheit* since American evangelicals have rarely valued the kind of community cohesion and attention to the wisdom of elders as Anabaptists have. Still, the interpretation of conversion as an act of yieldedness, as Daniel Kauffman articulated it, has important resonance within evangelical circles where "surrendering" to God's will has strong implications not only for the conversion event, but for leading a life of Christian obedience.[80] And while conservative interpretations of Christian marriage still emphasizes

---

77. Miller, *Culture for Service*, 82.

78. Ibid.

79. The title of a book published three decades ago serves notice of evangelicals' concern for authority and penchant for entrepreneurship: Quebedeaux, *By What Authority*. See also Owen, Wald, and Hill, "Authoritarian?"

80. Marsden, *Fundamentalism*, 68–71, 192–95.

traditional notions of female submission, the language of "mutual submission" has gained greater acceptance in recent decades.[81]

The awareness that the theme of submission has contemporary currency invites the children of modernity to revisit the significance of the question which Daniel Kauffman addressed by practicing and then rehearsing his two-word speech. Kauffman continued to remind himself and his readers that submission was a virtue. Nearly a half century following his conversion he edited the *Mennonite Cyclopedic Dictionary* and included an entry on "submission." The text offers more commentary than definition. Kauffman wrote, "The spirit of submission is one of the strongest traits of Christian character. Many regard it as a sign of weakness, but this erroneous view is probably due to the fact that they themselves are strangers to this Christian virtue."[82]

BIBLIOGRAPHY

Brunk, George R. "The Church." *Sword and Trumpet* 2.3 (1930) 13.

———. "Editorial." *Sword and Trumpet* 5.1 (1933) 2–4.

Bush, Perry. *Dancing with the Kobzar: Bluffton College and Mennonite Higher Education, 1899–1999*. Studies in Anabaptist and Mennonite History 38. Telford, PA: Pandora, 2000.

Dyck, Cornelius J. *An Introduction to Mennonite History: A Popular History of the Anabaptists and the Mennonites*. 2nd ed. Scottdale, PA: Herald, 1981; 3rd ed. Scottdale, PA: Herald, 1993.

Coakley, Sarah. *Powers and Submissions: Spirituality, Philosophy, and Gender*. Challenges in Contemporary Theology. Oxford, UK; Malden, MA: Blackwell, 2002.

Cochran, Pamela. *Evangelical Feminism: A History*. New York: New York University Press, 2005.

Cronk, Sandra. "Gelassenheit: The Rites of the Redemptive Process in Old Order Amish and Old Order Mennonite Communities." *The Mennonite Quarterly Review* 55 (1981) 5–44.

Dyck, Cornelius J., editor. *An Introduction To Mennonite History: A Popular History Of The Anabaptists And The Mennonites*. 2nd ed. Scottdale, PA: Herald, 1981.

Epp, Frank H. *Mennonites in Canada, 1786–1920: The History of a Separate People*. Mennonites in Canada 1. Toronto: Macmillan of Canada, 1974.

———. *Mennonites in Canada, 1920–1940: A People's Struggle for Survival*. Mennonites in Canada 2. Scottdale, PA: Herald, 1982.

Erb, Paul. *South Central Frontiers: A History of the South Central Mennonite Conference*. Studies in Anabaptist and Mennonite History 17. Scottdale, PA: Herald, 1974.

---

81. Cochran, *Evangelical Feminism*.

82. Kauffman, ed., *Mennonite Cyclopedic Dictionary* s.v. "Submission."

Erb, Paul, and Leonard Gross. "Kauffman, Daniel (1865-1944)." *Global Anabaptist Mennonite Encyclopedia Online*, 1989. No pages. Online: http://www.gameo.org/encyclopedia/contents/K386ME.html.

Friedmann, Robert. "Gelassenheit." *Global Anabaptist Mennonite Encyclopedia Online*, 1955. No pages. Online: http://www.gameo.org/encyclopedia/contents/G448.html.

Gingerich, Alice K. *Life and Times of Daniel Kauffman*. Scottdale, PA: Herald, 1954.

George, Timothy. *Theology of the Reformers*. Nashville: Broadman, 1988.

Gross, Leonard. "The Doctrinal Era of the Mennonite Church." *The Mennonite Quarterly Review* 60 (1986) 58–82.

Hauerwas, Stanley, and Samuel Wells. "How the Church Managed before There Was Ethics." In *The Blackwell Companion to Christian Ethics*, edited by Stanley Hauerwas and Samuel Wells, 37–50. Malden, MA: Blackwell, 2004.

Hostetler, Beulah Stauffer. *American Mennonites and Protestant Movements: A Community Paradigm*. Studies in Anabaptist and Mennonite History 28. Scottdale, PA: Herald, 1987.

Jencks, Christopher, and David Riesman. *The Academic Revolution*. Garden City, NY: Doubleday, 1968.

Juhnke, James C. "Gemeindechristentum and Bible Doctrine: Two Mennonite Visions of the Early Twentieth Century." *The Mennonite Quarterly Review* 57 (1983) 206–21.

———. *Vision, Doctrine, War: Mennonite Identity and Organization in America, 1890–1930*. The Mennonite Experience in America 3. Scottdale, PA: Herald, 1989.

Kauffman, Daniel, editor. *Bible Doctrine: A Treatise on the Great Doctrines of the Bible Pertaining to God, Angels, Satan, the Church, and the Salvation, Duties and Destiny of Man*. Scottdale, PA: Mennonite House, 1914.

———. *The Conservative Viewpoint: A Message to the Members of the Mennonite Church*. Scottdale, PA: Mennonite House, 1918.

———, editor. *Doctrines of the Bible: A Brief Discussion of the Teachings of God's Word*. Scottdale, PA: Mennonite House, 1928.

———. *Fifty Years in the Mennonite Church, 1890–1940*. Scottdale, PA: Mennonite House, 1941.

———. *Manual of Bible Doctrines*. Elkhart, IN: Mennonite, 1898.

———, editor. *Mennonite Cyclopedic Dictionary: A Compendium of the Doctrines, History, Activities, Literature, and Environments of the Mennonite Church, Especially in America*. Scottdale, PA: Mennonite House, 1937.

Klaassen, Walter. *Anabaptism: Neither Catholic nor Protestant*. 3rd ed. Kitchener, ON: Pandora, 2001.

Kniss, Fred. *Disquiet in the Land: Cultural Conflict in American Mennonite Communities*. New Brunswick, NJ: Rutgers University Press, 1997.

Kraus, C. Norman. "American Mennonites and the Bible, 1750–1950." *The Mennonite Quarterly Review* 41 (1967) 309–29.

———. "Evangelicalism: A Mennonite Critique." In *The Variety of American Evangelicalism*, edited by Donald W. Dayton and Robert K. Johnston, 184–203. Downers Grove, IL: InterVarsity, 1991.

Marsden, George M. *Fundamentalism and American Culture*. 2nd ed. Oxford: Oxford University Press, 2006.

Miller, Susan Fisher. *Culture for Service: A History of Goshen College, 1894–1994*. Goshen, IN: Goshen College, 1994.

Mitchell, Mark T. "Michael Polanyi and Michael Oakeshott: Common Ground, Uncommon Foundations." *Tradition & Discovery: The Polanyi Society Periodical* 28. 2 (2002) 23–34. Online: http://www.missouriwestern.edu/orgs/polanyi/tad%20web%20archive/tad28-2/tad28-2-pg23-34-pdf.pdf.

———. "Personal Participation: Michael Polanyi, Eric Voegelin, and the Indispensability of Faith." *Journal of Religious Ethics* 33 (2005) 65–89.

Murray, Stuart. *Biblical Interpretation in the Anabaptist Tradition*. Studies in the Believers Church Tradition 3. Kitchener, ON: Pandora, 2000.

Owen, Dennis E., Kenneth D. Wald, and Samuel S. Hill. "Authoritarian or Authority-Minded? The Cognitive Commitments of Fundamentalists and the Christian Right." *Religion and American Culture: A Journal of Interpretation* 1 (1991) 73–100.

Pellman, Hubert R. *Eastern Mennonite College, 1917–1967: A History*. Harrisonburg, VA: Eastern Mennonite College, 1967.

Polanyi, Michael. *Personal Knowledge: Towards a Post-Critical Philosophy*. Chicago: University of Chicago Press, 1958.

Quebedeaux, Richard. *By What Authority: The Rise of Personality Cults in American Christianity*. San Francisco: Harper & Row, 1982.

Ramseyer, J. Mark. Review of *Culture for Service*, by Susan Fisher Miller. *The Mennonite Quarterly Review* 70 (1996) 349–51.

Schlabach, Theron F. *Gospel Versus Gospel: Mission and the Mennonite Church, 1863–1944*. Studies in Anabaptist and Mennonite History 21. Scottdale, PA: Herald, 1980.

———. "Mennonites, Revivalism, Modernity: 1683–1850." *Church History* 48 (1979) 398–415.

———. "Reveille for *Die Stillen Im Lande*: A Stir among Mennonites in the Late Nineteenth Century—Awakening or Quickening? Revival or Acculturation? Anabaptist or What?" *The Mennonite Quarterly Review* 51 (1977) 213–26.

———. *War, Peace, and Social Conscience: Guy F. Hershberger and Mennonite Ethics*. Studies in Anabaptist and Mennonite History 45. Scottdale, PA: Herald, 2009.

Shenk, Sara Wenger. *Anabaptist Ways of Knowing: A Conversation About Tradition-Based Critical Education*. Telford, PA: Cascadia, 2003.

Smith, C. Henry. *Mennonite Country Boy: The Early Years of C. Henry Smith*. Newton, KS: Faith &Life, 1962.

———. *Mennonites in History*. Scottdale, PA: Mennonite Book and Tract Society, 1907.

Snyder, C. Arnold. *Following in the Footsteps of Christ: The Anabaptist Tradition*. Traditions of Christian Spirituality 18. Maryknoll, NY: Orbis, 2004.

Stout, Jeffrey. *The Flight from Authority: Religion, Morality, and the Quest for Autonomy*. Revisions: A Series of Books on Ethics 1, edited by Stanley Hauerwas and Alasdair MacIntyre. Notre Dame: University of Notre Dame Press, 1981.

Toews, Paul. *Mennonites in American Society, 1930–1970: Modernity and the Persistence of Religious Community*. The Mennonite Experience in America 4. Scottdale, PA: Herald, 1996.

Weaver, J. Denny. *Keeping Salvation Ethical: Mennonite and Amish Atonement Theology in the Late Nineteenth Century*. Studies in Anabaptist and Mennonite History 35. Scottdale, PA: Herald, 1997.

Yoder, Nathan E. "Mennonite Fundamentalism: Shaping an Identity for an American Context." PhD diss., University of Notre Dame, 1999.

———. "Mennonite Scholars and Mennonite Fundamentalism." *Journal of Mennonite Studies* 23 (2005) 111–22.

6

A Cord of Many Strands

Reexamining Grace Brethren Identity and the Fundamentalism of Alva J. McClain

M. M. Norris

ONE MORNING IN THE winter of 1968, a Winona Lake (Indiana) garbage truck routinely picked up a stack of boxes outside the home of Alva J. and Josephine McClain.[1] Placed on the curb by Josephine soon after her husband's death, the boxes contained all the personal papers and files of Alva that she could find.[2] Unfortunately, in an effort to make sure her husband would be remembered only for his public achievements and theological works, Mrs. McClain jeopardized the ability of later historians to create an authentic portrayal of the founder of Grace Theological Seminary—which would become, along with Dallas Theological Seminary, one of the most influential bastions of dispensationalism in America. The remnants of McClain's personal life that survived this purge represent an interesting assort-

---

1. I would like to thank Jared Burkholder for engaging with me in many stimulating discussions over the content of this essay and for his vital assistance in completing the chapter. I also wish to acknowledge several students who have helped to process the Alva J. McClain and Louis S. Bauman papers: Catherine Marshall, Brandy Allen, Joel Zakahi, Carrie Halquist, and Tory Sears. Their work has been vital. I am equally grateful to Corey Grandstaff who spent numerous hours transcribing interviews and to Charles Johnson who read a draft of this essay and offered helpful comments. In addition, Lauren Cartwright provided exceptional assistance in the office, allowing me to work more diligently on this project.

2. Darr, interview; Kent, interview.

ment of documents, pictures, and other random items that fit neatly in just two medium-sized archival boxes.³

Needless to say, rather than preserve the legacy of McClain, the dearth of manuscript sources have actually served to obscure the life of the individual who may have had the most influence on early Grace Brethren identity. Indeed, historians within Grace Brethren circles have varied in their assessments of McClain's significance. While some are nothing short of hagiography, others demonstrate more sophistication. The most common approach to interpreting McClain, however, is one that utilizes the dualism of the Fundamentalist-Modernist Debates. This parallels popular perceptions within the fellowship, where this dualism has also played a significant role for identity formation. Although members of the Fellowship of Grace Brethren Churches (FGBC) have a vague awareness of certain historic Brethren distinctives, such as nonresistance and nonconformity to the world, for many, their identity as evangelicals overshadows this awareness. Indeed, the most conservative members of the FGBC—those who may be described as fundamentalists, in fact believe they are preserving authentic Brethrenism through their adherence to rigid theological and political conservatism. This understanding is reinforced by the belief that Ashland seminary had "gone liberal" in the 1930s and that McClain and his coreligionists needed to separate in order to retain their purity. While this interpretation is seductive, it is largely a misunderstanding. Indeed, it has created a skewed picture of McClain—one that oversimplifies his life and career by implying that he was nothing more than a typical fundamentalist and that under his guidance, Grace Theological Seminary, as well as the congregations that identified with the seminary, moved steadily and inevitably away from their Anabaptist traditions and preserved orthodoxy by adopting wholesale American fundamentalism. It also fails to ascribe a sense of agency to McClain, who was not simply acted upon, but actively forged his own theological identity.

This essay seeks a more nuanced interpretation that accounts for the complexities and tensions that existed in the early years of the Grace Brethren movement as represented within the life of McClain

---

3. The Letters and Papers of Alva J. McClain (hereafter LPAJM) are housed in the Morgan Library Archives and Special Collections (hereafter MLASC), Grace College and Theological Seminary, Winona Lake, IN.

and illustrated by the events that led to the founding of Grace Theological Seminary in 1937. Specifically, this chapter argues that McClain fashioned a synthesis of varied and, at times, even conflicting streams—a cord of eclectic theological, cultural, and historical strands that would form the basis not only for Grace Theological Seminary, but for the identity of the FGBC as well. This identity included significant elements of American fundamentalism to be sure, but amounted to a more diverse synthesis than is popularly understood.

GRACE BRETHREN IDENTITY IN HISTORICAL PERSPECTIVE

Since the German beginnings of (Schwarzenau) Brethrenism in 1708 and the migration of this small religious group to America soon after, the Brethren movement has produced several branches.[4] The movement itself was the result of the same kind of eclecticism that characterized McClain. Indeed, Brethrenism included components of Reformed thought, the warm spirituality of Pietism, as well as the Anabaptist virtues of nonconformity and nonresistance.[5] Major splits in the late nineteenth century resulted in three American denominations: the Old German Baptist Brethren, which was established in 1881; the "progressives," who organized the Brethren Church in 1882–1883; and the largest group, the "conservatives," who would eventually become the Church of the Brethren. The progressivism of the Brethren Church became evident after the 1882 split as the group embraced various elements and religious trends of nineteenth-century America. Many adopted the latest trends in education, supported the temperance movement, missions, evangelical revivalism, and dressed themselves in contemporary garb.[6]

---

4. For denominational histories of the Brethren, consult Brumbaugh, *German Baptist Brethren*; Holsinger, *History of the Tunkers*; and Ronk, *History the Brethren Church*. For primary source collections, see Sappington, *Brethren in the New Nation*; Durnbaugh, *European Origins*; and Durnbaugh, *Brethren in Colonial America*.

5. Stoffer, *Background and Development*, 5, 83.

6. The adjectives "conservative" and "progressive" are somewhat distinct in the Anabaptist context, most often referring, as in this piece, to degrees of separation from mainstream American culture. Conservatives remained more distinct from the larger society while progressives were more apt to adopt various features of it. On conservatives and progressives in the Brethren tradition, see Brethren Encyclopedia (hereafter BE) I, 298–305; BE II, 1061.

The religious heritage of the McClain family was situated within the progressive branch—the Brethren Church. Alva J. McClain, or "Mick," as he was known to friends and family, was born in 1888 to Walter Scott McClain (of Scottish descent) and Mary Ellen Gnagey (Swiss German, Pennsylvania Dutch ancestry). Walter was ordained to the ministry in the Brethren Church by the Brethren leader, Henry R. Holsinger, and Mary was a sister of A. D. Gnagey, a leader who helped organize the Brethren Church and who also served as an editor of the *Brethren Evangelist*.[7] The McClain family moved to Sunnyside, Washington in 1900 when McClain was twelve—just after the territory was opened up to settlers. Following his education, McClain eventually landed a teaching position at the Brethren Church's flagship institution of higher education, Ashland Seminary (Ashland, OH). After teaching at Ashland for twelve years, however, McClain became embroiled in controversy that resulted in a particularly ugly and painful denominational divorce. He left Ashland in 1937 to start Grace Theological Seminary, which was established at its current location in Winona Lake, Indiana. Over four decades later, the congregations that identified with the new seminary officially organized themselves as the FGBC in 1982.

In considering the historiography of the Grace Brethren movement, it is telling that in an alcove on the second floor of Morgan Library on the campus of Grace College and Seminary, one can find a re-creation of McClain's office from the 1940s, including his original desk, furniture, and personal library. Needless to say, McClain has been memorialized on campus, and, not surprisingly, the earliest treatments of McClain's life and ministry have a strong hagiographic tone. This is typified by Norman B. Rohrer's book, *A Saint in Glory Stands: The Story of Alva J. McClain, Founder of Grace Theological Seminary*. Rohrer's saintly account of McClain seems to have been influenced by Homer Kent, Sr., who was among the exodus from Ashland Seminary and joined McClain at Grace. Written in 1958, Kent's *Conquering Frontiers: A History of the Brethren Church* was an uncritical history of the Brethren movement that culminated with the Grace group, which Kent believed embodied the most authentic expression of the Brethren tradition. *Conquering Frontiers* thus exemplified the optimism of the first generation, when the founders exhibited the aura of youthful

---

7. BE II, 772.

heroism and focused determination. These feelings were bolstered by the fact that at its inception both the fellowship and the college experienced consistent growth while Ashland Seminary languished for several years after the split. Also contributing to Kent's confidence was the fact that Dispensationalists had begun to flock to Grace Seminary, which was becoming nationally known as a rival to Dallas Theological Seminary. In short, he epitomized the exuberant spirit of the founding leaders, who saw the conquering hand of God in their endeavors.[8]

This sense of confidence was sustained through the Cold War but was severely tested in the 1980s when the FGBC experienced its own schism. Primarily the result of unresolved tensions and controversy over baptism, a sizable group dissented under the leadership of Flood Geology guru John Whitcomb and later took the name Conservative Fellowship of Grace Brethren Churches.[9] In the wake of the split, seminary enrollment dropped alarmingly, and the fellowship hit a period of stagnation and loss of purpose. Within this context, David Plaster, FGBC leader and Grace College and Seminary's academic dean, updated and revised Kent's work. He released *Finding Our Focus: A History of the Grace Brethren Church* in 2003, as the fellowship entered a new millennium. Within the pages of *Finding our Focus*, the natural confidence so prevalent in Kent's work and exuded in the first generation of leadership is gone. Though still optimistic, Plaster's confidence seems forced as he sought to narrate a history which would help the FGBC relocate its sense of purpose.[10] The shared thread that has run through all of these interpretations, and in fact, has always resonated

---

8. Kent, *Conquering Frontiers* (first published in 1958). Homer Austin Kent Sr. (1898–1981) was born in Hiram, OH and moved with his family in 1912 to Long Beach, CA where he heard the preaching of Louis S. Bauman and joined the First Brethren Congregation in 1914. He sat in McClain's Sunday school class and attended the Bible Institute of Los Angeles (diploma, 1919), Xenia Theological Seminary (ThM, 1923), Ashland College (BA, 1925) and Grace Theological Seminary (ThD, 1948). From 1925–1940 he was pastor of the First Brethren Church in Washington, DC after which he became professor of practical theology and church at Grace Seminary until 1969. He was vice-president of Grace Schools from 1962–1969. BE II, 688.

9. Flood Geology, which would become popular among fundamentalists, refers to the notion that the majority of the geological record can be explained through the effects of Noah's flood, which was interpreted as literal and worldwide. As mentioned below, Whitcomb became a leading proponent of this new alternative to mainstream geological understanding.

10. Plaster, *Finding Our Focus*.

among members of the FGBC, is the notion that the divide between Ashland Seminary and Grace Seminary was simply a split between theological modernism (Ashland) and fundamentalism (Grace).

Among historians of the Brethren Church, a similar version of this dualistic approach has also been prevalent. Albert T. Ronk, for example, who witnessed the events of the split, implies that McClain and his circle were captured by American fundamentalism and when the "true" Brethren banished McClain and others from Ashland for insubordination, the troublemakers left to found the fundamentalist Grace Theological Seminary.[11] Ronk's work, *History of the Brethren Church*, has been expanded by other denominational historians including Dale Stoffer and Dennis Martin.[12] Ironically then, both sides have claimed the mantel of true Brethrenism by distancing themselves from the opposing faction, forging their identity, in large part, by using the "fundamentalist" or "liberal" label to demonize the other side and define themselves by what they are not.

This traditional narrative, though, has not gone unchallenged. Indeed, there have been a variety of interpretations among Grace Brethren historians in recent years. Robert Clouse, for example, has brought a more critical understanding of the influence of fundamentalism and is more attuned to the complexities that existed in the early years of the fellowship and the divisions that surfaced in later decades.[13] Equally helpful is Jerry Young's dissertation (Dallas Theological Seminary), written in the mid 1990s, which examined a representative congregation from among the churches that identified with Grace Seminary and one that remained loyal to Ashland several decades after the split. It is ironic that Young found few doctrinal differences, and he concluded that the Ashland/Grace split was based

---

11. Ronk, *History of the Brethren*, 395–47. Scholarship pertaining to Mennonite fundamentalism can be helpful in understanding Brethren fundamentalism. Nathan Yoder suggests that "interaction" is a more helpful theme than "infiltration." Yoder has observed, "The focus on Mennonites' interacting with fundamentalism offers an alternative to infiltration motifs which represent fundamentalism as acting upon and even victimizing immigrant groups." See abstract in Yoder, "Mennonite Fundamentalism."

12. Stoffer, *Background and Development*; Stoffer, *Gleam of Shinning Hope*; and Martin, "Law and Grace."

13. See Clouse, "Brethren and Modernity," 205; Clouse, "*Fellowship*," 101–14; Clouse, "Changes and Partings," 180–98.

on shades of theological degrees rather than a result of significant doctrinal divisions.[14]

The most recent FGBC history is Todd Scoles' *Reforming the Household: The Quest of the Grace Brethren Church*. Scoles was a graduate of Ashland Seminary who became a noteworthy pastor in the FGBC. He also served recently as a member of the Board of Trustees for Grace College and Seminary. In his analysis, Scoles suggests that the FGBC left behind significant portions of its Brethren heritage and, like Plaster, is apprehensive about the future of the fellowship. Scoles' narrative points to the hope, however, that the FGBC could be "reformed" if its members hold firm to tradition, embracing the ordinances of threefold communion and threefold baptism.[15] With these works serving as the historiographical context, we turn to the multiple strands that coalesced in the life and career of McClain and that inform the identity of the FGBC.

PROGRESSIVE AND CONSERVATIVE STRANDS

While much of the papers and documents from McClain's life and career were lost after his death, a small collection has survived. Many of these sources still allow us to see McClain in a more authentic light than the hagiography of his denominational biographers. Among these sources are photographs that chronicle McClain's teenage years when he abandoned his family's Brethrenism for more youthful pursuits. During these years McClain was taken with athletics. Indeed, he started a football team and then led it to victory playing quarterback in 1905, 1906, and 1907.[16] One photograph captures McClain's adolescent spirit particularly well—in a championship pose from the 1906 season, McClain and three other teammates revel in a display of male bravado by proudly sporting their athletic protectors around their necks.[17]

---

14. Young, "Relationship"; Young, interview.

15. Scoles, *Restoring the Household*. The core of this work comes from his dissertation: "Power of the Ordinances." Tragically, Plaster, Scoles, and Young all died in 2010. This left Clouse, who retired from Indiana University several years earlier (though still a Grace Brethren Pastor) as the sole surviving Grace Brethren historian.

16. See Rohrer, *Saint in Glory*.

17. LPAJM, MLASC.

Other documents begin to reveal the multiple strands and even the conflicted nature of McClain's theological synthesis. McClain embodied the conflicting impulses within the Brethren Church's progressivism, for example. On the one hand, he embraced the stock Anabaptist virtue of nonconformity to the world as he gravitated toward cultural conservatism during the 1930s when he was still on the faculty at Ashland Seminary. For example, scraps of paper among his letters and photographs indicate that he made efforts to keep tabs on worldly behavior and heterodoxy throughout the campus. Indeed, it even appears that on one occasion, McClain circulated a packet of papers labeled "Rules and Regulation of Ashland College Faculty" in order to provide opportunity for individuals to report incidents of questionable behavior. At the top of the first page, the following was written in bold letters: "*Be* sure to return to me—*A. J. Mc.*" Another page, labeled simply "Vincent," lists four points of gossip: "1) Mrs. Stead ridiculed two girls for wanting to go to church to hear [Louis] Bauman instead of attending party. 2) Mrs. Stead spoke slightly of the Day of Prayer 3) Girls compelled to attend house councils where the proposition of Theater parties are discussed and 4) Some girls remark they had some religion when [they] came to dormitory but lost it since coming here."[18] McClain was likely gathering evidence to be used in his battle against worldliness and modernism.[19]

On the other hand, he was a progressive, which meant he rejected the traditionalism of the conservative Brethren he observed as a child. This was likely owing in part to painful memories of controversies that may have contributed to his personal demons later in life. In response to an unnamed colleague who accused McClain of contentiousness that contradicted the meek spirit of the Brethren tradition, McClain, with unveiled sarcasm, retorted:

> Do you know that I remember the days of our division? Do you know that I remember my dear old father and mother going to the business meeting in the Conservative church and there listening to the dear, "very sweet spirited" old Brethren

---

18. "Vincent" likely refers to the person who provided these tidbits of gossip. (In the original, emphasis was added with underscoring rather than italics as it is reproduced here.)

19. Many recent studies go beyond post-colonialism and demonstrate the importance of taking personal agency seriously. For one example, consult Young, *Indianness of Christianity*.

fighting like dogs and cats until three o'clock in the morning as to whether or not a sister might wear a sailor hat? As a result of one of these all night meetings, I had two sisters expelled from that church? "Very sweet spirited" indeed! Do you know that my father was expelled because he had his life insured? Do you know that a judge in Springfield, Illinois, once told me that those "very sweet spirited" Brethren expelled him from that church for parting his hair on the side? Do you know that I had relatives expelled from that church for wearing suspenders to hold up their pants? "Very sweet spirited" Brethren indeed![20]

More than demonstrating his childhood experience with denominational controversy, this letter illustrates McClain's cynicism toward the conservative Brethren and what he perceived as the legalism that plagued them.

McClain's educational journey also represented progressive impulses. (Regardless of the approach, higher education—whether the liberal arts model or even the Bible institute model—was inherently progressive within the context of the Brethren tradition, where any form of higher education might be considered worldly.) He cobbled together an undergraduate education, which stretched out for over fifteen years between 1908 and 1925, and he attended schools across the spectrum of educational approaches. McClain experienced the openness of a liberal arts approach at the University of Washington in 1908. Here he took a range of courses that included German, Latin, and various offerings in the biological and physical sciences.[21] Later, during the 1915–1916 school year he took sociology and ethics at Antioch College, a progressive institution that was among the first schools in the country to provide equal educational opportunities to women and African Americans, even the first to appoint a woman to its faculty and board of trustees.[22]

In contrast to his experiences at Washington University and Antioch College, however, McClain spent a semester, during the fall of 1914 at the Bible Institute of Los Angeles (later Biola College), where he embraced the Bible college approach while taking typical Bible

---

20. McClain to "George" (undated), LPAJM, Miscellany, folder 36, MLASC.

21. Edwin N. Stone (registrar) to Alva J. McClain, 26 August 1916, LPAJM, MLASC. (He attended each course 5 days a week for at least 45 minutes per a class so these were very rigorous classes with a seat time much above the normal semester.)

22. See Antioch College website.

institute classes such as homiletics, missions, and doctrine.²³ Though his time at Los Angeles was short, it would have lasting effects largely owing to the fact that he became acquainted with the fundamentalist leader Reuben A. Torrey (1856–1928). McClain often quoted Torrey in his theological works and kept copies of Torrey's works, including his systematic theology, in his personal library. Indeed, the future Grace Seminary course offerings were heavily influenced by the Bible institute model.²⁴

Even before he completed his undergraduate degree, McClain began attending classes at Xenia Theological Seminary (Ohio), where he took seminary courses in systematic theology, Biblical Studies, and comparative religions.²⁵ Then, after a six-year hiatus from his educational pursuits, during which he served as pastor at the first Brethren church in Philadelphia and taught apologetics at Philadelphia School of the Bible, McClain enrolled at Occidental College (Los Angeles), another liberal arts institution, in order to finish his BA. Here he took classes on logic, Latin, and classical literature, which paralleled the classes he took previously at Washington University and Antioch College, and finally graduated in 1925 with a BA in Philosophy and a minor in Political Science. (After his undergraduate degree was completed from Occidental, Xenia granted him an MA in theology the same year.)

Similar tensions between conservative and progressive tendencies can be seen in McClain's estimation of human civilization and learning. He could be quite pessimistic about the cultures that humans had fashioned. In his theology lectures, for example, he taught that various features of civilization, particularly the arts, originated with the descendents of Cain, which he dismissed simply as the "bad line." McClain postulated that the descendents of Seth stood fast in their worship of God but the line of Cain chose not to worship God and therefore became distracted by the arts and their efforts to build human civilization.²⁶ In contrast to this, however, McClain respected

---

23. McClain Term Certificate, The Bible College of Los Angeles, 18 September 1914, LPAJM, MLASC.

24. Manahan, interview. See also the Grace Seminary catalogues, MLASC.

25. Transcripts, Xenia United Presbyterian Theological Seminary, 1914–17, LPAJM, MLASC.

26. McClain, "Theology Notes," 1939, 26, MLASC.

the scientific disciplines. He believed, for example, that the command in Genesis that humans were to subdue the earth, included scientific inquiry and that ". . . the men of science are carrying out the mandate of God."[27]

Regarding his views on origins, this high view of science allowed him to synthesize biblical teachings with contemporary science in a way that resembled the views of many Protestants in the nineteenth century.[28] While Grace Theological Seminary as well as the college would later become a national center for young earth creationism, it is important to note that McClain was not a proponent of young earth interpretations. Instead, he subscribed to the "gap theory," which attempted to embrace both mainstream science and a literal view of Genesis chapter one.[29] Thus he disagreed with another prominent Grace Seminary professor, John Whitcomb, who was, along with Henry Morris, largely responsible for creating the belief, popular within many fundamentalist circles, that young earth creationism and Flood Geology were the only legitimate frameworks through which conservative Christians could interpret Genesis. In reality, not all fundamentalists believed in a young earth, and the diversity of views among the early faculty of Grace Seminary reflected the diversity of the larger fundamentalist movement, which made room for proponents of the Gap Theory as well as the Day-Age Theory.[30] It is ironic

---

27. Ibid., 23.

28. Barry Hankins has argued convincingly that Protestants in the nineteenth century were much more adept at integrating evolutionary science and the Bible than were twentieth century evangelicals, many of whom were conditioned by popular creationists to adopt a "warfare model," or the belief that science and the Bible were at odds. See Hankins, *American Evangelicals*, 51–67.

29. This theory proposes that a chronological gap exists in Genesis 1:1 between the phrase "In the Beginning God created the heavens and the earth" and the next sentence, "Now the earth was without form and void." Gap theorists believe that chaos erupted after the Devil was banished from heaven, and God therefore created earth anew and placed it under the supervision of Adam and Eve. McClain and many of his generation felt that reason and science led them to endorse both. The Scofield Bible also endorsed the Gap Theory as did other conservative Christians such as William Jennings Bryan and Bob Jones Sr. to name a few.

30. Hankins has observed, for example, that the twelve volume *Fundamentals* (1915), which played a significant part in defining the fundamentalist movement, included a spectrum of positions from those who were "open to evolution" to those who were adamantly opposed to it. See Hankins, *American Evangelicals*, 58–9. While Whitcomb and Morris popularized Flood Geology with the release of *The Genesis*

that although McClain had a low view of the arts, he had a broader view of science than would later generations of fundamentalists, including many at the seminary he founded.

THE SYSTEMATIZING STRAND OF FUNDAMENTALISM

While McClain's background and thought were comprised of more than simply a fundamentalist reaction to modernism, the fundamentalist movement did play a significant role in the direction his theology would take and the religious identity of the seminary he founded. One of the ways this is most clearly seen is in his adoption of (Calvinist) dispensationalism and the tendency therein to bring doctrinal order out of what he perceived to be the theological laxity of Brethrenism's non-creedalism.[31] McClain's desire to bring increasing degrees of systematization to the Brethren circles in which he was involved can be seen in a number of examples.

First, McClain gravitated toward Calvinist dispensationalism while in seminary, and this became increasingly important for him. This theological orientation was first nurtured at Xenia Seminary in Ohio, a Presbyterian institution with strong conservative leanings. Completing an MA in theology from Xenia even while he was still finishing his undergraduate degree, this seminary training would leave an indelible mark on McClain.[32] A Presbyterian Seminary may seem like an odd fit for someone such as McClain, whose upbringing was thoroughly Anabaptist, but McClain may have felt a connection between his father's Scottish ancestry and Xenia's Scots-Irish Presbyterianism. Probably more significant, however, was Xenia's

---

Flood in 1961, they borrowed heavily from Seventh Day Adventists, such as Ellen White and James McCready Price. Proponents of the Day-Age Theory held that the "days" of creation did not represent 24-hour periods of time, but rather long "ages" that accounted for the geological record. While much of this discussion can be found in Hankins, *American Evangelicals*, 49–82, the standard history of creationism is Numbers, *The Creationists*.

31. Non-creedalism is the belief that all creeds are limited and that the full truth for faith and practice lies only in the Scriptures; thus, proponents of non-creedalism eschewed written creeds and statements of faith.

32. Transcript, Occidental College, 21 February 1961; Bessie M. Burrows (registrar), Pittsburgh Theological Seminary (formerly Xenia), 9 June 1961, LPAJM, MLASC.

connection with prominent leaders within dispensationalist circles. For example, its president was prominent fundamentalist William G. Moorhead, who died the year McClain enrolled, though his larger-than-life persona continued at the institution. Moorehead was a Calvinist and post-tribulation premillennial dispensationalist and was an editor of the *Scofield Bible*. McClain, who later would himself become an editor of the *New Scofield Bible*, referred to him extensively in his writings.[33] It is important not to underestimate McClain's reliance on the Reformed theology he imbibed at Xenia. As a student, he studied the Princetonian A. A. Hodge's *Outlines of Theology*, and when he taught at Ashland he used E. H. Bancroft's *Christian Theology*, a textbook that drew heavily from Hodge and was both Reformed and dispensational.[34]

Second, McClain's dispensationalism included an increasing fascination with premillennial eschatology—a predictable consequence which was solidified through the Bible and prophecy conference movement.[35] Eschatological concerns were especially reinforced through the guidance of Louis S. Bauman (1875–1950), who would eventually join the faculty at Grace Seminary soon after it was founded and was himself a militant opponent of modernism with a bent toward doctrinal precision.[36] Although at one time Bauman was a postmillennialist, he converted to premillennialism after being attracted to the Bible Prophecy movement during the fundamentalist era. After embracing premillennialism, Bauman became active in prophecy circles, interpreting missions through eschatological lenses and traveling as a popular evangelist and speaker on biblical prophecy. Experiencing conversion at one of Bauman's prophecy conferences, McClain inher-

33. See for example, McClain, *Greatness*, 141, 166, 276n.

34. Stoffer, "Background and Development, 589, 605, 696. Hodge, *Outlines of Theology*. Bancroft, *Christian Theology*. For further influence see Strong, *Systematic Theology*. McClain's copies of all three of these systematic theologies are still extant. MLASC.

35. On fundamentalism, evangelicalism, and eschatology, see Marsden, *Fundamentalism*, 43–71, 141–52; and Hankins, *American Evangelicals*, 83–104.

36. Bauman was the son of Brethren pastor and evangelist William J. H. Bauman who helped organize the Brethren Church at Dayton, OH, in 1883. Bauman's second marriage was to Mary Melissa Wageman in 1898. She was ordained as an elder in 1900 by the Missionary Board. She took her husband's place in the pulpit during his times as traveling evangelist and was noted as being a fine speaker. See BE I, 96–97. Bauman's own penchant for systematizing can be seen in his, *Faith Once Delivered*.

ited a penchant for prophetic speculation.[37] During the Second World War, for example, both Bauman and McClain were convinced that Mussolini was the anti-Christ prophesied in the book of Revelation.[38]

Later, during his days as a student, McClain followed Bauman in helping to steer the Brethren Church toward more doctrinal codification. The two were part of a 1916 General Conference committee, which Bauman chaired, created to discuss the fundamental doctrines of the church. While McClain affirmed the committee's emphasis on the infallibility of Scripture "as originally given," he was disappointed that it did not mention the virgin birth or the deity of Christ. Foreshadowing McClain's later efforts, his concerns were always to bring greater levels of doctrinal definition to the church.

In 1918, McClain succeeded Bauman as pastor of the first Brethren church in Philadelphia. However, after several conversations with young men of the church who had attended Ashland Seminary—the denomination's training institution—McClain grew concerned about what he perceived to be the seminary's theological laxity. With surprising audacity, McClain wrote directly to Ashland's president, Edwin R. Jacobs, questioning his orthodoxy. Surprised to be subjected to such scrutiny by the young upstart pastor, Jacobs provided a calculated response meant to appease McClain's concerns. McClain fired back a nine-page single-spaced letter, however, in which he charged Jacobs with being loose in his theology, demanding more detailed clarification on several specific theological positions. McClain's letter provides a clear vision of the theological reform he believed the Brethren Church needed:

> This is all the more necessary since the Brethren church had never seen fit to declare her position on Christian truths. She has said that the New Testament is her creed and let it go at that. Such a position was fine as long as we had to deal only with the simple child-like faith of our fathers. If it was in the Book they accepted it as the last Word of Truth. But that day is

37. Bauman's influence on McClain cannot be overstated. For McClain's conversion, see the dedication in McClain, *Daniel's Prophecy*, which reads: "To LOUIS S. BAUMAN with Gratitude and Affection Whose Sound Instruction in the Prophecies of Daniel in the Year of 1911 Led Me to See the Saving Grace and Glory of Messiah the Prince." McClain also attended the Bible Institute of Los Angeles, Xenia, and Occidental as a result of Bauman's recommendation.

38. Stoffer, *German Baptist Brethren*, 727 n. 126; McClain, *The Jewish Problem*, passim.

past forever. Today our young men are being trained in various institutions whose main distinction in some cases is an invidious opposition to historic and evangelical Christianity. And the pity of it is that the Brethren church *lacking a systematized statement of Christian truth*, failed to ground them firmly in the truth when they were in our care.[39]

Though McClain presented an overly simplistic view of Brethren theology in this letter, his response to Jacobs provides a clear view of McClain's mind. He was the systematizer who felt that he needed to bring sophistication and maturity to the Brethren tradition, especially in order to defend it against theological modernism.

McClain's concerns for greater systematization of Brethren doctrine and practice as a means to safeguard the fundamentals of orthodoxy certainly reflected broader trends. In 1918, leaders of The World's Christian Fundamentals Association (WCFA), including R. A. Torrey and William Bell Riley, for example, held a planning session in Torrey's summer home on the Montrose Bible Conference meeting grounds (PA). Here, the WCFA changed its focus from prophecy to the fundamentals of the faith, and it advocated increased numbers of Bible conferences and the founding of Bible colleges.[40] These were heady and exciting times for fundamentalists. In the wake of the Great War, the optimism of western modernists was severely checked by the dark realities of human conflict. Fundamentalists were thus emboldened and seemed justified both in their pretribulation prophecy and also in their counter-culture emphases. With this new sense of a divine mandate, Riley could, with some credibility afforded to him by his peers, predict that this new fundamentalist movement would eclipse even the influence of Martin Luther in his stand against Roman Catholicism.[41] Many in the Brethren Church, such as Bauman and McClain, were energized by the excitement of the times and believed God's mandate to battle modernism applied to the Brethren tradition as much as it did to larger denominations and para-church organizations.

Thus by 1919, McClain's primary emphasis, like that of the WCFA, shifted from eschatological concerns to preserving Christian

---

39. McClain to Dr. Jacobs, 3 June 1919, LPAJM, folder 37, MLASC (italics added).
40. Beale, *Pursuit of Purity*, 97–109.
41. Peterson, "WCFA," 515–16.

orthodoxy against modernism. Feeling threatened by modernism, global events, and the growing momentum of post war ecumenism, the Brethren Church's National Ministerial Association decided to codify Brethren doctrine and distinctives—something that ran counter to the non-creedal orientation of Brethren tradition, but which seemed acceptable in light of the times. In 1921, McClain was appointed chair of a twenty-five member committee that would draft a new statement.[42]

The committee's work was collected and published as the "Message of the Brethren Ministry" (1921). The "Message" affirmed the Brethren Church's 1916 endorsement of the verbal plenary inspiration of the Bible as well as the denomination's motto, "The Bible, the Whole Bible, and Nothing but the Bible." It also included general orthodox statements on theology and practices, including the traditional Brethren commitments against Christian participation in war ("carnal strife") and the swearing of oaths; it also reaffirmed believer's baptism by trine immersion, feetwashing, and anointing of the sick. Not all controversy over the extent to which theology and practice should be defined disappeared, but it was evident that the systematizing efforts of McClain and Bauman had won the day—Brethren fundamentalism was born. Those with modernist leanings either left the denomination or conformed to the prevailing turn toward fundamentalism.

Thus over a decade *before* the split that resulted in McClain's founding of Grace Seminary, it is evident that Brethren Church actually endorsed a fundamentalist orientation and was not a bastion of modernism as some have more recently believed. Then, giving their stamp of approval to McClain's systematizing efforts, Ashland Seminary appointed him Professor of Theology in 1925, just a few months after the sensational Scopes Trial in Dayton, Tennessee. For his part, McClain was initially satisfied with the spiritual pulse of Ashland, writing in 1927, "I believe firmly in the future of Ashland College and also in its present . . . it offers to anyone a splendid opportunity for Christian service and a career. The written and spoken word of President Jacobs certainly leaves no doubt as to the attitude of the institution toward Christian faith and life."[43]

42. Martin, "Law and Grace," 81.

43. McClain, *Brethren Evangelist*, 1 October 1927, 3, 12; 25 June 1927, 3 (quoted in Martin, "Law and Grace," 94–95).

McClain's approach to Christian education shifted toward more doctrinal rigidity, however, perhaps due in part to a short stint at the Bible Institute of Los Angeles where he taught from 1927–1929. This shift would become problematic after coming back to Ashland. While later in his career he embraced a liberal arts approach, this adjustment in his teaching reflected an anti-intellectual suspicion of critical thinking and modern academic trends. McClain resented, for example, the fact that undergraduate professors at Ashland, who sought to challenge students to think critically, often raised questions or allowed for discussions that he believed ran counter to his own efforts to inculcate his graduate students with theological truth. He found he often needed to push those students who had come to the seminary through the college toward narrower definitions of orthodoxy, a mindset that can be seen throughout his personal papers. At least at this point in his career, McClain not only challenged students to imbibe a rigid interpretation of truth, but began a campaign to require all faculty members at Ashland to sign on to the 1921 "Message of the Brethren Ministry," which he had earlier written along with the others on the ministerial committee.

Many at Ashland resented McClain's narrow educational approach, preferring the more traditional non-creedalism. By the 1930s tensions began to escalate—so much so that in 1937 McClain, along with Herman Hoyt, was asked to leave Ashland. After their removal, McClain, Hoyt, and their circle founded the new Grace Theological Seminary with ideals that included a Bible-centered curriculum, a competent and believing scholarship, a spiritual and prayer-charged environment, a missionary and evangelistic spirit, a pre-millennial hope and viewpoint, a spirit-filled and separated life, as well as an expository preaching and teaching ministry.[44]

Though the seminary was chartered in Ohio, it soon moved to Winona Lake, Indiana, a location that would hold strategic significance and would become largely responsible for the new seminary's fundamentalist identity. Winona Lake had become, by the 1930s, a nationally-known center for the fundamentalist movement supported by leading personalities such as Billy and Helen ("Ma") Sunday and the aging and former presidential candidate, William Jennings Bryan. Winona Lake was also a center for fundamentalist parachurch

---

44. Ibid. See Seminary brochure, "Grace Theological Seminary," LPAJM, MLASC.

organizations such as Youth for Christ, led by the young Billy Graham as well as a hub for Bible and Prophecy conferences. The Winona Lake Bible Conference Association and Grace Seminary quickly became welcome allies, providing Grace Seminary with a national platform that would bring it into mainstream fundamentalism.[45]

As president of the new Grace Theological Seminary, McClain continued to guide the school in a precisionist direction, expanding the contents of the "Message of the Brethren Ministry" with numerous proof-texts and more precise definitions. Influence from the Bible and Prophecy conference is clearly evident, and not surprisingly, the statement is rooted in premillennialism and a literalist hermeneutic.[46] This revised statement of faith would form the basis of a new faith covenant, which all Grace Seminary faculty members were soon required to sign.

McClain's ongoing penchant for systematizing is clearly seen in his writing as well, such as in his booklet, *Bible Truths*, which he published in 1950. Though this was geared to Sunday schools rather than a college or seminary audience, it reveals McClain's simplistic pedagogical approach. Essentially a catechism, the booklet includes twenty-eight Christian themes, including everything from "The Bible" to the "New Heaven and Earth." Under each theme is a series of questions such as: "What name does the Bible give to its own writings?" or "What will come to pass after the judgment of the wicked?" Under each question is one main verse written out that serves as the answer, often along with several minor references. Sunday school students were to recite these in class until they were able to memorize them, which McClain noted would provide systematic Bible instruction for Brethren Sunday school students.[47]

McClain's systematic approach also found expression in his magnum opus, *The Greatness of the Kingdom*, which he intended to

---

45 Winona Lake had earlier become a Chautauqua, based on the original model in New York. The idea was to bring recreation, culture, and Christianity to less cultured areas in western America. The Winona Lake Chautauqua suffered severely during the Great Depression, and by the late 1930s it actively sought out the new seminary and asked its leaders to relocate to Winona Lake. No critical history of Winona Lake is yet to be produced, but for a useful popular work, see Gaddis and Huffman, *Winona Lake*. I am also indebted to Steve Grill, director of the Reneker Museum of Winona Lake History, for his expertise on these matters.

46. Whitcomb, *History of Grace*, 6–7.

47. McClain, *Bible Truths*, passim.

be the first volume in a masterful seven-volume systematic theology, but which was cut short by his death. Altogether jettisoning Brethren non-creedalism, in *The Greatness* McClain sought to systematize the Christian faith by integrating Calvinism and dispensationalism. He emphasized the direct sovereignty of God in supervising the seven dispensations, for example, while using a Kingdom motif as his overarching theme. Published in 1959, the first (and only) volume that was finished, *The Greatness* met with mixed reviews. For some reviewers, it was predictable dispensationalist fare, but for others, particularly those within the dispensationalist camp, the work was lauded as a successful integration of Calvinist and dispensational approaches that provided ammunition against modernism. Ironically, McClain's approach was methodologically modern, incorporating a strong sense of linear progress and attempting to approach the Bible with scientific precision. This can be seen as well in his commentary of the book of Daniel, which McClain believed comprised a "mathematical demonstration" for understanding eschatology.[48]

So while many within Grace Brethren circles assume the schism at Ashland and the ensuring separation of the "Grace group" was a contest that pitted McClain's fundamentalist orthodoxy against Ashland's liberalism, this is largely a product of reactionary misinterpretation. It certainly is true that McClain was influenced by American fundamentalism and that his epistemological and pedagogical approach was representative of fundamentalist posturing. And it is also true that after relocating to Indiana, the seminary would solidify its fundamentalist identity. But as we have indicated above, McClain and his associates had already won the day in the 1920s. After having vanquished the enemy of modernism with the 1921 "Message of the Brethren," Brethren fundamentalists reached for familiar weapons in their arsenal and within a generation turned on each other. By the time of the split in 1937, the doctrinal differences between Ashland and those who would form the "Grace group" were almost indiscernible. Jerry Young has suggested, for example, that with regard to Calvinism, the two groups differed on only one half point of the traditional five points of Calvinism—merely the way the doctrine of the "perseverance of the saints" should be articulated. In fact, Ashland changed little after McClain was expelled in 1937. Calvinist dispensationalism continued

48. McClain, *Daniel's Prophecy*, 5.

to be represented at Ashland Seminary within, for example, the course "Assurance of Salvation of the Believer," which was still being taught several years after the split. Additionally, Ashland retained committed fundamentalist faculty members.[49]

Rather than a controversy over orthodox doctrine, the 1937 split was rooted in divergent attitudes about the best approach to Christian higher education. McClain had adopted the systematizing and pedagogical framework of fundamentalist leaders, such as R. A. Torrey and the Bible Institute movement, which rooted Christian higher education in efforts to train future Christian leaders who would uphold narrow definitions of orthodoxy in an effort to resist the forces of modernism. This would take place largely through a process of simple Bible and theological instruction, which McClain believed was crucial for seminary training. This agenda, however, did not sit well with the administration at Ashland who favored an approach that valued a greater measure of academic freedom, openness, and engagement with mainstream society.[50]

THE ANABAPTIST AND PIETIST STRANDS

Just as it is an oversimplification to interpret the split between Ashland and those who would establish Grace Seminary as a contest over theological orthodoxy, it would be a mistake to assume that McClain's fundamentalism simply replaced his Brethren loyalties. The founding generation did not believe themselves to be leaving the Brethren tradition or their Anabaptist and pietist heritage. Rather, they believed their new seminary remained squarely inside the Brethren stream.[51] Indeed, McClain, Bauman, and others such

---

49. See Martin, "Law and Grace," 173.

50. We should note here, as mentioned earlier, that at the end of the day, both the Ashland and Grace factions were progressive when compared to more traditional Brethren who rejected higher education altogether. For the Ashland group, progressive thinking was embodied in a liberal arts approach to education; for the Grace group, it was an adoption of the Bible institute model, which at the time was also an innovative approach.

51. Pietism is difficult to define since it encompassed a wide range of theological orientations and historic movements. In general, however, pietism emerged in England and continental Europe, particularly Germany, as a response to Protestant scholasticism and the state churches of the seventeenth century. It embraced an ex-

as Charles Ashman and Homer Kent were not dissatisfied with Ashland for its adherence to a Brethren identity, but rather were concerned that it was not Brethren enough.[52] They believed that Ashland's Brethrenism was being eroded by those who were affiliated with the seminary who did not belong to the Brethren Church, for example. They claimed that Ashland's new constitution of 1937 gave the trustees, who were not all Brethren, too much control of the institution. Thus one of the original goals for Grace Theological Seminary, at least during the planning stages, was for its Board of Trustees and faculty members to be comprised entirely of Brethren Church members who were also married to Brethren spouses.[53]

For McClain, American fundamentalism represented a means to enhance the Anabaptist tradition, fashioning it for his contemporary context. While in hindsight, it seems clear that McClain and those in his circle chose a trajectory that would, in later generations, bring Grace College and Seminary as well as the FGBC more fully in alignment with American evangelicalism than with Anabaptism or pietism, this reflects more the transformations of later decades, particularly those of the Cold War era, than the loyalties of McClain and the founding generation.

Indeed, the shifting focus of the "Grace group" had clear precedent within the Anabaptist and pietist traditions. McClain's emphasis on biblical authority, for example, was certainly consistent with these traditions, even if fundamentalism's literalist hermeneutic was not.[54] What is more, the turn toward American evangelicalism was, at least in

---

periential approach to Christian faith that emphasized "heart religion," an intimate sense of community among believers, and active Christian service. On the development and distinctive features of pietism, see Brown, *Pietism*, as well as the helpful introduction by Lindberg in *Pietist Theologians*. For a (contested) treatment of the relationship between Anabaptism and pietism, see Friedmann, *Mennonite Piety*. Consult John Roth's essay in this volume for a critical assessment of Friedmann's thesis and its implications for Anabaptist-Mennonite historiography.

52. For biographical information on Charles Ashman consult BE I, 68.

53. To these ends the "Grace group" founded the Brethren Biblical Seminary Association in Ohio in early June of 1937. Later that year they founded Grace Theological Seminary of the Brethren Church, though they soon moved to Winona Lake under the shortened title of Grace Theological Seminary. See brochure, "New Seminary," LPAJM, MLASC.

54. Brown cites pietism as a "back-to-the-Bible movement." See especially Brown, *Pietism*, 46–56.

general terms, in line with pietism's evangelical identity.[55] Additionally, eschatological speculation enamored many pietist movements as well as certain radical Anabaptists just as it did McClain and his circle.[56] Even dispensationalism, though it became a hallmark of American fundamentalism, had at least some roots in pietism.[57] McClain and his circle also remained committed to what are perhaps the two most important distinctives both for historic Anabaptism and pietism: nonviolence and nonconformity to the world.

Regarding nonconformity to the world, McClain and Bauman were concerned that this Anabaptist virtue was also becoming compromised at Ashland. What disturbed McClain the most was the prevalence of such worldliness among students and faculty—that they engaged in dancing, card playing, and smoking. While it is tempting to see these concerns as evidence of McClain's acquiescence to fundamentalism, the opposition to worldly living had always been a hallmark feature of the Brethren tradition. As mentioned above, McClain sought to document worldly activities at Ashland through his own observation as well as the reports of others.[58] He recorded scornfully that students were smoking in dormitories, joining in worldly "fraternities," and indulging in theater shows and movies.[59] He even used the college newspaper, *The Collegian*, to document worldliness, clipping out items that smacked of worldliness, including one piece that made light of necking in parked cars by advising male students to remove their hats to "facilitate matters." McClain also kept the playbill from a Shakespeare production, possibly as further evidence of worldliness.[60]

---

55. On the confluence of pietism and evangelicalism, consult O'Malley, *Early Evangelicalism*; Lovelace, *Cotton Mather*; and Noll, *Rise of Evangelicalism*.

56. On eschatology in pietism, consult Lindberg, *Pietist Theologians*, 8–12, 35–36, 94–95, 154–56, 235–36.

57. Brown sees one source for dispensationalism in the Pietist Johann Bengel, who, according to Brown, begins "a line" that begins with Bengel and "extends through Darby and Scofield." Of course dispensationalism in its developed form begins with John Nelson Darby and the Plymouth Brethren, who were pietists in a nineteenth century English context. On the rise of Darby, consult Durnbaugh, *Believers' Church*, 161–72.

58. Delbert Flora to McClain, LPAJM, "1930" folder, 44, MLASC. Flora indicated to the obviously interested McClain that he is dismayed that several of the seminary boys have joined "a fraternity which indulges in dancing, card playing, smoking, etc."

59. LPAJM, "1930" folder, miscellany, 23 and 49, MLASC.

60. Ibid.

Charles Ashman joined in the effort, even writing angrily to then President Charles Anspach, declaring with horror that the seminary was not only allowing, but also promoting, worldly movies and theatrical productions. Ashman also charged the seminary with tacitly approving the tobacco industry by employing and retaining instructors who "openly and defiantly smoke cigarettes." He went so far as to declare that Ashland could not continue to call itself a Christian college that affirmed nonconformity to the world while such pastimes were permitted. When Anspach's reply failed to satisfy Ashman and McClain, they published an open letter to the president in which they reprimanded Anspach himself for attending movies and endorsing the vulgarity in the college newspaper.[61]

Not surprisingly, McClain codified the Anabaptist notion of separation from the world in the Grace Seminary statement of faith, which was explicit about the matter: ". . . since our Christian citizenship is in heaven, as the children of God we should walk in separation from this present world, having no fellowship with its evil ways . . . abstaining from all worldly amusements and unclean habits which defile mind and body . . ."[62] Grace Seminary also retained strong endorsement of the traditional Brethren ordinances of three-fold communion and trine immersion as well as the traditional Anabaptist opposition to oath taking.[63] It is clear that McClain considered himself fully

61. Ibid., "1936" folder, 49.

62. Whitcomb, *History of Grace*, 7. Separation from the world also seems to have taken on shades of political relevance in McClain's *The Greatness of the Kingdom*, which reads like a Cold War isolationist, anti-communist document. McClain wrote in this work in 1959: "A certain measure of isolationism could become the right kind of internationalism in the long run." See McClain, *Greatness*, 73.

63. The three-fold communion involves feet washing, the bread and the cup, and the love feast. These are symbolic of the past, present, and future aspect of salvation. Trine immersion is a form of baptism in which the believer kneels in a relatively shallow pool of water and is baptized three times forward in the name of the Father, Son, and Holy Spirit. Debate over the ordinances contributed to the ways the Ashland and Grace parties interpreted the schism. While the Ashland group condemned the "Grace Group" for "cheap grace" or antinomianism, the "Grace group" condemned Ashland for viewing these ordinances as necessary for salvation, or salvation "by works." This was the chief reason for naming the new seminary "Grace." In actuality, their views of these distinctives were very similar. Ashland emphasized the ordinances as necessary for responsible believers, and the "Grace group" emphasized the symbolic nature of the ordinances. Both sides believed in the classic Protestant doctrine of salvation by grace through faith alone. A similar dynamic played out among Mennonites as well. See the essays by John Roth and Jared S. Burkholder in this volume.

situated within the Brethren tradition and did not hesitate to defend his Brethren identity as he did in 1934 in response to accusations that he was not teaching the authentic Brethren faith. McClain believed the purity of his Brethren faith was evidenced by his commitment to the whole Bible, the fact that he had brought communion to the national conference and even was committed to opposing oath taking, which many others in Brethren circles were neglecting.[64]

Perhaps one of the strongest evidences of the Anabaptist stream can be found in McClain, Bauman, and Ashman's commitment to nonviolence as found in Jesus' teaching on the Sermon on the Mount. Not surprisingly, McClain's adoption of a dispensational approach led him to de-emphasize the Sermon on the Mount at least in comparison with others in the Anabaptist tradition. Like many dispensationalists, McClain believed the Sermon on the Mount provided a window into the future Millennial Kingdom when a literal Jerusalem will be restored. It is important to note, however, that McClain did not believe that the teachings of Jesus in these passages had no relevance or bearing on Christian living in the present. While in *The Greatness*, he would later admit that the ideals expressed in the Sermon on the Mount were radical, often impractical, and would not be fully realized until the millennium, McClain's personal commitment to nonviolence and nonconformity indicates that he believed Christians were not completely released from these teachings.[65] Indeed, as mentioned above, McClain's "The Message of the Brethren Ministry" affirmed nonviolence and other Anabaptist distinctives, and he remained committed in his opposition to Christian participation in war in the 1937 statement of faith for Grace Seminary, to which all faculty members were required to subscribe.

---

64. See N. V. Letherman to McClain and McClain's response, LPAJM, "1934" folder, 47, MLASC. McClain's opposition to oath taking can also be seen in a treatise he wrote against the Masons, largely because they took secret oaths.

65. McClain wrote, "By practical-minded men it has sometimes been argued that Christ's moral principles are so idealistic that they are not only impossible of realization, but that even to attempt to follow them may prove dangerous in the present world of reality. And such objections are not altogether without justification . . . And the conclusion seems inescapable that, short of heaven and the eternal state, only in a Kingdom of God on earth, where the outworking of the wrong desires of men is under external and immediate control, can the Golden Rule become *fully* a practical principle for all human action." See McClain, *Greatness*, 289.

This commitment would become especially relevant in just two years as the German war machine invaded Poland, setting in motion the events that plunged Europe into the Second World War. In 1941, anticipating the possibility of American involvement, McClain joined with Mennonites, members of the Church of the Brethren, and others in resisting Christian participation in the growing conflict. That same year, McClain sent notification to all Brethren pastors in the "Grace group" about their position on non-resistance and how to respond to impending war. He noted: "I am enclosing information which our pastors should study carefully so that they may counsel Brethren men intelligently. Also below I am passing on to you excerpts from letters received here from Church of the Brethren officials." McClain included a document of "Procedures for Inducting men into civilian Public Service Camps after They have been Placed in Class IV E."[66]

In an official tract meant to instruct the Grace Brethren constituency in how to respond to the Second World War, the authors use, in fact, the teachings of Jesus in strong defense of non-combatant roles. The tract cites the teachings of Jesus from the gospel of John: "My kingdom is not of this world. If my kingdom were of this world then my servants would fight."[67] The tract also quoted from the Sermon on the Mount: "Love your enemies, bless them that cure you, do good to them that hate you, and pray for them which spitefully use you, and persecute you; that ye may be the children of your Father which is in heaven; for he maketh the sun to rise on the evil and on the good, and sendeth the rain on the just and on the unjust."[68]

McClain was not alone among the founding generation of Grace Seminary in this commitment to the Anabaptist ideal of nonviolence.

---

66. "Grace Brethren and World War II."

67. John 18:36.

68. Matthew 5:44–45. Undated tract in "Grace Brethren and World War II." While the early Grace Brethren affirmed the position that Christians should fulfill their national obligations during wartime through filling non-combatant roles, some opened the door for the existence of weaker positions on nonviolence. For example, it is clear that some Grace Brethren writers did not want to be called "pacifists" because it was associated with leftist or perhaps even communist reasons for opposing war. One source stated, "A Pacifist is one who is against war in every form. He is against his government engaging in war. He does not necessarily take this stand from Christian principles. In fact many Pacifists are not Christians at all. Some are Communists. Brethren are not Pacifists." See "Brethren Church and War," in, "Grace Brethren and World War II."

Charles Ashman, for example, a prominent leader of the Grace group, wrote defiantly:

> Now, when the war drums roll, what should brethren do? Some doubtless will do as they did during the World War. They forgot all about the Brethren teachings and yielded to the mania for war. Some Brethren are strong for peace in times of peace but just as strong for war in times of war. But, real Brethren will declare, "We must obey God rather than man." They will take their stand on the Word of God! They will refuse to bear arms! They will be willing to take the consequences and, if needs be, "suffer reproach for the sake of Christ."[69]

Additionally, in a tract published by the Brethren Conference of Southern California in May of 1941, Ashman and Bauman laid out the historic Brethren position from the early eighteenth century, included a section on the biblical basis and authority, gave advice to the conscientious objector and selective service, and provided a copy of "The Message of the Brethren Ministry." This included the statement: "The Christian should 'be not conformed to this world' but 'be transformed by the renewing of the mind'; should not engage in carnal strife and should 'swear not at all.'" Scripture passages include Jesus' Sermon on the Mount as well as a host of other Old Testament and New Testament passages.[70] Thus it is clear that the founding generation did not believe their dispensationalism to negate the ideals of nonviolence found within the Sermon on the Mount.

CONCLUSION

In reflecting on the life and career of Alva J. McClain, the schism at Ashland Seminary, and the subsequent founding of Grace Theological Seminary, we can safely say that these events warrant an analysis that accounts for the complexity that existed. This essay represents a modest attempt to do just that. Rather than perpetuate a dualistic interpretation that operates with simple fundamentalist or liberal categories, this essay has suggested that the context of Grace Theological Seminary and the earliest identity of what became the FGBC was

---

69. Ashman, "War Drums," 3.
70. Ashman and Bauman, "Brethren Church and War."

an eclectic synthesis of varied theological and cultural strands, and Grace Seminary was as much the product of conflicting approaches to Christian education as it was a fundamentalist response to theological liberalism. As the person primarily responsible for establishing this new branch of the Brethren tradition, McClain himself represented various internal tensions. While it is clear that he adopted much from American fundamentalism, he had both conservative and progressive tendencies and retained a sense of Brethren identity and heritage. In essence, his was a fundamentalism adapted for a uniquely Brethren context.

BIBLIOGRAPHY

Antioch College Mission and History. No pages. Online: http://antiochcollege.org/aboutmission_and_history.html.

Bancroft, E. H. *Christian Theology: Systematic and Biblical*. Bible School Park, NY: Echoes, 1925.

Bauman, L. S. *The Faith Once for all Delivered Unto the Saints*. 9th ed. Winona Lake, IN: BMH, 1977.

Beale, David O. *In Pursuit of Purity: American Fundamentalism Since 1850*. Greenville, SC: Unusual, 1986.

Brown, William Adams. *Christian Theology in Outline*. New York: Scribner's, 1907.

Brown, Dale. *Understanding Pietism*. Rev. ed. Nappanee, IN: Evangel, 1996.

Brumbaugh, Martin Grove. *A History of the Brethren*. Mount Morris, IL: Brethren, 1899.

Clouse, Robert G. "Brethren and Modernity: Change and Development in the Progressive/Grace Church." *Brethren Life and Thought* (Summer 1988) 205.

———. "Changes and Partings: Division in the Progressive/Grace Brethren Church." *Brethren Life and Thought* (Fall 1997) 180–98.

———. "Fellowship of Grace Brethren Churches." In *Meet the Brethren*, edited by Donald F. Durnbaugh, 101–14. Philadelphia, PA: Brethren Encyclopedia, 1995.

Darr, William. 2010. Interview with author. October.

Dictionary of the Presbyterian & Reformed Tradition in America. Gen. ed. D. G. Hart, consulting ed. Mark A. Noll, Downers Grove, IL: InterVarsity, 1999.

Dixon, A. C., R. A. Torrey, et al. *The Fundamentals: A Testimony to the Truth*. Los Angeles: The Bible Institute of Los Angeles, 1917.

Durnbaugh, Donald F. *The Believers' Church: The History and Character of Radical Protestantism*. New York: Macmillan, 1970.

———, editor. *The Brethren in Colonial America: A Source Book on the Transplantation and Development of the Church of the Brethren in the Eighteenth Century*. Elgin IL: The Brethren, 1967.

———, editor. *European Origins of the Brethren: A Source Book on the Beginnings of the Church of the Brethren in the Early Eighteenth Century*. Elgin, IL: The Brethren, 1958.

———. *Meet the Brethren*. Elgin, IL: The Brethren for the Brethren Encyclopedia, 1984.
Durnbaugh, Donald F., and Dale V. Ulrich, editors. *The Brethren Encyclopedia*. 4 vols. 3rd ed. Philadelphia, PA: The Brethren Encyclopedia, 2005.
Friedman, Robert. *Mennonite Piety through the Centuries: Its Genius and its Literature*. Reprint. Eugene, OR: Wipf & Stock, 1998.
Gaddis, Vincent H., and Jasper A. Huffman. *The Story of Winona Lake: A Memory and a Vision*. Winona Lake, IN: Self-published, 1960.
"The Grace Brethren and World War II, A collection of Documents." Compiled by William Darr. Winona Lake, IN: Grace College, 2003. Unpublished.
Grill, Steve. 2010. Interview with author. October.
Hankins, Barry. *American Evangelicals: A Contemporary History of a Mainstream Religious Movement*. Plymouth, UK: Rowman & Littlefield, 2009.
Hodge, A. A. *Outlines of Theology: Rewritten and Enlarged*. New York: Hodder & Stoughton, George H. Doran Company, 1878. [McClain's copy.]
Holsinger, Henry R. *History of the Tunkers and the Brethren Church*. Lathrop, CA: Pacific, 1901.
Kent, Homer A. *Conquering Frontiers: A History of the Brethren Church*. Rev. ed. Winona Lake, IN: BMH, 1972 [1st ed., 1958].
———. 2007. Interview with author. October 22.
Lindberg, Carter. *The Pietist Theologians: An Introduction to Theology in the Seventh and Eighteenth Centuries*. Malden, MA: Blackwell, 2005.
Manahan, Ronald. 2010. Interview with author. September.
Lovelace, Richard R. *The American Pietism of Cotton Mather: Origins of American Evangelicalism*. Eugene, OR: Wipf & Stock, 2007.
Marsden, George M. *Fundamentalism and American Culture: The Shaping of Twentieth-Century Evangelicalism, 1870–1925*. New York: Oxford University Press, 1980.
———. *Reforming Fundamentalism: Fuller Seminary and the New Evangelicalism*. Grand Rapids: Eerdmans, 1995.
Martin, Dennis. "Law and Grace: The Progressive Brethren and Fundamentalism." Wheaton College. 1973. Wheaton, IL. [Independent study presented to Dr. David Maas, unpublished.]
McClain, Alva J. *Bible Truths*. Winona Lake, IN: BMH, 1979 [1st ed., 1950].
———. "The Book of Daniel." Class notes 1937–1938, unpublished. Morgan Library Archives and Special Collections. Winona Lake, IN.
———. *Daniel's Prophecy of the Seventy Weeks*. 6th ed. Grand Rapids: Zondervan, 1940.
———. *The Greatness of the Kingdom*. Chicago: Moody, 1979.
———. Letters and Papers of Alva J. McClain. Morgan Library Archives and Special Collections. Winona Lake, IN: Grace College.
———. "Theology Notes." 2 vols. Winona Lake, IN: Grace College, unpublished. [Bound, taken by a student of his in the 1950s. Vol. 1: "Notes for Inspiration, God, Christ, Holy Spirit, God and the World, and Angels. Vol. 2: "Man, Salvation, Kingdom, Church, and Eschatology."]
———. "1939 Theology Notes." Winona Lake, IN: Grace College, unpublished. [Bound, taken by an unnamed student in 1939.]
Noll, Mark. *The Rise of Evangelicalism: The Age of Edwards, Whitefield and the Wesleys*. Downers Grove, IL: InterVarsity, 2003.

Numbers, Ronald L. *The Creationists: The Evolution of Scientific Creationism*. Berkeley: University of California Press, 1992.

O'Malley, Steven. *Early German-American Evangelicalism: Pietist Sources on Discipleship and Sanctification*. Lanham, MD: Scarecrow, 1995.

Peterson, Kurt W. "World's Christian Fundamentals Association." In *Encyclopedia of Fundamentalism*, edited by Brenda Brasher, 515-16. New York: Routledge, 2001.

Plaster, David R. *Finding Our Focus: A History of the Grace Brethren Church*. Winona Lake, IN: BMH, 2003. [A revision and continuation of *Conquering Frontiers* by Dr. Homer A. Kent, Sr.]

Reid, Daniel G., et al., editors. *Concise Dictionary of Christianity in America*. Downers Grove, IL: InterVarsity, 1995.

Rohrer, Norman B. *A Saint in Glory Stands: The Story of Alva J. McClain, Founder of Grace Theological Seminary*. Winona Lake, IN: BMH, 1986.

Ronk, Albert R. *History of the Brethren Church*. Ashland, OH: Brethren, 1968.

Sappington, Roger E., editor. *The Brethren in the New Nation: A Source Book on the Development of the Church of the Brethren, 1785-1865*. Elgin, IL: The Brethren, 1976.

Scoles, Todd. "The Power of the Ordinances to Strengthen a Common Identity and Mission for the FGBC." DMin diss., Ashland Theological Seminary, 2006.

———. *Restoring the Household: The Quest of the Grace Brethren Church*. Winona Lake, IN: BMH, 2008.

Stoffer, Dale R. *Background and Development of Brethren Doctrines, 1650-1987*. 2 vols. Philadelphia: The Brethren Encyclopedia, 1989.

———. "The Background and Development of Thought and Practice in the German Baptist Brethren (Dunker) and the Brethren (Progressive) Churches (c. 1650-1979)." 2 vols. PhD diss., Fuller Theological Seminary, School of Theology, 1980.

———. "A Gleam of Shining Hope:" *The Story of Theological Education and Christian Witness at Ashland Theological Seminary (1906-2006) and Ashland College/University (1878-2006)*. Ashland, OH: Ashland Theological Seminary, 2007.

Strong, Augustus Hopkins. *Systematic Theology: A Compendium and Commonplace-Book*. Philadelphia: Judson, 1912.

Whitcomb, John C., editor. *The History of Grace Theological Seminary 1931-1951*. Winona Lake, IN: Grace College, 1951.

Whitcomb, John C., and Henry M. Morris. *The Genesis Flood: The Biblical Record and its Scientific Implications*. Philadelphia: Presbyterian and Reformed, 1961.

Yoder, C. F. *God's Means of Grace*. Elgin, IL: Brethren, 1908.

Yoder, Nathan Emerson. "Mennonite Fundamentalism: Shaping an Identity for the American Context." PhD diss., University of Notre Dame, 1999.

Young, Jerry. "The Relationship Between Local Grace Brethren Churches and Their Denominational Leadership." DMin diss., Dallas Theological Seminary, 1996.

———. 2009. Interview with author. July 30.

Young, Richard Fox. *India and the Indianness of Christianity: Essays on Understanding—Historical, Theological, and Bibliographical—in Honor of Robert Eric Frykenberg*. Grand Rapids: Eerdmans, 2009.

7

Misfits and Fundamentalists

The Question of Evangelicalism and Defection among Lancaster and Franconia Mennonites

Jared S. Burkholder

In 1933, THE SWORD and Trumpet, arguably the most militant outlet of popular Mennonite fundamentalist sentiment, printed an article entitled "Fundamentals and Fundamentalists," which assessed the strengths and weaknesses of American fundamentalism.[1] Within the article, the editors placed a cartoon with the caption, "Strengthening Others and Weakening Us" that pictured two building projects. On one street corner was a Mennonite church building still under construction while across the street stood a partially completed church labeled "The Undenominational Interdenominational Antidenominational Churches." Clearly meant to portray a sense of competition, workers are depicted carrying all manner of lumber and supplies from the Mennonite construction site to the other side of the street. With lament, one of the Mennonite workers declares, "Stop, Brethren! Why are you carrying our building material over there? They have plenty already that belongs to us—and workers too—we can't spare anymore."

---

1. Stauffer, "Fundamentals and Fundamentalists," 16–20. Since I deal with fundamentalism as it existed both inside and outside Mennonite communities, I will specify either "Mennonite" fundamentalism or "American" fundamentalism.

Cartoons such as this one, most of which were drawn by Ernest G. Gehman, were standard fare within the pages of *The Sword and Trumpet*, which was printed under the editorial guidance of George R. Brunk.[2] The competing building projects Gehman depicted demonstrates well the threat that many Mennonite leaders associated with the growing number of nondenominational fundamentalist churches in America. As the accompanying critique of the fundamentalist movement argued, American fundamentalism was to be applauded for its stance against theological modernism, but it also represented a competing religious movement that did not uphold traditional Anabaptist teachings such as nonconformity and nonresistance.[3] Perhaps even more troubling, it threatened to lure the faithful away from their Mennonite congregations.

While Brunk's *Sword and Trumpet* was published in Harrisburg, Virginia, Mennonite leaders in eastern Pennsylvania were similarly troubled by the increasing influence of non-Mennonite congregations and ministries, many of which were associated with the fundamentalist movement and often were "undenominational" or "interdenominational" in nature. Their fears were not completely unfounded since many Mennonites were, in fact, attracted to the growing network of fundamentalist Bible conferences, periodicals, and radio broadcasts between 1930 and 1950. And in some cases, new nondenominational congregations were formed and included members who had defected from Mennonite circles.[4]

---

2. George R. Brunk (1871–1938) was a popular evangelist in the Mennonite Church (MC) in Virginia and served several years as a board member for Eastern Mennonite College. He founded *The Sword and Trumpet* in 1927 and edited it until his death in 1938. Brunk is distinguished from his son, George R. Brunk II, who led a series of Mennonite Revivals in the 1950s. For more on Brunk, Sr., see the essays by Benjamin Wetzel and Nathan Yoder in the present volume.

3. See also Studer, "Is Fundamentalism Enough?" 486–87; Bender, "Outside Influences," 48.

4. On dissent within the Lancaster Conference during this period, due largely to fundamentalism, see Ruth, *Earth*, 1049–52. On similar trends within the Franconia Conference, see Ruth, *Maintaining*, 478–534. Numerous nondenominational congregations formed during this era. Most had generic names. Some remained Mennonite, while others did not. In addition to the two congregations specifically addressed in this chapter, other congregations relevant to this study would include, but are not limited to, Mount Calvary Church and The Gospel Tabernacle (Elizabethtown, PA), Grace Bible Church (Souderton, PA), Limerick Bible Church (Limerick, PA), Calvary Independent Church (Lancaster, PA), Monterey Mennonite

These trends have, of course, significant relevance to the historical relationship between evangelicalism and Anabaptism since the history of fundamentalism and American evangelicalism are interconnected.[5] Regarding this relationship, the traditional historiography on Mennonite fundamentalism has often interpreted fundamentalism, and therefore evangelicalism, primarily as an outside and corrupting phenomenon. Although the historiography has become more nuanced in recent years, Anabaptism and fundamentalism have, in some cases, been defined as existing in polar opposition to each other.[6] Without minimizing the significant distinctions of both traditions and the influence that did take place, it is important to emphasize that the fundamentalist phenomenon developed as much *within* American Mennonite communities as it did outside of them, which is illustrated well by the voices of ardent anti-modernists like George R. Brunk and the contributors to *The Sword and Trumpet*.

Indeed, this chapter examines a clash of two competing forms of fundamentalism that took place between 1935 and 1955—a distinctly Mennonite version that developed within the Lancaster and Franconia Mennonite Conferences, which are the oldest as well as the largest eastern Pennsylvania conferences; and the more mainstream, transdenominational American version whose influence helped to shape various groups of evangelical "misfits" who eventually defected from the Mennonite ranks.[7] I argue that in the case of these two Mennonite conferences, Mennonite fundamentalism was both an internal response to modernity and one that simultaneously opposed the broader, non-Mennonite fundamentalism that was gaining momentum in America during the same period. Therefore, the defection that took place was due as much to the uncompromising nature of these competing fundamentalisms, as to the incompatibility of the larger evangelical and Anabaptist traditions.[8]

Church (Lancaster, PA) and Neffsville Mennonite Church (Neffsville, PA).

5. For the interconnected role of fundamentalism within the larger history of American evangelicalism, see Hankins, *American Evangelicals*, 19–48; Sweeney, *Evangelical Story*, 155–80.

6. See, for example, Kauffman and Driedger, *Mennonite Mosaic*, 253–55.

7. "Conferences" refer to administrative branches or divisions among American Mennonites.

8. There are interesting parallels between this thesis and the conclusions of Richard T. Hughes who has recently argued that American fundamentalists have in-

The discussion below focuses first on the militant conservatism of the Lancaster and Franconia Mennonite conferences and the leadership structures that created a fundamentalist orientation. Second, it uses two episodes of dissent, both of which resulted in new, nondenominational congregations, as case studies that illustrate the intersection of and ensuing competition between Mennonite fundamentalism and its more mainstream cousin. We begin, however, with a brief description of several relevant historiographical trends.

THE HISTORIOGRAPHICAL CONTEXT

Fundamentalism can be defined either historically or comparatively, and I make use of both approaches in this essay.[9] Historically, American fundamentalism was a distinctly Protestant movement that emerged as a response to theological modernism culminating in the 1920s and 1930s. In its early stages, the movement fought its battles with liberalism within America's denominations, attempting to stave off modernist infiltration. Having lost these battles, fundamentalists withdrew but regrouped, forming a dynamic and revitalized network of personalities, congregations and organizations during the 1930s and 1940s. Since the 1970s, fundamentalism has increasingly been cast in a comparative light, defined as a "phenomenon" that can potentially become manifest in any religious community. In this sense, fundamentalism has become a category of analysis that may be applied across the spectrum of both world religions and local religious communities. It can include theological or cultural forms of conservatism and often has elements of both.

Critical assessment of fundamentalism within the Mennonite context began in the 1970s with the graduate work of Rodney Sawatsky (Princeton University) and Beulah Hostetler (University

---

creasingly seen themselves in eschatological competition with Islamists, or Muslim fundamentalists. See Hughes, *Christian America*. The sense of competition that American fundamentalists have felt with regard to Islam is also illustrated in Kidd, *Christians and Islam*, 96–164.

9. The standard treatment of fundamentalism in its historical American context remains Marsden, *Fundamentalism*. For a thorough analysis of fundamentalism as a comparative phenomenon, see the multivolume "Fundamentalisms Project" edited by Appleby and Marty.

of Pennsylvania) who both completed dissertations in 1977.[10] Sawatsky focused on the (Old) Mennonite Church as a whole and especially the controversy over modernism at Goshen College. In this regard, he concluded that the emergence of fundamentalism within the Mennonite context was a direct result of infiltration from non-Mennonite, Protestant fundamentalism that existed within the broader American culture. Hostetler concentrated on the Franconia Conference primarily, arguing that the cultural and theological traditionalism of this eastern Pennsylvania conference proved a successful bulwark against the kind of infiltration Sawatsky described. While examining two different contexts, Sawatsky and Hostetler primarily defined fundamentalism as foreign to or outside the Mennonite tradition as well as something that became a corrosive influence on Anabaptist distinctiveness. Both the Sawatsky and Hostetler dissertations were published, becoming accessible nearly the same time as another large study: Theron F. Schlabach's *Gospel vs. Gospel: Mission and the Mennonite Church, 1863-1944*. Taking the same interpretation as Sawatsky and Hostetler, Schlabach argued that in the context of Mennonite efforts for mission, both at home and abroad, fundamentalism was an outside, corrosive influence that took Mennonites "quite a distance ... from their own historic understandings."[11]

The fact that this era was dominated by what Nathan Yoder has called an "infiltration" thesis is not surprising, given the propensity of Mennonite historians and sociologists to use one acculturation theory or another to interpret many of the changes within Mennonite communities. Yet more recent scholarship has complicated this historiographical narrative. In his 1999 dissertation (Notre Dame), Yoder, like Sawatsky two decades earlier, focused on the (Old) Mennonite Church and the events at Goshen. But in re-examining the record, Yoder argued for a more complex interpretation, concluding that Mennonite fundamentalism developed as a corollary to the broader American version and that it originated *within* the Mennonite tradition in America. As such, conservative Mennonites, rather than

---

10. Consult Sawatsky, "The Influence of Fundamentalism" as well as "History and Ideology." See also Hostetler, "Franconia Mennonite Conference" and *American Mennonites*.

11 Schlabach, *Gospel Versus Gospel*, 115.

being victims of outside infiltration, successfully adapted features of American fundamentalism for a uniquely Anabaptist context.[12]

It should be noted that all of these authors recognize that Mennonite fundamentalism was not monolithic. There was a great variety of fundamentalist thinking among Mennonites. They differed in their stance toward non-Mennonite fundamentalists in their views on eschatology, current affairs, and the degree of militancy that was appropriate. Indeed, Sawatsky even created a complex typology of Mennonite fundamentalists, placing prominent Mennonite leaders in various categories based on their attitudes and theological positions.[13] All Mennonite fundamentalists, however, were staunchly traditionalist; and some conservative Mennonite leaders opposed American fundamentalism, even as they shared a similar response to modernity and an orientation that mirrored non-Mennonite fundamentalists. In terms of this essay, Yoder's analysis is especially helpful because it establishes explicit precedent for the existence of a distinctly Mennonite form of fundamentalism that was a product of, and inherent to, a particular Mennonite environment.[14]

This notion is also supported by recent trends in religious studies, where scholars have embraced the comparative study of fundamentalism. There are admitted difficulties with applying fundamentalism as a broad and comparative category, but R. Scott Appleby and Martin Marty have made a convincing case for its utility.[15] Fundamentalisms, they argue, represent particular forms of religiosity that have emerged in parallel fashion within a variety of contexts, and which share a concerted, if selective, rejection of modernity. In their opposition to modern social and religious trends, fundamentalisms often exhibit a cluster of characteristics. Among these are a bent toward authoritative leadership patterns, a strong desire to preserve the perceived traditions of the past, an emphasis on traditional interpretations of Scripture, as well as expectations that the faithful will conform to rigid behavioral standards. Inherent in this is the notion that a fundamen-

---

12. Yoder, "Mennonite Fundamentalism."

13. Sawatsky, "Fundamentalism, Liberalism, and Anabaptism."

14. For more on fundamentalism, modernism, and the Mennonite response, see Benjamin Wetzel's essay in this volume.

15. For a rationale for the term, see Marty and Appleby, *Fundamentalism Observed*, viii–ix.

talist "mentality" is often as much a result of internal factors as it is a product of external infiltration.[16]

Particularly relevant to a study of fundamentalism among American Anabaptists is the fact that Appleby and Marty draw a distinction between fundamentalism and mere traditionalism. While there are any number of Anabaptist groups that have been or continue to be staunchly traditionalist, they lack the activist impulse. Their response to the modern world has been to recede from it, often in a desire only to be left alone. But what sets fundamentalism apart from traditionalism is a drive to engage the modern world, even as they oppose it; a "reactive" desire to take back lost ground. "Fundamentalists begin as traditionalists who perceive some challenge or threat to their core identity, both social and personal . . . they react, they fight back with great innovative power."[17]

LANCASTER AND FRANCONIA STYLE FUNDAMENTALISM

During the first half of the twentieth century, Lancaster and Franconia conference bishops gravitated toward the kind of fundamentalism Marty and Appleby describe. These leaders resisted the period of institutional development and innovation that was taking place among the Midwestern conferences, charting a reactionary course that exhibited many features of the fundamentalist mentality.[18] In so doing, they sought to construct a bulwark against the influences of popular fundamentalism as well as the "neo-evangelicalism" that began to emerge around midcentury.[19] Reaching into the past, conference leaders made use of the traditional values of a strong and cohesive community, a quest for order, and robust church discipline that was codified within a heritage of "keeping house" and safeguarding the "right fellowship."[20]

16. Definitions for the Fundamentalisms Project are specifically addressed in the introduction of Marty and Appleby, vol. 1: *Fundamentalisms Observed*, and vol. 5: *Fundamentalisms Comprehended*, 399–444.

17. Marty and Appleby, *Fundamentalism Observed*, viii–ix.

18. On the "Awakening" or "Quickening" among the Midwestern Mennonites, see Juhnke, *Vision, Doctrine, War*, 107.

19. On "neo-evangelicalism," consult Sweeney, *Evangelical Story*, 155–80. For the Franconia Mennonite response to modernity, see especially Hostetler, *American Mennonites*, 245–71.

20. For the way this emphasis was applied among eastern Pennsylvania

Going beyond mere traditionalism, Lancaster and Franconia leaders fostered a culture of "aggresso-conservatism" that was unique to the eastern conferences.[21] They were not as concerned about theology, for example, as were Mennonite fundamentalists of the Midwest. Although theological modernism existed to a small degree among Midwestern Mennonites, it never gained any real traction among Mennonites in eastern Pennsylvania. Consequently, there was nothing akin to the controversy that took place at Goshen College, during which conservatives purged the college of faculty members with modernist leanings in 1923. Nor were the Lancaster and Franconia Conferences engaged in the broader Protestant circles in which many Midwestern Mennonites participated. With the exception of a few Lancaster leaders such as Bishop John H. Mosemann, who published articles against theological modernism, they did not participate side by side with other Protestants in the larger battles, as did John Horsch, or adopt the more extreme militant rhetoric of Brunk's *Sword and Trumpet*.[22]

The Lancaster and Franconia strain of fundamentalism was more concerned with the dangers of cultural accommodation than with theological modernism. These attitudes were rooted in the traditional Anabaptist emphasis on the centrality of discipleship and the community's role in caring for and disciplining members of the church as well as defending the church's standards of behavior.[23] Since discipleship was part and parcel of Christian salvation, Lancaster and Franconia bishops believed it was their duty to preserve the integrity of the church and the saliency of its mission. In 1932, for example, Lancaster bishop Noah Risser warned his flock that they would "need to hold fast to the faith" by retaining a commitment to distinctive Anabaptist cultural elements such as feet washing and

---

Mennonites, see Ruth, *Earth* and *Maintaining* throughout.

21. Daniel Kauffman used this term to identify the way his circle of midwestern Mennonites synthesized their activist program with a strong rejection of modernity. Although not originating within the eastern Pennsylvania context, I nevertheless utilize the term here to refer to the Lancaster and Franconia conferences' zeal for tradition. On the original use of "aggresso-conservatism," see Yoder, "Mennonite Fundamentalism."

22. Examples would include Horsch, *Failure of Modernism*; Mosemann, "Fundamentalism versus Modernism."

23. On the importance of discipleship in the Anabaptist tradition, see Snyder, *Anabaptist History*, 88.

the "devotional covering" so that the emphasis on non-conformity to the world would not be "lost."²⁴

The cultural conservatism of the eastern bishops provided the foundation for a fundamentalist mentality that permeated the leadership for several decades and found expression in a number of areas. One of the most visible was renewed efforts in the 1930s to codify plain dress standards, which conference leaders declared was a specific effort to stem the tide of worldliness.²⁵ Plain clothes signified a public rejection of worldly living as well as represented a yearning for continuity with the past, when worldliness had not been such a threat.²⁶ Yet this idealized past was something of an illusion, at least with respect to plain dress. Though some Pennsylvania Mennonites in the nineteenth century dressed in distinctly Mennonite attire, plain clothes did not become particularly stylized until the twentieth century, and the emphasis on conforming to standards of dress took on greater significance as the threats of the modern world facilitated more reactionary attitudes. This stronger emphasis often had great affect on local Mennonites, especially young people. Indeed, some local preachers—those of an especially rigid minority, such as Samuel K. Landis—even implied that that if young people refused to submit to the dress standards, they might face the terrors of hell.²⁷ The Franconia Conference followed suit, increasingly equating conformity to plain dress standards with identification with the church and a signal they would submit to conference authority.²⁸ The bishops of the Lancaster and Franconia Conferences took measures to ensure conformity with regard to other symbols of worldliness as well. They restricted the use of radios, sought to curtail certain forms of music, and prohibited such

---

24. Burkholder, "Fundamentalism," 41.

25. Lancaster Bishop Board minutes, 11–12 April 1935. See also Ruth, *Earth*, 839–45.

26. Marty and Appleby, *Fundamentalisms Observed*, ix–x. Marty and Appleby refer to this dualism as "Moral Manicheanism," in *Fundamentalisms Comprehended*, 406–7. Fundamentalists work to reclaim the perceived purity of the past—"an actual or imagined ideal." In an effort to shore up their identity, they will clarify boundaries, often operating with a dualistic mentality that safeguards the essential components of authentic faith.

27. Ruth, *Earth*, 844–45.

28. Ruth, *Maintaining*, 460–62, 480.

practices as taking out life insurance policies and exchanging wedding rings, all of which were viewed as worldly or unscriptural.

Efforts to safeguard the aggresso-conservative ethic of the Lancaster and Franconia Conferences were implemented through an increasingly centralized and hierarchical authority structure.[29] While "benevolent leaders" could be found among the Lancaster Conference's leadership, historian John Ruth paints a picture of austerity, "stern voices," and "authoritarian" bishops who appealed to the Anabaptist virtue of yieldedness (*Gelassenheit*) to enforce conference expectations.[30] Individual bishops were responsible for particular "districts" within the conference and therefore exercised leadership over the local ministers in a particular region. Bishops alone were responsible for administering certain ordinances, such as baptisms, communion, and ordinations. Senior members of the Bishop Board, as it was called among Lancaster Mennonites and the equivalent Executive Committee of Franconia, commanded strong respect and often represented the most concerted efforts to stave off modern encroachment. Among midwestern Mennonites, the eastern bishops were disparaged for their pharisaic reputation—Lancaster's bishops, for example, were sometimes referred to as the "Lancaster Sanhedrin."[31]

The "domineering" defender of tradition, Bishop Jacob Brubacher, for example, ushered the Lancaster Conference into the twentieth century, setting the conservative tone even as the new century brought many changes to American life. Overshadowing the Lancaster leadership well into his seventies, Brubacher gained a reputation for strong discipline and rigid enforcement of conference standards against the "enemy" of worldliness, whether it was preaching on the themes of "Doctrine and Obedience" or condemning modern society in Mennonite periodicals. Typical of his style, in 1912, Brubacher called for a renewed battle against the "monster" of worldly compromise, admonishing readers of the *Gospel Herald* to remain steadfast in nonconformity with an "indomitable will" and "united

---

29. Marty and Appleby, *Fundamentalisms Comprehended*, 408. Marty and Appleby suggest, "The division of power and bureaucracy is viewed as weakening the position and commitment to the fundamentals."

30. For a more positive application of yieldedness, see Nathan Yoder's essay in the present volume.

31. On this reputation, see Schlabach, *Peace, Faith, Nation*, 298–309.

front."³² Also concerned for transmitting these conservative values to younger generations, bishops such as Brubacher especially sought to safeguard young people from the evils of the world and to inspire them to be baptized early and commit themselves to the conservative Mennonite way.³³

In the 1920 and 1930s, when Protestant fundamentalists outside Mennonite circles were doing "battle royal" against the threats of modernity, the Lancaster and Franconia conference bishops fought their own battles, even assuming matters of church discipline that in earlier decades might have been left to individual congregations or the conference mission board.³⁴ Matters regarding standards for the members of their constituency were decided among themselves during bishop and executive committee meetings and disciplinary measures were also handled at such meetings. Harold Bender once compared the eastern bishops with "high-church" liturgical traditions. While the bishops in other conferences operated with a stronger sense of democracy, the eastern bishops retained the "sole right to initiate legislation" and to dictate decisions.³⁵ While biannual conference meetings were open to all ordained members, only the bishops were permitted to attend pre-conference assemblies in which the agenda was determined. Bishop board meetings created regulations as needed and also restated their rulings when the circumstances required. Although they sought to restore wayward members, they maintained a commitment to discipline those who would not comply.

The resolutions of the bishop board and executive committee were published yearly and disseminated in a small book known as the "Rules and Discipline."³⁶ The book was symbolic of the bishops' authority and the expectations of church members to comply. Indeed, the book was regularly employed to safeguard the purity of church membership, particularly in the context of celebrating the Lord's Supper. Mennonite communion was open only to members of the Mennonite faith and only to those in good standing with the con-

---

32. Quoted in Ruth, *Earth*, 832. On Brubacher, see Ruth, *Earth*, 821–22, 831–32, 834–35.
33. Ibid., 835.
34. Ibid., 881.
35. Bender, "Office of Bishop," 128–32.
36. On the Rules and Discipline, see Nolt, "Church Discipline," 1–16.

ference. To ensure conformity to the printed Rules and Discipline, meetings were held prior to communion, usually a week or two in advance. During these meetings, known as preparatory services, council meetings, or inquiry meetings, a bishop was present who read publically the Rules and Discipline while church members would examine their inner spiritual condition. The services also included a sermon that might admonish the congregation to stay committed to the standards and regulations of the conference. To close these meetings, the congregation was separated by gender and members would be asked individually to affirm their consent to the order and discipline of the conference.

Increasingly, the Bishop Board believed it was necessary to impose new resolutions and to "silence" members without congregational consent, which would have been required in earlier generations.[37] Some in the Franconia Conference were also influenced by the conservative Eastern Mennonite School. Graduates came back to eastern Pennsylvania resolute to combine their commitment to a conservative ethos with a commitment for active participation in service and outreach.[38] As in Lancaster, Franconia's elder and more traditional bishops, such as Abraham Clemmer, held sway, but younger bishops, such as John Lapp and Arthur Ruth also remained resolute in enforcing the teachings and regulations of the Franconia Conference.[39] Given the aggresso-conservative ethos of Lancaster's and Franconia's leaders, it is not surprising that any influence from the broader, American fundamentalist movement would be resisted just as staunchly as any modernist threat. Despite the efforts of conservative Mennonites, however, American fundamentalism did prove attractive to many.

MENNONITE MISFITS

Regrouping in the decades after the sensational Scopes Trial (1925), American fundamentalists bounced back with new vitality. In a surge of organizational energy, fundamentalists capitalized on internal networks of charismatic personalities, conference meetings, and

---

37. Ruth, *Earth*, 891–93.
38. Ruth, *Maintaining*, 480.
39. Ibid, 510–11.

parachurch organizations, and in the process marshaled the power of the media to unite their efforts and proclaim the evangelical message.[40] The dynamism of popular fundamentalism extended into the 1950s even as a new generation of "neo-evangelicals" was forming. The growing popularity of fundamentalism and evangelicalism was attractive to many Americans at a time when traditional Protestantism still felt plagued by theological modernism and foreign threats to the American way of life loomed large. Eastern Pennsylvania's Mennonite communities were no exception. The 1930s and 1940s witnessed an increase in participation in non-Mennonite fundamentalist networks and the adoption of theological views that were part and parcel of the broader fundamentalist movement in America. The section below examines the development of two movements of dissent in which popular fundamentalism played a significant role. These movements each culminated in the formation of independent Mennonite congregations that eventually moved completely out of the Anabaptist tradition, dropping "Mennonite" from their names.[41] The congregations were initially organized as Calvary Mennonite Church (1950) and Congregational Mennonite Church (1951). Calvary separated from the Franconia Conference while Congregational separated from the Lancaster Conference.[42]

---

40. For a discussion of the Scopes Trial within the larger historiography of fundamentalism, see Hankins, 49–82. A full treatment of the rebirth of fundamentalism after 1925 can be found in Carpenter, *Revive Us Again*.

41. Although these congregations would move easily into the "new" evangelical subculture that formed after 1950, I use "fundamentalism" more often than "evangelicalism" or "neo-evangelicalism" since these instances of dissent emerged out of the popular fundamentalism of the 1930s and 1940s (described by Joel Carpenter in *Revive us Again*).

42. Since I was raised in one of these congregations and my wife in the other, both of us had the curious experience of feeling caught between the evangelical and Anabaptist traditions. I had opportunity to make sense of this personal history through an MA thesis, which I completed at Trinity Evangelical Divinity School in 2000. It argued that American fundamentalism was, ironically, an empowering force, providing opportunity for progressive Mennonites of the Lancaster and Franconia Conferences to engage in broader religious circles. See Burkholder, "Fundamentalism." Subsequent articles related to these congregations are Burkholder, "Evangelicalism, Fundamentalism, and Religious Dissent"; Burkholder, "Origins of Calvary Mennonite Church." This essay represents further development in my thinking on these issues.

Both dissenting movements formed under the leadership of individual ministers. John Hiestand (1909-1992), who led the "Congregational" group out of the Lancaster Conference, had been critical of Mennonite authority since the 1930s.[43] He was ordained in 1938 as minister for the Marietta Mission congregation. As a gifted speaker, Hiestand was a popular evangelist who traveled the local circuit of Mennonite revival and evangelistic services. In 1935, even before his ordination, he sent a letter to the Lancaster bishops criticizing their position on special music. In 1944, Hiestand led a group of fifteen petitioners who called for a revival of sorts that would include a fresh emphasis on evangelism and "our primary mission to a lost world." The petitioners also hoped to prod the bishops toward "a more tolerant attitude toward those who are unable to give full support to the specifications of the Rules and Discipline."[44] In 1949, Hiestand also wrote a two page defense of one his teachers, Abram Gish, who had been suspended by the bishops for teaching the Scofield Bible Correspondence Course.[45] A final petition was sent to the bishops in 1951 in which Hiestand presented evidence that many others were dissatisfied with the "present form of church administration and emphasis."[46]

Like Hiestand, William Anders (b. 1915), who led the "Calvary" group, questioned the Mennonite leadership for quite some time before resigning his position.[47] Anders was minister at Towamencin Mennonite Church, in the Franconia Conference, and also witnessed the suspension of two of his teachers for disseminating teachings that were not in conformity with conference standards—in this case, the doctrine of eternal security.[48] Anders was similarly concerned with the relationship between conference regulations and evangelism as well as

---

43. On Hiestand, see Krabill, "John Shank Hiestand." On the split that produced Congregational Mennonite Church, aside from the author's work mentioned above, see Ruth, *Earth*, 1004, 1049-50; R. S. Burkholder, *Pathways*, 3-9.

44. Quoted in Burkholder, "Fundamentalism," 47. Hiestand Family Collection

45. Hiestand to the Lancaster Mennonite Bishop Board.

46. Minutes of the Lancaster Mennonite Conference Bishop Board (January 1950), Lancaster Mennonite Historical Society, Lancaster, PA (hereafter LMHS).

47. On Anders and the formation of Calvary Mennonite church, see the author's work mentioned above (note 41) as well as Lederach, *Seeking*, 73-78.

48. Minutes of the Franconia Mennonite Conference Executive Committee (20 March 1950), Mennonite Heritage Center, Harleysville, PA (hereafter MHC).

the emphasis placed on conformity. Another faction had formed at Blooming Glen Mennonite Church, also in the Franconia Conference, where members were dissatisfied with their minister. The group sent a petition to the bishops, requesting that the board provide their ministers with assistance.[49] But the group was impatient, and soon found camaraderie among Anders' faction at Towamencin.

In the twenty or so years leading up to the dissent led by Hiestand and Anders, influence from the broader fundamentalist movement proved to be a significant factor. In interviews with those who were active in these factions, individuals consistently cited interaction with American fundamentalism. One of the most significant factors was the Bible conference movement. Many Lancaster and Franconia Conference Mennonites drove to Bible conferences in Keswick, New Jersey, the Sandy Cove conference center on the Chesapeake Bay, Montrose Bible Conference in Pennsylvania, and Word of Life in New York. Here they heard fundamentalists and neo-evangelical preachers including George Palmer (founder of Sandy Cove Bible Conference) and Percy Crawford (founder of Youth for Christ.) In fact, John Hiestand attended non-Mennonite Bible conferences since the time he was a boy in the 1920s—something that "broadened his view of the church."[50] In 1949, while visiting relatives in Goshen, Hiestand even attended a Rodeheaver "song-fest" at Winona Lake (IN), a central hub within the fundamentalist Bible conference movement.[51] With their charismatic personalities, engaging messages, and mass appeal, fundamentalist preachers seemed to offer an attractive alternative to local Mennonite ministers who were chosen "by lot" and sometimes struggled to compete with the polished programs of non-Mennonite preachers.[52]

49. Petition letter from Blooming Glen Mennonite Church to the Franconia Mennonite Conference Executive Committee, Blooming Glen papers, MHC.

50. Kraybill, "John Shank Hiestand," 3.

51. Krabill to Hiestand. Burkholder, "Fundamentalism," 61. Homer Rodeheaver (1880–1955) was the popular song leader for the flamboyant evangelist Billy Sunday who made Winona Lake his headquarters in 1911. After Sunday died in 1935, Rodeheaver continued his music ministry in Sunday's Tabernacle.

52. Burkholder, "Fundamentalism," 76–77. Determining God's will through this process was the traditional method of choosing ministers (as well as bishops). A small group of laymen were nominated by the congregation and then selected through a lottery process designed to determine the man of God's choosing. While Mennonite tradition held that the arbitrary blessing of God and his Spirit was all

Replicating what they were experiencing at fundamentalist Bible conferences, a group of Franconia Mennonites began holding Bible conferences in 1942 at Highland Park Camp Meeting Grounds in Harleysville (PA). Here they secured popular speakers such as George Palmer, Clarence Didden, Layman Strauss, and Rowen Pierce.[53] Mennonite lay persons who attended these gatherings were enamored by the well-honed sermons of these seminary-trained speakers who seemed to be able to expound the Bible in ways that their Mennonite ministers could not.[54] In some cases, revivals and Bible conferences even became the catalyst for new, often nondenominational, congregations.[55]

A number of Lancaster and Franconia Conference Mennonites also listened regularly to mainstream radio broadcasts, which included such well-known fundamentalist and neo-evangelical programs as Billy Graham's *Hour of Decision,* Theodore Epp's *Back to the Bible,* Charles Fuller's *Old Fashioned Revival Hour,* Moody Bible Institute's *Radio School of the Bible,* George Palmer's *Morning Cheer,* Donald Grey Barnhouse's *Bible Study Hour,* and Percy Crawford's *Young People's Church of the Air.*[56]

One individual who joined Hiestand's congregation remembered listening to Fuller's *Old Fashioned Revival Hour* as a boy on Sunday afternoons even though these programs were strongly discouraged by the Lancaster Conference. Hiestand himself owned a radio, even though he sold it to his brother when he was ordained.[57] Members of Anders' congregation also tuned in, some listening to the *Morning Cheer* on a daily basis.[58] Anders approved and later attributed radio

---

that was needed for ordination— not seminary degrees, natural ability, a personal sense of calling, or even a salary—progressives sometimes doubted the validity of the practice.

53. Ibid., 64–65. Didden was a pastor from Limerick, PA; Strauss served at a Presbyterian church in Bristol, PA; Piece was a popular Bible teacher and pastor from Philadelphia.

54. For a fuller treatment of the participation of Lancaster and Franconia Mennonites in the Bible conference movement, see Burkholder, "Fundamentalism," 57–60.

55. For examples, Calvary Independent Church and Word of Life Chapel were organized in the wake of a series of Lancaster City revivals in 1951.

56. Burkholder, "Fundamentalism, " 72–77.

57. L. Miller, interview; Kraybill, "John Shank Hiestand," 15.

58. Gross, interview.

broadcasts as the most significant way that the fundamentalist "gospel of grace" was disseminated among his congregation.[59] As a result of their listening habits, many Mennonites also began to view the radio as a means of evangelism. A few began their own broadcasts, such as the popular William Detweiler, who was raised in the conservative Franconia Conference before moving to Ohio. Beginning his broadcasts in 1936, Detweiler was broadcasting on seven stations in four states within a decade and became a household name among more progressive Mennonites.[60]

Participation in fundamentalist Bible conferences, listening to evangelical radio broadcasts, and attending revivals dovetailed with other components of American fundamentalism, including study of the popular Scofield Bible and enrollment in correspondence courses organized under the direction of Moody Bible Institute. In the Lancaster area, Ezra Brubaker, who led a local gospel choir that included Hiestand and other influential founding members of Congregational Mennonite Church, took the Scofield course under Hiram Lefever, pastor of Elizabethtown's Gospel Tabernacle. Serving as a spiritual father figure, Brubaker shepherded the young men in his chorus and encouraged them to take the Scofield course as well. Brubaker encouraged Hiestand and another young Lancaster Conference Mennonite, Abram Gish, to enroll as well. Having completed the Scofield class, Gish himself began teaching it on Wednesday evenings at Hiestand's Marietta mission.[61]

With Gish serving as instructor, the Scofield Bible Correspondence Course became immensely popular. Starting out in 1944, Gish had over seventy students from at least twenty-five different families representing four Mennonite districts in the Lancaster Conference as well as individuals from non-Mennonite churches.[62] A gifted communicator, Gish added more Moody courses to his repertoire and continued teaching them for many years, eventually creating his own radio

---

59. Anders, interview. See also Steven M. Nolt's chapter in this volume.

60. On Detweiler, see Burkholder, "Fundamentalism," 66–72. On radio and American Mennonites, see Nolt, "Church Discipline, 1–16; E. Miller, "Use of the Radio," 131–48.

61. On Gish, the Scofield Bible Correspondence Course, and the Lancaster Conference, see Burkholder, "Fundamentalism," 92–100; R. S. Burkholder, *Pathways*, 7–8.

62. Ibid.

broadcast. Staunch opponents of the Scofield theological orientation, the Lancaster Conference silenced Gish for his teachings, but he soon had an invitation to become the pastor of Word of Life Chapel, a local nondenominational congregation, which began as a result of a series of evangelical revivals in Lancaster city. Throughout his career, Gish taught well over one thousand students, establishing classrooms in nearly a dozen towns, at two local colleges, and on three radio stations in eastern Pennsylvania. The Scofield Bible became a point of contact between American fundamentalism and Franconia Mennonites as well. Several members of Anders' Towamencin congregation had embraced the Scofield Bible in the 1930s. Other Mennonites in the Souderton area took the Scofield Correspondence Course at Grace Bible Church under Gerald Stover, the new congregation's pastor.

While the Lancaster and Franconia bishops forbade the Scofield Bible for its premillennial and dispensationalist orientation, those who began to use it found it difficult to understand why their Mennonite leaders rejected it, assuming their bishops were attempting to diminish access to the Bible and wanted to prevent laypeople from studying it on their own. While the Scofield correspondence courses made the Bible seem easily accessible, Mennonite ministers seemed backward and controlling, and this sentiment that was reinforced by at least one Mennonite leader who remarked that the Scofield Bible would give lay people the ability to "understand the scriptures better than the bishops."[63] But while these individuals may have thought this new way of Bible study simply provided a more effective approach to understanding Scripture, there is little question that it contributed to a doctrinal shift toward dispensationalism, which ran counter to traditional Mennonite teachings. Those who adopted dispensationalism, for example, often embraced the premillennialism that went with it—something that most Mennonites of the day rejected. Most, if not all, of the founding members of Calvary and Congregational affirmed their acceptance of dispensationalism and premillennialism, and as Abram Gish disseminated the new understandings, prophecy became a favorite topic among his preaching and teaching.[64]

---

63. Gish, interview.
64. Burkholder, "Fundamentalism," 97.

COMPETING FUNDAMENTALISMS

After 1930, Lancaster's aggresso-conservative rejection of both modernity and American fundamentalism became increasingly apparent, especially in response to Mennonite participation in these trends. Both the Lancaster and Franconia conference leaders took measures against avenues of fundamentalist and neo-evangelical influence. In Lancaster, for example, Noah Mack and Noah Risser, the elder bishops, led the charge along with younger bishops, including Amos Horst and Henry Lutz.[65] The Bishop Board had specified in 1935 that members were strictly prohibited from attending "Inter-Denominational Bible Conferences," since such conferences were organized by those who did not affirm traditional Mennonite teachings such as "Non-Resistance." They warned that, "Members who persist in attending such meetings, will bring themselves to a place, where their membership shall be questioned."[66]

The bishops took a similar posture with regard to the radio, which was both a symbol of modern worldliness and a medium for outside influence. The Franconia Conference prohibited the use of radios in 1931, asserting, "We as a conference protest against the evils of the radio. Preachers should not remain silent, but condemn the worldly, foolish as well as the heretical doctrines on the air and often tuned in by so called Christian people."[67] This decision was reaffirmed in 1937 after it became clear that a number of Mennonites were embracing the radio.[68]

In 1939, the young and influential J. Paul Graybill was ordained to the Lancaster Bishop Board and continued the assault on worldliness. Graybill was probably the most charismatic aggresso-conservative since Jacob Brubacher and quickly gained a reputation for his commitment to resist the encroachment of worldliness.[69] Graybill declared that a defensive strategy of preserving "every detail" of conference

---

65. On Mack, see Ruth, *Earth*, 939–41. On general leadership patterns during this period, see Ruth, *Earth*, 958–65.

66. Minutes of the Lancaster Mennonite Conference Bishop Board (11–12 April 1935), LMHS.

67. Minutes of the Franconia Mennonite Conference (1 October 1931), MHC.

68. Ibid. (7 October 1937), MHC.

69. On J. Paul Graybill, see Ruth, *Earth*, 908 and especially 968–69.

standards was not enough; the "offensive must be taken."[70] This stance was embodied through the creation of a new Mennonite periodical, the *Pastoral Messenger*, which Graybill edited. He hoped the new periodical would be an effective means of transmitting conservative commitments from the Bishop Board to the pew.[71]

In 1940, as the popularity of Mennonite radio personality William Detweiler continued to expand, the Lancaster Conference specifically condemned him "for coming into our district," doing "regular broadcasting," and "soliciting young members to assist him." Ironically, John Hiestand was one of those "young members"—serving for a time as the bookkeeper for Detweiler's ministry. They also called on the Ohio Conference to control the extent of Detweiler's influence in "the eastern Conferences."[72]

Dispensationalism and premillennialism also came under fire. Lancaster and Franconia leaders made use of local Mennonite publications, in which they condemned the evils of the Scofield Bible, dispensationalism, and premillennialism. Ira Landis also published a monograph attacking premillennialism, linking it directly to the doctrine of eternal security and "Ultra-dispensationalism." For Landis and other traditional Mennonites, "once saved, always saved" flew in the face of Mennonite humility. It was also linked with the Calvinist teachings of unconditional election, and for Landis it opened the door for antinomianism—it was conducive to "carefree" living. Focusing on the warning passages in Hebrews, Landis asserted "there is much assurance and encouragement [in the book of Hebrews] but no room for the present-day doctrine of eternal security, whether in seed or in full bloom . . . We have seen the heinousness of this false doctrine gone to seed in the church and our message to Israel. God will hold us accountable for the souls we deceive and are thus forever lost."[73]

---

70. Ruth, *Earth*, 968. It should be noted that Graybill is a good example of the way fundamentalists often make use of a selective rejection of modernity, for while Graybill was staunchly opposed to modern influences, he introduced innovations that included summer Bible schools and a Christian school just outside of Lancaster City. Such efforts were not to become modernized; quite the opposite, they were attempts to protect young people from the evils of worldliness.

71. Ruth, *Earth*, 968.

72. Minutes of the Lancaster Mennonite Conference Bishop Board (Spring, 1940), LMHS.

73. Landis, *Faith of our Fathers*, 199, 208.

Conservatives in the Lancaster and Franconia Conferences continued to attack the Scofield Bible. Graybill's *Pastoral Messenger*, for example, printed an article condemning the Bible, which, the author lamented, had become "one of the most popular Bibles used in our Lancaster Conference." The article argued that Scofield was mixing the poison of dispensationalism into the food and drink of Pennsylvania's Mennonites and called for a complete rejection of this version of the Bible "as one of the means by which we may help to halt this eating canker of fractional gospel truth which is subverting, if not shipwrecking, souls."[74]

Those Mennonites who embraced elements of American fundamentalism increasingly found it difficult to tolerate the rigidity of their bishops. Believing they had been awakened to a more authentic spirituality, they imbued their cause with greater religious and theological significance. They charged the bishops with legalism, asserting that they cared more about conforming to misguided traditions than true Christian faith. Years later, they were still prone to see themselves in the same light as the Protestant reformers who freed Christians from the overbearing bishops of the Roman church. Considering themselves victims of their own overbearing bishops, they claimed the moral high ground, claiming, with a sense of superiority, the doctrine of grace in the midst of legalism.[75] They accused their Mennonite leadership of placing conference regulations on the same level as Scripture or even that the "rules and regulations obscured many biblical truths." One person remembered, "Although I learned many Bible stories and meaningful Scripture growing up and even joined the church and was baptized, I never grew as a Christian or had a personal relationship with Christ. I always felt since I was a 'member in good standing' that was all there was . . . Only after we attended meetings that stressed knowing Christ personally, did I see that continuing in the old Mennonite church would not help me grow as a Christian."[76]

Confidence in their "personal relationship" with Christ was reinforced through the teaching of eternal security. For traditionalist Mennonites, this confidence was presumptuous. It failed to take

---

74. Shank, "What is wrong," 224–25.

75. Burkholder, "Fundamentalism," 113. On competing perceptions of grace and legalism, consult the essays by M. M. Norris as well as John Roth in this volume.

76. Clemens, response to questionnaire, March 1999.

seriously the warning passages in Scripture and contradicted the Mennonite emphasis on humility and discipleship.[77] Yet many of the dispensationalist preachers to which these Mennonites were attracted were Calvinists and taught that those who were saved could rest with the assurance that resulted in divine election.[78] One member commented that eternal security "took time for us to grasp . . . and we spent much time discussing it" [in the Scofield Bible Correspondence course until it] "became a part of us."

These "misfits" also believed that the demands of the Lancaster and Franconia Conferences were prohibitive for their evangelistic efforts. Lancaster and Franconia Mennonites supported multiple efforts of missions and evangelism, yet progressives believed that these efforts would be more effective if they could leave behind the prohibitions against special music and the radio as well as let go of cultural oddities such as plain dress. Not surprisingly, mission congregations were most prone to tensions over evangelism. Often existing on the geographical and administrative edge of the conference, mission congregations sometimes pushed the boundaries of conference regulations. They tended to favor more expedient methods and at the same time enjoyed a greater level of autonomy. Hiestand's first experience in ministry was in the context of the Marietta mission congregation, and evangelism was an important part of his ministry. In addition to the regular evangelistic services he held at Marietta and throughout the Lancaster Conference, Hiestand used Brubacker's men's chorus as a means of evangelism. While the choir sung at outdoor programs, with a sound system strapped to a car and wired into the battery, Hiestand would take the microphone and intersperse evangelistic preaching with the songs.[79] But the chorus had to tread lightly. Such music was rarely permitted within the context of Sunday services. On some occasions they were permitted to sing but had to sit in the front pew with their backs to the congregation as they sang. Other times they sang

---

77. Burkholder, "Fundamentalism," 108–12.

78. The notes for Jude 1 in the Scofield Bible were clear about eternal security: "Assurance is the believer's full conviction that, through the work of Christ alone, received by faith, he is in possession of salvation in which he will be eternally kept. And this assurance rests only upon the Scripture promises to him who believes."

79. L. Miller, interview.

from the back of the meeting house. On other occasions they simply ignored conference regulations altogether.[80]

In the Franconia Conference, tensions over evangelism also surfaced, with progressives pushing for greater leniency as a means to increase evangelistic effectiveness. At the Rockyridge mission congregation, for example, some believed the expectations to adhere to the plain dress standards were hindrances to outreach. Visitors might come once, they observed, but after realizing the expectations of the Mennonite church would not return. Other members of the Rockyridge congregation, such as Leon Horst, who eventually joined Anders' group of defectors, worked in the business world and believed that the standards of the Franconia Conference were a barrier to outreach. Employed by a local company that made women's hosiery, Horst often traveled to New York City on business, where he felt awkward going to business meetings in his plain Mennonite suit. Eventually he purchased a conventional suit for his business dealings but continued to wear his plain attire to church—something that made him feel hypocritical. How could he wear his stylish suit to work and yet expect those who converted through the mission congregation to begin wearing the plain Mennonite suit? Caught in anguish, Horst sought the advice of one of the itinerant Mennonite evangelists from outside the conference, who encouraged him to leave his plain coat behind. The same evening Horst went to the evangelistic services in his business suit, defying conference regulations as well the expectations of his minster.[81]

FROM ONE FUNDAMENTALISM TO ANOTHER

By 1950, both Anders and Hiestand had become seriously estranged from their Mennonite leaders. Although the Franconia bishops held out at least some hope of reconciliation with Anders and his group, this never materialized. In May 1950, Anders submitted his resignation, complaining that "Discipline is before doctrine . . . and our rules and discipline have taken the place of Christ in our program."[82]

80. Burkholder, "Fundamentalism," 130.
81. Horst, interview.
82. Minutes of the Franconia Mennonite Conference Executive Committee (4 May 1950), MHC; William Anders, Letter of Resignation (19 March 1950),

Within the year, Anders would oversee the formation of Calvary Mennonite Church.

Reconciliation did not materialize between the Lancaster Conference and Hiestand's group either. A few months after Anders' resignation, Hiestand declared his intent to leave the Lancaster Conference. In response, a contingent of bishops traveled to the Marietta mission on Sunday, September 9, to "take charge of the services at Marietta."[83] Later that month, Hiestand and his supporters, which were most of his mission congregation, began meeting at a local community center. Soon thereafter, the group began construction of Congregational Mennonite Church, and Hiestand began a radio ministry, *The Crusade for Christ Hour*, which was modeled after Detweiler's broadcasts and the fundamentalist programming he had come to embrace.[84]

Somehow Hiestand and Anders learned about each other and their similar experiences. Within a year, they began meeting together along with members from two other congregations that had formed under similar circumstances. They contemplated creating a new Mennonite conference, perhaps an eastern branch of the Ohio Conference, and also met with representatives from the (Old) Mennonite General Conference. These meetings failed to bring about any new Mennonite conference or new Anabaptist affiliation, however. Calvary Mennonite Church and Congregational Mennonite Church remained independent, and eventually both congregations dropped the Mennonite distinction and moved thoroughly into the evangelical world, becoming "nondenominational."

On one level the dissent of Congregational and Calvary confirms the reality of the nondenominational threat depicted in the *Sword and Trumpet* cartoon referenced at the opening of this chapter. It is tempting, therefore, to interpret these defections as evidence of the corrosive influence of evangelicalism. Indeed, just a few years after these defections, Harold Bender called fundamentalism one of the "greatest dangers" that threatened American Mennonites.[85] Yet, as this chapter

---

Towamencin Papers, MHC.

83. Minutes of the Lancaster Mennonite Conference Bishop Board (August 1951), LMHS.

84. On Hiestand's radio broadcasts, see Burkholder, "Fundamentalism," 132–35.

85. Bender, "Outside Influences," 48.

has argued, the fact that these Mennonite misfits and the leaders of the Lancaster and Franconia Conferences failed to find a workable solution may best be explained by the fundamentalist mentality that permeated both sides of these schisms. Even as they were moving toward significant cultural changes that commenced in the 1960s, the Lancaster and Franconia Conferences were still permeated by decades of aggresso-conservative activism that found its expression, at least in part, in opposition to American fundamentalism. In like manner, those caught up in evangelical dissent framed their struggle as one that pitted the fundamentals of free grace, personal salvation, and expedient evangelism against legalism, "works salvation," and missional narrow-mindedness. Regardless of the theological and cultural disagreements that did indeed exist, the uncompromising fundamentalist mentality on both sides made any kind of creative solution impossible. Ironically, these defections may have had more to do with a shared, albeit competing, fundamentalist orientation and less to do with the incompatibility of evangelicalism and Anabaptism.[86]

BIBLIOGRAPHY

Anders, William. 1999. Interview with author. Recording in author's possession. March 2.

———. "Letter of Resignation." 19 March 1950. Towamencin Papers, Mennonite Heritage Center. Harleysville, PA.

Bender, Harold S. "The Office of Bishop in Anabaptist-Mennonite History." *The Mennonite Quarterly Review* 30 (1956) 120–27.

———. "Outside Influences on Mennonite Thought." *Mennonite Life*, January 1955, 45–8.

Blooming Glen Mennonite Church to the Franconia Mennonite Conference Executive Committee. Date unknown. Blooming Glen papers, Mennonite Heritage Center. Harleysville, PA.

Burkholder, Jared S. "Evangelicalism, Fundamentalism, and Religious Dissent in the Lancaster and Franconia Mennonite Conferences, Part I: The Roots of Congregational Mennonite Church, 1930–1955." *Pennsylvania Mennonite Heritage* 24.3 (2001) 2–13.

———. "Evangelicalism, Fundamentalism, and Religious Dissent in the Lancaster and Franconia Mennonite Conferences, Part II: The Separation and Organization of Calvary Mennonite Church, 1930–1955." *Pennsylvania Mennonite Heritage* 24.4 (2001) 2–17.

86. I wish to thank Barry Hankins and Carolyn Wenger, who reviewed a draft of this essay and offered helpful comments, as well as the staff at the Mennonite Historical Library at Goshen College for their research assistance.

---. "Fundamentalism and Freedom: The Story of Congregational Mennonite Church and Calvary Mennonite Church, 1935–1955." MA thesis, Trinity Evangelical Divinity School, 2000.

---. "The Origins of Calvary Mennonite Church, Souderton, Pennsylvania." *Mennonite Historians of Eastern Pennsylvania Quarterly* 5.1 (Spring 2002) 2–6.

Burkholder, Roy S. *Pathways to Renewal: A Narrative History of Neffsville Mennonite Church, 1952–2002.* Lititz, PA: author, 2002.

Carpenter, Joel A. *Revive Us Again: The Reawakening of American Fundamentalism.* New York: Oxford, 1997.

Clemens, Kay. Response to questionnaire. March 1999. In the author's possession.

Franconia Mennonite Conference. "Executive Committee Minutes." 1931–1950. Mennonite Heritage Center, Harleysville, PA.

Gish, Martin. 1999. Interview with author. Recording in author's possession. March 5.

Gross, Mary. 1999. Interview with author. Recording in author's possession. March 2.

Hankins, Barry. *American Evangelicals: A Contemporary History of a Mainstream Religious Movement.* Lanham, MD: Rowman & Littlefield, 2009.

Hiestand, John S. Letter to the Lancaster Mennonite Bishop Board, 1949 [exact date unknown]. Hiestand Family Collection. In the possession of Roy S. Burkholder, Lititz, PA.

Horsch, John. *The Failure of Modernism: A Reply to Harry Emerson Fosdick.* Chicago: The Bible Institute Colportage Association, 1925.

Horst, Leon. 1999. Interview with author. Recording in author's possession. July 10.

Hostetler, Beulah Stauffer. *American Mennonites and Protestant Movements: A Community Paradigm.* Scottdale, PA: Herald, 1987.

---. "Franconia Mennonite Conference and American Protestant Movements 1840–1940." PhD diss., University of Pennsylvania, 1977.

Hughes, Richard T. *Christian America and the Kingdom of God.* Champaign, IL: University of Illinois Press, 2009.

Juhnke, James C. *Vision, Doctrine, War: Mennonite Identity and Organization in America, 1890–1930.* The Mennonite Experience in America 3. Scottdale, PA: Herald, 1989.

Kauffman, J. Howard, and Leo Driedger. *The Mennonite Mosaic: Identity and Modernization.* Scottdale, PA: Herald, 1991.

Kidd, Thomas S. *American Christians and Islam: Evangelical Culture and Muslims from the Colonial Period to the Age of Terror.* Princeton, NJ: Princeton University Press, 2009.

Krabill, Russell R. "John Shank Hiestand, 1909–1992: Mennonite Minister and Founder of the Congregational Bible Church." Elkhart, IN: author, 1992.

---. Letter to John S. Hiestand. 25 July 1949. Hiestand Family Collection. In the possession of Roy S. Burkholder, Lititz, PA.

Lancaster Mennonite Conference. "Bishop Board Minutes." 1935–1951. Lancaster Mennonite Historical Society, Lancaster, PA.

Landis, Ira D. *The Faith of our Fathers on Eschatology.* Lititz, PA: author, 1946.

Lederach, Paul M. *Seeking What Cannot be Seen: The Blooming Glen Mennonite Congregation 250 Years: 1753–2003.* Blooming Glen, PA: Blooming Glen Mennonite Church, 2003.

Marty, Martin E., and R. Scott Appleby. *Fundamentalism Observed.* Chicago: The University of Chicago Press, 1991.

———. *Fundamentalisms Comprehended*. Chicago: The University of Chicago Press, 2004.
Miller, Ernest E. "Use of the Radio Among the Mennonites of Indian-Michigan Conference." *The Mennonite Quarterly Review* 14 (1940) 131–48.
Miller, Lloyd. 1999. Interview with author. Recording in author's possession. July 20.
Moseman, John H. "Fundamentalism versus Modernism." *The Sword and Trumpet* 1.1, January 1929, 20–21.
Nolt, Steven M. "Church Discipline in the Lancaster Mennonite Conference: The Printed Rules and Discipline, 1881–1968" *Pennsylvania Mennonite Heritage* 15 (1992) 1–16.
Ruth, John L. *The Earth is the Lord's: A Narrative History of the Lancaster Mennonite Conference*. Scottdale, PA: Herald, 2001.
———. *Maintaining the Right Fellowship: A Narrative Account of Life in the Oldest Mennonite Community in North America*. Scottdale, PA: Herald, 1984.
Sawatsky, Rodney. "Fundamentalism, Liberalism, and Anabaptism: Mennonite Choices in the 1920's and 1930's." Unpublished paper, 4 December 1978. Lancaster Mennonite Historical Society. Lancaster, PA.
———. "History and Ideology: American Mennonite Identity Definition through History." PhD diss., Princeton University, 1977.
———. *History and Ideology: American Mennonite Identity Definition through History*. Kitchener, ON: Pandora, 2005.
———. "The Influence of Fundamentalism on Mennonite Nonresistance 1908–1944." MA thesis, University of Minnesota, 1973.
Schlabach, Theron F. *Gospel Versus Gospel: Mission and the Mennonite Church, 1863–1944*. Scottdale, PA: Herald, 1980.
———. *Peace, Faith, Nation: Mennonites and Amish in Nineteenth-century America*. Scottdale, PA: Herald, 1988.
Shank, Aaron M. "What is Wrong with the Scofield Bible?" *Gospel Herald*, 11 March 1952, 224–25.
Snyder, C. Arnold. *Anabaptist History and Theology*. Kitchener, ON: Pandora, 1995.
Sweeney, Douglas A. *The American Evangelical Story: A History of the Movement*. Grand Rapids: Baker Academic, 2005.
Stauffer, J. L. "Fundamentals and Fundamentalists." *The Sword and Trumpet* 5.2 (1933) 16–20.
Studer, Gerald C. "Is Fundamentalism Enough?" *Gospel Herald*, 25 May 1948, 486.
Yoder, Nathan Emerson. "Mennonite Fundamentalism: Shaping an Identity for an American Context" PhD diss., University of Notre Dame, 1999.

PART III

Intersecting Concerns

*Anabaptist and Evangelical
Public Witness*

Introduction to Part III

As part of their shared activist impulse, evangelicals and Anabaptists have both maintained a commitment to a robust public witness. Such a public witness, broadly construed, includes a number of intersecting concerns: evangelism, missions, and a host of social and political issues. As the following chapters describe, these intersecting and overlapping concerns create both moments of tension and moments of creative synthesis between these two traditions.

One early experiment in maintaining an evangelical Anabaptist public witness was the Mennonite Brethren in Christ, which consolidated several Anabaptist groups, all of which had evangelical leanings, and would eventually become part of what is now the Missionary Church. Matthew Eaton and Joel Boehner explore the founding of the Mennonite Brethren in Christ and its attempt to integrate evangelicalism and Anabaptism. They focus specifically on the ethical question of war as represented in the *Gospel Banner*, the official serial of the Mennonite Brethren in Christ. Eaton and Boehner argue that the early history of this American denomination demonstrates that evangelicalism and Anabaptism can successfully coexist in a single institution and actually enhance the distinct identity of both traditions by mutually reinforcing the primary concerns of each: nonviolence for Anabaptism and missions for evangelicalism. At the same time, they document how such a creative synthesis can be a tenuous one, with the possibility of one side of the synthesis overwhelming the other.

Unfortunately, historical discussions of Anabaptism and evangelicalism in North America have tended to focus primarily—if not at times exclusively—on white males. The following two chapters, by Felipe Hinojosa and David Swartz, offer helpful correctives to that trend by discussing the relationship of Anabaptism and evangelicalism with special attention to Latinas/os and women, respectively. Hinojosa further examines Mennonite missions by focusing specifically on missionary activity among Mexican Americans in South Texas after World War II. Amid a hotbed of religious competition, Mennonites adopted many of the same outreach methods as evangelicals. But it was the work of the Mennonite Voluntary Service, Hinojosa argues, that ultimately proved more attractive and provided the means for forging the religious identity of these Mexican Americans as both *evangélicos* and *anabautistas*.

Just as missions at times has been a unifying concern between evangelicals and Anabaptists, so too has the realm of politics, especially between socially progressive Anabaptists and the so-called "evangelical left." Highlighting major figures from the 1960s onward, David Swartz and Geoff Bowden each place the Anabaptist-evangelical relationship in its political context. Swartz offers a compelling analysis of the evangelical left that challenges traditional interpretations of the Anabaptist-evangelical relationship. While Anabaptist historians at times portrayed Anabaptists as the victims of evangelicalism's corrupting influences, Swartz demonstrates that among left-of-center evangelicals, Anabaptists have exerted a surprising degree of influence. He notably traces, for example, the influence of Anabaptist author and activist Doris Longacre on the simple living movement as well as the work of Lareta Halteman Finger and a number of other Anabaptist women and men to enable the rise of evangelical feminism in the late 1970s. Swartz also suggests strong continuity between 1970s thinkers and activists such as Ron Sider and John Howard Yoder and contemporary neo-Anabaptist evangelicals such as Gregory Boyd and Shane Claiborne.

Shifting from the historical to the theoretical, Bowden picks up where Swartz leaves off—by examining the "political theologies" of two poles of the evangelical-Anabaptist spectrum, Francis Schaeffer and John Howard Yoder, before examining Jim Wallis' attempt at a middle ground—in order to elucidate some of the key points in which tension between these two traditions has existed. While he ultimately endorses Yoder's approach, Bowden concludes by calling for renewed discussion between Christians on the right and the left about how to witness faithfully to God's redemptive activity in the political sphere.

8

Practicing Peace, Embracing Evangelism

Missional Tensions in the Mennonite Brethren in Christ Church

MATTHEW EATON and JOEL BOEHNER

INTRODUCTION

THE MISSIONARY CHURCH USA, an evangelical denomination, finds its beginnings in the confluence of Anabaptism and late nineteenth-century revivalism. The Mennonite Brethren in Christ Church (MBIC), a precursor to the United Missionary Church (UMC) and Missionary Church, began in large part due to a Mennonite preacher from Ohio with a bold, bass voice—Daniel Brenneman. As a reluctant founder of the MBIC, Brenneman's life as an otherwise traditional Mennonite was changed as he began to embrace aspects of religious practice theretofore reserved for revivals. His religious concerns would come to characterize much of the early life of the MBIC as a denomination seeking to do the Lord's work through the simultaneous pursuit of peace and evangelism.

At age twenty-two, Daniel Brenneman, by his own account, was brought under deep conviction of sin and guilt, repented of his sins, experienced the joy of forgiveness, yielded himself to the Lord's service, and united with the Church of his fathers, the Mennonite

Church, in Fairfield County, Ohio. In this same year he would also be married and ordained. At age thirty, Brenneman moved his family to Elkhart County, Indiana to "spend and be spent in the work of Him who has so evidently called me into His service."[1] However, Brenneman's willingness to hold church services in both German and English and to incorporate multi-part singing, each of which were accepted elements of Mennonite practice in Ohio, put him at odds with the local bishop for the similarity of these practices to the protracted meetings of the revivalists.

At thirty-eight Brenneman would co-lead the first Mennonite protracted camp meeting with J. F. Funk and two years later, in 1874, he would be excommunicated from the Mennonite church.[2] Yet, importantly, Brenneman was not the only Mennonite preacher renewed by an emphasis on personal salvation and drawn to the practices of multi-part singing, testimony meetings, and English preaching. Brenneman found himself along with Solomon Eby, J. F. Funk, and J. A. Krupp as a part of the progressive element of the Mennonite church, all of whom would eventually be formally expelled from the church for disagreement over method. Although these methods brought more emotion into the corporate worship experience of the church, Brenneman's move to embrace them seems to be quite deliberate as he traveled on multiple occasions to Port Elgin, Ontario to observe and evaluate the similar revival practices of Solomon Eby, who emphasized "holiness" teaching and religious experience.

Though Brenneman in Indiana and Eby in Ontario are two of the figures in this Mennonite movement of progressive practice who are most available to the contemporary Missionary Church, this phenomenon of Mennonite preachers getting excommunicated for embracing the enthusiastic practices of the revivalists extended to other states—such as Pennsylvania, Ohio, and Michigan—as well as to other communities within Indiana and Ontario. Being excommunicated from the church into which he was baptized would remain a source

---

1. Brenneman, "Letter to C. Henry Smith," 42.

2. The telling of the origins of the MBIC in this essay differs from the popular, oral history often told in Missionary Church and Mennonite circles, which tends to cast Brenneman as a solitary, brash innovator happily leaving his Mennonitism behind. Rather we see Brenneman at the fore of a larger religious trend of Mennonites embracing revivalism and as a self-identifying Mennonite who also deeply embraced evangelical concerns.

of sorrow for Daniel Brenneman to the end of his days, yet this occasion gave Brenneman cause to reflect on where these "sheep without the fold"[3] might find fellowship. From the Dunkard Brethren to the Quakers, Free Methodists, and the Evangelical Association, even when some common ground was found, there would inevitably be elements of practice or belief that made a complete union inviable. For example, while the Evangelical Association would have been a good fit with the progressive methods of the newly excommunicated Mennonites, and they impressed Brenneman with their hospitality, some of the barriers to finding fully contented fellowship in the midst of the Evangelical Association included the sanctioned practice of infant baptism and the toleration of warfare. According to Brenneman, "Thus we were led to feel that 'in union there is strength,' and that in order to be successful in the work of the Lord, there needed to be organized effort upon the basis of a union of sentiment founded upon the word of the Lord, and hence labored to accomplish this end."[4] Thus, the best place for these "displaced" Mennonites seemed to be with one another.

To this end, the Mennonite Brethren in Christ Church was officially formed in 1883 out of the Evangelical United Mennonites and the Brethren in Christ. But the brief, conglomerating institutional affiliations of the forebears of the MBIC suggest that excommunicated Mennonites throughout the Great Lakes region were often looking for fellowship with one another. The Evangelical United Mennonites were formed in 1879 out of the Evangelical Mennonites of Pennsylvania and the United Mennonites.[5] The United Mennonites were formed out of the Reforming Mennonite Society and the New Mennonite Church of Canada West in 1875.[6] The trend of Mennonites excommunicated for their methods clustering together reached something of a terminus in the MBIC which, once formed, bound together excommunicated Mennonite groups in Ontario, Indiana, Ohio, and Pennsylvania.

One such binding force of the early MBIC was the *Gospel Banner*, which was founded in 1878 by Daniel Brenneman, five years before the MBIC proper came to be. The *Gospel Banner* would serve as the "denominational organ" of the MBIC and the UMC from the 1870s up

---

3. Brenneman, "Letter," 49.
4. Ibid., 50.
5. Huffman, *History of the Mennonite Brethren in Christ Church*, 77.
6. Ibid., 59.

through the 1960s, performing the simultaneous functions of newsletter, catechetical tool, and tract. Recognizing the importance of the *Gospel Banner* as well as its ability to illustrate the development of the MBIC, we use it here as a major source for our conclusions in this essay.

The newly formed not quite Mennonite but Mennonite and not quite evangelical but evangelical MBIC found itself with the dual emphases of spreading the gospel and bringing new believers into the church while maintaining traditional Anabaptist positions on baptism, war, and simplicity. Of particular interest in this essay is the articulation of the peace position within the MBIC, which stands as a litmus test for how Anabaptist this newly formed evangelical church would remain. Discussions in the *Gospel Banner* regarding the proper Christian attitude toward war reveal a denomination that, for a time, would hold in tandem both a robustly evangelistic agenda and an Anabaptist position on war.

1880–1900

Daniel Brenneman once described the Anabaptist and evangelical calling of the MBIC: "Nearly half a century ago, there came a crisis in our dear old Mennonite Church, in which some of us had for years been identified as members and ministers of the Gospel. Conviction increased upon our consciences that as a non-resistant church (whose principles and doctrines we so highly appreciated), we were largely wanting in earnest effort to more vigorously pursue these—to us—sacred principles and doctrines, at home and abroad."[7] As this calling was realized, new beliefs and new believers would mix with long-held beliefs and older believers as the MBIC conducted revivals and camp meetings that brought many new believers into the church. Yet as natural as such a situation may seem for an evangelical church, it was at the time actually quite remarkable for a Mennonite denomination to be so successful in bringing in people new to the faith who were not other Mennonites. Mennonite historian John Wenger said of the MBIC, "They actually win converts from non-Mennonite homes. In this respect the Mennonite Brethren in Christ have more nearly recaptured the Anabaptist vision of 1525–30 than

---

7. Brenneman, "Origin of the *Gospel Banner*," 10.

any other branch of Mennonites."⁸ Also significant about the MBIC's robust evangelistic agenda was that it represented a near complete departure from the old Mennonite way of living the Christian life, which focused almost exclusively on the preservation of the community. So, as new beliefs and new believers flowed into the church, the theological composition as well as the ethnic composition of members became increasingly American and less distinctly Mennonite. Yet non-resistance remained.⁹

The first article to appear in the *Gospel Banner* on the subject of war reflects the varied theological composition in the MBIC. This article, titled "Wesley's View on War," consists of passages gleaned from Wesley's writings and speaks to the strong Methodist streak that runs through this denomination as well as the desire to reconcile outside doctrines to inside doctrines.¹⁰ Here, the article makes reference to Wesley's condemnation of war: "Now, who can reconcile war, I will not say to religion, but to any degree of reason or common sense?" This critique of war appeals to common sense and civility among the nations. The concern was that power should not be seen as determining what is right. Even though this argument is not exactly the stuff that Anabaptist non-resistance is made of, it seems that a disapproval of war was good enough when it came to incorporating Wesleyan-holiness doctrine.

The nature of the MBIC's incorporation of Wesleyan-holiness doctrine is apparent in an article that features a letter from a young Methodist minister who bemoans the "principles of [the] war demon" that are upheld by his fellow Methodist preachers around the nation.¹¹ This article also touches on the most enduring and dominant argument for non-resistance in the *Gospel Banner*, namely that the principles of war are at variance with Christianity—that there is a fundamental incongruity between participation in war and the proper Christian life as determined by the Word. A recurring rhetorical question is, "How could a Christian participate in War while behaving as a Christian should?" Specifically, the article probed, "Is there a Christian way of

---

8. Wenger, *Glimpses of Mennonite History and Doctrine*, 123.

9. For a preliminary analysis of this era in the MBIC on which this section builds, see Boehner, "Into the World," 4–19.

10. Wesley, "Wesley's View on War," 3.

11. Graham, "Noble Resolution," 34.

burning villages?"[12] Often argument of incongruity would make reference to those portions of Scripture that exemplify Christ's teaching on war and peace. The MBIC held to a reading of Romans 13 that allowed for Christians to opt out of endorsing their civil government. This interpretation provided a biblical foundation for the MBIC's conception of the proper relationship between Christians and their government.

However, as important as Romans 13 might have been for the biblical justification of the Christian's proper relationship to government, in the 1880s the issue lacked the urgency that would accompany it if the nation had been in a time of war. The main concern of the MBIC in the 1880s is less on enforcing a proper relationship with the civil government and more on nurturing and teaching the body of believers, new and old; hence, the importance placed upon a proper reading of Scripture. It would even seem that there are ties between non-resistance and holiness as non-resistance can be taken to exemplify sinlessness in the face of trial and temptation. In this sense non-resistance fit rather naturally into the holiness influence of these revival-driven years. Non-resistance was also vital in a new way as this exemplification of the peace witness was purposefully extended beyond the insular community.

During these early years of the denomination the doctrine of non-resistance remained despite the inclusion of non-Mennonite theology and believers in the MBIC, as non-resistance was reconciled with the newer theologies that came with revivalism and increased immersion in American culture. Non-resistance complemented and reinforced the Church's primary concerns of living a holy life and spreading the gospel; and as interest increasingly turned to places both close to home and abroad as mission fields, the manner in which new evangelistic opportunities were presented invited comment and re-evaluation of doctrine as well as action. As early as 1884, one year after the MBIC officially came into being, a young woman in her early twenties named Janet Douglas was recognized by the MBIC as the church's first "mission worker."[13] Janet Douglas and other City Mission workers, mostly women, labored for the Lord in urban centers in Michigan, Ohio, Northern Indiana, and Ontario. Involvement in urban life brought the MBIC face-to-face with challenges to pacifism, namely the increased

12. "Fair Test," 87.
13. Lageer, *Merging Streams*, 75.

possibility of crime and violence. MBIC responses to these challenges fit squarely within traditional Anabaptist doctrine, as expressed in the Schleitheim and Dordrecht confessions, and involved recognizing the use of the sword by the civil magistracy.

With the onset of the Spanish-American War, the MBIC struggled to understand the role of the U.S.A. and themselves within the expanding empire of the United States. As it was earlier, a prime concern of the MBIC was still with outreach even as they maintained a strong grasp on the importance of the doctrine of non-resistance and the peace witness. The Spanish-American War was certainly not explicitly endorsed in the *Gospel Banner* but neither was it denounced outright. Rather the expansion of the American empire, though not necessarily tied to the expansion of God's kingdom, was recognized as making new mission fields possible. New mission fields, it appears, could be to the MBIC a redeeming quality of this war. Christian Nysewander completes this gospel spreading allegory by equating salvation with "celestial liberty" and renaming missions "celestial imperialism."[14] This article, though allegorical, does serve to describe the prevailing concept of missions. The odd paradox of militant peace and imperialistic freedom that this idea represents is quite striking, and it seems that this paradox is meant to both subvert imperialism by presenting a higher kind of imperialism and, in a way, to give imperialism its due for the opportunities that now exist for the expansion of God's kingdom.

This discussion of war and non-resistance at the end of the nineteenth century addressed the proper way to engage the world more broadly than before. Non-resistance remained the proper personal manifestation of a Christian's contact with the world, but this era of expansion brought new and different concerns to the larger church body. The drive to spread the gospel brought the MBIC into contact with new people and places; and as the MBIC encountered the realities of life in an urban setting, they called on their Mennonite heritage to guide their actions and thought. As the Mennonites of the MBIC labored to bring the gospel to the world, they also strived to remain peaceful and pure. Mennonite principles and Wesleyan-holiness teaching dynamically reinforced each other in these years, and actively engaging the world in an urban setting brought the MBIC back to some

14. Nysewander, "Imperialism," 4.

of Anabaptism's earlier guiding principles. The Spanish-American War provided new missions opportunities for this outward-looking Anabaptist denomination as the "rusty old gates" of the Pacific islands opened, and the MBIC stepped further into the world.[15]

1900–1925

During the period surrounding World War I (1900–1925), we see continued development of an evangelical emphasis on outreach and a traditional Anabaptist emphasis on peace—and the clearest overlap between the two in the MBIC. Though the *Gospel Banner* cannot tell us the whole story of what is happening in the MBIC, it is clear that during this period many see evangelism and peace as intimately connected even if this idea is articulated in various ways.

In this period, there are essentially three ways in which the *Gospel Banner* speaks of peace and war. Most commonly, the authors describe war as (1) an aberration of the will of God in which no one may justifiably participate.[16] In these articles there are no redemptive qualities in armed conflict, and war is portrayed as an absolute evil.[17] Alternatively, there are some voices in the *Gospel Banner* which suggest (2) that God does not cause or support war but both allows and subversively uses war for a greater good.[18] War is still sinful, and Christians are by no means allowed to participate, but God may providentially bring about the divine will through these international conflicts. Finally, there is a minority voice asserting (3) that God may indeed not merely cause wars, but that God may also use them in a positive way to accomplish the divine will. This thinking is found most often within a dispensationalist framework of history,[19] though there are examples within the *Gospel Banner* supporting the idea that

---

15. Ibid.

16. One more example of a potentially divergent view where war is permissible for those outside the church is found in Hygema, "Spiritual Vaccination," 3.

17. See, e.g., "Is the Lord in War?" 10; Yoder, "Shall We Fight?" 3. Many more such references could be produced.

18. This is seen, e.g., in an interpretation of the Russo-Japanese (1904–1905), where Russia is seen as disciplined for persecuting Jews. Hallman, "War in the East," 1. For an example during the World War I period, see, "Peace not War," 5.

19. See Brenneman, "Carnal Warfare," 3; Coate, "Should Christians Engage in War?" 2.

God may indeed continue to ordain and positively use war regardless of time period. War in this view may be the will of God to open up new avenues for the spread of the gospel.[20]

Just as there were differing understandings of the nature of peace, there were different justifications for this position. The most common reason cited for the evil nature of war was that it simply contradicted the nature of God as seen through the person of Jesus Christ. This is the foundation of all non-resistant thought throughout the history of the MBIC. In addition to the moral and religious reasons for condemning war, much of the rationale is highly pragmatic. A second line of thought for the illegitimacy of war often cited during this period of the *Gospel Banner* is that it simply costs too much and is not a reasonable or practical way of settling conflict. The reasoning here approaches the liberal pacifism that is prominent between the world wars, though pragmatic concerns among the MBIC are often connected to religious and moral views and are thus typically not the sole or primary reasons for refusing to condone violence.

Often, the religious/pragmatic condemnation of war approaches the topic from the perspective of evangelism and mission. As evangelism is at the heart of MBIC thought and history, it is not surprising that it makes its way into the traditional Anabaptist polemic against the practice of war. While there are a few dissenting voices concerning this position, the dominant view expressed in the *Gospel Banner* at this time is that war fundamentally undercuts mission.

As mentioned above, there are places where the *Gospel Banner* condemns war on pragmatic grounds for wasting valuable resources on illegitimate solutions to solve conflict. However, these pragmatic grounds for condemning war often contain an underlying missional logic. The pragmatic critique of violence is largely made in light of the perceived need for worldwide mission to spread the gospel. A paradigmatic example of this type of critique comes from C. H. Brunner: "The folly of building warships that cost $15,000,000 apiece! What a waste of money! Enough money [is] spent on one of the modern type super-dreadnoughts to support 40,000 missionaries for one year and build 1,000 churches . . . One single discharge from one of our big guns costs more than 100 barrels of flour to feed the poor or as much as it costs to support two missionaries for one year. . . . Even the

---

20. Woodring, "War in the Old and New Testaments," 3.

preservation of peace in this age is very expensive."[21] The attitude here is clear: resources should be put into humanitarian aide and endeavors worthy of the gospel. It may not be that Brunner literally thought this money should be spent by the U.S. on funding the mission of the church, though several authors in the *Gospel Banner* during this period believe that there is a call for the U.S. to obey the teachings of Jesus. Regardless of the literal meaning of passages like these, the message is clear: war violates the spirit of mission and evangelism, which seeks to bring hope and humanitarian aide to the world instead of death and destruction.

Another helpful example illustrating this convergence of evangelistic fervor and an Anabaptist peace witness comes from W. R. Grout's *Gospel Banner* essay, "The Origin of War."[22] In Grout's thinking, war is completely at odds with mission because it does not lead to the life and hope of the gospel. War does the exact opposite of what mission and evangelism does. War brings death, while mission brings life. Violence potentially damns one to hell, while evangelism leads to the inheritance of eternal life. Grout sums up his view towards war and mission as follows: "War is an element that Satan must delight in; for it often cuts off, in their sins, more souls in a day, than by natural death, he can hope to grasp in many years."[23] Missional logic, according to many *Gospel Banner* authors, rejects the logic of force and war. Evangelistic mission is Christ's paradigm for world influence, and the only hope the earth has for lasting peace.[24]

To be accurate to the sources, however, it must be mentioned that there are a few articles in the *Gospel Banner* during this time that potentially dissent from this position. The clearest example of this comes from Richard Woodring's turn of the century article, "War in the Old and New Testament." Woodring's position is that war potentially opens up avenues for the church to extend the gospel to new realms. In these cases, it is not that war is good, but that God may use war to open up

---

21. Brunner, "War," 5.
22. Grout, "Origin of War," 4.
23. Ibid.
24. For the multitude of ways the MBIC envisions coming peace see, e.g., "Christ and War," 5; Brunner, "Editorial," 1; "Cry of Humanity Against War," 9; "A Waste of Life and Money," 5; "In Time of Peace Prepare for War," 6; Hoy, "Justifiable Preparedness," 4; Campbell, "Militarism and Schools," 3; Brenneman, "Gigantic Insanity," 4; Huffman, "Can the American Conscience be Conscripted?" 2–3.

the mission field. In this sense, God uses war to further the Kingdom. There is a missional reading of war here that moves toward a justification of violence for the sake of evangelism, even though Woodring still paradoxically condemns those who participate in conflict. Logic of this type is sparse in the *Gospel Banner* at this time, but its presence is nevertheless significant, as is shows a clear, early example of MBIC members questioning the absolute pacifism of their tradition for the sake of evangelism.

1925–1945

Throughout the periods surrounding the Spanish-American War and World War I, there is solid convergence between a traditional Anabaptist emphasis on peace and an evangelical focus on outreach. Indeed, with few exceptions, the two have gone hand in hand. This robust profession of pacifism and outreach would continue in the *Gospel Banner* during the period surrounding World War II, under the editorial guidance of J. A. Huffman. There is, however, more going on within the MBIC regarding a shifting attitude toward war than what is seen in the *Gospel Banner*. Nevertheless, peace and evangelical activism continue to play a major role in the MBIC for the next two decades. A favorite phrase of Huffman's describing this convergence of Anabaptist and evangelical influences was "super-resistance," a lifestyle that overcomes the power of evil and violence with love as opposed to coercive, violent force. Super-resistance is a move toward a more active peace witness that is not simply concerned with the purity and holiness of the church, but is rather intimately engaged with the world in which it seeks to effect change. In this final period surveyed, we continue to see peace and evangelism connected, though the way this is articulated shifts. Here, with evangelism retaining importance throughout, the emphasis shifts from missions and war to the need for discipleship and education regarding practiced peace among converts in the MBIC.

One such voice for non-resistance education was T. D. Gehret whose interest in such education is framed by the view that "The predictions of Scripture concerning end times are being fulfilled."[25] This

---

25. Gehret, "Carnal Weapons," 2.

end times fervor contributes to a kind of non-resistance of complete withdrawal from the world. However, even though Gehret calls for much separation between Christians and the world, he still calls for active witnessing: "We are 'ambassadors for Christ,' and we have but one object and that is to witness for Christ."[26] For Gehret it would seem that the non-resistant life could be a way of witnessing for Christ, but the utility of the peace witness as an evangelical tool in this climate of apocalyptic urgency is effectively undermined by the belief that the end was so near that a pious faithfulness in the peace witness rather than the evangelical utility of the active peace witness was paramount. So though several in the MBIC are calling for increased non-resistance education, not all are accessing this doctrine with the same perspective as to its function in the church.

Another example of this emphasis on non-resistance education is a speech given at an MBIC youth conference, which thoroughly argues for the incongruity of participation in war and the Christian Life.[27] The usual rhetorical techniques of definition, exegesis, quotes from famous people, and appeals to common sense are evident in the speech, but in addition to these rhetorical strategies, Clayton Severn makes an explicit appeal to tradition and identity and in doing so publicizes the only name in the *Gospel Banner* unmistakably associated with suffering persecution for living out pacifist convictions. Orval Brenneman is upheld as an example of a man who endured in faithfulness and obedience despite persecution surrounding his conscription into World War I. Yet Orval Brenneman was just one of many MBIC members who refused military service in World War I. According to Huffman, even though the church was not prepared for the test that conscription would pose, "It was rare exception when a young man volunteered for army service, and it was not general that so-called 'non-combatant' service was accepted. Most of the young men either secured farm furloughs, thus rendering service of a non-military nature, or where no favorable action could be secured, paid the price of their non-resistant attitude by suffering segregation in military camps or serving sentence in federal prisons."[28] Yet when Severn's speech was given—the late 1930s—another war was on the horizon, and church

---

26. Ibid.
27. Severn, "Should Christians Bear Arms?" 11.
28. Huffman, *History of the Mennonite Brethren in Christ Church*, 164–65.

membership was growing, especially with new, non-Mennonite converts.[29] At this critical juncture, catechizing new believers in the proper attitude toward war becomes an especially pressing matter for those committed to non-resistance as an entailment of discipleship.

If conscription for World War I caught the MBIC unawares, it would seem that they, in spite of a largely favorable outcome in terms of practice, learned from this lesson, for in the lead up to World War II the MBIC took a proactive approach to educating its members. This education included outside Mennonite and Quaker voices that contended for the civilian service option and the non-combatant option respectively. A Mennonite from outside the MBIC, John Horsch, argues in the *Gospel Banner* that serving as a non-combatant is, in principle, identical to regular military service.[30] The non-combatant option, nonetheless, was also endorsed in the *Gospel Banner*. Articles endorsing non-combatant military service express a distinct reverence for America: "I want no one within the sound of my voice to feel that I am casting any reflection upon our national government. I praise God for the power that has made and preserved the United States a democratic nation."[31] More absolutist stances toward Christian participation in war also appear: "I can't have anything to do with war, even if I am drafted."[32] Thus, the *Gospel Banner* reflects the gamut of pacifist responses to World War II conscription. The MBIC's official stance would address all of these positions.

"A Description of the Selective Service Act of 1940" appears in the *Gospel Banner* less than one month after it was signed into law.[33] The nuts and bolts of the bill are spelled out in this reprint from the Peace Committee of the Mennonite Church to which Huffman adds some observations and suggestions:

---

29. The evangelistic program of the MBIC can be partially illustrated through a survey of the population growth of the MBIC from 1900–1968. From 1900–1951 the MBIC grew from 5,020 members to 13,920 members. In 1955, the numbers decrease to 10,233 as a result of losing the Pennsylvania conference over doctrinal matters but increase to 11,871 members in 1968. These statistics are taken from the minutes of the General Conference meeting that typically took place every four years.

30. Horsch, "So-Called Non-Combatant Military Service," 5.

31. Ditmer, "Position of a Young Man in Case of War," 1.

32. Eikenberry, "If I am Drafted—What Then?" 9.

33. Huffman, "Description of the Selective Service Act of 1940," 2.

> That there are two CO options, non-combatant service and civilian service, is cause for thanks. No provision was requested or granted for an 'absolutist' position because 'there is some obligation owed by every citizen to his country at all times.' A 'quiet, unassuming, and prayerful, but positive manner' along with the advantage of having been raised in a non-resistant faith are ways of dealing with the misunderstandings and persecution that should be expected by those requesting civilian service. Nonetheless, in a climate of war hysteria, conscientious objectors should be prepared to suffer.[34]

Later, Huffman will explicitly endorse the civilian service option, arguing that serving in a non-combatant role too closely associates the CO with the practice of making war.[35] Thus, the MBIC's official stance on the proper manner of service for draftees in World War II was civilian service. Yet despite relatively greater proactive non-resistance and selective service education in the lead up to World War II, in 1943, the MBIC, consisting of 12,860 total members, saw a mere 81 serve in civilian service capacity.[36]

It should be noted that, as valuable as the material from the *Gospel Banner* is, these numbers suggest there are clear limitations to what it can tell us about the character of the MBIC/UMC regarding attitudes toward war and peace. The attitudes expressed in the *Gospel Banner* reflect strongly the convictions of its editors. Thus, the articles printed in the *Gospel Banner*, largely in support of non-resistance, cannot attest to the overall position of the church as a whole, but to the position of some of the leadership in the MBIC. While evidence in the *Gospel Banner* is sparse regarding a divergence of opinion, at least until the post-World War II era, evidence of unrest is present in A. B. Yoder's editor's report to the 1943 General Conference. Yoder, in his last year as editor of the *Gospel Banner*, reports that "the war situation has presented to the Editor some very perplexing problems, due to the difference of opinions on the war question as held

---

34. Ibid.

35. Huffman, "Christian and War," 6. See also Gehman, "Christian's Attitude Toward War," 3.

36. Gehret and Wolf, *Proceedings of the Mennonite Brethren in Christ Church*, 68. Fifty Canadian MBIC members opted for alternative service, and thirty-one Americans opted for civilian service.

by our different Conferences. It is my opinion as Editor of the *Gospel Banner* that the Church paper should stand out against those things that destroy life rather than save it."[37] Clearly, as editor of the *Gospel Banner*, Yoder's agenda was to promote a position of non-resistance. Thus, the character of the *Gospel Banner*, at least under Yoder's time as editor, but clearly under others as well, reflected a position of non-resistance despite this not being a universally shared conviction in the church. Apparently by 1943 there was a strong enough rejection of non-resistance that Yoder experienced notable tension regarding the position advocated by the *Gospel Banner*. The most we can say for sure is that by the mid 1940s, the character of the church was undergoing a dramatic shift in opinion on the war question even as the evangelical emphases of the church remained.

CONCLUSION

While we cannot fully respond to the question of what led the MBIC/UMC to eventually reject their Anabaptist peace witness, we make a tentative suggestion here—that, despite the earlier symmetry between peace and evangelism, eventually an underlying tension found in the context of mid-twentieth century America led to the MBIC's move away from practiced peace. In this context, a strongly patriotic, national culture ultimately shaped the evangelistic agenda of the MBIC such that a traditional Anabaptist peace stance was no longer a boon to evangelical efforts but a barrier.[38]

37. Ibid., 11.

38. The issue of Anabaptist-Mennonite identity loss, especially in terms of a practiced peace, has been discussed elsewhere in relation to other particular Mennonite groups. Some, such as Rodney Sawasky and Theron Schlabach, argue that fundamentalism had infiltrated Mennonitism leading to an eventual demise of its Anabaptist identity. Others, such as Nathan Yoder, make the case that it is not as simple as a fundamentalist influence changing the identity of some Mennonite churches; he argues, rather, that there were other internal issues that allowed Anabaptist distinctives to fall by the wayside. While there are certainly some commonalities between the MBIC and the other Mennonite groups who have been researched more thoroughly, it remains to be seen whether there are significant parallels between these Mennonite groups and the MBIC. More comparative work between the MBIC and other Mennonite groups is needed to establish any substantive link. As such links may be formed, a mitigating factor is the degree to which the MBIC was, in fact, fundamentalist. To this end it would seem that their evangelical and Anabaptist concerns

It is hardly necessary to establish the fact that the MBIC/UMC holds the call of the Great Commission as foundational to their organization as a church. The founders of what would become the MBIC/UMC were heavily influenced by Wesleyan and Keswickian holiness revival movements sweeping across North America in the late nineteenth century.[39] Through tent meetings, itinerant evangelism, the creation of mission schools, missions abroad, and urban ministry, the MBIC was centrally focused on "winning souls." While revivalism at the end of the nineteenth and into the twentieth century is not a monolithic ideology, it is clear that "soul winning" was at the heart of the movement.[40] In describing one group of American revivalists, George Marsden writes, "A major element in the movement, well developed in nineteenth century revivalism, was the subordination of all other concerns . . . to soul-saving and practical Christianity."[41] While there were clearly concerns other than simply "soul-winning" in the revivalist and holiness movements, evangelism took pride of place. The *Gospel Banner*, for example, is filled with appeals to holy living, which were to characterize the believer after new birth. The gospel was to be preached to the world bringing with it a call to conversion that would radically alter one's relationship to sin. This emphasis on evangelism provides a scenario where the salvation of one's soul takes precedence over all else, with holiness to follow from true conversions. Practiced peace came to be understood in this context as a manifestation of personal holiness, yet as "soul winning" emerged as the primary emphasis of the MBIC/UMC, practiced peace became one of many manifestations of holiness in the believer's life. As holiness teaching, then, fell out of favor to a more mainstream evangelical teaching emphasis after World War II, practiced peace all but disappears from the popular life of the denomination.

One such indication of a shift toward a brand of Christianity more palatable to mainstream America is the 1947 name change when the Mennonite Brethren in Christ Church became the United Missionary

---

prevent them from fitting the fundamentalist label fully. See, e.g., Sawatsky, *History and Ideology*; Schlabach, *Gospel Versus Gospel*; Yoder, "Mennonite Fundamentalism."

39. See also Huffman, *History of the Mennonite Brethren in Christ*; Lageer, *Merging Streams*, 17–23, 32–64, for the early history of the MBIC.

40. On the polyphonic character of revivalism, see Marsden, *Fundamentalism and American Culture*, 43–48.

41. Ibid., 43.

Church. Motivating this name change was a perceived need to present the gospel apart from a tradition so fundamentally grounded in practiced peace. To become Mennonite could have been seen by potential converts in this period as being un-American due to the traditional Anabaptist-Mennonite rejection of violence and military service. In a period of patriotic fervor to be expected during war time, it seems quite reasonable for a church whose primary focus is evangelism to attempt to remove any barriers to the potential conversion of "lost souls."[42] There is clear evidence of persecution of groups who refused to support this and other wars. The MBIC of the World War I period endured such persecution, but by World War II the popular will of the MBIC expressed itself as men overwhelmingly chose military service over conscientious objector status. At the time of the name change many people within the MBIC were embracing this national spirit, while also expressing fear that potential converts would reject the gospel from a group associated with non-resistance. Despite substantial catechetical efforts to maintain a peace emphasis, despite the demonstrated historic success of peace and evangelism working together, and despite the theoretical theological congruence of these two emphases, the MBIC/UMC ultimately divorced itself from a robust peace witness. Thus, as the members of the MBIC began to more fully embrace the concerns of the nation, and as new converts who already embraced such concerns entered the church from non-Mennonite homes, the identity of the MBIC/UMC continued to change.

The eventual fracturing of the peace witness in the MBIC/UMC is poignantly evident in what could almost be a conversation through time. Early MBIC leader, Jacob Shantz, writes, "Dear Christian Reader, if you are yet influenced with the idea that warfare is right and the duty of the Christian, read faithfully the Gospel of Christ and you will find no passage that sanctions or commands such a thing."[43] The message here is clear: The gospel teaches that Christians should not participate in war. Yet, as seen in the name change in 1947, the momentum of the church regarding war and peace continued to shift. In 1966 a letter from a soldier and presumed UMC church member

---

42. For a discussion of the name change, see Lageer, *Merging Streams*, 305–16, esp. 307. Lageer asserts that the MBIC name "was not conducive to church expansion" (307).

43. Shantz, "Can a Christian Engage in Warfare?" 2.

fighting in the Vietnam War appears in the *Gospel Banner*: "Dear Loved Ones . . . I don't know if I should say this or not, but I trust you will understand. I'm happy to be a Marine. I feel the job I am doing will help my family and my church. Many people asked me why I wanted to go to Vietnam or if I didn't think the war was crazy. Well, I'm not here for Mike Peffley so much. It's for Mother, Pat, and Linda. I don't want anything to happen to them or my country. My family means everything in the world to me."[44] Receiving at least the passing endorsement of the denomination, Peffley's letter home demonstrates how defense of family and national interests are now understood to be appropriate priorities in the life of a disciple. This view epitomizes the post-World War II institutional shift away from the evangelical peace witness of Brenneman, Shantz, and numerous other voices in the church and toward a more mainstream American evangelicalism.

In spite of this later shift away from the evangelical peace witness of the early MBIC faithful, which is in part due to the privileging of an evangelical emphasis, an unequivocally global approach to missions and evangelism, it appears, can bring the importance of practiced peace back into relevance within the denomination. Even late in the *Gospel Banner*'s history and well into the period beyond which the MBIC/UMC can be considered a peace church, a voice identifying the necessary convergence of peace and mission comes from J. A. Toews:

> It is our deep conviction that one of the chief reasons for the church's failure in world evangelization has been her inconsistency and compromise in the question of war. Almost insuperable barriers have been raised for missionary efforts as a result of this tragic compromise of the church's call and calling. Sometimes the question arises in our mind whether the church has not destroyed as many lives by her participation in the wars of the world as she has saved through all her missionary efforts.[45]

Despite not being a member of the UMC, Toews' comments are endorsed by some of the UMC, giving a final witness in the *Gospel Banner* that the dual emphases of peace and evangelism do not have to be abandoned for the UMC to carry out its mission. Though the UMC can no longer be considered a peace church, the presence of this

---

44. Peffley, "Written on the Way to Vietnam," 7.
45. Toews, "Christian and War," 10.

article indicates that there are likely still some who refuse to embrace war while maintaining a radical call to mission. Toews' comments, like those above, embrace both a Mennonite-holiness peace ethic and a fervent call to spread the gospel to the ends of the earth. War, in all of these voices, contradicts the missional logic that the MBIC/UMC had embraced so long ago. Peace and evangelism could have partnered more dynamically in the mission of the church, but in the MBIC/UMC and her current manifestation, the Missionary Church, this partnership is characterized by a distinct privileging of evangelism over and above a practiced peace.

BIBLIOGRAPHY

Boehner, Joel. "Into the World: How War and Missions Transformed the Early Mennonite Brethren in Christ Church, 1880–1900." *Reflections* 8.2 (2004) 4–19.

Brenneman, Daniel. "Letter From Daniel Brenneman to C. Henry Smith." *Reflections* 6 (2002) 41–50.

———. "The Origin of the *Gospel Banner*." *Gospel Banner*, 25 October 1917, 10.

Brenneman, T. H. "Carnal Warfare: Should a Christian Engage in It?" *Gospel Banner*, 11 November 1915, 3.

———. "Gigantic Insanity." *Gospel Banner*, 28 August 1919, 4.

Brunner, C. H. "Editorial." *Gospel Banner*, 25 November 1909, 1.

———. "War." *Gospel Banner*, 8 February 1912, 5.

Campbell, Gertrude. "Militarism and Schools." *Gospel Banner*, 15 February 1917, 3.

"Christ and War." *Gospel Banner*, 21 October 1905, 5.

Coate, Lowell H. "Should Christians Engage in War?" *Gospel Banner*, 13 January 1921, 2.

"The Cry of Humanity Against War." *Gospel Banner*, 11 March 1909, 7, 9.

Ditmer, R. P. "Position of a Young Man in Case of War." *Gospel Banner*, 9 November 1939, 1.

Eikenberry, Lorrell S. "If I am Drafted—What Then?" *Gospel Banner*, 18 January 1940, 9.

"Fair Test." *Gospel Banner*, 1 June 1881, 87.

Gehret T. D., and N. G. Wolf, editors. *Proceedings of the Mennonite Brethren in Christ Church: Fourteenth General Conference, 1943*. Kitchner, Ontario, 1943.

Gehret, Timothy D. "Carnal Weapons." *Gospel Banner*, March 1931, 2.

Gehman, Wilbert. "Christian's Attitude Toward War." *Gospel Banner*, 2 April 1942, 3.

Graham, W. Q. A. "A Noble Resolution." *Gospel Banner*, 1 March 1880, 34.

Grout, W. R. "The Origin of War." *Gospel Banner*, 19 January 1922, 4.

Hallman, Henry. "The War in the East." *Gospel Banner*, 15 July 1905, 1.

Horsch, John. "So-Called Non-Combatant Military Service." *Gospel Banner*, 22 June 1939, 5.

Hoy, George W. "Justifiable Preparedness." *Gospel Banner*, 30 March 1916, 4.

Huffman, J. A. "Can the American Conscience Be Conscripted?" *Gospel Banner*, 30 October 1919, 2–3.

———. "Christian and War." *Gospel Banner*, 12 February 1942, 6.

———. "Description of the Selective Service Act of 1940." *Gospel Banner*, 3 October 1940, 2.

———. *History of the Mennonite Brethren in Christ Church*. New Carlisle, OH: Bethel, 1920.

Hygema, Jacob. "Spiritual Vaccination." *Gospel Banner*, 7 March 1918, 3.

"In Time of Peace Prepare for War." *Gospel Banner*, 4 February 1915, 6.

"Is the Lord in War?" *Gospel Banner*, 10 October 1903, 10.

Lageer, Eileen. *Merging Streams: Story of the Missionary Church*. Elkhart, IN: Bethel, 1979.

Marsden, George. *Fundamentalism and American Culture*. New York: Oxford University Press, 2006.

Nysewander, Christian. "Imperialism." *Gospel Banner*, 3 November 1900, 4.

"Peace not War." *Gospel Banner*, 1 July 1915, 5.

Peffley, Michael. "Written on the Way to Vietnam." *Gospel Banner*, 27 January 1966, 7.

Sawatsky, Rodney. *History and Ideology: American Mennonite Identity Definition through History*. Anabaptist and Mennonite Studies 5. Kitchener, ON: Pandora, 2005.

Schlabach, Theron F. *Gospel Versus Gospel: Mission and the Mennonite Church, 1863–1944*. Studies in Anabaptist and Mennonite History 21. Scottdale, PA: Herald, 1980.

Severn, Clayton W. "Should Christians Bear Arms?" *Gospel Banner*, 10 February 1938, 11.

Shantz, Jacob Y. "Can a Christian Engage in Warfare?" *Gospel Banner*, April 1879, 2.

Toews, J. A. "The Christian and War." *Gospel Banner*, 29 December 1966, 10.

"A Waste of Life and Money." *Gospel Banner*, 14 May 1914, 5.

Wenger, John C. *Glimpses of Mennonite History and Doctrine*. Scottdale, PA: Herald, 1959.

Wesley, John. "Wesley's View on War." *Gospel Banner*, August 1878, 3.

Woodring, Richard. "War in the Old and New Testaments." *Gospel Banner*, 13 October 1900, 3.

Yoder, A. B. "Shall We Fight?" *Gospel Banner*, 17 January 1918, 3.

Yoder, Nathan E. "Mennonite Fundamentalism: Shaping an Identity for an American Context." PhD diss., University of Notre Dame, 1999.

9

"Pool Tables are the Devil's Playground"

Forging an Evangélico-Anabautista Identity in South Texas

Felipe Hinojosa

ON THE MORNING OF March 10, 1936, in Pennsylvania, Mennonite missionaries T. K. Hershey and William G. Detweiler loaded their Ford V-8, bid farewell to their families, and began their trip to the U.S./Mexico borderlands. Their trip, although somewhat late in the missionary timeline, continued a long tradition of missionary activity among the ethnic Mexican population in the Southwest dating back to the latter part of the nineteenth century.[1] From Texas to California, Hershey and Detweiler surveyed the Southwest in hopes of beginning a mission among the growing population of ethnic Mexicans.[2] After traveling more than seven thousand miles, the missionary duo decided the South Texas region (just south of San Antonio) represented the ideal spot, as there resided a "good class of Mexicans, mostly pure

---

1. For more on Protestant missionary efforts in the Borderlands, see Walker-Jones, *Protestantism,* and Martínez, *Sea La Luz.*

2. In this essay I use the term "ethnic Mexican" to describe the Mexican population in the Southwest, regardless of citizenship. This does not suggest that the Mexican origin population was not a racialized group in the Southwest. For more on this term see Gutierrez, *Walls and Mirrors.* I use Mexican American when identifying the population in Mathis, TX, and Latina/o when identifying people of Latin American descent in the Mennonite church.

Mexicans not Spanish Americans, which are harder to reach."[3] For Hershey and Detweiler the desire to evangelize the borderlands represented more than their own missionary zeal, but also a belief that the Mennonite church as a whole was not doing enough to spread the Gospel message. Shortly before their trip, Detweiler expressed his frustration to Hershey: "I do believe that the greatest sin that we as a Mennonite church are guilty of is the failure to render greater obedience to the Great Commission."[4]

Detweiler's frustrations over the lack of evangelical zeal within the Mennonite church highlights a very real tension between those who desired to remain "the quiet in the land" and those who believed in the evangelical mission of the church.[5] As important as this discussion was to the entire church leadership, I suggest that it cannot be understood without the voices of those who formed part of the growing evangelical mission of the church—Mexican Americans in South Texas. Defining the relationship between evangelicalism and Anabaptism, in other words, did not remain the sole domain of Mennonite missionaries.

Although the story of Protestant missions in the U.S./Mexico borderlands is familiar to Latina/o religious studies scholars, the case of Mennonite missionaries presents a new set of questions over the relationship between Anabaptism and evangelicalism. Historically, scholars of Anabaptism have described this movement as a "third way" alternative to either evangelical or Catholic Christianity.[6] But the distinctions have not always been so clear, especially when considering the history of Latina/o Mennonites. When Mennonite missionaries entered Mexican American neighborhoods in South Texas, for example, they did so as unapologetic evangelicals. Yet their message included distinctive Anabaptist teachings, such as pacifism and the importance of community service, which naturally shaped the

---

3. Thirtieth Annual Report, Mennonite Board of Missions and Charities (hereafter MBMC), 10–12 May 1936.

4. The "Great Commission" in Christian communities signifies the call to evangelical work to those who do not "know Christ." William G. Detweiler, file: T. K. Hershey, Box 4, Hist. Mss 1–114. Mennonite Church (hereafter MC) USA Archives, Goshen, IN.

5. For more discussion on the identifier, "the quiet of the land," see Bush, *Two Kingdoms*, 18–29.

6. See, for example, Klaasan, *Anabaptism*, 1–10.

religious identity of the Mexican American congregations they established. As this chapter demonstrates, however, Latina/o Mennonites actively forged an evangelical and Anabaptist identity that was unique to their communities—one that better reflected their own cultural and ethnic context.

The fact that Mexican Americans in South Texas forged this unique identity is representative of the broader Latina/o experience. From mainline groups to rural Mennonites, Latinas/os have historically shifted the confines of religious practices in ways that better reflect not only their ethnic identity, but their understanding of the Bible and theology.[7] Historically, this process has forged a unique religious identity for Latinas/os throughout the Southwest and Latin America as *"los evangélicos."* Indeed, as religious historian Gastón Espinosa correctly asserts, "most Latino Protestants regardless of family grouping see themselves as *Evangélicos* in the Spanish-speaking community."[8] Identifying as an *evangélico* has thus served as a way to unite the multiple traditions and theological orientations that exist within both mainline Protestant and Pentecostal communities.

It is important to emphasize here that the Spanish use of *evangélico* carries different connotations than the popular English version, "evangelical." As is the case with African American evangelical traditions, Latina/o Pentecostal and mainline Protestants have their own history, which in this context speaks to the importance of race, citizenship, and culture along with religious devotion, spirituality, and church missions.[9] One clear example of this comes from the 1980s when many Latino churches (Catholic and Protestant) served as "sanctuary churches" where Central American refugees found rest and a warm meal before continuing their trek north.[10] Many churches continue to serve in this way and in the process present a new way

---

7. Consult Garcia-Treto and Brackenridge, *Iglesia Presbiteriana*; Martínez, *Sea La Luz*; Barton, *Methodists, Presbyterians, Baptists*.

8. Religious historian, Gastón Espinosa, in his introduction to the book *Rethinking Latino/a Religion* correctly identifies Latina/o Mennonites as an "evangelical" group because of their religious patterns of worship and evangelism similar to their evangelical counterparts. See especially page 37.

9. Martínez and Scott, *Los Evangélicos*, xxi; Espinosa, "History and Theory," 69–100.

10. One of those churches was *Iglesia Menonita del Cordero* in Brownsville, TX, where I grew up, which in the late 1980s provided refuge for hundreds of Central American immigrants making their way north.

to think about the politics of immigration and biblical concepts of justice. For this reason, scholars like Juan F. Martínez suggest that Latina/o Protestantism is situated within the borderlands of religion and is often defined as much by its surrounding landscapes, language, and culture as by its theology. Other scholars like David Maldonado, Jr., suggest that the difference lies more along the lines of culture and religious identity than on theological differences between whites and Latinas/os.[11] In other words, "*evangélico*," is not simply a Spanish language version of "evangelical," but instead a religious and cultural movement defined as much by the politics of race and citizenship as by the theology of the "Great Commission."

Understanding the particular history of *evangélicos* in the U.S., therefore, requires scholars to seriously consider Peter Goodwin Heltzel's call for "a new genealogy of evangelicalism."[12] As he argues in his book *Jesus and Justice*, the problem with popular definitions of evangelicalism is that they often do not go far enough in engaging social and cultural politics. In other words, there is rarely a socially contextualized definition of evangelicalism that explores the contradictions and complexities of this religious movement. Doing so, Heltzel argues, might help clarify how the varying strands of evangelicalism formed and developed within the religious histories of marginalized groups like Latinos, African Americans, Native Americans, and Asian Americans.

With an eye toward mapping out a "new genealogy of evangelicalism," this essay examines how the relationship between evangelicalism and Anabaptism played out among the Mexican American population in the small town of Mathis, Texas, after World War II. Mathis was like many small towns in Texas that practiced Jim Crow segregation, prohibited alcohol within its city limits, and, as the local newspaper highlighted, held constant revivals as itinerant preach-

---

11. Martinez, *Sea La Luz*, 149; David Maldonado, Jr., suggests that "while the English word Evangelical primarily has a theological meaning, the Spanish term *evangélico* is used to distinguish Protestant from Roman Catholic identity. "Evangélicos" include non-Catholic Christians from a wide spectrum of theological orientations. The distinction connotes more than doctrinal, theological, or liturgical differences from the Roman Catholic Church. It includes many social, cultural, and identity issues related to having a Protestant identity within a Roman Catholic community. Maldonado, "Protestantes: An Introduction," 10.

12. Heltzel, *Jesus & Justice*, 7–11.

ers visited this small town.[13] Between the 1940s and 1960s, the small town of Mathis was a hotbed of religious activity as Baptists, Pentecostals, Methodists, and Catholics all competed for Mexican American souls. For Mennonite missionaries, religious competition forced them to appropriate many of the approaches of their religious counterparts in order to meet their evangelical impulse to "save souls."[14] They did this by hosting church revivals and requiring that new converts refrain from supposed vices such as dancing, Mexican music, alcohol, tobacco, movies, make-up, shorts, and pool tables. But religious revivals and devotional requirements did not match the attention that the new Voluntary Service (VS) program garnered in 1952. Modeled after the governmental Civilian Public Service program in Puerto Rico during World War II, VS captured the attention of Mexican Americans in Mathis by organizing programs that addressed the educational and healthcare needs of the local community. Mennonite volunteers accomplished this all while being careful not to disturb the racial geography and politics in Mathis.

However, as this essay demonstrates, this two-tier approach of "saving souls" and "patching roofs" did more than increase the number of people in church. It also raised important questions for Mexican Americans around ethnicity, pacifism, and religious identity. Becoming Mennonite often hinged on accepting the central tenets of both John 3:16 and the Sermon on the Mount, but it did not necessarily express a new religious identity where ethnicity takes a back seat to religion. In other words, ethnic identity, even with conversion to a new faith, never yielded to a more powerful religious identity. The racialized realities of Mexican Americans in South Texas often required that religious and ethnic identities coexist and change even as contexts changed. And even with the historic

---

13. *The Mathis News*, 19 September 1946, Issue over dry status in Mathis. "A county wide election has been called for Saturday, October 5 on the question of prohibition in our county." *The Mathis News*, 11 October 1946, "At the vote the county remained wet while Mathis in a vote of 226 dry-195 wet, remained dry."

14. This essay focuses on one particular Mennonite group, the Mennonite Church (MC, or Old Mennonites), which represents one of the oldest Mennonite groups, of Swiss/South German descent in the U.S. While other Mennonite groups, like the General Conference Mennonite church (GCMC) and the Mennonite Brethren (MB) were also involved in missions to Spanish-speaking populations, this essay focuses on the Mennonite Church as it had the largest number of Latinas/os and because it later served as the denominational home for *Iglesia Menonita Hispana*.

link to Anabaptism, becoming Mennonite—in a Mexican American context—meant that one was an *aleluya*, a Mexican American who was also an *evangélico*.[15] As this essay argues, these questions and intersections, which were often raised at late night basketball games or late night church services, helped forge how Mexican Americans thought about their ethnic and religious identities as both *evangélicos* and *Anabautistas*, especially as the rumblings of the Chicano movement loomed large in the late 1960s.[16]

THE RELIGIOUS PREDICAMENT OF MENNONITES IN SOUTH TEXAS

In the late 1930s Lupe De León, Sr., moved his family to Mathis for reasons similar to other Mexican American families making the move—work opportunities. The family worked the fields, and as the eldest son Lupe De León, Jr., commented, "I hated that work with a passion."[17] For the De León family, Mathis was a strategic town. Before Mathis became an agricultural giant in the 1930s, it was mostly a farming and ranching area. However, when the De León family moved to the area, it was the center of agricultural activity, and it had one of the largest populations of migrant farm workers in the nation.

The Chamber of Commerce in Mathis boasted that "Mathis Is as Good as the Best and Better Than the Rest."[18] Mathis' claim to fame revolved around the production of crops like spinach, onion, carrots, cabbage, and of course, cotton.[19] Between about 1935 and 1970, the Vahlsing corporation loomed large in Mathis, hiring Mexican workers and shipping vegetables across the country.[20] Vahlsing controlled

15. "*Aleluya*" was often a term used by Mexican American Catholics toward Mexican American Protestants who Catholics felt always had their hands up in the air singing "aleluya." According to David Maldonado, Jr., the term "aleluya" was often experienced as a form of teasing by Mexican American Catholics to their Protestant counterparts. See Maldonado, *Crossing Guadalupe Street*, 13.

16. See Martinez and Scott, *Los Evangélicos*; Maldonado, *Protestantes/Protestants*.

17. Lupe De León, Jr., interview.

18. Guthrie, *San Patricio County*, 98.

19. "Mathis making steady progress as trucking center," *The Mathis News*, 10 April 1942; "Vahlsing's Interests Growth Parallels Mathis' Gain," *The Mathis News*, 17 October 1952.

20. Guthrie, *San Patricio County*, 98.

his empire from New York and transformed the small community of Mathis into a major hub for the distribution of staple crops.[21] The migration of Mexican Americans to Mathis from surrounding communities prompted the Mennonite Board of Missions and Charities (MBMC) to rethink its mission strategy. This meant leaving the small towns of Normanna and Tuleta, where T. K. Hershey and William Detweiler first established the mission, in search of greener pastures in the upstart agricultural community of Mathis.[22] In addition to establishing a mission outpost in Mathis, MBMC started the Voluntary Service (VS) program and by 1952 counted its first three volunteers. VS came on the heels of the Civilian Public Service (CPS) in Puerto Rico and served as an alternative to military service for Mennonite conscientious objectors, which in the post-World War II era the government labeled as I-W men and women. Whereas CPS in Puerto Rico received its funding and administrative direction from the U.S. government, VS was a church program administered by MBMC.[23]

The transformation of Mathis from a farming and ranching community to a major vegetable producer increased the desire of religious leaders to hold religious revivals in the area. With a population nearing six thousand in the 1950s, Mathis had its share of Protestant denominations, including Baptists, Pentecostals, Methodists, Presbyterians, as well as Catholics—all of which had some form of ministry to the Mexican American population. The local newspaper, *The Mathis News*, frequently promoted "tent revivals" organized by Protestant denominations in the area.[24] Every week a new evangelist from the Baptist, Pentecostal, or Methodist tradition came to Mathis to bring salvation to the growing number of Mexican American farm workers. Religious revivals in Mathis were only a small part of a larger movement in the religious landscapes of postwar America. According to historian Kevin M. Schultz, religion served "as a common cause

---

21. *The Mathis News*, 10 April 1942.

22. Forty-fourth Annual Meeting of the Mennonite Board of Missions and Charities, 10–13 June 1950. The outreach to Mexicans in places like Falfurrias, Tuleta, Normanna, and Helena ceased to exist by 1948.

23. Bush, *Two Kingdoms*, 165–66.

24. In my research of "The Mathis News," which sits in piles at the newspaper office in Mathis, I was amazed to find tent revivals being announced almost on a weekly basis. These events were mostly put on by the local Protestant denominations, including, albeit grudgingly, Mennonites.

in the Cold War against communism."[25] Billy Graham revivals and Pentecostal tent meetings dominated the U.S. landscape as religion became an important marker of identity.[26]

For the most part Mennonite missionaries stayed away from the revival circuit. Excited revivals, loud music, and loud preaching did not appeal to missionaries who continued to debate the use of musical instruments in church and for the most part sang in four part harmonies. By the 1950s, however, Mennonites could no longer avoid the growing popularity of revivals across the country. The religious fervor sweeping the nation, promoted most fervently by evangelists like Billy Graham, captured the imagination of Mennonites as well, and many in church leadership began to view evangelical missions in the U.S. as critically important, if not more so, than foreign missions.

In addition to this religious awakening, demographic shifts were another major reason Mennonites paid particular attention to missions in the U.S. and the Latino community in particular. In the 1950s thousands of Puerto Ricans migrated to New York City and Chicago in large numbers, in what historians have called "the Great Migration."[27] Mennonites took note. "Tens of thousands of Puerto Ricans are coming to the states annually," wrote Nelson Kauffman, "and immigrants from other countries are coming in large numbers and are unevangelized."[28] Kauffman was referencing not only Puerto Ricans in New York, but also the steadily growing numbers of ethnic Mexicans all along the Southwest. As leader of the Mennonite Board of Missions and Charities (MBMC), Kauffman feared that ignoring rapidly changing demographics among the Latino population carried grave consequences for the future of the Mennonite church. The challenge and mere scope of the missionary focus on U.S. soil moved Kauffman to place much of the responsibility on white Mennonite congregations: "The time is here when every congregation of our church should recognize that it *is* a mission church instead of being interested only in *having* a mission church."[29] What followed was the most direct and focused approach to church mission programs aimed

---

25. Consult Schultz, "Religion as Identity," and Prothero, *American Jesus*, 117.
26. Prothero, *American Jesus*, 117.
27. See Virginia Sanchez-Korrol, *Colonia to Community*, 211–18.
28. Kauffman, "Broadening Our Witness."
29. Ibid. Emphasis added.

at Latino communities, from New York to South Texas, in the history of the Mennonite church.

In South Texas, Mennonite missionary Elvin Snyder shared Kauffman's concern for church growth among Mexican Americans. Before the establishment of the VS program, many shared a common sentiment that in Mathis, "the mission program is operating at a minimum and doing little more than competing with Baptists, Pentecostals, and Catholics in trying to get folks to come to Sunday school and church services."[30] It became clear, then, that attracting Mexican Americans to their particular group required appropriating the tenets of mainline Protestant and Pentecostal missionaries. Nelson Kauffman even agreed that Mennonites might "find a great deal in common with the objectives and . . . work of other evangelical groups."[31]

What emerged, then, was a two-tier approach that blended the evangelical styles of mainline Protestant groups with a social services strategy that had served Mennonites well during their CPS days in Puerto Rico. In some cases, Mennonites even took to the migrant trail working alongside Mexican American migrants who worked in the hot and dusty fields of South and West Texas. As a way to maintain contact with newly converted families who were not able to participate in church services year round, Mennonites took to the fields working by day and providing Bible studies a few nights a week for migrant farm workers. One Mexican American family in particular, the Saldivar family, whose work often took them as far away as Minnesota, often served as missionaries in the cotton fields of South Texas bringing families to church for the Sunday and Wednesday services.[32] After several years of this, support from local Mexican Americans and Mennonites in denominational leadership approved the establishment of a church building. In January 1955 they broke ground in Mathis' west side for the *Iglesia Menonita del Calvario*. At its height the Mennonite church in Mathis attracted two hundred Mexican Americans every Sunday morning.[33] For white Mennonites in South Texas, it was a goal reached

30. Snyder, "Mennonite Witness."
31. Kauffman, "Workshop for workers."
32. Conrad, "Calvary Mennonite Church," 161.
33. MBMC Annual Meetings, Church census records between 1952–1968. IV-6-3, MC USA Archives, Goshen, IN.

only by a VS program that provided more that evangelical services, but also social services in order to better compete with mainline Protestants and Pentecostals for Mexican American souls.

VOLUNTARY SERVICE: MEXICAN AMERICAN PERCEPTIONS AND IDENTITY

The VS program in Mathis became a popular destination point for many young white Mennonites. The lure of serving in a "foreign" context without leaving the U.S. was an appealing possibility for many. As one volunteer noted, working in Mathis felt "as much like foreign work as one can get without going outside of the United States."[34] The three central programs of VS came about from the actual needs of Mexican Americans in Mathis—maternity care, kindergarten education, and vacation Bible school. But before any of these programs actually launched, the Mennonite volunteers moving in to Mathis' west side—the Mexican side of town—captured the attention of young children in the neighborhood.

"They came with their long and plain colored dresses and long sleeves," remembered Rosario Gonzalez, "and I started dressing like them as well because I saw it and thought are we supposed to wear that?" Since the VSers were the only white people living on Mathis' west side, their arrival and friendliness seemed quite strange to Rosario. Growing up in Mathis, even as a little girl, Rosario clearly understood her place as a Mexican American. "In Mathis they didn't greet us and we didn't greet them (Anglos), they did their thing and we, well, we were shy, but when the volunteers arrived they showed us no prejudice."[35]

As a way to build trust with local Mexican American families, volunteers opened their homes and invited families to share a meal on Sunday afternoons. One of the first families to accept this invitation was the same De León family who had moved to Mathis ten years earlier. The children, Perfecta, Lupe, and other siblings, began attending vacation Bible school with the VSers after a Mennonite missionary provided the family with a bag of groceries during a particularly dif-

---

34. "Blank Notes," *La Voz de Mathis Newsletter*.
35. Vallejo, interview.

ficult time for the family. The Sunday afternoon meals, remembered Perfecta, introduced the family to the delicious bread VSers baked: "well, we had never eaten rolls and bread and the first time we went my sisters ate the entire loaf of bread with butter and they thought it was funny, but my mother was fuming."[36] Initially there was tremendous excitement about the VSers. They attracted other Mexican American children to participate in craft sessions, activities on Saturdays, and Bible studies. The Gonzalez family benefited as they opened their little store during these times to sell candy to the children. The volunteers taught Rosario's mother how to bake doughnuts and cakes, which were a huge hit, while Rosario's father taught the volunteers how to prepare and roast a pig.

In the 1950s, the plain dressed Mennonite volunteers entered a segregated world where Mexican Americans were relegated to poor working and living conditions, segregated housing, education, cemeteries, and a poor healthcare system. VSers quickly learned that Mexican Americans, who were more accustomed to blank stares and the arrogant apathy of local Anglos, received their good deeds with a certain level of suspicion. But they also knew that their work as both missionaries and social service agents positioned them quite favorably against the racism in Mathis. In Mathis, where segregation and religion were practiced in communion, most Protestant denominations conducted separate services for Anglos and Mexican Americans. Mennonites were an anomaly, however. They were some of the first Anglos to live and commiserate with Mexican Americans on the west side of town. They organized a church where Anglos and Mexican Americans worshipped together and where Spanish was spoken. "Through the unit members' (VSers) quiet work with all racial groups," wrote Boyd Nelson (secretary for Mennonite Board of Relief and Service), "in the community, the maternity home's service to all racial groups, and the kindergarten and construction program operating integratedly, the unit has been effective at bringing community integration at the church level."[37]

For many of the children who first attended the Mennonite church, the pleasant behavior of Anglos came as a shock. "I really did not understand why they were so nice," recalled Perfecta, "because

---

36. Perfecta De León, interview.
37. Nelson, "Relief and Service."

white people in Mathis were so mean—they would spit at us and treat us badly and didn't let us play with them."[38] This does not suggest that Mennonites were above racial prejudice, but it does point to the unique circumstances that Mennonites created within Mathis' religious economy. The social work of Mennonites, for example, even during the fears of communist conspiracies rampant in the 1950s, did not garner the suspicion from the Anglo community in Mathis. Anglos accepted what the Mennonites did as long as they remained on the west side and practiced church missions and did not preach social change. To that end, Mennonite volunteers obeyed the local racial codes and positioned themselves as the parents of lost children. Doing so allowed the VS program to work in areas of social well-being without raising the ire of local Anglos.

The other side of that coin, however, was that while VSers maintained a "friendly paternalism" with Mexican Americans, they nonetheless operated from a safe distance so as to not disrupt the power hierarchy, especially along the lines of gender. Mennonite missionaries and the VS program kept strict guidelines about interracial dating by prohibiting VSers from forging strong relationships, especially between young white women who were reminded to "be friendly to everyone, but single boys." It also limited any activities that brought boys and girls together. VS women were warned: "for a clear Christian testimony and in view of the differences in Latin and Anglo cultures it is advised that you refrain from activities with the opposite sex."[39] But the warnings extended beyond simply being culturally appropriate in South Texas. In the nearby town of Premont, where VSers also held vacation Bible school, one of the more eager participants of VS programs, Ted Chapa, remembered how Mennonites "would come and they would preach to us and live in our community . . . but if one of their sons or daughters wanted to marry a Mexicano or Mexicana that was a no-no and they would open the Bible and explain why that should not happen."[40] Regardless of these warnings, however, relationships developed between white Mennonite volunteers and Mexican Americans that caught the ire of many white Mennonites in leadership.[41]

38. Perfecta De León, interview.
39. See "Group Living Guides."
40. Chapa, interview.
41. Moreover, in order to keep gender groups separate, VSers often practiced

VACATION BIBLE SCHOOLS

Of the programs that the VS program organized, the summer vacation Bible schools were by far the most popular events in Mathis. They attracted nearly one hundred and sixty children every day for the five day-long Bible school.[42] Large numbers like this did not escape the eye of local religious leaders. According to Mennonite missionary T. K. Hershey, children were often warned by the Catholic priest not to attend the Mennonite Bible schools. "A little girl told us," wrote Hershey, "that she could not come anymore because the priest had pulled her ears and pinched her cheeks and arms and told her that she could not attend our bible school under threat of excommunication."[43] The following year the Catholic church planned its own religious school in order to sway young people away from the vacation Bible schools organized by Mennonites and other Protestants in the area. "They [Catholics]," wrote Weldon Martin, "even became bold enough to send a delegation to take from our school the Catholic children."[44]

The protests raised by Catholic leaders highlight the fears some had of losing large numbers of Mexican American children, and thus families, to the new missionaries in town. According to a report titled "Major Problems the Unit Faces," VSers complained that Catholic "sisters" often warned families that their sins would not be forgiven if they continued to send their children to the Mennonite vacation Bible schools. Yet even as VSers launched complaints against Catholic fears, they cloaked their concerns around an evangelical message that labeled Catholicism a hindrance in "reaching them [Mexican Americans] with the True Light." The report even suggested that the evangelical message of Mennonites in Mathis was not being effective

---

harsh discipline on the children who they felt did not receive enough at home. And they consistently strategized over how to "win over" Mexican Americans from Catholicism. One VSer, Savilla Ebersole, did not follow the strict guidelines for punishment. As a result, tensions developed with several of her fellow VSers, and she became a "problem" for apparently believing that the MVS form of harsh discipline on the children in Mathis reflected poorly on their Christian mission. Ironically, VS workers were jealous at the fact that Ebersole made lasting connections with people, especially the young women. See Horst, "Visit to Mathis."

42. Weldon and Martin, "Expanding Mission-Service."
43. Hershey, "Vineyard of God."
44. J. Weldon Martin, "Advances in South Texas."

at luring Mexican Americans away from Catholicism.[45] Similar incidents occurred in the Mennonite mission in Puerto Rico around the same time. There Mennonites reported that Catholics often stood at the entrance of the church in order to persuade people to leave the evangelical church. In some cases, firecrackers were set off to disrupt Mennonite church services.[46]

But the fears constituted more than simply another religious challenge for Catholic leaders in South Texas. Mennonite VSers represented an interesting blend of evangelical methods and cultural idiosyncrasies that attracted and intrigued Mexican Americans. For Mexican American children, attending vacation Bible schools and interacting closely with VSers provided an in-depth glimpse into the cultural idiosyncrasies of white Mennonites. While many children like Rosario Gonzalez and Perfecta and Lupe De León did accept Mennonite religious teachings, this conversion did not fundamentally shift their perception of being Mexican Americans as much as it changed how they lived out cultural norms and practices. For example, popular leisure activities among Mexican Americans such as dancing or going to the movies were prohibited in the newly converted household, as it was in any Protestant home during this era. What made the Mennonite experience different, and what became most relevant to young Mexican American girls especially, found its expression through the body. Becoming Mennonite meant no shorts, no short sleeves, and a conservative dress that mirrored how Mennonites themselves dressed; no dancing, no listening to Mexican rhythms, and of course, no make-up.[47] This represented a fundamental shift for most families, like Rosario's, which often enjoyed dancing in surrounding *ranchitos* around Mathis. As a musician, Rosario's father gave up his craft because being a musician meant being at dances that often lasted the entire night. "When we came to town and met the missionaries and my dad stopped playing and my mom stopped using make-up,"

---

45. "Major Problems the Unit Face" IV-19-7, Relief & Service. There is some evidence that some Mexican American families did not allow their children to attend Mennonite church or club activities. One VSer remarked, "The cake turned out real nice and Kass had a contact with the girl whose parents will not let their children come to club or church." See Seitz, "Monthly Report."

46. Nissley "Witnesses."

47. Perfecta De León, interview.

noted Rosario, "because we saw how the Mennonites lived and the example they gave us . . . I never used make-up because of the VSers."[48]

The VSers became for many young Mexican American children models of how to live a Christian life. They were white, seemed not to worry about financial needs, dressed simply, and were always willing to hang out and play games with the young children. But religious expectations often played themselves out differently for young Mexican American boys and girls. While for girls it expressed itself through the body with dress styles and lack of facial make-up, for boys it meant staying clear from perceived vices like military service, drinking alcohol, dancing, smoking, secular music, and of course, hanging out in pool halls, which according to white Mennonites were "the devil's playground." The life of Lupe De León, Jr., older brother to Perfecta, provides a particularly clear view for understanding the religious expectations of Mennonites, but more importantly, how the relationship between evangelicalism and Anabaptism remained a central part of Mexican American religious identity.

Lupe's life was typical of many Mexican Americans growing up in 1950s Mathis. He was the son of a World War II veteran, belonged to a family of farm workers, and practiced the nominal Catholicism of his parents. Growing up, Lupe knew little about the religious faith into which he was born. However, that changed as Lupe attended the vacation Bibles schools offered by the various Protestant groups. His first foray into vacation Bible school came through the Mexican Mission of the Baptist church. The Baptist church often gathered large followings of young Mexican American children in search of alternatives to an otherwise dull summer. It was at the Baptist Bible school that Lupe and other children were presented with the Christian story from a Protestant perspective. "I, like many others who had no religious training," remembered Lupe, "was moved by this and accepted Christ, but after Bible school I didn't go back because we were Catholics."

In the end, however, it was the Mennonites who won De León's soul. They did this, according to De León, because of their relaxed demeanor, their willingness to sit in people's living rooms, and the basketball courts they erected, which provided a place to hang out and kill time. As insignificant as the Mennonite approach might seem, it directly countered the legacy of racism and segregation in Mathis.

48. Vallejo, interview.

Without knowing it, Mennonite VSers confronted an intense and racist milieu by their mere presence. No one knew this better than the Mexican American children that greeted the Mennonites. Even as a child, Lupe was keenly aware of the racially hostile environment in which he was living. But if Lupe's story is any indication, strong community ties on the Mexican side of town often moderated any feelings of inferiority. "I was always proud of who I was. A block away from my house we had a Mexican theatre and the radio stations would beam language programs; we had grocery stores, good mechanics, department stores . . . and we had no reason to go uptown to the white stores because we had everything in our community . . . I saw movies by Pedro Infante, Jorge Negrete, Cantinflas and I identified with them because I spoke Spanish."[49] This sense of identifying with what historian Arnoldo De León calls both *lo Mexicano y lo Americano* comprised an important part of De León's life as he and other children grew up in a racially hostile environment.[50] Navigating the delicate and often dangerous environment in Mathis opened new possibilities for children and youth to be not only recipients of a religious doctrine, but also active agents in questioning the central beliefs of Mennonite VSers. In other words, Mexican American children and youth, surprised as they were over the generosity of Mennonites, often questioned why Mennonites came to Mathis and why they assumed military service contradicted Christianity.

The Mennonite church, as a historic peace church, has throughout its history maintained a fairly strong position against war and military service. The VS program in Mathis represented another manifestation of how white Mennonites refused military service and instead practiced a combination of social work and evangelism in Latino communities. But in a community like Mathis, with a proud record of Mexican Americans who served in the U.S. military, the question of pacifism and non-resistance, especially for young Mexican

49. Lupe De León, interview.

50. This "bi-cultural" approach became popular in the 1980s with De León's, *The Tejano Community*. For De León, nineteenth century Tejanos had effectively negotiated both identities, *lo Mexicano y lo Americano*, simultaneously in order to survive virulent racism and the rapid economic and cultural changes occurring in Texas after 1836. Being bicultural did not mean abandoning Mexican values for Anglo ones; instead it signified the active approaches Tejanos took in adapting to their changing environment.

American boys whose fathers and uncles had just returned from World War II, seemed inauthentic. They were leery of pacifism and often asked pointed questions to the VSers about their commitment to peace: "What would you do if somebody was raping your sister?" The responses often failed to satisfy the minds of the young boys, but the pacifist ethic did make an impression on the lives of the young boys who interacted with Mennonite volunteers. Early on, the peacemaking ideals of VSers, caused Lupe to vacillate between the admiration he felt toward his father and other local war veterans and his cynical interest in Mennonite pacifism. At issue for Lupe was his loyalty to his father. He valued his father's service in World War II and especially admired the young veterans who returned in shiny uniforms, driving fancy cars, and with money in their pockets. "I would tell my dad that as soon as I'm 18 I'm going to join the army," Lupe remembered, "but my dad was always against the army; he used to tell me I didn't know the real army."

Juxtaposed to young veterans with shiny cars and slick fashions were VSers who wore faded blue jeans and white t-shirts. That fashion sense did not bring envious feelings, but it did peak his curiosity and forced him to question the politics behind those faded jeans. In the end the non-resistance talk by VSers in faded jeans caused Lupe and other teenage boys to reconsider their commitment to military service. In the early 1960s, with the Vietnam War looming large and many young men leaving home for war, Lupe and four friends (Ted Chapa, Raúl Hernandez, Samuel Hernandez, Israel De León) registered as conscientious objectors (CO).[51] The question of pacifism, and the decision to become a CO, was often negotiated over late night basketball games and long church services between young Mexican American boys and white VSers. For Lupe and his close friends, becoming Mennonite did not only mean accepting the tenets of John 3:16. It also signified a political decision that cut against existing notions of Mexican American manhood and citizenship. "In school we were graded and rated," remembered Lupe, "and we were rated as 'no good Mexicans' for the rest

---

51. When the draft initiated during Vietnam, Lupe and Samuel were given a pass based on their role as pastors. Ted, Israel, and Raul, on the other hand, were drafted but because of their CO status each participated in alternatives to military service. Ted served in a boy's home in Denver, Colorado. Israel, Lupe's younger brother, served in a nursing home in Maryland, and Raul worked in a hospital in Indiana.

of our lives. . . . The military was one way out."[52] Since the early part of the twentieth century, and especially since World War II, military service served as a marker for U.S. citizenship and authentic masculinity for Mexican American men.[53] In other words, becoming Mennonite for Mexican Americans in South Texas carried with it national and gendered consequences.

Soon after declaring CO status in order to avoid military service in Vietnam, Lupe's life took some unexpected turns. Like many teenagers his age, he rebelled against the church and even decided to leave South Texas. Six weeks before high school graduation, Lupe dropped out of high school to find work in order to help his family financially. The move took him away from the VS basketball courts and away from his religious beliefs. "I made a lot of bad choices," remembered Lupe. "I ended up being a thug, a *borracho*, and a fighter." Migrant work also took Lupe away from the familiar confines of South Texas to the beet fields of Minnesota. In Minnesota, Lupe and two of his closest friends, Raul and Samuel, attended a local Pentecostal church. Reaching out to the Pentecostal church (there was no Spanish-speaking Mennonite church in Minnesota) became one way that Lupe and his friends tried to reconnect with their religious backgrounds and understandings. But interestingly enough, his time in the small migrant Pentecostal church spurred on a vision that reconnected him to his Christian faith, but this time under the guise of Pentecostalism. "It was here that I got a vision. In the vision, I saw Jesus beckoning me to go to school in La Paz, Baja CA. And along with Raul we both left Mathis in the fall and went to Baja CA. We studied in Spanish and lived in poor conditions, and later Raul's brother Samuel Hernandez joined us as well. After we returned I married Seferina Garcia."[54] Lupe's own mini-pentecost directed him to a small evangelical Bible school in Mexico in order to prepare for what he felt was a strong calling to take on pastoral leadership. After a year in Mexico, he returned to South Texas and in 1965 became pastor of a Mennonite church in nearby Premont, TX. It was here where Lupe met other Mexican Americans in the church who along with him would help forge the future of Mexican American church leadership in the Mennonite church: Ted Chapa,

52. Lupe De León, interview.
53. See Oropeza, *¡Raza Si, Guerra No!*, 1–10.
54. Lupe De León, interview.

Criselda Garza, Manuela Garcia, and Chuy Navarro. Each one had connections to the Mennonite missions in South Texas and together, they helped organize the leadership group, South Texas Mennonite Church Council (STMCC). Shortly after beginning his pastoral duties in Premont, Lupe was given an opportunity to continue his education at Hesston College, a Mennonite college in Kansas. In 1966, with the Vietnam War in high gear and rumblings of an emerging Chicano movement, Lupe and his young family moved to Kansas.

It did not take long for Lupe to begin challenging all he had considered sacred as a Mennonite once he arrived at Hesston College. No longer a child enjoying the Kool-Aid and cookies at Mennonite vacation Bible schools, Lupe was irritated by the hypocrisy he encountered on the campus of Hesston College during the tumultuous 1960s, especially respecting the ideals of non-resistance and peacemaking he remembered VSers preaching in South Texas. "In Hesston College," Lupe recalled, "many of the Mennonite boys were driving around in hemi-charged cars, living like the devil and hiding behind the skirt of the church. If I have friends dying in Vietnam then why are these Mennonite boys having such a good time?"[55] This became even more personal when he received word that two boys from Mathis were killed in combat.

The reverence he had for the Mennonite church in general and VSers in particular also began to fade amidst the stark realities of his own identity in relation to white Mennonites. Most notably, Lupe identified a double standard he believed existed between what he and his community were taught by Mennonites and how white Mennonite youth actually behaved within their own ethnic enclave. For example, as a child Lupe remembered the clear admonishments against pool halls and yet Hesston College had several pool tables. "Here in Mathis we were told we couldn't buy anything on Sundays because it was the Lord's day," Lupe remembered, "no soda, no *raspas*, and I go to Hesston and Mennonite businesses were open for business . . . and so all of those things prompted me to become an activist."[56]

For Lupe it became clear that the rules and regulations Mennonites and VSers insisted they practice were nothing more than cultural mores set up to evangelize the Mexican American commu-

55. Lupe De León, interview.
56. Ibid.

nity in Mathis. There was little doubt that he admired the work of VSers, and especially the time they devoted to his own life, but as he caught wind of the antiwar protests and later the Chicano movement, he questioned his own political and theological leanings as a Mexican American Mennonite from South Texas. If legalistic positions against pool halls or doing business on Sundays were mere smoke screens, then how committed could he remain to Mennonite pacifism? How would he reconcile the secular nature of the Chicano movement with his own religious convictions? And while these were deeply personal questions, they represented a broader shift as Mexican Americans in South Texas began to question the role of VSers and the VS program as Mennonite churches slowly took root.

QUESTIONING THE ROLE OF VS IN SOUTH TEXAS

By 1964 the VS program had stretched into the surrounding communities of Robstown, Corpus Christi, and Alice where a total of two hundred students attended the increasingly popular vacation Bible schools. But in addition to an expanding program, the late 1960s brought major questions over the relationship of Anglo leadership and the emerging Mexican American leaders of the newly organized STMCC. Church leaders like Howard J. Zehr of the South Central Conference, of which churches in South Texas were members, questioned the threat VS posed to developing Mexican American leaders in South Texas. "Personally I have been deeply concerned for the indigenous church in Texas . . . Lupe De León definitely feels that the church is too much Anglo and that Latins are happy to have it that way."[57] The notion that "Latins are happy to have it that way" concerned not only Lupe and other South Texas leaders, but white Mennonites in conference and denominational leadership in Kansas and Indiana. Out of this concern came the idea to transfer total ownership of the VS program to local pastors and local churches. The transfer of power was bad news for all white Mennonites in South Texas as local Mexican American leaders, including Lupe, claimed in 1966 that "the Anglo person tends to bring a problem into the Latin community."[58] This

---

57. Howard Zehr to John Lehman, 27 April 1966.
58. Lehman, "Administrative Visit."

shift in local power was not unique to Mennonites. Many religious groups during this era faced growing criticism from civil rights activists for the legacy of racism and paternalism in communities of color where white missionaries had operated.

By 1968 Jake and Rachel Snyder had finished their VS term in Mathis and no VS personnel planned to follow. While the VS program did not end here, it did begin to rethink how it operated amidst growing tensions surrounding the Chicano movement in Mathis and surrounding South Texas communities. Most notably were the political showdowns in Mathis in 1965 when two Mexican Americans were elected to the City Council for the first time in the town's history.[59] In nearby Crystal City, under the leadership of Chicano movement leader José Angel Gutierrez, Mexican Americans also won important political seats in 1965. The Crystal City and Mathis races both garnered the attention of *The New York Times*, which reported that "the elections are important as symbols of Latin muscle-flexing in communities where Mexican-Americans have large majorities."[60] While Crystal City remained in the national spotlight as a beacon of Mexican American political strength, Mathis carefully mounted an organized movement for change that, as *The New York Times* reported, "kept itself free from outside influences, raising a one thousand dollar campaign fund in nickels and dimes over a period of seven months."[61] This carefully crafted movement in Mathis, which placed Mexican Americans in political power, only reaffirmed the need for VSers to step aside and allow Mexican American Mennonites to take leadership of their own churches. The mood had indeed changed and the time seemed ripe for Mexican Americans to practice and lead their own style of being Mennonite in South Texas.

As in the early 1950s when the missionary strategy changed to incorporate social services and establish VS, the late 1960s brought out a critique against white VS workers who operated in paternalistic ways

59. Mario Robles was actually the first elected in 1963. But the victory that brought Manuel Chavez and Joe Ramirez into office was seen as an historic victory in Mathis. Conversely, *The New York Times* reported that Robles' victory was "designed to offset an attempt by Mexican-Americans to form a party." *The New York Times*, 7 April 1965, 19. Accessed through ProQuest Historical Newspapers, *The New York Times*.

60. *The New York Times*, 4 April 1965, 47.

61. Ibid.

and often failed to foster or encourage Mexican American leadership. At one committee meeting in South Texas, several Mexican American leaders, now in their late teens, noted that "the Anglo person tends to bring a problem into the Latin community."[62] What made this shift even more powerful was that the critique came from the same kids who played basketball on VS courts and attended countless vacation Bible schools during those hot summers in Mathis—Lupe and Seferina De León, Ted Chapa, Criselda Garza, Samuel Hernandez, and others. Many of the young leaders of the newly organized South Texas Mennonite Church Council (STMCC) believed that bringing in outside missionaries denied Mexican American leaders the empowerment to lead their own churches. All of the STMCC leaders would go on to hold leadership positions within the Mennonite church in the 1970s and 1980s. This included Lupe who, ironically, became a central leader of Mennonite mission programs in the U.S. It would not be long before the character of the churches began to change as more incorporated "Pentecostal" styles of music and carefully negotiated between notions of pacifism and peacemaking that better reflected their own context. The children of the VS program, who listened to frequent citations of John 3:16 and snacked on Kool-Aid and cookies, were now positioned quite well to fashion their own religious styles somewhere between Anabaptism and evangelicalism.

This essay began with the journey of T. K. Hershey and William Detweiler from Pennsylvania to the Southwest Borderlands. The trip came in response to what some within the Mennonite church believed was a major fault of the church—the lack of attention on the "Great Commission." No program represented this debate any more clearly, I suggest, than the VS programs that launched in the U.S. after the second World War. Mennonites, eager to reconcile their "quiet in the land" politics with evangelical fervor, instituted the VS program in South Texas both as a result of the success of CPS in Puerto Rico and as a way to sidestep direct competition with evangelical groups in South Texas. The idea worked to some extent, and the program enjoys some success to date. But more importantly were the questions and religious identities Mexican Americans fashioned in response to VS programs and evangelically minded Mennonites. Most importantly, Mennonite ideas of peace and non-resistance often placed Mexican Americans in

---

62. Lehman, "Administrative Visit."

a difficult position, choosing between a new theological understanding and a strong history of military service that also came loaded with questions of citizenship and gender. The case of Lupe De León in particular highlights this tension. From being a registered conscientious objector to questioning pacifism during his years at Hesston College, Lupe represented much of the angst Mexican American Mennonites felt over their new faith. Since the 1960s, Mexican American and Latina/o Mennonites have struggled with how best to negotiate the evangelical politics of John 3:16 with Anabaptist proclamations of peace and justice. These tensions have quietly affected the theological and historical positions of Latina/o Mennonites within American society, and suggest that the religious identities of these Mexican Americans have been shaped by the intersection of *evangélicos* and *Anabautistas* in profound ways.

BIBLIOGRAPHY

Banker, Mark T. *Presbyterian Missions and Cultural Interaction in the Far Southwest, 1850–1950*. Champaign, IL: University of Illinois Press, 1992.
Barton, Paul. *Hispanic Methodists, Presbyterians, and Baptists in Texas*. Austin: University of Texas Press, 2006.
"Blank Notes." La Voz de Mathis Newsletter, III-43-7. Calvary Mennonite Articles, 1948–1955. Mennonite Church USA Archives. Goshen, IN.
Bush, Perry. *Two Kingdoms, Two Loyalties: Mennonite Pacifism in Modern America*. Baltimore: Johns Hopkins University Press, 1998.
Chapa, Ted. 2007. Interview with author. Tape recording. January 25. San Antonio, TX.
Conrad, Paul. "Calvary Mennonite Church, Mathis, Texas." Fifty-third Annual Meeting of the Mennonite Board of Missions and Charities. 1959. Mennonite Church USA Archives. Goshen, IN.
De León, Arnoldo. *The Tejano Community, 1836–1900*. Dallas: Southern Methodist University Press, 1998.
De León, Lupe. 2007. Interview with author. Tape recording. June. Mathis, TX.
De León, Perfecta. 2006. Interview with author. Tape recording. December 28. Mathis, TX.
Detweiler, William G. Personal Papers. Mennonite Church USA Archives. Goshen, IN.
Espinosa, Gastón. "History and Theory in the Study of Mexican American Religions." In *Rethinking Latino(a) Religion and Identity*, edited by Miguel A. De La Torre and Gastón Espinosa, 69–100. Cleveland, OH: Pilgrim, 2006.
———. "Methodological Reflections on Social Science Research on Latino Religions." In *Rethinking Latino(a) Religion and Identity*, edited by Miguel A. De La Torre and Gastón Espinosa, 13–45. Cleveland, OH: Pilgrim, 2006.

Garcia-Treto, Francisco, and R. Douglas Brackenridge. *Iglesia Presbiteriana: A History of Presbyterians and Mexican Americans in the Southwest*. San Antonio: Trinity University Press, 1987.

"Group Living Guides for Mathis, Texas." IV-19-7 Relief and Service. Mennonite Church USA Archives. Goshen, IN.

Guthrie, Keith. *History of San Patricio County*. Wichita Falls, TX: Nortex, 1986.

Gutierrez, David. *Walls and Mirrors: Mexican Americans, Mexican Immigrants, and the Politics of Ethnicity*. Berkeley: University of California Press, 1995.

Heltzel, Peter Goodwin. *Jesus & Justice: Evangelicals, Race, and American Politics*. New Haven: Yale University Press, 2009.

Hershey, T. K. "The Vineyard of God in Mathis, Texas." Forty-ninth Annual Meeting of the Mennonite Board of Missions and Charities. Mennonite Church USA Archives. Goshen, IN.

Horst, Ray. "Visit to Mathis, Texas Unit." 26 July 1956. IV-19-7. Mennonite Church USA Archives. Goshen, IN.

Kauffman, Nelson E. "Broadening Our Witness to Meet Expanding Needs at Home." Fifty-first Annual Meeting of the Mennonite Board of Missions and Charities. Mennonite Church USA Archives. Goshen, IN.

———. "Workshop for workers with Spanish speaking people." March 1956 IV-16-21, "Latin America Strategy 1956–65." Mennonite Church USA Archives. Goshen, IN.

Klaasan, Walter. *Anabaptism: Neither Catholic nor Protestant*. Rev. ed. Waterloo, ON: Conrad, 1981.

Lehman, John. "Administrative Visit to South Texas." 31 October 1966. IV-19-7. Relief and Service. Mennonite Church USA Archives. Goshen, IN.

Maldonado, David, Jr., editor. *Crossing Guadalupe Street: Growing up Hispanic and Protestant*. Albuquerque: University of New Mexico Press, 2001.

———. *Protestants/Protestantes: Hispanic Christianity Within Mainline Traditions*. Nashville: Abingdon, 1999.

———. "Protestantes: An Introduction." In *Protestants/Protestantes: Hispanic Christianity Within Mainline Traditions*, edited by David Maldonado, Jr., 9–18. Nashville: Abingdon, 1999.

Martin, J. Weldon. "Advances in South Texas." Fiftieth Annual Meeting of the Mennonite Board of Missions and Charities. Mennonite Church USA. Archives, Goshen, IN.

Martin, J. Weldon., and Lorene Martin. "The Expanding Mission-Service Program at Mathis." Forty-eighth Annual Meeting of the Mennonite Board of Missions and Charities. Mennonite Church USA Archives. Goshen, IN.

Martínez, Juan F. *Sea La Luz: The Making of Mexican Protestantism in the American Southwest, 1829–1900*. Denton: University of North Texas Press, 2006.

Martínez, Juan F., and Lindy Scott, editors. *Los Evangélicos: Portraits of Latino Protestantism in the U.S.* Eugene, OR: Wipf & Stock, 2009.

Mathis News, The. 1942–1952. Housed in the newspaper office in Mathis, Texas. Accessed between 2007–2008.

Mennonite Board of Missions and Charities Annual Meetings and Reports, 1936–1968. Mennonite Church USA Archives. Goshen, IN.

Nelson, Boyd. "Relief and Service Builds Churches." Fifty-first Annual Meeting of the Mennonite Board of Missions and Charities. Mennonite Church USA Archives. Goshen, IN.

New York Times, The. April 1965.
Nissley, Addona. "We Are His Witnesses." Fifty-Second Annual Meeting of the Mennonite Board of Missions and Charities. Mennonite Church USA Archives. Goshen, IN.
Oropeza, Lorena. *¡Raza Si, Guerra No!: Chicano Protest and Patriotism During the Viet Nam War Era.* Berkeley: University of California Press, 2005.
Prothero, Stephen. *American Jesus: How the Son of God Became a National Icon.* New York: Farrar, Starus & Giroux, 2003.
Schultz, Kevin M. "Religion as Identity in Postwar America: The Last Serious Attempt to Put a Question on Religion in the United States Census." *The Journal of American History* 93.2 (2006) 359–84.
Sanchez-Korrol, Virginia. *From Colonia to Community: The History of Puerto Ricans in New York City.* Berkeley: University of California Press, 1983.
Seitz, Ken Jr. "Monthly Report for MRSC Service Units." 1 March 1961. IV-19-7. Mennonite Church USA Archives. Goshen, IN.
Snyder, Elvin. "A Brief History of the Mennonite Witness in Mathis, Texas." IV-19-7. Mennonite Church USA Archives. Goshen, IN.
Vallejo, Rosario. 2006. Interview with author. Tape recording. December 28. Mathis, Texas.
Walker-Jones, Randi. *Protestantism in the Sangre De Cristos, 1850–1920.* Albuquerque: University of New Mexico Press, 1991.
Zehr, Howard. "Letter to John Lehman." 27 April 1966, IV-19-7. Relief and Service. Mennonite Church USA Archives. Goshen, IN.

10

Re-Baptizing Evangelicalism

American Anabaptists and the 1970s Evangelical Left

DAVID R. SWARTZ

AT A YMCA HOTEL in Chicago on Thanksgiving weekend of 1973, a group of forty evangelical leaders confessed that they had failed to defend the social and economic rights of the poor, the oppressed, and minorities. In a document entitled "The Chicago Declaration," these leaders attacked an American "pathology of war," sexism, and materialism. They pledged to acknowledge God's "total claim upon the lives of his people." "We endorse no political ideology or party," signers continued, "but call our nation's leaders and people to that righteousness which exalts a nation." Final approval was given to the Declaration during a worship service on Sunday morning. When the vote had been tallied, Ron Sider, a Mennonite from Pennsylvania who initiated the gathering, rose to speak of "a deep sense of presence and guidance of the risen Lord." He then invited delegates to sing the Doxology, marking the end of a remarkable weekend of progressive politics and evangelical piety.[1]

Given the evangelical alliance with the Republican Party that came in the 1980s, this scene from 1973 seems anomalous. It can partly be explained, however, by the sociological and theological emergence of North American Mennonite and Brethren Anabaptists, who

---

1. Frank E. Gaebelein, Statement on Chicago Declaration, Folder "1973 Chicago Declaration," ESA Archives.

began to more fully integrate into the broader evangelical orbit in the postwar period. Many historians have entirely overlooked Anabaptist sectors of evangelicalism. Others, including many Mennonites themselves, have cast American Anabaptists as the victims of modernization and evangelical imperialism and consequently have not fully appreciated their reflexive influence on American evangelicalism. But the emergence of an evangelical left in the 1970s, in fact, featured a disproportionate number of Anabaptists and offers a counter-example to the dominant narrative of evangelical imperialism. As Sider organized the Thanksgiving Workshop, he wrote the following to theologian John Howard Yoder, who had just agreed to present a paper: "Thanks so much for giving this major address, which I hope, will be one further step in increasing Anabaptism's influence on contemporary evangelicals."[2]

Yoder and Sider were far more successful than they might have imagined. After the Workshop, a Reformed delegate commented about the ambition, energy, and nerve of the Anabaptist participants. "The most glamorous," he wrote, "were the neo-Anabaptists. Indeed it could be argued that every notion of a Coalition such as the group that signed the Chicago Declaration was theirs." Among the important contributors to the emerging evangelical left were Yoder, Mennonite author of the recently released *Politics of Jesus* (1972); Sider, son of a Brethren in Christ minister from Canada and author of *Rich Christians in an Age of Hunger* (1977); Doris Longacre, Mennonite activist for social justice and author of the *More with Less Cookbook* (1976); and a coterie of Anabaptist members of the Evangelical Women's Caucus. The stories of these activists extend the work of Perry Bush, who highlighted sustained points of contact between Mennonites and new evangelicals in the 1960s. In an article entitled "Anabaptism Born Again," Bush described a process of mutual exchange in which Mennonites came to be listed as "a legitimate evangelical subgroup" and evangelicals used Anabaptism as a "useable past." In this chapter, I amplify Bush's latter point, highlighting Anabaptism's profound

---

2. For scholarship that emphasizes American evangelicalism's influence on Anabaptists, see Weaver, *Keeping Salvation Ethical*; Toews, *Mennonites in American Society*; Calvin Redekop, *Leaving Anabaptism*. One of the exceptions to this trend is Roth, ed., *Engaging Anabaptism*. For "Anabaptism's influence on contemporary evangelicals," see Ron Sider to John Howard Yoder, 14 September 1973, Folder "Chicago Declaration Planning 1973," ESA Archives.

influence on the evangelical left during the 1970s. The participation of Yoder, Sider, and Longacre in campaigns for peace, internationalism, simple living, and egalitarianism highlight the diversity and fluidity of an evangelical tradition often caricatured as uniformly nationalistic, consumerist, and patriarchal. Their activities also suggest the importance of American Anabaptism in the field of religious history and point toward the continuing relevance of Anabaptism in contemporary evangelicalism.[3]

COMMUNITIES OF PEACE

John Howard Yoder, an Anabaptist theologian from the Mennonite heartland in rural Ohio, issued strong calls for peace within evangelicalism. As part of the Concern movement in the 1950s, he initially focused his efforts on sensitizing the Mennonite Church to issues of race, gender, and social structures. A growing ecumenical spirit, however, soon led Yoder and other Mennonites to, among other traditions, more broadly evangelical sites such as National Association of Evangelicals meetings. In 1963 thirty Mennonite and evangelical leaders participated in a two-day seminar about "The Evangelical Christian and Modern War" at Grace College in Winona Lake, Indiana. In 1964 Yoder questioned evangelicals for their reflexive support of the military. Christian soldiers, he wrote in the magazine of InterVarsity Christian Fellowship, a leading evangelical campus ministry, typically spoke of the armed forces as a place to advance professionally, to practice a life of piety in a disciplined environment, and to evangelize unbelievers. Rarely did they acknowledge "what a military experience is primarily for," which is "learning to kill." Evangelical participation in the armed forces inevitably resulted in a focus on personal piety at the expense of larger moral concerns. "A lack of sensitive ethical awareness to the meaning of the great social institutions of our time, of which the military is certainly the largest and most impersonal," wrote Yoder, "permits us to move through experiences such as a hitch in the army without even asking what it means morally. This is itself the besetting temptation of evangelicalism." Mennonites typically found

---

3. Bush, "Anabaptism Born Again," 26–47. For "neo-Anabaptists," see Calvin Theological Seminary speech by Marlin Van Eldernan, 5 December 1974, Folder 13, Box, ESA Collection, Billy Graham Center Archives.

these conversations constructive. In 1967 one of forty participants in a seminar on "Evangelicals in Social Action Peace Witness Seminar" held at Eastern Mennonite College reported that "something concrete and meaningful had occurred."[4]

Mennonites ramped up their criticisms in the late 1960s. In 1968 the pacifist Yoder marshaled just-war logic against the burgeoning war in Southeast Asia, telling tens of thousands of InterVarsity students that the Vietnam War manifestly failed to meet just-war conditions of just authority, legitimate cause, and just means. War, he continued, was not "a morally neutral event for which the Christian has no responsibility of decision." Nor was just war doctrine "a blank check for the government." A month later Yoder appealed to the students' evangelistic fervor, writing that "Only when we reject the politic-religious alliance of American religion with American politics can we hope to refute the Marxist and Muslim claim that Jesus is the tribal deity of the white westerner. For the military and political establishment this alliance may be welcome. But it is the death of mission." A vibrant debate over war, peace, evangelism, and Vietnam followed over the next year in the magazine's Letters section and then spilled over into Urbana 70, a massive InterVarsity missions convention. At Urbana 70 fifty Mennonite students and Myron Augsburger, the president of Eastern Mennonite College, continued Yoder's provocations. Before ten thousand evangelical students, Augsburger declared, "I am a global citizen. On a matter like the war in Vietnam I am a dove, without apology. Over and beyond that I believe there is something more in the New Testament, that I have not fulfilled my mission until I let it be understood by my brothers or neighbors in Vietnam, North and South, that I want them to know Jesus Christ and become my brothers in Christ. And I can't do that standing at one end of a gun barrel and they at the other."[5] The enthusiastic applause in response to Augsburger's words

---

4. On the Concern movement and Mennonite social responsibility, see Yoder, "Anabaptist Dissent"; Kaufman, "Nonresistance and Responsibility." On the growing interaction between Mennonites and evangelicals on matters of war and peace, see Yoder, "War, Peace and the Evangelical Challenge"; id., "Capital Punishment and the Bible," 3–10; id., "After Foreign Mission—What?" 12–13; id., "Christian and War"; id., "God Used It for Good," 28–29; id., "The Anabaptist Vision," 15–22; id., "Comments on 'War and the New Morality,'" 30; id., "Non-Baptist View of Southern Baptists," 219–228; id., "Price of Discipleship"; id., "Just War"; Bush, "Anabaptism Born Again," 35–37.

5. On Yoder and Augsburger at InterVarsity, see Yoder, "Vietnam: A Just War?"

revealed the resonance of the Anabaptist critique of Vietnam with significant numbers of evangelicals.

Coalitions between Anabaptists and evangelicals grew in the early 1970s. At Explo 72, a prominent evangelical youth rally staged in Dallas's Cotton Bowl by another campus parachurch organization called Campus Crusade, Mennonites allied with other evangelical dissenters. Members of the Post-American intentional community in Chicago and the Christian World Liberation Front from Berkeley, California, joined Mennonites from the Midwest and Colorado to condemn Campus Crusade's saluting of the flag and reciting of the Pledge of Allegiance. They criticized these acts of civic religion as a "truncated and domesticated gospel" perpetuated since the fourth-century Roman emperor Constantine. They set up literature booths and wore black armbands to protest the war. They quizzed Billy Graham at a press conference about his close ties with President Richard Nixon and his tacit approval of the war. They wore sandwich-board signs that read "The 300 Persons Killed by American Bombs Today Will Not Be Won in This Generation" (a variation of the convention's theme, "Win the World for Christ in This Generation"), "Choose This Day—Make Disciples or Make Bombs," and "Love your Enemies or Kill Your Enemies." During a military ceremony, they stood under the stadium's scoreboard, unfurled a banner—"Cross or Flag, Christ or Country," and chanted "Stop the War!" If most Explo participants did not join the protests, many did smile and said "Right On" or "Amen" as they walked by the booth.[6]

A year later many of the same principals met in Chicago for the Thanksgiving Workshop. When the Workshop threatened to focus exclusively around gender and racial concerns, Yoder hijacked the meeting and demanded attention to issues of peace. "Blacks have a paragraph they can redo; women have a word they can redo; but there is nothing at all about war," Yoder declared. "It contains something about the military-industrial complex being bad for the budget, but

---

1–3; id., "Vietnam: Another Option," 8–11; Augsburger, "Revolution and World Evangelism," 121–31.

6. On Explo, see "People's Christian Coalition—Newsletter No. 4," May 1972, in Box VII7, Folder "Peoples Christian Coalition Trinity," Sojourners Collection, WCSC; Richard K. Taylor, "Hopeful Stirrings among Evangelicals," *The Witness*, copy in Box IV3, Folder "News Releases and Post-American," Sojourners Collection, WCSC; Ediger, "Explo '72," 13; Fiske, "'Religious Woodstock'," 19.

nothing about it being bad for the Vietnamese." Yoder, supported by Ron Sider, on faculty at the Brethren in Christ-affiliated Messiah College; Jim Wallis, editor of the *Post-American*; Dale Brown, former moderator of the Church of the Brethren; and Myron Augsburger, president of Eastern Mennonite College, persuaded the delegates to insert the following into the Declaration: "We must challenge the misplaced trust of the nation in economic and military might—a proud trust that promotes a national pathology of war and violence which victimizes our neighbors at home and abroad." This statement, grounded in dissent toward the Vietnam War, helped cement a long-standing alliance between Anabaptists and an evangelical left.[7]

If Vietnam sparked this alliance, Yoder's magnum opus grounded it in rigorous Anabaptist theology. *The Politics of Jesus* (1972), an incisive exegesis of the Gospel of Luke and Paul's letter to the Romans, repudiated Niebuhrian realism, just war theory, and evangelical nationalism. Critiquing the Constantinian merging of church and state, Yoder argued against the Christian coercion of society. The state, to which Christians do not owe a reflexive obedience, is inherently corrupt, Yoder maintained, and entanglement in the state is fraught with danger and compromise. Be a faithful church, he urged, that does not resist evil with evil and that is willing to suffer for the sake of the gospel. The example of Jesus, which ought to be central to Christian social ethics, seemed to promote nonresistance and eliminate "utilitarian thinking, compromising in the short-run for a long-term goal." Jesus' greatest temptation was that of wielding political power, or as Yoder suggested at a conference at Calvin College, of becoming a Calvinist. Even Marlin Van Elderen, a Reformed critic of Yoder, conceded that *Politics of Jesus* "has become virtually required reading among [young evangelicals] and should lay to rest any vestiges of the notion that Anabaptist ethics is a simple-minded exercise in idealism not capable of being sustained by careful and informed reasoning."[8]

Drawing on his Mennonite heritage's long tradition of structured community life, Yoder offered a starkly non-Reformed model for political involvement. *Politics of Jesus* suggested that

---

7. Sider, "Historic Moment," 27.

8. Yoder, *Politics of Jesus*; id., "Persistence of the Constantinian Heresy," 4–5. On "utilitarian thinking," see Yoder, "Biblical Mandate for Evangelical Social Action," 86–114. For Reformed critiques of Yoder, see Van Elderen, "Evangelicals and Liberals," 151–55.

the communal church could serve as a social model to the world. Grounding political participation primarily through the Church, Yoder urged Christians to form countercultural communities that would feed the hungry, care for the sick, and speak prophetically to positions of power on behalf of the oppressed. Servanthood, grassroots action, and persuasion, rather than coercion, ought to characterize Christian politics. As an example of this approach, Yoder often cited his involvement with an ecumenical group of Christians who were trying to ameliorate the racially segregated community of Evanston, Illinois, in the 1960s. Most in the group found it self-evident that the ministers in the community ought to run for city council and lobby the mayor to adopt open housing policies. This would be the church discharging her social responsibility. But the conversation fell into disarray when someone pointed out that most of the real estate dealers and sellers of houses were members of the very Protestant churches that the ministers led. The problem, reported Yoder, was that the typical minister seemed "powerless to get his own members to take Christian ethics seriously without the coercion of government to get 'the church' as membership involved in lay professions to be less unchristian." More effort ought to be dedicated to discipleship at the church level, he suggested. Why should Christians expect other forces in society to be more effective and insightful than the "body of believers in their structured life together?" The primary social structure through which the gospel works to change other social structures, wrote Yoder, "is that of the Christian community."[9]

As a political strategy, Yoder's theology fit nicely with the approach of New Leftist evangelicals, who feared that working from within the system would compromise their ideals. A genre-bending book by Art Gish, a Church of the Brethren veteran of the civil rights and antiwar movements, in fact, explicitly linked Yoder's theology and American politics. In the aptly titled *The New Left and Christian Radicalism* (1970), a book used as a textbook at Trinity College in Deerfield, Illinois, and published by the evangelical Eerdmans Press, Gish urged evangelicals to merge the "old, old story" with the New Left. Gish argued that Vietnam, racism, and poverty exposed an "evil system that forces men to do evil deeds." "We reject," wrote Gish, "the

---

9. Yoder, "Biblical Mandate," 21–25; id., *Politics of Jesus*, 157.

bourgeois liberal contention that all change must be rational, orderly, and within the limits of the present system. The liberal believes that the tendency for progress is incorporated into the very nature of our institutions. Thus he is forced to believe that continual progress is being made, even while poverty, starvation, militarism, and racism are on the increase." Gish condemned this view as a naïve commitment to the "present system and a refusal to understand how disorderly, irrational, and violent the present system is." Moral and spiritual purity demanded resistance to a compromising liberalism.[10]

Gish, however, while echoing the Port Huron Statement's stress on political purity, authenticity, and stress on small, democratic structures, suggested an idiosyncratic interpretation of the movement. The New Left, he argued, was an ideological descendent of sixteenth-century Anabaptism. Like the contemporary political protest movement, sixteenth-century Anabaptism nurtured a two-kingdom dualism that sharply distinguished between the kingdom of the world and the kingdom of the church. Moreover, it built a socialist economy that "rejected selfish, capitalistic motives," embraced "the simple life," adopted nonviolence, and spurned political change from the top down. Anabaptists, who adhered to a "priesthood of all believers," had even engaged in an early form of "participatory democracy." The New Left, in refusing "to work through the magistrates to achieve their goals," resembled radical Christian faith in general and the Anabaptist tradition in particular. Gish sought "the recovery of the Anabaptist vision" for evangelicalism. Anabaptists, in the words of historian Perry Bush, offered evangelicals a "usable past."[11]

A host of evangelicals echoed these themes. Jim Wallis, founder of the People's Christian Coalition intentional community in Chicago, thundered against the Constantinian resemblances of modern America. Wallis frequently printed Yoder's writings and named him an associate editor of the *Post-American* tabloid. Fellow *Post-American* contributor and theologian Clark Pinnock lauded innovations such as freedom of conscience and the separation of church and state. These were "great principles . . . first enunciated by Anabaptists." Pinnock would later write that Anabaptist theology "facilitated the radicalization process by providing theological foundations." Evangelical New

---

10. Gish, *New Left*, 27, 49, 57, 66.
11. Ibid., 67, 71, 119; Bush, "Anabaptism Born Again," 27.

Leftists—Jim Wallis, Dale Brown, Art Gish, John Howard Yoder, Boyd Reese, John Alexander, and Joe Roos—and Anabaptist participants in the Thanksgiving Workshops of the mid-1970s were often one and the same. In *Politics* Yoder offered the evangelical left a respectable scholarly and theological rationale for their subversive engagement in American politics.[12]

Evangelical intentional communities, modeled on Yoder's formulation of the Christian Church as an engine and model of social justice, multiplied in the early 1970s. Reba Place, founded in 1957, was the first. A Mennonite intentional community/church of eighty members in Evanston, Illinois, Reba Place grew in a racially transitional neighborhood that soon filled with black residents. To ensure interdependence with each other and dependence on the provisions of God, members shared a common purse and refused to purchase automobile insurance. As Reba Place burgeoned in the 1970s, others followed their forms. The Christian World Liberation Front—described by Jim Wallis as "one of the few groups to emerge from the Jesus movement with a commitment to radical discipleship. It falls within the Anabaptist stream of church tradition"—regularly featured Yoder. Reba Place also served as an embodied ecclesiastical model of Anabaptism for the Post-Americans. The earliest issues of the *Post-American* magazine, of which Yoder was an associate editor, featured dozens of articles by Yoder, Gish, Dale Brown, and radical evangelicals who praised these sixteenth-century Anabaptists for their "costly faith" amid violent persecution. In 1971 the Post-Americans held "Summer Education-Action Seminars" in Chicago on "The Christian and the State," "American Civil Religion," and "War and U.S. Globalism." Yoder's *Politics of Jesus* and Gish's *New Left and Christian Radicalism* were required reading in these free university courses. In 1972 they lauded Reba Place's participation in a war tax refusal movement. In 1976 they distributed a twenty minute slideshow produced by the Mennonite Church denomination entitled "The Seduction of the Church" that decried American civil religion. As Mennonites shaped the Post-Americans, the Post-Americans in turn moved tens of thousands of young evangelical readers in an Anabaptist direction.[13]

12. For "great principles," see Pinnock, "Radical Reformation," 4–5. For "radicalization," see Pinnock quoted in Curry, "Biblical Politics and Foreign Policy," 51.

13. On Reba Place, see Dave and Neta Jackson, *Living Together*; id., "Question

The influence of Anabaptism extended well beyond the margins of evangelical intentional communities. Yoder was active internationally within the Latin American Theological Fraternity and the Lausanne Movement. The first edition of *Politics of Jesus*, published by the evangelical publisher William B. Eerdmans, sold more than seventy-five thousand copies and was translated into ten languages. Christian booksellers and Reformed opponents alike called *Politics* the most widely read political book in progressive evangelical circles. Senator Mark Hatfield read Yoder in the woods on a spiritual retreat, which led him to more firmly reject the Vietnam War and military escalation in general. Clark Pinnock, as associate editor of the *Post-American*, articulated the Anabaptist appeal for evangelicals like Wallis: "When it dawned upon us, we had the feeling of a second conversion. It was Christ-centered and Biblicist and so appealed to our evangelical instincts, but it was radical and subversive of every status quo and so confirmed the cultural alienation we felt." For many in the evangelical left revolting against the Vietnam War, Anabaptism offered a theological and historical precedent for their dissent. Dovetailing with the ethos of the sixties, an Anabaptist vision of communitarianism and peace profoundly shaped evangelical politics in the 1970s.[14]

---

about Insurance," 157–59. On praise for and contributions by Anabaptists in CWLF's *Right On*, see "Editor's Note," 31; Heinz, "American Fantasy," 4; Gill, "Toward a Radical Christian Identity"; id., "Interview with John Howard Yoder." For articles by Anabaptist authors, see Gish, "New Left and Christian Radicalism," 8; id., "Reconsideration," 12; Yoder, "Biblical Mandate," 21–25; id., Study notes on "Political Interpretations of John's Apocalypse," in Folder "XI1 Post-American—Internal," Wheaton College Archives; Pinnock, "Radical Reformation," 4–5; Yoder, "Original Revolution," 4–5, 15; Brown, "Powers," 3, 13. For "Summer Education-Action Seminars," see "Quest for Discipleship: A Summer Education-Action Seminar," in Box XI1, "Post-American—Internal," Sojourners Collection, WCA; Yoder, "Exodus," 26–29; id., "Martin Luther's Forgotten Vision," 66–70; id., "Persistence of the Constantinian Heresy," 4–5. On interactions with Reba Place, see "Signs of a New Order," 13; "Interview with Reba Place," 8–11.

14. On the Latin American Theological Fraternity, see Escobar, "Anabaptism and Radical Christianity," 75–88. On the influence and sales of *Politics of Jesus*, see Mott, "'The Politics of Jesus,'" 7–10; Mouw interview; Ellis, "Books for Young Evangelicals," 25. Pinnock quoted Curry, "Biblical Politics and Foreign Policy," 51.

GLOBAL JUSTICE

Ron Sider echoed Yoder's vision of peaceful communitarianism and extended Anabaptist influence to issues of global justice. Firmly ensconced in the close community of the nonconformist Brethren in Christ, a denomination equal parts Anabaptist and holiness, Sider grew up in the 1940s on a 275-acre farm in rural southern Ontario. His mother wore a prayer veiling; his cousin Roy Sider, an influential bishop, preached that it was wrong to vote; his family contributed money to the relief work of Mennonite Central Committee. Sider would go on to earn a PhD in European history from Yale University, spearhead a social concerns organization called Evangelicals for Social Action, and write a best-selling book entitled *Rich Christians in an Age of Hunger*. By the late 1960s, Sider, shaped by higher education and urban life in New Haven, Connecticut, had abandoned his tradition's social quietism. He extended Mennonite Central Committee's mandate beyond famine and relocation to a new consideration of global and economic structures. In doing so, he helped spark a new evangelical agenda of global justice and simple living.

Sider burst onto the broader evangelical scene in the early 1970s. Disillusioned with the passive conservatism of evangelicals during the civil rights movement and the Vietnam War, Sider stumped on behalf of the Democrat opponent of Richard Nixon. Evangelicals for McGovern, launched in 1972 just months before the national election, failed to rally evangelicals in significant numbers. It did, however, raise eyebrows and lead to a much larger progressive movement. A year later Sider convened the Thanksgiving Workshop on Evangelical Social Concerns, a meeting at which delegates denounced racism, sexism, economic injustice, and militarism. The resulting Chicago Declaration declared that evangelicals "dare no longer remain silent in the face of glaring social evil. . . . We acknowledge that God requires justice. But we have not proclaimed or demonstrated his justice to an unjust American society. Although the Lord calls us to defend the social and economic rights of the poor and the oppressed, we have mostly remained silent."

Few observers at the time noticed the large number of Anabaptist evangelicals who helped draft this text in Chicago. A year later at the second Thanksgiving Workshop, more people observed the presence of Art Gish, John Howard Yoder, Dale Brown, and Myron

Augsburger—as well as the activism of radical evangelicals such as Jim Wallis and John Alexander who were growing more sympathetic to Anabaptist views. These individuals dominated the caucus on "economic lifestyles," which produced a constellation of rather "startling" proposals: a graduated tithe that would increase as income increased; an additional 1 percent tithe meant for evangelical projects that would change "white attitudes and power structures"; a boycott of lawn fertilizer; a national day of fasting; one meatless day per week; and a commitment that a family of four live on an annual income of eight thousand dollars.[15]

Many of these proposals stemmed from a widely read 1972 article by Sider in InterVarsity's magazine. Urging students to embrace marginalization, Sider wrote that Christians should avoid excessive wealth and give generously to the needy. He urged them to increase giving beyond the standard 10 percent rate. As your income grows, Sider wrote, so should the proportion of your giving. This anti-prosperity gospel resonated with evangelicals in the midst of economic recession and oil embargoes, and he became a sought-after speaker across the nation. Sider's "graduated tithe" article itself swelled into a best-selling book on simple living and global injustice. *Rich Christians in an Age of Hunger*, which embodied Anabaptism's most influential contribution to evangelicalism in the postwar era, opened darkly. "Hunger and starvation stalk the land," intoned Sider. "Ten thousand persons died today because of inadequate food. One billion people are mentally retarded or physically deformed because of a poor diet. The problem, we know, is that the world's resources are not evenly distributed. North Americans live on an affluent island amid a sea of starving humanity." Maintaining current American policy, explained Sider, would lead the world toward global economic collapse.[16]

Rich Christians, however, was more of a moral indictment than an economic critique. Evangelicals should not take action merely to avoid economic collapse, Sider contended. They should take action because Christians have a moral obligation to right injustices. Evangelicals, he complained, all too often failed to do justice because of an inadequate

---

15. For "startling," see "Piety's Progress." For the complete text of these proposals, see "A Report on the Second Thanksgiving Workshop," 20 December 1974, in Box 3, Folder 13, ESA Collection, BGCA.

16. Sider, "Ministry of Affluence," 6–8; id., *Rich Christians*, 1, 172.

conception of sin. "Christians frequently restrict the scope of ethics to a narrow class of 'personal' sins," he explained. "they fail to preach about the sins of institutionalized racism, unjust economic structures and militaristic institutions which destroy people just as much as do alcohol and drugs." White flight from the cities to the suburbs, with the concomitant loss of resources from such a demographic shift, only exacerbated structural injustice embedded in the current economic and political system. Even the purchase of bananas, Sider continued, confronted evangelicals with moral questions. Why are bananas from Central America so much more inexpensive than apples from a neighboring state? They are cheaper, he answered, despite added shipping costs, because U.S. fruit conglomerates pay such unfair wages to Latin American workers. "If God's Word is true, then all of us who dwell in affluent nations are trapped in sin," Sider concluded. "We have profited from systematic injustice. . . . We are guilty of an outrageous offense against God and neighbor." Sider's incorporation of the language of sin offered a uniquely evangelical contribution to broader debates on global poverty.[17]

Sider concluded with a call to political action. The virtue in individual acts of economic penance, he suggested, would extrapolate if Christians banded together to transform foreign and domestic policy. "We must demand a foreign policy that unequivocally sides with the poor. If we truly believe that 'all men are created equal,' then our foreign policy must be redesigned to promote the interests of all people and not just the wealthy elites in developing countries or our own multinational corporations." Urging attention to the structures of world trade and the international debt crisis, he urged evangelicals to lobby Congress into dropping trade barriers of imports from developing countries and to devote more money to third-world nations than to the arms race. Sider also offered a striking global perspective. In an era when global hunger had not yet captivated the public's attention with images of Africans' distended bellies on television, *Rich Christians* presented an unrelenting international focus with stories from Africa and statistics from the Southern Hemisphere. Elsewhere, he lambasted Richard Nixon for a 1973 speech: "I have made this basic decision: In allocating the products of America's farms between markets abroad

---

17. Sider, *Rich Christians*, 163–65. On the language of sin, see Stafford, "Ron Sider's Unsettling Crusade," 18–22.

and those in the United States, we must put the American consumer first." "Such a statement may be good politics," rebutted Sider, "but it certainly is not good theology."

This last sentence from *Rich Christians* captures Sider's most enduring contribution to evangelicalism. In the midst of a dominant preoccupation with personal holiness among Billy Graham-style evangelicals, Sider sought to apply principles of faith on a structural level. This would play itself out in very diverse ways. Even the right-wing surge of the Moral Majority took some cues from Sider. Before that, Sider's critique of American materialism, imperialism, and social injustice helped launch the evangelical left. Whatever direction evangelical politics took, Sider helped catalyze the evangelical engagement of political structures with one's spiritual commitments.[18]

THEOLOGIES IN THE KITCHEN

If Sider's treatment of global injustice in *Rich Christians* was substantially theoretical, a second influential Anabaptist text was eminently practical. On the kitchen counters of many evangelicals in the 1970s lay a cookbook called *More with Less* and a simple living manual entitled *Living More with Less*, both printed by Mennonite publisher Herald Press. Ron Sider praised author Doris Longacre for providing "good concrete models" for the "astonishing numbers of people" who had responded to *Rich Christians*. In compiling five hundred thrifty, nutritious recipes, Longacre was constructing practical theology in the kitchen.[19]

Like Sider, Longacre nurtured a global perspective. After graduating from Goshen College (IN), she served with the relief agency Mennonite Central Committee (MCC). She managed a Language Study Center in Vietnam from 1964 to 1967 and worked in Indonesia from 1971 to 1972. When she returned to the United States, she

---

18. Sider, *Rich Christians*, 172. Sider's economic thought was complemented by several Mennonite economists working in evangelical circles. Observers called Norm Ewert, an economics professor at Wheaton, "another Ron Sider" who functioned as the "resident Anabaptist" and who "has had a profound influence on the campus." See Wally Kroeker to Ron Sider, 15 June 1978, Folder "1978," ESA Archives.

19. Longacre, *More with Less*; Longacre, *Living More with Less*. For praise of Longacre, see Sider, *Rich Christians*, 182; Sider, "Introduction," in Longacre, *Living More with Less*, 6–7.

became a frequent lecturer on world hunger and an assistant in the MCC division of Rural Development and Food Production. Her husband Paul Longacre became MCC coordinator for Food and Hunger Concerns.

These weighty concerns shaped *More with Less*. Longacre's cookbook, according to advertisements, boasted "delightful recipes that prove that when we reduce our need for heavily grain-fed meat, the superprocessed, and the sugary, we not only release resources for the hungry, but also protect our health and our pocketbooks." Recipes from Uganda, Mexico, Vietnam, and other corners of the globe filled the pages. Especially popular were "Brazilian Beans and Rice" offered by a contributor from Recife, Brazil, "Middle-Eastern Lentil Soup" from Egypt, and "Zucchini Omelet" from Lancaster County, Pennsylvania. "The average North American," explained Longacre, "uses five times as much grain per person yearly as does one of the two billion persons living in poor countries." *More with Less* was not vegetarian; Longacre knew that a meatless cookbook, like Frances Lappe's immensely popular and rigidly vegetarian *Diet for a Small Planet*, was not "realistic" for its intended audience of Mennonite farmers. She did, however, drastically cut meat ingredients to an intake level on par with third-world nations and eliminate instructions on roasting and carving meat. The cookbook's sequel—*Living More with Less*—offered critiques and suggestions from around the world on nearly every page of the lifestyle manual. In a chapter entitled "Learn from the World Community," Christians from around the world admonished American readers to build energy-efficient public transportation networks between towns and cities; to learn to cook simple, nutritious meals; to use fewer kitchen appliances; to recycle; to plant home and community gardens; and to value families and friendships above making money.[20]

More with Less held appeal for a wider readership in part because it applied a warm evangelical piety to its hard-edged critique of the American economy. In a cassette tape entitled "Entertaining Simply," Longacre told listeners, "Jesus frequently used mealtime settings to share and teach important values, build relationships, and celebrate events." Food, she suggested, could be used even to teach spiritual

---

20. File "IX-6-3 More with Less Cookbook, 1979–80" in Mennonite Central Committee Collection, Mennonite Church USA Archives, Goshen, IN; Longacre, *Living More with Less*, 30–36.

truths. In Scripture, Longacre reminded readers, "Jesus said, "I am the Bread of Life; I am the Water of Life; Man does not live by bread alone; as often as you eat this bread and drink this cup." She urged readers to read passages from Scripture and devotional books and to share stories of God's grace with one another before leaving the dinner table. Longacre urged readers to be intentional about building relationships when entertaining. She encouraged people while eating during meals to engage in self-disclosure and profound conversation; to read devotional or biblical literature aloud; to tell stories and experiences; and to share object lessons. This Yoderian emphasis on the Church as community translated well to evangelical circles.[21]

More with Less sold surprisingly well despite its preachy premise, unconventional recipes, and obscure Mennonite roots. Its expressions of evangelical piety and its perfectly timed release in the midst of global hunger awareness resonated with the public. Upon its release in 1976, sales boomed in Mennonite counties throughout Pennsylvania, Ohio, and Indiana. The cookbook soon spread within broader evangelicalism. The Southern Baptist Book Club ordered two thousand copies. A Methodist order of two thousand more followed. Within months, the publishers told Longacre that interest in her cookbook was "phenomenal." Sales reached sixty-eight thousand within the first year. The public read reviews in hundreds of newspapers, including the *Los Angeles Times* and the *Chicago Tribune*, and in dozens of evangelical journals such as *Eternity*, *National Courier*, *Vanguard*, *Right On*, *Sojourners*, and *The Other Side*. Catholics (who learned about it from Arthur Simon's *Bread for the World*), Christian World Liberation Front members in Berkeley, Covenant church members in Minnesota, and Christian Reformed members in Grand Rapids, Michigan, purchased thousands of copies. The Sojourners community in Washington, DC, which regularly prepared a sweet and sour soybean recipe from *More with Less*, invited Longacre to speak at a Wednesday evening worship service.[22]

21. On "sharing stories of God's grace," see "Seeds," 30.
22. Hansen, "From the Mennonites," G6. On Baptist and Methodist sales, see Paul Schrock to Doris Longacre, 18 November 1976, in Folder IX-6-3. MCC Collection, Mennonite Church Archives, Goshen, IN. On first-year sales and positive reviews, see Herald Press to Longacre, 8 April 1976; Herald Press to Longacre, 18 November 1976, in Folder IX-6-3, MCC Collection, MCA. On the diverse readership of *More with Less*, see LaVerne Triezenberg to Herald Press, 4 December 1980;

Praise for Longacre flooded in. She received letters from delighted housewives. "Those of my generation," wrote one, "felt themselves liberated from the gardening and 'from scratch' cooking and baking our mothers had known, to the delightfully packaged and processed foods of today's supermarkets, only to learn that our mothers were right, and to see our daughters return to bread baking. . . . My two daughters and my daughter-in-law are receiving *More with Less* cookbooks for Easter." Para-church and denominational leaders also praised Longacre and MCC. World Vision's Stanley Mooneyham wrote that "there is nobody in the country doing more to sensitize the conscience of North Americans." Senator Mark Hatfield praised her in a personal letter. "You have made a large contribution to the store of knowledge on world hunger," wrote Hatfield, "and what the individual can do to alleviate it." Longacre built a brand out with the expanded constituency. *Living More with Less* (1980), which recommended environmentally friendly cleaning solutions and offered tips on gardening, extended simple living beyond the kitchen. Fans listened to "More with Less" cassette tapes on topics such as "Entertaining Simply," "Combining Proteins to Get More with Less," "Theology in the Kitchen," and "How to Host a More with Less Workshop." Others held "hunger awareness dinners." By August 1980, just four years after its release, *More with Less* had entered its twenty-fourth printing with three hundred and fifty-five thousand copies in print.[23]

---

copy in author's possession, sent by mail from Herald Press archives in Scottdale, PA, in February 2006. Also see Virginia Hearn to David Swartz, 1 March 2006; Gallagher interview. On Longacre and Sojourners, see "Recipe of the Week," 1; Joyce Hollyday in *Sojourners Newsletter* (Fall 1978), in Folder VI1, "Sojourners Community," Sojourners Collection, WCA.

23. For evangelical praise of *More with Less*, see Doris Longacre to Jack Scott, 19 May 1976; Mark O. Hatfield to Doris Longacre, 4 March 1976; W. Stanley Mooneyham, 22 March 1976, copy in author's possession, received from Herald Press archives in February 2006. Longacre spoke at a Wednesday evening meeting of Sojourners in the fall of 1978. See Box VI1-VI3, Folder, "Community Newsletters, Fall 1978," Sojourners Collection, WCSC. On the cookbook's popularity at Gordon-Conwell Seminary, see Sider, "A Brief Report," 1 March 1978, in Folder "Discipleship Workshops," ESA Archives. On the spread of *More with Less* and "hunger awareness" dinners in Christian Reformed circles, see Treizenburg interview; Greidanus interview. On *More with Less* cassette tapes, see "Seeds," 30. For spin-offs of *More with Less*, see Longacre, *Living More with Less*; Van Beilen, *Hunger Awareness Dinners*; Friesen, *Living More with Less*. For sales figures, see Paul Schrock to Reg Toews, 15 June 1983, in Folder IX-6-3, MCC Collection, MCA.

Other Anabaptists and evangelicals piggybacked off Longacre's success. Sider collaborated with Walter and Ginny Hearn, evangelical writers and champions of simple living in Berkeley, California. The *Post-American* published a monthly column called "Simplicity." In *Beyond the Rat Race* (1973), a sequel of sorts to *The New Left and Christian Radicalism* (1970), brethren activist Art Gish sought to apply the "radical theology of revolution to life-style." He urged readers to get rid of televisions and radios, to quit washing their cars, to encourage men to wash dishes and women to fix cars, and to live in sharing communities. The simple life—its repudiation of materialism, its embrace of the family and healthy living—was a legitimate protest of the technocracy. *Beyond the Rat Race*, reprinted in 1981 and 2002 and recommended by John Howard Yoder in the first pages of later editions of *Politics of Jesus*, influenced CWLF, InterVarsity students, and racial activist John Alexander.[24]

The 1974 Lausanne Congress both reflected this Anabaptist influence and revealed the potential of the movement in broader evangelical circles. During the Congress, John Howard Yoder helped incite a wildcat "radical discipleship" caucus that challenged the politically conservative planners of the Congress. The resulting "Lausanne Covenant" stated, not unexpectedly, that "The goal should be, by all available means and at the earliest possible time, that every person will have the opportunity to hear, understand, and to receive the good news." Less expected were subsequent sentences that emphasized simple living and generosity toward the poor as an important element of evangelism. "We cannot hope to attain this goal without sacrifice," declared the Covenant. "All of us are shocked by the poverty of millions and disturbed by the injustices which cause it. Those of us who live in affluent circumstances accept our duty to develop a simple life-style in order to contribute more generously to both relief and evangelism." The Lausanne movement, very much in the evangelical mainstream, continued to stress simple living through the 1970s and 1980s. As the movement peaked in the late 1970s, an International Consultation on Simple Lifestyle released "Lausanne Occasional Paper 20: An Evangelical Commitment to Simple Life-Style." A proliferation

24. On the Hearns, see Sider, *Living More Simply*, 73–96; Russell, "Ph.D. Scrounges for a Living," 3. Also see Gish, *Beyond the Race Race*, 9, 37, 112–32; Gish, "Simplicity," 10. On Gish's influence with CWLF and Alexander, see Hearn interview; Olson interview; Gish, "Simplicity," 14–16.

of simple-living appeals supplemented the official pronouncements of the Lausanne consultations. Dozens of books and hundreds of articles, many of them written by Anabaptists, appeared in evangelical magazines such as *Christianity Today*, Evangelicals for Social Action's *Update*, InterVarsity's *HIS*, the *Post-American*, and *The Other Side*.[25]

The simple living movement touched evangelicals even at the highest levels of electoral politics. Senator Mark Hatfield, nudged by Anabaptists Jim Wallis, Longacre, and Sider, promoted action in Washington, DC. In the mid-1970s the senator attacked Nixon and Ford for inattention to global consultations on food and hunger. In 1975, after the World Food Conference in Rome, Hatfield held a press conference that turned out to be a hunger simulation, the latest rage among evangelical youth groups. Hatfield served journalists, others senators, staffers, and ambassadors a sixty-seven-calorie meal that cost eight cents, the very same meal that World Vision's president Stanley Mooneyham had seen Indians eating during a recent tour of the world's "hunger belt."

American Anabaptists thus buttressed the growing evangelical impulse to expand personal responsibility to corporate responsibility. Both Sider and Longacre urged attention to structural injustices: too-high tariff barriers imposed by affluent nations against poor nations, lack of involvement by poor nations in international economic agencies, corporate farming, global unemployment, unfair farm policy, and arms sales to third world dictators. After you cook simple, healthy meals, Longacre urged her readers, write letters to lawmakers: "The two realms—conserving resources at home and taking on economic and political issues—are as inseparable as the yolk and white of a scrambled egg." Anabaptist evangelicals interpreted the seventies in terms that evangelicals could understand. They cast simple living as evangelism and faithfulness to Jesus. For Hatfield, Mooneyham, and many others, the journey toward global concerns and simple living led through Pennsylvania Dutch country. The integration of Anabaptist

---

25. On the international consultation, see Alan Nichols, "Evangelical Commitment to Simple Life-Style," copy in Box 36, Folder 9, Lausanne Committee for World Evangelization, BGCA. For copies of the *Simple Lifestyle Newsletter*, see Box 36, Folder 15. Also see Eller, *Simple Life*; Gill, "Simple Life," 29–31; Rasmussen, "Simple Life," 381–83; Gaebelein, "Challenging Christians," 22–26; Morris, "Thinking Things Through," 60; Sider, "Does God Live in Glass Houses?" 14–19; Sider, *Living More Simply*; Sider, *Lifestyle in the Eighties*; Foster, *Freedom of Simplicity*.

champions of simplicity into the evangelical orbit catalyzed the simple living movement.[26]

EGALITARIANISM

Several dozen evangelical feminists added to Longacre's substantial Anabaptist influence. Many of them appeared at a series of meetings stemming out of the 1973 Chicago Declaration. Organizers of the first Workshop invited only six women, but those women, energetic and aghast at the "Eastern men's club" feel of the Workshop, jumpstarted a movement. Forming a tiny "women's caucus," they pushed through, against substantial resistance from some, a statement that appeared in the Chicago Declaration text itself. "We acknowledge that we have encouraged men to prideful domination and women to irresponsible passivity," the Declaration read. "So we call both men and women to mutual submission and active discipleship." They also lobbied for more inclusion in upcoming Workshops. Their efforts paid off as Sider fired off letters asking for ideas of women to invite, even urging that "men be willing to stay home to give wives a chance to attend conferences." In the end, the planning committee invited over sixty women. Over thirty, nearly all white, urban, professional, highly educated women came. In 1974 they established a formal organization called the Evangelical Women's Caucus (EWC), which immediately issued demands about inclusive language, women's ordination, Equal Rights Amendment, and equal employment opportunities in evangelical organizations. The Caucus also printed and distributed a directory of "evangelical feminists," produced study materials for churches, and launched several publications including

26. Longacre, *Living More with Less*, 26; Sider, *Living More Simply*, 14–15. On hunger simulations, see "Door Interview with Stanley Mooneyham," 12. For other global hunger simulations and "hunger clubs" in evangelical congregations and colleges, see Folder "Discipleship Workshops," ESA Archives. On the structural aspects of global hunger, see Mooneyham, *What Do You Say to a Hungry World?*; Sider, *Cry Justice!*; Simon, *Bread for the World*; Barnet, *The Lean Years*. Dozens of feature articles on hunger by Sider and others also appeared in all of the progressive and mainstream evangelical publications including *Christianity Today*, *Eternity*, *Wittenburg Door*, *Vanguard*, *HIS*, *The Other Side*, and *The Post-American*. For Southern Baptist interaction with Sider and other action to address global hunger in the late 1970s, see Boxes 36 and 51, "Christian Life Commission Resource Files," AR. 138-2, Southern Baptist Historical Library and Archives, Nashville, TN.

Daughters of Sarah, The EWC Update, and *Green Leaf.* Thus began the evangelical feminist movement.[27]

Anabaptists critically enabled the movement. They were not, to be sure, the only supporters of evangelical feminism. Evangelicals with a holiness background often pointed to a long legacy of women preachers in the nineteenth century. And many Anabaptists were not feminist. But some Mennonites, however, found a natural home in the Evangelical Women's Caucus. John Howard Yoder, for example, regularly attended early caucus meetings, the only man to do so. Willard Swartley, a New Testament scholar at Associated Mennonite Biblical Seminary (AMBS) in Elkhart, Indiana, wrote an influential book on hermeneutics entitled *Slavery, Sabbath, War, and Women* (1983), which mapped the overarching trajectory of "God's redemptive action, grace, and kingdom justice" through Scripture. Swartley contended that slavery, participation in war, and male headship were cultural artifacts of the Old Testament rather than proscriptions for modern life. The Seattle chapter of EWC studied it every Sunday evening for two months in 1983. David Augsburger, an associate professor of pastoral care and counseling at AMBS, likewise emphasized the egalitarian nature of the priesthood of all believers. In *EWC Update,* he wrote, "We are of equal worth. We each deserve the privilege of equal words. We can stand with each other, with the freedom to think, feel, and speak, horizontally, equally, levelly." Brethren pastor Art Gish sought to informalize or entirely drop "titles of distinction." He argued that "the use of titles means perpetuation of inequality and authoritarianism." Using "Mr." and "Mrs." created generational barriers. Using "pagan titles" like "professor" or "doctor" set people apart from others." Using "Reverend" violated the Anabaptist notion of the "priesthood of all believers."[28]

---

27. On the "Eastern men's club feel," see Hardesty, "Reflections," *The Chicago Declaration,* 123. Also see "Proposals from the Women's Caucus," November 1974, in Box 2, Folder 15, "Thanksgiving Workshop, Evangelicals for Social Action (1974): Action Proposals n.d.," ESA Collection, BGCA.

28. On holiness, see Lucille Sider Dayton, "Rise of Women in Evangelicalism"; Donald Dayton and Lucille Sider Dayton, "Women as Preachers," 4–7; Donald Dayton, *Discovering an Evangelical Heritage.* On Swartley, see Thompson, "Chapter and Verse," 12; Swartley, *Slavery, Sabbath, War, and Women.* Also see Augsburger, "Talking Up," 2; Gish, "Simplicity," 10.

Anabaptist women applied this egalitarian theory to gender. Lareta Halteman Finger, for example, grew up among Swiss-German Mennonites in rural southeastern Pennsylvania, where "culture was loading me with double messages." Her tradition, she wrote in the 1970s, "had an early history of radical nonconformism and leadership for both men and women. They had taken initiative in foreign missions and relief work. But that was all theory to me . . . What I actually *saw* were men and women acting out staid, traditional roles." She carried that cognitive dissonance into evangelical circles. She attended Gordon Divinity School near Boston in the mid-1960s and went on to attend an intentional evangelical community in Chicago called Austin Community Fellowship. By the late 1970s Halteman Finger had reached the highest levels of the evangelical feminist movement, serving on the executive council, the publications committee, and the mediations committee of the EWC. She was also editor of the Christian feminist journal *Daughters of Sarah* for nearly twenty years. She would later preach gender egalitarianism as a professor of New Testament at Messiah College in Grantham, Pennsylvania. For Halteman Finger, egalitarian Anabaptism offered a way out of a calcified Mennonite patriarchy into a broader evangelical world.[29]

Anabaptist precedents also inspired Ruth Schmidt, the daughter of a Mennonite minister from the Midwest. Schmidt believed that she "developed a resistance to what society teaches young women about their role in life" because of growing up in a "minority culture." "By being one of the oddballs of my class and surroundings," she later surmised, "I learned not to conform to society's dictates. . . . Unconsciously, I applied that principle of independence in other areas of life, chiefly in what I thought about my life as a woman in a sexist society and in a sexist church." She began to speak out, even in unfriendly contexts. Her influential 1971 article in *Christianity Today*, entitled "Second Class Citizenship in the Kingdom of God," abetted the evangelical feminist movement in its earliest stages. As a Spanish scholar, provost of Wheaton College (MA), and the first president of Agnes Scott College, Schmidt was very involved in the Greater Boston EWC chapter. She faithfully attended national EWC

---

29. On Halteman Finger, see Hearn, *Our Struggle to Serve*, 29, 35; "Reta Finger, Susie Stanley Join Executive Council," 7. Her husband Tom Finger, an Anabaptist theologian, would eventually publish *A Contemporary Anabaptist Theology*.

conventions, testifying about how "it was gloriously liberating to enjoy the company of other feminist believers, joining in worship, celebration, concern, and study."[30]

Reports such as these stirred other Anabaptists to join the growing EWC network. Lorraine Peters, who grew up in a Mennonite Brethren church on the Saskatchewan prairie, read *All We're Meant to Be*, a best-selling evangelical feminist book that successfully translated mainstream feminism into evangelical categories. Like Schmidt, Peters attended the first EWC convention. The 1975 meeting in Washington, DC, she reported, "was for me, akin to falling in love." Hymns "of freedom and liberty" from her Mennonite childhood came to life. "Suddenly I understood that life in Christ meant freedom for men and women alike," she wrote. "I was the most liberated and excited woman on earth." Peters, who served on the EWC nominating committee, and her husband John went on to present seminars in the 1980s on "Mutual Growth in Marriage in the Middle Years" and "Creative Parenting." Peters, in her participation in the evangelical left, embodied the new synchronicity of Anabaptist and evangelical orbits.[31]

The stories of Schmidt, Halteman Finger, and Peters represent dozens of other Anabaptist women. Neta Jackson, co-author of *Living Together in a World Falling Apart*, lived in the egalitarian intentional community Reba Place and interacted broadly with the evangelical left. Joyce Gladwell, mother of the best-selling pop sociologist Malcolm Gladwell and member of the EWC in the 1970s, bridged the evangelical world of British theologian-pastor John Stott and the Mennonite world of rural Ontario. Marilyn Peters, graduate of the Mennonite Brethren Biblical Seminary and a doctoral student in theology at Fuller Theological Seminary, hosted events of the San Joaquin Valley EWC chapter at Mennonite Community Church in Fresno, California. Bertha Beachy, manager of a Mennonite bookstore, joined the EWC from Goshen, Indiana. Lois Landis Shenk, author of *Out of Mighty Waters* and representative from the Lancaster Mennonite Conference Peace Commission and the Mennonite Central Committee Women's

---

30. Schmidt, "Second-Class Citizenship in the Kingdom of God," 13–14; Schmidt in Hearn, ed., *Our Struggle to Serve*, 101–8; "Dixie—and Presidency—Beckons Ruth Schmidt," 8; Schmidt, "Remembering Washington '75," 4–5.

31. Hardesty and Scanzoni, *All We're Meant to Be*; Lorraine Peters in Hearn, ed., *Our Struggle*, 73–82; Peters, "Remembering Washington '75," 4–5.

Task Force, joined EWC from Lancaster, Pennsylvania. Katie Funk Wiebe, an English professor at the Mennonite Brethren Tabor College in Hillsboro, Kansas, and speaker at a San Francisco Bay chapter of the EWC, researched the contributions made by Mennonite women on the mission field and during times of persecution. These women—and many others including Mary Gramberg, a founding member of the Central Valley EWC chapter and student at the MB Biblical Seminary; Joyce Shutt, a graduate of Bluffton College and chair of the committee of ministers at Fairfield Mennonite Church in Pennsylvania; Dorothy Friesen, a feminist Mennonite doing inner-city work in Elkhart, Indiana; Lucille Sider Dayton, sister of Ron Sider and scholar of nineteenth century holiness women preachers; Kathryn Klassen Neufeld, an MCC worker, clinical psychologist, and leader in EWC; Peggy Voth, an EWC member and pastor of a MB church in Alberta—disproportionately populated the EWC. Their activism and writings, steeped in an egalitarian Anabaptist tradition, significantly added to the ferment of evangelical feminism as it emerged in the 1970s.[32]

* * *

Common elements connected Yoder, Sider, Longacre, Halteman Finger, and other prominent Anabaptists to American evangelical groups. First, despite voicing criticism of evangelicalism, each nonetheless identified with evangelical theology. Each appreciated the seriousness with which the broader evangelical movement took the *evangel*, that is, the gospel of Jesus Christ. The work of Christ on the cross may have social implications, Yoder argued, but it primarily demanded personal transformation. "My purpose," he wrote in *Politics of Jesus*, "is not to reverse a prior error by claiming that justification is *only* social."[33] Evangelicals' unrelenting focus on Jesus, Yoder asserted, potentially could lead to a more vital, faithful spirituality than the

---

32. On Gladwell, see Hearn, *Our Struggle*, 38–49. On Marilyn Peters, see "Chapter and Verse," 10–11. On Landis Shenk, see "Members on the Move," 8. On Funk Wiebe, see Hearn, *Our Struggle*, 131–41; Karne, "Chapter and Verse," 3. On Gramberg, see "Members on the Move," 10. On Shutt, see Hearn, *Our Struggle*, 142–52. On Sider Dayton, see "Our Foremothers," 2. On Klassen Neufeld, see "Executive Council's Busy Session," 2; "Introducing . . .," 4. On Voth, see "Members on the Move," 10.

33. On this important point, see Nation, "Politics of Yoder," 44–45.

parsed, academic theology of Protestant liberalism. In the early 1970s, Yoder predicted that "evangelicalism's social action can outlast liberal activist fads."[34] Many evangelicals reciprocated by claiming Yoder as their own. In 2000 *Christianity Today* named *Politics of Jesus* as one of the ten most important religous books of the twentieth century.

Second, this fundamental theological resonance took fuller form as American Anabaptists, often denoted as the "quiet in the land," emerged out of ethnic enclaves in the 1950s and 1960s. Thousands of Mennonites joined Sider and Yoder in flocking to college, graduate school, and urban centers. Their increased social mobility brought them into closer contact with other religious bodies in America, perhaps none more than evangelicalism.[35]

American Anabaptists thus encountered evangelicalism at a particularly fortuitous moment. The 1970s—a decade rife with war protest, economic stagnation, and energy crises—marked the end of a liberal consensus. Progressive evangelicals, aghast both by the disintegration of a political tradition they were just starting to embrace and the vitality of an emerging religious right, looked to the historic tradition of Anabaptism for resources. They were a receptive audience for Yoder, Sider, Longacre, and Halteman Finger. In Yoder's *Politics of Jesus*, the evangelical left found a vision of the church as a community of peace that could address the problem of violence in the world. In Sider's *Rich Christians in an Age of Hunger*, they found a sharp critique of American materialism and global inequalities. In Longacre's *More with Less* cookbook, they learned that kitchens were moral spaces where a theology of simple living could be practiced. From Anabaptist women in the Evangelical Women's Caucus, they learned to apply the logic of the "priesthood of all believers" to gender. Anabaptists profoundly shaped the direction of the evangelical left in the 1970s.[36]

34. Yoder quoted in Marty, "Needed," 1–6.

35. On Yoder as an evangelical, see Nation, *John Howard Yoder*, xx. On the significance of *Politics of Jesus*, see "Books of the Century." On the social mobility of Mennonites in the postwar era, see Bush, *Two Kingdoms*; Miller, *Wise as Serpents*; Driedger and Kraybill, *Mennonite Peacemaking*.

36. To be sure, the kaleidoscopic evangelical left featured colorful diversity and multiple sources. Donald Dayton, for example, mined nineteenth-century holiness circles for a radical evangelical heritage. See Dayton, *Discovering an Evangelical Heritage*. Two-thirds world evangelicals offered critiques of American-style capitalism and politics. See Escobar, "Social Responsibility," 129–52; Costas, *The Church and Its Mission*. Reformed evangelicals, associated with Calvin College and the

Three decades later, a recapitulation of the 1970s encounter between evangelicals and Anabaptists is underway. Doris Longacre's *More with Less* cookbook, now in its forty-seventh printing, remains in print along with a new Herald Press cookbook promoting simple living. *Simply in Season*, written by Mennonites Mary Beth Lind and Cathleen Hockman-Wert, is also popular among broader evangelicals. An increasingly unpopular war disillusioned many evangelicals with George W. Bush. A deep economic recession and concerns about global warming are making evangelicals suspicious of unfettered free enterprise. Like the uncertain 1970s, several prominent evangelicals again stand at the intersection of evangelical and Anabaptist worlds. Shane Claiborne, founding member of The Simple Way intentional community, marshals Yoderian theology to take on conservative evangelical heavyweights such as Charles Colson. Greg Boyd, a megachurch pastor in metropolitan Minneapolis, regularly critiques American nationalism and the war in Iraq. At a time when many traditional Anabaptist denominations are declining in numbers and vitality, perhaps this renewed convergence will revitalize American Anabaptism as much as evangelicalism.[37]

BIBLIOGRAPHY

Augsburger, David. "Talking Up—Talking Down—Talking With." *EWC Update* 5 (1981) 2.
Augsburger, Myron. "Revolution and World Evangelism." In *Christ the Liberator*, edited by John Stott, 121–31. Downers Grove, IL: InterVarsity, 1971.
Barnet, Richard J. *The Lean Years: Politics in the Age of Scarcity*. New York: Simon & Schuster, 1980.
"Books of the Century." *Christianity Today*, 24 April 2000.
Boyd, Gregory. *The Myth of a Christian Nation: How the Quest for Political Power Is Destroying the Church*. Grand Rapids: Zondervan, 2005.
Brown, Dale. "The Powers: A Bible Study." *Post-American* 3 (1974) 3, 13.
Bush, Perry. "Anabaptism Born Again: Mennonites, New Evangelicals, and the Search for a Usable Past, 1950–1980." *Fides et Historia* 25 (1993) 26–47.
———. *Two Kingdoms, Two Loyalties: Mennonite Pacifism in Modern America*. Baltimore: Johns Hopkins University Press, 1998.

Reformed Journal, promoted a realist version of evangelical politics. See Mouw, *Political Evangelism*.

37. Claiborne, *Irresistible Revolution*; Claiborne, *Jesus for President*; Boyd, *Myth of a Christian Nation*; Lind and Hockman-Wert, *Simply in Season*. On the decline of Anabaptist denominations, see Kanagy, *Road Signs*.

"Chapter and Verse." *EWC Update* 9 (1985) 10–11.

Claiborne, Shane. *The Irresistible Revolution: Living as an Ordinary Radical*. Grand Rapids: Zondervan, 2006.

———. *Jesus for President: Politics for Ordinary Radicals*. Grand Rapids: Zondervan, 2008.

Costas, Orlando. *The Church and Its Mission: A Shattering Critique from the Third World*. Wheaton, IL: Tyndale, 1974.

Curry, Dean C. "Biblical Politics and Foreign Policy." In *Evangelicals and Foreign Policy: Four Perspectives*, edited by Michael Cromartie, 43–64. Lanham, MD: University Press of America, 1989.

Dayton, Donald W. *Discovering an Evangelical Heritage*. New York: Harper & Row, 1976.

Dayton, Donald W., and Lucille Sider Dayton. "Women as Preachers: Evangelical Precedents." *Christianity Today* 29 (1975) 4–7.

Dayton, Lucille Sider. "The Rise of Women in Evangelicalism." Unpublished manuscript, 1974.

"Dixie—and Presidency—Beckons Ruth Schmidt." *EWC Update* 6 (1982) 8.

Driedger, Leo, and Donald B. Kraybill. *Mennonite Peacemaking: From Quietism to Activism*. Scottdale, PA: Herald, 1994.

Ediger, Peter. "Explo '72." *Post-American* 1 (1972) 13.

"Editor's Note." *Post-American* 3 (1974) 31.

Eller, Vernard. *The Simple Life*. Grand Rapids: Eerdmans, 1983.

Ellis, Bill. "Books for Young Evangelicals." *Christian Booksellers Magazine* (1975) 25.

Escobar, Samuel. "Anabaptism and Radical Christianity." In *Engaging Anabaptism: Conversations with a Radical Tradition*, edited by John D. Roth, 75–88. Scottdale, PA: Herald, 2001.

———. "The Social Responsibility of the Church in Latin America." *Evangelical Missions Quarterly* 6 (1970) 129–52.

"Executive Council's Busy Session." *EWC Update* 7 (1983) 2.

Finger, Tom. *A Contemporary Anabaptist Theology: Biblical, Historical, Constructive*. Downers Grove, IL: InterVarsity, 2004.

Fiske, Edward B. "A 'Religious Woodstock' Draws 75,000." *New York Times*, 16 June 1972, 19.

Foster, Richard J. *Freedom of Simplicity*. New York: Harper & Row, 1981.

Friesen, Delores Histand. *Living More with Less: Study/Action Guide*. Scottdale, PA: Herald, 1981.

Gaebelein, Frank E. "Challenging Christians to the Simple Life." *Christianity Today* 22 (1979) 22–26.

Gill, David W. "The Simple Life." *Christianity Today* 18, 26 July 1974, 29–31.

———. "Toward a Radical Christian Identity." *Right On* 6 (1974).

———. Interview with John Howard Yoder. *Right On* 6 (1975).

Gish, Arthur G. *Beyond the Race Race*. Scottdale, PA: Herald, 1973.

———. *The New Left and Christian Radicalism*. Grand Rapids: Eerdmans, 1970.

———. "The New Left and Christian Radicalism." *Post-American* 1 (1971) 8.

———. "Reconsideration." *Post-American* 1 (1972) 12.

———. "Simplicity." *The Other Side* 9 (1973) 14–16.

———. "Simplicity." *Post-American* 1 (1972) 10.

Hansen, Barbara. "From the Mennonites: A Cookbook That's Critical of our Eating Habits." *Los Angeles Times*, 6 May 1976, G6.

Hardesty, Nancy and Letha Scanzoni. *All We're Meant to Be: A Biblical Approach to Women's Liberation*. Waco, TX: Word, 1975.
Hearn, Virginia, editor. *Our Struggle to Serve: The Stories of Fifteen Evangelical Women*. Waco, TX: Word, 1979.
Heinz, Donald. "An American Fantasy." *Right On* 6 (1974) 4.
"An Interview with Reba Place Fellowship." *Post-American* 2.4 (September–October 1973) 8–11.
"Introducing . . ." *EWC Update* 9 (1985) 4.
Jackson, Dave and Neta. *Living Together in a World Falling Apart*. Carol Stream, IL: Creation, 1974.
———. "A Question about Insurance." In *Living More Simply*, edited by Ronald J. Sider, 157–59. Downers Grove, IL: InterVarsity, 1980.
Kanagy, Conrad. *Road Signs for the Journey: A Profile of Mennonite Church USA*. Scottdale, PA: Herald, 2007.
Karne, Mary. "Chapter and Verse." *EWC Update* 5 (1981) 3.
Kaufman, Gordon. "Nonresistance and Responsibility." *Concern: A Pamphlet Series* 6 (1958).
Lind, Mary Beth, and Cathleen Hockman-Wert. *Simply in Season: A World Community Cookbook*. Scottdale, PA: Herald, 2005.
Longacre, Doris Janzen. *Living More with Less*. Scottdale, PA: Herald, 1980.
———. *More with Less*. Scottdale, PA: Herald, 1976.
Marty, Martin. "Needed: Revised Social Gospel." *Context*, 15 March 1974, 1–6.
"Members on the Move." *EWC Update* 6 (1982) 8.
"Members on the Move." *EWC Update* 7 (1983) 10.
Miller, Keith Graber. *Wise as Serpents, Innocent as Doves: American Mennonites Engage Washington*. Knoxville: University of Tennessee Press, 1996.
Mooneyham, W. Stanley. "Door Interview with Stanley Mooneyham." *Wittenburg Door* 23 (1975) 12.
———. *What Do You Say to a Hungry World?* Waco, TX: Word, 1975.
Morris, Leon. "Thinking Things Through: The Witness of the Church Is Adulterated by the Affluent Lifestyles of Its Members." *Christianity Today* 23.22, 21 September 1979, 60, 62.
Mott, Stephen Charles. "'The Politics of Jesus' and our Responsibilities." *Reformed Journal* 26 (1976) 7–10.
Mouw, Richard. *Political Evangelism*. Grand Rapids: Eerdmans, 1973.
Nation, Mark Thiessen. *John Howard Yoder: Mennonite Patience, Evangelical Witness, Catholic Convictions*. Grand Rapids: Eerdmans, 2006.
———. "The Politics of Yoder Regarding the *The Politics of Jesus*." In *Radical Ecumenicity: Pursuing Unity and Continuity after John Howard Yoder*, edited by John C. Nugent, 37–56. Abilene, TX: Abilene Christian University Press, 2010.
"Our Foremothers: Catherine Booth: Co-founder of the Salvation Army." *Daughters of Sarah* 1 (1974) 2.
Peters, Lorraine. "Remembering Washington '75." *EWC Update* 9 (1985) 4–5.
"Piety's Progress." *Christian Century* 41.45, 25 December 1974, 1214.
Pinnock, Clark. "The Radical Reformation." *Post-American* 1 (1972) 4–5.
Rasmussen, Larry L. "The Simple Life." *Religion in Life* 43 (1974) 381–83.
"Recipe of the Week." *Sojourners Weekly Update*, 1 December 1980, 1.
Redekop, Calvin. *Leaving Anabaptism: From Evangelical Mennonite Brethren to Fellowship of Evangelical Bible Churches*. Scottdale, PA: Herald, 1998.

"Reta Finger, Susie Stanley Join Executive Council." *EWC Update* 5 (1981) 7.

Roth, John D., editor. *Engaging Anabaptism: Conversations with a Radical Tradition.* Scottdale, PA: Herald, 2001.

Russell, Chandler. "Ph.D. Scrounges for a Living." *Los Angeles Times*, 1 December 1975, 3.

Schmidt, Ruth. "Remembering Washington '75." *EWC Update* 9 (1985) 4–5.

———. "Second-Class Citizenship in the Kingdom of God." *Christianity Today* 15 (1971) 13–14.

"Seeds." *Sojourners* 7 (1978) 30.

"Signs of a New Order." *Post-American* (Summer 1972) 13.

Sider, Ronald J. *Cry Justice! The Bible on Hunger and Poverty.* Downer's Grove, IL: InterVarsity, 1980.

———. "Does God Live in Glass Houses? Cautions against Ecclesiastical Elegance." *Christianity Today* 23 (1979) 14–19.

———. "An Historic Moment for Biblical Social Concern." In *The Chicago Declaration*, edited by Ronald J. Sider, 11–42. Carol Stream, IL: Creation, 1974.

———. *Lifestyle in the Eighties: An Evangelical Commitment to Simple Lifestyle.* Philadelphia: Westminster, 1982.

———. *Living More Simply: Biblical Principles & Practical Models.* Downers Grove, IL: InterVarsity, 1980.

———. "The Ministry of Affluence: A Graduated Tithe." *HIS* 32 (1972) 6–8.

———. *Rich Christians in an Age of Hunger: A Biblical Study.* Downers Grove, IL: InterVarsity, 1977.

Sider, Ronald J., editor. *The Chicago Declaration.* Carol Stream, IL: Creation, 1974.

Simon, Arthur. *Bread for the World.* New York: Paulist, 1975.

Stafford, Tim. "Ron Sider's Unsettling Crusade." *Christianity Today* 36 (1992) 18–22.

Swartley, Willard. *Slavery, Sabbath, War, and Women: Case Issues in Biblical Interpretation.* Scottdale, PA: Herald, 1983.

Thompson, Liz. "Chapter and Verse." *EWC Update* 7 (1983) 12.

Toews, Paul. *Mennonites in American Society, 1930–1970: Modernity and the Persistence of Religious Community.* Scottdale, PA: Herald, 1996.

Van Beilen, Aileen. *Hunger Awareness Dinners: A Planning Manual.* Scottdale, PA: Herald, 1978.

Van Elderen, Marlin J. "Evangelicals and Liberals: Is There a Common Ground?" *Christianity and Crisis* 34 (1974) 151–55.

Weaver, J. Denny. *Keeping Salvation Ethical: Mennonite and Amish Atonement Theology in the Late Nineteenth Century.* Scottdale, PA: Herald, 1997.

Yoder, John Howard. "After Foreign Mission—What?" *Christianity Today* 6 (1962) 12–13.

———. "The Anabaptist Dissent: The Logic of the Place of the Disciple in Society." *Concern: A Pamphlet Series* 1 (1954).

———. "The Anabaptist Vision." *The Asbury Seminarian* 21 (1967) 15–22.

———. "The Biblical Mandate." *Post-American* 3 (1974) 21–25.

———. "The Biblical Mandate for Evangelical Social Action." In *The Chicago Declaration*, edited by Ronald J. Sider, 86–114. Carol Stream, IL: Creation, 1974.

———. "Capital Punishment and the Bible." *Christianity Today* 4 (1960) 3–10.

———. "The Christian and War in the Perspective of Historical and Systematic Theology." Seminar study paper prepared for a conference on The Evangelical Christian and Modern War, 26–28 August 1963.

———. "Comments on 'War and the New Morality.'" *Reformed Journal* 18 (1968) 30.
———. "Exodus: Probing the Meaning of Liberation." *Sojourners* 5 (1976) 26–29.
———. "God Used It for Good." *HIS* 24 (1964) 28–29.
———. "An Interview with Reba Place Fellowship." *Post-American* 2 (1973) 8–11.
———. "Just War: Back to Economics." Lecture at Regent College, 1980.
———. "Martin Luther's Forgotten Vision." *The Other Side* 13 (1977) 66–70.
———. "A Non-Baptist View of Southern Baptists." *Review and Expositor* 67 (1970) 219–28.
———. "The Original Revolution." *Post-American* 2 (1973) 4–5, 15.
———. "The Persistence of the Constantinian Heresy." *Right On* 10 (1974) 4–5.
———. *The Politics of Jesus*. Grand Rapids: Eerdmans, 1972.
———. "The Price of Discipleship." Chapel address at Fuller Theological Seminary, January 1978.
———. "Vietnam: A Just War?" *HIS* 28 (1968) 1–3.
———. "Vietnam: Another Option." *HIS* 28 (1968) 8–11.
———. "War, Peace and the Evangelical Challenge." Unpublished presentation in Denver, CO, 19 April 1966.

Archives

Evangelicals for Social Action, Philadelphia, PA.
Billy Graham Center Archives, Wheaton, IL.
Wheaton College Special Collections, Wheaton, IL.
Mennonite Church USA Archives, Goshen, IN.
Herald Archives, Scottdale, PA.

Oral Interviews

Gallagher, Sharon. 2006. Interview with author. July 7. Berkeley, CA.
Greidanus, Morris and Alice. 2008. Interview with author. January 20. South Bend, IN.
Hearn, Walter and Ginny. 2006. Interview with author. July 9. Berkeley, CA.
Mouw, Richard. 2006. Interview with author. July 12. Pasadena, CA.
Olson, Mark. 2009. Interview with author. May 21. South Bend, IN.
Sider, Ronald J. 2005. Interview with author. August 9. Philadelphia, PA.
Treizenburg, Dan. 2007. Interview with author. April 19. South Bend, IN.

11

The Evangelical-Anabaptist Spectrum

The Political Theologies of Francis Schaeffer, John Howard Yoder, and Jim Wallis

GEOFFREY C. BOWDEN

INTRODUCTION

EVANGELICALISM'S PROPULSION INTO THE political spotlight in America probably has as much to do with developments in the larger American cultural and social context as it does with the theological, sociological, and economic dynamics of American evangelicalism. It is no coincidence that the late 1970s sees both the rise of the Religious Right and the resurgence of a political and intellectual conservatism welcoming of a religious bloc to the larger coalition. Oddly enough, we do not see major theological shifts occurring in evangelical theology that allow for this renewed emphasis on political activity. It is as if the political-theological impulse always existed latently, only waiting for the right political environment to manifest itself.

Anabaptists, on the other hand, have yet to organize and assert themselves as a bloc into the fray of American partisan politics, and we should probably not hold our breath. Given their historical theological separatism and the commitment to non-violence, it is no wonder that Anabaptists generally shy away from the political arena, a scene rife with power and compromise, neither of which is the currency of historic Anabaptism. Yet, beneath the infamous non-involvement, there exists a theology of the state and of Christian identity in light of the existence and activity of government. And while not many Anabaptists or evangelicals would probably describe their theologies as "political theologies," embedded within both of these traditions is a set of theological views that fit together in a variety of ways that would constitute theological perspectives on governmental institutions, political activity generally, and Christian involvement in that activity.

This essay does not explore evangelical or Anabaptist political theologies in general. Rather, it focuses on a small set of three thinkers who have held/hold influential positions in both evangelical and Anabaptist circles. As opposed to painting with a broad brush, the essay delves into the specifics of the theological writings of Francis Schaeffer, Jim Wallis, and John Howard Yoder, all of whom have articulated a theological vision of politics for the Christian citizen, and each of which pursues a distinct trajectory of political theology. Wallis' thinking is an amalgam of that of Schaeffer and Yoder, with subtle developmental currents, with the earlier Wallis sharing much of Yoder's ecclesiological "otherness" and the later Wallis adopting a politically engaged strategy akin to Schaeffer's mature position.[1]

Before beginning the analyses, I should explain what I mean by "political theology." Political theology is essentially thinking about politics, government, and citizenship from a theological perspective with largely theological language. It takes many forms and raises many questions about both theology and politics. It is a mistake to assume that political theology is simply taking policy positions that are compatible with or even mandated by Christian ethics. This is a part of political theology, but the discipline goes much deeper, often treading at the very doctrinal core of the Christian faith. Political theology is not simply the political wing of Christian theology; in its more

---

1. It should be noted at the outset that while the essay attempts to offer charitable interpretations of the texts chosen for analysis, the essay contains a normative thread that contends that, while the evangelical political theologies of Schaeffer and Wallis make positive contributions to thinking about politics from a Christian perspective, Yoder offers the most helpful theological framework simply because of its rootedness in the biblical narrative. I will not spend any time developing a "rubric" for assessing the superiority of one view over another, but will let the expositions develop dialogically, and it should become clear in that process why I think Yoder's view is the superior one.

sophisticated versions, it is the essence of Christian theology. But the extent to which this is so depends on the role that politics plays in a particular theological vision.

THE EVANGELICAL-ANABAPTIST SPECTRUM: SCHAEFFER AND YODER

Evangelicalism is a broad umbrella, to be sure, and any attempt to pin down "an evangelical political theology" would exclude many who find themselves under this umbrella. To avoid such an attempt, this essay will focus on one of the early pioneers of evangelical political theology in the twentieth century. Francis Schaeffer's influence on evangelical thinking and practice spans from correspondence with some of the most prominent evangelical thinkers of the era to a widely-disseminated video series viewed in even the smallest Sunday School classes.[2] But it was his later writings encouraging American evangelicals to launch headlong into what would become known as the "culture wars" by vigorously advocating for policy and legal positions commensurate with the Christian faith that would be Schaeffer's most enduring influence on evangelicalism. In that respect, Schaeffer will serve as a model of evangelical political theology in this essay.

The work of John Howard Yoder will represent Anabaptist political theology in this essay. There is no more prolific and influential Anabaptist theologian in the twentieth century, and as Wallis' political theology will make clear, a portion of Yoder's legacy is taking Anabaptist theology into the mainstream, directing and inspiring several generations of theologians. While Yoder attempts to challenge the political disengagement of his own tradition, the unique manner in which he reads the Scriptures renders his version of "engagement" much different than that of Schaeffer. Placing our political activity with a theoretical context shaped by an eschatology hewn out of the biblical narrative, Yoder rejects the need to be "politically relevant" in favor of faithfulness to the witness of the cross, a witness that can adopt a language that the world understands.

---

2. Schaeffer's dialogue with Mark Noll and George Marsden set some of the fault lines for future debates in evangelicalism. And I remember being in more than one Sunday School class of five to six people where we watched an installment of "How Should We Then Live?"

Francis Schaeffer and the Priority of God's Law

After moving to Switzerland to serve as a missionary for the Bible Presbyterian Church with his wife, Edith, Francis Schaeffer grew uncomfortable with the denomination's hostile engagements against the enemies of its fundamentalist doctrine. While affirming the doctrines themselves, Schaeffer concluded that "orthodox belief must travel hand in hand with demonstrative love" and not bellicosity toward those one disagrees with.[3] This set the stage for Schaeffer's transition from his "American fundamentalism" period to what historian Barry Hankins calls Schaeffer's "European evangelicalism" (stage two), most notable for the formation of the L'Abri community in the mountains of Switzerland, and Schaeffer's subsequent emergence (stage three) as a central figure in the rise of a politically-active evangelicalism in America.[4] It is this last stage of Schaeffer's ministry that is most relevant for this study, because it is during this period that he hones his message that authentic Christianity cannot be limited to the inner, spiritual life, but must be actively engaged with culture and even politics. Schaeffer's most systematic thinking about the relationship between the Christian life and the political arena is his *A Christian Manifesto*, published initially in 1981.

Schaeffer frames his analysis of the circumstances of Protestant Christianity in late twentieth-century America as a totalizing battle between two incompatible worldviews: Judeo-Christian Truth and humanism.[5] Christianity is true, for Schaeffer, in that it is "true to total reality—the total of what is, beginning with the central reality, the objective existence of the personal-infinite God."[6] Humanism, as explicated by the *Humanist Manifestos I* and *II*, situates the human being as the central reality of the cosmos, and the final reality of the universe is material. For Schaeffer, one must go beyond merely acknowledging the tension between these two perspectives to recognizing that they are all-encompassing systems of thought that are

---

3. Hamilton, "Dissatisfactions of Francis Schaeffer," 24.

4. Hankins, *Francis Schaeffer*, see especially ch. 2 and ch. 8.

5. Schaeffer often uses the term "Judeo-Christian" to refer to principles that both Christianity and Judaism hold in common and, hence, can be allies. However, he also uses the terms "Christianity" and "Christian," but does not imply that Judaism should be excluded from the point that he is making. I will try to stick closely with Schaeffer's particular usage of these terms in various contexts.

6. Schaeffer, *Christian Manifesto*, 19–20.

incompatible at their very core and, thus, natural enemies. The arena where these two "worldviews" clash most prominently is that of law and politics, though, regrettably, Christians have failed both to recognize this clash and to engage in the battle, a result that Schaeffer attributes to the Pietist movement under the leadership of P. J. Spener. The Pietist movement "made a sharp division between the 'spiritual' and the 'material' world—giving little, or no, importance to the 'material' world," and the politics and public morality issues that accompany the material world.[7] In order to prevent a cultural, moral, and intellectual victory for humanism, Christians must shun the Pietistic tendency to isolate the Christian faith from the public realm. In short, God cares that we act and how we act in society. However, the details of the manifestation of Christian activity in the public realm are a bit more complicated.

The fundamental importance of Christ for political society and policy comes with the economy of salvation in the crucifixion event. Schaeffer channels Henry de Bracton's "Judeo-Christian worldview" to contend that Christ's death for the sins of the world reveals that God prefers to use justice to regulate the world before the use of power: "Christ died that justice, rooted in what God is, would be the solution."[8] The political and constitutional implications of this are clear for Schaeffer: societies should be ruled by laws and not by men, to prevent the formation of tyranny or a "governmental elite." God's choosing to reconcile humankind to himself through the instrument of justice as opposed to brute force serves as a model for the construction of human societies that govern by laws, and not elite prerogative.

Schaeffer argues that the Christian worldview provides not only a model for the form of governance, but also some guidelines for the substance of the laws. A measure of justice emerges with the application of a uniform legal code for all, and not just those who are ruled. But justice is embodied to a fuller extent in a legal code that has "God's written Law, back through the New Testament to Moses' written Law" as its foundation.[9] The relationship between the Christian religion and civil society begins to take shape in Schaeffer's presentation. The Christian faith, or more specifically, the moral principles of

---

7. Ibid., 18–19.
8. Ibid., 28.
9. Ibid.

the Christian faith, is essential to establishing boundaries for human freedom, and the civil law must garner support from these principles to achieve the justice that is requisite to keeping society from collapsing on itself. Presumably, the details of this moral and legal code are the basics of the Ten Commandments, which must then be expanded to address the varieties of human activity.

These moral and legal principles must be differentiated from the doctrinal claims of Christianity, which should not be embodied in the legal code, lest we establish a theocracy, a regime-type that is theologically off-limits given the emergence of the church in the New Testament. Christians have an institution with the mission of spreading the gospel, and do not need state interference in that mission. We see the mistakes of an official alignment between church and state with the reign of Constantine:

> There have been times of very good government when this interrelationship of church and state has been present. But through the centuries it has caused great confusion between loyalty to the state and loyalty to Christ, between patriotism and being a Christian.
> We must not confuse the Kingdom of God with our country. To say it another way: "We should not wrap Christianity in our national flag."[10]

This is a rather odd argument from Schaeffer, considering that he spends a considerable amount of time in the early portions of *A Christian Manifesto* attempting to make the case that America has deep and important Christian roots, and that those roots have regrettably been supplanted by the "religion" of humanism. Furthermore, Christians, and especially Christian lawyers, should do everything that they can to challenge the onslaught of "sociological law," which is grounded on the premise that human beings are the measure of their own activities. The most pressing target of this legal warfare should be abortion laws, and particularly the U.S. Supreme Court's ruling in *Roe v. Wade*.

Christians must engage the political realm, first, to endeavor to reform the laws so that they are more in line with the principles of God's law.[11] If, however, the state becomes so corrupted that Christians

---

10. Ibid., 121.

11. Schaeffer quotes Matt 22:21, "Give to Caesar what is Caesar's, and to God

cannot in good conscience continue to endorse and/or obey its laws, the Christian then has the duty to be disobedient and may even be required to violently subvert the authority of the state. The duty that Christians are given to obey the state, which Schaeffer surmises from his reading of Romans 13:1–4, must be viewed within a larger moral and theological context: "God has ordained the state as a *delegated* authority; it is not autonomous. The state is to be an agent of justice, to restrain evil by punishing the wrongdoer, and to protect the good in society. When it does the reverse, *it has no proper authority*. It is then a usurped authority and as such it becomes lawless and is tyranny."[12] Schaeffer then mines intellectual history to construct a defense of armed revolution against a government that failed to base its laws on the Bible. John Knox, the famous Scotsman, becomes the hero of Schaeffer's intellectual history, going even further than the giants of the Protestant Reformation: "Whereas Reformers such as Martin Luther and John Calvin had reserved the right to rebellion to the civil rulers alone, Knox went further. He maintained that the common people had the right and duty to disobedience [sic] and rebellion if state officials ruled contrary to the Bible. To do otherwise would be rebellion against God."[13] Knox subsequently has a prominent influence on Samuel Rutherford, whom Schaeffer has already mysteriously elevated as the seminal influence on the American founders, especially the Christian John Witherspoon.[14] When the writers of the Declaration of Independence make the case for the dissolution of ties with Great Britain, Knox and Rutherford supply the Christian theology needed to bring the move in-line with God's law. John Locke's influence on the founders comes merely as a secularizer of the principles articulated

---

what is God's" as evidence that "civil government . . . stands under the Law of God." *Christian Manifesto*, 90.

12. Ibid., 91.

13. Ibid., 97.

14. Barry Hankins states, "Significantly, virtually no professional historian, Christian or secular, believes that Rutherford had significant influence on the American founding. Schaeffer's emphasis on Rutherford, therefore, is highly idiosyncratic, and it would probably be safe to say that whenever one sees a Christian author discussing Rutherford, the author probably has been influenced by Schaeffer and/or [John] Whitehead" (*Francis Schaeffer*, 199). For an instance of such a Christian author discussing the influence of Rutherford and others on the American founding see, Hall, *Genevan Reformation*, who also spent time at L'Abri.

earlier by Knox and Rutherford, namely that law ultimately has to be based on God's authority.

Schaeffer styles his *Christian Manifesto* as a call to action, but stops short of saying that Christians in America should now actively engage in resistance to the U.S. Government.[15] Other, less violent means of engagement should precede resistance. Schaeffer further rationalizes resistance to the government by forging a distinction between the office of the magistrate and the person that holds that office. One must always be subject to the office of the magistrate, even while one resists the person who holds that office. Much of the confusion issuing forth from Schaeffer's position stems from his unwillingness to give a more extended explication of what it means to "be subject" to governing authorities. From the context of Schaeffer's use of this term, it appears that he equates "being subject" with "being obedient," especially in those contexts where he juxtaposes "being subject" with "being resistant." At the very least, Schaeffer understands "being subject" as not being actively disobedient, which obviously includes not being violently resistant. To say the least, much of this discussion could do with considerable clarification. Nevertheless, Schaeffer seems to suggest that a Christian has the unqualified biblical duty to obey the state, stemming from both Romans 13:1–4 and 1 Peter 2, and to ensure its continued existence, because the state has a theological role to play at this current point in human history. However, this duty extends to the offices of the state, and not to the people who currently hold those offices.

Schaeffer's attempt to draw deep connections between the American founding and the Christian faith gives rise to several important implications. First, Schaeffer lets the concerns of government establish the framework for Christianity's influence on government. Government is concerned with law, justice, and order, all three of which rightly transcend the human being's natural desires, which often have a sinful cast. This transcendent law, which confers justice and order on the society that obeys this law, has a natural correlate in the Christian faith in the divine God that transcends the people of Israel in the Bible. God's interaction with the people of Israel is

---

15. My reading of Schaeffer concludes that when he uses the term "resistance" in the context of a citizen's obedience or disobedience to government, he is referencing some version of violent resistance. He does not seem to make much of "non-violent resistance" as an option.

through his transcendent law, which is periodically written down for the people and stands as a substitute for God's using his omnipotence to maintain justice and order. So, Schaeffer's first conclusion in his political theology is that God desires that societies be governed by law, and not the arbitrary use of force. Second, those laws must find their normativity in something that transcends human desires and the material world. Humanism makes the mistake of thinking that human beings and their desires are the guide to living, so rooting laws in the transcendent (God's law) obviates this mistake. Third, Schaeffer does not delve any deeper into the biblical narrative to provide further specificity to his conclusion that God's law should be the foundation of a society. Oddly, there is no real discussion of Jesus in Schaeffer's *Christian Manifesto*, nor is there an attempt to understand God's relationship with the nation of Israel, and the subsequent developments in the New Testament as a narrative, a story of God's interaction with his people. In this fashion, Schaeffer provides something of a model for Christian thinking about politics in his avoidance of talking about the specifics of Jesus' teachings, life, death, and resurrection. The more vaguely one envisions God and God's relationship to human government, the less one has to deal with the messy details of the Christian faith and the implications that may have for interacting with government. Hence, Schaeffer's formula: God governs Israel with his law, so Americans should govern their society by God's law. There may also be a historical reason for a non-narrative, Jesus-avoiding account of political theology: drawing a close connection between the American founders and the Christian faith would become much more difficult. The tendency to speak of God in vague, non-historical, non-narrative ways has the advantage of being able to link God to a much wider range of arguments and political positions, and makes engaging the public arena easier and disarming. More people will be willing to entertain arguments rooted in a vague notion of God's law than they will be to listen to arguments that emerge out of the biblical narrative of Jesus' interactions with the powers of his day.

Yoder and the Eschatological Politics of the Kingdom of God

On the surface, John Howard Yoder's understanding of the relationship between religion and politics, between the Christian and his or her government looks very similar to that of both Schaeffer and Wallis.

The Christian faith leads adherents to a certain set of moral positions, positions that Yoder, Schaeffer, and Wallis share to a large extent, and those adherents, whether collectively or individually, should find occasion to encourage government to align itself with some of the moral positions of the Christian faith.[16]

A reader might assume that, as the single Anabaptist in this comparison of evangelicals and Anabaptists in the area of political theology, Yoder is representative of the Anabaptist tradition as a whole. That would be a mistake. In many ways, Yoder is a traditional Anabaptist, committed to the centrality of the cross as salvific and as a model for Christian discipleship, advocating peace in every instance of conflict in which the Christian finds him or herself. But the nuances of Yoder's political theology reveal that he is surreptitiously attempting to rend Anabaptist communities away from their traditional separatism from the world, especially their non-involvement in social and political matters. In this regard, Yoder looks a lot like Schaeffer and Wallis, as all three desire to wrest pietistic Christians from their quietistic slumber and lead them to a more robust social consciousness. Christians cannot not pay attention to the world around them.[17]

This presentation of Yoder's political theology will begin at the end: eschatology.[18] When Jesus proclaimed that the Kingdom of God

---

16. It should be noted at the outset that while Wallis and Schaeffer both had seminary training and both continue/continued to study and seek the truth after seminary training, Yoder is the only one of the three who was trained as a professional theologian. His writings are generally not styled for popular consumption (they are often dense and written in the convoluted language of the discipline), and often his writings plunge the reader into particularized debates between Yoder and some of the giants of theology, noticeably Reinhold Niebuhr and Karl Barth in the writings on the topic of this essay. For a very helpful account of Yoder's life and intellectual influences, see Nation, *John Howard Yoder*, esp. ch. 1. A discussion of Yoder's interaction with Barth and his understanding of law and natural law is offered in Forrester, "John Howard Yoder," 407–12.

17. We have a host of evidence to suggest that Yoder was engaged in moral discussions about public issues. His refusal to simply be a "Mennonite theologian" or a "separatist" is evidenced in his profound engagement with the public issues of the day. For instance, on the issue of law, Thomas L. Shaffer provides accounts of Yoder's interaction with the law professors and students at the University of Notre Dame. See Shaffer, *Moral Memoranda*, and Shaffer in conversation with John Howard Yoder, "Anabaptist Law Schools," 65–76.

18. Anyone familiar with Yoder's corpus of work knows that he was a prolific writer. This brief excursus on his political theology will only address a few of his writings (as with Schaeffer and Wallis) that the author deems most apposite for pre-

was at hand, he restructured the notion of time for the people of God. While the Kingdom of God is an alternative political reality, as the early Wallis asserts, it also compels the Christian to adopt a new vision of the future of the world. Because Jesus inaugurated the Kingdom with his words and actions and because God's victory over death occurred in the resurrection, the fate of the powers and principalities of the Kingdom of the world is sealed, providing Christians with an assurance of the dominion of God over the earth and all that is in it and hope for the fullness of the Kingdom of God in the future. Yoder asserts that eschatology structures and gives meaning to all else that follows: "There is no significance to human effort and, strictly speaking, no history unless life can be seen in terms of ultimate goals. The *eschaton*, the 'Last Thing,' the End-Event, imparts to life a meaningfulness that it would not otherwise have."[19] The Christian faith must be viewed in the framework of a narrative, one that begins long before the incarnation of God in Christ and one that will continue long after the resurrection and ascension in the life and work of the Christian community. The life, teachings, and death of Jesus make far less sense as abstractions from this overarching narrative.

For Yoder, it is precisely in the eschatological narrative that Christians garner a social ethic and a model of Christian interaction with the powers of the world. The very idea of "peace," so routinely vilified as unrealistic and irresponsible, can only be properly understood within this eschatological narrative: "'Peace' describes the pacifist's hope, the goal in the light of which Christians act, the character of Christian actions, the ultimate divine certainly that lets the Christian position make sense; it does not describe the external appearance or the observable results of Christian behavior. This is what we mean by eschatology: a hope that, defying present frustration, defines a present

---

senting the basic structure of his political theology. In no way is this presentation meant to be exhaustive. While the same proviso could be offered for the sections on Wallis and Schaeffer, the massive body of literature that Yoder generated makes it most appropriate to place it here.

19. Yoder, "Peace Without Eschatology?" 145. The parallels of Yoder's political theology with Aristotelian and Thomistic moral theory should not be overlooked. We do not have much evidence to suggest that Yoder spent any significant amount of time reading Aristotle or Aquinas, but he seems to have adopted a remarkably similar insight at the outset of his project. As teleology defines our activity and pursuit of goods, so eschatology imbues the course of history with meaning and direction.

position in terms of the yet unseen goal that gives it meaning."[20] It is precisely because Christians have been given this hope that the future will manifest God's victory that was wrought in the gospel narrative that they can act as if that victory has already been secured. Governments that possess overwhelming force and economies that appear virtually untamable (even by governments!) now exist within a historical context in which they have no control over their ultimate destiny. They must submit to God's dominion.

But, obviously, the powers and principalities have not submitted to God's dominion. So, how are Christians to view the current epoch of human history, the current stage of the narrative before the final consummation of the Kingdom of God? Yoder uses the language of "two aeons" to describe a common time period in history (our current period, between "Pentecost and the Parousia") where there are two different moral realities. One reality, the Kingdom of the world, takes its moral cues from the past, while the other reality, the Kingdom of God, embodies a different, scandalous ethic. The former kingdom does not recognize the eschatological fate of both this period of time and the kingdom's moral commitments. Violence, power, and oppression may seem to be effective in the current realm, but that method of human interaction (and even interaction with the natural world) is doomed. The latter aeon is guided by eschatological hope rooted in the victory of the resurrection.

But how do these two aeons interact with one another, since both exist in the world as we know it now? Yoder provides the following sketch of the nature of God's dominion and the implications of God's victory over death and evil in the current phase of human history:

> Christ is not only the Head of the church; he is at the same time Lord of history, reigning at the right hand of God over the principalities and powers. The old aeon, representative of human history under the mark of sin, has also been brought under the reign of Christ (which is not identical with the consummate kingdom of God, 1 Cor. 15:24). The characteristic of the reign of Christ is that evil, without being blotted out, is channelized by God, in spite of itself, to serve God's purposes. Vengeance itself, the most characteristic manifestation of evil, instead of creating chaos as is its nature, is harnessed through the state in such a way as to preserve order and give room for

20. Ibid., 145.

the growth and work of the church. Vengeance is not thereby redeemed or made good; it is nonetheless rendered subservient to God's purposes, as an anticipation of the promised ultimate defeat of sin.[21]

As opposed to ridding the world of evil completely, a task that would no doubt require a purge akin to the flood or worse, God has chosen to slowly and methodically witness to his victory over the evil of the world by using the powers of the world, even though they are unaware of their being used, to create a suitable "space" for the people of God to witness to God's victory through the exercise of God's love. The extended quote above constitutes a succinct and revealing account of the theological purpose of the state. The state should not be viewed as a moral entity that exists outside the boundaries of Christ's lordship over the earth. It exists within the confines of Christ's reign, and hence, whenever it does either good or evil, those activities are "channeled" to the holy purposes of God, most notably for the sake of the church's work on earth. The specificity of the moral purposes of the state are outlined at various junctures in the Scriptures, summarized as follows: "The reign of Christ means for the state the obligation to serve God by encouraging the good and restraining evil, i.e., to serve peace, to preserve the social cohesion in which the leaven of the gospel can build the church, and also render the old aeon more tolerable."[22] Yoder's theological-moral vision is, in a sense, dualistic, in that the Christian ethic for the state is a function of the state's response to ethics of the Kingdom of God: "When God's will is communicated to man or men in their rebellion, neither God nor His ultimate will changes, but His current demands take into account the nonbelief of the addressee (just as any truly *personal* communication encounters the addressee where he is) and therefore stay within other limits of possibility."[23] Christians should not be violent, but the state is ordained to use the sword for the purpose of encouraging the good, punishing evil, and making the way for the peace of the gospel, because those who fill the offices and fulfill

21. Ibid., 149.

22. Ibid., 158–59.

23. Yoder, *Christian Witness to the State*, 32. I had a long conversation with Yoder several months before his death in which I suggested that he was a dualist in this sense. He rejected the appellation initially, but acceded to my argument in the end. However, this moral dualism should not be confused with a more rigid, ontological dualism between the realm of church and that of state, which Yoder ardently rejects.

the duties of the state are either unaware of the dictates of the Kingdom of God or are in knowing rebellion against them. Nevertheless, this moral dualism has a hierarchical structure, in which the purposes of the state exist for the sake of the purposes of the church. It is when the state understands itself as morally autonomous that it sinks further into rebellion against God's design.

Yoder's most famous work details the precise nature of how Christian interactions with the world find their impetus in the life, death, and resurrection of Christ. *The Politics of Jesus* argues that Jesus was presented with a variety of options for engaging the world, the most tempting of which was the so-called "Zealot-option." From his time in the desert being tempted to usurp governmental authority, to the populist fervor generated by the mass feedings, to the moral authority that could have been leveraged into real political power in the Temple cleansing episode, and finally to the spark of violent insurrection as Peter unsheathed his sword in the Garden of Gethsemane, Jesus rejected the option of assuming worldly power and ruling the Kingdom of God through violence.[24] This does not mean, however, that the Kingdom of God is a spiritual kingdom only, having no worldly manifestations. Rather, the Kingdom of God has a politics that accompanies it, a type of rule that uniquely typifies God's love for his creation, including those in his own image.

For Yoder, the substance of the politics of Jesus comes with the proclamation of the year of Jubilee that comes with the opening reading of the scroll of Isaiah in the temple in Galilee, after the temptation narrative. There are four specific provisions: "(1) leaving the soil fallow, (2) the remission of debts, (3) the liberation of slaves, (4) the return to each individual of his family's property."[25] The teachings, including the Sermon on the Mount, and the healings that occur throughout the remainder of the gospels are merely a further elucidation of the terms of the Jubilee. This set of political practices, centering on the "equation between the practice of Jubilee and the grace of God,"[26] counters the politics of the kingdom of the world. Yoder claims that, biblically, "[the powers] were part of the good creation of God. Society and

---

24. This interpretation comes to the fore in Yoder's brief reading of Luke's gospel, given in ch. 2, "The Kingdom Coming." See Yoder, *Politics of Jesus*, 21ff.

25. Yoder, *Politics of Jesus*, 60.

26. Ibid., 62.

history, even nature, would be impossible without regularity, system, order—and God has provided for this need."[27] But the powers have fallen, seeking to elevate themselves above the authority of God, seeking their own purposes through their own means: "These structures which were supposed to be our servants have become our masters and our guardians."[28] The politics of the Kingdom of God, embodied in the practice of Jubilee and succinctly summarized at various other places in the gospels, constitutes the in-breaking of God's rule in the midst of the rule of the powers of the world. It is an alternative to, and can, at times, be perceived as a threat to the kingdom of the world.

But it is more than Jesus' teachings that bring Yoder to this conclusion. The cross itself becomes the central metaphor for Christian political activity: "Christ is *agape*; self-giving, nonresistant love. At the cross this nonresistance, including the refusal to use political means of self-defense, found its ultimate revelation in the uncomplaining and forgiving death of the innocent at the hands of the guilty. This death reveals how God deals with evil; here is the only valid starting point for Christian pacifism or nonresistance. The cross is the extreme demonstration that *agape* seeks neither effectiveness nor justice and is willing to suffer any loss or seeming defeat for the sake of obedience.[29] It is this sort of rule that the world does not know. Violence, oppression, and mandated-worship of the political system,[30] if not the actual authorities themselves, seem to be the pattern of activity for the principalities and powers.

Because the state operates within the jurisdiction of Christ, Christians are liberated from being morally "responsible" for achieving the state's goals through the means available to the state. Yoder spent much of his early career challenging this notion of "responsibility" that was unchained from any larger theological vision, a notion embedded in a "Constantinian" vision of the world.[31] But Yoder does

27. Ibid., 141.

28. Ibid.

29. Yoder, "Peace without Eschatology?" 147.

30. This claim may seem a bit over-the-top for, say, the current political environment in America. But a closer look at the 2008 Presidential campaign reveals the extent to which the modern nation-state is elevated to the highest importance. Political leaders regularly proclaimed that America is the greatest hope for the future of the world.

31. See Yoder, "Peace without Eschatology?" 161ff., and Yoder, "Reinhold

not eschew all conceptions of Christian responsibility for the social order. Rather, he asserts, "The Christian's responsibility for defeating evil is to resist the temptation to meet it on its own terms. To crush the evil adversary is to be vanquished by him because it means accepting his standards."[32] Furthermore, the problem with the Constantinian understanding of responsibility "is not in affirming that there is a real Christian responsibility to and for the social order; it is rather in the (generally unexamined and unavowed) presuppositions that result in that responsibility's being defined from within the given order alone rather than from the gospel as it infringes upon the situation."[33]

The Christian's responsibility for the social order is to act as leaven in society for the sake of the gospel, witnessing to the in-breaking of God's kingdom and the liberation from the old epoch. While the state has a role to play in this period in salvation history, it is passing away, yielding to the dictates of the Kingdom of God. The "Christian witness to the state" is to call the state back to its purpose in this epoch, and to remind it that its purposes are subservient to the larger eschatological vision of God. A problem, as Yoder sees it, emerges when the church speaks to the state in the moral language of the Christian gospel, a language that the state does not speak. Grace, forgiveness, loving enemies, and not returning evil for evil make no sense to an institution with the habit of vanquishing its enemies. Therefore, the church must speak to state by using "middle-axioms": "These concepts will translate into meaningful and concrete terms the general relevance of the lordship of Christ for a given social ethical issue. They mediate between the general principles of Christological ethics and the concrete problems of political application."[34] So, for fundamental principles of Christian ethics, like non-violence, in Yoder's estimation, the church must always strive to lead the state to achieve the closest possible approximation to the Christian standard. Hence, "When we concede that the state cannot be expected to trust the Holy Spirit, . . . this does not mean that we shall ever completely accept the specific governmental

---

Niebuhr," 101–17.

32. Yoder, "Peace without Eschatology?" 152.

33. Ibid., 162.

34. Yoder, *Christian Witness to the State*, 32–33. Though Yoder dropped the language of "middle-axioms" in his subsequent work, the concept still persists throughout his later works.

violences in the way in which socially conservative Christianity has usually done." The practical upshot of this approach is this: "We do not ask of the government that it be nonresistant; we do, however, ask that it take the most just and the least violent action possible."[35] Hence, Yoder discusses a range of issues about which the church could, and perhaps should, witness to the state, issues ranging from economics to war.

JIM WALLIS AND THE POLITICS OF PROPHECY

Occupying the other end of the evangelical political spectrum from Schaeffer is Jim Wallis, the pastor of the Sojourner's Community in Washington, DC, a Christian community located in one of the most downtrodden neighborhoods in the nation's capital. That Wallis' politics surge to the left comes as no surprise to anyone who has encountered his writings or his personal story. Raised in Detroit, Wallis was largely a product of white, suburban, northern evangelicalism, that is, until he began to get to know the black community in Detroit as a young man. These encounters and friendships revolutionized the manner in which Wallis began to think about the nature of the gospel message and the calling to which Christians must heed. And while race is a critical component of Wallis' agenda for healing both Christian communities and American neighborhoods, the real issue goes even deeper for Wallis: poverty. It is through the conduit of poverty that Wallis begins to construct his political theology, largely because so much of the biblical narrative addresses the topic of financial resources and the lack thereof for essential parts of the people of Israel.[36] But Wallis' political engagement expands beyond poverty and race to encompass a range of issues, including war and budgeting.

Like most of the intellectually-inclined, Wallis' political theology goes through developmental stages, though not the same stages as

---

35. Yoder, *Christian Witness to the State*, 42.

36. The centrality of poverty as *the* Christian moral issue of our day for Wallis was confirmed in a recent interview. When asked whether abortion is the modern-day equivalent of slavery in William Wilberforce's day, Wallis responds in this fashion: "I don't think that abortion is the moral equivalent issue to slavery that Wilberforce dealt with. I think that poverty is the new slavery. Poverty and global inequality are the fundamental moral issues of our time. That's my judgment." See Olsen, "Where Jim Wallis Stands," 54.

Schaeffer's. Where Schaeffer moves from a stance of disengagement to one of engagement and influence, Wallis' early work is that of an active resistor/protester, often bordering on being separatist, and his later work takes the tone of a lobbyist, one seeking to influence power by garnering "a place at the table," as the saying goes. This discussion of Wallis' political theology focuses primarily on three major works, the last two of which share a similar developmental perspective. As with all developmental theses, the most interesting question is the one of continuity: Does the earlier work provide a foundation or launching point for the later work? Or does the later work constitute a complete break with the earlier work, a rejection of previously held positions? Regarding Wallis, there is clear continuity, but also subtle shifts in emphasis that make for interesting comparisons with Schaeffer, which will comprise the last portion of this section.

In the mid-1970s, Wallis wrote his most thorough accounting of political theology to date. *Agenda for Biblical People* presents a defense of an ethically serious and politically active church. The first task concerns the identity of the church, and it is here that the poor enter the stage most prominently. For Wallis, the modern evangelical church in America has grown all-too-mainstream: "A church of comfort, property, privilege, and position stands in sharp contrast with the biblical description of the people of God as aliens, exiles, sojourners, strangers, and pilgrims."[37] The identity of the church embodies an ethical maxim: The church is at once called to identify with the least privileged in society and to be comprised of the least privileged in society. A church of wealth that merely "ministers" to the dispossessed, but refuses to worship with them, either through conscious revulsion or simply as a by-product of constructing church buildings in affluent suburbs, fails to be the people of God at a very basic level.

It is this stark dividing line between those with means and those without that tracks the core theological/biblical distinction at the heart of Wallis' political theology. The Kingdom of God, inaugurated by Jesus' life, teachings, death, and resurrection, comprises the alternative to the kingdom of the world and all for which it stands:

> Jesus announced the beginning of the new order, preached repentance, and began immediately to call his disciples, saying, "Follow me and I will make you fishers of men." The call was to

37. Wallis, *Agenda*, 2.

absolute allegiance and obedient faith, and "they immediately left their nets and followed him." As always, former securities and attachments are left behind as the choice is made to follow Christ, as we "find" our life by "losing it" for the sake of the gospel. Then Christ began to go about healing the infirmities of the people, preaching the gospel of the kingdom, and teaching his disciples how the life to be found in the new order of Christ was at odds with the values of the world.[38]

Notice that Wallis' political theology doesn't begin with the question about how Christians should integrate themselves into the world given their commitment to certain "values" or theological propositions. Nor does Wallis begin with an account of the "path to salvation" that individuals pursue, which then prompts them to live a redeemed existence as individuals who engage the government at an individual level. Rather, Wallis begins with the fundamental theological reality of the establishment of a separate regime or rule: the Kingdom of God. This regime is wholly other from the worldly regimes we encounter daily, and it is by definition corporate, a separate body of people united by their willingness and desire to live under this different regime. Worldly power, whether it be governmental, commercial, or cultural, takes the establishment of the Kingdom of God as an affront to their own power, and so does not passively ignore the establishment of this regime. And rightly so, according to Wallis: "the gospel signals the end of the uncontested dominion of the principalities and powers of the world over people's lives."[39] No longer do God's people have to structure their lives according to the dictates of these powerful institutions.

To begin a brief comparison with Schaeffer's political theology, it is worth noting that both Wallis and Schaeffer stylize the political involvement of Christians as at least potentially adversarial. Schaeffer suggests that government can be good if it achieves God's ordained calling, but if it fails to achieve that calling, Christians may be called to resist government, perhaps even violently. Wallis, at the outset, imbues his political theology with an adversarial framework: the Kingdom of God as alternative to worldly power, supplanting worldly power for those who claim to be the people of God. The role of Christians, as members of the Kingdom of God, becomes to adopt a critical stance

38. Ibid., 18.
39. Ibid., 21.

toward government, rejecting the impulse to conform to the agenda of worldly powers, an impulse that far too many Christians act on. While admitting that government does indeed have a divine calling, Wallis argues that the biblical conclusion about government is one of fallenness: "Institutions, rather than functioning to serve and edify human life, have become distorted, dominating, and even demonic in character and function."[40] Governments are assigned a particular function in God's blueprint for the world (Col 1:15–17), a limited function, the boundaries of which the governments of the world refuse to recognize (Rom 8:38–45). The resulting situation calls for the establishment of the Kingdom of God to serve both as an alternative to the kingdoms of the world and as prophetic witness to those kingdoms, calling them back to their God-ordained purpose.[41]

Wallis contends that the church must exercise a "moral independence," refusing to let herself be co-opted by the powers of the world. One manner of maintaining this moral independence is to be a worshipping community, as "[w]orship is not to be conceived as ritual and ceremony apart from ethics, politics, and other parts of life. Instead, worship and praise become the *style of life* for the gathered community living in faithful obedience to the Word of God in the midst of the blasphemy of the fallen powers."[42] Another critical component to moral independence involves sources of moral authority. Where Schaeffer makes essentially no mention of the life and teachings of Jesus as the source for Christian moral activity, Wallis makes them the center. Wallis summarizes the theme of this moral existence in one word: servanthood.[43] If one were to characterize the critical difference between the evangelical left and the evangelical right in the realm of political theology, it concerns the manner in which, for the left, Jesus' life and teachings model not merely a moral existence, but a radically *political* existence in which power is redefined as serving others despite their potential hostile reaction or their inclination to take advantage of such generosity. Because this notion of power directly contradicts

---

40. Ibid., 43.

41. Wallis draws heavily upon John Howard Yoder, Hans Berkhof, and William Stringfellow at this juncture in the work. I note this to point out that it is precisely in regard to these ideas that Wallis' theology most closely resembles that of Yoder.

42. Wallis, *Agenda*, 47, 50.

43. Ibid., 88ff.

the operative notion of power in political and economic circles, the church's stance toward the world is necessarily going to be one of opposition and prophetic corrective.

In all of this, the evangelical left closely resembles Anabaptism.[44] If the world rejects the prophetic corrective or decides that the very existence of a community that fashions itself as a standing opposition to the *sine qua non* of worldly power is too much of a threat to allow it to continue to exist, the people of God are commanded to reject violence as a mode of engaging one's enemies. Wallis' pacifism is clear: "the Christian community must avoid the false assumption that the salvation and liberation of the world come through violence and force, that the means of the kingdom are compatible with the means of death."[45] Christians must not take this rejection of violence to be a rejection of conflict, for it is precisely in the midst of conflict that Christians should find themselves. Wallis endorses, if not incites, revolution, just not a violent one.

Wallis embraces the language of revolution to present his view on the nature of Christian engagement in politics. While he has made clear that the church needs to maintain moral independence, and that a portion of the method for achieving this is to worship and to live with the dispossessed, Wallis adheres to the view that the avenue for transforming the world, and perhaps for making substantial strides toward the full development of the kingdom is through traditional political routes. It is not enough to live and worship differently; Christians must be the prophetic voice to the principalities and powers on behalf of the poor and dispossessed to bring about the Christian revolution. We get a glimpse of this in his early work: "The task of the Christian revolution is not only to change and reform the economic and political facts and form of the world but to seek fundamental change in the very framework of a world system that needs to be continually examined and tested by the judgment of the Word of God."[46] The church must proclaim the lordship of Christ over the powers of the world, even though they fail to recognize his authority over them. Christ's lordship would involve the governments and economies of the world

---

44. On this point, see the essay by David Swartz in the present volume.
45. Ibid., 84.
46. Ibid., 96–97.

realigning themselves with the priorities of the Kingdom of God, favoring the dispossessed, the widowed, and the lame.

Before transitioning briefly to Wallis' later work, it should be noted that his penchant for political engagement, lobbying, and viewing the political arena as a main avenue for achieving the vision of the Kingdom of God is quite reserved in *Agenda for Biblical People*. Even if the governments of the world were to realign themselves with the principles of God's rule and view themselves as merely one tool whereby God rules this current realm, "[a]ll of these social changes will be temporary and limited in scope and, while they are important, will never satisfy the more absolute demands of the kingdom."[47] As opposed to a full-scale engagement with the powers of the world, Wallis proves cautious and somewhat reserved in advocating a *political* agenda for the church. While Christians must prophesy, the form of this prophecy is as of standing over against, and not necessarily working within the halls of power.

This last claim does not hold true in Wallis' later writings. Both *The Soul of Politics* and *God's Politics* leave the lofty heights of political theology behind, with very little mention of the Kingdom of God as an *alternative* political reality made manifest by the church. With these books, we see a shift, if not in his political theology generally, at least in emphasis. *The Soul of Politics* elevates a "prophetic spirituality" as the moral way forward for Christians, a spirituality rooted in the Hebrew prophets, Jesus, and the early church.[48] The fundamentals of this spirituality are a renewed commitment to economic equality, sharing land resources, eschewing violence, and caring for the "least of these." Already, Wallis presents his moral vision for the church in a starkly different fashion. Issues and issue politics emerge to the fore. He bypasses the theological structure that made sense of his earlier appeal to be an alternative community in favor of a Christian mode of interaction with government that seeks to reinvigorate biblical imperatives by thrusting them into the political arena.

Perhaps the key section of the book in understanding any sort of shift from his earlier to his later work is entitled "Can Politics Be Moral?"[49]—a question Wallis subtly answers in the affirmative. For

---

47. Ibid., 97.
48. Wallis, *Soul of Politics*, 38ff.
49. Ibid., ch. 2.

far too long Americans and especially American Christians have been cordoned in by the dualistic structure of American politics. Left versus right, liberal versus conservative, and east and west have held Christian thinking about politics captive. What ails Christian involvement in politics is a crisis of imagination, an ability to think about Christian approaches to social issues outside of the framework that the powers of the world offer us. A key to resolving this crisis and breaking free from the duality of our political thinking is to recover fresh approaches to moral issues, and for Wallis, that is precisely what a prophetic spirituality offers us. Along with shifting to an issues-based approach to framing Christian political engagement, Wallis now wants to affirm enthusiastically the need to "transform" and "take responsibility for" the political realm. The shift in Wallis' thinking is subtle, because he still uses biblical language to craft not only a new mode of interaction with government, but also to elevate some social issues to a higher importance than they currently attain. The shift is this: The covenant community that Wallis discusses is not the Christian church, but the body politic. He very shrewdly generalizes the moral and political theology of the gospel to be inclusive of other religious groups in the effort to transform the political realm, and he abandons the specifics of the church's opposition to the principalities and powers of the world in favor of a "moral politics" and a generalized covenant that provides redemption and reconciliation to anyone willing to embrace this moralized politics. While space constraints prohibit examining this shift in great detail, a comparison of Wallis' discussion of the centrality of Jesus in *Agenda for Biblical People* versus his virtual neglect of Jesus language in *The Soul of Politics* illustrates this shift well.

Wallis has removed himself from the "alternative political community" to enter into the world of advocacy politics and coalition-building. In other words, the reason Wallis abandons the narrative of the Christian church in favor of a more generalized "prophetic spirituality" is because he can attract larger numbers of (morally serious) people into a political coalition that can influence government in a way that Wallis now considers to be morally responsible. Wallis' audience is now different. And with the different audience comes a different political theology, one that is issues-based and embedded in a language that is religiously-inclusive. No longer are Jesus, Isaiah, and Amos simply characters in the narrative of God's people, they are moral exemplars and moral "sages" for any context and any body politic. One sees this even more forcefully in Wallis' *God's Politics: Why the Right Gets it Wrong and the Left Doesn't Get It*. Each section-title of this book begins with the phrase "Spiritual Values," increasingly the parlance of religious players in the political arena. To Wallis' credit, he does attempt to provide a more substantial account of what God desires of his people, but he does so without the narrative of the covenant and the context of the Christian church. As opposed to the rich political theology of *Agenda*, Wallis resorts to extracting biblical characters from their narrative contexts and placing them in current situations, as if the covenantal context has minimal moral influence.[50]

Wallis' strategy for political engagement spans both the evangelical left and right. The early Wallis seems less concerned about this engagement than the later Wallis, so there is a modicum of evidence to support a discontinuity thesis at the level of deep analysis (even though there is substantial continuity at the level of the political issues). But the later Wallis seems to take this approach: take the morally- and theologically-rich tradition of Christian political theology and dilute it to the point that you can appeal to a wide range of "religious people" and advocate a spectrum of "spiritual values" without the political messiness of the gospel.[51] This strategy will win one access to the halls of power (Wallis is no stranger to the power-elite in D.C. and receives the occasional invite to the White House), and will win one a voice in public discussions.

What is most worrisome about Wallis' political theology, especially the later instantiations, is that he seems very willing to use theological language in a fashion that is disconnected from the institution of the church and the narrative of Scripture and carelessly apply it to the "nation," or citizens, or government. When he begins to talk about the "covenant" that we have with each other—and it is clear that the covenant is not the biblical covenant but some sort of moral

---

50. See, e.g., Wallis' provocatively titled chapter, "Amos and Enron: What Scandalizes God?" in *God's Politics*.

51. There are some theologians who contend that the moral language of the church cannot be translated into the language of the world without compromising the witness of the gospel, and hence the church should not even attempt to engage in that dialogue. Stanley Hauerwas is perhaps the most prominent among these theologians.

covenant that Americans enter into—Wallis crosses a line that dangerously imperils the Christian witness by mixing the communities of the church and the state. And his doing so seems suspiciously linked to a wayward attempt to allow the concern to be "influential" in the political arena to trump the integrity of the Christian witness. To speak truthfully to the powers with the goal of having real influence, while also maintaining a theological rootedness in the specifics of Christian narrative, requires a fairly diligent balancing act that Wallis does not quite pull off.

CONCLUSION: YODER, SCHAEFFER, AND WALLIS

Yoder's call for Christians to pursue peace from within an eschatological theology asserts that God's rule has commenced and that the powers and principalities that characterized the old aeon, though they still exist, are passing away. Nevertheless, Christians must maintain hope for the future completion of God's rule by witnessing to that kingdom amidst the practices of the old aeon. It is precisely this narrative structure of biblical history that shapes the ethical dispositions of the people of God in their interactions with the government from the Anabaptist point of view, and it is this narrative structure that is absent from Schaeffer's political theology and from Wallis' later manifestations of his witness to the powers. If the church envisions herself in the midst of this story that has yet to come to completion but is on a generally defined trajectory that she believes concludes with God's final and full redemption of the earth and the faithful, the church is liberated in her interactions with the world, free to speak and act out of love and not essentially out of self-preservation. There is no need to cast the church's interactions with the government as constitutive of a battle for the moral fate of the cosmos. That victory has already been won in the cross and resurrection.

The most substantial difference between Schaeffer's evangelical political theology and Yoder's Anabaptist political theology resides in the place of the biblical narrative. For Schaeffer, the Bible plays a minimal role in structuring his thinking about politics, much less a narrative reading of the Bible in which contemporary Christians find themselves as characters in the long story. What little Scripture appears in Schaeffer's reading serves as a seedbed for principles upon which to build a political theology, as in culling a doctrine of the state from Romans 13. Further, Schaeffer gives no indication that Jesus' teachings, life, death, resurrection, or ascension serves any function in thinking about politics. Presumably, the model of political theology for Schaeffer is that politics is ancillary to the gospel itself, not central to the message. The core message of the gospel is that Jesus died so that individuals might be forgiven their sins and placed in right relationship with God, and that is the central function of Jesus' ministry, including his atoning death. Politics finds no purchase in that equation, and thus is relegated to the outskirts of Christian moral thinking where it finds its importance as an instrument that shapes personal morality. Politics creates law, and law affects morality, all of which comes after the justification wrought in the gospel in the economy of salvation. Hence, in Schaeffer's major work on Christian political thinking, Jesus is barely mentioned.

On the evangelical left, Wallis emerges as a bit of a mystery. His early work, before he was "influential," resembles that of Yoder, contextualizing Jesus, his teaching, and his sacrifice on the cross, in stark political terms. But even in Wallis' early work, he leaves space in his theory for a much more elevated role for government in the advancing of God's rule. In fact, he suggests that government can be a substantial vehicle for God's activity in the world, and hence Christians must steer government's activity toward those "values" embodied in the gospel, values that are very much advanced by Jesus' teachings. So, unlike Schaeffer, Wallis' political theology is rooted in Jesus, and Christian political activity takes a much more central role in the gospel message as a whole. Moreover, when comparing Yoder and Wallis, there are two possible interpretive options. First, it is clear that Wallis takes much of his early political theology from Yoder, and hence one sees a keen similarity between the two. On closer inspection, however, it appears that Wallis differs from Yoder in that Yoder eschews the notion that Christians must take responsibility for the social order to the extent that they begin to adopt the methods of the world to meet the demands of those responsibilities. Contrary to some interpretations or adaptations of Yoder's theology,[52] he does not advocate a separatism that hides from the world altogether. Rather, he opens up space for a notion of Christian social responsibility, but a responsibility that can only be met on the terms of the gospel. So when Wallis trades in his deep and reflective early political theology for his later shallow, generically religious discourse on "spiritual values" that are relevant to politics, I suspect that Yoder would cringe at Wallis' abandonment of the deep particularities of the gospel in favor of an autonomous set of "values" that seem no longer attached to the gospel narrative. Furthermore, Wallis appears willing to cross a line that Yoder shies away from by actively seeking a voice within contentious and partisan political debates over policy, a move that Wallis makes because he affords government a much larger role in the moral activity of God's kingdom. Wallis waters down his theology because a more nuanced and deep theology is too exclusive for the purposes of political discussion in a pluralistic society. While Wallis ultimately may be guided by the narrative of the Christian gospel, his political and moral language seems to have lost its connection with that narrative, settling for political influence in the corridors of power above a distinctively Christian voice in the public arena.

A second line of interpretation of Wallis, vis-à-vis Yoder's political theology, runs like this. Wallis' later books, which are clearly more generically religious and spiritual and less distinctively Christian, are an exercise in the use of Yoderian middle-axioms. Wallis knows that he cannot maximize his influence in the political arena by speaking Christian morality in distinctively Christian language. So he adapts that language to the task at hand, using what Yoder referred to as middle-axioms, casting policy positions that cohere with Christian morality in secular or at least watered-down religious language that non-adherents can understand, increasing the likelihood that the policy position will be viewed as a serious option and not a sectarian rant.

---

52. Stanley Hauerwas is the most notable advocate of Yoderian-style separatism that argues that Christians have no responsibilities for or to the social or political order and should hence simply "be the church." My interpretation of Yoder suggests that he would differ from Hauerwas on precisely this point, arguing that we do have some sort of responsibility to seek the good of the larger order, but Christians should seek that good according to the methods and substance of the gospel, which is precisely where I would see Yoder differing from Wallis.

I am inclined to think the first option is the more accurate interpretation of Wallis' thought, but am open to being convinced that the second one is viable. I would still argue that the second interpretation leaves Wallis open to certain sorts of temptations that result in his using the means of the state to achieve Christian moral goals, something that Yoder was wary of ever doing.

As is probably fairly obvious in my accounting of these three political theologies, I find myself in Yoder's camp and would consider him to be the standard-bearer on Christian political theology. But this essay only begins to compare the basics of evangelical and Anabaptist political theologies, from a very small number of sources. I am sure that evangelicals from both the left and the right would have a number of problems with Yoder's political theology (or at least my accounting of it), and I, for one, would welcome furthering that discussion in hopes that we could all be better witnesses of God's redemptive activity.

BIBLIOGRAPHY

Forrester, Duncan B. "John Howard Yoder (1927–1997): Commentary." In *The Teachings of Modern Protestantism on Law, Politics, & Human Nature*, edited by John Witte, Jr., and Mark A. Noll, 407–12. New York: Columbia University Press, 2007.

Hall, David W. *The Genevan Reformation and the American Founding*. Lanham, MD: Lexington, 2003.

Hamilton, Michael S. "The Dissatisfactions of Francis Schaeffer." *Christianity Today* 41.3 (1997) 22–30.

Hankins, Barry. *Francis Schaeffer and the Shaping of Evangelical America*. Grand Rapids: Eerdmans, 2008.

Nation, Mark Thiessen. *John Howard Yoder: Mennonite Patience, Evangelical Witness, Catholic Convictions*. Grand Rapids: Eerdmans, 2006.

Olsen, Ted. "Where Jim Wallis Stands: The Longtime Activist on Abortion, Gay Marriage, Iraq—and Biblical Orthodoxy." *Christianity Today* 52.5, (2008) 52–59.

Shaffer, Thomas L. "Anabaptist Law Schools." In *Faith and Law*, edited by Robert F. Cochran, Jr., 65–76. New York: New York University Press, 2008.

———. *Moral Memoranda from John Howard Yoder*. Eugene, OR: Wipf & Stock, 2002.

Schaeffer, Francis A. *A Christian Manifesto*. Westchester, IL: Crossway, 1982.

Wallis, Jim. *Agenda for Biblical People*. San Francisco: Harper & Row, 1984.

———. *God's Politics: Why the Right Gets It Wrong and the Left Doesn't Get It*. San Francisco: HarperSan Francisco, 2005.

———. *The Soul of Politics*. Maryknoll, NY: Orbis, 1994.

Yoder, John Howard. *The Christian Witness to the State*. Scottdale, PA: Herald, 2002.

———. "Peace Without Eschatology?" In *The Royal Priesthood: Essays Ecclesiological and Ecumenical,* by John Howard Yoder, ed. Michael G. Cartwright, 143–67. Grand Rapids: Eerdmans, 1994.

———. *The Politics of Jesus.* 2nd ed. Grand Rapids: Eerdmans, 1994.

———. "Reinhold Niebuhr and Christian Realism." *The Mennonite Quarterly Review* 29 (1955) 101–17.

PART IV

Intersecting Trajectories
Toward an Evangelical Anabaptist Theology and Praxis

Introduction to Part IV

THE CHAPTERS THUS FAR have described the historical intersections of evangelicalism and Anabaptism. In this fourth and final part, each chapter describes a potential trajectory for an emerging evangelical Anabaptism. Since some of the most foundational conversations between evangelicals and Anabaptists have involved questions of ethics and politics within the public arena, Timothy Paul Erdel begins this section where the third section left off: with a discussion of church-state issues in the context of America's ongoing culture wars. Some evangelicals have jumped at the possibility of exercising moral authority within American society, but Erdel argues that while Christians may have the legal right to try to "legislate morality," it may be impossible to do so without becoming entangled in the state's coercive power, which would be unacceptable for Anabaptists. Erdel thus explores the possibility of a non-coercive Christian witness in the public square, which might integrate evangelical social concerns with Anabaptist political sensibilities.

While ethical and political issues have dominated the evangelical-Anabaptist exchange over the last thirty years, a number of recent theological developments also provide fertile ground for further evangelical-Anabaptist dialogue. Perhaps one of the most hotly debated theological issues currently is the doctrine of the atonement. Unlike some of the ethical and political issues discussed in other chapters, there is no clear-cut evangelical or Anabaptist position on the atonement, and indeed, there is much cross-pollination between evangelical and Anabaptist thought on this issue. Many evangelicals and some Anabaptists remain convinced that satisfaction or penal substitution models constitute the only biblical or orthodox view, but this position is being challenged on multiple fronts. Some evangelicals, such as New Testament scholar Scot McKnight (*A Community Called Atonement*), argue for the use of a plurality of images and metaphors for the atonement. However, a growing number of scholars—evangelical and Anabaptist alike—are beginning to reject satisfaction or substitutionary models entirely. Anabaptist theologian J. Denny Weaver (*The Nonviolent Atonement*) has led this charge by arguing for a nonviolent, *Christus Victor* model of the atonement, which has sparked much debate among Anabaptists while at the same time resonating with the work of some prominent evangelical theologians, such as Gregory Boyd (*God at War*). In our penultimate chapter, Kirk R. MacGregor cuts through this debate, offering a creative synthesis of Anselmian satisfaction theory and nonviolent *Christus Victor* and exemplar themes. He does so while surprisingly maintaining a commitment to the classic evangelical doctrine of biblical inerrancy by offering penetrating analyses of standard biblical texts pertaining to the atonement that challenge traditional readings. Indeed, MacGregor's proffered solution challenges each end of the evangelical-Anabaptist spectrum, while drawing richly from them both.

Finally, David C. Cramer continues charting an evangelical Anabaptist path with a biblical reexamination of the question of war. While the majority of evangelicals have rejected the Anabaptist commitment to pacifism as unbiblical, Cramer believes that evangelicals should feel compelled by their commitment to Scripture to consider the pacifist position more carefully. His argument rests not on a discussion of just war theory or the merits of "redemptive violence" as is often the case. Rather, he asserts that this issue has more to do with traditional evangelical concerns regarding faith and Scripture than it does with violence per se. Appropriating John Howard Yoder's evangelical Anabaptist reading of Scripture as well as a fresh consideration of *sola fide* (faith alone) and *sola scriptura* (Scripture alone), Cramer beckons evangelicals to reopen this important topic that has long been central to Anabaptist teaching.

"Go Tell that Fox!"

Evangelical Anabaptist Reflections on Religion and the Public Square

Timothy Paul Erdel

INTRODUCTION

EVANGELICAL ANABAPTISM IS THE air I breathe, or the lens through which I view the world.[1] My family story and church background both provide countless examples of a sometimes messy conglomeration of these traditions.[2] Though holding to the convictions central to each tradition has always seemed natural to me, for some reason affirming both traditions simultaneously often has meant not fully having a home in either. I suspect that part of the reason may have to do

---

1. I am grateful to Sally Erdel, Cristian Mihut, Robby Prenkert, and David Schmidt for taking the time to read and comment on an earlier draft of this essay, which was first prepared for the ETS Ethics Consultation: Is Christian Ethics for Everyone, or Just for Christians?, at the 60th annual meeting of the Evangelical Theological Society, Rhode Island Convention Center, Providence, Rhode Island, 20 November 2008. The original subtitle for this essay was "Should Christian Values Guide Non-Christians? Could They if They Should?" Matthew Erdel kindly reviewed this present version, and David C. Cramer provided a number of helpful revisions at the last minute.

2. For more on my family story, see Erdel, "Not All Those Who Wander Are Lost," 35–42. For the story of my church background, see Erdel, "The Missionary Church," 60, 59; Erdel, "Holiness among the Mennonites," 5–42. Cf. the essay by Joel Boehner and Matthew Eaton in the present volume.

with politics. I further suspect that the reason not only has to do with these traditions' respective political positions, but perhaps even more so with their respective approaches to political engagement in the first place. Perhaps a couple of anecdotes will illustrate my suspicions.

The day before the 2008 U.S. presidential election,[3] I approached a bright and capable married student in one of my classes and encouraged him to start turning in his assignments, since he had submitted no written work for the class to that point in the semester, nor had he otherwise responded to my previous prodding, including a mid-term grade report of F. The student had, however, repeatedly requested prayer for the nation, given the then forthcoming elections. When I spoke to him yet again about the urgency of his overdue papers, he exclaimed, "I have just been too upset about [the prospect of] Obama [being elected] to do any work this semester!"

Two days later, I visited a local funeral home to give my condolences to a college staff member whose husband had just died after a long and difficult illness. As I extended my sympathies to her, she expressed her frustration and grief, saying that she wished she could have died with her husband. What I did not realize at first—in fact, what took me quite awhile to absorb—was that her dismay was, by her own emphatic testimony, not over the death of her husband, whose physical suffering was now over, but rather over the election of Barack Obama to the presidency of the United States![4]

One feature that linked both these Doomsday reactions, which a fuller recounting of the conversations would have made more explicit, was their use of apocalyptic language and imagery. Moreover, it was clear that, from the perspective of the people I was talking to, if Christian righteousness did not prevail at the ballot box, presumably as defined by such issues as the stated political party platforms on abortion and same-sex marriage, then the collapse of the world as we know it was at hand.[5]

---

3. 3 November 2008—the election took place on Tuesday, November 4.

4. I do not wish to be too harsh in re-telling this odd interchange, as grief can do strange things to people.

5. The prevalence of this sort of sentiment among some on our college campus led one of my professorial colleagues, Robby Prenkert, to facetiously suggest to one of his classes that everyone should vote for Barack Obama in order to guarantee the end of the age, and therefore, to hasten the Second Coming of Jesus Christ!

I work and teach at Bethel College, Mishawaka, Indiana,[6] a school with an interesting mix of religious roots and political allegiances. I have shared these two anecdotes from that campus *not* because I think we are a hopelessly naïve, anti-intellectual backwater, nor even particularly unusual among campuses in the Council for Christian Colleges and Universities, but in order to illustrate the passionate intermingling of religious beliefs with political convictions that I am quite certain occurs in other circles as well—including, I might add, secular ones where the phrase "ideological views" might be substituted for "religious beliefs," but with similarly bizarre effects.[7]

Bethel is a Christian college with roots in at least five distinct but overlapping Christian traditions: Anabaptist, Pietist, Wesleyan-holiness, and Keswickian-holiness, as well as a more broadly evangelical heritage.[8] Bethel College will also hire and tenure faculty members from other Christian traditions, including Roman Catholics, so long as they give vital personal testimony of their faith in Jesus Christ and willingly affirm the school's lifestyle covenant. From a political perspective, Bethel College clearly has the sort of Republican Party ethos often associated with conservative evangelicalism. One indication is that President George W. Bush chose Bethel College as a host site for a congressional campaign luncheon fundraiser.[9] Another is that John McCain and Sarah Palin subsequently won a mock election in 2008 with over 70 percent of the campus vote.[10]

There are, however, a number of other political cross-currents on campus. Of the two faculty members who actually hold local political office, one is a Republican, but the other is firmly and without

---

6. Bethel College, Mishawaka, Indiana is the liberal arts college of the Missionary Church, Inc. See also note 9 below.

7. Thus I could tell equally tragicomical stories from my years of studying and teaching in the context of major universities that are avowedly secular, contexts generally permeated by very different political sentiments. In my experience, political alarmists may be found among the intellectually elite at research universities as well as among those on the "margins" of higher education, i.e., in smaller religious institutions.

8. See, e.g., Erdel, "The Missionary Church"; Erdel, "Holiness among the Mennonites."

9. See the twin cover stories, Kinzel, "Opportunity of a Lifetime," 4–5, and "Bethel Rolls out the Red Carpet for President Bush," 6–7. The cover title was "World Changers: President Bush Visits Campus."

10. Gerand, "John McCain Wins Bethel Mock Election," 1.

apology a Democrat.¹¹ Some faculty reacted with similar apocalyptic Doomsday horror to the nomination of Sarah Palin as the Republican candidate for Vice-President as others on campus did to the subsequent election of Barack Obama. A small but vocal minority on and around campus even explicitly recognizes the influence of Anabaptist thought on their political outlook. During the same election season some students invited Mennonite historian John D. Roth of Goshen College to lecture on an Anabaptist case for conscientious political abstinence.[12] There is a growing neo-Anabaptist movement among recent graduates that calls itself, somewhat facetiously, "the Evangelical Anabaptist Revolution."[13]

I suspect that what the student and staff member who spoke to me were responding to were not nearly so much to any campus position or policy, which would be officially neutral on matters political, but to nearly hysterical communications that have circulated among evangelicals via such venues as the Internet, email, and religious broadcasting.[14] Among the tangle of opinions being purveyed are the convictions that form the following rough outline of an argument.

1. The United States is a Christian nation, one exceptional in its mission and calling.

2. Christians should actively seek to establish and enforce Christian

---

11. Mark J. Root, the Republican, is a two-term member of the St. Joseph County Council, while Thomas J. LaFountain, the Democrat, is a member of the South Bend City Council.

12. Roth, "Being Christian; Being Citizen," invited address, with panel discussion following on the topic "Should Christians Abstain from Voting?" David E. Schmidt rounded out the panel discussion.

13. If I am reading them correctly, they would appreciate such recent works as Boyd, *Myth of a Christian Nation*, and Carter, *Rethinking Christ and Culture*. Their leading voice, to this point, is David Charles Cramer, who has had his blog selected by *Christian Century* for their online *CC Blogs* network at http://cramercomments.blogspot.com/ and who has taken over the editorship of *Reflections*, the journal of the Missionary Church Historical Society. See, e.g., Yoder et al., "Younger Voices in the Missionary Church," 43–51. E.A.R.'s sometimes tongue-in-cheek attitude is epitomized by T-shirts they printed on which an image of Mennonite theologian John Howard Yoder was stylized to look like the famous Che Guevera "Viva la Revolución" image. A near cousin, but with somewhat Libertarian instincts, would be Missionary Church minister Bill Barnwell; see his former blog, "The Wilderness Crier" at http://www.billbarnwell.blogspot.com/.

14. See Martin, *With God on our Side*, and Hughes, *Christian America and the Kingdom of God*.

values within our Christian nation.

3. The electoral process is the appropriate means to accomplish such a goal, given that electing the right government office holders will more likely result in the appropriate political legislation, executive orders, and judicial appointments, since the latter will also more likely lead to correct interpretations of the United States Constitution, of the laws enacted by right-minded legislators, and of properly motivated executive orders.

4. Further loss of biblical values in our nation may be directly attributable to the loss of an election by the Republican party, which is clearly the only viable political party (at least at this time) in terms of enacting and supporting Christian values.

5. Thus, the rapid loss of Christian values that would all but inevitably follow from a Democratic party victory at the polls would in turn soon bring about the end of this present age.[15]

The foregoing anecdotes, however comical or sad, may still raise serious issues about faith and politics. For there are various ways to think about the place of religion in the public square. Whole journals are devoted to such matters.[16] In what follows, I propose to ruminate upon two related questions, and to do so from the perspective of a person who admits a Christian worldview deeply rooted in his own understanding of the teachings of Jesus, especially in the Sermon on the Mount.[17] The first question is, "Should Christian values guide secular society?" The second is, "Could Christian values guide secular society even if they should?"[18] In the anecdotes above, there was an assumed affirmative answer to both of these questions, but I argue that further Christian reflection offers reason for questioning that assumption. I reflect on two politically charged issues—abortion and same-sex marriage—in order draw out some of the implications of these questions.

---

15. In fact, a few went even beyond the foregoing and wondered out loud if Barack Obama could possibly be the Anti-Christ, so that the end really is at hand, hence the sarcastic jibe from my colleague to his students (see note 5 above).

16. *Journal of Church and State* and *First Things* are obvious examples.

17. Erdel, "Holiness among Mennonites"; Erdel, "Great Commission and God's Righteous Kingdom."

18. Sometimes important technical distinctions are made between values, ethics, and morals; but here I will use the terms, perhaps somewhat colloquially, as more or less synonymous.

Finally, after examining a narrative from Luke, I suggest that the *primary* tasks Christians have in this world are not political as typically understood.[19] According to this approach, Christians are called first and foremost to love God, each other, and our neighbors, who are defined as persons in need, and to make disciples of Jesus Christ even as we reach out in compassion to persons in need. Any overt political involvements are to be clearly subsidiary to and supportive of these primary calls.[20] While I do not presume to speak on behalf of either evangelicalism or Anabaptism in the following, it should be clear that my somewhat idiosyncratic reflections on these questions are deeply shaped by my roots in each. Perhaps, then, the following approach could be viewed as one possible model for an evangelical Anabaptist synthesis, drawing richly from each tradition but not fully embracing either at the expense of the other.

SHOULD CHRISTIAN VALUES GUIDE SECULAR SOCIETY?

Should Christian values guide secular society? My answer is an emphatic *"Yes!"* But this is at the same time in some sense qualified by all sorts of further observations that may seem to undermine the force of this positive response. Below are seven preliminary ruminations.

First, this strongly affirmative reply openly assumes a Christian perspective, indeed, a whole Christian worldview, though there may be some overlap with other theistic traditions. Since all persons are made in the image of God, whether we acknowledge that fact or not, and since God's values are part of the Creation order,[21] we flourish

---

19. "Political" here means active involvement in governmental or Republican/Democrat party politics. There is in currency a broader use of "political" connoting *any* kind of social involvement, including Christian worship and mission, which would of course encompass the primary tasks of Christians. In my conclusion I draw on this broader use. Cf. John Howard Yoder's titles, *Politics of Jesus, Discipleship as Political Responsibility*, and *Body Politics*.

20. Though this does not necessarily exclude the possibility that some individuals may have a calling to a political vocation.

21. Many have pointed out, for example, how the speaking of the Ten Words in Exodus 20 echoes the Creation Story in Genesis 1, thereby underscoring the link between the physical and the moral in the created order. One of my intuitions is that one need not come from a culture directly influenced by the formal teaching of the Ten Commandments to react negatively when one learns about others breaking them, thereby suggesting that there is some sense in which God has written his Law

as human beings when we obey the Law of God. I take it that these are deep and pervasive themes of Scripture that are echoed in many passages.[22] God's values represent the best moral option for everyone because they fit what we need to be and do if we are to experience the fullness of our potential as human beings made in the image of God. However, since secularists are not likely to accept this opening premise, I have probably limited my audience dramatically, even if they might ultimately be surprised by some of the positions which are a consequence of a Christian worldview, or at least of the worldview of this Christian.

Second, my general presumption, following a broadly Anabaptist and Wesleyan hermeneutic, is that there are distinctly Christian values that go beyond the Natural Law as presented in the created order, and even beyond common readings of the written Law of Moses. For Christian values are rooted in the sacrificial, divine love known in the New Covenant as *agapē*, a love demonstrated by the Incarnation, particularly by the humble service and sacrificial sufferings and death of Jesus Christ. The Old Covenant taught love for God and neighbor, but the New Covenant brings further insight when it stresses that the neighbor includes our enemy. We are to love our enemies even as Jesus loved us and endured the Crucifixion on our behalf while we were still his enemies. Thus the New Covenant makes much clearer what was at best latent in the Old Covenant.[23] At the very least, Christians tend to have a substantially different reading of the Hebrew Scriptures than do Jews and Muslims, and my general suggestion is that the difference is not merely theological, but should extend to the ethical domain as well, even though many others might tend to see more overlap in ethics between various religions and worldviews than in theology.

Third, such values as the love of enemy, I would suggest, make Christian values unique among other religions and worldviews. Virtually every high religion or great worldview promotes some version of the Silver Rule, namely, that we should not do to others what

---

on our hearts from the beginning, prior to the formal giving of the Law at Sinai. The problem, presumably, is that when we harden our hearts against this inherent moral knowledge, then God must write his Law on tablets of stone to underline our failure to embrace in joyous obedience what he originally gave us to guide us into full and abundant lives.

22. E.g., Ps. 1, 19, 119; Jer 17:7–8; Matt 7:24–27.
23. See Swartley, *Covenant of Peace*.

we would not want done to ourselves. But Jesus gives us the Golden Rule, urging us to seek the positive good of our neighbors, not just to avoid doing evil to them.[24]

This emphasis on positive, sacrificial love toward all persons is reiterated by many of the teachings of Jesus. A prime example would be the Story of the Good Samaritan in Luke 10:25–27. The robbers are clearly unjust. "What's yours is mine." But what fascinates us is the realization that by many ethical systems, the self-serving choices of the Priest and the Levite are perfectly just. "What's mine is mine." Yet all we have to do is hear the story for us to realize that such definitions of "justice" are wholly inadequate within a Christian worldview. The Good Samaritan who risks all to help his needy neighbor is clearly the right path to follow, one built on a deep *agapē* love. "What's mine is yours."

Fourth, presumably because of the effects of the Fall, even those moral intuitions that should be rooted in our beings as a part of the created order are not always as clear as one would hope apart from divine Revelation. Thus there may be ethical quandaries—for example, questions about the legitimacy or illegitimacy of certain attitudes (lust, hate, pride, envy) or of certain types of sexual relations (pre-marital or extra-marital)—that would be difficult to determine conclusively without an appeal to the clear teachings of Scripture.

Fifth, even if one grants all of the foregoing—the general Christian presuppositions and worldview, the uniqueness of Christian values in going beyond previous Revelation and beyond the best insights of other religions and worldviews, and also the need for appeals to Christian Scriptures to clarify moral intuitions—these may not be sufficient to answer another nagging question, that is, "*Which Christian ethic is being recommended to general society?*" Terms like Christian or biblical or evangelical or orthodox (or in the realm of ethics, orthopraxis) do not by themselves settle all sorts of potential disputes. The fact of the matter is that earnest, biblical Christians—evangelical Christians who affirm biblical inerrancy and various other technical demarcations of in-circle evangelical orthodoxy—may differ

---

24. Such an ethical view is by no means the only characteristic of Christianity that, I would argue, makes it unique among other religions and worldviews. See, e.g., Erdel, "'Tis So Sweet to Trust in Jesus," 21–41; cf. also id., "What Is My Epistemic Duty?"

dramatically in both their theoretical approaches to ethics and in their practical stances with respect to a wide range of moral problems.

For example, on the theoretical level, should one articulate Christian ethics primarily in terms of Natural Law, of obedience to Divine commands, of Christian virtue, of radical, sacrificial love, of some combination of the foregoing, or of some other approach to ethics? To what extent should Christian ethics draw on insights from essentially secular approaches to ethics, whether Platonic, Aristotelian, Humean, Kantian, Utilitarian, Nietzschean, or the like? What place might there be for theories that stress moral absolutes, or the apparent inevitability of relative applications, or hierarchical decision-making procedures such as identifying the "lesser evil" or the "greater good"?

If Christians are divided on the theoretical level, they diverge even more, if possible, in their responses to specific moral problems. One simple illustration of this is the number of books from different evangelical publishers which present multiple opposing views in response to pressing ethical (or doctrinal) questions under one editorial cover.[25] Specific moral questions include but are by no means limited to all sorts of issues related to the nature of a just society, to identifying preferred economic systems, to strategies for helping the poor, to proper relationships between Church and state, to the legitimacy of lethal force in war and peace, to befitting stewardship of the environment, to exploring justifiable approaches to bio-ethical research and practices, to the places, if any, for birth control and abortion, to guidelines for marriage and divorce, to the recognition of sexual boundaries, to models for gender relations, to the appropriate forms of Sabbath observance, to acceptable types of entertainment, to the admissibility of gambling, to the use or prohibition of tobacco or alcoholic beverages, and so forth.[26]

---

25. Zondervan, InterVarsity Press, and B&H are the publishers best known among evangelicals for this type of work; but others include Fortress Press, Kregel, Thomas Nelson, and even Blackwell. One of the earliest such volumes was Clouse, ed., *War: Four Christian Views*. The more doctrinally oriented titles may still have important ethical or meta-ethical implications; see, e.g., Basinger and Basinger, *Predestination & Free Will*, and Strickland, *Five Views on Law and Gospel*.

26. One way to illustrate the indefinite number of ethical topics that might be raised is to simply peruse the *Christian Reflection* series published by The Center for Christian Ethics, Baylor University, Waco, Texas, 2001– .

As a biblically informed pacifist, for example, my response to military policies might be rather different from that of a biblically informed just war theorist.[27] But is it really obvious that our very different approaches require that only one approach be correct *and* that the correct approach can be readily identified so as to be presented to others in a pluralistic society as *the* Christian position? I might be thoroughly convinced that my view is *the only correct* Christian stance; but, as my view is a minority one, it would seem a bit presumptuous of me to speak for Christians as a whole in a pluralistic society.

Sixth, none of the foregoing deals with admittedly difficult questions about Christian failures and hypocrisy. If it turned out that Christians did not (and perhaps even could not) maintain the values and standards that they were recommending to society at large, then surely there are serious doubts as to the legitimacy of their doing so, especially if such recommendations were being enforced by civil legislation, with punitive consequences for disobeying the law.[28] Then there is the long and sorry stream of evangelical leaders who have fallen from grace rather publicly; nor are they all televangelists from the Pentecostal or Charismatic side of the camp. Some were far from the limelight until their white collar crimes were made known.

Seventh, there are also questions as to just *how* Christians might go about persuading others to follow Christian morality, even if one could settle on *which* Christian morality is *the* Christian morality. Is there any reason to think that others would follow Christian ethics merely because Christian morality were shown by apologetic or political arguments to be the morally prudent thing to do? Or would something more than rational persuasion be needed? If so, might it entail social or governmental coercion, perhaps even the threat of law, or even of lethal force? Is it possible for Christians to transform secular society without resorting, even indirectly, to violence? But at this point it seems to me that we are approaching my second major question, namely, "Could Christian values guide secular society even if they should?"

---

27. See, e.g., Erdel, "Is Just War Still an Oxymoron?" 53–76.

28. See the anecdote by John Howard Yoder where Church leaders in Evanston, IL, discussed turning to the government to enforce policies that they were fearful of requiring of their own Church members, "The Biblical Mandate for Evangelical Social Action," 188. David Swartz also recalls this anecdote in his essay in the present volume.

COULD CHRISTIAN VALUES GUIDE SECULAR SOCIETY EVEN IF THEY SHOULD?

Even Christians have a hard time with a truly Christian ethic, with following the radical teachings of Jesus. That is why, of the twelve or so major Christian interpretations of the Sermon on the Mount, there is a sense in which one can divide the approaches into the one and the eleven. Nearly all interpretations in some sense soften the force of or even set aside the teachings of Jesus.[29] So presumably, when asking the question as to whether secular society should follow Christian values, there is simultaneously a recognition that it would be very unusual for those outside Christianity to consciously try to pattern their life on radically Christian values as taught, for example, in the Sermon on the Mount. If many Christians do not even try to follow the teachings of Jesus without some form of serious qualification, why would we expect anyone else to do so?

Nevertheless, one could point to rare examples, such as Mahatma Gandhi, who apparently did meditate on the Sermon on the Mount daily throughout his adult life, and who tried to incorporate and enact at least some of its basic principles in the social and political movements he led. But it still seems unlikely that many outside Christianity would even try to follow such principles across the board. Gandhi himself was somewhat selective in the way he followed the teachings of Jesus. Yet Gandhi does serve as an eloquent witness as to how far a professed non-Christian might actually go in following radical Christian values.

Could those outside the church really live what is essentially the "victorious Christian life"? From a theological standpoint, it would seem very unlikely they would or could do so, since they presumably lack both the intrinsic motivation (a loving response to God's unmerited grace—the forgiveness of sins and the gift of eternal life) and purifying power (the indwelling presence of the Holy Spirit, the Spirit of the Resurrected Christ) to do so. In fact, from the perspective of traditional Christian teachings, it is impossible to attain goodness or to live a holy life apart from the grace of God or without the indwelling and transforming power of the Holy Spirit, who convicts of sin, cleanses

---

29. See McArthur, *Understanding the Sermon on the Mount*, 105–48; cf. Erdel, "Holiness among Mennonites" and "Commission and Kingdom." Cf. also Bauman, *The Sermon on the Mount*, and Stassen and Gushee, *Kingdom Ethics*.

from sin, and makes holy. No one, I suspect, has ever proposed that if the United States is a Christian nation, we should enact laws that require us to turn the other cheek, to give our last garment, or to walk the extra mile.

The exalted ideals of the Sermon on the Mount notwithstanding, can someone who is not a true disciple of Jesus Christ even keep the basic commandments that are written into the created order and reiterated on stone tablets given to Moses? At first it might seem so, if we listen to the testimony of the Rich Young Ruler (Matt 19:16–30; Mark 10:17–31; Luke 18:18–30). But the call of Jesus to radical discipleship actually exposes an inability to keep any of the commands, for the Rich Ruler loves money more than God or the poor, thereby disclosing his failure to truly keep the spirit of either the divinely directed or the humanly oriented commands. Money is the idol he worships instead of the living God, and the love of money keeps him from loving his neighbor in need. Truly obeying the commands of God is impossible by human effort alone. "With human beings this is impossible, but with God all things are possible" (Matt 19:26b TNIV).

What is presumably really meant by the question of whether or not secular society should or could follow Christian values is something else. That is, should society follow those broadly theistic laws written into the created order (and presumably spelled out in the Ten Commandments in the context of more general Mosaic legislation) that will, if enforced and obeyed, restrain evil in general society? Should Christians therefore try to enact such laws with the general view that they will, if properly enforced, restrain the worst sorts of evils, with the possible added benefits that they would expose sin and the need for Christ, or even have a "sanctifying effect" on society as a whole?

I doubt that the so-called "blue laws" of Puritan New England ever really went much beyond a selective application of the Ten Commandments combined with local community ideals, even if some of the particular laws enacted by legislators went to absurd extremes in trying to accomplish said goal, such as dictating that only clergy could cross a river on Sunday, one of many such now laughable decrees that apparently lasted right on up to the twentieth century in Connecticut.[30] But that does illustrate a problem, namely,

---

30. I am relying here on the expertise of James E. Smith, who studied Sabbath

that modern attempts to implement certain Mosaic laws may give rise to absurd applications.[31]

There are many more theological reflections one could make, each one opening the potential for further commentary. One is that, unless one is such a strict theological determinist as to not even allow for philosophical compatibilism, one will acknowledge that God has from the beginning granted humans freedom of choice with respect to ethical decisions. At the same time, even one wrong choice is disastrous from a biblical perspective, while a pattern of deliberate, willfully wrong choices may lead to the degenerate state where God simply "gives over" persons to the idolatry and wickedness described in Romans chapter one, where persons who reject God become slaves to lifestyles characterized by unnatural desires that lead to death. Thus, there seems to be a fascinating dialectic throughout Scripture. On the one hand, there are the clear commands that identify sinful attitudes and actions as well as spelling out the accompanying judgments on those who flaunt God's will. On the other hand, there is the ultimate freedom God gives to people to choose and persist in pursuing abhorrent paths, despite those warnings and obstacles he places in their way.

Christians are not God, and we should be careful in what ways we try to be like God. But perhaps there is a bit of a lesson here, in that we should both encourage justice and righteousness (*dikaiosynē* covers both terms in the New Testament) and yet not totally prohibit moral free choice (if we even could). Would it be better to emphasize the difference between Christian and secular values by our witness and authentic lives rather than trying to *legislate* them?

And yet, who would not want legislation against murder, theft, and the like? Nevertheless, any attempt to enact and enforce Christian values through legislation is likely to raise the specter, especially from a secular perspective, of the Spanish Inquisition, of Calvin's Geneva Experiment, of the Puritan Revolution in England,

---

legislation extensively while doing research for his doctoral dissertation, i.e., "Enhancing the Worship of God," and who presented various anecdotes while making an oral presentation to the Missionary Church Historical Society, Bethel College, Mishawaka, Indiana, 5 April 2008.

31. See, e.g., Bush, "Debating Marriage," 31–49. As an aside, I suspect that, on close inspection, similar problems plague the proposals put forward by proponents of Christian Reconstructionism/Dominion Theology/Theonomy; cf., e.g., Rushdoony, *Institutes*.

or of misguided religious utopias: from the violent, polygamous Anabaptists in Münster to John Alexander Dowie's controversial and somewhat narcissistic—though at least inter-racial and pacifist—Christian Catholic Apostolic Church of Zion, Illinois, to Jim Jones and the suicidal People's Temple in Jonestown, Guyana.[32] The history of so-called Christian theocracies is not particularly encouraging and all too often entails horrible violence, as well as numerous other abuses. C. S. Lewis, no less, did not hesitate to pronounce, "Theocracy is the worst of all possible governments. . . . the worst corruption of all."[33] Even if a full-blown Theocracy is not in view, secular perceptions of Christian attempts to legislate Christian values rapidly generate fears of possible abuses in that direction.[34]

It seems to me, however, that, on a purely political level, where there is a Christian consensus, there is nothing particularly wrong with enshrining Christian values. In a liberal democracy, Christians certainly have the political right, *contra* John Rawls and many others, to promote and try to enact such laws as seem best to them for the entire population to follow.[35] They even have the right to do so if they are in a distinct minority, though their task would be much more difficult, since they would have to persuade the majority that it is in their best interest to do so.

One of the last times that there was a broad religious consensus in the U.S. on an issue—other than religious communities *temporarily* responding as one to a national crisis or catastrophe, whether brought on by enemy attack, economic collapse, or natural

---

32. On the People's Temple dystopia, see especially Naipaul, *Journey to Nowhere*.

33. Lewis, "Lilies That Fester," 40. Lewis makes clear, however, that he thought the era of Theocracy was probably over, and he instead feared a secular variation on it that he called *Charientocracy*, the rule of the "Cultured," a self-appointed elite with their own dogmas. He presumably did not envision the resurgence of Islam, nor even the rise of right-wing religious movements within the West such as Christian Reconstructionism, Dominion Theology, or Theonomy, though he did live into the establishment of Apartheid in South Africa, which merged theological and political visions.

34. My earnest evangelical colleague, Friends historian David Schmidt, only semi-facetiously suggests that we need the state outlined in Romans 13 to protect us from other professed Christians!

35. I find the general arguments of Christopher J. Eberle persuasive on this point; see Eberle, *Religious Convictions in Liberal Politics*. For a different perspective, see the appreciative but more critical analysis by Gaus, Review of *Religious Convictions in Liberal Politics*.

disaster—drawing together clear majorities of both religious conservatives and religious liberals over a sustained period of time, at least on the Protestant side, was the decades-long campaign against alcoholic consumption that culminated in Prohibition. When finally enacted, however, what the experiment with Prohibition then showed is the difficulty of enforcing public morality over the long term even with the full backing of the law, that is, if one loses the broader cultural consensus in favor of that morality.[36]

While there are clearly problems with trying to legislate morality, there is also a conundrum for anyone who simply dismisses a particular legislative proposal with the trite observation that, "You can't legislate morality." For all laws reflect some sort of values, so the notion that "You can't legislate morality" is in one sense blind to the axiology implicit in virtually any law. The question is not whether or not one can legislate value free laws, but whose values will be represented.

On the other side, even laws against the most heinous possible crimes (serial murder, rape and dismemberment, child abuse) do not stop them from happening; and if a society as a whole becomes callous toward some great evil, that evil can become deeply embedded in that society, and even publically celebrated, existing legislation to the contrary notwithstanding. A painful illustration of this fact would be found in the formerly popular postcards with carefully staged pictures of ordinary people, including children, in their Sunday best, who posed for photographs that would be sent by mail to relatives, friends, and acquaintances—each postcard celebrating one's personal yet very public identification with a gruesome local *lynching!*[37] Technically, laws on the books should have made the practice of lynching illegal, but a general consensus in favor of lynching, at least within certain communities across broad segments of the nation (as far north as

---

36. I once heard William F. Buckley tell an anecdote about the shifting tides of moral consensus, illustrating that our larger society tends to gain real insights in some areas even while it completely loses its bearings in others. He said that, when he was a boy, a strict New England mother would have told her family, who had been sailing on their yacht all day, to be good children and gather up the trash and throw it overboard before they headed for the harbor. A couple of generations later, Buckley observed, New England parents would be horrified by the potential damage to the environment caused by throwing trash overboard, but might now instead willfully ignore juveniles smoking marijuana or casually fornicating below deck during a similar family outing.

37. Smith, "Critic's Notebook"; see also Allen et al., *Without Sanctuary*.

Duluth, Minnesota), turned public, communal murder of racial minorities, particularly those of African descent, into a scofflaw.[38]

CURSORY COMMENTS ON TWO CONTEMPORARY CASE STUDIES

Evangelicals and Anabaptists each have their set of pet social issues but tend to have varying approaches as to how one should go about addressing these issues in the public square. For contemporary evangelicals, abortion and same-sex marriage are primary concerns, while for Anabaptists issues of peace and justice are primary. However, while Anabaptists have traditionally approached social issues in a non-coercive or "non-Constantinian" manner, evangelicals have tended toward more "Constantinian" approaches.[39] So it seems that there are differences between evangelicals and Anabaptists not only in the positions held and issues addressed, but also in their general approaches to addressing social issues. In the following case studies, I tease out these differences by addressing two of the primary issues of evangelical social concern but doing so with an appreciation for Anabaptist political sensibilities.

I strongly sympathize with those evangelicals who wish there were a way to once again make abortion illegal, because both I and they believe abortion is morally tantamount to murder, even if it is legally sanctioned, and think any civilized society should make murder illegal. But rather than trying to defend these evangelical views here, I will instead point to an interesting fact or two.

At the time of the infamous *Roe v. Wade* and *Doe v. Bolton* decisions handed down by the United States Supreme Court on January 22, 1973, the majority of Americans viewed abortion with a fair amount of horror, even though there was a sizable underground industry of abortion providers who catered to desperate women.[40] The Supreme

---

38. One is reminded of an observation frequently attributed to Émile Durkheim: "When mores are sufficient, laws are unnecessary; when mores are insufficient, laws are unenforceable."

39. For a discussion of the various kinds of Constantinianisms, old and new, as well as non-Constantinian alternatives, see Yoder, "Christ, the Hope of the World," 140–76.

40. I am not a woman; but I know there are hard cases, though they do not al-

Court decision and subsequent legislation together with court rulings sustaining and in some ways even extending the original edict seem to have shifted U.S. opinion significantly, however; so that, while most citizens once thought abortion immoral[41] and were aghast that it had been made legal by court fiat, many (perhaps even most) citizens now think that abortion is a moral right because it is by now a fairly longstanding legal one.[42] So legislation is not unimportant in shaping climate of opinion. If the Supreme Court decision were overturned, or there were a constitutional "Right to Life" amendment enacted, then public opinion might be shaped once more, at least in part, by the changing legal status of abortion.

But legislation is clearly not the whole story, because there are many examples of scofflaw situations, of laws on the books that proved unenforceable because there was no public will to obey or enforce them. Some are so ludicrous, such as laws against singing in the bathtub, that even though they may technically remain in legal codes, any attempt to enforce them would result in universal derision.[43] There are also scofflaw situations where the circumstances are much more serious. An example would be the latter stages of Prohibition, where, however important the source of the injunction (the *Constitution* itself), or however heroic attempts at enforcement by some officers of

---

ways turn out the way one might expect. Here is one: In 1896 a thirteen year old girl was raped at knife-point in Chester, Pennsylvania. Nine months later she gave birth to a baby girl. Baby Ethel grew up in difficult circumstances, bouncing from place to place. She ended up working in nightclubs around rough men. But one night people realized she could sing. Ethel Waters became one of the great blues singers of the twentieth century, the second African-American ever to be nominated for an Academy Award. She later became a Roman Catholic Christian, and then a lead soloist for Billy Graham. She sang her testimony, her signature solo, wherever she went, "His Eye Is on the Sparrow." I was one of many millions blessed by her ministry.

41. Their views were grounded not just on religious beliefs, but also such pre-Christian moral pillars as the Hippocratic Oath. There had also been a reaction, at least for awhile, against proponents of eugenics who had championed abortion, i.e., when the once fairly widespread enthusiasm for eugenics fell into at least temporary disfavor with the general public after some streams of the eugenics movement were linked to Nazi atrocities.

42. The social studies used to back these rough claims are sometimes conflicting, but a technical discussion of the history of public opinion polls about and other research into the general public's attitudes toward abortion will be set aside for the moment.

43. Cf. http://www.idiotlaws.com.

the law, the legal position did not by itself prove sufficient to sustain public opinion and support for the ban.

My own preliminary suggestion about the status of abortion in our society is that we have reached a stage where the battle for minds and hearts is much more important than the legal battle to end abortion. If we do not somehow win a broad and general consensus that abortion is a terribly wrong choice, then political and legal victories will mean far less than one might otherwise hope. A legal victory at this stage might invite little more than a scofflaw response, unless the penalties were so extremely harsh and thoroughly enforced that even the most ardent pro-life advocate might feel uneasy.

I am also sympathetic with those evangelicals opposed to same-sex marriage on moral and religious grounds,[44] but I am personally more ambivalent about the possibilities for convincing secular citizens that same-sex marriages are inappropriate than I am of convincing others that abortion is an evil.[45] My unproven intuition is that arguments in favor of ordering one's sexual life are more closely tied to specific religious teachings and convictions than are arguments about the sanctity of life.[46] A *prima facie* appeal can be made in support of this intuition by pointing to the fact that the U.S. founding documents repeatedly reference issues pertaining to life, but not to sexual practices.

---

44. I have been reading revisionist approaches to Scripture with respect to same-sex sexual relations (by scholars such as John Boswell, Robin Scroggs, and their heirs) as well as occasionally dialoguing with religious advocates of the legitimacy of same-sex sexual relationships, since the mid-1970s, most recently when Soul Force/Equality Ride visited the Bethel College campus on April 16, 2010. Attempts to examine biblical teachings were dismissed categorically as invoking "clobber passages" by Equality Riders, who proved uninterested in serious intellectual discussions about Scripture that day, despite their own pamphlets calling for revisionist interpretations.

45. Cf. Eberle, *Religious Convictions*; cf. also Kynes, "Marriage Debate," 187–203; and the *Manhattan Declaration*.

46. Though that is not to say that arguments can't be made for the former. See, e.g., evangelical philosopher Paul Copan, who devotes three thoughtful chapters to preparing lay Christians to speak to LGBTQ issues in *When God Goes to Starbucks*, 77–118. Evangelical Catholic Francis J. Beckwith, who seems to relish confrontation, writes lively and provocative counterarguments to proponents of same-sex marriages. See, e.g., Beckwith, "Street Theatre in the Bay Area." See also Beckwith, "Same-Sex Marriage and the Failure of Justificatory Liberalism." Beckwith participated, along with Marvin M. Ellison, J. Budziszewski, and Ronald E. Long, in a "Same-Sex Marriage Debate" at the American Academy of Religion in 2004 that appeared in *Philosophia Christi* 7.1 (2005) 7–58.

Furthermore, I have a second ambivalence. Is regularizing and regulating an evil a gain or a loss, or perhaps both? Take irregular heterosexual relationships as an example. While, from a biblical perspective, it would be better that men and women not enter into a sexual relationship without being married, might it not still be good to recognize and perhaps to some degree even privilege common-law marriages, that is, as opposed to treating all sexual relationships outside of formal ecclesiastical or civil marriages as equally bad?[47] *Mutatis mutandis*, would not tying same-sex couples in some form of civil union at least encourage and perhaps even enforce some levels of discipline on their lives that might not otherwise be present? Or would the effects actually run the other direction, as many fear, and further erode the sanctity of marriage? Still to use a more distant analogy, even if one is opposed to the manufacture and sale of distilled liquors, would it not be better to at least restrict how, where, when, and to whom they can be sold, especially given the now discarded public policy of legal Prohibition?

Another issue complicating matters is that it is easy for a culture to confuse religious and civil understandings of marriage, especially when both are attempting to regulate marriage. Once the state has entered the business of regulating marriages at all, then the state may presumably regulate as it sees fit, subject to the limitations of a liberal democracy, at least in the case of a country such as the United States. The people of the United States have already decided that all sorts of proposed marriages should be out of bounds, so the quarrel then becomes over which boundaries are legitimate and which are not. It seems that it would be better if there were a clearer demarcation between the views of the Church and the state when it comes to matrimony. The Church should not expect the state to uphold the standards for Christian marriage. That is for the Church to do.

There are, at the same time, still many reasons to be leery of the drive to legalize same-sex sexual relationships. For example, if religious "discrimination" against same-sex sexual relationships and advocacy becomes "discrimination" against a "civil right," then persecution (or at least a substantial loss of privileges currently taken almost for granted—say, in the tax code, or of student aid) might fall

---

47. See Dundas, "Morality and Marital Status of the Caribbean Common-Law Union."

upon courageous Christians (and their institutions) who denounce such sexual relationships as sinful. That is not an attractive prospect, though neither is persecution the worst fate that a Christian can face. In fact, if we take the Sermon on the Mount seriously, it is a normative one for Christians, something that we rejoice in while enduring, given the noble company we are placed in by suffering for the sake of *dikaiosynē*.

As noted earlier, and *contra* a host of thinkers, beginning with John Rawls, we do have the philosophical, ethical, and political right to put forward our views within a secular liberal democracy on *purely religious* grounds.[48] But the degree to which we should expend our energies trying to do so is not altogether clear to me.[49] It depends in part on how paradigmatic one takes the political life of Jesus to be for Christians in a modern, democratic society.

"GO TELL THAT FOX!"

Jesus is fearless when he responds to the intimidating warnings from Pharisees that Herod intends to kill him: "Go tell that fox!" (Luke 13:32). Jesus boldly proclaims what he is doing to advance the Kingdom of Heaven—casting out demons and healing the sick. He is resolute in his mission, which he fully realizes will take him to Jerusalem to die, but not at the hand of Herod. This curt, uncompromising, and courageous reply appears in the context of Lucan narratives that are filled with all sorts of political implications for earthly rulers, even though Jesus is pursuing and fulfilling the goals of a very different Kingdom.[50] Is the example of Jesus in Luke paradigmatic for us as well, or not?

Does the Kingdom of God require political engagement with the political kingdoms of this world, disengagement from them, or some other form of engagement with this world?[51] I suggest that nothing is

---

48. Eberle, *Religious Convictions*; cf. Wolterstorff, "How Social Justice Got to Me," 664–79, and Stout, "2007 Presidential Address," 533–44.

49. This is my primary ambivalence with the *Manhattan Declaration*, along with what may amount to implicit Constantinian assumptions behind the document.

50. The classic text which prompted discussion of this sort is Yoder, *Politics of Jesus*. Cf. Sloan, *Favorable Year of the Lord*.

51. Some of my own very preliminary views concerning political power are spelled out in Erdel, "Book of *Ruth* and Coetzee's *Age of Iron*."

likely to make a more powerful political statement than for Christians to pursue their primary callings, regardless of whatever else they might do as well. What are they? I trust most reading this essay know these callings well. As I stated in the introduction above, we are to love God, each other, and our neighbors, who are defined as persons in need, and to make disciples of Jesus Christ in obedience to the Great Commission, even as we reach out in compassion to persons in need. Any overt political involvements are to be clearly subsidiary to and supportive of these primary callings, though that does not necessarily exclude the possibility that some individuals may have a specific calling to a political vocation. William Wilberforce and his battle against slavery come to mind. For God calls people to many vocations, in part because such callings are part of his legitimate creation order, in part because these vocations may also be the means for furthering his Kingdom, though not, perhaps, in ways that the world would expect.[52]

I do not pretend to have answered the questions I have posed in this essay very well; but I would propose that there are far more questions, some of them harder yet to explore, that this essay, with its limitations of length (not to mention my own limitations), has not begun to address.

Here is one: To what extent may I, as a biblical pacifist, serve as a magistrate in a setting that presumes that a state has the right to use lethal force? Some of the earliest Christian writings proscribe the professions of painter or sculptor if they make idols; of soldiers if they would carry out an order to kill someone or if they bind themselves with an oath; of a governor, presumably because of the power of the sword; of a charioteer who would compete in games; of a gladiator; or of a brothel-keeper as all being positions incompatible with Church membership.[53]

Here is an even more important question. To what extent has this whole focus on politics been a misleading one? There are many domains of life, and it may be that the real power today is in the marketplace. Should not the values of the upside-down Kingdom be taken there? Could anyone but Christians themselves stop Christians

---

52. A calling to a certain vocation does not mean a validation of the way that vocation is typically conceived. See below.

53. Hippolytus of Rome, *Apostolic Tradition*, 16:1–16. The list given in the text above is illustrative and indicative, not systematic and exhaustive.

from carrying Christian values into the realm of business? More dramatically, should Christian values guide secularists too, even on Wall Street? That would indeed be a revolutionary turn of events.

The values of the Kingdom of God will create extreme challenges, no matter what domain we enter. It may be enough if we can remain loyal ambassadors of those values, unswerving in our commitment to the King. But if we are ambassadors, our message is not just for ourselves, but for those to whom we have been sent. And we are fairly unique as ambassadors, because we are ambassadors who often serve best the One who has sent us by humbly serving those who he has sent us to reach. Christian values should guide secular society, but in the long run those values cannot be sustained apart from the indwelling and empowering presence of the living God. Christian values cannot be sustained without Christian discipleship, both in our own lives, and in the lives of those we reach out to as we make disciples in obedience to the Great Commission.[54]

So, I would conclude, the best way to spread and support Christian values is to work toward making disciples. When we do so we should remember that the "teaching them to obey all things" of the Great Commission, a passage dear to evangelicals, is directly linked to the teachings of Jesus in the Sermon on the Mount, a passage at the heart of Anabaptist life.[55]

BIBLIOGRAPHY

Allen, James, Hilton Als, and Leon F. Litwack. *Without Sanctuary: Lynching Photography in America*. Foreword by John Lewis. Santa Fe, NM: Twin Palms, 2000.

Basinger, David, and Randall Basinger, editors. *Predestination & Free Will: Four Views of Divine Sovereignty & Human Freedom*, with John Feinberg, Norman Geisler, Bruce Reichenbach, and Clark Pinnock. Downers Grove, IL: InterVarsity, 1986.

Bauman, Clarence. *The Sermon on the Mount: The Modern Quest for Meaning*. Macon, GA: Mercer University Press, 1986.

---

54. Throughout his career John Howard Yoder attempted to articulate in various ways how Christians can be ambassadors in the public square without forsaking their primary calling to discipleship. See, e.g., Yoder, *Christian Witness to the State*; Yoder, *Body Politics*. See also Ellul, *Politics of God*.

55. See Erdel, "Commission and Kingdom."

Beckwith, Francis J. "Same-Sex Marriage and the Failure of Justificatory Liberalism." *First Things* 10 December 2008. No pages. Online: http://www.firstthings.com/onthesquare/2088/12/same-sex-marriage-and-the-fail.

———. "Street Theatre in the Bay Area: What Social Conservatives Should Do." *National Review* 26 February 2004. No pages. Online: http://old.nationalreview.com/comment/beckwith200402260920.asp.

Beckwith, Francis J., Marvin M. Ellison, J. Budziszewski, and Ronald E. Long. "Same-Sex Marriage Debate." Themed issue of *Philosophia Christi* 7 (2005) 7–58.

Boyd, Gregory A. *The Myth of a Christian Nation: How the Quest for Political Power Is Destroying the Church*. Grand Rapids: Zondervan, 2005.

Bush, Peter. "Debating Marriage: Marrying the Sister of a Deceased Wife and the Presbyterian Church in Canada." *Fides et Historia* 41.2 (2009) 31–49.

Carter, Craig A. *Rethinking: Christ and Culture: A Post-Christendom Perspective*. Grand Rapids: Brazos, 2006.

Clouse, Robert G., editor. *War: Four Christian Views*, with Herman A. Hoyt, Myron S. Augsburger, Arthur F. Holmes, and Harold O. J. Brown. Downers Grover, IL: InterVarsity, 1981.

Copan, Paul. *When God Goes to Starbucks: A Guide to Everyday Apologetics*. Grand Rapids: Baker, 2008.

Dundas, Leon A. "The Morality and Marital Status of the Caribbean Common-Law Union." MA thesis, Caribbean Graduate School of Theology, 1990.

Eberle, Christopher J. *Religious Convictions in Liberal Politics*. Cambridge: Cambridge University Press, 2002.

Ellul, Jacques. *The Politics of God and the Politics of Man*. Translated and edited by Geoffrey W. Bromiley. Grand Rapids: Eerdmans, 1972.

Erdel, Timothy Paul. "The Book of *Ruth* and Coetzee's *Age of Iron*: Marginal Women and Personal Virtue Midst Moral and Political Chaos." Paper presented at the 58th annual meeting of the Evangelical Theological Society, Washington, DC, 15 November 2006.

———. "The Great Commission and God's Righteous Kingdom." *Mission Focus: Annual Review* 16 (2008) 93–115.

———. "Holiness among the Mennonites." *Reflections* 10 (2008) 5–42.

———. "Is Just War Still an Oxymoron?" *Criswell Theological Review* 4.2 (2007) 53–76.

———. "The Missionary Church: From Radical Outcast to the Wild Child of Anabaptism." *Illinois Mennonite Heritage* 24.3 (1997) 60, 59 [guest commentary].

———. "Not All Those Who Wander Are Lost." *Reflections* 11 (2009) 35–42.

———. "'Tis So Sweet to Trust in Jesus': What a Comparative Analysis of Trust in Different Religious Traditions Suggests about the Uniqueness of Christian Faith." *Caribbean Journal of Evangelical Theology* 8 (2004) 21–41.

———. "What Is My Epistemic Duty Toward Religious Beliefs and Practices That Seem to Me, *prima facie*, to Be False, Immoral, or Otherwise Inadequate?" Paper presented at the Society of Christian Philosophy Midwest Division Annual Meeting, "Christian Philosophy and Religious Diversity," Lincoln Christian College and Seminary, Lincoln, IL, 8 April 2005.

Gaus, Christopher Gerald. Review of *Religious Convictions in Liberal Politics*, by Christopher Eberle. *Notre Dame Philosophical Reviews* 8 March 2008. No pages. Online: http://ndpr.nd.edu/review.cfm?id=1214.

Gerand, Chris. "John McCain Wins Bethel Mock Election." *Bethel Beacon* 62.2 (2008) 1.

Hippolytus of Rome, *Apostolic Tradition*. Formerly known as *Egyptian Church Order*.

Hughes, Richard T. *Christian America and the Kingdom of God*. Urbana: University of Illinois Press, 2009.

Kinzel, Erin. "Bethel Rolls out the Red Carpet for President Bush." *Bethel: The Magazine of Bethel College* 17.1 (2006) 6–7.

———. "Opportunity of a Lifetime: George W. Bush Becomes First Sitting President to Visit Bethel College." *Bethel: The Magazine of Bethel College* 17.1, (2006) 4–5.

Kynes, William L. "The Marriage Debate: A Public Theology of Marriage." *Trinity Journal* 28.2 (2007) 187–203.

Lewis, C. S. (Clive Staples). "Lilies That Fester." In *The World's Last Night: And Other Essays*, 31–49. New York: Harcourt, Brace & World, 1960.

Manhattan Declaration: A Call of Christian Conscience. Drafted 20 October 2009. Released 20 November 2009. No pages. Online: http://www.demossnews.com/manhattandeclaration.

Martin, William. *With God on our Side: The Rise of the Religious Right in America*. Rev. ed. New York: Broadway, 2005.

McArthur, Harvey K. *Understanding the Sermon on the Mount*. New York: Harper, 1960.

Naipaul, Shiva. *Journey to Nowhere: A New World Tragedy*. New York: Simon & Schuster, 1980. [British edition is *Black and White*. London: Hamish Hamilton, 1980.]

Roth, John D. "Being Christian; Being Citizen." Colloquium presentation, Miller-Moore Academic Center, Bethel College, Mishawaka, Indiana, 14 October 2008.

Rushdoony, Rousas John. *Institutes of Biblical Law*. Nutley, NJ: Craig, 1973.

Sloan, Robert B., Jr. *The Favorable Year of the Lord: A Study of Jubilary Theology in the Gospel of Luke*. Austin, TX: Schola, 1977.

Smith, James E. "Enhancing the Worship of God through Understanding and Hallowing the Lord's Day at Bethel Missionary Church in Goshen, Indiana." DWS thesis, The Robert E. Webber Institute for Worship Studies, Orange Park, Florida, 2007.

Smith, Robert. "Critic's Notebook: An Ugly Legacy Lives on, It's Glare Unsoftened by Age." *New York Times*, 13 January 2000. No pages. Online: http://query.nytimes.com/gst/fullpage.html?res=9C0DE3rdF143AF930A25752C0A9669C8B63&sec=&spon=&pagewanted=2#.

Stassen, Glen H., and David P. Gushee, *Kingdom Ethics: Following Jesus in Contemporary Context*. Downers Grove, IL: InterVarsity, 2003.

Stout, Jeffrey. "2007 Presidential Address: The Folly of Secularism." *Journal of the American Academy of Religion* 76 (2008) 533–44.

Strickland, Wayne G., editor. *Five Views on Law and Gospel*, with Greg L. Bahnsen, Walter C. Kaiser, Jr., Douglas J. Moo, Wayne G. Strickland, and Willem A. VanGemeren. Counterpoints. Grand Rapids, MI: Zondervan, 1996. [First published in 1993 as *The Law, the Gospel, and the Modern Christian*.]

Swartley, Willard M. *Covenant of Peace: The Missing Peace in New Testament Theology and Ethics*. Grand Rapids: Eerdmans, 2006.

Wolterstorff, Nicholas. "How Social Justice Got to Me and Why It Never Left." *Journal of the American Academy of Religion* 76 (2008) 664–679.

Yoder, John Howard. "The Biblical Mandate for Evangelical Social Action." In *For the Nations: Essays Evangelical and Public*, 180–98. Grand Rapids: Eerdmans, 1998.

———. *Body Politics: Five Practices of the Christian Community before the Watching World*. Scottdale, PA: Herald, 2001.

———. "Christ, the Hope of the World." In *The Original Revolution: Essays on Christian Pacifism*, 140–76. Scottdale, PA: Herald, 2003.

———. *The Christian Witness to the State*. Institute of Mennonite Studies 3. Newton, KS: Faith and Life, 1964. [Reprint ed., Scottdale, PA: Herald, 2002.]

———. *Discipleship as Political Responsibility*. Translated from German by Timothy J. Geddert. Scottdale, PA: Herald, 2003.

———. *The Politics of Jesus: Vicit Agnus Noster*. Grand Rapids: Eerdmans, 1972. [2nd edition, 1994].

Yoder, Matthew, et al. "Younger Voices in the Missionary Church." *Reflections* 11 (2009) 43–51.

Beyond Anselm

A Biblical and Evangelical Case for Nonviolent Atonement

KIRK R. MACGREGOR

INTRODUCTION TO THE PROBLEM: EVANGELICALS AND ANABAPTISTS ON ATONEMENT

FROM THE FIRST THIRD of the last century to the present, atonement theology has surfaced as a major area of contention between evangelicalism and historic peace churches in America. This tension solidified following the 1931 publication of Gustaf Aulén's *Christus Victor*, which earned wide acclaim as the definitive typology of atonement themes throughout church history. Aulén divided these themes into three categories: classical, satisfaction, and exemplar. By "classical" Aulén designated the theme, frequently expressed in the Patristic Church, of Jesus fighting against and defeating the evil powers of this world through the cross, which victory accomplished God's reconciliation of the world to himself. By "satisfaction" Aulén referenced the theme, originally formulated by the eleventh-century philosophical theologian Anselm, that Christ's death satisfied a precondition without whose fulfillment a holy God could not forgive sinners. By "exemplar" Aulén denoted the theme, first articulated by Anselm's twelfth century foil Abelard, that Jesus' crucifixion served as an example of the type of suffering Christians should be willing to endure for the sake of God's

Kingdom. For Aulén, these three themes could either stand alone as, or function as ingredients of, complete theories of the atonement.

Prior to 1931, it would be fair to say that, notwithstanding some important exceptions, the general rule saw evangelicals and Anabaptists employ two different unwritten "recipes" for understanding the suffering of Christ: penal substitutionary atonement and transformative identification. Delineated by Martin Luther and John Calvin, penal substitutionary atonement combined the classical and satisfaction themes by positing believers' victory over the forces of evil *through Jesus' vicarious death in their place*, which propitiated the wrath of God against their sins.[1] In contradistinction, transformative identification aimed to enable believers to remain faithful amidst persecution by combining the classical and exemplar themes. Stemming mainly from the writings of Balthasar Hubmaier, Peter Riedemann, and Pilgram Marpeck, this recipe posits believers' victory over the forces of evil *through spiritual transformation*, a transformation which occurs when believers identify themselves with Jesus by showing willingness to suffer unto death as Jesus did.[2]

Three interrelated observations deserve comment at this juncture. First, the evangelical recipe is primarily theoretical, while the Anabaptist recipe is primarily practical. Second, this contrast is due to the fact that for each community, there existed a need that its atonement theory met. For the evangelical community, coming as it did out of a university-driven Protestant Reformation with its academic roots in the Renaissance, the need amounted to an intellectual explanation of how humans could find relationship with an absolutely just God. For the Anabaptist community, which faced intense persecution throughout the early modern period from Protestants and Catholics alike, the need constituted moral suasion to remain faithful to the gospel of Christ when so doing spelled death. Third, for the sake of genuine discipleship of mind and strength, we stress that these intellectual

---

1. On this view, Satan never held any kind of ownership over human beings. Rather, by sinning against an infinitely good God, human beings incur a debt greater than their ability to repay; it is this debt alone that, by virtue of God's perfect justice, subjects them to eternal damnation.

2. On this view, prior to their transformation humans find themselves not under God's wrath but under Satan's ownership. Since God is perfectly loving, it is absurd to think that God needed Jesus' death in order to forgive sinners. Instead, in sinning humans voluntarily enslave themselves to Satan, the lord of sin.

and practical needs are equally legitimate and should both be met by any atonement models henceforth proposed.

Paradoxically, the unintended consequence of Aulén's work for evangelicals and Anabaptists in America was precisely the same: to lead both communities to excise from their atonement models the theme of believers' victory over the forces of evil. This surprising effect materialized because, in a capsule, Aulén did not merely historically document the three aforementioned atonement themes but also prescribed that the classical theory of the atonement—with its emphasis on Christ's victory over the demonic hordes who had enslaved humanity—should be elevated to prominence over against the satisfaction theory, the exemplar theory, and any combination theory. Although unproblematic in his native Europe, this decision evoked considerable controversy in North America, where evangelicals and Anabaptists were both intentionally distancing themselves from the Fundamentalist-Modernist controversy. On the one hand, among the most controversial assertions of Fundamentalism was its insistence on the literal role of Satan in the world, evidenced scripturally in demon-possession. On the other hand, among the most controversial assertions of Modernism was its denial of Satan's existence and subsequent reinterpretation of biblical narratives featuring the demonic in psychological and social terms. Thus evangelicals and Anabaptists could now neither accept nor reject the classical theory without setting themselves decisively on one side or the other of the raging controversy. Accordingly, evangelicals and Anabaptists in America bracketed the classical theory and so neglected all elements thereof in their subsequent constructions of the atonement.

The net result of the foregoing was to render most evangelical and Anabaptist atonement doctrines in America as monothematic from the outbreak of the Second World War until the end of the Cold War. During this period, the norm in American evangelicalism was a strictly forensic version of penal substitutionary atonement, while the norm in American Anabaptism was a strictly ethical version of transformative identification. Both sides were so entrenched in their respective positions that Colin Grant in 1986 and Colin Gunton in 1989 could report "the abandonment" of theological innovation on the atonement by both sides.[3] However, the last two decades have seen

---

3. Grant, "Abandonment of Atonement," 1–8; Gunton, *Actuality of the Atonement*, xi.

a renaissance of atonement studies, wherein more creative work has been done on the atonement by evangelicals and Anabaptists than at any time since the days of Anselm and Abelard.[4] The prevailing tides began to turn as a result of three challenges, the first undermining both penal substitutionary atonement and transformative identification, the second undermining the transformative view, and the third undermining the penal view.

First, a spate of feminist and womanist critiques charged the penal and transformative views with promoting abuse by those in positions of power and apathetic tolerance of abuse by its victims. On this critique, the penal view unthinkably made salvation the effect of two grand injustices: God the Father's commission of "cosmic child abuse" by crucifying his innocent Son, and the Son's refusal to escape from his abusive Father by willingly enduring Calvary. Similarly, the transformative view unthinkably made personal regeneration the fruit of an unholy alliance between glorifying the experience of Jesus' pointless execution at the hands of the Romans and consigning ourselves to suicidally embrace the same fate.

Second, the interdisciplinary work of historian and social philosopher René Girard indicted the transformative view with a fundamental misunderstanding of Jesus' death while at the same time bequeathing Anabaptists a new understanding of the cross more in line with their own tradition.[5] According to Girard's *tour de force*, the scapegoat theory of ritual violence, societies typically avert widespread internal conflict and thus preserve the social order by channeling innate human hostility toward a scapegoat. But for Girard, the Passion furnishes what no other scapegoat scenario does: it objectively discloses the innocence of the scapegoat, Jesus, and thereby unmasks the ritual violence associated with the scapegoat myth for the debacle that it is. Hence the Passion is not an act

---

4. While initially remarkable to those unacquainted with the contemporary theological landscape on atonement, my verdict is confirmed by Weaver (*Nonviolent Atonement*, 1), Jersak ("Nonviolent Identification," 22–25), Hardin ("Out of the Fog," 55–56), Rieger ("Good News for Postmodern Man," 378–86), and Beilby and Eddy (*Nature of the Atonement*, 9–11), among others.

5. Although Girard stands even more at variance with penal substitution than transformative identification, the fact that his research was sociological rather than exegetical rendered it of far greater force to American Anabaptists, many of whom employ social science as a lens for biblical interpretation, than to American evangelicals, who typically reject the hermeneutical value of social science.

to be emulated; rather, it is incontrovertible proof of the immorality of ritual violence, the antidote for the scapegoating plague endemic to human civilization, and so the necessary banner in working for social justice worldwide. Due to their foundational commitment to peace and social justice, American Anabaptists widely embraced Girard's proposed atonement revisioning.

Third, the disquiet felt by a strong minority of American evangelicals toward the majority American evangelical support for the war in Iraq and its concomitant American imperialism served as the greatest factor in the contemporary evangelical reconceptualization of the atonement. This somewhat counterintuitive situation materialized because of the either explicit or implicit appeal by evangelical backers of the George W. Bush administration to penal substitutionary atonement as the *sine qua non* presupposition for supporting the war.[6] The argument ran as follows. At the cross God the Father was justified in performing an act that by itself would have been unjust—exacting retributive punishment upon his Son for sins he did not commit—because it was the only way to accomplish human salvation. Thus, far from being immoral, the Father deserves praise and glory for using seemingly gratuitous violence because that violence accomplished the greater good; the end justified the means. According to the Bible, Christians are supposed to emulate God. But if God legitimately used seemingly gratuitous violence to accomplish the greater good, and if Christians are supposed to emulate God, then it follows that Christians can and should use gratuitous violence to accomplish greater goods. Therefore it mattered not that America's involvement in the Iraq war was based on the Bush administration's false charges of Iraq's possession of weapons of mass destruction and Iraq's collusion with Al-Qaeda. Yes, America's violence was gratuitous, but it was legitimated on the grounds of producing such greater goods as democracy and the spread of evangelical Christianity in the Middle East. For many evangelicals, the repugnance of this argument, seemingly inescapable given penal substitution, shone a spotlight on the previously unseen divine violence lurking at the heart of the penal view and its tragic logical consequences for Christian ethics.

---

6. One implicit appeal I have frequently heard in evangelical churches (most recently this past Memorial Day) is that, just as our troops died to give us physical and temporal life, so Jesus died to give us spiritual and eternal life.

That evangelicals were now challenging the penal view on the same score that Anabaptists always had—the problem of divine violence—brought many among these two communities into constructive dialogue, giving thinkers on each side a fresh appreciation of the strengths of the other side. The strengths of evangelicalism, as David Bebbington points out, may be summarized in four categories: conversionism, the notion that persons need to have their lives changed by Jesus in order to find salvation; activism, the manifestation of the gospel in individual and communal living; biblicism, a high view of the Bible as the inspired and infallible Word of God; and crucicentrism, an emphasis on Jesus' salvific work via the cross.[7] Matching these evangelical areas appealing to Anabaptists were four Anabaptist areas whose attractiveness to many evangelicals stood in stark contrast to the ugliness of the violence sanctioned by their coreligionists. First was a Christocentrism committed to following Jesus as well as worshiping him and to making Jesus' life and teachings, particularly the Sermon on the Mount, the starting point for biblical interpretation. Second, Christianity must disassociate itself from wealth, power, and status and instead embody good news to the poor, powerless, and persecuted. Third, churches must be committed communities of discipleship, friendship, mission, and mutual accountability where roles are related to spiritual gifts rather than gender and where believers alone receive baptism. Fourth, peace between God and humanity and between human beings constitutes the center of the gospel, such that spirituality is inextricably intertwined with prophetically engaging the political and economic arenas of our day as Jesus did in his.[8]

The resulting collaboration between evangelicals and Anabaptists has culminated in a plethora of books written from multiple *Ausgangspunkte* (starting points or points of departure), of which representative works include J. Denny Weaver's *The Nonviolent Atonement* (Anabaptist theology; 2001), Steve Chalke and Alan Mann's *The Lost Message of Jesus* (evangelical theology; 2003), Scot McKnight's *Jesus and His Death* (historical Jesus studies; 2005), the essay collection *Proclaiming the Scandal of the Cross*, edited by Mark Baker (practical theology; 2006), and S. Mark Heim's *Saved from Sacrifice: A*

---

7. Bebbington, *Dominance of Evangelicalism*, 23–40.

8. These four areas are adapted from the seven Core Convictions articulated by the Anabaptist Network in 1998 and then revised in 2006.

Theology of the Cross (integrative theology; 2006). Moreover, these *Ausgangspunkte* have converged in such significant forums as the 2005 London Symposium on the Theology of the Atonement and the 2007 Conference on Nonviolent Atonement (Akron, Pennsylvania), which latter meeting yielded the watershed collection of essays *Stricken by God?* edited by Brad Jersak and Michael Hardin (2007).

My present contribution to this ongoing discussion springs from the *Ausgangspunkt* of integrative theology, namely, the intersection of biblical, historical, and philosophical theology.[9] At this juncture a brief word about my personal history is in order. I stand with one foot in the evangelical tradition and the other foot in the Anabaptist tradition. Raised in a United Methodist Church shepherded by evangelical pastors in Defiance, Ohio, as an undergraduate at Miami University (Ohio) I was deeply engaged with Campus Crusade for Christ and attended a Bible church founded by two evangelical faculty members. I went on to do my master's work at Biola University, an evangelical university, and as a doctoral student at the University of Iowa I was highly involved with InterVarsity Graduate Christian Fellowship and attended an Evangelical Free Church. Regarding my Anabaptist heritage, I am descended on my mother's side (maiden name Speicher) from a long line of Brethren pastors reaching back to the German Brethren, who immigrated to the United States in 1729 under the leadership of Brethren founder Alexander Mack. Hence my parents did not baptize me as an infant but instilled in me the importance of believer's baptism, which I received after professing my faith before my United Methodist congregation at age fourteen. (As the merger between the Evangelical United Brethren Church and the Methodist Church, the United Methodist Church gives parents the option of having their infants baptized but does not require it.) With a lifelong interest in Anabaptist studies, the subject of my doctoral dissertation comprised sixteenth century Anabaptism's sole academic theologian, Balthasar Hubmaier (a 1512 ThD from Universität Ingolstadt under *doktorvater* John Eck).

As an evangelical, an Anabaptist, and an integrative theologian, I hold several distinct commitments whose conjunction may, for some,

---

9. Although this style of theology has a venerable history stretching back to Tertullian, the linguistic handle "integrative theology" was coined by Lewis and Demarest (*Integrative Theology*, 1:8–13) and has since gained currency.

be controversial. Per my evangelical identity, I am committed to the classic doctrine of biblical inerrancy and the grammatico-historical exegesis of Scripture. Per my Anabaptist identity, I am committed to the historical Jesus' conception and manifestation of the peaceful Kingdom of God, where God reigns over all spheres of life not as a haughty monarch but as a humble servant.[10] Per my identity as an integrative theologian, I am committed to the necessity of philosophical reflection in constructing probable solutions to doctrinal problems that cannot be solved by Scripture alone. Among such problems, I believe, is the solidification of an adequate atonement theory, the parts of which Scripture furnishes but does not combine. In other words, passages of Scripture addressing the same topic can be exegeted grammatico-historically to yield the distinct ideas that go to make up an adequate theory. But to turn these ideas from a disjointed list into a synthesized whole where we see how the ideas fit together, we need the God-given deliverances of reason, logic, and ethics.

In this chapter, therefore, I will employ the tools of the integrative theologian to sketch a model of the atonement that is faithful to both the evangelical tradition and the Anabaptist tradition. This model will be faithful to evangelicalism because it formulates all its ideas from grammatico-historical exegesis of Scripture, without avoiding or "explaining away" problematic passages. This model will also be faithful to Anabaptism because of its nonviolent character, namely, in its demonstration that the Bible (when grammatico-historically exegeted) precludes the notion that the atonement constituted the required appeasement of God the Father's infinite wrath against human sin via the human sacrifice of his sinless Son. Hence this model offers evangelicals a way to endorse nonviolence (i.e., divine and, derivatively, human nonviolence) and remain good evangelicals, and it offers Anabaptists a way to endorse biblical inerrancy (at least on the topic of the atonement) and remain good Anabaptists.[11] Moreover, the "recipe" it furnishes will include elements of the classical, satisfaction, and exemplar themes.

---

10. See the chapter on Jesus' conception of the Kingdom of God in my *Molinist-Anabaptist Systematic Theology*, 265–303.

11. Only a minority of contemporary Anabaptists hold to biblical inerrancy, largely due to their fear that inerrancy leads to a violent view of God and to the legitimation of violence between humans.

BIBLICAL THEOLOGY: THE IDEAS OF NONVIOLENT ATONEMENT THEORY

Grammatico-historical exegesis of the Bible yields seven broad ideas, which together comprise nonviolent atonement theory. We shall state each idea and then furnish its exegetical substantiation.

First, Jesus is the necessary means by which God forgives human sins. In the New Testament, this idea is often communicated via the technical terms *hilasmos* and *hilastērion*. According to Johannes Louw and Eugene Nida's authoritative *Greek-English Lexicon of the New Testament Based on Semantic Domains*, *hilasmos* and *hilastērion* mean "the means by which sins are forgiven—'the means of forgiveness, expiation.'"[12] The NRSV and NIV communicate this idea through the free translations "atoning sacrifice" and "sacrifice of atonement," while the RSV employs the more literal yet somewhat archaic "expiation." Although the conventional rendering of these terms is the KJV "propitiation" (retained in the NKJV, NASB, and ESV), Louw and Nida point out that this is a mistranslation: "Though some traditional translations render *hilastērion* as 'propitiation,' this involves a wrong interpretation of the term in question. Propitiation is essentially a process by which one does a favor to a person in order to make him or her favorably disposed, but in the NT God is never the object of propitiation since he is already on the side of the people. *Hilasmos* and *hilastērion* denote the means of forgiveness and not propitiation."[13] Surveying the texts in question, we shall italicize all phrases conveying *hilasmos* and *hilastērion* and translate these terms woodenly as *the means by which sins are forgiven* or *the means of forgiveness* for the sake of precision.

Thus Paul explained concerning Jesus, "God presented him as *a means by which sins are forgiven* through faith in him" (Rom 3:25). The Elder John concurred that Jesus "is *the means of forgiveness* for our sins, and not only for ours but also for the sins of the whole world" (1 John 2:2), a fact that exemplifies the *agapē* of God: "This is love: not that we loved God, but that he loved us and sent his Son as *the means of forgiveness* for our sins" (1 John 4:10). Here we call attention to a fact that is often overlooked: while these texts state that *Jesus himself*—namely, the *Logos*' incarnate life—was the necessary means by which God forgives sins, they neither state nor imply that Jesus' *death*

---

12. Louw and Nida, *Greek-English Lexicon*, 1:504.
13. Ibid.

in particular comprised the necessary means by which God forgives sins. Hence this first category, while proving that the Trinitarian God needed the incarnation in order to forgive human sin, provides no evidence either for or against the penal substitutionary assumption that God needed Jesus *to die* in order to forgive human sin. So at this juncture, the evangelical hallmark of biblicism remains compatible with the Anabaptist notion that the peaceful God revealed in Jesus is able to freely forgive sinners apart from Jesus' death.

Second, Jesus died "on behalf of," "because of," and "for the sake of" us and our sins.[14] While the Bible does not say Jesus died so that God could forgive our sins, it does affirm that our sins constituted the reason Jesus died. The quoted prepositional phrases woodenly translate the preposition *huper* when it takes a genitive object (the Greek words for "us" and "our sins" are always genitive when following *huper*), thus marking "a participant who is benefited by an event or on whose behalf an event takes place."[15] Virtually all Bible translations render *huper* as "for," which is certainly accurate but does not specify, as needed here, which nuances of this fluid English preposition are particularly in view. Thus we shall bring out these nuances in citing the pertinent verses, italicizing phrases that translate *huper*. The primitive Jerusalem creedal confession quoted by Paul maintained "that Christ died *on behalf of* our sins according to the Scriptures" (1 Cor 15:3). Paul declared that Jesus "loved me and gave himself *for the sake of* me" (Gal 2:20) and, through his ignominious crucifixion, "became a curse *on behalf of* us" (Gal 3:13), which demonstrates the divine *agapē*: "But God proves his love for us in this: While we were still sinners, Christ died *on behalf of* us" (Rom 5:8). Consequently, the evangelical emphasis upon crucicentrism emerges as exegetically secure.

Returning to the Anabaptist question of whether Jesus' career necessarily included his crucifixion for God to be able to forgive sins, we note that Paul never made this affirmation. Rather, Paul gave two reasons why Jesus died for our sake on behalf of our sins. According to Gal 1:4, Jesus "gave himself *on behalf of* our sins to set us free from the present evil age, according to the will of our God and Father." Here Paul professed that it was the Father's will for Jesus to die not so that he could forgive our sins but so that we would be set free from the present

14. Ibid., 1:781, 803; 2:251.
15. Ibid., 1:802–3.

evil age (*aiōn*), a topic to which we shall return. Further, according to 2 Cor 5:14-15, "Christ's love compels us because we are convinced that one died *for the sake of* all, and therefore all died. And he died *for the sake* of all, in order that those who live should no longer live *for the sake of* themselves but *for the sake of* him who died *for the sake of* them and was raised again." Hence Jesus died for our sake so that believers would live for his sake rather than for their own. On this score we find that Paul's teaching is in line not only with the Anabaptist commitment to peace but also with the evangelical commitments to conversionism (reason one) and activism (reason two).

Third, Jesus was sacrificed as our Passover lamb. Those who appropriate his sacrifice are reconciled to God and receive healing from his wounds as well as removal of sins (different from "forgiveness of sins"), healing, clear consciences, and peace through his blood. John the Baptist identified Jesus as "the Lamb of God who takes away the sins of the world" (John 1:29; cf. 1:36), and Paul confirmed that "indeed Christ, our Passover lamb, has been sacrificed" (1 Cor 5:7). In order to understand what this symbolism means, we need to explore Exod 12:1-30 to see precisely what the Passover lamb did and did not accomplish. Positively, the Israelites slew the Passover lamb and put its blood on the sides and tops of their doorframes to identify themselves as members of the community embracing God's covenant (and thus under God's protection) rather than the community rejecting God's covenant (and thus under God's wrath). In every home not so marked (namely, those of the Egyptians who rejected God's covenant despite repeated exposure to his miraculous power), God struck down the firstborn son (Exod 12:23). Negatively, the Passover lamb neither was punished for the Israelites' sins nor received the brunt of God's wrath in Israel's place. Instead, it formed the centerpiece of a God-given meal that identified people as within his covenant and thereby rightly related to him, exempt from judgment, and poised for deliverance. With this in mind, we are now in a position to understand the implications of Jesus' being our Passover lamb.

By appropriating Jesus' sacrifice through faith, we become part of the community with which God has made the new covenant, a covenant whose benefits include reconciliation to God, removal of sins, healing, clear consciences, and peace.[16] This resonates perfectly with

---

16. This, of course, is the meaning Jesus ascribed to the Lord's Supper at its insti-

the Anabaptist dedication to redemptive community. Commenting on Ezekiel's description of the benefits accruing to members of this community (36:25–26, 33), Paul wrote:

> Therefore, if anyone is in Christ—new being! The old things passed away; behold, everything has become new. All this is of God, *the one who reconciled us to himself through Christ* and gave us the ministry of reconciliation; that is, God was in Christ *reconciling the world to himself*, not reckoning their trespasses to them and having put in us the message of reconciliation. Therefore we are ambassadors on behalf of Christ, since God is making his appeal through us; we ask on behalf of Christ, *be reconciled to God* (2 Cor 5:17–21; emphasis added).

Here a number of points deserve comment. Through and in Christ, God reconciled the world to himself; note that the text does not say "God reconciled himself to the world." Although this latter sentiment is affirmed by penal substitution, it constitutes the inversion of the scriptural witness. That the direction of reconciliation is "us to God" and not "God to us" is emphasized elsewhere by Paul (Rom 5:10–11; Col 1:18–22). On the same score, it is us who were God's enemies; by contrast, the all-loving God has never been our enemy but cared for us so much that he reconciled us to himself. This reconciliation furnishes the basis for peace within the covenant community between all racial, gender, and ethnic groups (Eph 2:14–18).

A further reinforcement of evangelical crucicentrism, we find that Jesus' blood heals the damage caused by our sins, thereby making us "holy" in God's sight. Consequently Peter maintained, "He himself bore our sins in his body on the tree, so that we might die to sins and live for righteousness; by his wounds you have been healed" (1 Pet 2:24), where "bore" (*anēnenken*) entails enduring the brunt of something with patience and forgiveness. That Jesus endured our sins with patience and forgiveness on the cross is displayed by his repeated[17] prayer, "Father, forgive them, for they do not know what they are doing" (Luke 23:34), and is made explicit by the affirmation in Heb 12:2 that Jesus "endured the cross, despising its shame." Since Christ's blood

---

tution: "This is my blood of the covenant, which is being poured out *for the sake of many*" (Mark 14:24).

17. This was not a prayer Jesus offered once but many times, as evidenced by the use of the continuous-aspect imperfect verb *elegen* ("But Jesus *was continually saying/kept on saying*") rather than the finite-aspect aorist verb *eipen* ("But Jesus *said*").

healed us from the effects of our sins, everything we could justifiably feel guilty about is eradicated. Therefore, the book of Hebrews emphasizes that we can boldly approach God "with our hearts sprinkled clean from an evil conscience" (10:22).

Fourth, at the cross God neither punished nor forsook Jesus, even though Jesus' contemporaries thought God had. This idea is explicitly stated in Isaiah 53, the famous prophetic Servant song. Here Isaiah furnishes a word of hope to God's people, suffering in exile due to their disobedience of the divine covenant. Amidst their pain, God's Servant stands in absolute solidarity with his people, so totally identifying with their suffering at the hands of their tormentors that they might *falsely* conclude he was "stricken by God, smitten by him, and afflicted" (3), as though he were also under God's wrath. But Isaiah cautions that this conclusion would be incorrect. Our bracketed comments bring out the force of Isaiah's reasoning:

> He was despised and rejected by humans, *[Who rejected him? God? No, humans did.]*
> a man of sorrows and acquainted with infirmity.
> Like one from whom people hide their faces *[Who hid their face(s)? God? No, us.]*
> he was despised, and we held him of no account.
> Surely he bore our infirmities
> and carried our sorrows,
> yet we considered him stricken by God, *[Who thought this? We did.]*
> smitten by him, and afflicted. *[And was he?]*
> But he was pierced for our transgressions, *[No, our transgressions pierced him.]*
> he was crushed for our iniquities; *[It was our iniquities that crushed him.]*
> upon him was the punishment that brought us peace, *[Who punished him? We did. Yet what was his response? Peace, forgiveness, and reconciliation.]*
> and by his stripes we are healed. *[We wounded him, but he healed us.]* (3–5)[18]

Confirming that the Father was not pitted against his Son but was rather pleased with him at the cross, Isaiah affirmed that the suffering Servant "will see his seed and prolong his days, and the pleasure of

---

18. Adapted from Jersak, "Nonviolent Identification," 36.

Yahweh shall prosper in his hand" (10). He proceeded to report the attitude of Yahweh toward his Servant: "Therefore I will give him a portion among the great, and he will divide the spoils with the strong, because he poured out his life unto death and was numbered with the transgressors. For he bore the sin of many and made intercession for the transgressors" (12).

Although Jesus' words from the cross are often taken out of context to argue that the Father turned his face away from the Son, we need only recall that Jesus (and the New Testament in general) employed metalepsis when quoting the Hebrew Bible to prove that the opposite is true. In the words of Richard Hays' authoritative book on this subject, metalepsis is allusion "to an earlier text in a way that evokes resonances of the earlier text *beyond those explicitly cited*."[19] Thus when Jesus quotes a memorable line from a passage of Scripture, he is referring not merely to that line but using that line as a mnemonic device to recall the entire passage in the minds of his listeners. Jesus' so-called "cry of dereliction," "My God, my God, why have you forsaken me?" (Mark 15:34; Matt 27:46), is the opening line of Psalm 22, which foretold the death of the Messiah in precisely the way Jesus was dying and proceeded to give God's answer to the Messiah's complaint of forsakenness. The answer states: "For he has not despised or disdained the suffering of the afflicted one; *he has not hidden his face from him* but has listened to his cry for help" (24; emphasis added). Jesus drove the point home with his last words, "Father, into your hands I commit my spirit" (Luke 23:46), a quote from Psalm 31 that spelled out the Father's role at the cross in no uncertain terms. This messianic psalm explains: "Into your hands I commit my spirit; you have redeemed me, O Yahweh, faithful God. . . . I will be glad and rejoice in your steadfast love, because you saw my affliction and took heed of the anguish of my soul. . . . Praise be to Yahweh, for he showed his wonderful love to me when I was in a besieged city. In my alarm I had said, 'I am cut off from your sight!' Yet you heard my cry for mercy when I called to you for help" (5, 7, 21–22). Utterly exploding the notion that the Father turned his back on the Son, this psalm poignantly reveals the Father's wonderful love and encouragement for the Son as he suffered on the cross. Hence the Anabaptist repudiation

---

19. Hays, *Conversion of the Imagination*, 2, emphasis his.

of penal substitutionary atonement as effrontery to the character of God is exegetically verified.

Fifth, God in some way caused Jesus' death, laying our sins upon him and making his life a sacrificial offering. While the Bible rejects God's penal need for Jesus to die to make forgiveness possible, it affirms that God in some way caused his crucifixion. The reason I say "in some way" is because Scripture attributes to God not only events that he causes *in sensu diviso* (in the divided sense) but also events that he causes *in sensu composito* (in the composite sense). For the purposes of our discussion, let us assume that humans possess free choice. Then for God to cause something *in sensu diviso* means that, needing the occurrence of some event in order to accomplish a desired good, he positively wills for that event to take place and supernaturally intervenes in the world to set up the particular circumstances in which he foreknows humans would freely bring about that event.[20] For example, God "brought" the Israelites into the Promised Land *in sensu diviso* by miraculously parting the Red Sea (Exod 13:11; 14:26–30; Deut 6:10; Neh 9:23). By contrast, for God to cause something *in sensu composito* is to create an entire world despite his foreknowledge that, were he to create the world, humans therein would choose to carry out a sinful event that he does not positively will and for which he obviously does not supernaturally intervene to set up its particular circumstances.[21] In other words, although he did not directly cause it, God indirectly causes the event in the sense that if he had not created the world, the event would have never transpired. For example, God "incited" David to take a blasphemous census (2 Sam 24:1) *in sensu composito* by creating a world in which David freely performed this Satan-inspired deed (2 Chr 21:1).

Since Scripture does not differentiate between causation *in sensu diviso* and causation *in sensu composito*, the question of the manner in which God caused Jesus' death, delivering him up as an offering, can only be settled by joining philosophical reflection to biblical exegesis. That said, let us proceed to establish the *fact* of divine causation, regardless of its manner. Isaiah 53 plainly envisages concerning Jesus' death,

---

20. This causation is so called because, when we divide the world into its component moments, at some particular moment God supernaturally intervenes to ordain the occurrence of some particular event.

21. This causation is so called since God created the composite (an entire world) whose parts he knew would include the sinful event.

"Yahweh laid on him the iniquity of us all. . . . Yet it was Yahweh's will to crush him and cause him to suffer" (6, 10; cf. Heb 9:28). Similarly, New Testament texts containing words in the *paradidōmi/ekdotos* ("to hand or deliver over") semantic domain state that God handed or delivered Jesus over to death (Rom 8:32; 2 Cor 5:21; Acts 2:23; 3:18).

Sixth, Jesus, standing in the prophetic tradition of opposition to the corrupted sacrificial system, constituted the final High Priest who brought all Temple sacrifice to an end. Congruent with the Anabaptist obligation of protecting God's people from religious corruption, this sentiment is expressed in Jesus' repeated directive, "But go and learn what this means: 'I desire mercy and not sacrifice'" (Matt 9:13; 12:7). Such is a quotation of Yahweh's words in Hosea 6:6, which continues, "and the knowledge of God rather than burnt offerings." It is also entailed by Jesus' symbolic destruction of the Temple (Mark 11:15–19; Luke 19:45–48; Matt 21:12–17; John 2:13–22), often misunderstood as a cleansing of the Temple.[22] To understand why Jesus and his prophetic forebears regarded the sacrificial system as irreparable, we need first to grasp how its praxis departed from the divinely ordained Levitical model.

The first eight chapters of Leviticus delineate procedures for the various ritual sacrifices, to be offered at times of celebration and thanksgiving (Lev 7:12–15) and at times of inadvertent sin when restitution and restoration were impossible (Lev 4:1–6:7).[23] Despite these varying circumstances, the ritual sacrifice was practically the same. A perfect and healthy animal would be brought by the worshiper to the priest. The worshiper would place his or her hands on the head of the animal. It would then be slain by the priest, who scattered the animal's blood on and around the altar. These sacrifices made "atonement" for the worshiper (1:4; 4:20, 26, 31, 35; 5:6, 10, 13, 16, 18; 6:7; 7:7). Because identical sacrifices were prescribed in times of rejoicing, thanksgiving, and sin alike, it is impossible for said atonement to comprise ritualized blood payment for the satisfaction of guilt. The

---

22. That Jesus never intended to cleanse the Temple but rather symbolized its destruction has been demonstrated by scholars across the "liberal-moderate-conservative" theological spectrum. For respective examples representing each of these three stances see Crossan, *Who Killed Jesus*, 58–65; Sanders, *Jesus and Judaism*, 61–71; and Wright, *Jesus*, 418–28, 510–28.

23. My exegesis of Leviticus closely follows the analysis of Weaver, *Nonviolent Atonement*, 58–61.

idea of ritualized blood payment is also precluded by the fact that sin and guilt offerings dealt with unintentional sins; for even the gravest intentional sins, blood was not required. These severe sins were borne on Yom Kippur by the scapegoat, which, incidentally, was not killed but driven away from the camp into the wilderness (16:21–22).

Rather than blood payment, therefore, the key to understanding how Yahweh intended ritual sacrifice to atone for the worshiper is Leviticus 17:11, "For the life of the flesh is in the blood" (cf. 17:14; Gen 9:4; Deut 12:23). When we add this notion to the worshiper's identification with the sacrificial animal through laying on of hands, we discover that the priest's placement of the blood of the animal with which the worshiper is identified on the horns of the altar where God's definitive presence resided amounted to a ritual self-dedication and self-giving of the worshiper to God. This ritual was not a *quid pro quo* of slaying an animal in place of slaying a human being. Instead, the life of the animal (e.g., its blood), and with it the life of the worshiper, was given to God.

Despite this original purpose of personal commitment to Yahweh, by the eighth century BCE the Israelites subverted the sacrificial system by turning it into a *quid pro quo*; following their pagan neighbors, the Israelites believed they could violate the Mosaic Covenant as long as they "paid off" Yahweh through animal sacrifices at the Temple. In other words, the "sacrifice for grave sins" motif was *the Israelites' corruption of the sacrificial system*, not God's intent for the system (Mic 6:7–8; Isa 1:10–20; Jer 6:20; 7:22–23).[24] Thus the author of Hebrews noted that, according to rabbinic law (Oral Torah) but contrary to Mosaic Law (Written Torah), "without the shedding of blood there is no forgiveness" (9:22).[25]

In Hebrews, Jesus is the ultimate "High Priest" (2:17; 3:1; 4:14–15; 5:5, 10; 6:20; 8:1, 3) who brings about the reality to which the Levitical sacrificial system originally pointed, thereby consummating and concluding that system, and who subversively exposed the inefficacy of the corrupt Temple version of that system. Hence, as Hardin observes, of prime importance for the author of Hebrews is the subversion of the

---

24. Schwager, *Jesus in the Drama*, 180.

25. A reference to the oral tradition later transcribed as *Yoma* 1f; this sentiment is absent from the Hebrew Bible.

corrupt sacrificial system under the cover of sacrificial language.[26] In the "greater and perfect tabernacle" (9:11), of which the earthly Temple tabernacle is merely a "shadow" (8:5; 10:1), a person may only come to God via total dedication, that is, living perfectly through continual righteous behavior without any sin, thus literally serving as a living bodily sacrifice. To this the Levitical self-dedication to God through animal sacrifice legitimately pointed, not to a vicarious exchange for forgiveness of sins (9:9–10). Note the author's *reductio ad absurdum* of sacrificial animals vicariously removing people's sins and so perfecting them: "[T]he same sacrifices repeated endlessly year after year can never make perfect those who approach. Otherwise, would they not have stopped being offered? For the worshipers, cleansed once for all, would no longer have any consciousness of sin. But those sacrifices are a reminder of sin year after year. Thus it is impossible for the blood of bulls and goats to take away sins" (10:1–4). All this, avers the author of Hebrews, was expressed by the pre-incarnate Christ: "Sacrifices and offerings you have not desired, but a body you prepared for me; with burnt offerings and sin offerings you have taken no pleasure. . . . Here I am, as it is written about me in the scroll, I have come to do your will, O God" (10:5–7). Note Christ's insistence that God was never ultimately interested in dead animals but a human body that perfectly *lives* according to God's will. Through his perfect human life (7:26, 28), Christ forever stands as both High Priest and living sacrifice in the heavenly sanctuary, such that all who identify with Jesus by dedicating their lives to God through him are imputed his perfect righteousness and receive salvation (7:25; 10:14; 11:40; 12:23; Rom 12:1; 1 Cor 6:12–20). All this beautifully amplifies the evangelical emphasis on the necessity and salvific effects of personal conversion.

Our nonviolent atonement theory interlocks the evangelical stress on conversionism with the Anabaptist stress on Christocentrically following Jesus' nonviolent ethic. For the author of Hebrews, Jesus dismantled the violent misconception that God required sin to be repaid via blood sacrifice by allowing his enemies to kill him without a quest for vengeance (cf. Luke 23:34). While Abel's blood cried from the ground for vengeance (Gen 4:10), Jesus' blood "speaks a better word than the blood of Abel" (Heb 12:24), namely, "the introduction of a better hope through which we draw near to God" (Heb 7:19). After

26. Hardin, "Sacrificial Language in Hebrews," 106.

his perfect life was ended through judicial murder, Jesus took his shed blood into the heavenly tabernacle precisely to atone *for that blood*, that is, to atone for the debacle of its being shed. In this way, Jesus made peace between God (Father and Holy Spirit) and the fact of his crucifixion, a peace necessary so that God would not punish those responsible for it (namely, all humanity since each person chooses to participate in and perpetuate the domination system or *aiōn* that caused it). Thus paradoxically, unlike people's wrongful confidence in the blood of animals to remove sin, Jesus' blood cleansed our consciences from complicity in the very system that caused his death and thereby freed us to serve God (Heb 7:12–14; 10:19; cf. 1 Pet 1:18–19; 1 John 1:7; Rev 12:10–11).

Seventh, Jesus' death ransomed us from the aiōn *and for God.* In the New Testament, the *aiōn*, translated "age" and "world" and shorthand for the "Kingdom of the World," is the philosophical system of domination and oppression according to which the world typically operates. Modern colloquialisms like "look out for number one" and "might makes right" epitomize the *aiōn*, marked by self-centeredness on the individual level and tribalism on the group level; here one person or group attempts to exercise power over others by inflicting pain on those who threaten and defy its desires. Hence the *aiōn* enslaves people by using death as its most potent threat. Diametrically opposed to the *aiōn* is the *agapē*-centered Kingdom of God proclaimed by Jesus, into which the ransom freed us. The "new song" of Revelation 5:9–10 glorifies Christ "because you were slain and by your blood you ransomed *for* God persons *from* every tribe and language and people and nation [namely the *aiōn*] and made them a kingdom *for* God as well as priests" (emphasis and gloss added). As Jesus memorably told his disciples, "For even the Son of Man did not come to be served but to serve, and to give his life as a ransom for many" (Mark 10:45; cf. 1 Tim 2:6; Heb 2:14–17).

With these seven ideas on the table, we now avail ourselves of historical theology to mine past structural insights on how they may be harmonized.

HISTORICAL THEOLOGY: ANSELM AND FRIENDS

Here we redeem what is positive from the satisfaction model of Anselm and from reflections of other theologians on topics relevant to atonement theory. The first systematic study of the atonement in church history, Anselm's masterwork *Cur Deus Homo* (Why the God-Man?) inquired, "Why is a God-man necessary for the redemption of humankind? Why not an angel? A mere human? Or, apart from any life, could God have saved humanity simply by an act of omnipotence?" Anselm answered this question by positing that Christ rendered the "satisfaction" needed by himself and the other two persons of the Trinity in order to forgive creaturely sin. (It should be highlighted that Anselm did not regard the Father as punishing the Son for the sins of humanity in place of the guilty human perpetrators;[27] this was added to Anselm's theory by the Protestant Reformers.) Here we agree with Anselm, stipulating that Christ's life fulfilled the interrelated justice and holiness without which it would be logically impossible for a perfectly just and holy God (Lev 19:2; Deut 32:4) to forgive sinners.[28] Anselm rightly pointed out that God cannot overlook the sin and unholiness of persons without being unjust and unholy. At this point we must ask: what is sin and what is holiness?

Regarding sin, we follow Augustine in defining sin as a *privatio boni* (a privation or lack of good), which has no being in and of itself but exists only as a defect imposed by persons upon created entities, such as themselves, other persons, and other animate and inanimate realities in the universe. The opposite of sin is justice, namely, the doing of righteousness.[29] Such an understanding expresses in metaphysical terms the biblical view of sin as active rebellion or passive indifference toward God, toward social justice, or both—in other words, any deviation from the two supreme commandments to love God maximally and to love neighbor as oneself (Mark 12:30–31). Whenever humans violate these commandments, they incur damage (privation of good) to themselves, to one another, and to the natural order. Anselm

---

27. Anselm, *Cur Deus Homo*, 1.5.

28. This does not compromise God's omnipotence, since omnipotence means the ability to do anything logically possible and not the ability to actualize logical absurdities.

29. Such is precisely the meaning of the biblical terms for justice, namely, the Hebrew *tzedakah* and the Greek *dikaios*.

correctly observed that God is unable either to pretend this damage does not exist or to do nothing about it without himself committing injustice, or sinning. Moreover, this damage causes his creation to become unholy. For the essence of holiness is what we shall denominate "complete functional unity and integrity,"[30] that is, the conjunction of completeness, wholeness, soundness, and unity; but the damage of sin obviously destroys completeness and wholeness as well as breaking a sound or healthy creation into defective fragments. At this point the following relationship emerges: while justice is the means to holiness, sin is the means to unholiness. So for a holy God to be in relationship with created persons (along with the rest of the created order), those persons must be first made holy, bearing complete functional unity and integrity, lest God, by virtue of relations with incomplete beings (and so unholy relations), cease to be holy.

At this juncture of the argument, Anselm made the astute observation that humans cannot save themselves from this sinful and unholy condition. Transposing the most optimistic New Testament anthropology into philosophical terms, humanity was created with free choice, having the ability to do anything on the spectrum between the two poles of (1) living ultimately for self and (2) living ultimately for God and others. Poles (1) and (2) were originally equal in desirability. But in the Fall, humanity strengthened (1) to such a degree that, even though it remains possible to perform (2)-type actions, (1) grew tremendously more desirable for people and became their *modus operandi*. This strengthened (1) is what Paul terms the "flesh" or "sinful nature" (e.g., Rom 7:18). For persons in this condition, the vast majority of their actions are ultimately rooted in self-centeredness, even those that on the surface appear God-centered or other-centered, and those actions that are genuinely God-centered or other-centered amount to the exception proving the fleshly rule. Such persons, Jesus taught, are "once-born" and cannot enter the Kingdom of God (John 3:3). Since the soul, as the center of self-consciousness, can act upon the body but not upon itself, humans cannot "fix" their own souls and save themselves from this condition. As Anselm's contemporary Bernard of Clairvaux poignantly illustrated, humans living apart from God have dug for themselves a

---

30. MacGregor, *Molinist-Anabaptist Systematic Theology*, 159.

naturally inescapable pit and then have willingly fallen into it.[31] Thus we recognize the evangelical necessity of conversion.

Hence the necessity of a Redeemer becomes apparent, but what kind of a Redeemer is required to pull us from this pit? This all depends on the "depth" of the pit, namely, the extent of the damage we have imposed on ourselves. We again concur with Anselm that the gravity of any sin (i.e., the damage that it enacts upon the sinner) is proportional to the value of the being sinned against. But since God is a being of infinite value, any sin, as a violation of God's moral character, is of infinite gravity. Thus we find ourselves confronted with the sobering reality that, for each sin we commit, we inflict infinite (not simply humanly irreparable) harm upon ourselves, not to mention whatever finite harms we inflict upon others and the natural world. The infinite gravity of sin outweighs anything in the world, except God himself. In other words, since the damage humanity has inflicted upon itself is greater than all created things, it follows that the Redeemer must be capable of making an infinite satisfaction for such damage. Therefore, it is necessary for the redeemer to be God. But the Redeemer must also share in the human condition in order to transmit his restoring benefits to humanity, in accordance with the principle *quod non est assumptum non est sanatum* (what is not assumed is not saved). As a result, the Redeemer must also be human, yet himself without sin, so as not to deface the justice and holiness necessary to his deity, on which the infinite power of his saving work depends. Employing the language of twentieth-century philosophical theologian Paul Tillich, the Redeemer needs to be the bearer and inaugurator of the "new being" (2 Cor 5:17) or transfigured creation exemplified by essential or complete humanity—humanity that is whole, fully actualizing its potentialities to maximally love God and neighbor and so rightly related to God—under the conditions of earthly existence.[32] In other words, the Redeemer must create and empower the Anabaptist characteristics of social justice, community, and peace.

---

31. Bernard, *De gratia*, 208.
32. Tillich, *Systematic Theology*, 2:120–21.

PHILOSOPHICAL THEOLOGY: STRUCTURING SCRIPTURAL IDEAS

Going beyond Anselm, we now turn to philosophical theology to logically and coherently synthesize our biblical ideas with one another by means of the conceptual structures bequeathed to us by church history. To do this, we shall pick up our discussion of justice. If justice is the doing of righteousness, then it follows that justice is not retributive but reparative or restorative; thus the necessary and sufficient basis of God's justly forgiving sinners is the work through which all the damage caused by their sin will be repaired, namely, the life of the God-Man (our first biblical idea). Hence God was just in forgiving sinners before the Incarnation only because he foreknew that the Incarnation would occur. Conveying these sentiments, Paul declared that God carried out his saving work in Christ "to demonstrate his justice, because in his divine forbearance he had passed over the sins that were previously committed—he did it to demonstrate his justice at the present time, so as to be just and the justifier of those who have faith in Jesus" (Rom 3:25–27; cf. 1 John 1:9). Further, as N. T. Wright emphasizes, an integral part of Jesus' divinely ordained mission was to personally fulfill the vocation entrusted to Israel at Mount Sinai, that is, to be the light of the world by engaging in Spirit-powered loving service to the nations beyond itself and thereby inviting outsiders to join the community of God, a vocation that Israel had collectively failed to accomplish.[33] Jesus also intended to bring about in his own person Israel's true return from exile, namely, its liberation from the *aiōn* into the Kingdom of God. By reopening the gateway for all persons, regardless of ethnic heritage, to become part of the family of God, Jesus explicitly extended the abolition of exile to all humanity who wished to be grafted into the tree of Israel (Rom 11:17–24). Hence Jesus instituted a new entity, which he dubbed the *ekklēsia* (Matt 16:18; 18:17), the standard English translation of which, "church," hides its exactingly literal meaning: "the called-out-of-exile people," intended to include all *ethnē*, or ethnic groups (Matt 28:19).

The conjunction of full deity and full humanity powerfully reveals why Jesus, through his incarnate life, was able to set in motion an unstoppable and supernaturally powered Kingdom that is continually repairing, and will culminate by totally repairing, the damage of sin caused by humanity. Had Jesus simply been a sinless human, his

---

33. Wright, *Jesus*, 530–31.

life would possess only the finite power to preserve himself from the clutches of the *aiōn* and thus be impotent to heal any other person's infinitely deep wounds of sin. But since Jesus is also God, it follows logically that his incarnate life is of infinite value, rendering his ministry a work of supererogation, or possessing a power far above and beyond what is possible for a solely human life. Consequently, through his infinitely valuable divine-human Kingdom ministry, Jesus produced in time and space an endless storehouse of healing power (or, adapting medieval theological language, an infinite treasury of grace) forever accessible to any person who enters the Kingdom through the bond of personal commitment to him, that is, biblical faith. This indissoluble bond, depicted as the spiritual marriage between Christ and the believer in both Scripture and ecclesiastical tradition, puts to rest the Levitical system of dedication to God through the blood of animals, just as a physical marriage renders obsolete the necessity of getting engaged to one's significant other (our sixth biblical idea).

By virtue of this bond, Jesus' infinite restorative power, or "grace," automatically and constantly flows into each believer's soul from the moment of personal commitment, immediately healing all the believer's infinite wounds of sin as well as immediately canceling out and thereby negating the deleterious force of future sin before it may harm the soul. Recalling the two aforementioned poles on the spectrum of free choice, this grace strips (1) of its power and greatly empowers (2), so that living to carry out the desires of God becomes tremendously more desirable for the believer and constitutes his or her new *modus operandi*. This "soul operation" is what Jesus (John 3:3, 7), Paul (Titus 3:5), Peter (1 Pet 1:3, 23), and James (Jas 1:18) called "being born again" or "regeneration." Having been made holy, the believer's soul is a fit habitation for a holy God, who can now spiritually commune with the believer on earth (John 14:20–27; 17:22–23) and in Paradise upon the believer's death (2 Cor 5:6–9; Phil 1:21–24). The believer's body is made holy at the general resurrection, at which time a holy God commences physical communion with it (1 Cor 15:50–55). Also by virtue of this bond, at the general resurrection Jesus will pour out his infinite restorative power to heal all the damage believers inflicted on other humans and the rest of the created order, thus perfecting the physical universe and bringing about the "new heaven and new earth" (Rev 21:1; cf. Isa 65:17; 66:22). Since all the damage we did to our souls was healed at the moment of conversion, and since God foreknows that all the damage we did to our bodies, to other humans, and the rest of creation will be healed when Christ returns (the "restoration of all things" described by Acts 3:21), God in no way compromises his justice when he forgives our sins.

At this point we take up the question: Did God cause Jesus' death and lay our sins on him *in sensu diviso* or *in sensu composito*? The only answer compatible with the non-contradictory quality of an inerrant Bible is causation *in sensu composito*, which alone is consistent with our first and fourth biblical ideas and with the perfection of God in general. Such is easily verified through *reductio ad absurdum*. For if God caused Jesus' death *in sensu diviso*, then the crucifixion fulfilled a necessary divine condition without which God could not instantiate humanity's salvation. In that case, a monstrous human evil was necessary for God to accomplish the ultimate good. Not only would this undercut the omnipotence of God, who then could not perform the clearly logically possible state of affairs of forgiving humanity apart from the judicial murder of his second Person, but it would also destroy the justice of God, who would then be guilty of the supreme employment of ends to justify the means. But since God can accomplish all logically possible states of affairs[34] and, as an all-just being, could never ordain the greatest possible injustice—the crucifixion of one who deserved precisely the opposite treatment—to carry out good, it follows that Jesus' crucifixion was not essential to God's forgiveness of sins. The same conclusion is reached by reflecting on Jesus' words, "Father, forgive them, for they do not know what they are doing" (Luke 23:34). If God caused Jesus' death *in sensu diviso*, the Father would be forgiving us for something without which the Father could not forgive us of anything. Since we sinfully crucified Jesus, our sin paid for our sin. All this, of course, is nonsense (Rom 3:8; 6:1–2). Hence it is not the case that a wrathful Father required the ultimate human sacrifice of his innocent Son to forgive humanity, nor was violence in any way necessary for the justice or holiness of God to be satisfied (our fourth biblical idea).

---

34. Since we have already assumed that God created humans with free choice, any logically possible state of affairs would need to be compatible with human free decisions. Thus, for the purposes of this discussion, logically possible states of affairs are the same as feasible states of affairs, which categories would not be identical apart from our assumption.

On the contrary, such violence stands as testimony to the depths of wickedness in the human heart and was ultimately engineered by Satan. If the Jewish religious aristocracy had received Jesus' teaching and Israel had adopted his way of being the light of the world, then humanity would no less have been redeemed from sin. Thus we see that penal substitutionary theory puts the emphasis of Jesus' redemptive work in the wrong place: what God required for humanity's redemption was Jesus' literal embodiment of the Kingdom of God, regardless of how we responded to it, and not our negative reaction of brutally executing him. In other words, Jesus' role as Savior was not predicated upon inciting others to crucify him. So it was not Jesus' crucifixion that invested his embodied Kingdom with value, but his embodied Kingdom that, consistently with his ability to take the greatest evils and invert them (Rom 8:28; Eph 1:11), brought good out of his crucifixion (cf. 1 Cor 1:27–28). Since God had foreknowledge that if he, as the Second Person of the Trinity, were to incarnate the Kingdom, the Jewish and Roman political leaders would freely crucify him, and yet God chose to become incarnate, God caused Jesus' death *in sensu composito* (our fifth biblical idea). This entails, in Jersak's words, that the *"Father's foreknowledge and willingness to overturn our wicked intentions through forgiveness and resurrection is neither an endorsement of our murderous act nor divine complicity in it. Rather, it testifies to God's power to redeem."*[35]

Because our sins—the sins of the world (*aiōn*) in which we all willingly participate—caused the crucifixion, Jesus literally died because of, on behalf of, and for the sake of our sins and hence died because of us. Jesus bore the full brunt of our sins, as we sinfully arrested, flogged, spit upon, scourged, tortured, and executed him. Jesus also died on behalf of and for the sake of us because he humbly endured our wrath instead of invoking the wrath of God upon us (our second biblical idea). Jesus said precisely this to Peter: "Put your sword away, for all who take the sword shall die by the sword. Do you think that I cannot appeal to my Father, who will at once put at my disposal more than twelve legions of angels? But how then would the Scriptures be fulfilled, which say it must happen in this way?" (Matt 26:52–54; cf. John 18:36). Had Jesus called down the divine wrath, we would be forever lost to the *aiōn* and objects of eternal death. But by not calling

---

35. Jersak, "Nonviolent Identification," 28; emphasis his.

it down and instead dying as the lamb silent before its slaughterers, Jesus' death ransomed us from the *aiōn* and afforded us the opportunity to come to God (our seventh biblical idea). Here we see the classical motif of Jesus defeating the dark forces of the *aiōn* and accomplishing God's reconciliation of the world to himself at the cross. Just as the Passover lamb saved Israel from God's wrath in Egypt, so Jesus, our Passover lamb, saved humanity from God's wrath at the cross. Even more astonishingly, all who accept the forgiveness Jesus offered by enduring the cross—the forgiveness proven by his blood—are reconciled to God and can appropriate all the benefits of Jesus' incarnate life, including removal of sins, healing, a clear conscience, and peace (our third biblical idea). Believers are then called to follow Jesus to the point of the cross, thereby joining Jesus not in a pointless death but in a death that nullifies death. We therefore also perceive the exemplar motif, as Jesus stands as the ultimate example of commitment to God.

CONCLUSION: A "RECIPE" FOR NONVIOLENT ATONEMENT THEORY

We finally arrive at a "recipe" for nonviolent atonement theory organized around the notions of non-punitive sacrifice, divine causation *in sensu composito*, and restorative justice.

Regarding atonement as non-punitive sacrifice, we take Anselm's emphasis on the fallen human condition and extend it to show that humanity, not God, is ultimately responsible for the death of Jesus. At the cross, God neither punished nor forsook Jesus. Thus the crucifixion is not a blood payment from Jesus to the Father but rather Jesus' sacrifice both of devotion to the Father (i.e., faithfulness to his Kingdom vocation to the point of death) and of love to us (i.e., choosing to forgivingly endure our depravity instead of calling down the Father's wrath upon us). The function of non-punitive sacrifice is to emphasize that Jesus as sacrifice stands at the center of the atonement and to preserve a strong sense of human depravity—the evangelical hallmarks of crucicentrism and conversionism—while averting the problems Anabaptists rightfully find with penal substitutionary theory.

Regarding atonement as divine causation *in sensu composito*, we affirm the fact that God caused the crucifixion, and we submit this fact as logically necessary given God's creation of our world. The function of divine causation *in sensu composito* is twofold. In evangelical fashion, it brings biblical teaching to the fore by acknowledging the Father's role in the crucifixion. In Anabaptist fashion, it logically discloses the Father's role as indirectly, not directly, causing the crucifixion, thus absolving the Father of doing violence to the Son.

Regarding atonement as restorative justice, we maintain that Jesus' life, not death, is the essential component in our redemption. We thus amplify the Anselmian necessity of the God-Man and reveal that, through his work, humanity is reconciled to God (not the other way around). As a result of embracing this reconciliation, believers are ransomed from the *aiōn* to which they had enslaved themselves. Here, *pro* evangelicalism, Jesus and the biblical text are front and center. But, *pro* Anabaptism, we shift the penal theory's focus from Jesus' death to his incarnate life and shift the ransom theory's focus from ameliorating Satan to breaking our self-inflicted bonds of worldly slavery. These shifts shine new light on restoration and reconciliation, thus engaging with transformational theory and appealing to the Anabaptist concern for justice.

In sum, the fidelity of our nonviolent atonement theory to the plain meaning of the inerrant scriptural text commends it to all evangelicals, and its fidelity to Jesus' peaceful Kingdom of God commends it to all Anabaptists.[36]

BIBLIOGRAPHY

Anselm. *Cur Deus Homo?* Reprint ed. London: Griffith & Farran, 2010.
Bebbington, David W. *The Dominance of Evangelicalism: The Age of Spurgeon and Moody*. Downers Grove, IL: InterVarsity, 2005.
Beilby, James, and Paul R. Eddy, editors. *The Nature of the Atonement: Four Views*. Downers Grove, IL: InterVarsity, 2006.
Bernard de Clairvaux. *De gratia et libero arbitrio*. In *Sämtliche Werke lateinisch/ deutsch*, 153–256. Innsbruck: Tyrolia-Verlag, 1990.
Crossan, John Dominic. *Who Killed Jesus?* San Francisco: HarperSan Francisco, 1995.
Grant, Colin. "The Abandonment of Atonement." *King's Theological Review* 9 (1986) 1–8.

---

36. Many thanks to Jared Burkholder for proposing the arrangement of the conclusion and for many other helpful suggestions on this chapter.

Gunton, Colin E. *The Actuality of the Atonement*. Grand Rapids: Eerdmans, 1989.
Hardin, Michael. "Out of the Fog: New Horizons for Atonement Theory." In *Stricken by God? Nonviolent Identification and the Victory of Christ*, edited by Brad Jersak and Hardin, 54–76. Grand Rapids: Eerdmans, 2007.
———. "Sacrificial Language in Hebrews: Reappraising René Girard." In *Violence Renounced: René Girard, Biblical Studies, and Peacemaking*, edited by Willard M. Swartley, 103–19. Telford, PA: Pandora, 2000.
Hays, Richard B. *The Conversion of the Imagination*. Grand Rapids: Eerdmans, 2005.
Jersak, Brad. "Nonviolent Identification and the Victory of Christ." In *Stricken by God? Nonviolent Identification and the Victory of Christ*, edited by Brad Jersak and Michael Hardin, 18–53. Grand Rapids: Eerdmans, 2007.
Lewis, Gordon R., and Bruce A. Demarest. *Integrative Theology*. 3 vols. Grand Rapids: Zondervan, 1996.
Louw, Johannes P., and Eugene A. Nida. *Greek-English Lexicon of the New Testament Based on Semantic Domains*. 2 vols. New York: United Bible Societies, 1989.
MacGregor, Kirk R. *A Molinist-Anabaptist Systematic Theology*. Lanham, MD: University Press of America, 2007.
Rieger, Nathan. "Good News for Postmodern Man: *Christus Victor* in the Lucan Kerygma." In *Stricken by God? Nonviolent Identification and the Victory of Christ*, edited by Brad Jersak and Michael Hardin, 378–404. Grand Rapids: Eerdmans, 2007.
Sanders, E. P. *Jesus and Judaism*. Minneapolis: Fortress, 1985.
Schwager, Raymund. *Jesus in the Drama of Salvation*. New York: Crossroad, 1999.
Tillich, Paul. *Systematic Theology*. 3 vols. Chicago: University of Chicago Press, 1967.
Weaver, J. Denny. *The Nonviolent Atonement*. Grand Rapids: Eerdmans, 2001.
Wright, N. T. *Jesus and the Victory of God*. Minneapolis: Fortress, 1996.

14

Evangelical Hermeneutics, Anabaptist Ethics

John Howard Yoder, the Solas, *and the Question of War*

David C. Cramer

It is significant . . . that statements of the peace church position have not received serious brotherly attention from non-pacifist evangelicals. There has been little serious effort on the part of non-pacifist evangelicals to explain the compatibility of war with Christianity.

—*John Howard Yoder*[1]

Some trust in chariots and some in horses,
but we trust in the name of YHWH our God.

—*Psalm 20:7*[2]

INTRODUCTION

As the essays in this volume demonstrate, evangelicalism is far from a homogenous block. Yet it is safe to say that by and large American evangelicals have tended to be dismissive of pacifism as a normative stance for the Christian.[3] On the other hand, while this vol-

---

1. Yoder, "Contemporary Evangelical Revival," 85–86.

2. All Scripture quotations are from the New International Version (NIV) unless otherwise noted. The Hebrew name for God, YHWH, has been used instead of the NIV's "the Lord," derived from the Septuagint (LXX).

3. The exceptions to this generalization often include Anabaptist or Anabaptist-

ume also attests to the diversity within Anabaptism, the normativity of Christian pacifism constitutes perhaps the most notable emphasis of historic and contemporary Anabaptism.[4] So whatever else their points of convergence historically and theologically, the question of the legitimacy of military violence by followers of Jesus Christ remains an ongoing point of contention between these two groups.[5] I say that American evangelicals have tended to be "dismissive" of pacifism because, as the above epigraph by John Howard Yoder indicates, for the most part it is not as though evangelicals have carefully considered the case for pacifism and found it wanting; rather, they have failed to seriously consider the case for pacifism at all.[6] From my own experience in evangelical contexts,[7] I propose that this dismissal of pacifism is based

---

influenced evangelicals, such as Ron Sider's Evangelicals for Social Action and Jim Wallis's Sojourners. See Swartz, "Left Behind"; Swartz, Evangelicalism Re-Baptized in the present volume. The question of the historical links between American evangelicalism and pacifism is a more complex one that will not be addressed here. In his fascinating study of the history of American evangelicalism, Donald Dayton argues convincingly that the standard account of American evangelicalism as a conservative, traditionalist branch of Christianity fails to take into account the influence of its early holiness roots, which were often socially radical for their day on issues such as pacifism, abolitionism, and feminism. Dayton calls the standard account of American evangelicalism the result of the "Presbyterianization of evangelical historiography," which tends to obscure the actual history for theological reasons ("Yet Another Layer," 87–110).

4. See point six of the "Shared Convictions" of the Mennonite World Conference, adopting in 2006: "The Spirit of Jesus empowers us to trust God in all areas of life so we become peacemakers who renounce violence, love our enemies, seek justice, and share our possessions with those in need."

5. Though my discussion is framed in terms of pacifism versus military violence, it is not my intention to downplay the importance of nonviolence in other nonmilitary contexts. Addressing these other contexts would simply take us well beyond the scope of the present essay. However, for a penetrating discussion of the use of violence for family protection, see Yoder, *What Would You Do?*

6. My Bethel College colleague, Jim Stump, pointed out to me that this quote is reminiscent of the famous G. K. Chesterton quote: "The Christian ideal has not been tried and found wanting; it has been found difficult and left untried."

7. That is to say, the majority of my church experience: childhood at Community Gospel Church in Bremen, Indiana; adolescence and college years in the Missionary Church (see Boehner and Eaton, "Practicing Peace, Embracing Evangelism," in the present volume, which explains the history of the Missionary Church and the irony of her being considered evangelical rather than Anabaptist); college at the evangelical Bethel College in Mishawaka, Indiana; seminary at Trinity Evangelical Divinity School in Deerfield, Illinois; a three year stint during seminary at the Korean evangelical New Community Presbyterian Church in Chicago, Illinois; and finally

not on the weight of a specific counter-position, such as the just war theory, but rather on the assumed logical outworking of an evangelical biblical hermeneutic. It is believed by non-pacifist evangelicals that a faithful reading of Scripture through the lens of the foundational Reformation doctrines—the so-called *solas*—is incompatible with a pacifist conviction.[8] In turn, many Anabaptists have concluded: So much the worse for the *solas*! Because pacifism is so firmly rooted in the Anabaptist understanding of the gospel of Jesus Christ, it is argued that anything inconsistent with that gospel—including even certain Reformation doctrines—will need to be jettisoned.[9]

It is precisely at this seeming impasse that the work of the late evangelical Anabaptist theologian John Howard Yoder is so valuable.[10] Rather than accepting the assumed dichotomy between fidelity to Scripture and fidelity to the gospel of peace, Yoder sought to demonstrate that the gospel of peace finds its basis squarely in Scripture. And rather than developing a "canon within the canon" as Anabaptist theologians are often accused (and sometimes guilty) of doing, Yoder sought to show that the gospel of peace stands in continuity with the witness of the entire canon of Scripture. Yoder's work, spanning half a century, is multifaceted and voluminous, as his style was to engage specific questions as they arose in specific contexts, and as he was in-

---

ministerial licensure in the Missionary Church and a return to Bethel College to teach. Indeed, I am much more familiar with—and in some ways more comfortable in—evangelical contexts than Anabaptist ones, despite my growing identification with Anabaptist ethical-theological commitments.

8. So, for example, outspoken evangelical Reformed leader, Mark Driscoll, has pointedly stated that "A pacifist has a lot of difficulty reconciling pacifism with scripture" (quoted in Lanham, "Mark Driscoll"). See also, Nix, "The Evangelical and War," 133–46.

9. See, e.g., Stoltzfus, "Nonviolent Jesus, Violent God?" 29–46, who argues that the Old Testament depiction of God needs to be radically altered to fit an Anabaptist understanding of nonviolence.

10. Some might find it surprising to see Yoder referred to as "evangelical." However, see the numerous writings on Yoder by Nation, including, "John Howard Yoder: Mennonite, Evangelical, Catholic," 357–70, esp. 364–66; "John H. Yoder, Ecumenical Neo-Anabaptist," 1–23; *John Howard Yoder*, xx–xxi; cf. Swartz, "Evangelicalism Re-Baptized." For his own part, Yoder seemed ambivalent about being considered "evangelical" because of some of the baggage that often comes with that term. Nevertheless, he did considerable work in evangelical contexts and wrote from an evangelical posture rightly understood as "having to do with being bearers of good news to the world" (*For the Nations*, 7), as the subtitle of the book from which that quote is drawn indicates: *Essays Public & Evangelical*.

vited to speak and write in a vast array of contexts. It would thus be impossible in such a short essay to try to exposit Yoder's reading of Scripture.[11] Neither is it my aim to add to the ever-growing body of Yoder scholarship.[12] Rather, in what follows I trace and develop one major strand of Yoder's reading of Scripture that has strong continuity with evangelical commitments. In so doing I hope to demonstrate one way in which an evangelical hermeneutic and an Anabaptist ethic may peacefully coexist. But first I must explain further why they are so often thought to be at odds.

EVANGELICAL HERMENEUTICS AND THE QUESTION OF WAR

Evangelicals do not have a well-articulated position on war. While many evangelicals give lip service to just war theory, it is typically not developed and articulated as carefully and comprehensively among evangelicals as it has been among other branches of Christianity.[13] The result is that, whereas Christians who have begun to take the just war tradition seriously have curbed their support for modern wars deemed unjust,[14] many American evangelicals have gone in the other

---

11. Happily such exposition has been attempted by Yoder scholars much abler than myself. See, e.g., Nation, "Politics of Yoder," 37–56; Kissling, "Yoder's Reading of the Old Testament," 129–47; Nugent, "Biblical Warfare Revisited," 167–84; Murphy, "Yoder's Systematic Defense," 45–68.

12. Three recent collections of Yoder scholarship include *Power and Practices*, *Radical Ecumenicity*, and *New Yoder*. For a review of these three collections, see my essay, "Inheriting Yoder Faithfully," 133–46.

13. A recent example of an attempt to take the just war tradition seriously by a United Methodist theological ethicist is Bell, *Just War as Christian Discipleship*.

14. Wilhelm Wille notes, "Most churches have not discarded the just-war doctrine . . . but are, at least, committed to interpret it in the strictest possible way . . . Therefore, a broad ecumenical coalition including the Roman Catholics could denounce the last Iraq war and, though unable to stop it, thoroughly de-legitimised that outburst of organized violence" ("Ambivalence," 239). Likewise, Catholic theologian Todd Whitmore notes that the Vatican has been accused by neoconservatives of being pacifist for refusing to support the Iraq war, while in reality the Vatican was simply applying the just war criteria to a clearly unjust war ("Lesser Evil," 69). For an argument for the convergence of just war theory and pacifism, see Friesen, "Peacemaking," 161–80. Many pacifists, however, view the just war tradition as yet another way for Christians to legitimize the warfare of their nation-states. See, e.g., Erdel, "Is Just War Still an Oxymoron?" 53–76. Though at times Yoder engaged the just war tradition sympathetically, on the whole his evaluation of the just war tradition is negative. See, e.g., Yoder, *When War is Unjust*; Yoder, "How Many Ways

extreme and given *de facto* support of just about every recent U.S. military venture. In our post-9/11 world, it seems that unless and until evangelicals formulate a more robust position on war, this *de facto* support will continue.[15]

In order for a position on war to be accepted within evangelicalism, it will need to comport with the broadly defining characteristics of evangelicalism. But because evangelicalism is a varied and living phenomenon, it is difficult to state without remainder precisely what those defining characteristics are. Theologically a good place to start with a definition of evangelicalism might be the Reformation *solas*: *sola scriptura* ("Scripture alone"), *sola fide* ("faith alone"), *sola gratia* ("grace alone"), *solus Christus* ("Christ alone"), and *soli Deo gloria* ("glory to God alone"). While all five of these *solas* might be included in a more comprehensive definition of evangelicalism, the first two best characterize evangelical distinctiveness.[16] *Sola scriptura* might be considered the primary hermeneutical principle of the Reformation (of which modern evangelicalism is arguably an heir), while *sola fide* is the primary doctrine derived from that hermeneutic.[17] In other words, one might say that Luther's discovery of the doctrine of "justification by faith" was predicated on his recovery of the doctrine of Scripture as the only uniquely authoritative source of Christian truth.[18] Thus,

---

are There to Think Morally about War?" 83–107; Yoder, *War of the Lamb*, esp. 89, 95–102, 109–16; Pfeil, "Yoder's Pedagogical Approach," 181–88.

15. See Durham, "Evangelical Protestantism," 145–58. See also Barnwell, "Halt," 22–24. Barnwell notes that after a group of influential evangelical leaders wrote a letter to President Bush supporting a preemptive strike on Iraq in 2002, "Their flock followed: in the runup to war, polls found that 69 percent of evangelical Christians supported the action—10 percentage points higher than the general population" (22).

16. The other three *solas*, which are less controversial and thus more readily accepted by other Christian traditions, are thereby not as distinctive of evangelical thought as the two under consideration here.

17. For a more nuanced discussion of the relationship between *sola scriptura* and evangelicalism, see Allert, "Trying to Conserve?" 327–48. Unfortunately, though the article is quite informative, Allert is unfairly dismissive of early Anabaptist applications of *sola scriptura*. For a better discussion of early Anabaptist hermeneutics, including their application of *sola scriptura*, see Roth, "Community," 51–64; cf. Yoder, "Hermeneutics," 291–308; Kraus, "American Mennonites," 309–29.

18. I am, of course, offering a somewhat caricatured account of the development of Luther's thought, which would need to be further nuanced by Luther scholars (among which I am not included).

despite evangelicalism's diversity on a host of theological doctrines and ethical commitments, its unifying core remains these two *solas*.[19] When a theological tradition holds convictions that contradict one of these *solas*, it is thereby considered outside the bounds of evangelicalism.[20] Conversely, when one's theological position is in line with these two *solas*, it can be considered—at least *prima facie*—within the bounds of evangelicalism. When analyzing evangelical attitudes toward war, then, it is helpful to understand them in reference to these fundamental evangelical commitments. For example, in his survey of the uses of the Bible in U.S. wars, evangelical New Testament scholar and ethicist Alan Johnson reasons that for evangelicals "the Bible is the primary source and final authority for moral guidance on any issue that calls for a specific moral judgment. Christian attitude toward war is just such a moral judgment."[21] And while Johnson's attitude toward the use of Scripture to justify war is ambivalent at best,[22] evangelical philosopher Richard Mouw—in conversation with Yoder and his pacifist colleague Stanley Hauerwas—uses the authority of Scripture as a direct rationale for his non-pacifist stance. Mouw concedes that when the debate between pacifists and non-pacifists focuses solely on Jesus' teachings and example, the non-pacifist will have "some awkward moments." However, Mouw insists that "this sense of awkwardness does not succeed in shaking our basic confidence that the use of lethal violence is on occasion morally justified. We want an understanding of the Sermon on the Mount which fits into what we take to be the overall sense of the Scriptures. This involves not only looking

---

19. I am well aware of other ways of defining evangelicalism that are in currency. Evangelical ethicist Wyndy Corbin Reuschling briefly surveys a number of attempts in *Reviving Evangelical Ethics*, 15–24. As far as I can tell, all such definitions minimally include an insistence on the authority of Scripture and the importance of a personal faith commitment, which closely parallel the two *solas* under consideration here.

20. So, for example, when the Evangelical Theological Society discussed whether or not to expel those members who held to the position of Open Theism, the debate centered not on the theology per se but on whether such theology was "incompatible with [biblical] inerrancy." See Koop, "Closing the Door."

21. Johnson, "Bible and War," 169.

22. Johnson concludes, "[I]n recent years most of the serious Biblical reflection in this country [the U.S.] on a theology of war has come from the pacifist tradition. This does not as such mean that this tradition is correct or more Biblical, but the fact of this imbalance remains" ("Bible and War," 181).

at Jesus' teachings in the light of the Old Testament, but also in relationship to the apostolic witness and the life of the early church."[23] In other words, while Mouw admits that an exclusive focus on Jesus' life and teachings—a canon within the canon—might offer *prima facie* support for pacifism, these considerations are overridden by an affirmation of the authority of the entirety of Scripture, including the Old Testament, which Mouw believes offers significant support for military violence.

Likewise, non-pacifist evangelicals worry that making pacifism normative for Christians leads to a perfectionism or legalism that contradicts the fundamental Reformation doctrine of *sola fide*—that faith alone, and not works, is constitutive of salvation.[24] This concern was expressed forcefully in the middle of the twentieth century by one of Yoder's most common foils, Reinhold Niebuhr: "I take the Reformation doctrine of 'justification by faith' seriously and I observe that the spiritual ground upon which our modern pacifism has grown is a sectarian perfectionism that hasn't the slightest idea of what the Reformation meant by its doctrine of 'justification by faith.'"[25] According to Niebuhr's critique, pacifists not only reject *sola fide*; they haven't "the slightest idea" what it even means. Clearly if such a charge were true, Anabaptists (and other Peace Churches) would be excluded

---

23. Mouw, "Christianity and Pacifism," 106. Cf. Hauerwas, "Pacifism," 99–104; Yoder, "Consistent Alternative View," 112–20. These three articles were first presented at a plenary session of the Eastern Regional Meeting of the Society of Christian Philosophers at the University of Notre Dame on 8–10 March 1984. Mouw and Yoder would have ongoing dialogue over the years regarding Anabaptist and Reformed visions of evangelical ethics. See, e.g., Mouw and Yoder, "Evangelical Ethics," 121–37. Cf. Mouw's more recent statement: "I am no pacifist. I support campaigns against international terrorism and favor using our military for restoring justice. But I reserve the right also to criticize my government if I think they are misusing their power. . . . I take this view because I believe strongly in democracy. But even more important, I take it because I worry about the ever-present threat of idolatry" (Mouw, *Praying*, 119). See Mouw, "Violence," 159–71.

24. Given evangelicals' insistence on other moral stances, such as celibacy outside of heterosexual marriage or abstaining from abortion for any reason, one wonders how genuine this concern really is—or whether it simply makes a convenient way of ignoring certain uncomfortable New Testament teachings regarding nonviolence.

25. Niebuhr, "Open Letter," 269; quoted in Hauerwas, *With the Grain*, 95. Niebuhr was, of course, no evangelical. However, his view here is representative of current evangelical attitudes. Indeed, Niebuhr seems to have had a deep impact on evangelical thought regarding the "necessity" of war.

from evangelicalism *a priori* in virtue of their implicit rejection of one of evangelicalism's core doctrines.[26]

But is it necessary for Anabaptists—those who trace their lineage back to the Radical Reformation—to consciously or unconsciously reject these core Reformation commitments in order to remain committed to Christian pacifism?[27] Must Anabaptists simply fail to take Scripture as seriously as evangelicals? Or in focusing so much on Jesus' ethical imperatives, must they undermine the biblical importance of faith? To each of these questions, Yoder responds with a resounding *No!*

A YODERIAN READING OF BIBLICAL FAITH

John Howard Yoder made no claims to being a biblical scholar.[28] Nevertheless, his most famous work, *The Politics of Jesus*, was a watershed moment for biblical studies at the time of its publication in 1972. The book is a sustained argument that Jesus' life and teachings constitute a particular, normative Christian social ethic and that such a "messianic ethic" is congruent with the entire witness of Scripture. *Politics of Jesus* is also Yoder's most widely read book among evangelicals, even being nominated by the flagship evangelical magazine *Christianity Today* as one of the ten most important books of the twentieth century. Unfortunately, many evangelicals who have (mis)read *Politics of Jesus* have assumed because of its popularity

---

26. Yoder responds directly to the standard Protestant charge that his biblical pacifism contradicts "Justification by Grace through Faith" in chapter 11 of *Politics of Jesus* bearing that name.

27. Baptist historian William Estep argues that in their basic theological commitments, the sixteenth-century Anabaptists were actually *more* consistent than the Magisterial Reformers. According to Estep, this is especially true of *sola scriptura* and *sola fide*. Estep writes, "Within the Reformation no group took more seriously the principle of *sola Scriptura* in matters of doctrine and discipline than did the true Anabaptists. In this regard the Reformation stance of the Anabaptists is unequivocal" (*Anabaptist Story*, 190). Later in the same chapter Estep writes, "The Reformation text, 'The just shall live by faith,' became for the Anabaptists a vital truth.... For them faith was the means of a new life in Christ Jesus, the new birth of the Holy Spirit. This concept was emphasized by every Anabaptist theologian" (196–97).

28. Yoder may have been overly modest. New Testament scholar Richard Hays praises the sophistication of Yoder's exegetical work in *Politics of Jesus*. See Hays, *Moral Vision*, 239–53.

that it was Yoder's definitive statement on biblical pacifism.[29] Having perhaps found certain arguments in the book wanting, they have assumed that if the definitive statement on biblical pacifism by the foremost Christian pacifist is found wanting, then they can finally shake the proverbial dust from their sandals and move on. As it turns out, however, *Politics of Jesus* was never intended to be Yoder's definitive statement on pacifism any more than his dozen or so other books and myriad essays on the topic.[30] Rather, *Politics of Jesus* is simply the most famous instance of Yoder's lifelong experiment with rethinking the logic of violence that is so often taken for granted by Christians. As long as there were contexts and communities in which the necessity of violence was assumed, Yoder never assumed that his experiment was over—certainly not with the publication of *Politics of Jesus* and not even by his untimely death in 1997.

In what follows I continue Yoder's experiment by drawing often implicitly and sometimes explicitly on Yoder's work to develop a "Yoderian" sketch of the biblical concept of faith and its relevance to the question of war.[31] In doing so I have no intention of offering the definitive word on biblical faith or on biblical violence or even to offer an original reading of the text per se.[32] Rather, my modest goal is to prod evangelicals who—given their core faith commitments—currently assume the necessity of violence to begin to rethink that necessity. On the other hand, I hope to prod Anabaptists who—given their core faith commitments—currently assume the necessity of dismissing the biblical text to begin to rethink that necessity as well. What I believe we find when applying the evangelical hermeneutic of *sola scriptura* and *sola fide* to the question of war is that on the whole the

---

29. For Yoder's discussion of all the ways his *Politics of Jesus* was misunderstood, see *To Hear the Word*, 47–70.

30. See, e.g., Yoder, *Nevertheless*; Yoder, *Original Revolution*; Yoder, *Discipleship as Political Responsibility*; Yoder, *He Came Preaching Peace*; Yoder, *War of the Lamb*; Gwyn et al., *Declaration on Peace*. Yoder's bibliography is around fifty pages long and growing. See Nation, *Comprehensive Bibliography*; Nation, "Supplement, 472–91."

31. Where I don't quote Yoder directly, I will reference his works where a fuller discussion of the biblical passage or theme can be found.

32. Indeed, one colleague noted that though my reading of the biblical story is common among Anabaptists, for some reason it has not received much attention among evangelicals. Willard Swartley identifies a similar disparity in New Testament studies in his work, *Covenant of Peace*, appendix 1. Cf. Swartley, *Slavery, Sabbath, War, and Women*.

results comport much better with an Anabaptist pacifist position than with the standard evangelical support of state-sanctioned violence.

Faith as Trust

The biblical concept of faith was central to Yoder's reading of Scripture. However, unlike modern notions of faith as primarily cognitive assent to religious propositions or an inward subjective feeling,[33] Yoder understood the New Testament concept of faith, or *pistis*, to carry a more volitional connotation in Scripture. Yoder's understanding of faith is affirmed by prominent New Testament scholar, Richard B. Hays, who argues convincingly that in Paul's thought *pistis* is better understood as "trust." According to Hays, one of Paul's main themes in Romans is that "those who stand in a right relation to God are those who hear and trust what God has spoken."[34] Hays discusses Paul's contrast between the trust (*pistis*) of Abraham and the lack of trust (*apistia*) of the Israelites. Contrary to some understandings of Reformation thought, Paul's message is not primarily about an abstract faith that

---

33. That is, in the Thomistic form as an intellectual assent to a set of divinely revealed doctrinal propositions or in the fideistic, existentialist, or pragmatic views represented by Pascal, Kierkegaard, and William James, respectively. For a critical discussion of a number of modern views of faith, see Hick, *Faith and Knowledge*. For a discussion of Hick's understanding of faith, see my "Nonevidentialism"; see also Cramer, "John Hick."

34. Hays, "Salvation by Trust?" 219. Cf. Hay, "Pistis," 461–76; Waetjen, "Trust," 446–54. Incidentally, this understanding of *pistis* as trust seems to fit with either the subjective or objective reading of the hotly debated term *pistis Christou*. For a fuller discussion of *pistis* (and *pistis Christou*) in New Testament theology, see Hays, *Faith of Jesus Christ*. For a comparison between contemporary views of *pistis* and sixteenth-century Protestant and Anabaptist views, see Eaton, "Anabaptist Covenantal Soteriology," 67–93; Eaton, "Anabaptist Soteriology." In email correspondence (13 August 2010), Mark Thiessen Nation suggested that my argument would benefit from more explicit interaction with the recent Pauline scholarship of Hays, Michael Gorman, and N. T. Wright, which share affinities with Yoder's work in *Politics of Jesus* and elsewhere. While I appreciate Nation's suggestion, I have nevertheless avoided tying my argument to this scholarship as I am aware that the so-called "new perspective" is every bit as controversial among some evangelicals as is the question of pacifism. While I too am sympathetic with the new perspective(s), which is not really as "new" as some think, I am not convinced that one's perspective on Paul need determine one's perspective on warfare. However, for tantalizing suggestions of the connections between Yoder's and Wright's work, see Nation, "Politics of Yoder," 51–53 (notes 11, 19, 29, 41). For further connections between Yoder's work and the new perspective(s) on Paul, see Yoder, *Jewish-Christian Schism Revisited*, esp. 34, 94, 101–2, 116–17, 211.

can be distinguished from ethical conduct; rather, his message is that "[t]hose who receive this good news respond to it in turn with trust. Their *pistis*, which is prefigured in the Old Testament story of Abraham, becomes shaped by the pattern of Jesus' own faith-obedience."[35] The believer's response of faith or trust (*pistis*) is predicated precisely on her recognition of God's faithfulness or trustworthiness (*pistis*). Moreover, for Yoder the theme of trust is precisely that which binds the Old Testament to the New. Just as Abraham's trust in God was demonstrated by his obedience to the point of sacrificing his son's life, so too Jesus' trust is demonstrated by his obedience to the point of sacrificing his own life—a model which in turn becomes the pattern for all Christ-followers.

In Old Testament Hebrew, the concept of *'emunah* or faith/trust is intimately tied not only etymologically but also theologically to that of *'emet* or faithfulness/trustworthiness.[36] Just as the New Testament Greek uses the same root word, *pistis*, to describe human trust and God's trustworthiness, so too in the Hebrew of the Old Testament, God's people are to trust (*'aman*) in God because of God's trustworthiness (*'emet*). Indeed, in God's very self-revelation to Moses on Sinai, God uses this latter term,[37] which is then invoked time and again throughout the rest of the Old Testament in pleas for or remembrances of God's trustworthiness to his people.[38]

Trust in the Old Testament Narrative

In surveying the biblical narrative, we find that having faith—that is, *trusting*—in God is indeed a key scriptural motif, unifying the Old Testament with the New. We find as early as Genesis 22 God's test of Abraham's trust when asked to sacrifice his only son Isaac. Yoder reasons, "What then was the test put to Abraham? . . . The wider story itself makes clear, as does the analysis of Hebrews (ch. 11), that the

---

35. Hays, "Salvation by Trust?," 120.

36. Of this Hebrew term Old Testament scholar Eugene Carpenter states, "The word used in Habakkuk to assert that the righteous should live by their faith was the Hebrew word *'emunah*. This word means 'firmness,' 'steadfastness,' 'fidelity,' 'faithfulness,' 'faith.' It is clearly a powerful and important word. This word is derived from the verbal root, *'aman*, meaning 'to confirm,' 'to support,' 'to be confirmed,' and 'to trust'" (Carpenter and Comfort, *Holman Treasury*, 56).

37. Exod 34:6.

38. For the most striking example, see Ps 86:15.

issue for Abraham was whether to trust his God for his survival."[39] This theme of trust is again highlighted in the narrative of Israel's exodus from Egypt and her subsequent wilderness wanderings. Exodus 14:31 states that "when the Israelites saw the great power YHWH displayed against the Egyptians, the people feared YHWH and put their trust[40] in him and in Moses his servant." Israel's trust in God does not last long, however, so that by the time they reach the Promised Land and God tells them to take possession of it, they turn back in fear. Moses' charge to the Israelites is damning: "But you rebelled against the command of YHWH your God. You did not trust[41] him or obey him."[42]

We thus find that by the time we arrive at the infamous conquest narratives, rather than finding any kind of pro-militaristic apologetic as is commonly assumed, the central theme is instead that of trusting YHWH. Indeed, when reading the scriptural narrative through what Hays calls "a hermeneutic of trust,"[43] we find—somewhat paradoxically and contrary to initial appearances—that Israel's war narratives are decisively anti-militaristic.[44] What could be more absurd, from a military standpoint, than marching around an enemy city and blowing trumpets (Josh 6)? Or reducing one's army from thirty-two thousand to three hundred before going into battle (Judg 7)? Or having an untrained shepherd boy fight with a slingshot against a highly trained, heavily armored soldier for the fate of the nation (1 Sam 17)? Even Goliath recognizes the absurdity of Israel's "military strategy," asking, "Am I a dog, that you come at me with sticks?"[45] David's response, though admittedly violent, is nevertheless paradigmatic of what it means for Israel to trust in God rather than in their military might:

> You come against me with sword and spear and javelin, but I come against you in the name of YHWH Almighty, the God of the armies of Israel, whom you have defied. This day YHWH will hand you over to me, and I'll strike you down and cut

39. Yoder, "If Abraham is Our Father," 96.
40. MT: *ya'amînû*; LXX: *episteusan*.
41. MT: *he'emantem*; LXX: *episteusate*.
42. Deut 9:23.
43. Hays, "Salvation by Trust?" 219. Hays uses this phrase in a slightly different context with a slightly different connotation but would undoubtedly approve of its appropriation here.
44. See Yoder, *Politics of Jesus*, chapter 4, "God Will Fight for Us."
45. 1 Sam 17:43.

off your head. Today I will give the carcasses of the Philistine army to the birds of the air and the beasts of the earth, and the whole world will know that there is a God in Israel. All those gathered here will know that it is not by sword or spear that YHWH saves; for the battle is YHWH's, and he will give all of you into our hands.[46]

In this record of David's battle cry, the writer subverts a militaristic reading of Israel's history by stating that "*YHWH* will hand you over to me" and that "it is *not* by sword or spear that YHWH saves." Even when the Old Testament depicts graphic violence, then, it does not endorse military warfare.

This juxtaposition of the themes of trusting in God with an intentional subversion of reliance on military strength is prominent in the Psalms as well. Consider the following passages:

> Some trust in chariots and some in horses,
> but we trust in the name of YHWH our God.[47]

> YHWH is my strength and my shield;
> my heart trusts in him, and I am helped.[48]

> I do not trust in my bow,
> my sword does not bring me victory;
> but you give us victory over our enemies,
> you put our adversaries to shame.
> In God we make our boast all day long,
> and we will praise your name forever.[49]

> O house of Israel, trust in YHWH—
> he is their help and shield.
> O house of Aaron, trust in YHWH—
> he is their help and shield.
> You who fear him, trust in YHWH—
> he is their help and shield.[50]

> Do not put your trust in princes,

---

46. 1 Sam 17:45–47.

47. Ps 20:7. In a number of these Psalms, the word *baṭaḥ* is used instead of *'aman* for "trust." These two terms are closely related, however, as is evidenced by their parallel usage in Ps 78:22: "for they did not believe [*he'emînnû*] in God or trust [*bāṭ^eḥû*] in his deliverance."

48. Ps 28:7.

49. Ps 44:6–8.

50. Ps 115:9–11.

> in mortal men, who cannot save.
> When their spirit departs, they return to the ground;
> on that very day their plans come to nothing.[51]

These passages are representative rather than exhaustive.[52] Nevertheless, they illustrate the point that the psalmists, often assumed to be focused on vengeance and violence, have little time for nationalistic military agendas, focusing instead on putting faith in the deliverance that comes from God.

The Old Testament prophets likewise develop the contrast between trusting in God and relying on one's military—blessing Israel or Judah when they do the former but cursing them when they do the latter:

> Woe to those who go down to Egypt for help,
> who rely on horses,
> who trust in the multitude of their chariots
> and in the great strength of their horsemen,
> but do not look to the Holy One of Israel,
> or seek help from YHWH.[53]

> But I will rescue you on that day, declares YHWH; you will not be handed over to those you fear. I will save you; you will not fall by the sword but will escape with your life, because you trust in me, declares YHWH.[54]

> But you have planted wickedness,
> you have reaped evil,
> you have eaten the fruit of deception.
> Because you have depended on your own strength
> and on your many warriors,
> the roar of battle will rise against your people,
> so that all your fortresses will be devastated—
> as Shalman devastated Beth Arbel on the day of battle,
> when mothers were dashed to the ground with their children.[55]

---

51. Ps 146:3–4.

52. See Lind, *Yahweh is a Warrior*, for further discussion of these and other Old Testament passages. Yoder draws heavily from Lind's work in his discussion of the Old Testament.

53. Isa 31:1.

54. Jer 39:17–18.

55. Hos 10:13–14.

One of the major reasons for the prophets' condemnation of Israel and Judah was their reliance on their own military strength and international alliances rather than trusting in God—the latter of which may have even meant surrendering to their attackers rather than defending themselves militarily.[56] Yoder summarizes well the prophets' message regarding warfare: "These later interpreters do not derive from the [holy war] tradition, 'Israel slaughtered the Amalekites and therefore we should put to death all the enemies of God.' The point made by the prophets is rather, 'Jahweh has always taken care of us in the past; should we not be able to trust His providence for the immediate future?' Its impact in those later prophetic proclamations was to work *against* the development of a military caste, military alliances, and political designs based on the availability of military power."[57]

So while there may still be outlying questions regarding God's commands for violent action towards certain peoples early in Israel's history,[58] the Old Testament message nevertheless fails to come anywhere near offering support for national military campaigns analogous to what we find in the U.S. today. Instead we find in the Old Testament that when God's people rely on their own military strength,

---

56. A major question that will not be addressed here is to what extent the prophets should be read as a development of or even a departure from the earlier Old Testament writings or to what extent they should be read as complementary. For a recent attempt at answering this question, see Hughes, *Christian America*, especially chapter two, "The Witness of the Hebrew Bible." See my online review of Hughes's book, where I support Hughes's main thesis but note that, unlike Yoder, Hughes is too quickly dismissive of scriptural texts that do not comport with his main thesis. Cf. Yoder, "Wars of Joshua," 67–75.

57. Yoder, "If Abraham is Our Father," 99 (italics original). Cf. Yoder, "See How They Go," 183–204.

58. Indeed, a number of important questions have been bracketed in this paper, including how to understand the progressive element of revelation from the Old to the New Testament; the issue of divine violence in regards to Old Testament depictions of God's direct annihilation of peoples through flood and fire as well as God's delegated annihilation of peoples through other peoples, including Israel and Assyria; and debates over violent versus nonviolent atonement theories (though, on this last question, see the essay by Kirk MacGregor in the present volume). While these are each important questions in their own right, how one answers these questions need not affect the main lines of my argument, which is predicated on faith in YHWH as described in the narrative of Scripture itself rather than on an answer to any one of these second order theological questions. Such an approach follows what Yoder describes as "Biblical Realism" in his posthumously published work, *To Hear the Word*, esp. 57, 79–81, 125–44.

they thereby forfeit their trust in God. It seems that, even in the Old Testament, it is impossible to trust in both God and the sword. Indeed, God warns the Israelites when they ask for a king that a king will amass a cavalry of horses and chariots, require the Israelite men to participate in war, and tax the people to support his military campaigns—a prophecy that is fulfilled no later than the reign of Solomon. As the text makes clear, the Israelite kings acted this way not out of God's design but because they wanted to be like every other nation.[59]

In his book, *Choosing Against War: A Christian View*, Mennonite historian John D. Roth offers a fitting summary of the message of trust in the Old Testament and its application for twenty-first century American Christians:

> If we Christians in North America truly wish to claim the national motto "In God We Trust," then let us be honest about the subtle ways in which patriotism redirects our trust away from God to the nation, to its leaders, to military might, and to our own self-interest.... The only biblical example of a political entity uniquely associated with God's will and purpose was that of Israel in the Old Testament, the descendants of Abraham whom God promised to make into "a great nation" (Gen. 12:2). But even in the case of the Children of Israel, scriptures make it clear that their primary identity as a people was defined by their *trust in God* and explicitly *not* in the strength of their armies, the power of their kings, or even the boundaries of their territory.[60]

As this passage suggests, American Christians must ask which reading is more faithful to the witness of the Old Testament as read through the hermeneutic of *sola scriptura* and *sole fide*. Is it the standard evangelical reading, represented by non-pacifist evangelicals such as Mouw, who argue that because the Old Testament endorses violence at certain points, American Christians can therefore support the U.S. military in its various campaigns? Or could it be Yoder's evangelical Anabaptist reading, which argues that trusting in God entails refusing

---

59. 1 Sam 8:10–18; cf. Deut 17:14–20; 1 Kgs 10:26–29; 2 Chr 1:14–17; 9:25–28. See Yoder, "Wars of Joshua," 69–70.

60. Roth, *Choosing against War*, 136–37 (italics original). Cf. Erdel, "Rationality of Christian Faith," esp. chap. 4, "The Rationality of Christian Trust," 138–94; Erdel, "Simply Believing."

Trust in New Testament Teaching

When we come to the New Testament, we find that rather than encountering a radically new message, we encounter one largely continuous with the trajectory of the Old Testament message as read through a hermeneutic of trust. In Jesus' Sermon on the Mount (Matthew 5–7), we find not a foreign code of stringent ethical imperatives but a description of what life looks like when one has placed full trust in the goodness of her heavenly Father. When one has faith in the coming Kingdom, one considers herself blessed when faced with persecution. When one trusts God for her daily provisions, one is empowered to respond to unjust exploitation with kindness and generosity rather than retaliation. One is able to pray for her enemy rather than exacting retributive justice when one trusts that the universe is under the care of a God who treats enemies with love as well.[61]

Jesus not only taught this kind of radical trust; he exemplified it in his life. As Jesus hung on the cross, his mockers spoke better than they knew: "He saved others, but he can't save himself! He's the King of Israel! Let him come down now from the cross, and we will believe in him. *He trusts in God*. Let God rescue him now if he wants him, for he said, 'I am the Son of God.'"[62] Because of Jesus' radical trust in God's providence, he refused to take any kind of action to save himself or take the easy way out. His trust led to his humiliating death on a Roman cross. But his trust was vindicated three days later by his resurrection.[63]

The message of the New Testament is best read not merely as a call to believe certain propositions about Christ's death and resurrection but to have the same kind of trust (*pistis*) in Christ that Christ had in the Father. Before facing his own death, Jesus instructed his disciples: "Do not let your hearts be troubled. Trust in God; trust also in me."[64] Trusting God empowers Christ-followers to have the same attitude "as that of Christ Jesus," who "humbled himself and

---

61. See Yoder, "Political Axioms of the Sermon on the Mount," 34–51.
62. Matt 27:42–43 (italics mine).
63. See Yoder, "If Christ is Truly Lord," 52–84; Yoder, "Jesus," 77–82.
64. John 14:1.

became obedient to death—even death on a cross," as Paul writes the Philippian church.[65] Trusting God empowers Christ-followers to "live at peace with everyone," to "not take revenge" but "leave room for God's wrath," to feed hungry enemies, and to "overcome evil with good," as Paul writes to the church in Rome.[66] Trusting God empowers Christ-followers to submit to governing authorities rather than trying to take the law into their own hands, knowing that all power is ultimately derived from the same God who has their best interests in mind, as Paul continues in his message to Rome and Peter echoes in his message to the Diaspora.[67] These latter passages are, of course, often mined as proof-texts for Christian participation in the military, but as Yoder argues, such a reading would have been completely foreign and unthinkable to the original recipients who were facing persecution from the pagan Roman Empire. Rather, it is precisely because Christ-followers trust that the outcome of history is governed by God's providence and not the result of their own devices that they are empowered to relinquish the reigns of history over to God rather than striving for political power.[68]

Trusting God even empowers Christ-followers to face persecution and death, as the author of Hebrews commends. Yoder writes of Hebrews 11–12: "Faith is . . . the willingness to accept the apparently ineffective path of obedience, trusting in God for the results. Faith, even in Hebrews 11:1f., does not mean doctrinal acquiescence to unproved affirmations, but the same trust in God which Christ initiated and perfected in itself (12:3)."[69] Finally, instead of attempting to control the course of history, trusting God empowers Christ-followers to worship the conquering Lion, who is also the slain Lamb, as John records in his Apocalypse (another text strangely misread as support for Christian participation in the military).[70] In short, trusting God empowers Christ-followers to actually follow Christ.

---

65. Phil 2:5, 8. See Yoder, *Politics of Jesus*, 234–36.

66. Rom 12:18–21.

67. Rom 13:1–7; 1 Peter 2:13–17.

68. See Yoder, *Politics of Jesus*, chapter 10, "Let Every Soul Be Subject: Romans 13 and the Authority of the State."

69. Yoder, "Christ," 63.

70. See Yoder, *Politics of Jesus*, chapter 12, "War of the Lamb," and Yoder's posthumous work, *War of the Lamb*.

EVANGELICAL HERMENEUTICS, ANABAPTIST ETHICS

After our brief survey of the biblical narrative as read through an evangelical hermeneutic of trust, we should not be surprised to find Yoder appealing to evangelical commitments—such as *sola scriptura* and *sola fide*—in his interaction with evangelicals on the question of war. In his essay, "The Contemporary Evangelical Revival and the Peace Churches," that is precisely what we find. In this essay, portions of which were first presented at the 1966 convention of the National Association of Evangelicals, Yoder argues that evangelicalism cannot make sense of its own core commitments without adopting a peace stance, stating that "the peace church vision is itself the logically consistent form of evangelical revival."[71] Yoder explains that "each of the elements of evangelical identity itself calls for a Christian peacemaking witness.... If one looks clearly at the moral and spiritual value of what evangelicalism claims to be saying, one cannot explain not being a pacifist."[72] Yoder continues by delineating the various elements of evangelical identity, which we have identified above: "vital personal faith" and "Scripture as the authority for change."[73] After listing a few further characteristics of evangelicalism, such as its emphasis on world missions, Yoder continues: "There is the trust in providence and the coming kingdom which enables us to renounce the temptation to make history come out right by means of violence. This trust may not mean that discussing practicality is irrelevant, but it does mean that effectiveness is not the first or last word in weighing what we are to do about conflict."[74] For Yoder, *sola scriptura* and *sola fide*—when understood rightly—point decisively toward a pacifist commitment for Christians.

In the volume in which Yoder's article appeared, *Mission and the Peace Witness: The Gospel and Christian Discipleship*, a number of other evangelically-minded Anabaptist theologians and practitioners reflect on the possibilities of an evangelical Anabaptism—or an Anabaptist evangelicalism. Almost without exception they also appeal to the kind of evangelical hermeneutic outlined above. So, for example, Sjouke Voolstra argues in his essay, "The Search for a Biblical

71. Yoder, "Contemporary Evangelical Revival," 79.
72. Ibid., 80.
73. Ibid., 80–81.
74. Ibid., 83.

Peace Testimony," that rather than providing a major break from the thought patterns of the Old Testament, "the New Testament is a continuation and a specific interpretation of certain Old Testament thought patterns, such as when it speaks of the life of Jesus as God's strength in weakness, even in suffering."[75] According to Voolstra, Christ's power in weakness "is with a person who implicitly keeps faith in the covenant that the God of Israel makes with all people, even to the point of suffering and in doing so causes peace and justice to flourish around him."[76] For Voolstra, then, Old and New Testament alike teach the imperative of a faith in God that is demonstrated by a willingness to suffer rather than resort to violence. Likewise, in his essay, "Shalom is the Mission," James Metzler argues that "very early in redemption history, shalom indicated God's movement from chaos and bondage into orderliness and freedom; however, it was a relationship that was grounded in His people's response, trust, and faithfulness. Instead of viewing the Israelites' journey to Canaan (as well as the period of the judges) as being the dark ages, we really should see this period as the Old Testament's golden age when God's rule among His people was most dynamic and direct."[77] Rather than avoiding or deemphasizing the conquest narratives, Metzler finds in them the epitome of the biblical message of trust. Later Metzler describes the relationship between our trust in God and our response of obedience: "This is what Hebrews 11 calls faith: acknowledging God as Ruler by ordering our values and lifestyles accordingly. . . . [S]halom can only come in a trusting relationship and a loyal commitment both to God and to His people around us."[78] For Metzler, pacifism is not an ethical add-on or attempted perfectionism; it constitutes the heart of one's faith response to the Lord.

In his essay, "A Call for Evangelical Nonviolence," the always provocative Ronald Sider takes the standard evangelical arguments against Anabaptist commitments and turns them back on evangelicals. Of evangelicals' arguments from *sola scriptura*, Sider writes: "I am convinced that an evangelical commitment to biblical authority leads finally to nonviolence. . . . If evangelicals really believe that Jesus is

75. Voolstra, "Search," 32.
76. Ibid., 32–33.
77. Metzler, "Shalom," 38.
78. Ibid., 48.

Lord and that canonical Scripture is binding, then surely there is only one possibility. If Scripture calls us to love our enemies as Jesus loved His enemies at the cross, we must either accept the way of nonviolence or abandon our affirmation of scriptural authority."[79] Likewise, Sider writes of *sola fide*: "If we reject the biblical imperative to follow Jesus at this point, we in effect express *disbelief* about the validity of God's way of reconciling enemies. But to do that is to express *disbelief* about the atonement itself."[80] Yet, instead of finding trusting belief among evangelicals, Sider finds the pragmatic arguments of Niebuhr's "realism."[81]

Finally, in the concluding essay of the volume, "Mennonite Missions and the Christian Peace Witness," Robert Ramseyer reflects on the kenosis hymn of Philippians 2:6–11, arguing that this passage "leaves no possibility of having faith in the Jesus Christ who is revealed in the New Testament without being committed to walking where He walked in the way of peace, because the Jesus Christ of the New Testament is a real Person who lived and walked in the same world in which we have been placed."[82] In short, Ramseyer, as with these other Anabaptist thinkers, urges that one's evangelical faith is vacuous if it does not take the shape of the nonviolent love that Jesus commanded in his teaching, exemplified in his life and death, and made possible in his resurrection.

It seems to me that the reflections on the nature of biblical faith on the part of these Anabaptist thinkers demonstrably belie the caricature of Anabaptist ethics as legalistically perfectionist or as working fast and loose with the Old Testament in an attempt to support their Marcionic reading of the Gospels. Instead, it turns out that even the title of the present essay is misleading. For Yoder and these other Anabaptist thinkers, there is no "Anabaptist ethic" that can be abstracted from an "evangelical hermeneutic." Rather, a faithful evangelical reading of Scripture highlights the biblical necessity of the believer's trusting response to a trustworthy God. Such trust is betrayed when Christians rely on ever-increasing military strength for

---

79. Sider, "Evangelical Nonviolence," 55–56. Cf. Sider, *Non-violence*.

80. Ibid., 57 (italics mine).

81. Sider writes, "Most evangelicals probably agree with Reinhold Niebuhr that in a world infested with well-armed Hitlers, Stalins, and colonialists, persons and nations that follow the way of the cross get wiped out. So one must sadly and repentantly fight wars for the sake of peace" (ibid., 59).

82. Ramseyer, "Mennonite Missions," 127–28 (italics mine).

protection. Instead, trust may involve suffering, persecution, and even martyrdom rather than taking recourse to the sword.

CONCLUSION

In this essay I have addressed two common evangelical objections to the Anabaptist commitment to pacifism: (1) that a pacifist commitment stands in tension with a commitment to biblical authority, thus undermining the evangelical doctrine of *sola scriptura*; and (2) that a pacifist commitment ties an unnecessary ethical burden to the faith, thus undermining the evangelical doctrine of *sola fide*. Using John Howard Yoder as my guide, I argued that when the biblical notion of faith is rightly understood in terms of a trusting response to a trustworthy God, these objections to pacifism prove to be unfounded. Christian pacifism is seen to be perfectly consistent with core evangelical commitments. And if the above reading of the narrative and teaching of Scripture is correct, one might even be able to make the stronger claim that placing one's trust in God necessarily precludes reliance on military strength. I have no delusion, however, that this brief survey of the biblical material is by any means conclusive. As stated above, the goal is not to be definitive but to continue the conversation. It is thus my hope that the above discussion may lead non-pacifist evangelicals simply to reconsider the basis for their acceptance of military violence. If their acceptance of military violence is due to the supposed logical outworking of their core evangelical commitment to the *solas*, I hope to have demonstrated that the latter need not entail the former.[83] Moreover, my hope is that the lines of argument developed above may remind Anabaptists of the evangelical nature of their pacifist commitments and thus suggest avenues for future dialogue. Instead of simply rehashing the well-worn arguments that divide Anabaptists from evangelicals, Anabaptists would do well to maintain focus on the historically evangelical nature of their faith. Such a focus might foster more fruitful dialogue between Anabaptists

---

83. Another "hidden" agenda that I might as well confess at this point is to introduce more evangelicals to Yoder's work. In my own experience I have found reading Yoder to strengthen my evangelical commitments even as it continually challenges them.

and evangelicals going forward on just how fundamentally pacifism fits among the core commitments of their shared biblical faith.[84]

BIBLIOGRAPHY

Allert, Craig D. "What Are We Trying to Conserve? Evangelicalism and *Sola Scriptura*." *Evangelical Quarterly* 76 (2004) 327–48.

Barnwell, Bill. "Halt, Christian Soldier: Evangelicals' Militant Tendencies Aren't Grounded in Church History or Scripture." *The American Conservative*, 6 November 2006, 22–24.

Bell, Daniel M., Jr. *Just War as Christian Discipleship: Recentering the Tradition in the Church Rather Than the State*. Grand Rapids: Brazos, 2009.

Bergen, Jeremy M., and Anthony G. Siegrist, editors. *Power and Practices: Engaging the Work of John Howard Yoder*. Scottdale, PA: Herald, 2009.

Carpenter, Eugene E., and Philip W. Comfort. *Holman Treasury of Key Bible Words*. Nashville: Broadman & Holman, 2000.

Cramer, David C. "Nonevidentialism, Pluralism, and Warrant: Plantinga, Hick, and the Epistemological Challenge of Religious Diversity." MA thesis, Trinity International University, 2009.

———. "Inheriting Yoder Faithfully: A Review of New Yoder Scholarship." *The Mennonite Quarterly Review* 85 (2011) 133–46.

———. "John Hick." In *The Internet Encyclopedia of Philosophy*. No pages. Online: http://www.iep.utm.edu/hick/.

———. Review of *Christian America and the Kingdom of God*, by Richard T. Hughes. No pages. Online: http://www.patheos.com/community/jesuscreed/2010/06/12/saturday-afternoon-book-review-david-cramer/.

Dayton, Donald W. "Yet Another Layer of the Onion: Or Opening the Ecumenical Door to Let the Riffraff in." *The Ecumenical Review* 40 (1988) 87–110.

Gwyn, Douglas, et al. *A Declaration on Peace: In God's People the World's Renewal Has Begun*. Scottdale, PA: Herald, 1991.

Durham, Martin. "Evangelical Protestantism and Foreign Policy in the United States after September 11." *Patterns of Prejudice* 38 (2004) 145–58.

Dula, Peter, and Chris K. Huebner, editors. *The New Yoder*. Eugene, OR: Cascade, 2010.

Eaton, Matthew. "Toward an Anabaptist Soteriology: An Assessment of the Soteriological Models of Martin Luther, Balthasar Hubmaier, and Leonhard Schiermer in Light of Contemporary Pauline Research." MA thesis, Associated Mennonite Biblical Seminary, 2009.

———. "Toward an Anabaptist Covenantal Soteriology: A Dialogue with Balthasar Hubmaier and Contemporary Pauline Scholarship." *The Mennonite Quarterly Review* 84 (2010) 67–93.

---

84. Thanks to the following friends who provided helpful comments at various stages of this essay's completion: Jared Burkholder, Tim Erdel, Mark Thiessen Nation, John Roth, Jim Stump, and the theological discussion group that met in the home of Chad Meister on 25 July 2010.

Erdel, Timothy Paul. "Is Just War Still An Oxymoron?" *Criswell Theological Review* 4 (2007) 53–76.

———. "The Rationality of the Christian Faith." PhD diss., University of Illinois at Urbana-Champaign, 2000.

———. "Simply Believing: Trusting (Luke 16:1–15)." Chapel address, Bethel College, Mishawaka, Indiana, 10 November 2008. No pages. Online video: http://www.bethelcollege.edu/studentlife/chapel/archive/?page=fall_08&play=yes&post=27&type=mov.

Estep, William R. *The Anabaptist Story: An Introduction to Sixteenth-Century Anabaptism*, 3rd ed. Grand Rapids: Eerdmans, 1996.

Friesen, Duane K. "Peacemaking as an Ethical Category: The Convergence of Pacifism and Just War." In *Ethics in the Nuclear Age: Strategy, Religious Studies, and the Churches*, edited by Todd Whitmore, 161–80. Dallas: Southern Methodist University Press, 1989.

Hauerwas, Stanley. "Pacifism: Some Philosophical Considerations." *Faith and Philosophy* 2 (1985) 99–104.

———. *With the Grain of the Universe: The Church's Witness and Natural Theology*. Grand Rapids: Brazos, 2001.

Hay, David M. "*Pistis* as 'Ground for Faith' in Hellenized Judaism and Paul." *Journal of Biblical Literature* 108 (1989) 461–76.

Hays, Richard B. *The Faith of Jesus Christ: The Narrative Substructure of Galatians 3:1–4:11*. 2nd ed. Grand Rapids: Eerdmans, 2002.

———. *The Moral Vision of the New Testament: Community, Cross, New Creation; A Contemporary Introduction to New Testament Ethics*. San Francisco: HarperCollins, 1996.

———. "Salvation by Trust? Reading the Bible Faithfully." *Christian Century* 114 (1997) 219.

Hick, John. *Faith and Knowledge*, 2nd ed. Ithaca: Cornell University Press, 1966.

Hughes, Richard T. *Christian America and the Kingdom of God*. Urbana: University of Illinois Press, 2009.

Johnson, Alan. "The Bible and War in America: An Historical Survey." *Journal of the Evangelical Theological Society* 28 (1985) 169.

Kissling, Paul J. "John Howard Yoder's Reading of the Old Testament and the Stone-Campbell Tradition." In *Radical Ecumenicity: Pursuing Unity and Continuity after John Howard Yoder*, edited by John C. Nugent, 129–47. Abilene, TX: Abilene Christian University Press, 2010.

Koop, Doug. "Closing the Door on Open Theists? ETS to examine whether Clark Pinnock and John Sanders Can Remain Members." *Christianity Today*. No pages. Online: http://www.christianitytoday.com/ct/2003/january/14.24.html?start=1.

Kraus, C. Norman. "American Mennonites and the Bible, 1750–1950." *The Mennonite Quarterly Review* 41 (1967) 309–29.

Lanham, Robert. "Mark Driscoll: 'Meek. Mild. As If.'" No pages. Online: http://www.evangelicalright.com/2006/10/mark_driscoll_meek_mild_as_if_1.html.

Lind, Millard. *Yahweh is a Warrior: The Theology of Warfare in Ancient Israel*. Scottdale, PA: Herald, 1980.

Mennonite World Conference, "Shared Convictions." No pages. Online: http://www.mwc-cmm.org/MWC/Councils/2006SharedConvictionsENG.pdf.

Metzler, James E. "Shalom is the Mission." In *Mission and the Peace Witness: The Gospel and Christian Discipleship*, edited by Robert L. Ramseyer, 36–51. Scottdale, PA: Herald, 1979.

Mouw, Richard. "Christianity and Pacifism." *Faith and Philosophy* 2 (1985) 105–11.

———. *Praying at Burger King*. Grand Rapids: Eerdmans, 2007.

———. "Violence and the Atonement." In *Must Christianity Be Violent? Reflections on History, Practice, and Theology*, edited by Kenneth R. Chase and Alan Jacobs, 159–71. Grand Rapids: Brazos, 2003.

Mouw, Richard, and John Howard Yoder. "Evangelical Ethics and the Anabaptist-Reformed Dialogue." *The Journal of Religious Ethics* 17 (1989) 121–37.

Murphy, Nancey. "John Howard Yoder's Systematic Defense of Christian Pacifism." In *The Wisdom of the Cross: Essays in Honor of John Howard Yoder*, edited by Stanley Hauerwas et al., 45–68. Grand Rapids: Eerdmans, 1999.

Nation, Mark Thiessen. *A Comprehensive Bibliography of the Writings of John Howard Yoder*. Goshen, IN: Mennonite Historical Society, 1997.

———. "John Howard Yoder: Mennonite, Evangelical, Catholic." *The Mennonite Quarterly Review* 77 (2003) 357–70.

———. *John Howard Yoder: Mennonite Patience, Evangelical Witness, Catholic Convictions*. Grand Rapids: Eerdmans, 2006.

———. "John H. Yoder, Ecumenical Neo-Anabaptist: A Biographical Sketch." In *The Wisdom of the Cross: Essays in Honor of John Howard Yoder*, edited by Stanley Hauerwas et al., 1–23. Grand Rapids: Eerdmans, 1999.

———. "The Politics of Yoder Regarding the Politics of Jesus: Recovering the Implicit in Yoder's Holistic Theology for Pacifism." In *Radical Ecumenicity: Pursuing Unity and Continuity after John Howard Yoder*, edited by John C. Nugent, 37–56. Abilene, TX: Abilene Christian University Press, 2010.

———. "Supplement to 'A Comprehensive Bibliography of the Writings of John Howard Yoder.'" In *The Wisdom of the Cross: Essays in Honor of John Howard Yoder*, edited by Stanley Hauerwas et al., 472–91. Grand Rapids: Eerdmans, 1999.

Niebuhr, Reinhold. "An Open Letter (to Richard Roberts)." In *Love and Justice: Selections from the Shorter Writings of Reinhold Niebuhr*, edited by D. B. Robertson, 267–71. New York: Meridian, 1967.

Nix, William E. "The Evangelical and War." *Journal of the Evangelical Theological Society* 13 (1970) 133–46.

Nugent, John C. "Biblical Warfare Revisited: Extending the Insights of John Howard Yoder." In *Power and Practices: Engaging the Work of John Howard Yoder*, edited by Jeremy M. Bergen and Anthony G. Siegrist, 167–84. Scottdale, PA: Herald, 2009.

Nugent, John C., ed. *Radical Ecumenicity: Pursuing Unity and Continuity after John Howard Yoder*. Abilene, TX: Abilene Christian University Press, 2010.

Pfeil, Margaret R. "John Howard Yoder's Pedagogical Approach: A Just War Tradition with Teeth and a Hermeneutic of Peace." *The Mennonite Quarterly Review* 76 (2002) 181–88.

Ramseyer, Robert L. "Mennonite Missions and the Christian Peace Witness." In *Mission and the Peace Witness: The Gospel and Christian Discipleship*, edited by Robert L. Ramseyer, 114–34. Scottdale, PA: Herald, 1979.

Ramseyer, Robert L., ed. *Mission and the Peace Witness: The Gospel and Christian Discipleship*. Scottdale, PA: Herald, 1979.

Reuschling, Wyndy Corbin. *Reviving Evangelical Ethics: The Promises and Pitfalls of Classic Models of Morality*. Grand Rapids: Brazos, 2008.

Roth, John D. *Choosing Against War: A Christian View; "A Love Stronger Than Our Fears."* Intercourse, PA: Good, 2002.

———. "Community as Conversation: A New Model of Anabaptist Hermeneutics." In *Anabaptist Currents: History in Conversation with the Present*, edited by Carl F. Bowman and Stephen L. Longenecker, 51–64. Bridgewater, VA: Penobscot, 1995.

Sider, Ronald J. "A Call for Evangelical Nonviolence." In *Mission and the Peace Witness: The Gospel and Christian Discipleship*, edited by Robert L. Ramseyer, 52–67. Scottdale, PA: Herald, 1979.

———. *Non-violence, The Invincible Weapon?* Dallas: Word, 1989.

Stoltzfus, Philip E. "Nonviolent Jesus, Violent God? A Critique of John Howard Yoder's Approach to Theological Construction." In *Power and Practices: Engaging the Work of John Howard Yoder*, edited by Jeremy M. Bergen and Anthony G. Siegrist, 29–46. Scottdale, PA: Herald, 2009.

Swartley, Willard. *Covenant of Peace: The Missing Peace in New Testament Theology and Ethics*. Grand Rapids: Eerdmans, 2006.

———. *Slavery, Sabbath, War, and Women: Case Issues in Biblical Interpretation*. Scottdale, PA: Herald, 1983.

Swartz, David R. "Left Behind: The Evangelical Left and the Limits of Evangelical Politics, 1965–1985." PhD diss., University of Notre Dame, 2008.

Voolstra, Sjouke. "The Search for a Biblical Peace Testimony." In *Mission and the Peace Witness: The Gospel and Christian Discipleship*, edited by Robert L. Ramseyer, 24–35. Scottdale, PA: Herald, 1979.

Waetjen, Herman C. "The Trust of Abraham and the Trust of Jesus Christ: Romans 1:17." *Currents in Theology and Mission* 30 (2003) 446–54.

Whitmore, Todd. "When the Lesser Evil is Not Good Enough: The Catholic Case for Not Voting." In *Electing Not to Vote: Christian Reflections on Reasons for Not Voting*, edited by Ted Lewis, 62–80. Eugene, OR: Cascade, 2008.

Wille, Wilhelm. "Ambivalence in the Christian Attitude to War and Peace." *International Review of Psychiatry* 19 (2007) 235–42.

Yoder, John Howard. "A Consistent Alternative View within the Just War Family." *Faith and Philosophy* 2 (1985) 112–20.

———. "The Contemporary Evangelical Revival and the Peace Churches." In *Mission and the Peace Witness: The Gospel and Christian Discipleship*, edited by Robert L. Ramseyer, 68–103. Scottdale, PA: Herald, 1979.

———. *Discipleship as Political Responsibility*. Translated from German by Timothy J. Geddert. Scottdale, PA: Herald, 2003.

———. "From the Wars of Joshua to Jewish Pacifism." In *The War of the Lamb: The Ethics of Nonviolence and Peacemaking*, edited by Glen Stassen et al., 67–75. Grand Rapids: Brazos, 2009.

———. *For the Nations: Essays Public & Evangelical*. Grand Rapids: Eerdmans, 1997.

———. *He Came Preaching Peace*. Scottdale, PA: Herald, 2004.

———. "The Hermeneutics of the Anabaptists." *The Mennonite Quarterly Review* 41 (1967) 291–308.

———. "How Many Ways Are There to Think Morally about War?" *The Journal of Law and Religion* 11 (1994) 83–107.

———. "If Abraham is Our Father." In *The Original Revolution: Essays on Christian Pacifism*, 85–104. Scottdale, PA: Herald, 2003.

———. "If Christ is Truly Lord." In *The Original Revolution: Essays on Christian Pacifism*, 52–84. Scottdale, PA: Herald, 2003.

———. "Jesus: A Model of Radical Political Action." In *The War of the Lamb: The Ethics of Nonviolence and Peacemaking*, edited by Glen Stassen et al., 77–82. Grand Rapids: Brazos, 2009.

———. *The Jewish-Christian Schism Revisited*. Scottdale, PA: Herald, 2008.

———. *Nevertheless: The Varieties and Shortcomings of Religious Pacifism*. Rev. ed. Scottdale, PA: Herald, 1992.

———. *The Original Revolution: Essays on Christian Pacifism*. Scottdale, PA: Herald, 2003.

———. "The Political Axioms of the Sermon on the Mount." In *The Original Revolution: Essays on Christian Pacifism*, 34–51. Scottdale, PA: Herald, 2003.

———. *The Politics of Jesus: Vicit Agnus Noster*. 2nd ed. Grand Rapids: Eerdmans, 1994.

———. "See How They Go with Their Face to the Sun." In *The Jewish-Christian Schism Revisited*, edited by Michael G. Cartwright and Peter Ochs, 183–204. Scottdale, PA: Herald, 2008.

———. *To Hear the Word*. Eugene, OR: Wipf & Stock, 2001.

———. *The War of the Lamb: The Ethics of Nonviolence and Peacemaking*. Edited by Glen Stassen et al. Grand Rapids: Brazos, 2009.

———. *What Would You Do? A Serious Answer to a Standard Question*. Rev. ed. Scottdale, PA: Herald, 1992.

———. *When War Is Unjust: Being Honest in Just War Thinking*. Rev. ed. Maryknoll, NY: Orbis, 1996.

Afterword

I COME FROM A BIG family where meals around the table always involved animated conversation, with plenty of stories, loud arguments, complaints, compliments, raucous laughter, and hot tears. These meals were presided over by Mom and Dad, who made it clear that they expected good manners (no talking with mouth full of food) and civil address (no shouting or rude interruptions). And we would never begin a meal until we bowed our heads to say thank you to the Giver of all good. To begin a meal—even to reach in on the sly to grab a crumb—was verboten. After the last straggler had finally arrived at table, we together first closed our eyes to remember who we were—a family at table, grateful for a warm meal. And then, all manner of conversation, disputation, and eager eating could commence.

The editors of this fine volume have set a rich feast for us. Like parental presiders, they have invited folks around a table for conversation. But rather than inviting only one family, they have invited two families to table—a blended family if you will, who when most truly themselves, have a whole lot in common. The editors made it clear from the beginning that because their personal faith journeys have been immeasurably enriched by both evangelical and Anabaptist expressions of faith, they want representatives of each family to talk to each other with mutual respect and renewed appreciation for the ennobling influence they have sometimes had and can again have on each other.

The conversation is critically important because when we have neglected to talk to each other in respectful ways, we have often resorted to simplistic, dismissive caricatures that highlight the negative characteristics of the other. In reality, the internal dynamics in each of our families is much more complex than meets the eye. Each of us stewards particular strengths and continually wrestles with proclivities that threaten to undermine the best that we strive to be.

Family names are helpful, but only in a limited way. They tend to obscure as much as they reveal about our particular identity. A family name serves to place people within a historical matrix, but it cannot begin to capture the complex variations on how we choose to live out our family identities in all sorts of fascinating combinations.

To their immense credit, the editors of *The Activist Impulse* have managed to energize a critical exploration of distinctive features that have sometimes characterized so-called evangelicals and Anabaptists. With balance and thoughtful examination, the conversation they engender demonstrates that these two families need each other. When they have acted in more oppositional ways, it has sometimes served to correct harmful extremes in the other. At the historical moments when they joined in common cause, their shared witness was powerfully renewed. An Anabaptist discipleship ethic and peace witness when seamlessly integrated with evangelical warmth of devotion and winsome confidence about Jesus as Savior and Lord has been potent good news to a watching world over and over.

The complexity of these multi-faceted family relationships only highlights the significance and necessity of the conversation this book invites. I applaud the editors' desire to bring evangelicals and Anabaptists together in renewed mutual appreciation and collaboration. The problems to be solved, the tasks to be undertaken, the needs of our world to be addressed are so enormous that we cannot afford to arrogantly or self-righteously go it alone. The authors are right on in their discernment that the time is now for together reclaiming the best of what we both are called to proclaim and live in a shared embodiment of the Gospel of Jesus Christ. Imagine how the watching world would notice if together we bowed our heads to say thank you to the Giver of all good—sharing the shalom of God with each other—and joined our efforts to bring good news to the poor, to proclaim release to the captives and recovery of sight to the blind, to let the oppressed go free, and to proclaim the year of the Lord's favor.

Sara Wenger Shenk
President
Associated Mennonite Biblical Seminary

Index

Abelard, Peter, 350, 353
abortion, 297, 308n36, 326, 329, 333, 340–42, 385n24
acculturation, 29, 30, 32, 53, 54, 189
Africa, 11, 18, 39, 274, 338n33
African American(s), 14, 74, 164, 239, 240, 341n40
agapē, 306, 331, 332, 358, 359, 368. *See also* love
Agnes Scott College, 283
Ainley, Stephen C., 107n14, 117, 124n90
aiōn, 360, 368, 372, 373, 375–77
alcohol, 240, 241, 251, 274, 333, 339
Alexander, John, 270, 273, 279, 338
Alliance of Evangelical Mennonite Congregations, 49
Al-Qaeda, 354
Alttäufer, 47
America, ix, 2, 14, 15, 16, 27, 81, 110, 130, 158, 173n45, 186, 187, 189, 197, 229, 231, 232, 243, 286, 292, 295, 299, 306n30, 309, 350, 352
    Central, 239, 239n10, 274
    as Christian nation, 75–77, 82–86, 88, 117–18, 120, 297, 328, 329, 336
    Constitution of, 84, 87, 88, 176, 296, 329, 341
    Latin, 237n2, 239, 271, 274
    North, 12–13, 19–23, 39, 46, 50n8, 53, 138, 215, 232, 352, 394
    Pledge of Allegiance to, 266
    United States of, vii, 14–16, 24, 31, 46n2, 49, 62, 75, 78, 83–84, 87, 124, 132, 223, 226, 229, 237, 238, 240, 241n14, 243, 244, 246, 258, 275, 326, 329, 336, 338, 340, 341, 342, 343, 356, 384n22, 393
Amish, 2n3, 12, 13, 19, 20, 22, 25, 48, 52n15, 62, 78, 122, 123
Amish Mennonites, 138, 140
Anabaptism (select topics)
    as "third way," 22, 105, 117, 119, 121–23, 125, 238
    neo-Anabaptists, 4, 23, 24, 36, 38n84, 77–80, 82, 83, 86, 89, 216, 263, 264n3, 328, 381n10
Anders, William, 101, 102, 198–202, 207, 208
Andrews, Thomas, 86
Angas, William Henry, 48
anointing with oil, 119, 121
Anselm, 324, 350, 353, 369–72, 376, 377
Anspach, Charles, 178
antinomianism, 378n63, 204
Antioch College, 164, 165
anti-prosperity gospel, 273
apartheid, 11, 338n33
apistia, 388. *See also* faith; *pistis*
apologetic, 334, 390, 165
Appleby, R. Scott, 188n9, 190, 191, 193

Index

archeology, 111
Aristotle, 302n19, 333
Ashland Theological Seminary, 157, 159–63, 168, 169, 171, 172–78, 181
Ashman, Charles, 176, 178, 179, 181
Associated Mennonite Biblical Seminary, 13, 55n21, 282
Association of Evangelical Mennonites, 49
atonement, 21, 54, 64, 112, 122, 123, 148, 323, 324, 350–58, 364–65, 367, 369, 376–77, 393n58, 399
  Christus Victor, 324, 350
  feminist views of, 353
  satisfaction theory of, 122, 323–24, 350–52, 357, 365, 369, 371
Augsburger, David, 282
Augsburger, Myron, 37, 265, 267
Augustine, 369
Aulén, Gustaf, 350–52
Austin Community Fellowship, 283

Back to the Bible, 200
Bailyn, Bernard, 83
Baker, Mark, 355
Bancroft, E. H., 168
Bancroft, George, 84
baptism
  believer's, 57–59, 171, 356
  immersion, 21, 171, 178
  infant, 19, 59, 219
Baptist Continental Missionary Society, 45
Barnhouse, Donald Grey, 200
Barton, David, 84–86
Bauman, Louis S., 156n1, 160n8, 163, 168–69, 170, 171, 175, 177, 179, 181
Baumgartner, Christen, 46
Beachy, Bertha, 284
Bebbington, David, 13n8, 14, 50n8, 355

Beecher, Henry Ward, 116
Bender, Daniel H., 131
Bender, Harold S., 50, 54, 111, 117, 118, 119n65, 142n47, 186n3, 195
  "Anabaptist Vision," 22, 23, 51, 124, 220, 265n4, 269, 271
  and non-Mennonite influences, 53, 208
Benedict, Wilbur D., 12
Berkeley, CA, 17, 266, 277, 279
Bethel College (Mishawaka, IN), xi, 327, 337n30, 342n44, 380–81
Bible, the, 47, 70, 74, 107, 141, 142, 172, 176n54, 179, 205, 239, 248, 356
  authority of, 13, 25, 28, 60–61, 384
  Bible conferences, 113, 114, 170, 173, 186, 199–201, 203
  doctrines of, 109, 112, 119–20, 133
  inerrancy of, 25–26, 28, 324, 332, 357, 357n11, 374, 384n20
  infallibility of, 139, 355
  (verbal plenary) inspiration of, 115, 171, 355, 385
  instruction of, 175
  interpretation of, 25, 60, 113, 139, 358–68, 386–400
  and law, 298–99
  and politics, 316
  and prophecy, 15, 168, 173
  and science, 166–67
  study of, 24, 26–28, 173–74, 202, 245, 247
  and violence, 354, 357, 384
Bible institute
  Briercrest, 30
  of Los Angeles (Biola), 160n8, 164, 172, 169n37
  model, 164–65
  Moody, 26, 113, 114, 200, 201
  movement, 175
  Prairie, 30

Bible Presbyterian Church, 295
Bible Study Hour, 200
birthday celebrations, 119
blood, 20, 64, 87, 120, 124, 143, 360–61, 361n16, 365–68, 373, 376
Blooming Glen Mennonite Church, 199
blue laws, 336
Bluffton College (University), xi, 107n14, 109, 114, 121, 140–41, 144, 285
Boone, Pat, 17
"born again," 1, 18, 373. *See also* conversion
Bowlin, Ota, 106, 136
Boyd, Gregory, 4n7, 12, 38, 216, 287, 324, 324n13
Boyd, Jonathan, 84
Brenneman, Daniel, 48, 217–19, 220, 224n19, 226n24, 234
Brenneman, Orval, 228
Brethren (select topics)
 Brethren in Christ, 11, 21, 24n41, 35n76, 36n77, 37n81, 39, 48, 77, 263, 267, 272
 Brethren Church, the, 158–63, 165, 168n36, 169–71, 176
 Brethren Evangelist, 159, 171n43
 Brethren Voluntary Service, 22
 Church of the Brethren, the, 28n49, 48, 77, 158, 180, 267, 268
 Dunkard Brethren, 21, 219
 Grace Brethren. See Fellowship of Grace Brethren Churches; Conservative Fellowship of Grace Brethren Churches
 Old German Baptist Brethren, 12, 22, 158
 River Brethren, 21
Brown, Dale, 176n51, 176n54, 177n57, 267, 270, 271n13, 272
Brubacher, Jacob, 194, 195, 203

Brubaker, Ezra, 201
Bruderschaft, 29, 32
Brunk, George R., Jr., 30–32
Brunk, George R., Sr., 111, 115–17, 119n67, 125, 130, 131, 141–145, 149, 186, 187, 192
Brunner, C. H., 225–26
Bryan, William Jennings, 116n50, 166n29, 172
Burke, Flannery, 86
Burkholder, Christian, 122
Burkholder, Oscar, 114
Bush, George W., 287, 327, 354
Bush, Perry, 81, 107n14, 263, 269
Bushnell, Horace, 106
Byers, Noah E., 107–8, 110, 114

Calvary Independent Church, 35, 186n4, 200n55
Calvary Mennonite Church (Mathis, TX), 245n32
Calvary Mennonite Church (Souderton, PA), 197, 198n47, 208
Calvin, John, 298, 337, 351
Calvin College, 267, 286n36
Calvin Theological Seminary, 264
Calvinism, 26, 35, 111, 117–18, 167–68, 174, 204, 206, 267
 anti-, 21n32
camp meetings, 141, 200, 218, 220
Campus Crusade for Christ, 266, 356
capitalism, 78, 286n36
card playing, 177
carnal strife, 171, 181. *See also* war
Carter, Craig, 77
Carter, Jimmy, 1, 18
catechism, 29, 32, 173
Catholicism, 14, 57, 61, 170, 249–51
CFAM radio, 32
Chalke, Steve, 355
Chapa, Ted, 248, 253, 254, 258
charismatic movement, 18, 39, 47, 334
charitable giving, 19

"Chicago Declaration," 262, 263, 272, 281
Chicago Tribune, 277
Chicano movement, 242, 255, 256, 257
child abuse, 339, 353
Climenhaga, Arthur, M., 11
Christendom, 79, 116
Christian and Missionary Alliance, 22
Christian Catholic Apostolic Church, 338
Christian Exponent, 116, 117, 144
Christian Monitor, 139
Christian Reformed, 277, 278n23
Christian salutation, 119, 121
Christian World Liberation Front, 266, 270, 277
Christianity Today, viii, 12, 17, 280, 281n26, 283, 286, 386
Christology, 112, 118, 124. See also Jesus
Church of God in Christ, Mennonite, 48
civil law, 297
civil religion, 270
Civil Rights movement, 87, 257, 268, 272
Civilian Public Service, 180, 229, 230, 241, 243
Claiborne, Shane, 4, 37, 51, 216, 287
Clarke, William Newton, 109
Clemmer, Abraham, 196
clothing style, 30, 139, 158, 164
  plain, 20, 24, 54, 193, 206, 207, 246–247, 250–51
Clouse, Robert, 161, 162n15, 333n25
coercion, 58, 267, 268, 334
Coffman, John S., 106, 113, 114, 121, 129, 131–33, 137, 138, 139, 141, 147
Collegian, The, 177
Colson, Charles, 287
communion, 17, 244
  three-fold, 178

See also Lord's Supper
Conference on Faith and History, xi
Conference on Nonviolent Atonement, 356
Congo Inland Mission, 49
Congregational Mennonite Church, 197, 198n43, 201, 208
Congregationalism, 142
conscientious objector, 23, 36, 181, 230, 233, 243, 253, 259
Conservative Fellowship of Grace Brethren Churches, 160
Conservative Mennonite Conference, 23, 24n41, 49
conservativism, 27, 103, 167, 182, 279
  aggresso-, 192, 194, 196, 203, 209
  conservative American Protestantism, 53
  conservative Brethren, 157, 158, 162–67
  conservative Christianity, 308
  conservative Christians, 17, 28, 76, 166
  conservative evangelicalism, 327
  conservative evangelicals, 3, 16, 23n40, 51n10, 53, 101, 102, 152, 287
  conservative Mennonites, 102, 109, 111, 113–14, 125, 130, 132, 135, 141, 144, 189–90, 192, 194–96, 201, 204, 205, 250
  conservative theology, 15
  and liberalism, 107n14, 314
  neoconservatives, 382
Constantine, 266, 297
consumerism, 78
Contemporary Christian Music, 11, 35
conversion(s), 2, 13, 30, 31–32, 46, 48, 50, 51, 53–54, 58, 59, 121, 130, 131, 133, 136–37, 147, 152, 153, 168, 232, 233, 241,

Index   413

250, 271, 360, 367, 371, 374, 376
council meetings. *See* preparatory services
Council of Christian Colleges and Universities, 37n81
Crawford, Percy B., 33, 199, 200
creation, views of, 166, 167n30
Crusade for Christ Hour, 208
culture wars, 2, 24, 294, 323

Dallas Theological Seminary, viii, 156, 160, 161
dancing, 177, 241, 250, 251
Defenseless Mennonite Church, 48, 49
Democracy, 84, 142, 143, 195, 229, 269, 338, 343, 344, 354, 385n23
Democratic Party, 272, 328, 329, 330n19
Detweiler, William G., 201, 204, 208, 237–38, 243, 258
devotional covering, 54, 119, 121, 193
Didden, Clarence, 200
Die Stille im Lande, 117
discipleship, 24, 28, 37, 38, 47, 52, 53, 54, 59, 101, 133n11, 192, 206, 227, 229, 268, 281, 301, 346, 351, 355, 408
  as political, 330n19, 347n54
  radical, 270, 279, 336
  workshops, 271n13, 278n23, 281n26
dispensationalism, 16n15, 26, 30, 102, 111, 113, 156, 167, 168, 174, 177, 181, 202, 204–5
Dissent, 80
divorce, 333
Dobson, James, 34
Doe v. Bolton, 340
Doerksen, Brian, 11
Dordrecht Confession, 25n44, 223
Douglas, Janet, 222

Dowie, Alexander, 338

Eastern Mennonite College/University, 37n81, 114, 134, 186n2, 265, 267
Eastern Mennonite School, 118, 137n32, 196
Eby, Benjamin, 21
Eby, John, 34–36
Eby, Solomon, 48, 218
ecclesiology, 46, 51, 54, 62
egalitarianism, 264, 281–85
Egly, Henry, 48
ekklēsia, 372. *See also* ecclesiology
Elkhart (IN), 131–32, 218, 282, 285
Elkhart Institute, 107, 131n5, 132, 133n12, 138
Engle, Jacob, 48
Episcopalian, 27
Epp, Frank, 29n54, 31, 32, 132n7, 135
Epp, Theodore, 200
Equal Rights Amendment, 281
eschatology
  and ethics, 302
  amillennialism, 113
  postmillennial(ism), 168
  premillennial(ism), 55, 111, 113, 114, 117, 168, 173, 202, 204
Espinosa, Gastón, 239
eternal security, 118, 198, 204–6
Eternity, 277, 281n26
ethics
  Anabaptist, 20, 54, 62, 67, 69, 78, 82, 105, 121–23, 145, 147–49, 267, 316, 352, 381n7, 382, 397–99, 408
  Christian, 268, 293, 307, 331–34, 335, 337, 344, 354
  ecclesial, 309, 311
  evangelical, 384, 385n23
  and faith, 389, 400
  and historiography, 79, 82, 90
  of Jesus, 367, 386, 395
  personal, 21, 145, 274

social, 302, 307, 323
two-kingdom, 146, 303–4
of war and peace, 215, 235, 253, 264, 382n13, 398
ethnicity, 3, 20, 24, 29–32, 37, 39, 59, 102, 221, 131, 221, 237, 239, 241–42, 244, 255, 286, 361, 372
evangelicalism (select topics)
Anglo-evangelicals, 20, 21
Evangelical Anabaptist Revolution, 328
Evangelical Association, 219
evangelical feminism, 216, 282–85, 380n3
Evangelical Free Church, 74, 356
Evangelical Mennonite Brethren Conference, 49
Evangelical Mennonite Church, 30, 48, 49
Evangelical Mennonite Conference, 49
Evangelical Theological Society, 17, 325n1, 384n20
Evangelical United Brethren Church, 356
Evangelical United Mennonites, 219
Evangelical Women's Caucus, 263, 281–82, 286
Evangelicals for McGovern, 272
Evangelicals for Social Action, 37n81, 272, 280, 282n27, 380n3
National Association of Evangelicals 17, 18n24, 50 n8, 264, 397
neo-evangelicals, 17, 191, 197, 199, 200, 203
Evangelisch-Taufgesinnter Gemeinde, 46
evangelism, 3, 24n41, 30, 133n11, 172, 198, 201, 206–7, 209, 215, 217, 220–22, 224–27, 229n29, 231–35, 239n8, 252, 265, 279, 280. *See also* missions
evangelist(s), viii, 33, 81, 136–37, 168, 199n51, 243, 244
Mennonite evangelist(s), 30, 51, 129, 186n2, 198, 207
televangelist(s), 18, 55, 334
Evans, William, 112
excommunication, 109, 249
Executive Committee (Franconia Mennonite Conference), 194–95, 198n48, 199n49, 207n82
Explo '72, 266

Fairfield Mennonite Church, 285
faith, 12, 26, 32, 59, 61, 62, 64, 66, 68, 69, 88, 102, 106, 107, 108, 137, 141, 147, 167n31, 169, 171, 174, 176n51, 179, 193n26, 205, 251, 254, 293, 294, 296, 299, 300–302, 356, 407
alone, 324, 383, 385
Anabaptist-Mennonite, 20, 24, 37, 47, 48, 51n10, 56, 58, 78, 123–24, 149, 192, 195, 220, 230, 241, 259, 269, 270, 387
and Scripture, 60, 79, 324, 372, 373, 386, 387, 389–401
evangelical, 3, 11, 13, 23, 38, 39, 275, 296–97, 327, 329, 384n19, 387
(un)faithful(ness), 23, 28, 39, 50n9, 61, 69, 120, 123, 143, 146–47, 186, 190, 216, 228, 233, 234, 267, 280, 285, 294, 311, 316, 351, 357, 363, 376, 381, 389, 398
fundamentals of, 115, 170
healing, 36
justification by, 383, 385, 386n26, 386n27
salvation through, 178n63, 206n78, 358, 360

statement of, 173, 178, 179
and tradition, 31
as trust, 388–96
Falwell, Jerry, 1, 24
Family News in Focus, 34
fasting, 273
feet washing, 119, 178n63, 192
Fellowship of Grace Brethren Churches, 102, 157, 160. *See also* Brethren church(es)
feudal system, 89
Finger, Lareta Halteman, 216, 283
Finney, Charles, 15
Five "Cs" of Historical Thinking, 86
Flood Geology, 160, 166. *See also* science
Fosdick, Harry Emerson, 106, 116
Fox-Genovese, Elizabeth, 94
Franconia Mennonite Conference, 187, 188, 189n10, 198n48, 199n49, 203n67, 207n82
Free Methodists, 27, 219
Friedmann, Robert, 51, 52n14
Friesen, Dorothy, 285
Froehlich, Samuel, 45–47
Fuller Theological Seminary, viii, 17, 284
Fuller, Charles, 16, 200
Fundamentalism, viii, 1, 5, 16–17, 23, 62, 101–2, 295
and the Brethren Church, 157–61, 167–75, 176, 177, 182
and Mennonites, 26, 53, 104–25, 129–32, 141–52, 185–209, 231n38
and modernism, 105, 111, 117, 125, 352
Funk, John F., 131, 133, 147–48, 218

Gandhi, Mahatma, 335
Gehman, Ernest G., 145, 186, 230n35
Gehret, T. D., 227–29
Gelassenheit, 52, 130, 149, 151, 152, 194. *See also* submission

gender, 196, 248, 259, 264, 266, 283, 285, 333, 355, 361
General Conference (Mennonite Brethren in Christ), 229n29, 230
General Conference Mennonite Church, 26, 104, 129n1, 140, 241n14
Genovese, Eugene, 94
Gerber, Christen, 45
German (language), 29–30, 46, 131n5, 138, 139, 146, 218
Germany, 48, 175n51
Girard, René, 353–54
Gish, Abram, 198, 201–2
Gish, Arthur (Art), 268–70, 272, 279, 282
Gladwell, Joyce, 284
Gladwell, Malcolm, 284
Gleason, Robert, 90
global justice, 272. *See also* social justice
globalism, 270
Gnagey, A. D., 159
Gnagey, Mary Ellen, 159
Golden Rule, the, 179n65, 332
Goode, Richard C., 78–79
Gordon Divinity School, 283
Goshen College, 1, 107–9, 132–33, 135, 139, 140, 144, 189,192, 209n86, 275, 328
Gospel Banner, 215, 219–21, 223–32, 234
Gospel Herald, 102, 104, 106, 113, 114n42, 115–18, 120, 133–34, 194
Gospel Tabernacle (Elizabethtown, PA), 186n4, 201
Gospel Witness, 106, 133
government, 38, 84, 222, 243, 293, 296–301, 329, 330n19, 338, 385n23
and coercion, 268, 334
and war, 180n68, 229, 265
church polity, 142

Christian relationship to, 222,
298–318
See also politics
Grace Bible Church, 186n4, 202
Grace College, 157n3, 159, 160, 162,
176, 264
Grace Theological Seminary, 102,
156–59, 160n8, 161, 166,
172–73, 176, 181
graduated tithe, 273
Graham, Billy, 17, 31, 50n8, 51, 173,
200, 244, 264n3, 266, 275,
341n40
Gramberg, Mary, 285
grammatico-historical exegesis,
357–58. *See also* the Bible
Grant, Colin, 352
Gray, James M., 114, 115n45
Graybill, J. Paul, 203–5
Great Commission, 232, 238, 240,
258, 329n17, 345, 346
Great Migration, 244
Green, Stanley, 39
Gross, Leonard, 105, 122
Grout, W. R., 226
Gunton, Colin, 352

hagiography, 157, 162
Hamilton, Alexander, 80
Hankins, Barry, 166n28, 209n86,
295, 298n14
Hardin, Michael, 356
Hart, Albert Bushnell, 83
Hartley, L. P., 89
Hartzler, J. E., 107–10, 114
Harvard University, 108, 139, 151
hate, 180, 332
Hatfield, Mark, 271, 278, 280
Hauerwas, Stanley, 59, 77–78,
134n14, 148–49, 315n51,
318n52, 384–85
Hays, Richard, 77, 363, 386n28
Hearn, Ginny, 279
Hearn, Walter, 279
Heim, S. Mark, 355

Heltzel, Peter Goodwin, 240
Henry, Carl F. H., 17
Herald Press, 1, 275, 277n22, 287
hermeneutics, 54, 60–61, 66, 282,
379, 382, 383n17, 397. *See
also* the Bible
Hershberger, Guy F., 23n38, 111
Hershey, T. K., 237, 238, 243, 249,
258
Hess, Anna Kauffman, 108
Hess, J. Daniel, 104
Hesston College, 114, 255, 259
Hiestand, John S., 101, 102, 198–201,
204, 206–8
higher criticism, 25, 26, 106, 112. *See
also* the Bible
higher education, 20, 95, 131, 132,
140, 147, 159, 164, 175, 272,
327n7
Highland Park Camp Meeting
Grounds, 200
hilasmos, 358
hilastērion, 358
historiography, 9, 52, 76–79, 82, 121,
159, 176n51, 187, 197n40,
380n3
Hockman-Wert, Cathleen, 287
Hodge, A. A., 168
Holdeman, John, 48
Holsinger, Henry R., 158–59
holy kiss. *See* Christian salutation
Holy Spirit, 14, 48, 60, 66, 68–69,
93, 178n63, 307, 335, 368,
386n27
Horsch, John, 107, 114, 115n45, 117,
135, 192, 229
Horst, Amos, 203
Horst, Leon, 207
hospitality, 10, 74, 76, 77, 91, 93, 95,
219
Hostetler, Beulah, 22n35, 105,
114n43, 118, 125, 133n11,
188, 189, 191n19
Hour of Decision, 200
Hoyt, Herman, 172

Hubmaier, Balthasar, 351, 356
Huffman, J. A., 173, 219n5, 226n24, 227–30, 232n39
Hunter, James Davison, 77n3, 78, 82, 86

Iglesia Menonita del Calvario, 245
immigration, 15, 18, 240
imperialism, 223, 263, 275, 354
Indiana University, 108, 162n15
individualism, 38, 59, 130, 138–40, 149n69
infiltration, 161n11, 188–91
injustice, 76, 78, 81, 272–75, 279, 280, 353, 370, 374
inquiry meetings. *See* preparatory services
internationalism, 178n62, 264. *See also* nationalism
Intervarsity Christian Fellowship, 264
Intervarsity Graduate Christian Fellowship, 356
Islam, 188, 338n33
Israel
 ancient, 299–300, 308, 360, 364, 366, 372, 375, 376, 388, 390–95, 398
 modern-day, 17, 204

Jacobs, Edwin R., 169–71
James, William, 108, 388n33
Jefferson, Thomas, 80
Jeremiah, David, 38
Jersak, Brad, 353n4, 356, 362n18, 375
Jerusalem, 179, 344, 359
Jesus, 25, 32n61, 57, 64, 68, 85, 129, 225, 254, 265, 270, 280, 300, 313, 314, 327, 358, 366, 367, 372, 373, 380n4, 408
 and nonviolent atonement, 122, 376–77
 body of, 64
 death (crucifixion) of, 296, 331, 350, 359, 364, 368, 374–77, 300, 302, 306, 309, 317, 331, 350, 351, 353, 354n6, 355, 358–65, 368, 374–76, 377, 395
 disciples (followers) of, 78, 330, 336, 345, 380
 example of, 267, 276, 331, 344, 355, 384, 389, 395, 399
 gospel of, 285, 317, 381, 408
 historical, 355, 357
 life of, 300, 302, 309, 311, 317, 344, 355, 359, 372, 377, 385, 386, 398
 resurrection of, 21, 25, 69, 107, 124, 300, 302, 303, 305, 309, 216, 317, 375, 395, 399
 return (second coming) of, viii, 326n5
 politics of, 24, 78, 305
 teachings of, 3, 19, 20, 26, 38, 74, 77, 119, 122, 124, 146, 179, 180, 181, 226, 277, 300, 301, 302, 306, 309, 311, 317, 329, 332, 335, 346, 355, 357n10, 365, 368, 370, 375, 384–85, 386, 395, 399
 virgin birth (incarnation) of, 65–70, 107, 111, 124, 169, 302, 331, 359, 372, 373
Jesus People, 18
Jews, 224n18, 331. *See also* Israel
Jones, Jim, 338
Joris, David, 124
Juhnke, James C., 109n22, 116n53, 117n57, 121n77, 125, 131n4, 134, 144n53, 145n56, 148n66, 191n18
justification, 383, 385. *See also* faith; salvation
Kauffman, Daniel, 101, 102, 106, 119n65, 137, 143, 144, 146, 149n69, 150–53, 192n21
 and Anabaptist distinctiveness 119–21, 122–25

418 Index

as compared to other Mennonite leaders, 113–18, 138–45
and fundamentalism, 112
and *Gelassenheit*, 130, 136–38, 150–53
historical perceptions of, 104–5, 129, 134–36
as institutional leader, 130–34
and modernism, 112–13
Kauffman, David, 106
Kauffman, Nelson, 244, 245
Kauffman, Sam, 106
Kazin, Michael, 80, 81
Kent, Homer, Jr., 176
Kent, Homer, Sr., 159
Keswickian holiness, 232, 327
King Herod, 344
Kingdom of God, the
and atonement, 368–77
and Christian ethics, 5, 38, 39, 52, 180, 282, 283, 297, 316, 318, 351, 357
and dispensationalism, viii, 173–74, 179
and missions, 223, 227
and politics, 300–313, 344–46
Klaassen, Walter, 55n22, 65n35, 66n36, 68n40, 146
Kleine Gemeinde, 30, 49
Knox, John, 298
Korean Presbyterians, 29, 380n7
Kraus, C. Norman, 1, 2n2, 17n18, 24n42, 53n17, 54, 56n23, 105, 107n14, 117, 118, 122n80, 132, 147n60
Kraybill, J. Nelson, 2n3, 13, 55n21, 199n50, 200n57, 286n35
Krupp, J. A., 218
Kyle, Richard, 38

L'Abri, 295, 298n14
LaGrand, James, 90
LaHaye, Tim, 17

Lancaster Mennonite Conference, 33, 198n46, 203n66, 204n72, 208n83, 284
Landis, Ira D., 111, 204
Landis, Samuel K., 193
Lapp, Frances, 276
Lapp, John, 196
Latin American Theological Fraternity, 271
Lausanne Congress on World Evangelization, 39
Lausanne Covenant, 279
lay preachers, 47
Lefever, Hiram, 201
Left Behind series, 55
legalism, 56, 66, 164, 205, 209, 385
legislation, 195, 329, 334, 336, 337, 339, 341
Lehman, Chester K., 121
Lewis, C. S., 338
liberal arts, 76, 90, 132, 164, 165, 172, 175n50, 327n6
liberalism, 3, 23, 107n10, 109n23, 110, 11n30, 114, 115, 174, 182, 188, 190n13, 269, 286
liberation, 12, 266, 270, 277–78, 305–7, 312, 316, 372
liberty, 53n15, 69, 84, 223, 284
life insurance, 119, 194
Limbaugh, Rush, 87
Lind, Mary Beth, 287
literalism, 25, 64, 113, 152, 226, 367, 375. *See also* the Bible
Locke, John, 298
London Symposium on the Theology of the Atonement, 356
Longacre, Doris, 216, 263, 264, 275, 287
Longacre, Paul, 276–81, 285, 286
Lord's Supper, 20, 66–69, 195, 360n16
Los Angeles Times, 277
Loucks, Aaron, 131
Louw, Johannes, 358
love

Index 419

among Christians, 70
and the discipline of history, 76, 80, 93
as Christian virtue, 76, 330, 345, 369, 371
as social ethic, 38, 54, 67, 71, 146, 180, 227, 266, 295, 306, 316, 331, 332, 333, 380n4, 399
Divine love, 304, 305, 331, 363, 395
expressed in the atonement, 47, 69, 358–60, 376
of money, 336
Lowenthal, David, 89
Luther, Martin, 51n13, 60, 62, 145, 170, 271n13, 298, 351, 383
Lutheran Church, 19, 48, 62, 63n32, 66
Lutz, Henry, 203
lynching, 339

MacArthur, John, 12
Machen, J. Gresham, 28, 110
Mack, Alexander, 48, 203, 356
Mack, Noah, 203
Madison, James, 80
magistrates, 269, 299, 345
Mainline Protestants, 239, 246
make-up, 87, 241, 250, 251
Maldonado, David, Jr., 240, 242n15
Mann, Alan, 355
Marpeck, Pilgram, 9, 65–70, 351
marriage, 29, 46, 121, 151, 168n36, 284, 326, 329, 333, 337n31, 340, 342, 373, 385n24
same-sex, 326, 329, 340, 342–43
Marsden, George M., 15n14, 16n15, 17n20, 29n53, 36n79, 86n20, 111n29, 112n33, 115n46, 115n46, 152n80, 168n35, 188n9, 232, 294n2
Martin, Dennis, 161
Martin, Weldon, 249
Martinez, Juan F., 237n1, 239n7, 240, 242n16

Marty, Martin, 190, 191, 193, 194
Marxism, 265
materialism, 78, 262, 275, 279, 286
Matthews, Shailer, 106
McCain, John, 327
McClain, Alva J., 101, 102, 156–69, 170–81
McClain, Josephine, 156
McClain, Walter Scott, 159
McKnight, Scot, 4, 37, 324, 355
McLaren, Brian, 37
Mennonite (select topics)
    Board of Education, 131, 134
    Board of Missions and Charities, 131, 238n3, 243, 244
    Brethren, 11, 18, 30, 38, 48, 59n27, 219n5, 241n14, 284, 285
    Brethren Biblical Seminary, 284
    Brethren in Christ, 49, 215, 217, 219, 220, 228n28, 230n36, 232
    Central Committee, 22, 36, 272, 275, 276n20, 284
    Church USA, 34, 35, 129n1, 276n20, 284
    Community Church (Fresno, CA), 284
    Disaster Service, 36
    General Conference, 106, 208
    Great Awakening, 129, 148
    Mission Network, 40
    Publishing House, 116, 139
    Voluntary Service, 216
Messiah College, 75, 77, 85, 111, 267, 283
Methodism, 22, 27, 219, 221, 239n7, 241, 243, 277, 356, 382n13
Metzler, James, 398
Mexican Americans, 216, 238, 239, 241–43, 245–52, 254, 256–59
Mexico, 29, 30, 32, 237, 238, 254, 276
Miami University, Ohio, 356
Middle East, 2, 276, 354

military, 36, 146, 259, 334, 380, 390–96, 399
  alternatives to, 22, 228–29, 243, 251–54,
  American, ix, 118, 233, 395
  and evangelicalism, 55, 264–67, 271, 383, 385, 385n23, 400
  -industrial complex, 266
militarism, 117, 120n71, 226n24, 269, 272, 274, 390, 391
Miller, Orie O., 27
Miller, Susan Fisher, 125, 135
miracles, 107
Missionary Church, 22, 49, 215, 217, 218, 235, 325n2, 327n6, 328n13, 337n30, 380n7, 381n7. *See also* Mennonite Brethren in Christ
missions, 3, 30, 165, 215–16, 239
  as a source of tension, 48, 53–54, 158, 206
  emphasis on conversion, 232
  and imperialism, 223–24
  and Mennonites, 131, 238, 242n14, 244, 248, 255, 283
  and peace witness, 227, 234, 397–99
  and premillennialism, 168
  Urbana convention, 265
Mitchell, Mark T., 150, 151
modernity, 130–32, 140, 145, 146–50, 153, 187, 190, 195, 203, 204n70
Montrose Bible Conference, 170, 199
Moody, Dwight, 15, 22
Mooneyham, Stanley, 278, 280, 281n26
Moorhead, William G., 168
Moral Majority, 1, 55, 275
Morris, Henry, 166
Morning Cheer, 200
Mosaic laws, 337
Mosemann, John H., 111, 114–16, 192
Mosiman, S. K., 114

Mouw, Richard, 384, 385, 394
movies, 178, 241, 250, 252
Mt. Zion Mennonite Church, 129
Münster, 46n2, 338
Murray, Stuart, 77, 147
music, 18, 33–36, 55, 119, 193, 198, 206, 241, 244, 250, 251, 258
Muslims, 188n8, 265, 331
Mussolini, 169

Nachfolge, 52
  See also discipleship
Nash, Gary, 83
National Ministerial Association (Brethren Church), 171
National Prayer Breakfast, 11
National Religious Broadcasters, 17
nationalism, 11, 24, 75, 77, 78, 82–83, 118, 287
Native Americans, 80, 240
Nazarenes, 27
Nazi party, 87, 341n41
Neufeld, Kathryn Klassen, 285
Neutäufer. See Evangelisch-Taufgesinnter Gemeinde
New Left, 268–71, 279
New Mennonite Church of Canada West, 219
Nida, Eugene, 358
Niebuhr, Reinhold, 385, 399, 267, 301n16, 307n31
Nixon, Richard M., 266, 272, 274, 280
nonconformity to the world, 20–22, 24, 46, 54, 119–21, 157, 158, 163, 177–79, 186, 194
non-creedalism, 123, 167, 171, 172, 174
nondenominational, viii, 133, 186, 188, 200, 202, 208
nonviolence
  as Anabaptist distinctive, 101, 177, 179–81, 215, 269
  as response to war, 2–3

and atonement theory, 122,
    357–69,
  biblical support for, 380–400
  See also pacifism; peace
Nysewander, Christian, 223

oath taking, 19, 46, 119, 171, 178,
    179, 345
Obama, Barak, 326, 328, 329n15
Occidental College, 165, 167n32,
    169n37
Ockenga, Harold J., 17, 23n40
Ohio Mennonite Conference, 204,
    208
Old Colony Mennonites, 12, 32 n61
Old Fashioned Revival Hour, 200
Old Order movements, 22, 25, 47 n5
ordinances, 47, 54, 69, 119, 162, 178,
    194
ordination, 60, 62, 137, 194, 200n52
  of women, 281
orthodoxy, conceptions of, 2, 77n3,
    89, 101, 107, 112, 125, 152,
    157, 169, 170–75, 332
Osler Mission Chapel, 12
Other Side, The, 277, 280, 281
Oyer, Noah, 111

pacifism
  and *agape*, 306
  biblical support for, 324, 381–400
  and evangelicals, 379–80
  historiography and, 77, 81
  and kingdom ethics, 312
  liberal, 225
  and missions, 222, 227, 238, 241,
    252–53, 256, 258–59
  See also peace
Palatinate, 48
Palin, Sarah, 327–28
Palmer, George, 199, 200
Panama Canal, 24
para-church organizations, 170
parenting, 284
Passion, 53, 84, 242, 327, 353

Passover, 360, 376
Pastor, Adam, 124
Pastoral Messenger, 204, 205
patriotism, ix, 22, 81, 83, 118, 267,
    297, 394
  See also nationalism
Patristic Church, 350
peace
  Anabaptist commitment to, 3, 38,
    71, 119, 181, 252, 253, 258,
    259, 284, 301–2, 304, 316,
    340, 350, 354, 371, 379
  and biblical teachings, 359–62,
    368
  and evangelical left, 264–66,
    271–72, 284, 286
  and evangelism, 217, 220, 222–35
  fundamentalist threat to, 23, 53
  "peace church historiography,"
    77–82
  with God, 31, 355
  peacemaking, 11, 255, 258,
    286n35, 380n4, 397
  and teachings of Jesus, 119, 357,
    376–77, 381, 396–99
Peace Conference (Lancaster
    Mennonite Conference), 33,
    198n46, 203n66, 204n72,
    208n83, 284
Peace Churches, 3, 77, 78, 82, 234,
    252, 350, 379, 385, 397
Pentecost, 69, 303
Pentecostalism, 1, 15, 16, 18, 39, 239,
    241, 243–46, 254, 258, 334
People's Christian Coalition, 266n6,
    269
People's Temple, 338
Peters, Isaac, 49
Peters, Lorraine, 284
Peters, Marilyn, 284, 285n32
Phi Beta Kappa, 138
Philadelphia School of the Bible, 165
Phillips, Dirk, 124
Pierce, Rowen, 200
pietism, 158, 176–77

and Anabaptism, 52–53
definition of, 175n51
and eschatology, 177n56
and evangelicalism, 177n55
mystical, 20
radical, 19
Pinnock, Clark, 269, 270n12, 271
pistis, 388, 389, 395. See also faith
Plaster, David, 160, 162
pluralism, 15, 59
Polanyi, Michael, 150–51
politics, 106, 120, 253, 258, 259, 265, 306, 308, 311–18, 323, 330
and historical method, 78–80
and social justice, 240, 262,
and evangelical left, 216, 268–75, 280
evangelical involvement in, 1–2, 18, 75,
Theological views of, 292–96, 300, 305–18, 326, 329, 344–46
See also government
Port Huron Statement, 269
Post-American, 266, 267, 269, 270, 271, 279, 280, 281
postponement theory, 111. See also dispensationalism
poverty, 81, 268, 269, 274, 279, 308
power
divine, 69, 93, 229, 335, 360, 371, 373, 375, 390, 396, 398
and nonviolence, 71, 221, 227, 393
of the state, 38, 80, 134, 257, 267, 293, 323, 344n51, 345, 385n23, 393, 396
within the church, 53n15, 107, 109, 135, 143, 145, 256–57
worldly power structures, 81, 248, 268, 273, 296, 300, 302–18, 350, 353, 355, 368, 394
See also politics; government

preaching, 19, 25, 30, 31, 34, 35, 45, 48, 49, 90, 106, 133, 141, 146, 172, 194, 202, 206, 218, 244, 255, 310
preparatory services, 196
Presbyterian, 22, 27, 29, 110, 167, 243, 295
pride, 83, 232, 281, 332
priesthood of all believers, 60, 269, 282, 286
progressive(s), 31, 32, 101, 107, 109, 130, 132, 138, 139, 144, 158, 159, 163, 164, 165, 182, 204, 206, 207, 216, 218, 219, 262, 271, 286
Progressive Era, 134
prohibition, 133n11, 137, 206, 333, 339, 341, 343
propaganda, 80, 81, 89, 142
prophecy conferences, 168, 173
protracted meetings, 133, 218 . See also revivalism
Puritans, 117, 336, 337

Quakers, 219, 229
quietism, 272

race, 239, 240, 264, 308
racism, 81, 247, 251, 252n50, 257, 268, 269, 272, 274
radio, 12, 23n40, 32–37, 84, 87, 186, 193, 200–203, 206, 208, 252, 279
Radio School of the Bible, 200
Ramsey, David, 83
Ramseyer, Robert, 3n4, 135n23, 399
rape, 339, 341n40
Rawls, John, 338, 344
Reagan, Ronald, 17
Reba Place, 270–71, 284
Reese, Boyd, 270
Reformation
children of, 9, 21, 57–58, 60–61, 70

doctrines of, 381, 383, 385–86,
386n27, 388
Protestant, 21, 23, 57, 63, 351
Radical, 19, 23, 51, 386
Reformed tradition, ix, 14–16, 19,
38n84, 45, 118, 158, 162, 168,
263, 267, 271, 277, 278n23,
286n36, 381n8, 385n23
Reformed Mennonites, 49,
Reforming Mennonite Society, 219
Reimer, Ben D., 18n25, 30–31
repentance, 45, 57, 217, 309
Republican Party, 84, 262, 327, 328,
329, 330n19
resurrection, general, 373
revivalism
and Anabaptists, 21–23, 29–32,
47–51, 106, 113, 129, 131,
133n11, 136, 145–47, 158,
186n2, 198, 200–202, 217–18,
220, 222, 232, 241, 244
as feature of Wesleyan-holiness,
14, 21
and evangelical heritage, ix,
14–15, 45, 240, 243–44
Riedemann, Peter, 351
Right On, 271n13, 277
Riley, William Bell, 170
Risser, Noah, 192, 203
Rockyridge Mennonite Mission, 207
Rodeheaver, Homer, 199
Roe v. Wade, 297, 340
Rohrer, Norman B., 159, 162n16
Ronk, Albert T., 158n4, 161
Roos, Joe, 270
Rosedale Bible College, 49
Roth, John D., 9, 45, 328, 394
"Rules and Discipline" (Lancaster
Mennonite Conference),
33n68, 35n73, 195–96, 198,
207
Russia
association with godlessness, 142,
225n18

Mennonite immigrants from, 29,
49, 59n27
Mennonites in, 46, 48, 59n27
Ruth, Arthur, 196
Rutherford, Samuel, 298–99

Sabbath observance, 333, 336n30
sacraments, 9, 57, 63–65, 67, 68, 77,
146. *See also* ordinances
sacrificial system, 365–67
salvation, 24, 45, 51, 223, 243, 296,
307, 310, 312, 317
assurance of, 12, 48, 175, 206
and conversion, 53, 218, 232,
and discipleship, 54, 105, 121–23,
148, 192,
theological views of, 57–59,
63–64, 66, 121, 178n63, 209,
353–55, 367, 374
sanctification, 45, 141
Sandy Cove Conference Center, 199
Schaeffer, Edith, 295
Schaeffer, Francis, 18n22, 216,
293–302, 308–11, 316–19,
Schlabach, Theron F., 20n31, 22n36,
25n45, 53, 54, 55, 63n32, 105,
107, 125, 131n4, 145n56, 189,
194n31, 231n38, 232n38
Schleiermacher, Friedrich, 106, 109
Schleitheim Confession, 223
Schmidt, Ruth, 283, 284
Schultz, Kevin M., 243
Schwarzenau, 20fn29, 158
Schwehn, Mark, 94
science
and modernism, 106–7, 110, 174
Darwinism, 112, 115
views of, 112, 166, 167
Scofield Reference Bible, 23fn40,
166fn29, 168, 201, 202, 204–5
New Scofield Bible, 168
Scofield Bible Correspondence
Course, 35, 198, 201, 202, 206
Scofield, C. I., 111, 177
Scoles, Todd, 162

Index

Scopes Trial, 171, 196, 197fn40
sectarian(ism), 13, 15, 22, 65, 131, 318, 385
Selective Service, 181, 229, 230
self-denial, 93, 119
Senger, Rudy, 116
separation
  from the world, 20, 30, 46, 120, 301, 152, 158fn6, 178, 228
  of church and state, 38, 269
separatism, ix, 292, 318
Sermon on the Mount, 20, 179, 180, 181, 241, 305, 329, 335, 336, 344, 346, 355, 384, 395. *See also* Jesus, teachings of
Severn, Clayton, 228
sexism, 262, 272, 283
sexual relations, 248, 332, 333, 342, 343, 343, 344, 385fn24
Shantz, Jacob, 233, 24
"Shaping Families," 35
Shenk, Lois Landis, 284
Shenk, Sara Wenger, 145fn57, 150
Shenk, Stanley C., 27
Shutt, Joyce, 285
Sider Dayton, Lucille, 282fn28, 285
Sider, Ronald J., 37, 216, 262, 263fn2, 267, 272, 275, 285, 380fn3
Sider, Roy, 272
Simons, Menno, 113fn36, 124, 131
simple living, 216, 264, 272, 273, 275, 278–81, 286, 287
slavery, 74, 80, 90, 93–95, 282, 305, 345, 352, 368, 377
Smith, Jacob B., 111
Smoker, George, 27
smoking, 178
Snyder, Elvin, 245
social justice, 3, 38, 74, 77, 81, 263, 270, 272, 323, 354, 369, 371
Société évangélique de Genève, 45
Sojourners, 266fn6, 271fn13, 277, 278, 380fn3
sola fide, 324, 383, 385, 386n27, 387, 397, 399, 400. *See also* faith;

Reformation, doctrines of; salvation
sola scriptura, 324, 383, 386n27, 387, 394, 397, 398, 400. *See also* the Bible; Reformation, doctrines of
South Africa, 11, 39, 338n33
South Texas Mennonite Church, 255–58
Southern Baptist(s), 277, 281fn26
Soviet Union, 29
Spener, Philipp Jakob, 296
spiritual renewal, 37, 39, 47
Spiritualists, 66
Stamp Act, 83
starvation, 269, 273
Stauffer, Jacob, 122
Stauffer, John L., 111, 113fn38, 114
Steiner, Menno Simons, 131
Stewart, Lyman, 110
Stewart, Milton, 110
Stoffer, Dale, 158fn5, 161, 168–69
Stott, John, 284
Stout, Jeffrey, 140, 344fn48
Stover, Gerald, 202
Strauss, Layman, 200
Stucky, Joseph, 49
Student Volunteer Movement, 22
submission
  and gender, 281
  as Anabaptist virtue, 130, 132, 136–38, 140–45, 149–53, 193
  to God's dominion, 303
  to earthly authorities, 396
Sunday school, 22, 29, 33, 173, 245, 294
Sunday, Billy, 172, 199fn51
Sunday, Helen (Ma), 172
Supreme Court, 297, 340, 341
surrender, 31, 130, 141–44, 151–52. *See also* submission.
Swartley, Willard, 61fn29, 282, 331fn 23, 387fn32
Swatsky, Rodney, 111, 112, 117fn56, 188–90

Swedish Baptists, 27
Swedish Covenanters, 29
Swindoll, Charles, 34
Switzerland, 19n28, 45–48, 51n13, 295
Sword and Trumpet, 115, 116, 141, 144, 185, 186, 187, 192, 208

Tabor College, 285
television, 33–35, 84, 274, 279. *See also* evangelist(s)
Ten Commandments, 297, 336
textual criticism, 107. *See also* the Bible
Thanksgiving Workshops, 263, 266, 270, 272
theater, 163, 177
theocracy, 297, 338
theology, x, 58–65, 74, 92, 149, 167, 169, 171, 192, 222, 275, 286, 287, 331
  Anabaptist-Mennonite, 13, 20, 21n32, 22, 23, 25, 38n84, 54, 66, 79, 122, 123, 267–70, 355
  atonement, 122, 123, 350
  biblical, 356, 358–68, 388n34
  Brethren, 170
  Catholic, 65
  Classical, 70
  conservative, 15
  dispensational, 36
  evangelical, 32, 39, 50, 51n10, 54, 285, 292, 355, 383–84, 384n20
  historical, 78, 79, 356, 369–71
  humility, 20
  integrative, 356
  Latina/o, 239–40
  modern, viii
  new, 106–8, 110, 112, 115
  Pentecostal, 15
  philosophical, 356, 372–76
  political, 216, 292–319
  practical, 160n8, 275, 355
  radical, 279

Reformed (Calvinist), 118, 168
sacramental, 9, 63
systematic, 28, 124, 165, 168n34, 174
theologian(s), xi, 3, 9, 38, 54, 65, 77, 78, 80, 82, 86, 106–7, 110, 121, 148, 150, 151, 264, 269, 283n29, 284, 294, 301n16, 324, 328n13, 350, 356, 369, 371, 381, 386n27, 397
two-kingdom, 3
of war, 384n22
Thut, John, 114
tithe, 273
tobacco, 178, 241, 333
Toews, J. A., 234–35
Toews, Paul, 140, 145fn56, 149fn69
Torrey, Rueben A., 112, 165, 170, 175
Tosh, John, 87, 88
Towamencin Mennonite Church, 198, 199, 202
transformative identification, 351–53
transubstantiation, 67
  See also Lord's Supper; sacraments
Trinity College (Deerfield, IL), 268
Trinity Evangelical Divinity School (Deerfield, IL), 197n42, 380n7

Union Theological Seminary, 109
United Methodist Church, 356
United Missionary Church, 217
University of Chicago, 108
University of Illinois, 138
University of Washington, 164

Vacation Bible School, 246, 248, 249–56, 258
Van Elderen, Marlin, 267
Vanguard, 277
Victorious Christian Life. *See* Keswickian holiness
Vineyard Fellowship, 11, 18

violence, 66, 71, 78, 81, 146, 148n66, 223, 225–27, 233, 267, 269, 270, 286, 298, 299, 306, 310, 334, 338, 355, 357n11, 367, 375, 387, 397
   biblical, 387, 390–94
   divine, 354, 357n11, 374, 377, 393n58
   domestic, 2
   of government (military), 38, 308, 354, 380, 380n4, 382n14, 385, 388, 400
   gratuitous, 354
   lethal, 384
   redemptive, 324
   rejection of, 303, 304, 312, 313, 380n4, 398
   ritual, 353–54
   See also nonviolence
voluntarism, 58–60
Voolstra, Sjouke, 397, 398
Voth, Peggy, 285

Wall, Aaron, 49
Wallis, Jim, 216, 267, 269–71, 273, 280, 293, 294, 300–302, 308–19, 380n3
war, ix, 2, 20, 22, 78, 81, 119, 171, 179, 181, 214, 252, 262, 270, 282, 286, 308, 324, 379, 382–84, 387, 388n34, 397, 399n81
   Civil, 74, 87, 88, 13
   Cold, 22, 160, 176, 178n62, 244, 352
   Great. *See* World War I
   Holy, 393
   Iraq, 354, 382n14, 287, 354, 383n15
   just, 265, 324, 334, 381, 382, 382n13, 382n14
   in Old Testament, 390–95
   and peace, 219–35, 266n4, 333
   post-, 243, 263, 273, 286n35
   Revolutionary, 75, 83–84, 87
   Spanish-American, 118, 223, 224, 227
   Vietnam, 36, 234, 253, 254, 255, 265, 266, 267, 268, 271, 272, 275, 276
   World War I, 22, 29, 89, 120, 137, 148n66, 170, 181, 224, 227–29, 233
   World War II, 22, 23, 27, 180, 216, 227, 229–30, 232–34, 240–41, 243, 251, 253–54, 258, 352
Warren, Mercy Otis, 84
Warren, Rick, 18
Washington, George, 80
WDAC, 33–37
Weapons of Mass Destruction, 354
Weaver, J. Denny, 21n32, 54, 105, 109n21, 121–23, 135, 148–49, 263n2, 324, 353n4, 355, 365n23
Wells, Samuel, 148
Wenger, Amos D., 111, 113, 116n53, 131,
Wenger, John C., 112n35, 113n36, 220, 221n8,
Wesley, John, 221
Wesleyan-holiness, 14, 21, 141, 221, 223, 232, 327, 331
Westminster Seminary, 26
Wheaton College, viii, 271n13, 33n69, 50n8, 275n18, 283
Whitcomb, John, 160, 166, 173n46, 178n62
Whitmer, Paul E., 108
Wiebe, Katie Funk, 285
Willimon, William H., 78
Wineburg, Sam, 91, 92
Winnipeg Bible College, 30
Winona Lake Bible Conference Association, 173
Witherspoon, John, 298
Women's Task Force, 284–85
Wood, Gordon, 86, 89
Woodring, Richard, 225n20, 226–27

Word of Life Chapel, 35, 200n55, 202
Word of Life Fellowship, 199
World Food Conference, 280
World Vision, 17, 278, 280
World's Christian Fundamentals Association, 170
worldliness, 33, 163, 177, 193–94, 203, 204n70
worldview, 295, 296, 329, 330–32
worship, ix, 11, 14, 18, 25, 48, 50n8, 55, 64, 67, 69, 146, 218, 239n8, 247, 284, 311, 312, 365–67
Wright, N. T., 372, 388
Wüst, Edward, 48

Xenia Theological Seminary, 160n8, 165, 167, 168, 169n37

Yale University, 272
Yoder, A. B., 224n17, 230–31
Yoder, John Howard, 3n6, 216, 324, 328n13, 330n19, 334n28, 340n39, 346n54
    and evangelical left, 263–72, 277, 279, 282, 285–87
    and "peace church historiography," 77–79, 82
    and political theology, 293, 294, 300–308, 311n41, 316–19
    Politics of Jesus, 23, 24, 77, 78, 263, 267, 270, 271, 279, 285, 286, 305, 344n50, 386, 387
    use of Scripture, 379–400
Yoder, Nathan E., 24n41, 102, 108–10, 116, 125, 131n5, 132n10, 141n44, 142n42, 144n54, 145n55, 161n11, 189, 231n38
Yoder, S. C., 111
Yom Kippur, 366
Young People's Church of the Air, 200
Young, Jerry, 161, 174
Youth for Christ, 17, 33, 50n8, 173, 199

Zehr, Howard J., 28n51, 256
Zinn, Howard, 80–81

www.ingramcontent.com/pod-product-compliance
Lightning Source LLC
Chambersburg PA
CBHW072116290426
44111CB00012B/1682